Sound Recording
Practice

Sound Recording Practice

Edited by

JOHN BORWICK

*FOR THE ASSOCIATION OF PROFESSIONAL
RECORDING STUDIOS*

THIRD EDITION

Oxford   New York
OXFORD UNIVERSITY PRESS
1987

Oxford University Press, Walton Street, Oxford OX2 6DP

Oxford New York Toronto
Delhi Bombay Calcutta Madras Karachi
Petaling Jaya Singapore Hong Kong Tokyo
Nairobi Dar es Salaam Cape Town
Melbourne Auckland

and associated companies in
Beirut Berlin Ibadan Nicosia

Oxford is a trade mark of Oxford University Press

Published in the United States
by Oxford University Press, New York

British Library Cataloguing in Publication Data
Sound recording practice: a handbook.—3rd ed.
1. Sound—Recording and reproducing
I. Borwick, John II. Association of
Professional Recording Studies
621.389'32   TK7881.4
ISBN 0–19–311927–7

Library of Congress Cataloging-in-Publication Data
Sound recording practice.
Includes index.
1. Sound—Recording and reproducing.   2. Sound
recording industry.   3. Magnetic recorders and recording.
I. Borwick, John.   II. Association of Professional
Studios.
TK7881.4.S68   1987   621.389'32   87–5692
ISBN 0–19–311927–7

Typeset, printed and bound in Great Britain by William Clowes Limited,
Beccles and London

Foreword

It is now over a decade since the first edition of *Sound Recording Practice* was published. During the time that has now elapsed, many things have changed whilst others have remained constant.

We now live in a world of digital audio, unheard of in those early days of analogue, and with it a technology for which the language alone needs a new dictionary. Who could have anticipated that the Compact Disc would be rapidly eroding the market share of the long-playing record, or that R-DAT would be challenging the domination of the conventional cassette? Who could have foreseen that the domestic environment would have replay facilities giving quality comparable to the master tape in the studio, or that mixing consoles would be fitted with such comprehensive computerization?

Throughout the entire recording and post-production chain we are always striving for improvements in quality. Some involve huge investments in new capital equipment, whilst others can be achieved through quite small changes in technique. The Association of Professional Recording Studios has always been determined that those committed to high standards should be kept aware of all the latest developments. The authors selected for this new edition are experts in their own fields, proving our determination that this book should remain the definitive textbook for those involved in professional sound recording. The keyword to success is professionalism: that never changes, a fact endorsed by the choice of John Borwick once again as editor. May this book give you many hours of informative reading.

KEN TOWNSEND (General Manager, Abbey Road Studios)
Chairman
Association of Professional Recording Studios

Editor's preface to third edition

The first edition of this multi-author handbook appeared in 1976 and was aimed at everyone interested in the technical and practical aspects of professional sound recording. For the second edition (1980) I approached the same authors, each an expert in his field, for an update. Except that two new chapters were needed to describe the emerging systems for digital recording and console automation, the coverage was basically the same as before.

In the past few years, however, technical developments have proceeded at such an accelerated pace in every branch of recording that the APRS has encouraged me to take an entirely new approach, so that this third edition is to all intents and purposes a completely new book. Most of the authors are new, and are chosen for their day to day involvement in the latest techniques and processes. Many of them also have experience in passing on their knowledge to others, for example at the annual APRS Studio Engineers Course held at the University of Surrey, the home of this country's only Tonmeister degree course. The result is not only a text which is highly readable but one which is as informative and as thoroughly up to date as our combined forces could make it.

JOHN BORWICK
Haslemere, Surrey

Contents

Technical introduction

The equipment

Recording techniques

The consumer product

Allied media

TECHNICAL INTRODUCTION

1

The programme chain

John Borwick

The making and marketing of a successful sound recording is so much a matter of team-work that it can almost be compared to a relay race. Each member of a relay team needs to have the right talents, training, and attitudes, and to be on top form on the day. He is solely responsible for his part of the race but must work hand in hand (almost literally) with his fellow team-mates at the point of handing over the baton.

In the same way, the chain of 'runners' who carry a sound recording on its way from the original conception and performance to the consumer must apply a fine balance of skills and experience whilst the recording is in their hands. But they will do a better job—particularly at the hand over points—if they understand the role of their colleagues throughout the entire programme chain.

Just to take one example, a disc-cutting engineer has to juggle with various physical limitations of the vinyl disc medium every time he cuts an LP master. This may bring in decisions affecting his choice of average cutting level, the bass roll-off, maximum treble level, and even the relative phase and crosstalk between left and right channels. When the record producer attends the disc-cutting session, these compromise decisions can be discussed and mutually arrived at to ensure that the artistic impact of the music is preserved as much as possible—provided that the producer and engineer understand each other's 'language'. (The final 'proof of the pudding' listening stage cannot be reached until test pressings are sent out by the factory, and then the producer and cutting engineer will almost certainly have to listen to these in different locations and on very different playback and loudspeaker systems.) In practice, the engineer will often be working on his own when making the tape-to-disc transfer, and so he will need to use his own judgement, based on experience of the sound-quality tastes or aspirations of the given producer or others like him.

It will obviously help if the balance engineer at the original recording and mix-down sessions knows enough about these disc-cutting restrictions to anticipate—and avoid—serious problems. He will need to adhere to standard peak levels on the session and master tapes, avoid high amplitudes at extreme bass frequencies where possible, and minimize out-of-phase components on stereo recordings, since this results in vertical motion of the cutting stylus.

The stages in record manufacture

Without confusing the issue by attempting to describe every possible variation met in practice, let us trace the typical sequence of stages in record manufacture. This will introduce the reader to the kinds of decisions and skills needed at each stage. A more detailed coverage will of course be found in the relevant specialist chapters which follow. At the time of writing, the vinyl disc is still hanging on as the most widespread 'music carrier' medium, though it is coming under increasing pressure from the rival tape cassette and Compact Disc formats.

In terms of programme planning, the tendency has been to treat the LP record as the primary source when deciding the lengths of sides, and let the cassette and CD versions follow suit. However, this fails to make full use of the longer playing times possible on these two media, so that extra items are sometimes added.

It will be convenient at this point to outline the manufacture of a typical long-playing record first, and then discuss the differences which apply to cassette and CD manufacture afterwards. Figures 1.1 and 1.2 show the usual sequence of stages.

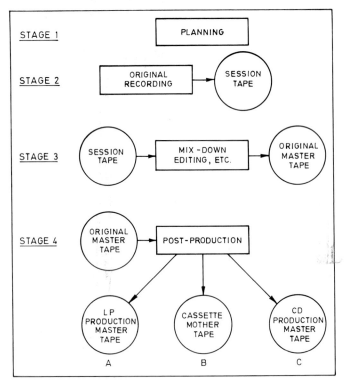

Fig. 1.1. Programme chain: stages 1–4

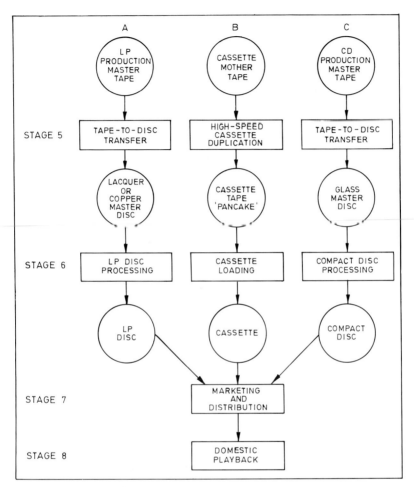

Fig. 1.2. Programme chain: stages 5–8

Vinyl disc manufacture

Stage 1: Planning

While mercenary considerations may be forgotten during the excitement of the music-making and recording sessions, it remains of first importance to realize that records must ultimately make money. The planning stage must therefore work towards this goal and include a close study of all the commercial aspects. The existing recorded repertoire must be surveyed before any given work is scheduled for recording. However popular the work is felt to be, its marketability must be coldly assessed in terms of the current record-buying climate, the suitability of the artists available, and even the image of the particular record label. Only when a reasonable guarantee of sufficient sales appears likely to make the venture worth while can the questions of dates, recording venue, contracts, and detailed costing be considered.

Stage 2: Original recording

As the musicians perform, the acoustic energy radiated by their instruments or voices, modified to some extent by the acoustic characteristics of the hall or studio, is converted into electrical energy by the microphone(s). This electrical signal is then amplified, mixed, and corrected as necessary at the control console and passed to the tape recorder. Here the electrical energy is converted to magnetic energy for storage and subsequent playback. The usual procedure is to record all takes and retakes (followed by any multitrack overdubs, etc.) so that this *Session Tape* contains all the programme material, leaving the final choice of best takes until later.

Already a number of variations to this basic scheme should be noted. For example, a number of audiophile record companies, seeking to eliminate as many sources of signal degradation as possible, have done away with the tape-recording stage. Instead, they record direct to disc, leap-frogging over the editing, mix-down, and tape-to-disc transfer stages to cut a whole LP side in a single once-for-all take. Also, there are now two competing systems of tape recording, analogue and digital. The former records a magnetic signal on the tape which is a close copy (or 'analogue') of the electrical signal waveform leaving the microphone. The latter first converts the electrical waveform into a series of on/off pulses and records these on the magnetic tape. The relative advantages and disadvantages of analogue and digital recording are discussed in some detail elsewhere in this book, and will be briefly referred to as they apply in this outline of the programme chain.

The best layout of the musicians in the studio calls for a good knowledge of the directional characteristics of each instrument, so that the sometimes conflicting needs of the performers and the microphones can be met. The hall or studio will presumably have been chosen because it has sympathetic acoustics. Even so, the amount of reverberation and its tonal quality (all reflecting and absorbing surfaces have an effect on the balance of frequencies in the sound) will need close study. Considerations of extraneous noise may also inhibit the freedom of choice in positioning of microphones.

The choice of microphone types, and their placement, subsequent mixing, frequency correction, and so on, involve techniques which vary considerably from engineer to engineer. Some guidelines are given in this book, though there are so many variable quantities that microphone balance is much more an art than a science. Control of the dynamic range, proper alignment of the tape machines, and even careful handling of the tapes are all matters which need scrupulous attention if the Session Tape is to attain optimum quality.

Stage 3: Editing, mix-down, etc.

A perfect take of a complete musical work is most unusual. Generally the best passages from several takes will be selected and edited together to form the *Original Master*. Also, particularly in pop recording, the Session Master will have been built up from several synchronized takes on multitrack tapes and will need to be mixed down or 'reduced' to a two-track version for production purposes.

While most of the value-judgements at this stage remain artistic ones, they depend for their realization on expert knowledge of the particular equipment and technical facilities available. The mere act of copying from the Session tape to an Original Master tape (in the general case where the Session tape, suitably edited, cannot go forward to production) creates a second-generation recording in which the signal-to-noise ratio will have been degraded. This is certainly true of analogue tapes, though noise reduction systems such as Dolby have done much to remove this potential source of increased noise. On the other hand, it is a principal benefit of digital recording that all copies are to all intents and purposes identical to the original.

It is important for the engineer making the Original Master to strive for optimum sound quality, and minimum noise, at this stage, since the recording is now at its peak and all subsequent processes must be expected to downgrade the quality to some degree. He must also take careful account of the problems inherent in disc cutting, as already mentioned. Proper regard for the question of phase really begins at the studio session and is a strong argument against multi-microphone and spaced microphone techniques. The exceptionally clean quality of sound sometimes heard on one-microphone tracks in pop recordings (and coincident-pair stereo recordings) is often remarked upon and can be attributed to the avoidance of spurious phase effects. Even the restrictions imposed by the consumer's playback equipment when the record is finally listened to and, hopefully, enjoyed should be borne in mind—perhaps by listening to smaller 'nearfield' loudspeakers as an alternative to the full-size studio monitors. If some important ingredient in the musical sounds is missing on the small speakers (and perhaps at a lower monitoring level), then correcting action might be advisable.

Stage 4: Post-production

In recent years, refinements in studio equipment and indeed in the results obtainable with advanced multitrack and digital techniques have led to a growth in post-production activities. Original Master Tapes are now seen to be capable of further refining or sweetening to optimize the sound quality on the *Production Master*. In addition, the existence in the market-place of competing vinyl disc, cassette tape, and Compact Disc formats has led to the need for separate Production Masters to be prepared for these three media, differing slightly in technical terms and also sometimes in the order and number of musical items within a given album. The major recording companies can usually accommodate this stage within their own studio complexes, whilst smaller companies tend to take their Original Master tapes along to a specialist post-production facility, where all the necessary final tweaking and assembly work can be undertaken (as described in Chapter 20) to present an ideal Production Master tailored specifically to meet the different demands of the LP or CD disc transfer processes or the high-speed cassette duplicating stage.

Stage 5A : Tape-to-disc Transfer

For the disc-cutting stage, the Production Master will hopefully have been optimized in terms of side lengths, dynamics, frequency, and phase response, but the cutting engineer will normally play the tape right through and set up the electronics of his cutting lathe as necessary to achieve the best cut he can. Then the tape is played and the electrical signals are used to drive the cutter head stylus on a disc-cutting lathe so that an equivalent (analogue) waveform is etched into the groove on a master disc. This disc is usually called a '*lacquer*', since the blank normally consists of a lacquer coating on an aluminium base (though the term 'acetate' is occasionally used in error as a hangover from older types of disc coating). There is nowadays another type of blank in use having a copper surface and used in the DMM (Direct Metal Mastering) technique, as described in Chapters 21 and 22.

Both types of blank disc require great care in terms of depth and level of cut. Limiting and compression may be necessary, despite attention to this factor at the studio, and such techniques as varigroove will be used to ensure the best compromise between recorded level and maximum duration per side. In the programme chain for manufacturing tape cassettes and Compact Discs, there is an equivalent transfer stage, as indicated in Figure 1.2, which will be described later.

Stage 6A : Vinyl disc processing

The lacquer disc is first sprayed with silver, to make it electrically conducting, and then put through a series of electroforming processes to produce successive metal-plated parts as follows:

(*a*) the *Master* (a negative, i.e. with ridges in place of grooves);
(*b*) the *Mother* (a positive);
(*c*) the *Stamper* (a negative), which is the moulding tool to be used in pressing out records from thermoplastic vinyl.

A pair of these metal stampers, one for each side of the record, is placed into the two plattens (or jaws) of an automatic press which, on closing, will mould a 'biscuit' of vinyl material into the final disc, or 'pressing' as it is sometimes called in the trade. The thermoplastic cycle of preheating, pressing, cooling, and releasing takes about 20 seconds. The discs are then trimmed and put into their sleeves. Cleanliness is obviously important throughout a pressing plant, as well as a vigilant programme of quality control checks to discover stamper wear or blemishes before a large number of wasted pressings is produced.

Stage 7: Marketing and distribution

Assuming that all the planning details were carried out as described under stage 1, the record company can now follow this up by proper attention to packaging the product (sleeve design, sleeve-note writing, booklet printing), marketing, distribution, and promotion. Suitable advertising will be necessary, and advance copies of the disc must be made available to reviewers and broadcasting organizations. Only in this way will a sufficient number of potential customers be alerted to the special attractions of this particular recording—and be persuaded to buy it.

Stage 8: Domestic playback

In the purchaser's home, the record player or hi-fi system reconverts the recorded waveforms into acoustic energy via the loudspeakers.

The sound waves will again be modified by the acoustic properties of the living-room, and there will be other restrictions because of the generally lower listening level, higher ambient noise level, and other domestic circumstances and distractions.

These factors should ideally have been allowed for at all earlier stages in the chain. For example, a slightly drier acoustic than the norm for a particular type of music may be aimed at to allow for the small amount of reverberation added by the listening-room. The full dynamic range of which the studio equipment may be capable will sometimes be compressed deliberately in acknowledgement of the narrower range usually found acceptable in most domestic situations or reproducible on much domestic equipment. In fact, the introduction of CD players has provided consumers with a wider dynamic range source than either LPs or cassettes, but the restrictions in terms of domestic ambient noise levels and maximum acceptable loudness still set a limit to what many home listeners would consider ideal.

No operating skills can be assumed on the part of the home user. Equipment and records must therefore be designed to be as foolproof as possible, and, where special instructions are needed as to choice of stylus type or record care, the record companies have a duty to educate users through dealer literature, sleeve notes, leaflets, etc. Even so, the quality of reproduction, and even the ability of the pickup stylus to track the groove securely, will vary from poor (with the simplest players) to remarkably good (with a top-flight hi-fi set-up). In the latter case, the domestic listener can indeed enjoy the full impact of modern recording techniques.

Pre-recorded cassette manufacture

The above sequence has charted the stages in the manufacture of vinyl discs. When it comes to the mass production of pre-recorded cassettes ('musicassettes'), stages 1–4 are broadly the same, but different procedures are followed at stages 5B and 6B, as indicated in the B sequence in Figure 1.2 and described in detail in Chapter 23.

Stage 5B: High-speed cassette duplication
The Production Master tape supplied from stage 4 to a tape-duplicating plant for stage 5B differs in several important ways from the straight Production Master tape supplied to the disc-cutting room for stage 5A.

It may be described as an *interim master* or *Mother* tape, and will have been specially equalized if necessary to accommodate the technical limits of the cassette system, Dolby B encoded, and so on. More particularly, it will consist of tape suitable for running on a high-speed 'sender' playback machine (at perhaps 32 or even 64 times normal speed). On receipt it will be formed into an endless loop and put into a 'loop bin' to be replayed over and over again non-stop. It therefore carries the two pairs of left/right tracks to form sides one and two on the final cassette (one pair recorded in the reverse direction).

The signals from the sender are relayed to a number of slave recorders loaded with large spools (or 'pancakes') of cassette tape, enough to record about twenty programmes separated by a special low-frequency cue tone.

Stage 6B: Cassette loading
The recorded tape pancakes are removed from the slaves and placed on machines known as 'loaders'. These are fully automatic, and continuously splice and spool the tape into empty cassette housings called 'C-zeros'. A sensor identifies the cue tone, stops the tape, and splices it on to the start leader tape before ejecting the loaded cassette. Labelling and packaging processes then follow.

Compact disc manufacture

Since the end of 1982, the record companies have had a third 'music carrier' to manufacture—the Compact Disc. This is potentially a very high-quality medium, and indeed the Production Master tape generated at the post-production stage (stage 4) for CD manufacture has generally to be recorded with even more precision (and less inherent noise) than those for LP and cassette. It is of course a digital tape, encoded to very strict standards and containing numerous code signals (in addition to the digital music tracks) identifying the beginning and end of each track, index points, total running time, and so on (see more detailed description in Chapters 20 and 24). The customer's CD player will scan all this information and display or act upon it as commanded.

Stage 5C: Tape-to-CD master disc transfer

The signals from the digital production master tape are fed to a special machine which converts the encoding format to the CD standards and passes the resulting train of pulses to a source of laser light. The laser beam is focused on to a precision glass disc coated with a light-sensitive material. The spiralling track (starting at the inner radius rather than the outer edge as on a vinyl disc) therefore consists of an interrupted series of extremely brief exposures to the light, and the disc can be 'developed' in a process similar to that used in ordinary photography. The exposed areas are left as tiny pits in the light-sensitive coating. An alternative method of CD master disc production using a modified version of the Direct Metal Mastering process can also be employed.

Stage 6C: Compact Disc processing

In a sequence of processes which bears a superficial resemblance to that used in vinyl disc manufacture, the glass disc is first vacuum-coated with silver to make it electrically conducting. Several electroforming processes follow, as with vinyl, to produce:

(a) the *Master* (a negative, i.e. with bumps in place of pits);
(b) the *Mother* (a positive);
(c) the *Stamper* (a negative).

Each stamper can be used to press out several thousand (one-sided) Compact Discs.

The resulting disc or 'pressing' of clear polycarbonate is still a long way from being a playable object (unlike the finished disc which emerges from a vinyl press). First the pitted surface has to be overlaid with a very thin reflective layer of aluminium, which will be scanned by the laser beam in the CD player to reproduce the pulse stream by on/off reflection on to a light-sensitive detector. This coating is applied by vacuum deposition and must be followed by a further coating process (still under the strictest clean-air conditions) in which a protective layer of clear lacquer is spread over the aluminium surface as a seal against damage or dust. The CD is then suitably labelled, passed through quality control, and packaged.

What about video?

Rapid expansions in the realms of television and pre-recorded video have made it impossible for recording studios to plan for sound-only productions without some reference to the parallel video markets. The pop video has become a powerful (and relatively expensive) method of audio disc promotion. Most broadcasting companies invest more money, and employ more personnel, in TV than in sound radio. The record companies are having to plan for increased production of video albums not to mention the CD-Video format.

These trends are likely to accelerate as more and better domestic formats appear in people's homes, and as satellite and cable systems increase the consumer's access to improved-quality entertainment media of all kinds. The Audio Engineering Society, formerly a basically sound-only institution, has added video aspects to most of its convention programmes. Figure 1.3 shows, for example, the audio/video chain which it used to organize the sessions at its May 1986 conference on 'Stereo Audio Technology for Television and Video'. A comparison between this chain and Figures 1.1 and 1.2 is instructive, and explains the many references to video throughout this book—not least in Chapters 26 (television), 27 (video), and 28 (film).

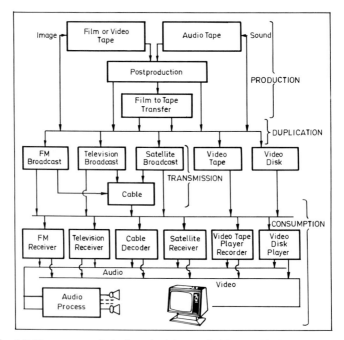

Fig. 1.3. Programme chain for television and video media (courtesy AES)

2

Basic electronics and acoustics
Allen Mornington-West

This chapter attempts to summarize some of the electrical and acoustical terms commonly found in the audio industry. There is not the space to cover any one item in depth, though there should be no great inaccuracy as a consequence.

Units

The basic units and symbols which make up the SI system of units (Système International d'Unités) are given in Appendix 1. The names of the units have often been derived from the names of past scientists and are in internationally agreed use. The wide range of values which these units may have requires an efficient scheme of notation. For example, the range of sound pressure levels (SPL) to which the human ear is sensitive extends to more than one million to one—from the threshold of hearing to the threshold of pain. Although the SPL at the threshold of hearing could be written as 0.000020 Pa, it is more usually written as 20 μ Pa. The μ stands for 'micro' and is a shorthand way of expressing the ratio of a millionth. The range of common multipliers is also given in Appendix 1. It can be seen that they rise in a ratio of a thousand to one.

Voltage, current, resistance, and power

Voltage is an electrical pressure in some ways analogous to the pressure of water, for example in a central heating system. Electrical current is thus analogous to the flow of water in such a system. The flow of electrical current is considered, by convention, to be from a positive voltage to a less positive one. In reality, the current in metal conductors is essentially the flow of small subatomic particles known as electrons. As these particles carry a negative charge, they will be attracted towards the more positive voltage, and thus move in a direction opposite to that in which the current is considered to flow.

Some circuit elements offer a high resistance to the flow of current (rather analogous to the use of thin pipes in a central heating system), whilst other elements will offer very little resistance. Some materials, for example most plastics, have such a high resistance to electrical current that they are referred to as insulators; this can be compared to the way that the pipes make sure that the water stays within them. Examples of good conductors (offering very low resistance) are most metals, the commonest being copper, the best being gold. In between these and the insulators are the materials such as carbon film, various metal oxides, and alloys of some metals (for example, nickel and chrome are used to produce nichrome resistance wire) which can be used to form resistors of a known value. Each of these materials has a range of properties (for example stability with respect to temperature, cost of manufacture, range of practical values) which affect their choice in a given application.

Ohm's Law, resistors in series and parallel

The relationship between voltage, current, and resistance is expressed by Ohm's Law:

$$V = I \times R$$

where V is the voltage (in volts) across the resistance R (in ohms) through which flows the current of I (amperes).

When resistors are placed in series in a circuit, that is to say the same current flows through each resistor (see Figure 2.1a), the total effective resistance is given by adding their resistances together. In the case of resistors in parallel, that is where the current is shared between the resistors (see Figure 2.1b), the effective resistance is given by taking the reciprocal of the sum of their conductances. Conductance (measured in siemens, symbol S) is simply the reciprocal of resistance and is the measure of how easily current flows. The proof of these relationships can be obtained through the use of Ohm's Law, bearing in mind that in the case of series resistors the current flowing through each resistor is the same and in the case of parallel resistors the voltage across each resistor is the same.

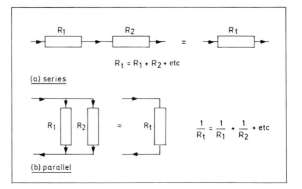

Fig. 2.1. Resistors (a) in series, (b) in parallel

As real conductors also exhibit some resistance, albeit small, it follows that the gauge of wire used for any particular purpose needs to be chosen with the current-carrying requirements borne in mind. Doubling the diameter of a conductor divides its resistance by a factor of four, and, for a given current, the voltage across a given length of conductor will fall by the same factor. The amount of resistance offered by different conductors is determined by their specific resistivity.

The resistance of real conductors (and resistors) is dependent additionally on temperature. For elemental metals the rise in resistance with temperature is, to a first approximation, linear: around 3000 parts per million per degree Celsius for copper, for example. Light bulbs, which generally use tungsten filaments, typically exhibit a cold resistance which is one-tenth of the resistance when fully working. Carbon, which is used in many resistor compositions, exhibits a falling resistance with a rise in temperature, typically 300 parts per million, but the value does depend on the process used to form the resistor.

Effects of electric current

There are two effects associated with the flow of electric current which should be noted here. The first is the *heating effect*, and the second is the formation of a *magnetic field*. The heat developed in a resistive load of R ohms having a voltage of V volts across it causing a current of I amps to flow is

$$P = V \times I \text{ watts}$$

Using Ohm's Law, this can also be written as

$$P = V^2/R \quad \text{or} \quad P = I^2 \times R$$

Heat is power, and is the measure of the rate of energy flow measured in joules/second. One joule will heat 0.24 g of water through 1° C. Note further that the power dissipated is independent of the direction of the current through the resistor.

The magnetic field which surrounds any conductor carrying current is used, for example, in moving coil meters where a lightweight coil is suspended in the fixed magnetic field produced from a permanent magnet. The strength of the magnetic field produced by the current flowing in the coil is dependent on the square of the number of turns of wire in the coil and linearly on the amount of current being passed through the coil. Most of the electromechanical meters use this magnetic effect of current. Therefore, when measuring the voltage in a circuit, the meter uses some of the current available from the circuit and thereby affects the reading. Similarly, using the meter to measure current involves a small voltage drop across the coil of the meter itself, and this too can affect the circuit. These are examples of loading effects. The ideal voltage meter would use negligible current for operation and the ideal current meter would cause a negligible voltage drop. If the meter is isolated from the circuit by appropriate buffering, then these ideals can be approached. If the voltage and current in a resistor can be measured, then the value of the resistance can be calculated from Ohm's Law.

Resistor marking

Resistors usually have their resistance value and manufacturing accuracy tolerance marked on them using a code of coloured bands (see Figure 2.2). Power and high-tolerance resistors usually have the value printed in numbers directly on the resistor. The colour code used is: 0 black, 1 brown, 2 red, 3 orange, 4 yellow, 5 green, 6 blue, 7 violet, 8 grey, 9 white.

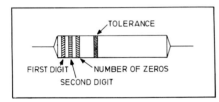

Fig. 2.2. Resistor colour codes

Practical power sources and loading

The currents which have been produced by the voltages referred to so far have been assumed to be unchanging with time. They are referred to as direct current (d.c.). A practical example of such a source of voltage is a battery. However, the battery cannot be taken as a model of a pure voltage generator. A simple model of a battery (see Figure 2.3) must include a small resistance (known as the battery's source resistance) in series with an ideal voltage source whose e.m.f. (electromotive force) is the voltage which would be measured by a meter which took no current from the battery during the measurement. The power which this battery can deliver into an external load is a maximum when the value of this load is equal to the source resistance. Half the available power is then dissipated in the external load and the other half heats up the battery. This is not the way that batteries or other power sources are usually operated but the principle is at the heart of what is referred to as impedance-matching.

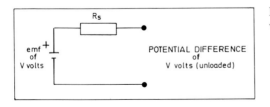

Fig. 2.3. Practical voltage source in which R_S is the source resistance

Alternating currents and voltages

Audio signals consist of voltages and currents which vary with time. The patterns of this variation (alternating currents or a.c.), if plotted against time, would provide a wide variety of waveshapes. Fortunately all waveshapes, however complex, can be considered as built out of sine waves (through the use of the Fourier series). Sine waves are easy to generate and are mathematically simple, and so it is sufficient to describe the response of a circuit to alternating currents by their use. The rate at which a sine waveshape repeats itself is known as its frequency (in cycles per second or hertz) and the time taken for one complete cycle is its period. Period is simply the reciprocal of frequency.

When an alternating voltage is applied to a resistor, the magnitude of the alternating current can be found using Ohm's Law. Similarly, the rules describing the series and parallel connection of resistors remain valid. In order that the power dissipated in a resistive load by an alternating current can be related to the same power developed by a d.c. source, the root-mean-square (r.m.s.) value is used. The r.m.s. value of a continuous sine wave is the square root of its peak value. Thus the r.m.s. value of a sine wave with a 2 V peak value is $\sqrt{2} = 1.414$ V.

An alternating voltage will not register a sensible reading on the usual electromechanical moving-coil meter, as the meter needle will simply twitch around the zero mark. Meters for direct indication of a.c. voltages do exist, such as moving-iron and thermocouple types. The method most often used involves converting the a.c. voltage into a d.c. one, through the use of a rectifier, and applying it to a conventional d.c. meter (see Figure 2.4). If this is all that is

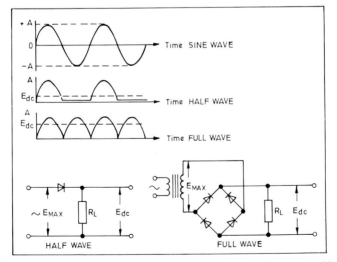

Fig. 2.4. Waveforms and circuit diagrams for half-wave and full-wave rectification of a sine wave

done, the meter indication will be that of the average value of the rectified signal and not the r.m.s value. Most general-purpose meters follow this principle and are usually calibrated to read the correct r.m.s. value for a sinusoid whilst responding to its average. For complex waveforms, quite severe errors can arise. Audio signals can be appreciably non-sinusoidal and may have crest factors of up to 10:1 (the crest factor is the ratio between the peak value of a signal and its average value). Figure 2.5 shows the relationship between the peak, r.m.s., and average values for a 10:1 square wave. The two commonest signal level meters used in audio, namely the volume unit (VU) meter and the peak programme meter (PPM), indicate approximately the average and the peak values of the audio signal respectively.

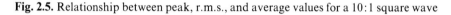

Fig. 2.5. Relationship between peak, r.m.s., and average values for a 10:1 square wave

Reactive components, capacitance, and inductance

Both capacitors and inductors can store energy and subsequently release it, capacitance as stress in a dielectric medium and inductance as flux in a permeable medium. At its simplest, a capacitor blocks d.c. whilst an inductor blocks a.c. Each will exhibit an impedance to electrical flow which depends on the frequency of the a.c. voltage applied and on the value of capacitance or inductance.

A simple capacitor can be thought of as two plates separated by a short distance (see Figure 2.6). The capacitance is dependent on the material between the plates, their area, and their separation. If a source of d.c. is connected to a capacitor value C via some value of resistor of value R, and the voltage across

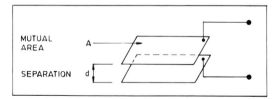

Fig. 2.6. Construction of an elementary capacitor: C is proportional to A/d

the capacitor is monitored, it will follow the form shown in Figure 2.7. The waveform of the current flow is the opposite. The current and voltage waveforms are thus not in step and the current is said to *lead* the voltage.

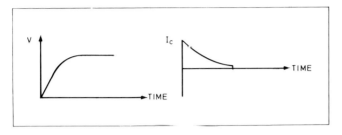

Fig. 2.7. Charging and discharging a capacitor

A similar state of affairs exists for inductors, and the waveform of the growth of current is similar to that for the growth of voltage in the case of capacitance. For an inductance the current *lags* the voltage (see Figure 2.8). A simple inductor can be considered as a coil of wire. The value of inductance is dependent on the square of the number of turns and the size of the coil. The changing magnetic flux caused by a changing current flowing through the coil creates a back e.m.f. in the coil. In a transformer a second coil shares this magnetic flux and thus develops an e.m.f. across its terminals. The magnitude of this secondary e.m.f. depends on the amount of the flux which is shared (the mutual inductance) and the ratio of the turns in the primary and secondary coils.

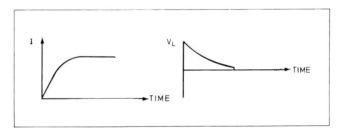

Fig. 2.8. Charging and discharging an inductor

Because the current and voltage waveforms of reactive components are not in phase, care is needed when working out their effective contribution to impedance in circuits. The contribution from a purely reactive element is known as reactance and is given the symbol X. The reactances, in ohms, of a capacitor and an inductor are:

$$X_C = \frac{1}{2\pi f C} \text{ for capacitance and } X_L = 2\pi f L \text{ for inductance.}$$

The expression $2\pi f$, where f is the frequency in hertz, is commonly replaced by ω (Greek omega).

In the case of a resistor and capacitor in series, it is clear that the same current must flow through both and that it must be in the same phase as the current going through the generator (see Figure 2.9). Therefore, in order that it is 90° ahead of the voltage across it, this voltage must lag that of the generator.

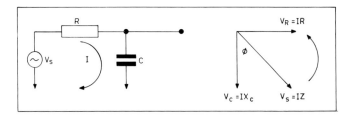

Fig. 2.9. Resistance and capacitance in series

The analysis of an inductance in series with a resistance is similar except that here, as the current in an inductor lags the voltage, and in order that the current through the resistor and the inductor should share the same phase it is necessary for the voltage across the inductor to lead the generator voltage.

Capacitances and inductances in series and parallel

The effect of joining capacitors in parallel is that of increasing the area of the capacitor plates. Thus

$$C_t = C_1 + C_2 + \text{etc.}$$

The net capacitance obtained by joining them in series is

$$\frac{1}{L_t} = \frac{1}{C_1} + \frac{1}{C_2} + \text{etc.}$$

and this can be appreciated by adding together their reactances in the same manner as performed for resistors in parallel. The total inductance obtained when inductors are placed in series is simply their sum:

$$L_t = L_1 + L_2 + \text{etc.}$$

and, in a similar fashion to resistors, the effective total inductance of a parallel connection is given by

$$\frac{1}{L_t} = \frac{1}{L_1} + \frac{1}{L_2} + \text{etc.}$$

When an inductance and a capacitance are placed in series or parallel, they form what is known as a tuned circuit (see Figure 2.10). The resonant frequency is the one where the reactances of the inductance and the capacitance are the same. It is given by

$$f = \frac{1}{2\pi\sqrt{LC}}$$

In the case of a series tuned circuit, the effective impedance at resonance tends to zero, and is limited only by the inevitable resistance involved in the windings of the inductance. A parallel tuned circuit has maximum impedance at resonance. There are good reasons for retaining tuned circuits in modern audio; indeed, some sound-balance technicians prefer the 'sound' of LC tuned circuit equalizers over the fully solid-state variety.

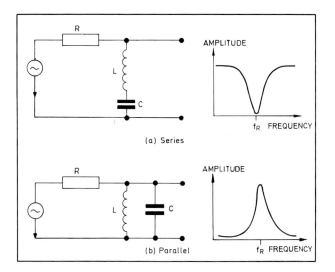

Fig. 2.10. Tuned circuits: (*a*) series, (*b*) parallel

Real components

All real components are in a sense impure. For example, a resistor can be better modelled as an ideal resistor in series with a small amount of inductance (due to the lead-out wires and the usually spiral shape of the resistance element itself), possibly shunted by (that is to say paralleled by) a small amount of stray capacitance. Real inductors are invariably accompanied by some resistance (due to the windings themselves) and by some self-capacitance; real capacitors may well be accompanied by a small amount of stray inductance, due mostly to the manner of manufacture. Just how important these stray effects will be depends on the frequency and accuracy at which the components are being used. Even a straight piece of wire has inductance and capacitance.

In addition, there will be other limitations placed on performance which reflect the materials and manufacturing methods used. Resistors come in a range of sizes and in a range of styles which fundamentally reflect their power-handling ability. Resistors can be considered, within their working range, as behaving linearly, and would seldom be suspected of being the cause of stray magnetic fields or of large amounts of distortion within, say, an amplifier.

Inductors intended to work in the audio band of frequencies (roughly from 20 Hz to 20 kHz) will use high-permeability core materials, such as ferrites and alloys of ferromagnetic metals, whose limit in terms of linear behaviour determines the maximum flux level which can exist in the core. The limit on the amount of power they can handle is in part controlled by the size of the core and the windings around it. A compromise is usually struck between weight and performance. In addition, audio-frequency inductors tend to be sensitive to stray magnetic fields, especially hum fields from mains power transformers.

There is a wide variety of materials and techniques used in capacitor manufacture. The maximum working voltage limit of capacitors is set by the ability of the dielectric to withstand the strain (dielectric strength). The dielectric is needed in order to multiply the 'open-air' value of capacitance, but dielectrics can be non-linear in a number of ways. The dielectric constant itself may be a function of the amount of electric stress in the capacitor, which usually varies with frequency. A dielectric material also tends to exhibit losses as the frequency is raised, thus causing the capacitor to increase its effective impedance. Finally, especially in both aluminium and tantalum electrolytic capacitors, the chemical processes employed during manufacture and the physics of the dielectric material itself (usually a metal oxide) can produce very small non-linear effects.

It is worth pointing out that a variety of effects can mar even the production of a satisfactory contact in a connector. Corrosion is the commonest cause of problems, and, although gold itself may be immune from attack by cigarette tar and spilt drinks, the congealed deposition certainly does not aid the process of creating proper electrical contact.

Logs and the decibel

It was pointed out above that the wide range of values which natural signals can take makes the use of a form of compressed notation desirable. A useful method of expressing powers is by the use of logarithms. The logarithm a of a positive real number x, with respect to a base b, can be expressed as $x = b^a$. The commonly used base is ten. The logarithm (abbreviated to log) of 1,000, for example, is 3. Adding logs is identical to multiplying together the two numbers which they represent (it is the principle behind the almost historic slide-rule), and subtracting logs is the same as division. As a negative logarithm represents a number less than one, and a positive logarithm a number greater than one, it can be seen that the log of one is zero, or, in other words, ten to the power of zero is one. Actually, any positive real number raised to the zeroth power is one.

The bel is a unit which expresses the ratio of two powers as a log (the base is assumed to be ten):

$$\text{Bel} = \log \frac{P_2}{P_1}$$

The bel turns out to be too large a unit in practice and so the decibel (dB) is defined as

$$\text{dB} = 10 \times \log \left(\frac{P_2}{P_1} \right)$$

Since the power delivered to a load can be expressed as $P = V^2/R$, then provided that the load (or source) resistances are identical the dB can be defined as

$$\text{dB} = 20 \times \log \left(\frac{V_2}{V_1} \right)$$

It is fundamentally an expression of the ratio of two power levels. In those environments where both the source and destination impedances are fixed at 600 ohms, the dB will still relate directly to a power ratio. However, since most measurements are performed on equipment and circuits whose output impedance is usually low (less than 100 ohms) and whose input impedance is reasonably high (greater than 10 k-ohms), and as (in addition to the difficulty of measuring power directly) the logarithmic scale is such a useful idea, it is usual within the audio industry to ignore this fact and to use the dB as an expression of voltage ratio. Thus a voltage ratio of 2:1 would be expressed as 6 dB, and so on. Table 2.1 shows how the first ± 10 dB relate to ratios. The dB always relates to ratios, and thus if we wish to use decibels to refer to an actual signal level we must agree upon a reference level. The level which is in common use in the audio industry relates to the voltage necessary to develop one milliwatt in a 600 ohm load (the unit is then referred to as dBm). This is 0.7746 volts, and the symbol dBu marks its use as a reference. It is worth commenting that other sections of the electronics industry use other references.

Gain (positive dB values) and attenuation (negative dB values) can now be expressed in decibels, and simple attenuating networks can be designed (see Figure 2.11). The simple resistor and reactance networks referred to above are examples of frequency-sensitive attenuators, and it is useful to bear in mind

TABLE 2.1. **Voltage ratios and the first ± 10 dB**

+dB	Gain ratio	−dB	Loss ratio
0	1.00	0	1.00
1	1.12	−1	0.89
2	1.26	−2	0.79
3	1.41	−3	0.71
4	1.58	−4	0.63
5	1.78	−5	0.56
6	2.00	−6	0.50
7	2.24	−7	0.45
8	2.51	−8	0.40
9	2.83	−9	0.36
10	3.16	−10	0.32

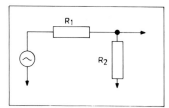

Fig. 2.11. A simple attenuator

that, at the frequency at which the reactance is equal to the resistance, the attenuation is 3 dB with respect to the input signal and the phase shift is 45°. These frequency-sensitive attenuators are better known as filters. High-pass filters block low frequencies whilst low-pass filters block high frequencies. Band-pass and band-stop filters can be simply realized by using resonant circuits.

It is important to realize that phase is related to the period of the signal and not directly to time. It is thus meaningless, for example, to consider that playing back a 1 kHz tone from a tape recorder one hour later is equivalent to 3.6 million degrees of phase shift! It, and the rest of the audio bandwidth of signals recorded at the same time, have simply been delayed. What might well be audible is the existence of any frequency-dependent non-uniformity in the delay (essentially this is group delay error, which does occur in analogue recordings). However, this error is sometimes expressed in phase terms when the response of complex filters is under discussion. The term 'linear phase response' implies that there is no group delay error within the system being discussed.

More about the transformer

A transformer cannot produce power gain; it merely handles the power available from the source connected to its input (usually referred to as the primary winding) and makes this available to a load connected to its output (the secondary winding). The ratio between the input and output voltages is dependent on the ratio of the turns, so a transformer with a turns ratio of, say, $N:1$ will produce an output voltage which is $1/N$ of the input. It will also reflect the impedance of the load on the secondary back to the primary so that, as far as the source signal is concerned, it sees a load whose value is N^2 times that of the secondary load. This is the property which is used in designing matching transformers, the aim being to make an input or an output impedance appear as a different value to some subsequent circuit or equipment. Any loss (or gain) in signal level can be corrected with an appropriate amplifier (or attenuator).

Transformers offer two other properties. The first is that of isolating the sending circuit from the receiving circuit (sometimes referred to as galvanic isolation). As the transformer primary and secondary circuits are insulated from each other, there is no direct connection between the two; thus there are no parts of the circuits which are common or shared. Most audio signals are referenced to a circuit's zero-volt rail (or its system ground), which is often, in turn, tied to mains earth. Equipments which share the same earth (or zero volt reference) should ideally be located close to each other.

The second property of a transformer is linked with the practice of balanced lines, and is its ability to reject common-mode signals (usually referred to as common-mode rejection ratio, CMRR). The two secondary output terminals can be thought of as providing a signal which is balanced about a centre point. This is sometimes an actual centre tap in the secondary of the transformer, as in a phantom microphone supply transformer, but commonly it is absent and the output signal from the transformer is considered as balanced and floating (floating because there is no connection from the centre tap to either send or receive zero reference). The advantage of operating a sound circuit in a balanced fashion, as distinct from a single-ended fashion (or unbalanced mode), is the much increased freedom from picking up unwanted electromagnetic interference due to stray signals coupling into the cable. This arises because, as any e.m.f. induced into the cable will be induced in the same polarity and magnitude into both of the cable's conductors, there will be no net resulting current in the circuit and thus no signal to be received at the secondary terminals of the receiving transformer. This rejection is not perfect, and it usually worsens with increasing frequency, partly because of capacitance effects within the transformer.

When designing and choosing transformers, it is necessary to bear in mind that the windings have resistance. The effect of this resistance can be taken into account by reflecting it (using the square or the reciprocal of the square of the transformer turns ratio, as appropriate), in order to lump both primary and secondary winding resistances as a single output resistance in series with the output of an ideal transformer. In addition to losses in the winding resistance, there are further losses due to eddy currents and hysteresis in the magnetically permeable core, which tend to increase with frequency.

Active devices

Most of the audio circuitry in use today is designed using semiconductor devices. Certain circuits still require the use of discrete devices, whilst others can utilize some of the many excellently performing integrated circuits (ICs) currently available. Much audio circuit design can be considered as broken down into a series of amplifier units (sometimes referred to as op-amps), and, although a detailed summary of discrete circuit design techniques is out of place here, a comment on the two commonest connections of the op-amp may be helpful (see Figure 2.12). The op-amp is not a universal panacea, because few practical op-amp realizations match the performance required of the ideal op-amp. The ideal is assumed to have infinite open loop gain (the gain when there is no negative feedback in use), infinitely high input impedance, infinitely low output impedance, negligible noise and distortion, and so on. One of the important parameters of an op-amp for handling audio signals is related to its frequency response, and this is its slew rate performance.

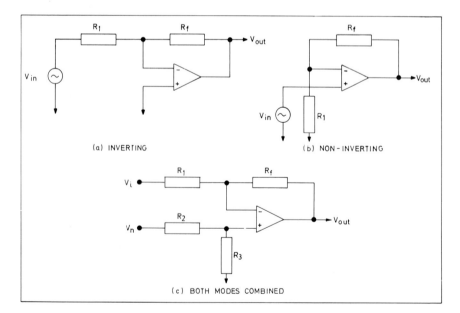

Fig. 2.12. Op-amp connections: (a) inverting, (b) non-inverting, (c) both modes combined

Noise

Any electrical noise present at the input to a mixing console will be amplified along with the required signal, and it is therefore desirable to keep this noise as low as possible. Desk designers usually arrange to place as much initial gain as possible in the first amplifier stage, and thus it is the noise performance of this which sets the limit on the system performance. In practice, all the usual real signal sources can be modelled as a generator in series with a source resistance, and it is the self-noise of this source resistance which sets the lower practical design limit. A good front-end design for a microphone pre-amplifier will increase this noise by only a small amount; a figure less than 1 dB would be considered very good, whilst a figure of up to 3 dB could be considered reasonable. In many practical situations of microphone use, the noise generated at the microphone output by the ambient acoustic noise of the recording environment will greatly exceed the self-noise of the microphone's source resistance. The self-noise of a resistor can be calculated, and is given by

$$E_{n.r.m.s.} = \sqrt{4kTBR}$$

where $E_{n.r.m.s.}$ is the r.m.s. noise voltage, k is Boltzmann's constant ($1.38\ 10^{-23}$), T is the temperature in degrees Kelvin, B is the bandwidth over which the noise is being calculated, R is the resistance in ohms.

For example, a 200 ohm source will have a self-noise of -129.7 dBu, and this will be gaussian (or equal-energy) white noise. Various weighting curves have been devised in order to relate the spectral characteristics of noise to the way in which the ear perceives it as annoying. Electrical noise measurements are usually carried out using the IEC468 (or CCIR) curve in conjunction with a quasi-peak-indicating metering system. It has been determined empirically that this approach produces a reading some 12.8 dB greater than that of the unweighted r.m.s. measurement. In calculating the noise the bandwidth is assumed to be sharply defined. In practice this is seldom achievable, and it can be shown that, providing the noise has a truly gaussian distribution of amplitudes, the effect of defining the bandwidth with first-order filters only is to increase the noise voltage measured by 1.96 dB.

Introduction to acoustics

Why do we bother with acoustics? The reason is that some characteristics of the sounds we hear are desirable and others are not. Thus we concern ourselves with isolation, room colouration, reverberation, mechanical rattles, and so on. But that's just the room. The study of acoustics also affects the design of the acoustic transducers, the microphones and the loudspeakers and their associated enclosures, their efficiency, their faithfulness, and to a lesser degree their individual foibles and characteristics. In order to appreciate some of the subtleties of the art we need to take a brief look at some of the ideas and terms used in the field of acoustics.

The nature of sound

Surrounding all of us on this earth is an atmosphere, mostly made up of nitrogen and oxygen. Although a gas, it still has has mass, and under the influence of gravitational pull this mass of air exerts a pressure which at sea level is approximately 100 kPa (15 pounds per square inch). The sounds which we hear are the result of very small variations in this static atmospheric pressure. These sound pressure changes travel through the air and can be referred to as sound waves. Note that it is the wave, or the disturbance in the atmosphere, which travels through the air. The successive compressions and rarefactions which comprise the longitudinal pressure wave essentially leave each particle of air in the same place after its passing. This mode of wave propagation is known as a longitudinal wave, and, by comparison, a wave travelling over the surface of water, as when a stone is dropped in a pond, is known as a transverse wave. We can appreciate this idea better if we consider the compressions and rarefactions found when a simple piston reciprocates in a tube (see Figure 2.13).

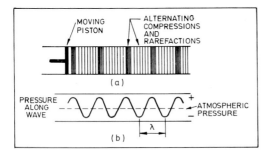

Fig. 2.13. Plane waves propagated along a tube (*a*) as an alternating air pressure (*b*) of wavelength λ

The speed of sound in a gas is dependent on the pressure and density of that gas:

$$c = \frac{\sqrt{1.4P}}{\rho}$$

where P is the atmospheric pressure, ρ is the density of air, c is the velocity in m/s.

Temperature also affects the speed, and, for air, the following relationship holds:

$$c = 332\sqrt{(1 + T/273)}$$

where T is the temperature in degrees Celsius.

For audio purposes the frequency range of interest is from 20 Hz to 20 kHz, a range of some ten octaves which covers acoustic wavelengths from 17 m to 17 mm. The wavelength, frequency, and velocity of sound are related:

$$c = f\lambda$$

where f is the frequency and λ is the wavelength.

Many a practical sound source can be considered, at least to an acceptable approximation, as a point source, or monopole, producing spherical acoustic waves (see Figure 2.14). The necessary approximation is that the dimensions of

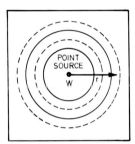

Fig. 2.14. A pulsating point source radiates spherical waves whose intensity falls off with distance according to the 'Inverse Square Law'

the sound source are small with respect to the wavelength of the sound being emitted. The direction of propagation is away from the centre of the sphere, unlike the plane wave of Figure 2.13 which travels in one direction only. The sound intensity from a point source depends on the distance from its centre:

$$I = \frac{W}{4\pi r^2}$$

where I is the intensity in W/m^2
  W is the acoustic power of the source
  r is the distance from its centre.

This 'Inverse Square Law' can be expressed as the SPL decreasing by 6 dB each time the distance from the source is doubled.

The combination of two monopoles back to back, but 180° out of phase (an unbaffled or open-backed loudspeaker, for example) gives rise to an acoustic dipole (see Figure 2.15). The dipole illustrates simple acoustic interference effects, as it is clear that, along the axis normal to the line joining the two sources, the soundfield produced by one of the monopole sources is cancelled by that produced by the other. More complex examples of the effect of constructive

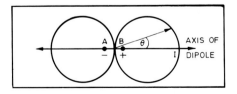

Fig. 2.15. The formation of a dipole source from two spaced monopoles (or point sources) A and B 180° out of phase. Intensity at any angle θ is $I \cos \theta$

and destructive interference are its use in acoustic lenses and its presence as an undesirable effect when sound waves are refracted and when discrete reflections cause interference with the direct wanted sounds. The extra complexities are due to the real environment where there are acoustic obstructions which prevent a true free field from existing.

Measuring sound

The easiest descriptor of the intensity of a sound which we can measure is its sound pressure. Other pointers to a sound's intensity, such as the magnitude of particle movement or particle velocity, are best arrived at by measuring the sound pressure. The amplitudes of particle movement for the range of audible sounds is quite small and spans the range from a few mm for loud sounds (which are likely to cause damage to the ear) down to movements of 100 pm (pico-metre), which are associated with sounds at the limit of audibility. We can express the ratio of two sound pressures using the dB, and we can use a dB scale as an absolute scale (thus defining the sound pressure level or SPL) if we first define an acceptable reference. The quietest sounds which can usually be sensed by the average young adult are around 20 μPa, and this sound pressure is used as a reference level. Figure 2.16 gives some idea as to how SPLs are related to some common sound sources.

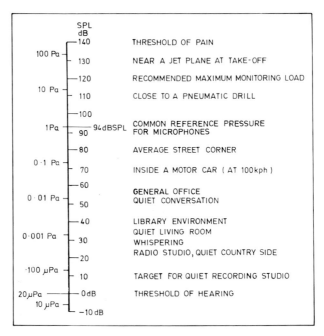

Fig. 2.16. Sound pressure levels for various typical sources

If we consider SPL to be analogous to voltage and the resultant particle velocity analogous to current, then it is understandable that there will also be acoustic impedance (the impedance of air is around 415 rayls). For any other than a plane progressive wave, this impedance will possess a reactive part, and this also implies that there will be acoustic analogues of inductance and capacitance. This becomes important in loudspeaker design, for example, where full consideration needs to be given to the proper acoustic loading of drive units. This is especially so in the design of horn-loaded enclosures where the high pressure changes (accompanied by small movements of air) are transformed to small pressure movements (and large movements of air) at the mouth of the horn.

The vented cabinet is a particular application of the Helmholtz resonator, in which the natural resonant frequency of the enclosure is designed to assist the drive unit's efficiency at low frequencies. It has the disadvantage that, at frequencies below this resonance, the drive unit is essentially not loaded and may be prone to damage from very low-frequency signals. In the case of a simple Helmholtz resonator (see Figure 5.9 in Chapter 5) the resonant frequency is given by

$$f = \left(\frac{c}{2\pi}\right)\sqrt{\frac{S}{lV}}$$

where V is the volume of the cavity (m³)
$\quad l$ is the length of the neck (m)
$\quad S$ is the cross-sectional area of the neck (m²).

Loudness

Difficulties arise when describing the loudness of a sound. Loudness is a subjective characteristic largely due to the ear's decidedly non-linear response to both level and frequency. Both the phon (a phon is the level numerically equal to the intensity level of a 1,000 Hz tone that is judged equally loud) and the sone (a sone is equal to the loudness of any sound having the loudness level of 40 phons) are encountered in subjective measurements.

Energy

An acoustic wave contains energy (the amount of energy crossing unit area normal to the direction of propagation in unit time is defined as the intensity). As ever, it can be expressed in dB provided that there is a suitable reference level ($10^{-12} W/m^2$ is used by convention). A large orchestra produces around 10 W and a whisper around 1 nW, and it is not surprising that the 50 MW produced by a Saturn rocket is damaging to the ear! The measurement of sound power is not a simple matter and it requires measurement of both SPL and particle velocity, generally using a special twin-microphone technique.

Acoustic noise measurements

In making measurements of acoustic noise, account is taken of the ear's frequency response by the use of various weighting curves. The curve most in use within the studio environment is the A-weighting curve (see Figure 2.17), whose results are quoted in dB(A). It bears resemblance to the mirror image of

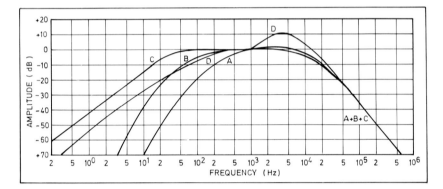

Fig. 2.17. Standard weighting curves for sound level measurements. Curve *A* is the one most used in studio acoustics work

the ear's response at around 55 phons and is the most commonly used where a single figure describing noise is acceptable. However, a single-figure result gives no detail as to the frequency composition of the noise, and a more detailed description requires the use of octave or even third-octave filters in the measurement circuit. Measurements thus obtained may be then compared to particular performance requirements, such as those embodied in noise rating (NR) and noise criterion (NC) curves.

Continual exposure to high SPLs and to high levels of impulsive noise (for example) can give rise to significant hearing impairment, the degree of which depends on the overall exposure. In essence, the damage rises rapidly for exposure to levels above around 90 dB for a significant fraction of a day. To express the exposure, the Leq is defined as the equivalent steady sound level (in dB(A)) which would produce the same A-weighted sound energy over a stated period of time (usually 8 hours) as the time-varying sound. For example, the 90 dB Leq limit would be reached in 4 hours at a SPL of 96 dB, and at 120 dB an exposure of only 15 minutes is needed.

Real rooms

Real rooms contain surfaces which are neither perfect reflectors nor perfect absorbers of sound. Thus the sound from a sound source may bounce around the walls of the room many times before its SPL has died to inaudibility. This is the essence of reverberation. The ear appears to take reflections occurring within the first 30 ms or so of the direct sound as enhancing the level of the source sound, whereas sounds occurring after some 50 ms tend to be discerned as discrete reflections or echoes. The detailed structure of these reflections gives each acoustic environment its particular character.

Reverberation

After the ambient noise level, the reverberation time of a room is perhaps its most important characteristic. Reverberation time (RT) is defined as the time taken for a steady-state sound to die down to one-thousandth (-60 dB) of its initial steady-state SPL when the source energy is cut. The decay is usually linear when plotted using a logarithmic scale for amplitude and a linear one for time. The RT of a room does not necessarily indicate how the room will sound, as there is no simple figure of merit which can be relied on. The traces obtained in making RT measurements do need to be carefully interpreted, and, with the appropriate techniques, many of the room's acoustic mechanisms can be investigated.

Conventionally, reverberation time measurements are made by exciting a room with band-limited pink noise (see Figure 2.18). (Pink noise is noise whose energy content is inversely proportional to frequency thus giving rise to a 3 dB/

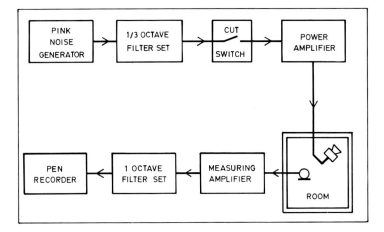

Fig. 2.18. Usual pen plotting arrangement for measuring reverberation time

octave or 10 dB/decade slope, whereas white noise is a broad band noise with constant energy per unit of frequency.) The noise is shut off and a high-speed pen plotter used to plot the logarithm of the decay envelope of the sound. A special protractor is used from which the slope of the decay can be read directly as RT. The trouble is that, with isolated pen traces, the consistent patterns in room behaviour are hard to spot and most usually go unnoticed. Methods which average successive traces at each given frequency produce decay traces in which the random elements of room behaviour are averaged out and the dominant patterns become more prominent. The technique, employed in tools like the IBA ARK (Automated Reverberation Kit) and the BBC ART (Automatic Reverberation Timer), can be useful in unravelling misbehaviour in the room's far reverberant field.

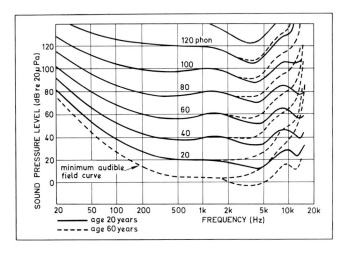

Fig. 2.19. Equal loudness contours for pure tones (Robinson and Dadson)

There are techniques which allow examination of the clusters of initial reflections which come from the surfaces of various objects, and features of the room close to the path between loudspeaker and listener. Haas showed that reflections of a sound which arrived at the ear within 30 ms (and usually at a similar level) were integrated in the ear and, as a consequence, were perceived as part of one louder sound. On the other hand, reflections which arrived later tended to be perceived as discrete reflections (Haas Effect). The techniques employed in time-delay spectrometry (TDS) allow analysis of such reflections, with the result that it is often possible to identify the group of early reflections which may be causing problems. The room radius is defined as the distance from the sound source where the level of the source sound (which merges with that from the reflections) and the reverberant field are equal.

The ear

The ear is a remarkable sensor: it can withstand sound pressures above 10 Pa and yet still detect pressures as low as 10 μPa. At such low levels, the movement of the ear drum (in the ear's most sensitive frequency range of 1 kHz to 5 kHz) is around 10^{-11} m, approximately 10 pm (picometer) or around a tenth of the diameter of a hydrogen molecule. However, the ear's frequency response is not flat, and it also varies considerably with SPL. This is usually expressed in the Robinson–Dadson or Fletcher–Munson curves (see Figure 2.19). The biology of the mechanism of human hearing appears to be very complex, and the models which have been invoked in the many hypotheses do not fully account for all the ear's abilities. The ear is not simply a frequency-selective sensor, and its analytical power appears to be neurologically distributed.

3

Digital theory

Allen Mornington-West

The analogue signal

The sounds which we hear come to the ear as a continuously changing variation in the ambient atmospheric pressure. These small changes are the very ones which we aim to pick up using a microphone. The output of the microphone is an electrical signal (voltage) which is related to the pressure changes which move the microphone diaphragm. This signal is thus an analogue of the originating pressure changes, and hence it is referred to as an analogue (sometimes spelt analog) signal. The principal characteristic of an analogue signal is that it is continuous in time and that there are thus no discontinuities. Indeed, if we use a conventional oscilloscope to trace out the shape of the signal's size or amplitude with respect to time then we might see something such as Figure 3.1. This trace we would refer to as its wave shape. We can

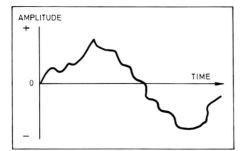

Fig. 3.1. Complex wave shape typical of music, speech, or noise signals. Notice that time is drawn along the horizontal axis and signal amplitude on the vertical axis

contrast this shape with the mathematically much simpler one of a sine wave, as in Figure 3.2.

It is conventionally and conveniently claimed that the bandwidth of frequencies occupied by analogue audio signals covers the range from 20 Hz to 20 kHz. This range of frequencies might appear to be quite generous, as there are a great many satisfied listeners with medium-wave radio receivers. Yet such receivers rarely have a bandwidth extending beyond 3 kHz, and those with responses 3 dB down at 1 kHz are far from uncommon! It is worth commenting that even modern pop music has progressively less amplitude at higher frequencies (see Figure 3.3).

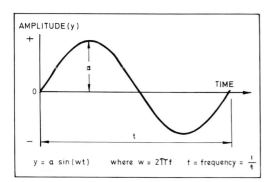

Fig. 3.2. The sine-wave shape typical of a single-frequency electronic oscillator or tuning-fork. The sine function is a repetitive one with a period of $t = 1/f$

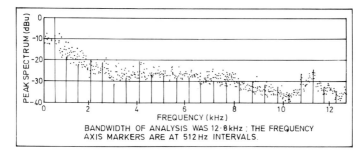

Fig. 3.3. Typical peak spectrum of pop music (first two tracks of the Dire Straits CD *Brothers in Arms*). The peak spectrum is a plot of the maximum amplitude in each of the 12.8 Hz frequency bands

Analogue processing

The simplest control over an analogue signal is probably amplitude control by a fader. A fader acts as a multiplier, and if the value that the fader represents is less than one (less than unity) then the signal at its output will be attenuated. We shall see the consequences of this later when we consider simple digital signal processing. Of course a fader acts on the whole bandwidth of the signal uniformly. If we wish to alter the balance of frequency components in the analogue signal, we must use the reactive components referred to in Chapter 2. For example, a simple low-pass filter (Figure 3.4) clearly has the capacitive element acting as a frequency-dependent attenuator, and it might thus be correctly suspected that we shall again need to use multipliers in order to create filtering action when working on the audio signal in the digital domain.

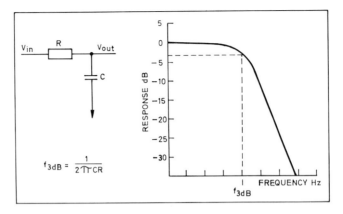

Fig. 3.4. A simple analogue low-pass filter and its response. The -3 dB point is at a frequency of $f=\frac{1}{2}\pi CR$, and the response falls off at a rate of 6 dB per octave (20 dB per decade)

Whilst we are still in the analogue domain, it is worth noting some typical figures concerning dynamic range and distortion. For studios we can note that current quiet studios can have a background noise characteristic close to NR15 (see Chapter 5). Although it is important to note that the spectrum of the noise is very bass-heavy, the NR15 curve does imply that the SPL around the 1 kHz octave is about 15 dB. This is quieter than most studio microphone and pre-amplifier combinations, whose output noise (when related to SPL) is around 30 dB. This does not set an absolute lower limit of audibility because the human ear has the ability to detect the presence of musical noises when they are well below the wide-band noise level. By comparison, the loud noises encountered in the act of recording might lie at sound levels of 130 dB. If a margin of 20 dB is allowed for future improvements in technology and acoustics, the total acoustic dynamic range is of the order of 120 dB. A professional analogue sound recorder might, under similar considerations, display a dynamic range of some 65 dB prior to the application of noise reduction. The use of noise reduction could add up to 25 dB to this figure, thus producing a total dynamic range of 90 dB. The third major limiting item in the studio environment is the mixing desk. Its dynamic range is greatly determined by the number of channels being summed and their gain: 32 channels set to the same gain can be expected to add at least 15 dB to the noise floor of a mixing desk, if the output gain is left untouched. Should all those channels be active with different signals passing through each, then the output level will also rise by 15 dB. If channels which are not in use are muted (good practice) then the dynamic range of the signal from the desk is independent of the number of channels available and could be around 110 dB.

The digital signal

The digital signal is a representation of the analogue signal by a string of numbers. The numbers will, in their turn, be represented by groups of pulses, and this method of describing a signal is one of the types of pulse code modulation (PCM). Early theoretical work on aspects of PCM dates from the late 1930s, and a comprehensive evaluation, arising from work carried out at Bell Telephone Laboratories, was published in 1948 by Oliver, Pierce, and Shannon.

The essence of the digitizing process is the deriving of the strings of numbers through the twin processes of sampling and quantizing. Sampling is rather like freezing the signal at a moment in time, and is the process which results in what is called the 'discrete signal', because the signal has been caught at a discrete point in time. Quantizing, which is a process applied to this frozen signal, is like measuring the size of the signal to the nearest whole number of measurement units. These processes, of stopping the signal and measuring it, are accompanied by effects and limitations of the practical world, and it will be worth taking a brief look at some of the more important of these.

Sampling

A simplified diagram of a typical sampling circuit is shown in Figure 3.5. The three elements of the sampling circuit are the switch, a capacitor in which to

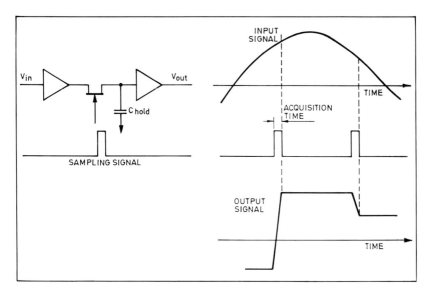

Fig. 3.5. Simplified sampling circuit and the associated wave shapes

store the sample, and a buffer amplifier. The switch is usually a FET, but a common technique for high-speed sampling uses a diode bridge arrangement. At the instant of sampling, the switch is closed and the value of the input analogue signal is applied to the capacitor. A very short time later, the switch is opened. The capacitor voltage should now be that at the instant of sampling, and the output of the buffer amplifier is a usable copy of it.

The simplest way to reconstruct the signal would be to arrange that the points representing the samples are simply joined up (Figure 3.6). However, should the rate of sampling with respect to the signal frequency be reduced, we shall approach the rate at which the number of samples per input cycle is not enough to describe the input signal adequately. Figure 3.7 shows the situation close to the limit, where the sampling rate (f_s) is a little more than twice the input signal rate. If the samples took place at say the zero crossing of the signal, then there would be no net output.

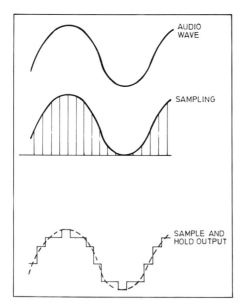

Fig. 3.6. A well-sampled waveform

Figure 3.8a shows the situation when f_s is less than twice the input signal rate. In Figure 3.8b it can be seen how a reconstructed waveform would appear at a different sampling frequency. This illustration of the limit of the sampling rate is the essence of Shannon's sampling theorem. Signal frequencies which are greater than $f_s/2$ will appear folded back into the spectrum occupied by the wanted signal (this is the essence of Nyquist's theorem). These are called aliases, and, once they have been created, they are indistinguishable from the wanted

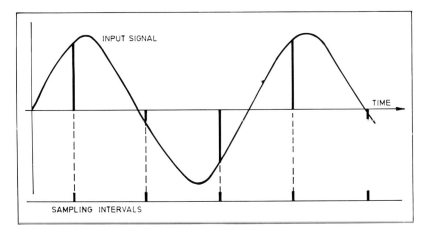

Fig. 3.7. A waveform sampled at just more than twice the input signal frequency

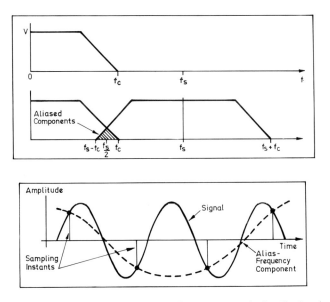

Fig. 3.8. Sampling at less than twice the signal frequency results in aliasing (overlapping of higher-order spectra) and produces a low-frequency sinusoid or alias-frequency component

signal and cannot be removed. Thus it is necessary to remove all frequencies greater than $f_s/2$. Limitations of filter design (principally the difficulty of producing an infinitely fast cut-off rate) dictate that, for practical purposes, the sampling rate is a little more (10–25 per cent) than twice the required bandwidth.

This folding back, or aliasing, can be viewed from another angle. It is necessary to recognize that the ideal sampling waveform has a spectrum which extends to infinity (Figure 3.9). As the process of sampling is similar to multiplying the signal by the sampling waveform, the spectrum of the result (Figure 3.10) will also be repetitive. The requirement for the sampling rate to

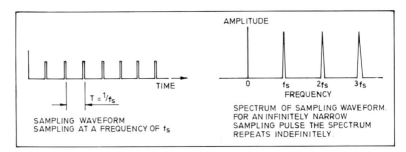

Fig. 3.9. Waveform and spectrum of a sampling signal

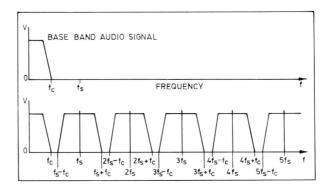

Fig. 3.10. Spectrum of a sampled signal

be at least twice the signal frequency can be seen as the need to avoid the difference frequency sideband, $f_s - f_c$, from entering the part of the spectrum occupied by the original signal. A more visual example of the creation of aliases is the appearance of backwards-rotating spoked wheels in cinema Westerns, as the stage-coach pulls away.

There is a tight constraint on the length of time (acquisition time) which can be taken in gathering each sample if it is to be considered accurate (shown in Figure 3.11 as total aperture error). An even tighter restriction is placed on the variation in time (aperture uncertainty) between successive sampling points. For a 20 kHz sine wave (arguably representing the worst case of a full amplitude signal at the top of the audio band) the acquisition time will usually be around 1 μs in order not to incur a large aperture loss, and the aperture uncertainty less

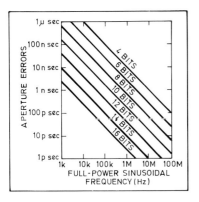

Fig. 3.11. Allowable aperture errors

than 80 ps if the signal is to be sampled to an accuracy of one part in 100,000 of the full-scale value. Other sources of error within the sampling process are due to the switching transient, feedthrough of the applied signal, droop of the sampled signal on the storage capacitor after the sampling switch has opened, dielectric storage performance of the storage capacitor, and so on.

Despite these sources of error, it is not the sampling process which is responsible for the overall noise and distortion performance in high-quality audio systems, as we shall see later. Further, a full-scale signal at the top of the band is an exceedingly rare, and probably unmusical, signal. Plots of the spectrum of musical signals indicate that the level of audio components at around 20 kHz is generally more than 30 dB lower than the level within the first 500 Hz of the audio band (see again Figure 3.3).

To reconstruct the signal, one could present it to a suitable low-pass filter which would remove all of the higher-frequency components. Alternatively, the sampled value can be held in what is called a zero-order hold circuit, until the next sample is supplied, following this stage with an appropriate low-pass filter. The consequence of forming this series of pulses from the samples is that the spectrum of the input signal is modified by a $\sin(x)/x$ shape (Figure 3.12), which

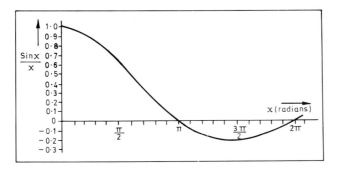

Fig. 3.12. Shape of the sin $(x)/x$ curve

effectively causes a linear phase roll-off of the sampled signal of about 4 dB at a frequency of $f_s/2$. The steps in this waveform, and the sin $(x)/x$ loss, can be dealt with by the low-pass filter. In order to recover the signal fully from the sampled waveform, the ideal response of this filter has an impulse response as shown in Figure 3.13.

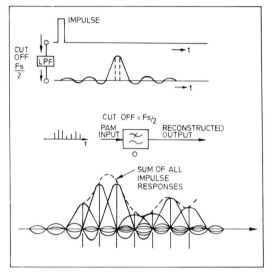

Fig. 3.13. Ideal reconstruction filter impulse response. Each impulse is converted to a sin $(x)/x$ wave and these are added in the filter to produce the continuous output (a sequence of pulse amplitude modulated impulses)

However, proper reconstruction will occur only if the input to the filter is a train of impulses of negligible width (and thus infinitesimally small energy). Under these conditions, the succession of impulses from the filter will add up to reconstitute the original waveform. However, real-world samples have finite duration (and finite energy) and are usually lengthened to last for some fraction of the sample period. The result is an aperture loss shown, for some common values of aperture ratio, in Figure 3.14. It is not necessary to make up for sin $(x)/x$ loss by analogue filtering since there is a clever way of doing this digitally, which is used in some Compact Disc players. This is part of the reason why aperture correction for d/a converters is not performed at the encoding stage.

Quantizing

Perhaps the easiest way to understand the operation of a quantizer is to apply a linear ramp to a converter and examine the resulting digital output (Figure 3.15). Notice that, as the input rises, the output goes up in steps and so the

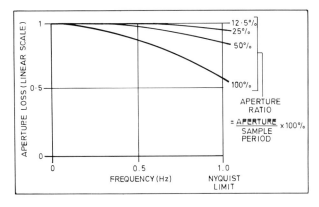

Fig. 3.14. Plots of aperture loss against aperture ratio

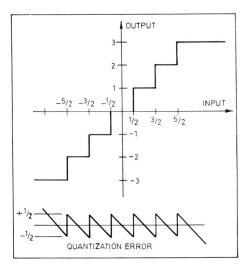

Fig. 3.15. Quantizing: showing a linear ramp's quantized output and its quantization error

difference between input and output takes on a saw-tooth shape. This error is referred to as quantization error (also called quantization noise, granular noise, or distortion). The error can be reduced by increasing the fineness of the steps, but there are limits to the fineness of resolution which can be imposed—if not by cost then by technology. The error is really a distortion, as it is correlated, in a complex manner, to the input signal. Figure 3.16 shows the error associated with quantizing a sine wave, and it is clear that, at least by eye, the error waveform, though complex, is well related to the originating signal. It is only for complex signals that the correlations in the errors approach a randomness similar to that of noise and the term quantization noise can be properly used.

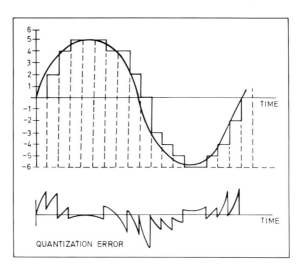

Fig. 3.16. Waveform of the quantization error for a sine wave

A particularly annoying instance of high quantization noise occurs when a very low-level signal is just crossing the first quantization level. If the signal were a sine wave, then the output from the quantizer would be a square wave. All the higher harmonics could then be called distortion components. This performance is particularly annoying when low-level, low-frequency tones decay into the noise. They are accompanied at first by noise, and as they decay towards the minimum quantizable level the noise progressively becomes more correlated to the input signal and thus noticeable as distortion. Luckily there is a neat trick which can improve matters without requiring a potentially expensive increase in the quantizer's resolution. It involves the addition of random noise to the signal about to be quantized, at a level such that its peak-to-peak amplitude is approximately one quantizing level. This noise 'dithers' the input signal so that the output is no longer a square wave (Figure 3.17). In a digital audio system this approach leads to a loss of some 4 dB in dynamic range, but it does result, paradoxically, in the pleasurable existence of the audio signal below the system noise floor.

So far the quantizers have been assumed to be linear, that is an n per cent change in input results, give or take the quantizing error, in an n per cent change in output. Non-linear quantizers are in use, particularly in telephony but also in some domestic audio equipment.

Numbering

So far we have considered the quantizing process but without stating what sort of numbers we shall be using. The most useful number scheme to use is

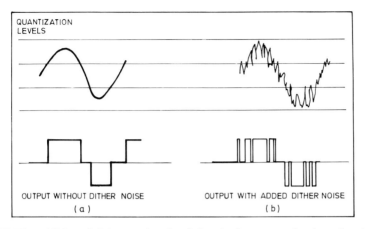

Fig. 3.17. The addition of dither to a low-level signal prior to quantization: showing (*a*) a sine wave around one quantization level in amplitude and its quantized output; (*b*) the same but with dither noise added to the sine wave

undoubtedly a binary one, counting using the base of two. The binary scheme is useful because the two possible digits, 1 and 0, can be represented in many ways. They can also be respectively described as on and off, high and low, true and not true, mark and space, and so on. As there are only two digits, counting up presents very little problem as the rules are simple:

1. Adding two zeros produces a zero
2. Adding a one and a zero produces a one
3. Adding two ones produces a zero and a one to carry into the next column.

Table 3.1 shows the counting sequence for a straight binary count from zero through to 8, and for some of the commoner coding schemes.

However, a pure binary count has no provision for negative numbers, and there does need to be some provision because the audio signal, with which we are concerned, can take on values that range from negative through to positive. Thus we need some way of describing a negative number. We could do this by setting a sign bit for negative numbers at the most significant bit (msb) position (Table 3.1(*b*)), but there will then be two numbers which represent the zero state. Or we could do it by setting the msb for all positive numbers which will make the most negative number in the series zero. This scheme, called 'offset binary' (Table 3.1(*d*)), has a drawback when it comes to signal processing. For example, adding two negative numbers together could result in a positive number!

The scheme adopted is called 'twos complement' (Table 3.1(*c*)) and is similar to the offset binary code except that the msb has been inverted. Twos complement code offers a very simple method of performing subtraction by the

TABLE 3.1. **Binary Counting Codes**

(a) Signed decimal	(b) Binary plus sign	(c) Twos complement	(d) Offset binary	(e) Grey code	(f) Unsigned decimal	(g) Hexadecimal notation
7	0111	0111	1111	1000	15	F
6	0110	0110	1110	1001	14	E
5	0101	0101	1101	1011	13	D
4	0100	0100	1100	1010	12	C
3	0011	0011	1011	1110	11	B
2	0010	0010	1010	1111	10	A
1	0001	0001	1001	1101	9	9
0 / −0	{ 0000 / 1000 }	0000	1000	1100	8	8
−1	1001	1111	0111	0100	7	7
−2	1010	1110	0110	0101	6	6
−3	1011	1101	0101	0111	5	5
−4	1100	1100	0100	0110	4	4
−5	1101	1011	0011	0010	3	3
−6	1110	1010	0010	0011	2	2
−7	1111	1001	0001	0001	1	1
−8	—	1000	0000	0000	0	0

tidy method of adding the negative of the number to be subtracted. There are many ways of forming the twos complement of a number, but the one which is most used in digital arithmetic is performed by taking the ones complement (inverting each bit in the number) and adding a one to the least significant bit (lsb) position. Interestingly, reconversion to an offset binary number requires the same process.

Another coding scheme which is commonly found in digital audio systems is called the 'Grey code' (Table 3.1(e)). In this code the counting is arranged so that at each count only one of the bit positions changes state. This code finds extensive use in control position sensors and shaft encoders, where it is essential that the inevitable skew of a mechanical assembly is not responsible for any miscounting.

In a linear code, each bit position can be thought of as marking the presence (or absence, if it is a zero) of a power of two. Thus in Table 3.1 column 2 (counting the lsb column as zero) marks the presence of 2^2, that is whether there is a four in the overall binary number. Similarly, column 1 marks the number of 2^1, or two. Finally, the zeroth column marks the presence or not of 2^0, or one. Thus each extra bit position which is used doubles the range of numbers which can be expressed. For an n-bit system the maximum signal-to-noise ratio (r.m.s.

signal to r.m.s. noise) is given by:

$$SNR[r.m.s.]dBu = 6n + 1.8$$

A 16-bit linear system can thus produce a dynamic range of 97.8 dB, assuming that everything is perfect. For reasons such as the addition of dither and imperfections within the conversion process, a practical value of SNR is of the order of 92 dB. As the use of the CCIR 468 weighting filter worsens noise measurements by about 8.6 dB and the use of a PPM-type meter worsens the noise measurement by around 4.2 dB, the dynamic range (measured weighted using a PPM-type meter) could be quoted as 85 dB. This is comparable to the dynamic range achieved by a high-quality analogue tape system relying on noise reduction systems.

Arithmetic

Figure 3.18 illustrates some simple sums in twos complement binary arithmetic. Note that, because only four bit positions have been defined, any carries have no extra column in which to be placed and have been neglected. There are two rules which need to be recognized in order to avoid an erroneous answer due to overflow or underflow:

1. If, when adding two positive numbers, the msb position is set then the sum has overflowed.
2. If, when adding two negative numbers, there is a carry bit coming from the msb, then the sum has underflowed.

In digital signal processing these conditions need to be trapped, and the output set to the fully negative or positive value, or some very peculiar noises can result. The process of handling overflow and underflow is equivalent to clipping an analogue signal.

Multiplying binary numbers is also relatively simple (see Figure 3.19). A one times any number will return the same number, whilst a zero times any number returns zero. Also, to multiply a number by two simply requires a left shift of all of the bits in that number. A zero is placed in the now vacated lsb position. Division by a power of two is similarly a matter of shifting, this time to the right. If the width of the binary number is not adequate, then the lsb will be lost in the division. Note that an n-bit number times an m-bit multiplier can require up to $n+m$ bits to cope with the full precision of the answer.

Although additions can be accomplished at speed, their repetition does lengthen the time needed to perform a multiplication. So-called parallel or combinatorial multipliers, which can form a 32-bit product from two 16-bit words within 140 ns, are readily available. The division operation is relatively rare in digital signal processing. If division by a constant is called for, it can be thought of as multiplication by a number less than unity; it is then necessary to

Basic addition in $\bar{2}$ is easy:

two positive numbers:

```
  0 1 0 1          +5
  0 0 1 0     +    +2
  0 1 1 1          +7
```

a positive number and a small negative number:

```
      0 1 0 1          +5
    +1 1 1 0     +     -2
 (1) 0 0 1 1          +3
```
carry is disregarded.

a positive number and a larger negative number:

```
      1 0 0 1          -7
    + 0 0 1 1     +    +3
      1 1 0 0          -4
```

two negative numbers:

```
  1 1 0 1          -3
  1 0 1 1     +    -5
  1 0 0 0          -8
```
carry is disregarded.

The carry is disregarded, but a change in the sign column occurring when two numbers of the same sign are operated on means overflow or underflow has occurred.

Subtraction in the twos complement system is merely a matter of finding the $\bar{2}$ of the subtrahend (including the sign bit) and then adding it to the minuend:

```
      0 1 0 1          +5
      1 1 0 0     +    -4
 (1) 0 0 0 1          +1
     carry is         carry is
     disregarded.     disregarded.
```

Fig. 3.18. Simple sums in twos complement arithmetic

```
      1 0 0 1     9    multiplicand
      1 0 1 1    11    multiplier
      1 0 0 1
    1 0 0 1             partial products
  0 0 0 0
1 0 0 1
1 1 0 0 0 1 1    99    product
```

Note. When negative numbers are multiplied they need to be converted into positive numbers and the sign bit, the msb, is handled separately. It will be used to indicate the sign of the answer. The example shows the shift and add technique, as the multiplicand is essentially shifted in position and added to the product if the corresponding bit position in the multiplier is a one. Each shift of the multiplicand is equivalent to doubling its value.

Fig. 3.19. Multiplying two positive numbers

come to an understanding as to where, within an equipment, the binary point is. It is usual to consider the digitized input signal as filling the range between +1 and −1, and to arrange that all multipliers or coefficients are also within this range. Division by a varying number can, in general, be done only by the time-consuming process of repeated trial subtractions in a manner entirely analogous to the way that longhand division is carried out on ordinary decimal numbers. Multiplication by a figure greater than unity then requires left-shifting of the initial product, and this feature is usually available in digital signal processing (DSP) hardware. Most DSP hardware has to resort to a modification of the straightforward binary representation. The reason is to do with the limitations of the hardware available. Multipliers which handle 16-bit inputs will usually produce a 32-bit answer. In order not to lose the detail in subsequent processing, a greater word width is needed. In digital audio this is often 24 bits; the extra bits can be handled as an exponent. The format is known as 'floating point' by analogy to the decimal system of numbers. Multiplication of numbers in exponent form requires that their exponents are merely added together, along with any change required as a result of the proper multiplication of the mantissa. The exponents could be handled by circuitry extra to the multipliers.

Faders and filters

Just as analogue processing could be seen to depend implicitly on multiplication, so the world of DSP relies explicitly on the power of a multiplier. The elemental outlines of a fader and a simple first-order low-pass filter are shown in Figure 3.20.

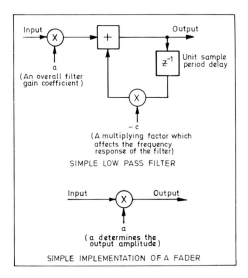

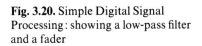

Fig. 3.20. Simple Digital Signal Processing: showing a low-pass filter and a fader

The fader is simply the action of a multiplier on the audio signal. A 16-bit by 16-bit multiply can result in a 32-bit product which will need to be rounded off for practical purposes (rather than truncated), perhaps to a 16-bit output. Rounding off is usually achieved digitally by adding a pseudo-random number to the lsb and lower bits, as this also effectively applies dither to the output sample. The addition of dither is needed as the rounding-off process is essentially a form of quantization even though it is accomplished digitally. A similar action is needed for the output of the simple low-pass filter. Note that, just as the spectrum of the input audio signal is periodic as a consequence of sampling, so the filter also has a periodic response and it does not form a precise analogy with the analogue equivalent.

There are two main classes of digital filter, the finite impulse response (FIR) and the infinite impulse response (IIR) types. They also have other names: FIR filters are also known as linear phase and transversal filters, while IIR filters also go by the name of recursive filters. It is more usual to find IIR filters in audio DSP. They are versatile and economical on processing power, but do require accurately calculated coefficients. The key features of a digital filter are the unit delay, the multiplier, and the adder. The unit delay lasts exactly one sample period. Sometimes also written in shorthand as z^{-1}, it is achieved simply by referring to the memory locations where successive samples have been stored. The multiplying and the adding (more usually referred to as a multiplier and accumulator or MAC) functions are the only ones needed to perform digital signal processing.

A more general type of filter is common in digital audio processing (see Figure 3.21). The structure of it does not change when different filter types are required. Characteristics such as shelving cut and boost, low-pass filters, mid-range cut

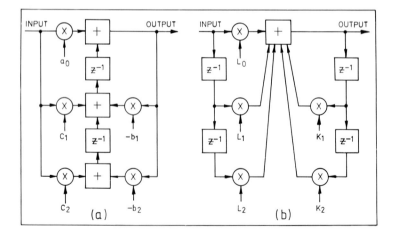

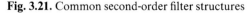

Fig. 3.21. Common second-order filter structures

and boost, and so on, are all achieved by operating the same structure but with different coefficients. The subtle difference between them is that in (*a*) the multipliers are associated with three separate accumulations and two delays, whilst (*b*) uses only one accumulation but requires four delays. The best filter structure to use depends not only on the characteristics of the hardware in use but, in a more subtle manner, on the performance details of the structure under special conditions of input and coefficient values.

For metering purposes the digital signal needs to be rectified; the negative part of a twos complement number is converted to offset binary by reapplying the twos complement conversion process. Note that the spectrum of the signal has now been doubled and rectified signal components of fundamentals higher than 10 kHz (in a 20 kHz system) will be aliased. In order to create attack and decay characteristics, filtering is needed. The output of the filtering can be applied directly to a suitable digital display or it can be converted to an analogue signal and applied to a conventional meter. The metering law can be defined digitally either by calculation or by use of a look-up table.

Digital reverberation

Digital reverberators can be viewed as collections of very complex filters. One particular architecture splits up the creation of early reflections and subsequent reverberation (see Figure 3.22). The filter-like structure of the early reflection and subsequent reverberation generators is shown in Figure 3.23.

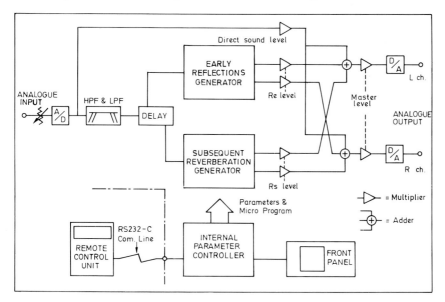

Fig. 3.22. Block diagram of a digital reverberator

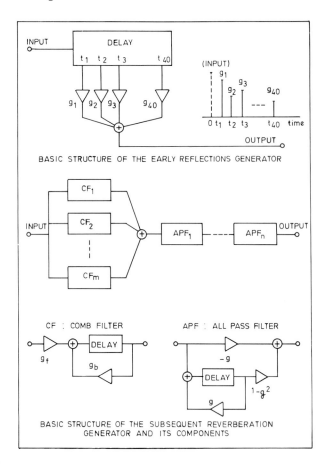

Fig. 3.23. Structures of the early and subsequent reflections generators

The rate at which the digital signal processing computations need to be done is fast, as all of the work must be carried out each time within one sampling period. For a mixing desk channel incorporating a four-band parametric equalizer in addition to eight auxiliaries, monitor and output fader, and panning, something of the order of 2.3 million computation cycles per second will be needed. This high speed is beyond the ability of ordinary microprocessors, and special processors are required.

Another aspect of DSP that requires mentioning is the need for the retention of as much precision (or word width) as possible. If, for example, we were to truncate the 32-bit output of a calculation to 16 bits then we would lose the detail in the lower 16 bits. This creates a worst-case error nearly equal to the size of the lsb, and makes the result only as good as 15-bit accuracy. The situation is a little better if we round up by adding a one to the 17th bit and then truncating the result at the 16th bit. That process creates only a worst-case error of approximately $\frac{1}{2}$ lsb, and, in general, it has to be done before the final digital output is presented to the output d/a converter. However, if there is more computation needed, then the errors in the output word will accumulate in proportion to the square root of the number of processes involved. Typically, the intermediate results in audio DSP are between 20 and 32 bits long, although 24 bits is usual. Another reason for maintaining the precision of intermediate results is that the complex matter of limit cycle oscillation is more easily avoided.

There are other, wider aspects of digital audio which have much to do with the philosophies underlying the way in which audio signals are controlled. Now that fully digitally controlled desks are available, the plangent prognostications of prior pundits can be put to the pungent proof of practicality.

Digital components

All the binary arithmetic described so far requires some hardware to make it happen. Although some of the hardware needed is fairly fearsome in complexity, all of it can be analysed as compositions of three basic functions, AND, OR, and inversion. As the only two states in a binary world can be expressed as 1 or 0, it is clear that the opposite of a one is its inverse, zero. A 'truth table' shows how a gate's output relates to its input (see Figure 3.24).

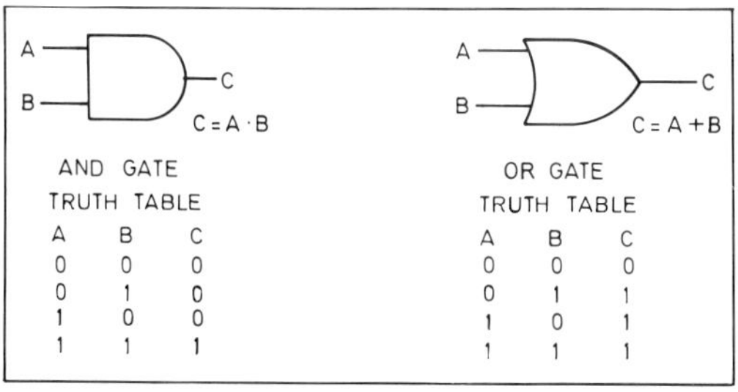

Fig. 3.24. The symbols, truth tables, and Boolean algebraic expressions for AND and OR gates

There is an algebra, called Boolean algebra, which can be used to relate the required output of a logic system to its inputs, and it is a powerful design tool. Rather than trying to design a logic function from truth tables, the algebra can be used to formulate and manipulate statements which define the logical relationship of inputs and outputs. The use of the invert function on the AND and OR functions turns them into NAND and NOR respectively, and their truth tables are shown in Figure 3.25.

There is one final common simple function which is derived from the other functions and is known as an 'exclusive or' (EXOR) gate (see Figure 3.26). It has the useful property of being usable as a controlled inverter; if one input is held high, the output will be the inverse of the other input. In combination with

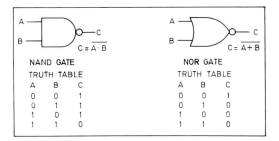

Fig. 3.25. The symbols, truth tables, and Boolean algebraic expressions for NAND and NOR gates

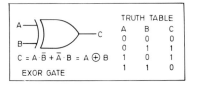

Fig. 3.26. The symbol, truth table, and Boolean algebraic expression for an 'exclusive or' (EXOR) gate

an AND gate it forms a half adder. A full adder is needed in order also to handle a carry as an input. Cumulative delays from previous stages of adders handling a wide word can be lengthy, and a modified form of adder with a look-ahead carry is used.

A simple combination of two NOR gates (two NAND gates can also be used but the sense of the logic will be inverted) will form an elementary one-bit memory or latch. The addition of a further two AND gates will form the JK flip-flop which can be used in most counters, latches, and registers (see Figure 3.27).

Multipliers are not so easily made, and much ingenuity has been expended in trying to achieve both speed and economy. A shift-and-add type of multiplier (an implementation of Booth's algorithm) is too slow for DSP work, and the technique is mostly used within the software in microprocessors, where the slowness of speed can be tolerated. Nowadays multipliers can be implemented as a single chip containing an array of three-bit adders which can perform a 16×16 bit multiply in typically less than 150 ns.

Further advances have led to two interesting developments. The first is the high-speed full arithmetic processor chips which are designed to be used as a co-processor in conjunction with a conventional microprocessor. The second is the emergence of true DSP chips, such as the Texas TMS32020, which can perform all the processes required in DSP. Like other dedicated DSP chips, they contain their own multiplier, arithmetic logic unit (ALU), program memory, and address sequencer. In due course it is likely that chips designed specifically for digital audio use will be produced and become freely available.

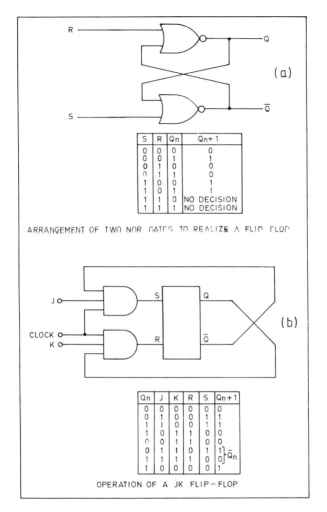

ARRANGEMENT OF TWO NOR GATES TO REALIZE A FLIP FLOP

S	R	Qn	Qn+1
0	0	0	0
0	0	1	1
0	1	0	0
0	1	1	0
1	0	0	1
1	0	1	1
1	1	0	NO DECISION
1	1	1	NO DECISION

Qn	J	K	R	S	Qn+1
0	0	0	0	0	0
0	1	0	0	1	1
1	1	0	0	1	1
1	0	1	1	0	0
0	0	1	1	0	0
0	1	1	0	1	1 } $\overline{Q_n}$
1	1	1	1	0	0 }
1	0	0	0	0	1

OPERATION OF A JK FLIP – FLOP

Fig. 3.27. (*a*) Cross-coupled NOR gates produce a set/reset (SR) flip-flop, whilst (*b*) the addition of two AND gates yields the JK flip-flop which changes state only when it is clocked

Logic families

There are many logic families in use these days, grouped into two main divisions. The first is the bipolar group, whose active elements use NPN (and occasionally the slightly slower PNP) transistors. Its main advantage has been its speed, and its major disadvantages are the power requirement and the area of silicon (the 'real estate' in the jargon) needed per function. The second group uses FETs as the active element, either in P and N channel complementary forms or as NMOS (and in the past the slower technology of PMOS) FETs. In general the FET-based families have a very much lower static power consumption than that of the bipolar families. However, the power dissipated by logic does depend on the frequency at which it is being worked, and, within a practical circuit, power is needed to charge and discharge all the inevitable stray capacitances. A word of caution: just because a logic family is characterized for a 5 V rail does not mean that it can be freely mixed with members from other 5 V families. Three main points need to be borne in mind. The first is speed, the second is the drive capability, and the third is whether the logic thresholds are compatible.

The first major division is the bipolar group typified by TTL (Transistor Transistor Logic). Historically developed in the 1960s from RTL and DTL families, the group identity is given by the use of 74xxnn-type part numbers. In general, as newer members of the TTL group were developed, the speed–power product fell. Thus TTL switched in 10 ns using 10 mW of power, whilst LSTTL (Law Power Schottky Transistor Transistor Logic) switched in 10 ns using 2 mW. Further modern developments give rise to the AS and ALS ranges (A stands for 'Advanced').

Somewhat faster speeds using bipolar techniques are obtained with ECL (Emitter Coupled Logic), where sub-nanosecond (picosecond) speeds around 300 ps are found. The two main families are the 10,000 (10 K) and 100,000 (100 K) series. Both of these use a -5.2 V supply and thus need a special interface to work with the TTL families. With high-speed logic, circuit layout becomes important, as 100 mm of track can introduce as much delay as a single 100 K series gate.

In order to maintain TTL compatibility but achieve ECL speeds, some specialized LSI (large-scale integration) chips employ a hybrid scheme where the input and output of the chip is at TTL levels whilst the function within the chip is effected using ECL technology. Impressive performances are heralded by designs such as the AMD29300 32-bit slice processor which can perform a 32-bit multiply within 70 ns. However, it is likely that this performance will be overtaken by the advances in high-speed CMOS technology. Gallium Arsenide (GaAs) technology can produce yet faster speeds, although at the time of writing only a limited range of devices is available, such as a counter capable of working up to 3 GHz.

The second major group is based on the use of MOS transistors. Originating in the late 1960s, CMOS (Complementary Metal Oxide On Silicon) devices were adopted widely in the mid-1970s when the 4000 series of devices was established. Standard CMOS parts will work on a range of supplies from 3 V through to 15 V. In general, the higher the operating voltage the faster the device, and a typical switching speed for a 5 V supply is around 250 ns. However, the static power consumption is low at a maximum of 1.25 μW per gate at room temperature, which is less than a millionth of the power required to run a LSTTL gate.

Developments in CMOS processing have produced parts with switching speeds close to those of LSTTL whilst using CMOS power levels. The new family has followed 74-series pin-outs and is generally known as the 74HC series. Much of the promise of high-speed low-power digital signal processing is based on the performance of high-speed CMOS techniques within LSI. Most microprocessors and dynamic memory chips are still made using the NMOS technology. Though NMOS has a poorer power–speed product than CMOS, it does require a simpler fabrication process. Increasingly, though, new devices tend to use CMOS technology.

Microprocessors

An easy way of categorizing microprocessors is in terms of the number of bits handled by the data bus. The largest volume of sales is still made in four-bit microprocessors, whose main use is in simple controllers and display drivers such as might be found in a washing machine or microwave oven. The majority of controllers found in low-volume applications, such as auto-locators and synchronizers, are likely to be using eight-bit microprocessors. The Z80, 6502, 6809, and 8080 are typical chip numbers.

True 16-bit processors, like the 8086 family, are commonly found in personal computers and controllers where there is a need to handle 16-bit wide data. Processors handling data in 32-bit wide words, such as the MC68020, NS32000, 80386, and the T414 transputer, are becoming common. They are used extensively in products such as multi-user systems and graphics terminals.

The processor types so far mentioned are, with rare exceptions, far too slow to be considered for use in digital audio processing. Mostly it is due to the way in which conventional microprocessor architectures handle and process a wide variety of instructions. Although a high-speed multiplier chip or a maths co-processor can be used as peripherals to a fast conventional microprocessor, there are at present two main ways of achieving suitable speeds in purpose-designed processors. The first is to build a specialized processing unit using bit slice techniques, which allows a little freedom in the determination of instructions. The second is to use one of the emergent DSP chips.

A bit slice approach to design is rather like arranging, in parallel, a group of processors whose individual word width is quite small. The typical word width, as used by the AMD2900 family, is four bits; 16-bit-wide slices (usually called word slice processors) are also becoming available. A principal advantage of the bit slice approach is the ease with which the data and instruction word widths can be expanded. For example, in the BBC COPAS-2 design the internal data word width is 24 bits whilst the instruction word width is 56 bits. The wide instruction word width provides a method whereby the processor can speed up the instruction rate by executing several different types of instruction within one system clock cycle. The bit slice approach will require the addition of a multiplier chip, and extra circuitry is needed in order to ensure that the use of a 16-bit multiplier does not force unnecessary truncation of the data word width. This can be overcome by adopting a floating-point representation for the data and handling the exponent separately.

The second approach is the DSP chip. There is now a choice of chips, all of which handle data in 16-bit wide words. Apart from the Texas Instruments TMS320 family mentioned above, those with offerings include ITT (the UDP101 is specially designed for audio DSP), STC (DSP-128), and Fujitsu (the MB8764 is claimed to be faster than the TMS320 series). A disadvantage of the current 16-bit DSP chips is that the data bus is only 16 bits wide. This forces a limit on the accuracy of arithmetic, for, although the internal MAC can return with a 32-bit product, its inputs are still limited to 16 bits and in simple systems truncation is inevitable. Newcomers to the market include the Analog Devices ADSP2100 (which is claimed to be five times faster than the TMS32020 and six times faster than the DSP128) and the National Semiconductor LM32900 series.

The DSP chip can perform the functions required of a fader and of simple equalization with ease. As the price of the chips falls (in quantity the TMS32020 is expected to cost $40, whilst the UDP101 is intended to cost only $10 in very high volume (1985/6 prices)), there is a possibility of using one processor per channel.

One complication for both approaches is the implementation of a digital audio limiter/compressor. Extra circuitry is needed in order to find the logarithm of the audio level so that a gain-controlling word can be derived. The digital implementation of a desk's routing matrix on to a time-shared parallel data bus is also not a trivial problem. In addition to incorporation into highly flexible signal processing units, DSP-chip-based designs are likely to find application in performing dedicated tasks such as sampling frequency conversion or interpolation.

Sampling Conversion

This is a non-trivial highly specific filtering process, and in all of the present-day approaches it requires intensive computation. The Stüder approach requires something of the order of 7×10^6 multiplications per second per stereo channel, but will convert an input sampled at one frequency into an output at an arbitrary, not necessarily constant, sampling rate. It is not cheap but it does provide a high-quality conversion (the process loses 2 dB of system dynamic range) which is better than could be achieved by converting to analogue and redigitizing.

The detailed manner in which the sampling frequency converter works is quite complex, and a simple analogy will have to suffice here. The input sequence of samples, or the input grid (see Figure 3.28) is digitally resampled at a new rate, the conversion grid. The output sequence of samples, the output

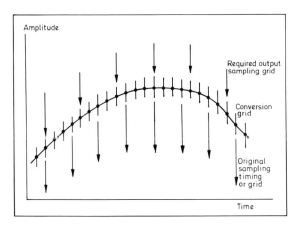

Fig. 3.28. Sampling rate conversion by means of a conversion grid

grid, is selected from the conversion grid at a rate which satisfies the required output sample rate. This is a diagram of a conceptual approach; the sampling rate of the conversion grid is around 1.5 GHz! Note that, in this simple model, resampling the signal at a lower rate could lead to the generation of aliases. In order to create the conversion grid to the accuracy required of 16-bit digital audio, the conversion grid needs to be 2^{15} (32,768) times the input sample rate or at around 1.5 GHz. Filters working at this rate are unrealistic and a method is adopted which considerably lightens the computational load. It is as if the only points on the conversion grid which are actually computed are those around which an output sample will be required. As the ratio of input to output sample rate is calculated over some time, there is a finite rate at which the output sequence of samples can keep track of changing sample rates. In other respects there is still the same need for stability of the sampling frequencies, if accuracy is not to be degraded any more than is inherent in the processing. A similar problem occurs when digitized audio signals at the same nominal sampling frequency are required to be processed together. A simpler tactic of sampling rate synchronization can be adopted provided that the difference between the sampling frequencies is no greater than ± 1 part in 10^5. The approach involves collecting incoming samples in a buffer store at the incoming sampling rate and reading them out at the receiving system's sampling rate. If the buffer store should become too full (or too empty) samples are discarded (or duplicated) at points where the audio signal level is quiet.

Digital interfaces

Within modern and foreseeable studio practice, there are at least four major types of digital interface. As only one of these caters for digital audio data, the other three are primarily concerned with the transmission of digital control information. They are:

1. The RS group: this includes the venerable RS232C and RS423, and the RS485 group in which is found the RS422.
2. The general-purpose interface bus (GPIB), also known as IEC 625 in Europe; the American equivalents are known as IEE 488 and HP-IB and are almost identical save for the connector specification.
3. The Musical Instrument Digital Interface (MIDI): discussed in Chapter 18.
4. The AES/EBU digital audio interface: for serial transmission of linearly represented digital audio data.

A few words on each of these standards is in order.

The RS group is summarized in Table 3.2. The information is sent in bit serial form, usually in words of seven or eight bits, preceded by synchronization or start bits and followed by parity and stop bits. In this system a mark is a low voltage and a space is a high one. Physical interface to the standard is easy, and there are many sources of the necessary chips. Most equipments using it will be microprocessor-driven. However, hooking up to an RS232C port is not always easy because considerable confusion can arise in determining which of the admissible signalling conventions is being used and how it is being implemented.

The GPIB group (to use the European name) are all very similar and deal with a byte serial bidirectional link, up to fifteen different pieces of equipment may be connected to the 16-line bus. Data is transmitted on eight of the lines at rates up to 1 megabyte per second, while hand-shaking and bus management signals are transmitted on the other eight lines. The maximum length of the bus is 20 m. Communication is carried out between talkers and listeners under the supervision of a controller. Although there can only be one controller, other devices may be both listener and talker, that is able to receive data or to send it. Physical interface to the bus is by readily available integrated circuits (ICs), but a useful interface requires a microprocessor. It is used, for example, on the Calrec assignable desk.

MIDI: the bus owes its ascendancy to the growth of digitally controlled music synthesizers. Certain studio outboard equipment, such as digital reverberators, can be controlled using the interface. The interface is a derivative of the RS232 serial bus, but it does differ. The baud rate is defined as 31.25 kbaud, which is a non-standard rate. Further, the bus does not support a communications protocol such as the data terminal ready (DTR) or clear to send (CTS) of the RS232C interface. Finally, in order that ground loops can be avoided, the receiving

TABLE 3.2. **Salient Features of the RS Type of Communication Standards**

Parameter	RS232	RS423	RS422
Mode of operation	Single-Ended	Single-Ended	Differential
Number of drivers and receivers allowed on line	1 Driver 1 Receiver	1 Driver 10 Receivers	1 Driver 10 Receivers
Maximum cable length (ft)	50	4000	4000
Maximum data rate (Bns sec)	20 K	100 K	10 M
Maximum common-mode voltage	±25 V	±6 V	+6 V −0.25 V
Driver output signal	±5 V min ±15 V max	±3.6 V min ±6.0 V max	±2 V min
Driver load	3 kΩ–7 kΩ	450 Ω min	100 Ω
Driver slew rate	30 V μs max	* Controlled * Determined by cable length & data rate	N/A
Drive output resistance (high Z state)	Power on N/A Power off 300Ω	N/A ±100 μA max at = 6 V	N/A ±100 μA max −0.25 V ≤ Vcm ≤ 6 V
Receiver resistance	3 kΩ–7 kΩ	>4 kΩ	>4 kΩ
Receiver sensitivity	±3 V	±200 mV	±200 mV −7 V ≤ Vcm ≤ 7 V

equipment must provide optical isolation. The commands and data are sent as eight-bit words to one of sixteen possible receiving channels. It is becoming widely used in areas other than the original area of application in music synthesizers.

The AES/EBU interface defines the frame and block structure for the serial transmission of two channels of periodically sampled and linearly quantized digital audio data from one transmitter to one or more receivers. The driver and receiver technology is similar to the RS422 balanced drive standard except that, in order to satisfy the EBU, the receiver should be transformer-coupled (optical coupling could be used but it is not specified) in order to achieve d.c. isolation.

The signal format comprises:

blocks which contain 192 frames,
frames which contain two subframes, *A* and *B*,
subframes which contain 32 time slots:
Four bits of sync which also allow definition of the start of a block (and

also the start of subframe *A*) or the start of subframe *A* only or the start of subframe *B*.

Four bits for auxiliary audio bits or other data.

Twenty bits for linearly quantized audio data.

Four data bits named as validity bit, user data bit, channel status bit, parity bit.

Figure 3.29 shows the construction. The 192 frames thus contain 192 bits of channel status and user data per channel. This is transmitted at the same rate as the sampling frequency and constitutes a prodigiously large amount of data. The format of the channel status bit sequence is well defined, whereas that for the user bit is not defined. It is not yet clear which of several possible strategies would be followed should the editing of such audio data be carried out when the edit point does not coincide with a block boundary. A similar problem exists where streams of blocks arrive independently at some equipment interface for further processing. The task may not just be a matter of synchronizing the individual samples but also one of synchronizing blocks and keeping track of the data which is held in the channel status and users bits.

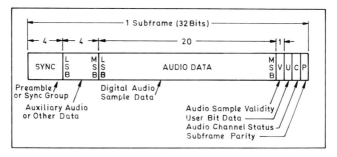

Fig. 3.29. Subframe, frame, and block make-up of the AES/EBU interface

Analogue-to-digital converters

A variety of techniques exist for converting an analogue quantity into digits, and most studios will have equipment, of one sort or another, which incorporates one of the techniques to be described. Some of the techniques simply cannot perform to a 50 kHz sampling rate and 16-bit quantization standard, but that will not have ruled out their use in other applications where the performance criteria are different.

Counter-based techniques

Perhaps amongst the easiest to grasp is that of the kind shown in Figure 3.30. At the start of conversion, the counter is started and an analogue ramp generator

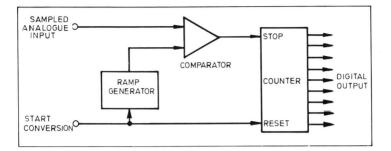

Fig. 3.30. A simple ramp converter

starts climbing. The comparator will change state when the ramp has reached the same voltage as the input sampled voltage, and this stops the counter. The size of the count indicates the size of the analogue sample. As a variation, the ramp could be generated digitally, but the principle is the same. The length of time required for conversion is substantial. For an input equivalent to the maximum count, the counter will have had to count through each of its values. If it were to attempt to reach 16-bit resolution, it would mean counting through 2^{16} (65,536) values, and, if this were required to happen at 50 k samples per second, the clock rate would need to be around 3.3 GHz—which is slightly unrealistic. None the less, it formed the essence of techniques used in early studio delay effects units and in some broadcast sound distribution equipment.

Related to this technique is the dual slope converter which is commonly found in most digital multimeters. Its strong points are its accuracy and cheapness, and its weak point is the slow speed of conversion. Figure 3.31 gives an outline of the converter. The operation cycle starts with $S1$ closing and $S4$ opened. The input voltage is integrated for n clock periods, where n is usually the maximum count of the counter. During this time the polarity of the signal

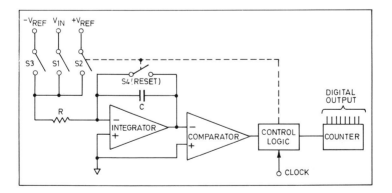

Fig. 3.31. Dual slope converter (the action of the switches is referred to in the text)

can be detected. At the end of the first integration cycle $S1$ is opened and, depending on the polarity, either $S3$ or $S2$ is closed. The counter again counts up from zero but this time it is stopped by the comparator when the integrator output reaches 0 V. The count is then proportional to the input voltage.

The delta modulator method of conversion belongs to a class of integrating-type converters. Figure 3.32 gives a block diagram of a simple delta modulator principle. Note that the output is information regarding the slope of the input signal and not its actual amplitude. Thus to achieve a word which describes the input signal amplitude it is necessary to integrate the output of the modulator. This can readily be done digitally using simple counting techniques.

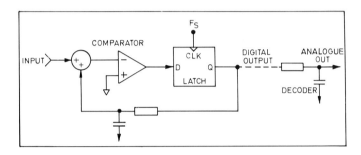

Fig. 3.32. Simple delta modulator and decoder

The analogue input signal is compared to the feedback signal coming from the output of the integrator formed by R and C. The comparator is essentially a one-bit quantizer. The output is converted to a stream of pulses by the D-type flip-flop (acting here as a zero-order hold), which is clocked at some suitable high rate. The output of the flip-flop drives the integrator. The decoder need only consist of a similar integrator. The emergent bit stream can be converted into a more conventional parallel word by counting, over some suitable number of clock periods, the difference between the number of mark periods and space periods at the output of the zero-order hold. This number is used to modify the net number achieved in the previous counting period. There is thus a lot of similarity, in respect of the limitations on the speed of conversion, between this technique and the more blatant counting approaches. However, if some modifications are made to the coding rules, such as transmitting special bits in the serial bit stream in order to indicate that the rate at which the net count is changing, then the system approaches the bounds of usefulness. Developments along similar lines lead to the dbx and Dolby approaches to adaptive delta modulation pulse code modulation (ADPCM).

A two-stage approach is taken in the Sony 16-bit ADC and DACs which are used in the PCM-F1 and CD equipments. The first stage sets the nine more significant bits of the eventual output by counting the time taken for a coarse constant current to charge a capacitor to a voltage just less than the input sampled signal. The second stage sets the seven less significant bits by a similar comparison, using an integrating current which is exactly $\frac{1}{127}$ the value of the coarse current. The technique has some similarities with the straightforward counting types of converter, with the difference that it involves a two-stage process.

Flash converters

The next obvious approach is to compare the analogue signal to an array of references, each one of which is set to a unique quantization value. The outputs of the comparators are combined to form the required output word. Figure 3.33 shows how simple the block diagram can be. The technique is capable of being very fast but has the disadvantage that an n-bit output requires 2^n comparators. This would be an impractical number for 16-bit conversion but is quite a

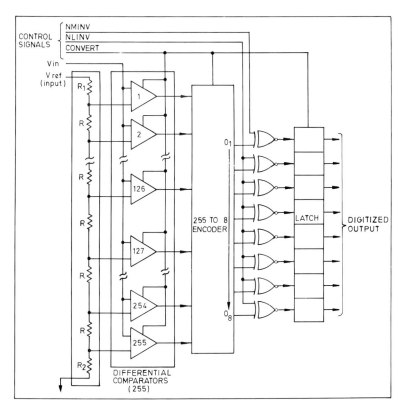

Fig. 3.33. Flash converter diagram

practical proposition for an eight-bit converter as only 255 comparators are needed. Eight-bit flash converters are extensively used in digitizing video signals. Further, a recent development uses a four-bit flash quantizer in a rather special form of converter which achieves an 18-bit resolution within an audio bandwidth. We shall mention this later.

Successive approximation

This is the commonest approach to digitizing audio signals. In Figure 3.34 the general layout of a converter is shown, whilst Figure 3.35 shows the typical waveforms involved, with successive approximation in progress. In the first clock period the most significant bit (msb) of the successive approximation register (SAR) is set. The resulting output of the digital-to-analogue converter (DAC) is compared to the input. If the input is greater, then the msb value is kept. The next clock cycle sets the next most significant bit, and a similar comparison is made. The process is repeated until all the bits have been set and tried.

For an *n*-bit conversion only *n* clock cycles are needed; thus a 16-bit conversion at a 50 kHz rate requires an 800 kHz clock rate. This is a practical rate and 16-bit performance can be approached.

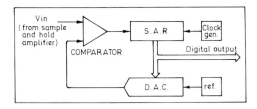

Fig. 3.34. Principal features of a successive approximation converter

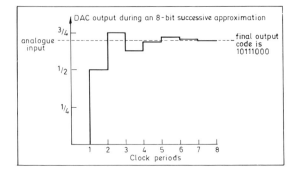

Fig. 3.35. Successive approximation in progress

Digital-to-analogue conversion

Just as an ADC could be made using counters, so can a DAC. Simply allow an integrator to charge up for a time proportional to the value of the digital word. This method is not much used because it is slow, and the most common technique in use relies on the switching of binary weighted currents.

The R-2R ladder

The approach requires only two resistor values R and twice R. As Figure 3.36 shows, the $2R$ elements are grounded by the switches either to $0V$ or to the virtual earth at the summing junction of the output op-amp. The resistors need to be trimmed to an accuracy better than one part in 2^n (0.0015 per cent for a 16-bit converter). In addition, they need to have matching temperature coefficients and be stable. The operation is based on the binary division of current as it flows down the ladder. The incoming digital data switches the binary weighted currents either to the summing junction, which is a virtual earth, or to ground. An input voltage is needed in order to generate a stable current so that the device can be used as an audio DAC. This is usually a highly stable, very quiet voltage source and is often referred to as a 'voltage reference'. However, there is no reason why some varying signal, such as an audio signal, cannot be used as the voltage source. The output of the DAC would then be a copy of the incoming audio signal but at a level determined by the digital data presented to the DAC. DACs which can be used in this way are called multiplying DACs (MDACs) and can be employed, for example, in digitally controlled faders.

A common, and inescapable, problem with parallel-input DACs is the glitch which is produced as the input data word is changed. The causes of the glitch include data bit skew and the different switching times of the individual switches in the DAC itself. As the sizes of the glitches differ for different digital inputs, they cannot be easily filtered out and instead are removed by deglitching.

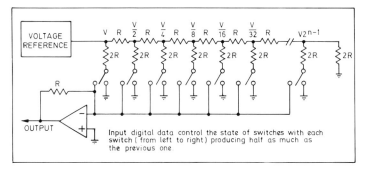

Fig. 3.36. R-2R ladder type of digital-to-analogue converter

This is usually performed by the zero-order hold circuit, and, as glitch-free switching is very difficult to achieve, most deglitchers essentially replace the varying timing and size of the input glitch for a regular constant-sized one which is more easily filtered out.

The use of an MDAC to control audio level is not without its problems, although the technique is important enough for specially designed logarithmically weighted MDACs to be produced. However, it is not the glitching problem which is mostly responsible for the audible defect, as this is usually well masked by the audio signal itself. The problem is most noticeable when a change in audio level, due to a change in the digital input, occurs at the peak of the audio waveform. A step change in the audio output is created. It is this step which can be heard. Amongst the techniques for reducing its effect is that of arranging for gain changes to occur only at zero crossing-points of the input audio signal.

Not all MDACs can be used successfully in this way as audio attenuators. The alternative approach to generating and switching binary weighted currents is shown in Figure 3.37. The use of an active current source is an advantage in terms of switching speed, and DACs using them are usually found in digital video environments. A mixture of the two approaches to generating binary weighted currents is used in some 16-bit digital audio DACs.

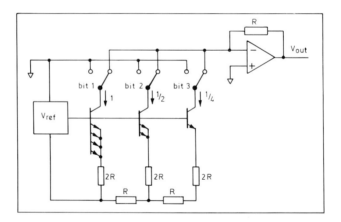

Fig. 3.37. A current-switching DAC (only three bits are shown)

An important variation on the binary weighted current converter is found in many CD players. The technique achieves 14-bit linearity without expensive trimming of the current sources integrated on the chip by means of what is referred to as dynamic element matching. The performance is exploited by the oversampling approach to the problems of digital-to-analogue conversion which Philips have pioneered.

Other conversion approaches

Floating-point converters

The floating-point (also called the flying-comma) converter produces an output which is made up of two different parts: the exponent and the mantissa. The exponent part may be thought of as representing the gain applied to the sample prior to quantization by a standard ADC. The output of the ADC becomes the mantissa. Figure 3.38 shows the main elements. Usually the gains are in multiples of 6 dB, so, for example, a three-bit exponent is able to describe a gain range of 42 dB. The conversion of the floating-point word into the commoner

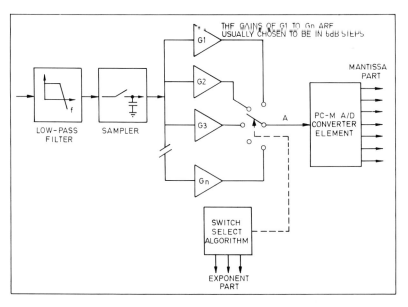

Fig. 3.38. Block diagram of a generalized floating-point conversion system

fixed-point representation requires the mantissa to be shifted as many spaces to the right as is indicated by the value of the exponent. The technique allows the use of, say, a ten-bit converter with an intrinsic range of approximately 60 dB, to cover a range of over 100 dB. The penalty is that the quantization noise changes with the signal level because the signal level causes changes in the gain of the converter. This results in noise modulation (one of the defects of conventional analogue magnetic tape recording) which produces audible defects if the resolution in the mantissa is inadequate. As a consequence, there exists the need to define the ratio of signal-to-quantization-noise in the presence of the signal (see Figure 3.39).

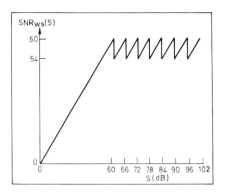

Fig. 3.39. Plot of the signal-to-noise ratio in the presence of signal for a floating-point converter. The one implied here uses a three-bit exponent and a ten-bit mantissa

Floating-point representation is used within many DSP environments in order that the full dynamic range of a calculated result may be retained. The disadvantage of the representation is that for output purposes, including the AES/EBU interface, a conversion must be carried out in order to produce a fixed-point word.

Because an incoming sample can be validly represented in a combination of exponents and mantissas, and because the converter must be able to change gain across the full range of its capability within the time span of one sample, there exists the need to define the algorithm by which the correct exponent value should be chosen. There are three main ways of doing this: instantaneous, syllabic, and block.

Full accuracy, in terms of monotonicity and linearity, is difficult to achieve if the gain range of the converter is permitted to change at each sample. The stability required of amplifiers, resistor networks, and switches is such that it is probably as easy to design a full-word-width linear converter anyway. In addition, the noise modulation can become objectionable for high-performance audio work, though the technique is used extensively in telephony. The decision as to the correct gain range could also be made over the duration of say 100 to 300 ms. This would be called a syllabic floating-point.

NICAM

In a block-type converter the sampled audio is typically presented to a standard full-range converter which, in the NICAM system used in broadcasting, for example, is 14 bits. A block of samples (typically 32 samples or 1 ms worth of samples in NICAM-3) is scanned, and the largest sample in the block determines the range for the block. The samples within the block are transmitted to ten-bit resolution with respect to the largest word within that block.

Oversampling conversion

Philips CD players use an oversampling technique in their DACs. Recent work describes the performance of a digital audio ADC with 18-bit resolution.

The use of a conventional R-2R type ADC places stringent demands on the recovery filter performance. The Philips approach involves resampling the digital audio signal at a frequency four times higher than the original sampling rate. For CD players this is 176.4 kHz and is achieved by a special digital filter chip. The higher sampling rate eases the design constraints on the reconstruction filter but it also allows the output digital word to be rounded off to 14-bit accuracy whilst still maintaining an analogue output with 16-bit resolution. This apparently paradoxical behaviour can be explained by the fact that the quantizing noise is now spread over four times the original audio bandwidth. As only a quarter of this band up to 20 kHz is relevant, the noise power in the audio band is now only a quarter of the total. The signal-to-quantizing-noise ratio is thus 6 dB greater than would be expected from a 14-bit system. A further 7 dB increase in signal-to-noise ratio is achieved by the process called noise-shaping, in which the error created when the output is rounded off to a 14-bit word is fed back to the next sample. The digital output drives a 14-bit ADC but the net performance is that of a 16-bit system. The DAC output is followed by a simple minimum-phase filter in order to remove the sample frequency components from 176.4 kHz upwards.

Similar oversampling and noise-shaping techniques are used, in conjunction with a specialized form of delta sigma modulator, in an oversampling ADC. A high-speed four-bit flash conversion of the error signal in the delta–sigma modulator is carried out at a 6.14 MHz rate. The digital output is subjected to complex filtering in order to achieve an output at a sampling frequency of 48 kHz with an effective resolution of 18 bits. Incidentally, the process also performs the necessary anti-alias filtering in the digital domain, thus avoiding the imperfections, in both frequency and time response, which accompany analogue anti-alias filtering.

Digital recording

The first aspect of digital audio recording to be noted is the sheer size of the amount of data. For example, the data rate of CD (including formatting and error protection overheads) is 4.3218 Mbits/s, which results in an hour's worth of recording requiring 15.56 gigabits of storage. The requirement of a multi-channel recorder will be proportionally higher. Non-mechanical storage media have been investigated but they are still neither economical nor practical. The largest random access memory chip (RAM) to date can hold 1 Mbit. Winchester disc drives can reasonably be expected to hold around 3 gigabits (1986) but are not an economic proposition as a replacement for tape-based systems. Magnetic tape is still the preferred medium for multi-track work where long-term storage of the master recording is required. However, magnetic-disc-based systems which can essentially emulate the performance of a short length of multitrack tape are finding use, particularly in post-production areas.

Ideally, there are only two magnetic states recorded on the tape. The record current is simply reversed in direction in order to create the required flux reversals. On replay, these transitions in polarity produce a pulse in the replay head, the size of which is dependent on the rate of change of the flux. It is the timing of successive transitions that is important, and a major feature of a digital data channel is that the signal-to-noise ratio need only lie in the range 21–30 dB—after all, the replay processing has only to decide whether the replayed signal was a one or a zero. The effect of noise is to introduce an error into this decision process, and it is more effective to provide error correction than it is to increase the signal-to-noise ratio (see Figure 3.40).

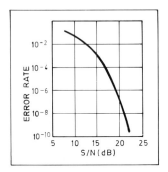

Fig. 3.40. The relationship between error rate and signal-to-random-noise ratio. The signal is assumed peak-to-peak and the noise is r.m.s. measured

The packing density of information on tape is typically around 40,000 bits per inch, and the dominant cause of errors is dropouts. These may be caused by dirt between the tape and the heads or by defects in the tape's magnetic coating. A dropout only 0.5 mm long will cause a burst of errors nearly 800 bits long. The separation of the tape from the replay head causes a loss of signal amplitude at a rate of 55 dB per wavelength of separation, and a fine dust particle only 1 μm in size will cause complete loss of replayed information. There are two main phases in handling errors: first they must be detected, and then they must be concealed or corrected. These stages can be accomplished only by adding more bits to the data already present. These extra bits may increase the number of bits by up to 50 per cent.

The magnetic tape medium has no d.c. response but the raw data (which is in the form of a non-return-to-zero (NRZ) code) does have significant energy around d.c. In order to preserve the timing information and to aid accurate data recovery, it is necessary (especially for non-rotary head recorders) for the data to be further encoded to match the characteristics of the recording channel. It is also useful if the encoding rule also enables easy recovery of the basic data clock rate during replay, whilst at the same time making economical use of tape. Of the many coding schemes in use, the three commoner ones in the digital audio arena are the HDM-1 scheme used in DASH format recorders, the EFM scheme used in the CD system, and MFM (also known as modified frequency modulation and self-clocking Manchester coding), which is common in floppy and hard magnetic discs and in the AES/EBU digital audio interface. The replay signal is fed to a data separator which produces both the clock and the data outputs.

The two main types of recording format in use are stationary-head and rotary-head. The rotary-head formats have usually been centred on the use of a video recorder. Thus the organization of the data on to tape has been dictated by the details of television standards. Indeed, the choice of sampling frequency used for CD is related to the constraints imposed by television. The digital audio signal, plus its associated error protection bits, is usually recorded on to modified video recorders without further encoding, a technique known as non-return-to-zero (NRZ).

Stationary head recorders employ multiple tracks in order to maximize the use of tape area, and currently are the only way of achieving 24- and 32-track recorders. Editing can be simpler than is possible with modified video recorders as the error protection schemes in use are strong enough to withstand the damage caused when mechanical cut edits are carried out. However, there is by no means the same degree of flexibility in a mechanical edit on a digital tape as there is in an analogue one, and the future of editing digital recordings lies firmly in the techniques of electronic editing. This is an approach which has been in common use for video editing for some time.

Magnetic-disc-based systems are emerging as a viable alternative to the tape recorder in some areas. The length of the audio recording is greatly limited by the capacity of the disc pack—to perhaps ten minutes of fully digitized stereo audio signal. A correspondingly shorter time is available if the digital audio format is rearranged to emulate, say, 16 tracks. Through the use of large buffers of RAM, editing becomes a matter of organizing the seek and access techniques of the disc-drive heads. Thus the original digital recording does not need to be altered during editing and, of course, access to any part of the piece of music can be instantaneous as no tape rewind and relocation time is required.

In the future other forms of digital storage may emerge. Optical techniques may be refined to produce the anticipated recordable CD, and perhaps, a long way into the future, holographic techniques remain a distinct possibility.

Error detection

The choice of an error protection scheme needs to be made after consideration of the error-generating characteristics of the recording medium. Most errors in magnetic recording will arise in bursts, and so schemes which can handle bursts of corrupted data are preferred over those which can handle isolated randomly spaced errors.

The simplest scheme used to detect errors is called 'parity'. The data word to be protected is scanned, an extra bit is added on to the word, and it is set to a one or zero in order that the number of ones in the whole word is an even number (called even parity); see Figure 3.41. Parity can only indicate when an odd number of errors has occurred and it cannot indicate which bit is in error. Failure of a parity check is thus an indication that some further action should be taken.

	data	even parity	
Input A	10110101	1	correct
Input B	01011010	0	
Output A	10010101	1	incorrect, parity check fails
Output B	01011110	0	

Fig. 3.41. The principle behind simple parity checking

A more complex detection technique is the cyclic redundancy check (CRC), in which a checkword is added to the data word in order to make it an integral multiple of a known divisor. This has enough power to detect all errors whose burst length, in bits, does not exceed the checkword length. Developments of CRC techniques permit the location of the error to be determined. As in any one-bit position there can be only one of two states, so that knowledge of the position of the error automatically indicates the correct setting at that bit position.

The most common codes in digital audio use, however, are developments of the CRC approach to detection applied to whole words, and are known as Reed–Solomon codes. These are a class of block codes which have been devised to handle burst errors and their correction efficiently. Further improvement in the robustness comes about through interleaving the code words. The effectiveness of the technique relies on distributing a long-burst error over a longer length of data, such that it appears as an apparently random sprinkling of much smaller-burst errors each of which can be easily detected and corrected (see Figure 3.42). The process is refined in the cross-interleave Reed–Solomon coding used in CD. The *X*s mark the location of words assumed to have been corrupted. After de-interleave, the errors are distributed throughout the sequence of words.

The DASH format, however, uses a similar cross-interleave method but employs a development of the simple parity technique in which two sets of parity code words are created. The first, known as P code, is formed before the interleaving process, and the second, known as Q code, is formed after the process.

Having detected that a particular word is in error, it is necessary to decide

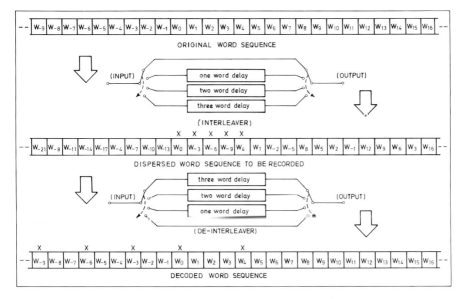

Fig. 3.42. Interleave and de-interleave

what to do about it. If the correct value of the word can be deduced then it can be fully corrected. It will then appear at the output of the digital audio system as if it had never suffered any deprivation. Where the correct value of the word cannot be deduced, but is known to be in error, it can be replaced either by the last known good word or by the average of two good words on either side of it. This latter process is known as interpolation and is a form of error concealment. Other forms of interpolation (another example of digital filtering) involving many previous correct samples are not much in use at present. If the severity of the burst of errors is such that no suitable samples exist in order to perform interpolation, then the commonest strategy adopted is to mute the output. This will usually take the form of a rapid fadeout to silence until a correctable sequence of samples is again available.

The correction power of these codes is fairly formidable. For three of the common digital audio formats they are as shown in Table 3.3.

TABLE 3.3. **Typical Correction Powers**

Format type	Full correction	Concealment	
		Good	Marginal
EIAJ	rotary head	4,096 bits	—	8,192
DASH	stationary head	8,640 bits	33,982	83,232
CD	optical disc	3,874 bits	13,282	15,495

The random error correctability of various coding techniques is shown in Figure 3.43.

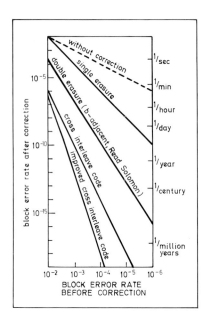

Fig. 3.43. Random error correctability of various codes

Digital Terminology

Analogue (or analog)	A continuous signal representing the variation of some physical event with the passage of time.
Bit	Short for binary digit.
Baud	The number of bits per second used to transmit a digital signal. It includes the signalling information such as the stop and start bits, and so the number of data bits actually sent per second is less than the baud rate.
Byte	A digital word comprising eight bits.
Nybble (*sic*)	A digital word comprising four bits.
Word	A digital word the size of which is dependent on the processor handling capacity. In digital audio processing this is commonly 24 bits.
Digital	Represented by a number.
Digital signal	A group of digital words which represent an analogue signal.
DSP	Digital Signal Processing; processing a digital signal using digital computing techniques.
Quantizing	Measurement of a signal amplitude to the nearest whole number of quantizing intervals or steps.

Quantizing noise	The ineluctable error resulting from the act of quantizing. The difference between the original signal and its quantized equivalent is unwanted noise or distortion.

For example, for a signal quantized by a perfect n-bit converter the peak value of the maximum signal will be $2^{(n-1)} \times Q$ and the maximum sine wave signal that could be passed is thus $Q \times 2^{(n-1)} \sqrt{2}$. We can estimate the quantization error energy by taking the energy for a given error X and multiplying it by the probability of this energy occurring $\Pr(x)dX$. The integral between $\pm Q/2$ of $X^2 \Pr(X)dX$ for all possible values of error gives the error energy. This, when transformed into a voltage, works out to the 'known' equation $\mathrm{SNR[dBu]} = 6.02 \times n + 1.76$.

Dither	A low-level random signal, added to the analogue signal prior to sampling and quantizing, which acts as if to spread the highly correlated quantization noise across the audio spectrum. It results in low-level signals being quantized more linearly. Low-level signals can thus be encoded below the apparent noise floor of the system.

A very important need for dither arises at the output of a DSP unit when the output word is required to be rounded down to 16 bits. A small pseudo-random binary number is added to the full-range digital audio word at bit positions 17 downwards and the top 16 bits of the digital word are output. Forming a 16-bit result from a longer word (usually called *truncation*), by simply taking the top 16 bits without even rounding up, is a process identical to quantizing an already sampled signal and is thus subject to the same limitation when the signal is represented by the bits at the lsb end of the 16-bit word. Adding a pseudo-random number, with a peak value equal to half an lsb (in this case up to and including the 17th bit), is analogous to the addition of random noise to the sampled signal during the original digitizing process.

Binary	A signal represented as one of two possible states.
Gate	A basic item of logic hardware. There are really only two gates, AND and OR. With the addition of the negation or inversion operation, all the other types of gate can be formed. These include NAND, NOR, EXCLUSIVE OR types.
ADC	Analogue-to-digital converter.
DAC	Digital-to-analogue converter.
Interface	A catch-all word for describing the way items of equipment need to talk to each other. An interface can be implemented in either software or hardware or a combination of both.
Hardware	The physical nuts and bolts, gates and connectors, transformers and chips, which comprise equipment.
Chip	A plentiful component of impoverished deserts (the silicon in sand) which is processed in order to enhance its semiconductor nature and thus provide transistors, microprocessors, and so on.

Microprocessor	A chip which is capable of executing a program.
Software	A program written for a microprocessor or other computing device. Sometimes used to refer to the recorded music.
Firmware	A program for a computing device which is resident within the equipment. It is not usually modifiable and forms part of what is known as the operating system. It may be held (stored) in ROM (usually an EPROM) or on a magnetic disc.
EPROM	Erasable Programmable Read Only Memory. Usually erased by short-wavelength UV light; other types include EEPROMs which are erasable electrically. Their main characteristic is that they can be read from many times faster than they can be written to. PROMs may be programmed only once, by the chip manufacturer in what is often referred to as a silicon foundry.
RAM	Random Access Memory. There are two main types—static and dynamic.
Flip-flop	A general term for a circuit which can be configured to behave as a latch, a counter, or a register. Sometimes loosely called a *bistable*.
Monostable	Related to a bistable, but produces an output which, when triggered, is present only for some definable time.
Alias	Sideband created when an analogue signal is sampled. If the sampling frequency is not more than twice the highest frequency component of the signal, then the alias will appear within the bandwidth of the signal.
Sampling	Freezing or capturing the amplitude of a signal at some constant rate.
Anti-alias filter	A filter which will ideally remove from a signal all components above some critical frequency. These filters are difficult to design as they must provide a high cut-off rate with minimal group delay distortion.
Parity	The primeval error detection technique. The number of ones in a word are added up. The answer will be either odd or even. The parity bit is an extra bit which is appended to the word in order to make the sum of all the bits either even (even parity) or odd (odd parity). This simple process can detect the existence of any odd number of errors but it cannot point to where the error is and thus cannot correct it.
Domain	Often heard in phrases such as the digital domain, the analogue domain, and so on. It is simply a way of stating what aspect of a signal is of fundamental interest.
Monotonicity	When the input to a converter (a/d or d/a) is increased, then the output should also increase. This is known as monotonic performance, and for 16-bit audio quality converters it is difficult to achieve.
Dynamic range	This is the ratio, in dB, between the peak level of a signal (at, say, the level of 3 per cent distortion) and the noise floor

associated with it (measured here as the quasi-peak CCIR weighted noise unless otherwise mentioned).

Discrete
A signal is described as discrete when it has been sampled and quantized. It is a single, discrete point, whereas, by comparison, the analogue signal is continuous.

Recursive filters
Also known as IIR response filters, they are a common form of filter in audio DSP because of their speed. It typically takes only five MAC operations to perform a DSP equivalent of the analogue state variable filter. However, IIR filters are sensitive to the values of the coefficients used and can produce limit cycle oscillations with certain combinations of filter structure and values of coefficients.

FIR filters
Also known as transversal filters, they form the other main class of digital filter (there is a third class, a hybrid, called lattice filters). FIR filters can produce linear phase response (low or zero group delay error), unlike IIR filters. They do delay the signal more because of the larger number of stages involved, and this severely limits the rate at which groups of samples can be handled by a processor. A FIR design is used in the Philips approach to the d/a converter in their CD players.

Limit cycles
An affliction of IIR filter types; certain structures are more prone to the problem. It is a condition in which the output of a filter is an oscillation, often at a low amplitude, which is caused by a particular circumstance of the input sample sequence and the coefficient values. Sometimes the problem arises through not being able to implement sufficient precision in the coefficients.

Port
A term used in electronic engineering to indicate a terminal or point from which a signal can be received (output port) or to which it can be sent (input port). Clearly there can also be bidirectional ports. The port might consist of several points (or lines) in parallel. Port is also used as a verb, and it then refers to the preparation and subsequent debugging of software which has been written on one system and is required to work on a different system.

COPAS
Computer for Processing Audio Signals. An interesting development pioneered by G. McNally at the BBC. The Mk 2 system underpins the development of the Neve DSP desk system.

Deglitcher
As the input code to a DAC is increased or decreased by small changes, it passes through what are known as major and minor transitions. The most major transition occurs at half scale (around zero volts for an audio signal) and is the point at which all bits change state. If, at major transitions, the switches of the DAC differ in their switching rates, then, for a short time, the DAC output will be a very different value. These short-term spikes or glitches are very difficult to remove by filtering. A deglitcher is a device which either removes them or at least makes them all the same. It usually comprises a fast sample-and-hold circuit which holds the output constant until the DAC

switches have settled. The function is usually combined with the DAC output zero-order hold function.

A law and μ law   Descriptions of the quantizing law used in two similar non-linear ADCs. Fundamentally suited to telecomms use, the A law is in use in Europe and the μ law is used in the USA. The encoding performance yields a dynamic range of a twelve-bit linear encoder but uses only eight bits. The encoding law is part of the intrinsic chip design but is also describable mathematically. Manufacturers' data books will reveal more.

Shannon and Nyquist   Shannon's paper, 'Communication in the Presence of Noise', Proc IRE vol. 37 January 1947, comes long after Nyquist's 'Certain Topics in Telegraph Transmission', Trans AIEE April 1928. Both papers can be related to sampling. Shannon said that a signal can be completely defined if sampled at more than twice the required signal bandwidth. Nyquist said that so long as this is so there will be no aliasing.

Complement   Two forms of complement are used here:

Ones complement is another way of saying that each bit in a digital word is inverted. Thus a one becomes a zero and a zero becomes a one.

Twos complement of a number is formed by taking its ones complement and adding 1 to the lsb. For example: to form the twos complement of 0110, first take the one complement 1001, and then add a one to the lsb 0001, which gives the result 1010.

You can play with complements using ordinary decimal numbers: nines complement is the equivalent of the binary ones complement and tens complement is the equivalent of twos complement.

Cyclic redundancy   A form of error detection. It works by adding, to a digital word, a number known as the checkword which will make the total an integral multiple of some dividing factor. In decoding, the replay information is divided by that factor, and, if there is no error, there will be no remainder and the original digital word will be able to be produced by subtracting the checkword. If an m-bit cyclic redundancy checkword (CRC) is added to a k-bit long data word, the code word formed will be $n = m + k$ bits long.

The technique can detect all burst errors of m-bits or less, and the misdetection of a burst error longer than m-bits is $2^{(m+1)}$. Clearly the longer the checkword the greater the detection ability, but the redundancy overhead is also increased. The division by the polynomial factor is achieved using a shift register with feedback.

4

Studio planning and installation
Andy Munro

Studio planning encompasses many disciplines, including some not immediately associated with the business and operation of recording studios. Installation is simply the execution of the planned schedule of works, and success or failure is almost entirely a result of the technical competence and experience of the studio 'designer'.

The word 'studio' is taken generally to mean any area associated with the technical or artistic procedures involved in the recording process. It may be argued that, to some clients, the quality of a studio's facilities in terms of catering and recreation are just as important as the quality of the studio acoustics or mixing console. However, a successful studio design is invariably the result of interpreting the exact requirements of the client, who presumably (but by no means always) has an equal understanding of his own (and his customers') recording and business philosophy.

The first step in the planning procedure is always the client's brief, assuming that there exists a normal client–designer relationship. Should a studio owner decide to perform the role of designer or utilize the expertise of his own staff, then the procedure remains essentially the same, although there will be many decisions which will necessitate outside help, if only for reasons of legality. The decision to appoint a studio designer and, with more difficulty, which type of designer to choose, does not lie within the scope of this chapter. However, it is hoped that the reader placed in such a position will be better able to judge his requirements for a particular project through awareness of the various disciplines involved.

The design brief

The brief for the design of a new studio can be broken into four main areas for the purposes of initial planning:

1. Establishing the studio format

Apart from the obvious requirements regarding format, it should be established that the studio is intended to provide a particular technical facility and that any present or future needs are fully understood. For example, the requirement may be a 24-track room suitable for recording mainly electronic music but with the need for overdubbing vocals and single acoustic instruments. There may be additional requirements for synthesizer programming and other 'off line' activities as well as for copy and duplication facilities. This description of a fairly typical contemporary studio could conceivably materialize into a 50 m² home 'workshop' or a complex electronic music and mix-down facility covering 250 m² and costing £1 million. The format, therefore, must include a detailed analysis of the type of equipment envisaged, the precise nature of the material intended for production, and an analysis of the requirements of clients, engineers, and producers.

2. Outline budget

No studio facility can be successfully designed without a thorough understanding of the capital cost requirements in relation to the intended use and revenue of the business. There are relatively few situations where studios are not subject to some form of fiscal analysis and it is essential to work within precise cost constraints from the outset. Costs can be divided into three distinct categories:

1. Building and fixed plant
2. Equipment and facilities
3. Operational costs and overheads.

At the feasibility stage of any project, the designer should present the client with such information as will enable both capital and running costs to be established. The client should also make the designer fully aware of all cost constraints from the beginning, so that all upper limits can be agreed.

It is the responsibility of the designer to set out the benefits and aesthetic requirements of various levels of expenditure, giving as much value for money as possible and a scale of expenditure priorities. An example of poor design would be where the reception desk cost more than the chairs for the engineer and producer.

3. Building requirements

Having established the format and budget, the requirements for a suitable building are logical in terms of space and cost. Additional factors must be considered, and these fall into five categories:

(a) Geographical location: may be important for many reasons including proximity of clients (e.g. Soho for film work); by contrast, a rural location might be chosen for peace and tranquillity.

(b) Environmental considerations: studios are invariably places which function in isolation from their immediate environment. It is therefore important that the outside world should not impose itself on the studio in terms

of noise, pollution, or interference. It would not be advisable to build a studio under a railway arch, or next to a glue factory or a first-division football ground. The fact that people sometimes do is testimony to the unfailing optimism of the music industry!

(c) Aesthetic appeal: is sadly neglected in the planning of most studios. Cost is the usual excuse for this, but in reality it is often simply a lack of imagination and design. The successful conversion of derelict dockside warehouses in London and Liverpool is a perfect example of industrial renovation and architectural enterprise.

(d) Planning restrictions: take many forms and are intended to prevent an individual or company from establishing an entity or activity which will detract from the balance and well-being of the locality and its occupants. The fact that a well-planned studio makes virtually no impact at all on its environment is a source of constant amazement to planning officers who invariably expect to contend with noise, heavy traffic, and undesirable aliens disguised as musicians. This having been said, do not expect to turn a Victorian listed church into a multi-studio and business complex without a considerable amount of persuasion, often involving meetings in draughty community halls trying to convince local pensioners that they have less to fear from a recording centre than from almost any other commercial activity. One factor which can cause considerable problems is that of an hours-of-use restriction. In residential areas it is common for commercial activity to be prohibited at night.

As in all matters relating to planning, no approach should be made without consulting a local surveyor or architect with a view to identifying possible pitfalls.

(e) Building regulations: often overlap both planning requirements and are basically related to public safety. Areas of particular concern to studio planning are:

Fire regulations and means of escape
Floor loading and structural safety
Suitability of materials and building methods.

In all but the most basic of studio projects, it is necessary to appoint a qualified structural engineer in order to satisfy by calculation any local statutory regulations.

Having satisfied all the preceding requirements, the preliminary feasibility work can be started, assuming that a suitable building is available or proposed. It is at this stage that a direct relationship can be established between the area and expenditure in terms of unit cost per square metre. The final costing should reflect the decisions and approach taken at this stage, and will make the difference between satisfactory completion and a project that simply runs out of money.

4. *Market Research*

There has been an explosion in the audio recording industry in recent years, prompted by an increased demand in almost every market sector. The complex interaction between the record, broadcasting, and cinematograph industries has fuelled the growth in specialist facilities and studios capable of providing a wide range of technical expertise in addition to the traditional concept of music album production.

In any growing industry it is difficult to predict precise market trends but it should be an essential step in any proposed new venture to analyse and examine the degree of commercial viability of the project. One thing is certain: assuming a static demand, for every new and technically advanced facility which is brought into service there must be a pruning of existing outdated studios in order to maintain equilibrium. For this reason, established successful studios are constantly updating and improving their facilities in order to avoid what is best described as the 'leap-frog effect'.

Feasibility study

If we can assume that the project has passed through the initial critical analysis contained in the briefing stage, it then becomes necessary to carry out a detailed feasibility study. Assuming that a suitable building space has been found, a full survey should be carried out and drawings produced at 1:50 scale. From these the designer and/or client should prepare accurate presentations of the studio areas at 1:50 in order to establish the suitability of the space.

At this point the designer will have initial discussions with various consultants concerning primarily the acoustic performance, structural requirements, services such as ventilation and electrics, and possibly interior design. The degree of involvement of specialists in any of these areas will depend on the complexity of the project and the existence of particularly difficult design situations.

It must be said that in most cases the acoustic requirements will take precedence in the decision-making process, although if such decisions are taken in isolation the results will invariably be aesthetically disappointing. Following agreement of a basic scheme, full costing should be carried out from a set of 1:100 drawings together with sufficient information as deemed necessary by the various consultants. It is the acceptance of this costing which marks the transition of the project from feasibility to full appointment and contract.

Appointments and contracts

It is now necessary to agree on the following appointments, again allowing for the actual scale of the project:

(a) Architect and/or project manager
(b) Structural and services consultants
(c) Acoustic designer/consultant
(d) Quantity surveyor
(e) Interior designer.

Some or all of these functions may overlap or be dispensed with by agreement with the client. Most specialist studio design companies offer a degree of rationulization of the individual roles, based on a thorough knowledge of their craft. When a studio owner attempts to fulfil some of these roles himself, this invariably ends in less than satisfactory results with little, or even a negative, cost advantage.

However, the client will probably have a reasonable idea of the required studio performance in terms of existing, comparable facilities, together with a firm opinion on what is right or wrong with such operations. A strongly expressed desire for such things as natural lighting or a feeling of openness (or possibly intimacy) will indicate to the designer a sense of the direction in which to proceed.

Acoustic requirements must be defined very precisely, as there is no area of discussion more open to ambiguity and evasive definitions. There is a precedent for acoustic design being enveloped in marketing concepts, much as in the way 'designer' clothes are packaged. The advantages of this are difficult to see, except to clients who literally have no sense of uniqueness or individuality, and to whom the concept of a packaged product offers some sense of safety.

Unfortunately, the laws of acoustics are such that even relatively standardized design systems can lead to widely differing results. It is equally gratifying, frustrating, and stimulating to find that it seems impossible to quantify the acoustic performance of rooms. The first concerted efforts to do just this were made by Beranek in the USA, by relating precise acoustic measurements in concert halls to the subjective appraisal of performances given in the same auditoria. Although several basic design criteria were established, subsequent projects proved that there were undoubtedly several 'missing links' to providing the 'perfect acoustic environment'.

There is, without doubt, a growing awareness of the possible improvements that are being made in acoustic design through an understanding of the complex relationship between time, energy, and frequency as perceived by the musical observer. Works carried out by such brilliant individuals as R. C. Heyser, M. Schroeder, and V. Pentz all concentrate on the overriding importance of the time domain in the qualitative assessment of acoustic performance. Several aspects of acoustic specification will be defined later in this chapter.

The completion of the feasibility stage of design will have several immediate effects. First, all specialists will either be given full appointment, or retention will cease. There are important legal considerations to take into account, all of which should be explored by the architect or designer. Full legal responsibility can be established only through precise procedures, and it is important that any client makes himself aware of the protection or lack of it afforded by professional liability and indemnity. It is equally important that the designer satisfies himself of the integrity and solvency of the client, as in many ways the designer carries the greater risk.

In law any contract which is deemed to be valid must satisfy these simple criteria:

Agreement: definition and evidence of terms
Certainty: evidence of acceptance by both parties
Consideration: evidence of benefit to both parties
Capacity: invalidation due to age or insanity
Consent: both parties must freely consent
Legality of objects: the contract must not constitute an illegal act
Object: the object of the contract must be possible
Formality: sometimes a contract must be written to be valid.

When one has presented the full feasibility study and obtained consent to proceed, after making all necessary amendments and adjustments, the following information will be required:

(a) Full production drawings at 1:20. These will be distributed to all consultants with instructions regarding the information required.

(b) Full instructions to the quantity surveyor in order to verify and establish the project budget. Any cost variations not anticipated at the feasibility stage must be referred to the client, excepting of course minor 'swings and roundabouts' fluctuations.

(c) Statutory consents must be obtained from all relevant authorities such as planning, fire, pollution, offices, building, and electrical supply. Outline approvals, obtained at the feasibility stage, should ensure that this stage will be a formality unless significant design changes occur.

(d) Agreement of professional fees. It is standard architectural practice to base all professional design fees on the RIBA percentage scale. In the event that a complete design–build package has been negotiated in advance, this will be irrelevant. It is hard to imagine any other industry where the client agrees to pay for something to be built before it has been designed, but this does sometimes occur in the recording industry.

It is the purpose of architectural design to ensure that the client will receive the most appropriate service for every aspect of his building. Whenever possible, competitive tender will be sought for each phase of the work involved, and payment will ensue only upon satisfactory completion of the work. The design–build approach often involves advance payment for work, which in all legal senses is extremely risky. Ultimately, the client should satisfy himself of the risk and exposure to which he is committed, but there can be little doubt than an independent designer–client relationship, with separate appointment of contractors, offers the greatest degree of protection to all concerned.

Design fees should be paid in stages according to the contracts finalized at this stage of the project. Any cost adjustments resulting from savings during the main contract will be adjusted on completion.

As production information flows into the design office, it is important to establish a formal series of drawings issues. This prevents specialists working with outdated information as the design progresses. For example, a decision to move technical ducting may require the repositioning of air-conditioning ducts, which may interfere with acoustic treatment. Such breakdowns in information exchange can turn a site during contract into an extremely unpleasant environment, where nobody trusts the information available. It is the function of the designer to provide fully co-ordinated information to all concerned. This is one of the two most important, even crucial, aspects of any project. The other is the appointment of the building main contractor.

Whereas the feasibility stage of a project must satisfy client, backers, investors, and bankers, the production stage of the design must produce sufficiently accurate information for persons totally uninvolved in the design process to comprehend fully and appreciate exactly what is required and expected. There will be aspects of the work which are so specialized that nominated subcontractors must be appointed. Typical areas for this approach will be computer installations, specialist acoustic materials supply, and monitor systems. In these cases, negotiations and appointment will be discussed with the client and negotiated directly with the individuals concerned.

The appointment of the main contractor would always ideally be the subject of competitive tender, but, for the following reasons, this may not be the case:

(a) The client may wish to negotiate with a single known contractor
(b) Time may prevent a full tender procedure
(c) Design cost constraints may not allow full production of tender information
(d) A geographical constraint may dictate a properly managed package format.

Where full tender procedure is used, every care must be exercised to ensure that the contractors invited to quote are sufficiently equipped and experienced to carry out the work. It has been said that there is no such thing as a specialist acoustic builder, just good builders and bad builders. It is true!

Following successful tender, the appointed builder must agree to the standard form of contract chosen for the purpose. This will include discussions on damages in the event that the contract is not completed according to schedule. Considering the high cost of delays to opening a studio, the builder must be fully satisfied that he can meet the completion date specified.

Prior to appointment of the contractor, a detailed briefing should be given to the client in order to agree formal acceptance. It should also be pointed out to the client that, on appointment, the architect must act as mediator and arbitrator to both sides. This is particularly important in the matter of issuing stage payment certificates.

Prior to commencing the contract, the appointed contractor must submit a schedule of works. This will enable all specialists to plan site visits and their own time slots as required. Regular site meetings are an essential part of all building programmes, and they make possible an exchange of information with the minimum of paperwork. Minutes of site meetings should be distributed to all present, with actionable items highlighted for the individuals concerned. At each subsequent meeting, previous minutes should be discussed and results measured. Failure to take action on the agreed procedures may invoke penalties and ultimately lead to the dismissal of the persons responsible.

A standard form of building contract in use in this country is published by the Joint Contracts Tribunal (JCT) and is accepted by all professional bodies, including chartered surveyors, engineers, and architects. There are nineteen standard documents published by JCT, covering everything from minor works to multi-million-pound developments. Contract law outside the UK will inevitably differ and interested parties should consult with a local architect.

When working outside the protection of a formal contract, both parties should adhere to the law of simple contract as previously discussed. No contract can be expected to run perfectly from start to finish, and some provision must be made for variations. Technical revisions, unforeseen site difficulties, and changes of mind may all cause prolongation or increased quantities and costs. Extensions and additional instructions should be issued in written form, with agreement obtained from both client and contractor.

Stages of completion are subject to inspection, and, following discussions regarding defects and remedial action, certificates are issued to authorize payment in full. It is usual to negotiate a retention by the client for a fixed period, in order to ensure rapid attention to defects occurring in the initial period of occupation.

Aspects of the project

Having covered the broad scope of the design and contract procedure, it is advisable to discuss in detail some specific aspects of each part of the project. A complete list is beyond the scope of this chapter, but the most important aspects are outlined below.

1. Acoustic isolation

There is a great deal of misunderstanding about isolation in studios, but there are really only three requirements.

(a) Isolation from the outside environment: the traditionally accepted ambient noise level inside recording areas is NC15, and within monitoring areas NC20–5 is often specified (see Chapter 5). In practice these levels can be achieved in central city areas only by elaborate floating structures designed to give isolation down to 25 Hz.

The efficiency of a resiliently mounted structure is frequency dependent and defined thus:

$$\text{Efficiency (\%)} = 100 \times \left(1 - \frac{1}{(R^2 - 1)}\right)$$

where R is the ratio of the forcing frequency and the natural frequency.

The natural frequency of a resilient mount under load is given by:

$$Fn = \frac{947}{\sqrt{d}}$$

where d is the static deflection under load.

It can be seen that without additional damping such resilient systems can become unstable if the forcing frequency is equal to the natural frequency. It is therefore imperative that such systems are both damped and have a natural frequency of at least half the lowest significant exciting frequency.

(b) Isolation between rooms inside the studio complex: can be defined simply at the design stage by predicting sound levels in one area and the required background noise in another. For example, if the monitor system in the control room generates boundary levels of 120 dB, and a small adjacent studio is required to record speech with a noise floor of 20 dB, the required isolation would be approaching 100 dB.

Such a situation would represent poor design in that 100 dB of isolation would involve extremely expensive structures, whereas a simple planning decision could relocate the voice studio to another part of the complex. The creation of buffer zones and sound locks is far cheaper than lead-lined double-skin structural shells. Acoustic doors and windows are expensive items and should be minimized through similar zoning.

To emphasize the difficulty of achieving isolation to the order of 100 dB, the requirement by Mass Law alone (see Chapter 5) would be for three sheets of 15 mm float glass, each independently mounted, with no direct air coupling between them. This is not impossible, but is certainly at the limits of technical achievement.

(c) Reduction of noise generated inside the complex: internally generated noise consists of services such as ventilation, equipment with mechanical movement, and fan cooling systems. With the advent of digital recording, there is a tendency to place tape recorders in separate clean-air environments, with the added advantage of reducing noise in the control room. Similarly, amplifiers and computer racks should be installed in a separate technical area (machine room).

Noise transmitted through air-conditioning ducts must be attenuated before it enters critical areas. Low-velocity air supply will eliminate noise caused by turbulence, but this will increase the cross-sectional area requirements for ductwork and grilles. Typical design figures are 1 m/sec for grille velocity and ten changes of air per hour for medium-sized rooms. Air-conditioning contractors should give written performance specifications for every room, based on a brief provided by the designer.

2. Room acoustics

As this subject is dealt with in the next chapter, it is only necessary to elaborate here on aspects relating to planning and execution.

The acoustics of both recording rooms and control rooms must be discussed at great length in order to establish a final specification. Control room designs, as previously mentioned, have often been shrouded in marketing jargon rather than involving specific criteria.

The simple requirements are as follows:

(a) Control room: (i) There should be sufficient area at the mixing console for engineer and producer to hear a faithful representation of the material replayed through the monitor system.

(ii) The monitor system should deliver a faithful representation of the signal applied to it in terms of level, frequency and phase response, harmonic distortion, and impulse response. Should the system require equalization to perform correctly, there should be true minimum-phase correlation between the amplitude and phase response.

(iii) The ratio between direct and reflected energy in the room should be sufficient to maintain accurate stereo imaging and tracking of the sound balance. At this point it should be noted that the D/R ratio will be affected by the acoustic Q of the monitor system, with higher values of Q increasing D/R.

(iv) The total decay time of the room should not be so long as to prevent distinct perception of reverberation and time delay applied to the recorded signal itself. The exact value as measured by the traditional RT60 method should be between 0.2 and 0.3 sec at middle and high frequencies, rising gradually below the 125–150 Hz band.

(v) Standing waves in the room should be sufficiently damped and distributed as uniformly as possible across the audio spectrum. Tuned narrow-band absorption may be introduced to reduce particular modes.

(vi) The reflections making up the reverberant soundfield should be as diffuse as possible in order to eliminate 'hot spots'. This is particularly important in large control rooms where the rear of the room is used by musicians, the object being to extend the area over which accurate monitoring is maintained.

(b) Studio: Whereas the control room environment should be designed to give neutral listening conditions, the studio is very much part of the performance being recorded. It affects not only the direct sound quality but also the way in which the musicians deliver their performance and their attitude to it. It therefore follows that the studio acoustics should optimize the feel and musicality of the instruments being recorded.

For orchestral work this involves recreating the atmosphere of the concert platform. A room of 400 m² and a minimum height of 6 m would be required to provide the best reverberant conditions. For pop, rock, and jazz recording there is a distinct trend to use acoustics as a form of enhancement, making drums and guitars sound particularly bright and expansive. There is also the requirement for a completely dry sound to which signal processing can be added at a later stage.

The fashion of designing large studios, made small again by large areas of absorbent trapping, seems largely out of favour. The advantages of inverse square-law sound propagation in such rooms is largely outweighed by the oppressive, unnatural feeling imparted to the musicians and their instruments.

3. Acoustic construction

Attention to detail is the main consideration in studio building. Every aspect of good isolation goes against the grain of traditional building practice, in the sense that most structures need to be held apart rather than together. This said, it is quality of workmanship which matters in the end, and building contractors should always be chosen for this reason above all.

The main elements of the building programme will be contained in the schedule of works, an example of which is shown in Figure 4.1. It can be seen that many operations must take place in sequence, which requires precise timing if delays or congestion are to be avoided. Off-site fabrication of woodwork, finishing panels, and audio looms is essential if projects are to be completed within the kind of time-scales shown even for small to medium-sized studios.

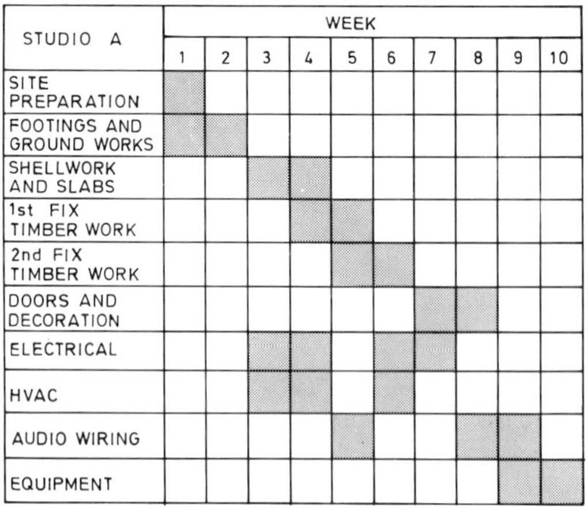

STUDIO A	WEEK									
	1	2	3	4	5	6	7	8	9	10
SITE PREPARATION	░									
FOOTINGS AND GROUND WORKS		░								
SHELLWORK AND SLABS			░	░						
1st FIX TIMBER WORK				░	░					
2nd FIX TIMBER WORK						░	░			
DOORS AND DECORATION								░	░	
ELECTRICAL			░	░						
HVAC			░	░	░					
AUDIO WIRING						░	░		░	
EQUIPMENT									░	░

Fig. 4.1. Example of a schedule of works

4. Air-conditioning

One aspect of studio design frequently underestimated is the cooling requirements of men and machines in a sealed enclosure. For all but the smallest studio, a three-phase supply is required, providing anything up to 100 amps per phase, even for an average-sized complex.

The precise cooling load for a control room depends largely on the equipment power consumption and the rate of airflow into the room for a given outside air temperature. The standard of thermal insulation in studios is usually very high and therefore the only way of maintaining normal room temperature is by controlled cooling. As previously mentioned, the air-conditioning contractor should be briefed as to the required operating conditions, and asked to provide limits of such operation under adverse environment conditions. It is not unusual for the HVAC cost to represent up to 25 per cent of the total building budget.

5. Other services

(a) Electrical installation: This represents a relatively straightforward part of the design and installation programme, although timing is often critical. Wiring should always be designed with future requirements in mind, allowing easy access to ducts and junction boxes. Several important points should be noted, such as the total power requirement per phase. Single-phase systems should be configured so that air-conditioning is supplied via a separate 'head'. Distribution of phases should avoid potential high-voltage links.

Provision of a high-conductivity technical earth is often desirable, but is by no means essential in areas with normal electricity supply. The practice of removing the mains earth from equipment is not advisable—in fact in most cases it is probably illegal.

Lighting requirements for studios fall into both technical and aesthetic areas, but it will be the job of the chosen electrical contractor to carry out the installation. Typical allocations for electrical wiring would be 5–10 per cent of the building budget, provided that an existing supply is adjacent to the studio.

(b) Audio installation: The subject of audio, and possibly video, systems could easily fill another chapter, but several basic rules will prevent the wiring of the studio equipment becoming a nightmare.

(i) Plan the wiring in advance with every termination numbered, and number every cable during installation.

(ii) Decide and maintain a shielding convention. Do not confuse shielding with earthing—they perform different functions.

(iii) Use suitable grades of connector and cable for permanent and demountable interfacing, with optimum matching of pin numbers.

(iv) Always provide suitable trunking and cable access with ample room for replacement and updating. The minimum trunking cross-section for interfacing a modern multitrack console is 400 cm².

(v) Avoid parallel runs of audio and electrical wiring. A suitable convention is to supply electrical wiring from high level vertically, and to run audio at low level horizontally.

(vi) Allow ample 'Christmas tree' terminations inside fixed racks to provide easy installation of outboard equipment.

(vii) Provide termination on all studio panels for MIDI, foldback, and ties. When establishing a formal tender procedure for the audio installation, it is important to establish the exact method proposed by each company—the cheapest is rarely the best.

Typical wiring budgets form 10 per cent of the main contract. Some companies quote installation based on 10 per cent of the equipment budget, but this method is not accurate enough for budgets in excess of £100,000.

Final installation

On completion of all contractual work, the equipment is finally installed in its normal working position. Some equipment must be terminated *in situ* and therefore the wiring team will remain on site during this phase.

Some equipment will be installed by the manufacturer, although this is unusual. Responsibility for acoustic measurements and system testing must remain with the designer and his technical associates. The following is a typical check-list for a control room:

Test absolute polarity of all signal paths.
Test noise and hum levels through main signal paths.
Check patch-bay for correct identification.
Check all systems for RF interference.

Test monitor systems for correct operation under standard conditions (1 W at 1 m). Check impedance.

Test absolute system frequency response from microphone input to monitor output, together with phase and distortion.

The precise method of verifying the acoustic performance in the control room and studio will vary with the test equipment available and the chosen methods of the acoustician. The following represents the minimum list of acoustic measurements which should be taken:

Nearfield monitor response, left and right, using pink noise and third-octave real-time analysis.

Monitor response at the mixing console, left and right, then summed.

The sum level of noise should increase by between 3 and 6 dB depending on the symmetry of the reverberant soundfield and the value of the direct/reflected energy ratio.

Any decrease in level must represent a phase problem and should be investigated.

If suitable equipment is available, a full set of measurements utilizing time delay spectrometry should be taken with particular emphasis on the following: Energy–Time Curves (ETC), Energy–Frequency curves (EFC), Phase–Frequency curves (PFC), Frequency–Time curves (FTC).

TDS as a standard method of measurement has been limited in the past to relatively cumbersome and expensive hardware and has therefore been slow in gaining wide acceptance. This situation will change over the next few years thanks to the introduction of compact microprocessor-driven analysers with friendly software. Examples of TDS measurements are given in Figures 4.2–4.5.

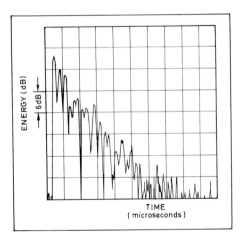

Fig. 4.2. Typical TDS measurement of energy–time response

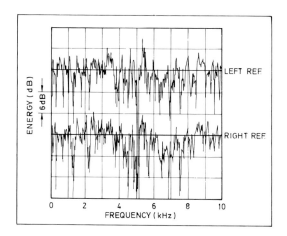

Fig. 4.3. Typical TDS measurement of energy–frequency response

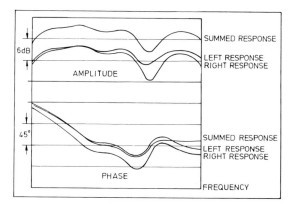

Fig. 4.4. Typical TDS measurement of amplitude and phase response

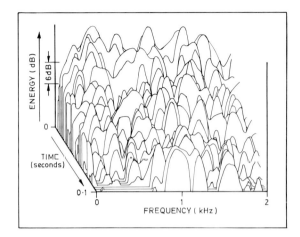

Fig. 4.5. Typical TDS three-dimensional plot of time–energy–frequency response

Summary

It may appear from the preceding pages that planning and installation have more to do with contracts and paperwork than designing. Although this may be largely the case, the scope for imaginative, progressive thought is still what makes the difference between the mundane and the exceptional. Also, there can be no better test of a studio than the sound it creates and the finished recorded product; the most important tools of the studio designer are ears and imagination.

5

Studio acoustics

Alex Burd

The aim of sound recording practice as described throughout this book is to enable the practitioners of the techniques commonly used to create a more or less permanent record of sound—which may or may not exist as an entity.

If the studio is the first link in the chain, which of course it will not be in the case of location recording, then the environment must assist the performers or the engineers (or both) to create the desired final product. While location recording can provide an environment which is unrivalled in the stimulation it brings to the performer, few locations these days can provide the quiet uninterrupted conditions which are necessary for economic recording. This chapter aims to describe the principles of acoustic design, together with the audible consequences of the design decisions that are taken. Various classes of studio, control room, and other technical rooms may need to be created to satisfy the manifold demands of clients. No one type of room can be expected to be suitable for all programme material, but certain fundamental considerations remain constant for all types.

Principles

In order to understand more clearly the interactions of sound with the structure which forms the studio, it is worth looking briefly at certain aspects of the generation and propagation of the sound. Sound is a pressure wave (see Figure 5.1) which is generated naturally by the movement of surface—strings or skins, amongst others—or the variation of airflow in a tube past an obstruction—as in

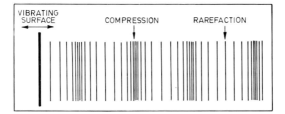

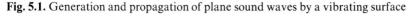

Fig. 5.1. Generation and propagation of plane sound waves by a vibrating surface

woodwind, brass, or vocals. These are the natural sources of sound, for which a studio and its acoustics will be important. Of course, the ever-growing family of synthesizers and electronic keyboards have no audible existence until the loudspeaker converts them into sound, and in these cases what used to be known as the control room will be the hub of all activities.

The sound waves cover the entire audible frequency spectrum from 20 to 20,000 Hz, and a corresponding range of wavelengths from those of the low frequencies which are comparable with the dimensions of entire buildings (15 m) down to 15 mm for the highest frequencies. This large range leads to fundamental differences in the type of interaction between the sound and the physical parts of the studio. The loudness of sounds is related to the amplitude of the pressure variations in the air and the corresponding amplitudes of vibration set up in the ear. The effect varies with frequency, the ear being at its most sensitive at frequencies around 1.4 kHz, where a practical limit to the useful increase of sensitivity is set by the random molecular motion of air particles.

Most musical sounds have their origins in a simple harmonic motion—a single frequency with harmonic overtones; the particular overtones selected and their relative intensities are the governing factors of the quality of sound. Starting transients and cut-offs also influence our judgement as to the instrument producing the sounds.

When the sound waves strike the boundaries of the studio, part of their energy is converted into vibration of the surface, while the remainder is reflected back into the studio. Of the vibrational energy in the structure, i.e. that which is not reflected, a part may be dissipated as heat (absorbed), while the remainder is transmitted through the material and re-radiated on the far side.

The amount of sound which is reflected is a function of the impedance mismatch at the boundary. Heavy materials have a large mass reactance, and only a small part of the acoustic energy is converted into vibrational energy. The impedance of the surface increases both with increase of the mass of the surface and with higher frequencies, and this gives rise to the so-called 'Mass Law' for sound insulating materials which will be referred to later. The simple Mass Law behaviour is found in most materials over a frequency range which is bounded by resonances of various types; at the resonance frequencies, the impedance of the material changes radically, and therefore related characteristics, such as sound insulation, will also be seen to show large variations.

If the reflected sound inside the studio is examined in more detail, it may be seen that under some conditions—flat surfaces whose dimensions are large compared with the wavelength of sound, for instance—specular reflection of the source waves will result. A limited number of discrete images will thus be found, and the resulting soundfield will show large variations from position to position. At the opposite extreme, rough surfaces having protuberances which are comparable with the wavelength will give rise to a large number of reflected waves scattered randomly in all directions, a condition which is known as a diffuse soundfield.

Porous or fibrous materials represent a special case, in which little sound will be reflected from the surface and large amounts of energy may be dissipated within the structure of the material by viscous flow in the interstices. These types of material will be seen to be particularly useful as acoustic absorbing materials. If no solid skin exists, then a large part of the incident energy will pass straight through such materials.

Background noise

The single most important design decision which has to be taken relates to the background noise levels which are necessary for each category of recording. This decision will have consequences on the acceptability of the site chosen for the premises and on the type of structure that is needed to exclude or contain the noise (although these first two considerations are related and interact with each other), and the implications for the building services can also be extremely expensive (as discussed in Chapter 4).

While noise levels can be described by single-figure descriptors (dB(A), NR, or PNC levels, etc.), it is essential for design purposes to look at the entire spectrum of noise—possibly even extended beyond the frequency range which is generally considered in architectural or environmental acoustics; architects may consider only a range from 100 to 3,150 Hz; environmental considerations will typically extend from 31.5 Hz to 10 kHz.

Noise spectra are most commonly expressed these days as Noise Rating criterion curves, as shown in Figure 5.2. These curves are the standardized form

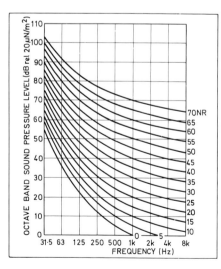

Fig. 5.2. Noise rating (NR) curves

approved by the International Organisation for Standardisation as a derivative of many other families which have existed in the past. The curves relate octave-band sound pressure levels to the centre frequencies of the bands; note that if one-third octave sound levels are used the entire curve will be shifted 5 dB downwards. Each curve is given a numerical value corresponding to the octave-band level at 1 kHz.

The shape of the curve bears some resemblance to the ear's equal loudness response (see Fig. 2.19, page 34). The human hearing system is generally less sensitive at low frequencies. The curves do not follow the ear's response in detail, and a sound whose spectrum follows an NR contour accurately will actually sound hissy. The shape of the curves varies at different sound levels—the higher the sound levels the flatter the curve—and in this respect also the curves follow the behaviour of the human ear.

Studio noise levels used to lie in the region NR 15–NR 25, depending on the requirements of different types of programme. Such sound levels were audible on many types of programme and required a certain discipline on the part of the programme originators. In recent years there has been a steady improvement in the recording techniques available and in the quality of equipment available even on the domestic market. The growth of the market in Compact Discs is perhaps the major factor in this respect. Studio background noise levels for the more critical types of programme have had to respond to these requirements, and NR 10 may be taken as the current norm for the best-quality recording studios equipped with digital recording machines, and therefore having the potential to achieve signal-to-(recording) noise levels 80 dB or greater. Some specialized studios may achieve even lower levels than NR 10, but this is uncommon in UK practice.

Sound levels are usually determined with a precision sound-level meter, with which a time and a spatial averaging of the noise level will be carried out. Where more than one noise level exists, the total sound level may be the quantity to be specified; any tonal or intermittent characteristics in the noise render it more obtrusive, and if such characteristics exist they must be at a level 5–10 dB lower than the continuous noise. An alternative approach specifies the continuous sound level—probably arising from the ventilation system—and uses this level to mask other intrusive noises. These have to be attenuated to a lower level than the specified continuous level in order that they will be inaudible and not raise the measured level by more than 1 dB. (As will be seen later, this approach may give savings in expensive areas of design.)

The design of a ventilation system to achieve such low levels requires great attention to detail: efficient anti-vibration measures to isolate all moving or vibrating parts; duct silencers at critical points; reduction of air velocities through the system, together with many other similar precautions.

Noise arising external to the building (traffic, aircraft, trains, etc.) or from other parts of the building (offices, other studios) have to be measured or estimated, and the steps necessary to attenuate these are described in the next section.

Sound insulation

The prevention of external noises penetrating into our quiet studio depends on a combined use of sound insulation techniques together with structural isolation measures.

As was seen above, the ability of a wall to reflect, that is not to transmit, energy is largely related to its surface density (mass per unit area in kg/m^2); see Figure 5.3. Within the so-called Mass Law region, the insulating properties of the surface increase by a theoretical 6 dB per octave (i.e. each doubling of the

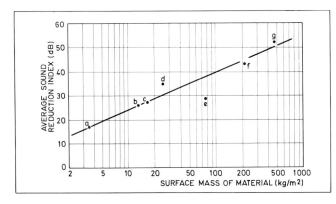

Fig. 5.3. Average Sound Reduction Index of various materials as a function of their surface mass. The materials are: (*a*) 6 mm plywood, (*b*) 18 mm chipboard, (*c*) 6 mm glass, (*d*) 11 mm plywood with lead bonded (absence of resonances improves SRI), (*e*) 50 mm wood wool with 2 × 12 mm plaster (serious resonances degrade SRI), (*f*) 112 mm brick with 12 mm plaster, (*g*) 225 mm brick with 2 × 12 mm plaster

frequency); equally, at a given frequency, the insulation properties will increase by a further 6 dB for each doubling of the surface density. The extent of the Mass Law region is restricted by many resonances in the partition governed by the various stiffnesses associated with the material (see Figure 5.4). At resonance, the severity of the reduction in the sound insulation will depend on the damping present; this damping may be the internal damping of the material or it may be added externally. The effect of the resonances is to reduce the theoretical dB/octave variation to a practical 5 dB/octave.

Various single-figure derivatives of the measured sound insulation values can be calculated, the simplest being the mean of the one-third octave values between 100 and 3,150 Hz. This corresponds to the normal range of interest for domestic situations but may be inadequate in many studio applications if the

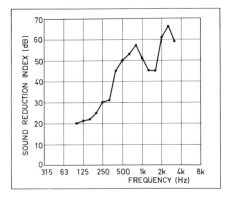

Fig. 5.4. Resonance (coincidence effect) in glass with low internal damping

resonances are designed to occur just above or below the defined frequency range in order to optimize the single-figure value.

Simple Mass Law constructions are usable up to mean sound reduction indices of 50–55 dB; above this value, the mass becomes excessive and leads to a cumulative thickening of all walls and foundations. Multiple-leaf constructions are necessary for higher values, the spacing between the leaves governing the frequency range within which a useful increase occurs. Where the spacing between the leaves is a fraction of a wavelength, the two leaves will behave as a single Mass Law partition. With rising frequency, a progressive improvement is found which depends on the spacing, and on the acoustic absorption within the cavity, until at high frequencies the SRI may increase at 10 dB/octave, indicating that the two leaves are acting independently. The presence of more than one panel introduces additional resonances, the most important of which occurs when the two panels move in anti-phase.

For the higher values of sound insulation at which multiple skins are required, flanking of the designed structure by any continuous walls or floor slabs can become a serious problem. It will frequently be necessary to introduce isolation joints in ground slabs, elastomeric pads beneath walls, and, in the limit, the isolated 'box-in-box' construction shown in Figure 5.5. Where the lowest internal noise levels are required, and high levels of external vibration exist on the site, often arising from underground trains, it may be necessary to isolate an entire building by constructing it on rubber bearing pads.

In certain cases it has proved advantageous to use a combination of massive structures, which may be in the load-bearing elements of the building, and construct the isolated rooms of lighter framed construction. In such cases it is necessary to take account of the sound absorption which will result from the lightweight panels.

This is not the place to enter into details of sound insulation, but a few representative examples may serve to show the wide range of values required and to indicate the types of construction that are used.

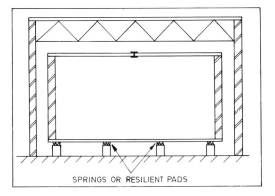

Fig. 5.5. Isolated box-in-box construction

In a typical studio centre, the roof may be required to exclude aircraft noise, and an average sound level difference of 70 dB may be specified. A structure to achieve such a value could be an inner roof of 150 mm reinforced concrete, supporting on resilient pads a second, lighter skin of wood wool slabs with suitable waterproofing and weather protection.

Walls to exclude traffic noise will have to achieve at least 65 dB average sound level difference. One possible construction is a cavity wall having two leaves of 225 mm brickwork and a cavity of 100 mm minimum. Some degree of structural isolation will be necessary to minimize flanking transmission through the ground slab.

Control room windows, to achieve compatible results, must be of heavy glass, and an air-space of minimum depth 200 mm with absorptive reveals is necessary. It is essential that the two glasses are of different thicknesses—say 8 mm and 12 mm—to ensure different resonance frequencies.

Where ventilation ducts or other services pass through a sound insulating partition, it is of course necessary to ensure that the sound level difference by that path does not degrade the overall insulation. The use of attenuators, commonly called 'crosstalk silencers', is the answer in the case of ventilation ductwork, while other cable ducts can be packed with sandbags or bags filled with mineral wool.

Acoustic quality

Having constructed the shell of a studio which is not subject to interference by noise from either external or internal sources, it is now necessary to ensure that it sounds 'right' to those who use it—both artists and engineers. The sound that is heard live in a studio, or at a microphone output before processing, is a combination of the direct sound from the source together with a multiplicity of reflections from the surfaces of the studio and from the furnishings and fittings.

When a short sharp sound is produced in the studio, it is possible to display electronically the pattern of reflections which results; this display is known as the impulse response. In the early part of such a display, shown in Figure 5.6, the first signal, which has travelled direct from source to microphone, can be

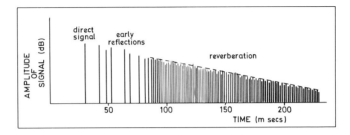

Fig. 5.6. Impulse response of an auditorium

seen, followed by several discrete reflections from floor, ceiling, walls, and furniture which are spaced apart by time intervals of a few milliseconds. After a time which will be a function of the size of the studio, the reflections are seen to arrive so close together that it is impossible to separate them. These later signals arise from multiple reflections within the studio, and, since energy will be lost from the sound wave each time it is reflected by a surface, the sound amplitude will gradually die away. This region, known as the reverberation, was the first part of the characteristic of sound in an enclosure to be systematically studied. It probably remains the most important single feature of the soundfield, although current research in concert halls is demonstrating the importance of the early sound, both in the aural judgement of the size of a room and also in defining subjective characteristics of the soundfield.

Within a room there exist regular series of standing waves arising from the reflection of sound by the major surfaces of the room; these are known as the natural modes or eigentones of the room. Figure 5.7 shows the three lowest modes which can exist between a pair of plane-parallel surfaces. The modes

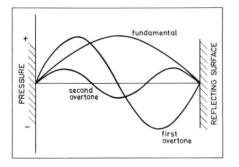

Fig. 5.7. Modes of vibration (eigentones) between two parallel reflecting surfaces

arising from the three pairs of opposing surfaces in a rectangular room comprise what are known as the axial modes of the room. The other series are the tangential modes, in which two pairs of surfaces contribute, and the oblique modes, which involve all three pairs of surfaces. The axial modes have been shown to be the most significant by virtue of the energy they carry and the longer duration of their decay.

An undue concentration of modes in one frequency region will often be heard as an accentuation of sounds around that region. By analogy with optical terminology, in which light of a particular colour arises from an electromagnetic vibration of a particular frequency, such an emphasis is called colouration. Colouration of the sound in a room results when modes are widely spaced, typically when one mode or one group of modes is separated by about 20 Hz from the adjacent modes, and when that frequency region is excited by a source of sound. This effect therefore tends to be associated with small rooms, where the lower-order modes are in the audible frequency range.

If two (or more) dimensions of a room are the same, or a simple multiple of each other, then their axial mode series will be the same or will have many common terms. The chances of colouration being audible are therefore increased and the acoustic designer's aim of a uniform distribution of sound is made more difficult to achieve.

In small rooms, the lowest frequencies in the axial modal series lie in the speech frequency region and are spaced well apart in frequency. The twenty lowest modes calculated for an echo room whose dimensions were adjusted to distribute the modes are shown in Table 5.1. For comparison, the modal frequencies of a well-known and highly coloured speech enclosure—a telephone booth—are also shown.

At first sight it might appear that these problems would be resolved by constructing non-rectangular rooms, a solution which has often been proposed. In practice, however, the room still has its eigentones and audible acoustic effects still result.

One important example of a standing wave is the regular series of reflections set up between a pair of plane-parallel reflecting surfaces. This is known as a flutter echo. This type of response is particularly apparent in an otherwise dead room, and can result from comparatively small areas such as control room windows or doors. The cure for a flutter echo may be to add more absorption, to make the surface diffusing, or to angle one of the surfaces relative to the other.

The decay of the soundfield in a room was studied by Sabine in the early part of this century. He noted that the reverberation time was a function of the volume of the room and of the total amount of absorption that it contained. He derived the relationship

$$T = \frac{0.161\ V}{\bar{\alpha}S}$$

where T is the reverberation time, RT (sec)
V is the volume of the room (m³)
S is the surface area of the room (m²)
$\bar{a}$ is the average absorption coefficient.

The reverberation time is defined as the time taken for the sound to die away to one-millionth of its original energy (60 dB), although, of course, measurements are seldom possible over such a wide range. The average absorption coefficient is obtained by adding together all the individual items of absorption and dividing by the total area:

$$\bar{\alpha} = \frac{1}{S}\{\alpha_1 S_1 + \alpha_2 S_2 + \dots\}$$

where S_1 is the area of material of absorption α_1, etc. The above formula assumes a continuous absorption of sound, whereas with the exception of air

TABLE 5.1. **Modal Frequencies of Two Rooms**

Room 1 (echo room)[a]				Room 2 (telephone booth)[b]			
n_x	n_y	n_z	Frequency (Hz)	n_x	n_y	n_z	Frequency (Hz)
1	0	0	34.02	0	0	1	76.22
0	1	0	43.20	0	0	2	152.44
1	1	0	54.99	0	1	0	201.77
0	0	1	56.15	1	0	0	211.73
1	0	1	65.65	0	1	1	215.68
2	0	0	68.08	1	0	1	225.03
0	1	1	70.85	0	0	3	228.67
1	1	1	78.59	0	1	2	252.88
2	1	0	80.63	1	0	2	260.90
0	2	0	86.44	1	1	0	292.47
2	0	1	88.25	1	1	1	302.24
1	2	0	92.89	0	0	4	304.89
2	1	1	98.25	0	1	3	304.96
3	0	0	102.00	1	0	3	311.64
0	2	1	103.08	1	1	2	329.81
1	2	1	108.54	0	1	4	365.60
2	2	0	110.03	1	0	4	371.20
0	0	2	112.30	1	1	3	371.25
1	0	2	117.34	0	0	5	381.11
0	1	2	120.32				

Note: a Length (x) 5.03 m; Breadth (y) 3.96 m; Height (z) 3.05 m.
b Length (x) 0.81 m; Breadth (y) 0.85 m; Height (z) 2.25 m.

absorption, the removal of energy is a discontinuous process occurring each time a wavefront is reflected from a surface.

Modifications to the formula have been made by later researchers, the most successful being that by Eyring in 1930 which allows for the discontinuous absorption and gives a greatly improved agreement with measured values at low reverberation times (high absorption coefficients):

$$T = \frac{0.161\ V}{-S \log_e (1 - \bar{\alpha}) + 4\ mV}$$

The 4 mV factor accounts for air absorption, which is significant at high frequencies and in rooms of large volume.

As was mentioned earlier, physical roughness of a wall surface will cause diffuse reflections of a sound wave; the size of the roughness determines the frequency at which the effect becomes noticeable, and it will be necessary to introduce projections of 200–300 mm in order to be effective for low frequencies. It has been shown that varying the absorbing characteristics of the surface can be equally effective in creating diffuse reflections, and it is therefore usual in studio design to distribute and intersperse the different types of acoustic absorbing material.

In addition to control of the general reverberant conditions, it may be necessary to eliminate strong reflections of sound from hard surfaces which can interfere with the direct sound at the microphone and cause a comb-filter distortion. The most common example of this effect is found in speech studios where interference results between the direct sound and that reflected from the table and/or script. A similar audible effect results when a free-standing loudspeaker is placed near to a reflecting wall or corner. The reflecting surface may also create difficulties in otherwise dead studios where pick-up by a microphone can lead to unwanted broadening of the stereo image.

Acoustic absorbers

It is necessary to adjust the absorbing characteristics of all studios in order to achieve the correct acoustic conditions. To this end, materials which absorb sound in particular frequency ranges have to be selected in the correct amounts and installed in the optimum positions. Acoustic absorbers operate by dissipating energy as heat, either in internal losses in vibrating materials or as viscous losses due to air movement in porous materials. The main categories of acoustic absorbers are described here.

1. Panel or 'membrane' absorbers

When a panel or membrane of a mechanically lossy material is excited into vibration by sound waves, energy will be dissipated. If such a panel comprises the exposed face of a closed box, a low-frequency resonator is formed; the resonance frequency is controlled by the mass of the panel and the combined stiffness of the material itself and the enclosed volume of air. Thus variation of the weight of the material, or of the volume of the air-space, will adjust the frequency at which maximum absorption occurs. In most cases it will be necessary to introduce additional damping into the box in the form of porous material; this must be mounted directly behind the membrane, since this is the position at which the particle velocity is at its greatest.

An extremely efficient form of membrane absorber developed in the BBC Research Department used bituminous roofing felt as the membrane. This material has a low inherent stiffness, and a considerable variation of resonance frequency results from alteration to the depth of the air-space. Results for this type of absorber are shown in Figure 5.8. Most other thin panel materials will act in the same fashion, but usually without achieving comparable bandwidths of absorption or allowing adjustment over a comparable frequency range.

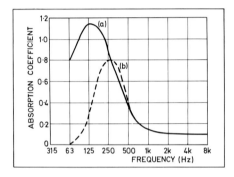

Fig. 5.8. Absorption coefficients of membrane absorbers with various air-space depths: (*a*) 300 mm, (*b*) 25 mm

2. Helmholtz resonators

An alternative resonant absorber for use at low frequencies is formed when an enclosed volume of air is coupled to the studio through a 'neck'. This form of resonator is well known to anyone who has blown over the neck of a bottle (see Figure 5.9). The resonance results from the movement of the mass of air contained in the neck, controlled by the stiffness of the enclosed volume of air.

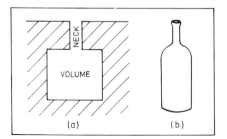

Fig. 5.9. Helmholtz resonator: (*a*) theoretical, (*b*) practical

The frequency is governed by the volume of air and by the size of the neck, so that tuning can be accomplished by changing one or the other. It will always be necessary to add a resistive material to the neck, to ensure absorption of energy over a useful bandwidth. Such absorbers have been used on occasions to damp out particular low-frequency modes in small rooms.

3. Porous absorbers

The greatest range of absorbing materials lies within this general classification; mineral wools and hanging curtains, wood wool slabs, and unplastered blockwork walls all dissipate energy by viscous loss in their pores. Provided the material is sufficiently dense, efficient absorption will result at high frequencies. As the thickness of the material is increased, the absorption will extend to lower frequencies; to some extent the same effect results from increasing the density of the material, but this may lead to increased surface reflection at higher frequences.

The first maximum in the absorption occurs at a frequency for which the thickness of the material is about one-eighth of a wavelength; doubling the thickness will lower this frequency by one octave. Progressive doubling of the thickness of absorbing material becomes expensive, and it is useful to note that there is not a great loss of efficiency if a layer of porous material is backed by an air-space to give the same total depth. Results typical of the behaviour of such porous absorbers are shown in Figure 5.10.

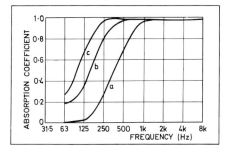

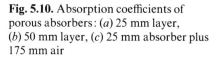

Fig. 5.10. Absorption coefficients of porous absorbers: (a) 25 mm layer, (b) 50 mm layer, (c) 25 mm absorber plus 175 mm air

The absorbing characteristics of this type of absorber can be modified by the use of a perforated facing material. Perforation providing a distributed open area of 25 per cent or greater will not significantly modify the absorber characteristic within the normal audio-frequency range. Reduction of the open area will cause a progressive cut-off of high-frequency absorption. When low-percentage perforations are reached (say 5 per cent or less) the behaviour is more like that of a surface containing a large number of Helmholtz resonators in which the perforation acts as the neck and the appropriate part of the space behind each perforation acts as the enclosed volume. Resonance absorption characteristics in the range 70–1,000 Hz can be produced by selecting the appropriate perforation and depth of air-space; typical results for absorbers which have been produced as a range of manufactured modular absorbers are shown in Figure 5.11.

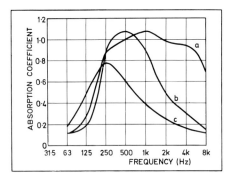

Fig. 5.11. Absorption coefficients of perforated faced absorbers: (*a*) 25%, (*b*) 5%, (*c*) 0.5% perforated face

Acoustic Design: Studios

The principles, and their practical implications, can now be applied to the design of the infinite variety of studios, control rooms, mix-down rooms, edit rooms, etc., which can exist. Only a few examples can be described, but these may be used as the models for many more similar rooms.

Music studios

A limited number of studios are still built to accommodate the activities of groups of classical musicians. This terms is used, for want of a better one, to describe a conventionally balanced group—a symphony orchestra, a chamber orchestra, or a string quartet, for example. The music created by such a group is already internally balanced and can be recorded on a single microphone (or stereo pair) without the addition of any spot microphones.

For such a musical group, the performing space constitutes an important part of the performance. The size and shape of the studio must allow the musicians to hear one another clearly in order that they may maintain an ensemble and adjust their balance one to another. Beyond this point, the acoustic characteristics of the studio should complement the sounds of the instruments to allow the individual sounds to blend and build up a warm, full tone. These and similar aspects of the studio design are important if the musicians are to give of their best, although to some extent modern technology can overcome the deficiencies of a less than perfect studio in the quality of the final output.

These requirements have implications for the dimensions of the studio as well as its purely acoustic characteristics. Orchestral musicians require a minimum of 2–3 m^2 of floor-space each, but it is also desirable that the walls of the studio should not be unduly close. The ceiling height has also been shown to be important for the larger orchestral groups, with an optimum of 9–10 m above floor level to give reflections over the whole orchestra after a suitable time delay. Given these requirements, it is generally found that studios range from 10,000 m³ for symphonic studios to 1,000 m³ for small recital studios.

Having determined the volume to accommodate the required number of musicians, an estimate of the required reverberation time can be obtained from published information such as that in Figure 5.12. However, although the size of the studio is clearly related to the anticipated use through the given numbers of musicians, some additional account may need to be taken of the type of music, if this is specific; thus romantic-style symphonic music will benefit from a longer reverberation time of 2.0–2.5 seconds, whilst chamber music, which developed in more intimate surroundings with closely textured scoring, can be better suited to a shorter reverberation time.

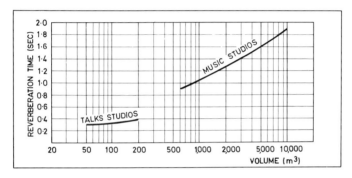

Fig. 5.12. Recommended reverberation times for broadcasting studios (courtesy BBC)

Opinions differ to some extent on the shape of the reverberation time/ frequency characteristic. UK practice has generally favoured a flat curve, but others feel that a rise at low frequencies—such as is normal in concert halls— can give added warmth. Only limited areas of designed absorption will be required to achieve the desired reverberation characteristics, though additional measures may have to be taken to increase the diffusion by shaping the surfaces appropriately.

Light music studios

The radio orchestra was undoubtedly the first step in the development of multi-microphone techniques; correct internal balance of the orchestra is no longer automatically necessary, the balance being achieved by the engineer in the control room rather than by the conductor, and the final recorded sound may be quite different from the real sound in the studio.

Under these conditions, the natural acoustics of the studio are no longer so directly relevant, and the aim has become that of ensuring good separation between the various instrumental groups. The reverberation time of the studio can be reduced to a reasonably low value which musicians still find acceptable; in addition, the widespread use of screens, partly absorbing and partly visually transparent, can help to provide the necessary separation.

Pop music studios

Pop music studios are the logical extension of the light music studios mentioned above. The studios are made as dead as possible and microphones are brought as close as practicable to the individual instruments. While all the musicians might still play at one time, it becomes necessary to strive for separation between the individual microphones. However, in the now popular technique of split-session recordings, it has become possible to record in an environment which suits the individual instruments without any necessity to deaden the space artificially. The use of gating circuits to limit the duration of the pick-up from percussive instruments gives a comparative freedom from the traditional necessity for dead drum booths.

Acoustic design in pop studios has become a more creative subject and a wide variation in the acoustic characteristics can be seen in recent designs.

Small studios (talks, DJ, demo)

The acoustic design of small studios (see Plates 1 and 2) has to make allowance for the widely distributed modal standing waves pattern. A fairly dead acoustic

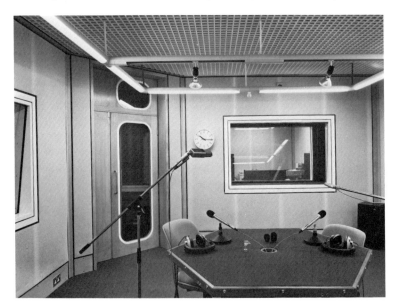

Plate 1. Studio at County Sound local radio station, Guildford (Photo: Jo Reid and John Peck)

Plate 2. Presentation studio at County Sound local radio station, Guildford (Photo: Jo Reid and John Peck)

response is normally desirable, and the use of large amounts of acoustic absorbing material gives the possibility of damping the more troublesome modes adequately. Problems do occur if the treatment is not well distributed, and a design aim which ensures that the average absorption coefficients of each pair of surfaces are similar (difference not greater than a factor of 1.4) has been found to be adequate. Control of the low-frequency reverberation is the greatest problem, and some increase of RT below 200 Hz has been found to be compatible with many types of material.

Television studios

Television studios are designed to be acoustically dead, as this is the condition which can be compatible with the widest range of programme requirements, the most critical of which may be the simulation of outdoor conditions. All the available surfaces are therefore treated with broad-band absorbing finishes of mineral fibre over a 200 mm air-space, which usually houses additional low-frequency panel absorption over an area of up to one-third of the total amount of treatment.

A recent design incorporated 100 mm screeded wood wool planks, as both the exposed acoustic absorbing face and as an isolated sound-attenuating inner lining. The larger (600 m²) production studio in this development is designed with music in mind and includes an electroacoustic artificial reverberation system. With this system—the Multi-channel Reverberation (MCR) system by Philips—the reverberation time can be varied between 0.8 and 1.4 seconds. The studio has proved successful for music productions but has also used the electroacoustic enhancement for a variety of other programme types.

Control rooms, monitoring, mix-down, etc.

The acoustic design of control rooms has, over the years, produced innumerable variations, each based on a new philosophy. However, there are some points of agreement between many of the designers.

Traditionally, control rooms were small and had the potential to introduce audible colourations. This, together with the knowledge that more critical judgements could be made in non-reverberant conditions, led to the inclusion of a reasonable amount of sound-absorbing material. Rooms have grown larger over the years because of the increase in the physical size of mixing consoles, the proliferation of ancillary equipment, and, recently, the translation of much of the keyboard and synthesizer activity into the control room for direct injection.

Reverberation time may not be the prime variable, but it is usual to find that the amount of acoustical absorbing material present reduces the RT to around 0.2–0.4 seconds. Any lack of left/right symmetry—either physical or acoustical—can upset the stereo balance, and this requirement will often dictate the relative positions of studio window and mixing console.

Beyond this point design philosophies vary. In broadcasting it is usual to find that the acoustic absorption is distributed within the room in order to create diffuse conditions which give a greater uniformity within the room. This approach is followed by the recent EBU Technical Recommendation on "Acoustical Properties of Control Rooms and Listening Rooms for the Assessment of Broadcast Programmes".

There are two current approaches to the idea of a live-end, dead-end design. In one the sound originates from the live end of the room and is completely absorbed at the rear of the room after a single pass by the head of the engineer.

In the alternative approach, the reflective end of the room is behind the engineer and the pattern of reflections is designed to complement the early impulse response of the origination.

THE EQUIPMENT

6

Microphones
John Borwick

The programme chain as described in Chapter 1 begins with one or more microphones and ends with one or more loudspeakers (the usual number is two, suitably spaced to produce the stereo effect of musicians arranged more or less naturally across an arc). Microphones and loudspeakers belong to the large family of 'transducers', that is devices whose job is is to convert energy from one form to another.

The microphone converts acoustical energy into electrical energy, whilst the loudspeaker, interestingly enough, does the same job in reverse, converting electrical energy (supplied as an electric current) back into acoustical energy (radiated as sound waves). Other examples of reciprocal transducing devices are to be found in the recording/reproducing chain. A tape recording head, for example, converts electrical energy into magnetic energy, whilst a tape playback head does the reverse. (Indeed, a single head is used on the majority of cheaper domestic tape machines, simply switched according to which function is required at the time.) A disc cutter converts electrical energy into mechanical vibration of the stylus, and leaves a 'record' of the sound waves embossed into a groove in the master disc surface; the gramophone pickup stylus retraces this waveform, and its vibrations are used to generate an electric current. Again, the laser source which 'cuts' a track of digital pits on the photo-resist surface of a Compact Disc master converts electrical energy into light energy, whilst the light-sensitive device in a CD player, which receives the reflected laser beam, reverses the transducing process and converts light energy into a usable electric current.

The transducing action in a microphone can be seen as comprising two stages, though of course they happen simultaneously:

(a) the changes in air pressure due to sound waves set a light diaphragm into mechanical motion,
(b) the vibrations of the diaphragm are used to generate an alternating voltage.

The acoustical/mechanical conversion

For the first stage, two basic methods can be used to produce mechanical vibration from the action of sound waves. The most simple method is called

119

pressure operation and has the diaphragm open to the air on one side only, with its back effectively enclosed (Figure 6.1). The diaphragm will then tend to move inwards and outwards as the instantaneous air pressure alternates above and below the normal atmospheric value.

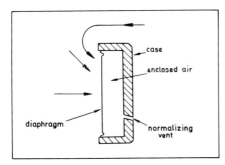

Fig. 6.1. Typical construction of a pressure-operated microphone

Such a pressure-operated microphone is theoretically non-directional (the preferred term is 'omnidirectional'), since pressure is a scalar rather than a vector quantity; the tendency for diaphragm movement will be the same regardless of the direction from which the sound waves are coming. The graph (polar diagram) of the microphone's output voltage for a given level of acoustic pressure variation in a given plane will therefore be a circle (and a three-dimensional plot would yield a sphere with the microphone at the centre).

In practice, however, the physical size of the microphone causes it to act as an obstacle to sound waves at higher frequencies (shorter wavelengths). The waves then tend to be reflected, with a boosting effect for front incident sounds and attenuation of sounds arriving at the back and sides. The family of directivity patterns for different frequencies therefore looks like the example in Figure 6.2, with the circular, omnidirectional pick-up pattern for low frequencies progressively narrowing and becoming front-biased as the frequency is increased.

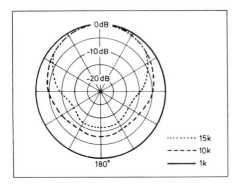

Fig. 6.2. Family of polar diagrams for a pressure-operated (nominally omnidirectional) microphone, showing the progressive narrowing of the response at higher frequencies

This changing frequency response at oblique angles has obvious practical consequences. Knowing that an omnidirectional microphone has its maximum high-frequency response on axis enables a user to tilt or offset the microphone angle in situations where a slight softening of the treble is desirable. Note that the family of curves is related solely to the ratio D/λ, where D is the microphone diameter and λ is the wavelength. Reducing the size of the microphone and mounting the diaphragm at the end of a narrow cylindrical case, for example, will raise the frequency limit for omnidirectional response.

The second method used to produce mechanical vibrations in response to the acoustical energy in sound waves is called *pressure-gradient* (or sometimes *velocity*) operation. In this method, the diaphragm is open to the air on both sides so that the force acting on it at any instant is due to the pressure difference or gradient at the two faces. As is shown in Figure 6.3a, this will be a maximum

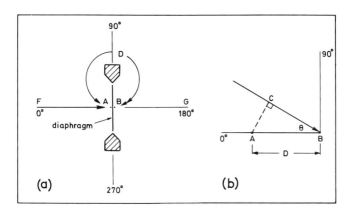

Fig. 6.3. Pressure-gradient operation: (a) front and back of diaphragm are effectively distance D apart, (b) distance reduces according to $D \cos \theta$ for oblique incidence

for normal incidence on the axis at 0° and 180°, when the extra path length for sounds to reach the back of the diaphragm is a maximum D. It will diminish at increasing off-axis angles, falling to a theoretical zero at 90° and 270°. Plotting such a response over the full 360° produces the familiar figure-of-eight graph shown in Figure 6.4. In mathematical terms, this is a graph of the expression $Y = X\cos\theta$, where Y is the sensitivity (response) at a given angle θ and X is the maximum sensitivity on axis. In practice, X is proportional to the distance which a sound incident at 0° must travel around the mounting or case to reach the remote face of the diaphragm (shown as D in Figure 6.3b), which explains why the voltage output from a pressure-gradient microphone is in effect proportional to sound particle velocity.

Many modern microphones are designed to combine the pressure and pressure-gradient principles of operation in specific proportions to provide

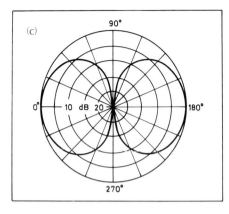

Fig. 6.4. Figure-of-eight polar diagram for pressure-gradient microphone

directivity patterns intermediate between the circle (omnidirectional) and the figure-of-eight (bidirectional). The sensitivity at any angle will then be given by the expression $Y = Z + X\cos\theta$, where Z is the sensitivity of the pressure-operated element and $X\cos\theta$ represents the contribution of the pressure-gradient element as before.

In the special case where $Z = X$, i.e. the pressure and PG elements are of equal axial sensitivity, the directivity pattern is heart-shaped and therefore referred to as a *cardioid*. The derivation of a cardioid pattern by simple addition of circle and figure-of-eight patterns having the same maximum sensitivity is illustrated in Figure 6.5.

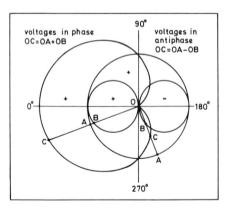

Fig. 6.5. Derivation of cardioid by combining a circle and a figure-of-eight of the same sensitivity

By choosing different relative values for Z and X, it is possible to derive other patterns which in effect look like unsymmetrical figures-of-eight. The two most common are shown in Figure 6.6. The *hypercardioid* results from values $Z =$

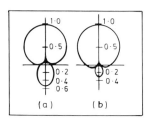

Fig. 6.6. Other common polar diagrams:
(*a*) hypercardioid, (*b*) supercardioid

0.25 and $X = 0.75$; the *supercardioid* has $Z = 0.375$ and $X = 0.625$. It will be seen that these patterns give better attentuation of sounds at 90° than the cardioid, which is the best choice, however, when rejection of sounds from behind the microphone (at 180°) is a main requirement. The attenuations in dB at 90° and 180° for the five directivity patterns so far mentioned are summarized in Figure 6.7.

CHARACTERISTIC	OMNI-DIRECTIONAL	CARDIOID	SUPER-CARDIOID	HYPER-CARDIOID	BI-DIRECTIONAL
POLAR RESPONSE PATTERN	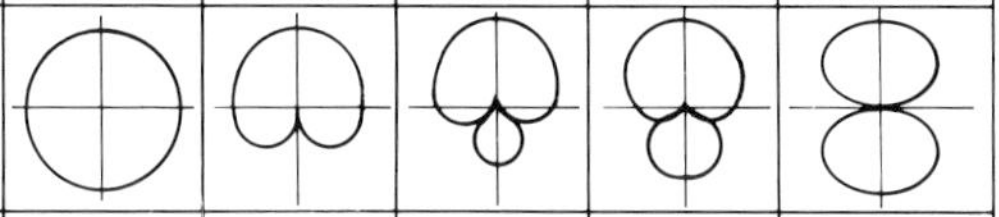				
POLAR EQUATION	1	$.5 + .5 \cos \theta$	$.375 + .625 \cos \theta$	$.25 + .75 \cos \theta$	$\cos \theta$
RELATIVE OUTPUT AT 90° (dB)	0	-6	-8.6	-12	$-\infty$
RELATIVE OUTPUT AT 180° (dB)	0	$-\infty$	-11.7	-6	0
ANGLE AT WHICH OUTPUT = 0	—	180°	126°	110°	90°
DISTANCE FACTOR (DF)	1	1.7	1.9	2	1.7

Fig. 6.7. A comparison of the five most common directivity patterns

There is also a useful differentiation in practical terms of the total amount of the soundfield picked up by these different microphone types. The omnidirectional microphone picks up all the ambient sound (direct sound plus reverberation), whereas the figure-of-eight and cardioid pick up only one-third. This means that these can be positioned 1.7 times further from the musicians for a given balance of direct-to-reverberant sound (see Figure 6.8). The supercardioid and hypercardioid can be set back even further, at 1.9 and 2.0 times respectively. It should be borne in mind that these diagrams aand distance values are the theoretical ones. In general, there is the same tendency for values to change at high frequencies due to microphone case dimensions as was mentioned in the case of the omni microphone.

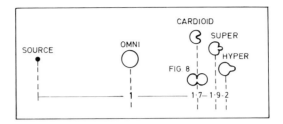

Fig. 6.8. Distance factors for different microphone types, giving the same ratio of direct-to-reverberant sounds

Effects of distance on frequency response

The distance between the microphone and the sound source has a number of important effects on the frequency response, particularly in the case of PG-operated microphones.

At short distances where the sound radiation may still be regarded as consisting of spherical waves (say at one-wavelength distance or less) the low-frequency response becomes severely accentuated. This is called the *proximity effect* and is illustrated in Figure 6.9. There is practically no such bass tip-up with omni microphones, which partly explains why these are favoured for close working, except that some vocalists (from Bing Crosby onwards) have found that some bass boost gives an added warmth to their sound. Of course, bass equalization can be applied to diminish any undesirable effects when PG microphones have to be used at short distances (such as in BBC talk studios).

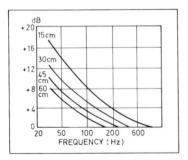

Fig. 6.9. Proximity effect: showing the bass tip-up to be expected at various close distances from a pressure-gradient-operated microphone

Another effect comes into play when large distances are used in a hall or studio. At all distances, the total output of a microphone is not due simply to the direct sound arriving on axis. It is made up of the sum of the direct sound (for which the axial *free-field* frequency response curve applies) and the numerous reflected sounds which arrive, after various time delays, more or less equally from all directions. A microphone's response to this reflected off-axis sound is called its *diffuse-field* response. Ideally this should run parallel to the free-field response curve, simply being at a lower signal level due to the attenuation with distance. Changing the microphone distance will then give the balance engineer a means of altering the apparent balance between direct and reverberant sound without materially affecting the balance of frequencies. This result is achieved in the better-quality PG microphones.

In pressure (omni) microphones, however, the diffuse-field response curve always shows a distinct falling off in treble response compared with the axial free-field response (due to the narrowing directivity illustrated in Figure 6.2). Some designers face up to this need for compromise by giving the axial response a degree of top lift; others go for a flat frontal response and leave it to the balance engineer to introduce some treble EQ on distant balances where necessary. The Brüel and Kjaer omni microphones are supplied with alternative front grilles for close and distant working (see Figure 6.10).

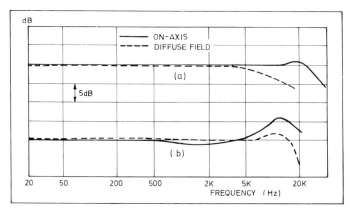

Fig. 6.10. Use of a special grille to optimize response of an omni microphone, either (*a*) for close working or (*b*) distant working in the diffuse field (courtesy Brüel and Kjaer)

Microphones for stereo

Ever since the launch of stereo records around 1958, the vast majority of music recordings have been made in two-channel stereo using a variety of microphone techniques where the directivity pattern is a vital factor. Some of these may be summarized as follows.

Coincident pair (Blumlein)

This technique uses a pair of identical directional microphones placed as nearly as possible in the same point in space. There is therefore minimum time-of-arrival difference at the two capsules, and the whole of the directional (stereo) information relies on the controlled intensity difference between the two microphone outputs. The method appeals to purists, because it avoids phasing problems and gives a more or less ideal spread over the standard 60° listening arc. It also has the benefit of historical respectability, since it was described in detail by A. D. Blumlein, who pioneered stereophonic recording in his famous Patent No. 394325 as long ago as 1931.

If the two microphones are set at 90° to each other (the usual arrangement), various acceptance angles—which will be reduced to the listening 60° arc on replay—are achieved depending on which directivity pattern is in use. Blumlein described the effect of using crossed figures-of-eight, which give a 90° acceptance angle, and this arrangement remains a favourite, but Figure 6.11 also shows the acceptance ange for two other patterns, hypercardioid and cardioid.

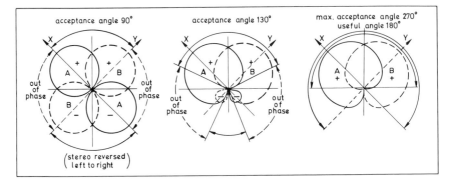

Fig. 6.11. Polar characteristics and acceptance angles for coincident pairs of figure-of-eight, hypercardioid, and cardioid microphones set at a mutual angle of 90°

MS stereo

This technique again uses coincident microphones, one of which is a Middle component microphone (usually cardioid or omni) pointing straight ahead. The other is a figure-of-eight Side component microphone arranged laterally (see Figure 6.12). The microphone outputs are processed by a sum-and-difference

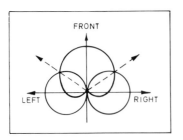

Fig. 6.12. MS stereo arrangement using a cardioid M component and a figure-of-eight S component

network to produce conventional left and right signals, making use of the fact that the two lobes of the figure-of-eight are in opposite phase.

Many variations are possible, the MS system being particularly attractive to broadcasters because it gives ideal compatibility with mono transmissions—simple addition of the left/right signals gives the M signal alone:

$$(M+S)+(M-S) = 2M.$$

Near coincident pair

Several systems have been evolved with the microphone pair spaced a short distance apart, with or without a physical baffle between them. These include the ORTF method of the French Broadcasting Organization, and various binaural recording systems using a real or stylized dummy head as the baffle. The latter technique of course succeeds best on headphone listening, when uncanny directional realism can sometimes be reproduced in all planes.

Spaced pair

A widely spaced pair of omni or other type of microphones (1–5 m apart) gives well-differentiated stereo but needs care if odd phase cancellations and a 'hole in the middle' effect are to be avoided, the latter caused by the lack of any microphone aimed directly at the centre stage (where soloists are often located). A solution often employed is to add a third microphone at the centre to control the apparent width and give improved focus on the centre image.

Multi-microphone stereo

It is also common practice to mix together a number of (mono or stereo) microphones, either recording them all at a single take or one or two at a time during a number of overdub multitrack sessions. Then the engineer has the responsibility of panning each source to that part of the stereo arc which seems to give the most artistic result. In pop recording there are no hard-and-fast rules, but for the classical repertoire it is usually best to employ a basic stereo pair out front and then pan each spot microphone until the spotlighted instrument appears in the same position across the stereo stage as it does in the overall stereo pair balance.

The mechanical/electrical conversion

A vibrating diaphragm can be made to generate a proportionate voltage using a number of transducer principles. These include piezo-electric (crystal and ceramic), contact resistance (carbon), thermal, ionic, magnetic (moving-coil and ribbon), and electrostatic (condenser and electret). Only the magnetic and electrostatic types are found in professional sound recording studios, and so the others will be left out of this discussion.

Magnetic or 'dynamic' microphones rely on the electromagnetic interaction between the field of a powerful permanent magnet and a moving conductor. In the moving-coil type, a coil of wire is fixed to the back of the diaphragm and is free to move in the circular gap of an annular magnet/polepiece assembly (see Figure 6.13a). Diaphragm motion results in the coil cutting through the magnetic field so that an electric current is induced in the coil. Impedance is low and therefore a step-up transformer may be built into the microphone. Even so, the sensitivity (voltage out for a given acoustic pressure level) is relatively low, but this is not a serious limitation in the applications for which moving-coils are commonly used, namely hand-held for vocals or interviews, lavalier types, and close balance of percussion instruments. They are well suited to this kind of application because their main resonance is mid-frequency and well damped, making them fairly impervious to wind and mechanical interference. Most moving-coils are pressure-operated and therefore omnidirectional, but more sophisticated cardioid or unidirectional models are also common.

Ribbon microphones use the same principle as moving-coils but have a thin strip (usually of aluminium leaf) doing double duty as diaphragm and conductor. The ribbon is only a few μm thick by 2–4 mm wide and is corrugated and held under light tension in the gap between specially shaped magnetic polepieces (see Figure 6.13b). The impedance is very low and so a built-in transformer is essential. Weighing only about 0.2 mg, the ribbon has an excellent transient response and a smooth frequency coverage, but it is very sensitive to wind noise and external vibrations, which restricts the situations in which it can be used. The open construction means that ribbon microphones are normally pressure-gradient-operated to give the classic figure-of-eight directivity pattern, but a few designs partially enclose one face of the ribbon or introduce an acoustical delay network (as in some condenser microphones) to produce cardioid or similar patterns.

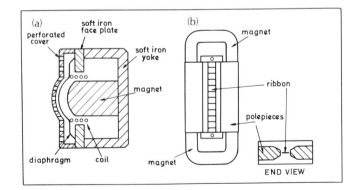

Fig. 6.13. Typical construction of (*a*) moving-coil and (*b*) ribbon microphones

Electrostatic microphones (otherwise called 'capacitor' or 'condenser') are now the type most commonly used in professional recording. This has come about despite the fact that they are difficult, and therefore expensive, to make and often need care in handling, storage and exposure to climatic extremes.

The thin, 1–10 μm, diaphragm is made of metal or metallized plastic film and supported around its rim at a small distance (5–50 μm) from the thicker metal backplate (see Figure 6.14). The thin diaphragm and fixed backplate therefore form the two electrodes of a simple capacitor and are oppositely charged by the application of a polarizing voltage. Vibrations of the diaphragm in response to the changing air pressure due to sound waves cause the spacing and therefore the capacitance of the two-plate condenser to alternate about its mean value, and this is used to generate the required output voltage. The very high (capacitative) impedance of the microphone capsule makes it impracticable to use a direct cable feed. A built-in head amplifier very close to the capsule is therefore essential, as much for impedance matching as for voltage gain. However, as an amplifier is obligatory, the output sensitivity and impedance can be optimized to suit the standard circuits used in professional applications.

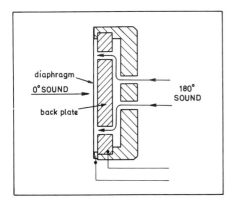

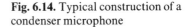

Fig. 6.14. Typical construction of a condenser microphone

The output of a condenser microphone is proportional to the d.c. polarizing voltage applied, and so simple switching of the value of this voltage can be used to give a range of directivity patterns from a single microphone (see Plate 3). In Figure 6.15a, for example, the microphone consists in effect of two cardioid capsules back to back. The polarizing voltage to one of the diaphragms (on the right in the diagram) is fixed at +60 V with respect to the common backplate to give a forward-facing cardioid response. The voltage to the second diaphragm can be switched from −60 V through 0 V to +60 V, and, since the a.c. signal outputs of the two capsules are connected in parallel through capacitor C, the five polar diagrams of Figure 6.15b can be obtained. In the centre position 3, for example, the rear diaphragm is at 0 V and contributes no signal, leaving the

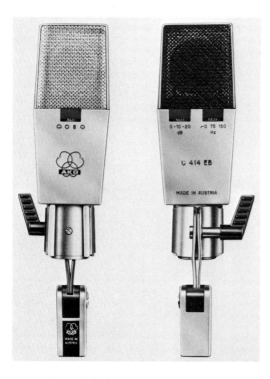

Plate 3. Electrostatic microphone showing switching for four directivity patterns (left), sensitivity and bass roll-off (right) (Photo: AKG)

forward cardioid in operation. In position 1, the two contributions are equal but in opposite phase to give a figure-of-eight response, and so on. Remote-controlled switching is of course perfectly possible, with a greater number of switch positions or a continuously variable potentiometer if required.

It is clearly a disadvantage that the condenser microphone requires a separate source of d.c. power both to polarize the plates and energize the built-in amplifier (though a 'phantom power' system usually supplies the required voltage along the signal cable). This situation has been met in part in recent years by the development of *electret microphones*, in which the diaphragm is made from a permanently polarized electret foil membrane. This has reduced the cost of manufacture and somewhat extended the freedom of application, since electret microphones can be very light and small in size. A low-voltage (battery) supply is still needed for the amplifier but the high-voltage polarizing source is eliminated. Note, however, that this also removes the possibility of variable-directivity switching with electret microphones.

Microphone sensitivity

The electrical output from a microphone for a given sound pressure level (defined as the sensitivity) should clearly be as high as possible, to provide a high signal-to-noise ratio (even more important now that digital recording and

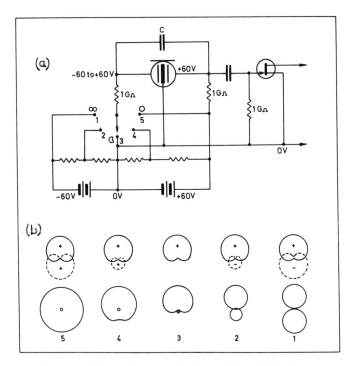

Fig. 6.15. Variable directivity: (*a*) basic switching with a double-diaphragm condenser microphone, (*b*) the polar diagrams for the five switch positions

the Compact Disc have greatly reduced other sources of inherent background noise). The word 'noise' is used here to mean electrical noise, interference, mechanical handling, cable rubbing, and indeed all the unwelcome accompaniments to the desired signal before it reaches the microphone input sockets on the control console.

In practice, the microphones used in professional recording vary widely in sensitivity, and it does not help that several different ways are used to specify this parameter in manufacturers' specifications. The IEC and British Standards method is to specify the voltage output per pascal (a sound pressure unit equal to 10 microbars) measured under open circuit conditions: a typical value would be 8.0 mV/Pa. The generally accepted threshold of hearing at 1,000 Hz corresponds to a pressure of 20×10^{-4} Pa, and Sound Pressure Level (SPL) in dB with reference to this threshold is frequently used instead of pressure in Pa. On the SPL scale, 1 Pa = 94 dB SPL, which corresponds to quite a loud sound. In a commonly used method of specifying sensitivity, the reference SPL is 74 dB, which is about the level of speech at 20 cm (and equals 0.1 Pa or 1 microbar); the sensitivity is given in terms of the voltage output level (in dB ref. 1 V, or sometimes 0.775 V).

Some manufacturers also quote an overload or *maximum SPL* for which the total harmonic distortion from the microphone reaches a stated value (say 0.5 per cent). As an indication of the microphone's *inherent noise*, the rated equivalent SPL which would give the same output voltage as the inherent noise is often quoted, and this can be either unweighted (measured via a meter flat from 20 Hz to 20 kHz) or weighted to the IEC A curve and given as a dBA value. Subtracting the equivalent noise level from the maximum SPL gives the microphone's total dynamic range. For example, if noise SPL is 14 dB and overload SPL is 134 dB (both very good values) the dynamic range is 120 dB.

Special microphones

A whole range of microphones designed to meet the needs of special applications has evolved over the years, and some of these will be described briefly.

Ultradirectional microphones

The need for higher directivity than can be got from cardioid or supercardioid microphones arises in such long-distance recording situations as sport, bird-song, and environments with high ambient noise, as in some television situations where the microphone must be kept away from the scene in shot. An early approach to this problem was to construct a parabolic reflector of say 0.5 or 1.0 m diameter and mount the microphone at the focal point. This effectively concentrates the parallel rays of sound arriving on axis and discriminates against sounds from other directions. It is unwieldy, however, and ceases to be effective for low-frequency sounds where the wavelength is equal to or greater than the reflector diameter.

A more versatile solution is the line or 'shot-gun' microphone, in which the microphone capsule is mounted at the end of a thin pipe having holes spaced along its length. Acoustic delay elements ensure that only the sounds arriving on the gun axis reach the capsule in phase and therefore add together to produce the desired narrow-angle response.

Boundary effect or PZM microphones

A recent development seeks to avoid the interference effect when sounds are reflected on to a microphone from a nearby surface, producing the well-known comb-filter type of distortion, as cancellation nulls appear at the frequency for which the spacing is $\frac{1}{4}$ wavelength and its harmonics. Provided that the microphone diaphragm can be mounted very close to a primary reflecting surface, the incident and reflected waves will be in phase and reinforce each other.

The boundary layer or pressure zone microphones (PZM) based on this idea have a small pressure-operated capsule mounted into a flat plate which can be laid on the floor or taped to a wall or lectern. The capsule receives the direct and reflected wave simultaneously and can have a consistently smooth frequency response over a whole hemisphere. A cardioid version also exists.

Direction-sensing microphones

An extension of the boundary microphone idea has led to the production of direction-sensing microphones. These have two cardioid capsules back to back feeding a special mixer unit. This senses the ratio of sound from the two capsules and gates 'on' the appropriate signal for which the talker is within $\pm 60°$ of the axis.

Contact microphones

Transducer elements which can convert the physical vibrations of an instrument string or body directly to an electrical signal have been in use for many years in electronic guitars, keyboards, and other instruments. A more recent move has been towards the use of a contact capacity transducer in the form of a very thin (1 mm) tape supplied in various lengths. This can be applied to the curved surface of a double bass or drum casing, and gives a very high ratio of instrument pick-up to ambient sounds.

Wireless microphones

Where complete freedom from the trailing microphone cable is needed, in complicated stage or TV shows for example, a radio microphone can provide the answer. This employs a conventional hand-held or (concealed) tie-pin/lavalier microphone attached to a miniature radio transmitter worn by the user. A special receiver is tuned to the transmitter frequency and produces an audio output signal suitable for feeding into the normal line input of the control console. Several radio microphones may be used at once, tuned to different radio frequencies. There are also 'diversity reception' systems in which the microphone signal is picked up by more than one receiver and automatic switching reduces the risks of fading as the artist moves around.

Soundfield microphone

Whilst the four-channel quadraphonic recordings promoted in the 1970s failed to secure a wide public following—due partly to the confusing parallel promotion of several competing non-compatible encoding systems and partly to the poor sound imaging which resulted—a small band of researchers continues to search for a commercially viable surround sound system. Very acceptable results can be demonstrated using the Ambisonics system, and a by-product of this research has been the Soundfield microphone. This consists of four microphone capsules arranged in a regular tetrahedron inside a single casing and orientated in such a way as to capture all the directional information needed to reproduce (through a suitable array of four or more loudspeakers) the full $360°$ three-dimensional soundfield.

This surround-sound application has still failed to attract a substantial show of interest from the major record companies or broadcasters, though film and video producers are now actively pursuing three-dimensional soundtracks. However, the Soundfield microphone has proved to be extremely versatile as a tool in two-channel stereo recording. The remote-control unit allows the engineer to steer the microphone's directivity and alter the stereo width and such other parameters as direct-to-reverberant sound balance, apparent height, and so on.

7

Mixing consoles: Analogue

Richard Swettenham

In order to cover all the features likely to be met in consoles for recording use, this chapter will describe the units and systems found in a typical console for multitrack recording, considered mainly from the operational rather than the engineering design point of view. By way of illustration, Figure 7.1 shows a typical controls layout for one channel of a simple console and Figure 7.2 illustrates the flow diagram for the input module of a similar console. A modern console having extensive computer-assisted mixing facilities is illustrated in Plate 4.

Microphone inputs

The main factors of importance here are: source and input impedances, noise in relation to gain, and gain range and headroom. The majority of studio microphones have nominal impedances in the range of 150–300 ohms, and for practical purposes may be regarded as 200 ohms. Almost all capacitor microphones fall into this group, though some have provision for internal connection for 50 ohms. This gives half the output voltage, which is sometimes useful to avoid overloading the input of equipment basically intended for use with low-level dynamic microphones. With the average studio console it is not useful or desirable.

Some dynamic microphones are still supplied in the 30–60 ohms impedance range. Hence some older consoles had a '50–200 ohm' input switch which varied the input transformer ratio to give extra step-up, with the intention of improving signal-to-noise ratio. However, with most input amplifier designs the noise at high gain will be related to the source impedance presented to the input (seen after the transformer, if there is one). So, though the transformer appears to give 'free gain' the advantage in fact may be small. Current practice is simply to regard the lower-impedance microphones as less sensitive types.

The impedance seen by the microphone is also important, because a dynamic microphone is not a pure resistive source and its impedance, particularly at high frequencies, may be somewhat higher than the stated value. If it were noticeably loaded, this might well degrade the frequency response. Hence microphones of all types are intended to be used as unloaded voltage generators and their

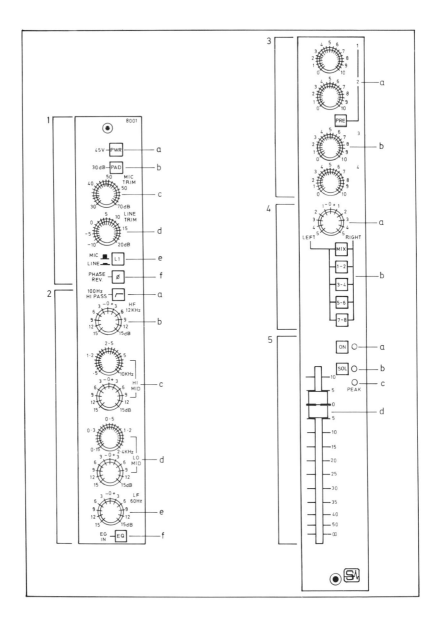

Fig. 7.1. Typical layout of controls, showing 1. channel input section (furthest from the operator), 2. equalization, 3. auxiliary, 4. routing, 5. channel status (nearest the operator) (Soundcraft Series 800)

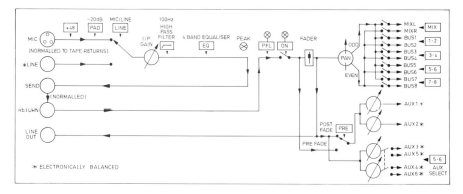

Fig. 7.2. Typical flow diagram (Soundcraft Series 500)

Plate 4. Typical modular console designed for stereo broadcasting with computer assistance (Photo: Solid State Logic)

published response curves are taken in this way. Standard recommended practice, therefore, is for the impedance looking into the microphone input of the console to be at least five times that of the microphone, that is 1 k ohms or higher over the whole frequency range, and this value must also be unaffected by any feedback gain change or the introduction of input pads.

Noise

In comparing manufacturers' specifications, it is essential to compare the stated test conditions and regard with caution any figures which do not state them clearly. Noise is normally specified at maximum gain, and is stated either as 'equivalent input noise' or 'noise figure'. Equivalent input noise is the noise measured at the amplifier output in dBu (dB relative to 0.775 V) plus the amplifier and transformer voltage gain in dB when the input is terminated with a resistor of the normal microphone value (usually 200 ohms). Note that a 600 ohm source, sometimes specified, will produce an apparently worse figure, and a 30 ohm source (sometimes not mentioned) an apparently better figure.

Example: Noise measured -57 dBu, gain 70 dB,
Equivalent Input Noise $= -127$ dB.

The Noise Figure is the amount by which the Equivalent Input Noise is higher than the thermal noise of a 200 ohm (or other specified) resistor. Here the source value is part of the calculation, so the above ambiguity is avoided. It is also necessary to state the bandwidth of measurement, or the weighting network used, and the type of voltage-measuring instrument. A nominal 'r.m.s.' microvoltmeter will give a lower reading on noise than a peak instrument such as a PPM.

The above figures give a measure of the quietness of a microphone amplifier at highest gain. As the gain is reduced, the noise will reduce at first in proportion to the gain, but then tend to level off towards a certain minimum noise at low gains (Figure 7.3). The Noise Figure in top-class designs has been very close to

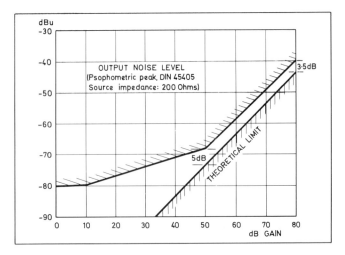

Fig. 7.3. Noise level limits for microphone amplifiers (Nordic Broadcasting Authorities' recommendations)

theoretical limits for some years, but the general improvement in amplifier devices has meant that the noise/gain relationship can now be maintained down to much lower gains.

Input gain range

The microphone circuit requires the widest range of gain adjustment in the whole audio system. On the one hand a ribbon microphone over a clavichord may call for all possible gain; on the other, a capacitor in front of a bass drum may well deliver 0 dB or more to the console. In the past, many strategies combining negative feedback with attentuation, and even the switching in and out of amplifier blocks, have been used to cover the whole range. An available input gain of 80 dB used to be considered necessary in broadcasting consoles, but when it is realised that this means a peak signal-to-noise ratio of worse than 55 dB it becomes obvious that this is hardly usable in modern recording. General practice seems to have settled on a gain range of 20–70 dB, with a balanced pad at the input giving a further loss of 20 dB.

Overload margin

The maximum voltage output available from a microphone amplifier will depend simply on the supply voltages, as in all other amplifiers in the console. Yet the designer has to consider whether extra headroom should be provided for unexpected high-level input peaks by arranging the gain structure to give a lower 'normal' output level from the first amplifier and making it up later in the system after a level control. Some broadcasting specifications demand this, having in mind the unrehearsed live programme situation, but in the music studio it is less of a problem. In the case of a microphone amplifier with transformer input, when the gain is low and input level high (as with close miking of loud instruments with capacitor microphones), harmonic distortion may appear, due to saturation of the transformer, particularly at low frequencies, though the output level is normal. This may be avoided by switching in the resistive pad mentioned above (which is always in front of the transformer). Sometimes it may be desirable to put in a pad and then put back a few steps of gain.

It has taken some years for the transformerless (electronically balanced) microphone amplifier to reach noise performance comparable with transformer types, but it can provide virtually perfect frequency and transient response. Yet there remains a case, here if nowhere else in the console, for the retention of the transformer, less for obtaining gain than as an isolating device. The all-electronic circuit has to be carefully trimmed to reject any common-mode (audio pair to earth) signals from being amplified, and protected against excessive voltages damaging the input circuit. Large electrolytic capacitors are also required to isolate the phantom power supplies for capacitor microphones.

Phantom power supply

Phantom-operated capacitor microphones (as mentioned in Chapter 6) fall into two groups: those which utilise about 48 V d.c. directly for polarisation and have amplifier powering, and those which generate operating voltages by an oscillator–rectifier arrangement from any available supply from 9 V upwards, with phantom splitting resistors chosen according to supply voltage. Since a console may have to supply microphones of both types, the built-in supply will be 48 V and the resistor value chosen for the microphone type which draws the greatest current. The 'true 48 V' types draw very little current, so there is minimal voltage drop.

Gain settings

The key to the correct setting of microphone amplifier gain, with respect both to noise and overload margin, is to keep the channel fader at the intended 'normal' setting (e.g. 10 dB from maximum) when the channel is contributing a signal to the mix that produces a peak-level indication. This assumes of course that the group master fader is also at normal.

A useful approach to the correct situation is to set all faders to normal on rehearsal and attempt to produce a plausible balance on the microphone gain controls. It should be realized that any downward movement of the fader from this position, other than to reduce the amount of that channel heard in the mix, is eating into the available headroom. If restoring any fader to the reference mark causes the level meter to go over peak, then microphone gain must be reduced. An LED overload warning light is commonly found in input channels, and desirably these should respond to pre-set warning levels detected both before and after the equalizer.

Filters and phase reversal

A phase-reversal switch, operating on both microphone and line inputs, and a low-frequency cut-off filter are normally found in each channel. High-frequency filters are common, but not universal. The filters have a slope of 12 or 18 dB per octave from the turnover frequency, and are usually switched into circuit only when required.

The LF cut-off filter has considerable use since the normal response specification of 20 Hz to 20 kHz is usable only under ideal conditions. More often it is necessary to curtail the response below the lowest fundamental note of an instrument to cut off air-conditioning rumble, vibration of microphone stands, and hum from guitar amplifiers. High-frequency filtering is less necessary in live recording, but may be useful to cut off overspill, say from cymbals picked up on a microphone covering a bass instrument whose harmonics do not come far up the frequency range. Typically, switched LF filters will operate at 40, 80, 120, and 180 Hz, and HF filters at 12, 8, 6, and 4 kHz. Filters with 'sliding' turnover frequency are now available in many consoles; these can be moved up from about 15 Hz to say 350 Hz, and from 25 kHz down to say 3 kHz (see Figure 7.4).

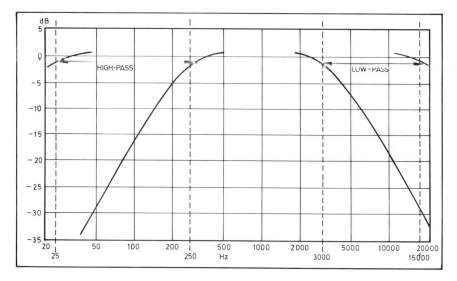

Fig. 7.4. Variable high-pass and low-pass filters

Equalizers

The very simplest equalizers found in mixing consoles provide high and low-frequency shelving curves similar to the treble and bass controls of domestic equipment (Figures 7.5 and 7.6), plus a mid-range lift or cut at various switchable frequencies from about 500 Hz to 6 kHz (Figure 7.7). This is often called a 'presence' control as its effect is to make the signal affected stand out in the balance, as if closer to the microphone. If applied in an exaggerated way, it will give a hard metallic effect which destroys realism. The mid-frequency dip, called in European terminology 'absence', has the contrary effect. It is used to reduce those parts of the range of an instrument which 'stick out' too prominently in a mix, or to counteract in remixing the excessive use of 'presence' in the original recording.

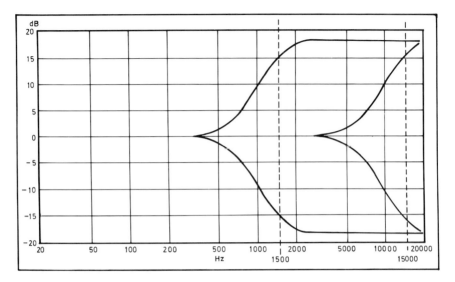

Fig. 7.5. Shelving treble EQ at −3 dB frequencies of 1.5 and 15 kHz

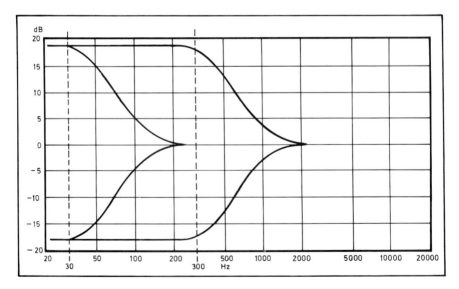

Fig. 7.6. Shelving bass EQ at −3 dB frequencies of 30 and 300 Hz (approx.)

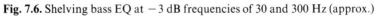

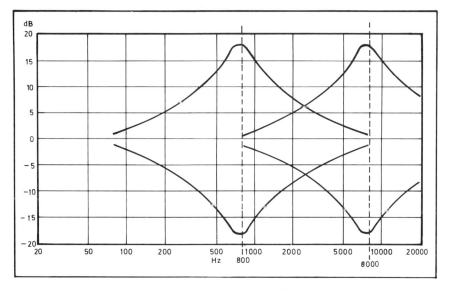

Fig. 7.7. Mid-range EQ at centre frequencies of 800 and 8,000 Hz (approx.)

It will be obvious that a normal shelving bass lift, which levels off and continues at a raised level down to the bottom end of the frequency range (Figure 7.6), will exaggerate any hum or rumble present in the input, which will in turn call for a low cut-off filter. For this reason, there is a strong case for bass boost to take the form of a fairly broad resonant curve (Figure 7.8), so that if the 200–300 Hz region, say, is lifted to 'warm up' a male voice or a cello the response will have returned to flat by about 60 Hz, and need not then be curtailed. Likewise, high-frequency shelf lift (Figure 7.5) should be used very sparingly, to avoid exaggeration of mechanical noises from close-miked instruments or the lifting of microphone amplifier hiss.

For many years, equalizer controls had precisely calibrated steps of both level and frequency in the interest of returning to repeatable settings, and because circuit design with inductors etc, required it. But engineers came to prefer continuously variable adjustment, and the most common preference today is for the so-called parametric equalizer (see Figure 7.9). In these units the frequency spectrum is usually divided into four regions. The frequency of peak or trough in each region is continuously tuneable by a potentiometer. The amplitude of the peak is also continuously variable, and lastly the sharpness or bandwidth of the peak (known as 'Q') may be varied in steps or even continuously. The frequency regions may overlap, any one region having a ratio of highest to lowest frequency of say 20:1, though even wider is possible. The highest and lowest regions may be switched from a peak to a shelf form. All this can require up to twelve knobs per channel, consuming a great deal of panel space. With

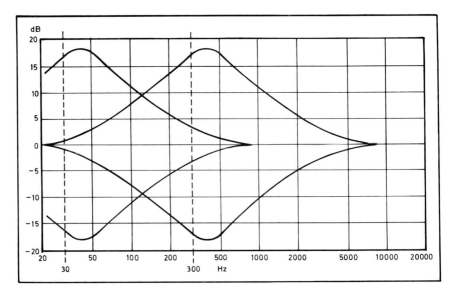

Fig. 7.8. Bass EQ using a broad peak at 30 and 300 Hz (approx.)

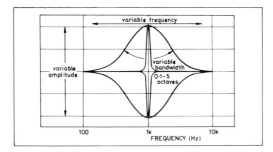

Fig. 7.9. Range of control in one section of a parametric equalizer

such equalizers it is possible to produce very strange and exaggerated effects, and it is important to bear in mind exactly what one is trying to achieve and proceed very logically in setting the controls.

An equalizer is designed to have the same maximum output level as the other amplifiers in the console. With its controls at flat, it will not overload sooner than the microphone amplifier. But with any considerable amount of boost applied to a region where full level is coming from the source, more of the headroom at the equalizer output will be taken up. It will naturally 'sound louder', and one will tend to pull down the fader. However, since the fader comes after the EQ, it may be better to reduce the input gain instead.

Insert points

Break-in points are customarily provided in each channel before and after the equalizer (and sometimes also after the fader), at which an outboard processing element can be inserted. The signal path may simply be led out via normalled jacks, but it is commoner today to have a switch in the channel for each insert point so that the effect of the inserted device can be compared with that of 'straight through', or the device can be switched in and out on cue. To reduce the number of jacks in a large console, the switch may be arranged to select one of the possible break-in positions and bring it out through a single pair of jacks. Wherever possible, levels are arranged so that all the insert points through a console are at standard line level.

The channel fader

For many years, the straight-line slide fader has been almost universal in studio consoles, except for a small percentage of quadrant lever types which are basically the same internally. The stud construction with precision resistors once used has been replaced by continuous tracks of conductive plastic. At first there was concern about lack of accuracy of calibration or stereo matching, but trimming techniques have now been established to control the law as closely as desired.

Considerations in the choice of a fader are smooth physical feel, freedom from electrical noise, minimum breakthrough of signal with the fader fully closed, and susceptibility to damage by dust and liquids spilt on the console. A switch may be fitted at the 'off' position to start remote machines, mute loudspeakers, or illuminate signal lights. A further switch known as 'overpress' is sometimes fitted, which is operated by pressing the knob past the 'off' position. This can turn on the pre-fade listen circuit, or possibly change over the channel input between two sources.

PFL, AFL, and Solo

The pre-fade listen (PFL) circuit provides a means to check (a) that the correct signal is present at the correct level, before opening a fader, and (b) to verify the technical quality of an input signal at a standard listening level without disturbing the recording balance. This signal from one or more channels may either appear on a small speaker in the console or be substituted for the main monitor signal, which is momentarily muted.

The after-fader listen (AFL) circuit is exactly the same, but takes its signal from the output of the fader, and is therefore heard at a level proportional to its level in the mix. Either PFL or AFL will enable the operator to judge how much 'overspill' from other instruments is entering any studio microphone. In

American terminology, AFL is sometimes called Solo or Audition, and the Solo as usually referred to was earlier called 'Solo-in-Place'. In AFL, the selected signal is heard by itself, usually in mono, and without the echo return which may be associated with it. Solo operates by muting all channels whose solo buttons are not pressed, so that those soloed are still heard at their proper levels and stereo positions in the mix, and with their proper echo, if the echo returns are excepted from being muted. Use of Solo during recording would destroy the mix, so provision is usually made to disable Solo or convert it to AFL when recording, though the Solo enable/disable switch is sometimes used as a means of muting and unmuting a group of channels during a take.

Auxiliary sends from channel

A signal may be taken off before or after the channel fader via switches and level controls to feed echo and effects and foldback ('cue' or artist headphone) mixes. Foldback is normally taken before the fader so that it is unaffected by balance changes. Echo send usually follows the fader, though a pre–post fader switch is often provided. In consoles for general-purpose broadcasting or recording use, no distinction is generally made between echo and foldback, and each auxiliary feed will have a pre-fade, off, post-fade switch. A channel direct output jack may also be provided after the fader to access individual channels. A broadcast-type console, where only occasional multitrack recording is required, may have an output taken from before the fader via a level trim control and buffer amplifier.

Stereo panning

In the early days of stereo, a relationship was established between the proportion of signal level fed to two loudspeakers and the apparent position of the sound source (Figure 7.10). If the levels to left and right are controlled according to these curves, the sum of the power outputs from the two speakers will remain constant, so that when a source is panned from one speaker to the other the loudness will not vary. To produce the exact curves, a double-stud potentiometer was originally used with precision resistors on as many steps as practicable. An acceptable approximation is made nowadays with linear continuous pots and fixed resistors.

While the 3 dB loss in the centre produces constant acoustic level from a pair of loudspeakers, if the two identical − 3 dB signals are added electically further on in the system to produce a mono output the voltage will be doubled, and the mono will therefore be 3 dB higher with the pan-pot central than with the pot to one side. (The same will happen if the stereo recording is combined to mono in a playback system.) A 6 dB loss at the mid-point would remove this effect, but produce an apparent level dip in the centre on stereo. Where mono results

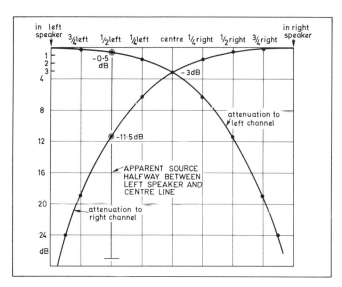

Fig. 7.10. Pan-pot law: the attenuator will give constant loudness for a single source panned across a pair of loudspeakers

are still considered important, as in broadcasting, a compromise value of 4.5 dB at the mid-point may be adopted.

Various provisions were made in console design for the short-lived requirements of quadraphony. These are mostly redundant, except that one useful by-product, the 'front–back' pan-pot, has found a new use. If the 'back' outputs, left and right, are regarded as 'stereo output no. 2', and the front–back pots are initially set to half-way, two stereo mixes are obtained, which can be separately recorded. Initially they are the same, but by altering the 'front–back' ratio one may be given, say, a touch more of vocal, solo instrument, or echo return, or have one channel, say commentary voice-over, turned off altogether. Mixing on the faders then proceeds normally, listening to stereo no. 1, and the versions are compared afterwards. There is also a possible new use for the 'joystick' in preparing tracks for cinema surround-sound, directing the signal to left, centre, right, and surround.

Channel routing to groups

For multitrack recording, the ability to send any input channel to any tape track is essential. Basically this is a simple matter of switching, but care in design is necessary to minimize crosstalk between tracks, assure reliability, and to give a self-evident presentation of routing in the minimum space.

Initially, rotary switches selected the channel output to any one of the available groups. If it was desired to record stereo pairs of signals on adjacent tracks, the switching in of the pan-pot also connected a second switch-bank to the next higher-numbered group, that is selection of '1' plus 'Pan in' gave panning between groups 1 and 2, and so on. Sometimes two switches were provided, leading to odd- and even-numbered groups (as in Figure 7.2).

Early in the development of multitrack recording it was felt necessary to be able to route an input simultaneously to any or all tracks. The standard way of doing this is by latching push-buttons, often with illuminated caps. The pan-pot, if inserted, operates between two sets of buttons, again leading to odd- and even-numbered groups. The push-button system was excellent for up to 16 tracks, with numbered button caps, but with 24 or more outputs it consumes a great deal of panel space. Hence buttons have been reduced to the minimum possible size, with LED indication. In some lower-priced consoles the number of buttons is halved and labelled '1–2', etc., with further 'odd–even' switches.

Besides occupying space, this vast number of buttons had been a serious cost element in large consoles and a source of worry about contact reliability in polluted atmospheres. Until recently there has not been an economic alternative, due to the cost per cross-point of any other method. Technical problems with sold-state switching elements have also taken time to overcome. Logic-operated systems are now coming into use, in which numbers representing the channel and the destination are keyed in to latch reed relays or solid-state switches, at the same time giving a visual indication of the routing established. This also gives the possibility of memorizing and recalling complete sets of console assignments. The addressing arrangements must include secure latching against accidental alteration of routing by power supply disturbances, and memory is commonly preserved by battery backup against power interruption.

Free grouping

This term is sometimes met in the description of medium-sized consoles, particularly for broadcast use. It means that any channel may be designated as a group controller over several other input channels, or over several groups as a final output. Several channels are directed to a mixing bus, which is then picked up as an input source by the 'group' channel. The output of this channel, and of other 'group master' channels, will then be combined on another mixing bus, and the last channel will pick up this bus and will thus control the overall main output. Switching of inputs and outputs is so arranged that a channel cannot pick up its own output (Figure 7.11). This principle originated in standard broadcast consoles where varying programme use demanded something other than a fixed number and position of permanent group master faders. A form of the same principle is now common in the 'in-line' multitrack console. Here the

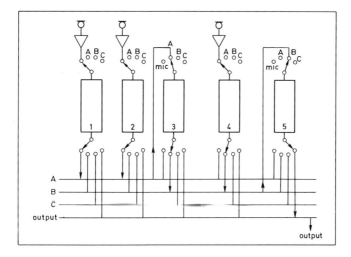

Fig. 7.11. Free grouping mixer principle: 1 and 2 are routed to subgroup *A*, which is controlled by 3. Output of 3 goes to *B*, as does independent input 4. *C* is not in use at present. Group *B* is controlled overall by 5, which is designated as the source of the main output

mixing amplifier of a group is physically located in the channel module of the same number, so a 'group' switch permits the fader, equalizer, etc. of the channel to be inserted in the group instead of controlling an input.

Voltage-controlled amplifier grouping

Group fader control was made very much more flexible by the availability of the voltage-controlled amplifier. In spite of some initial weaknesses, VCAs have for some years offered fully acceptable quality standards for top-class consoles. The VCA takes the place of the audio fader in the input channel, and its gain is controlled by a sum of d.c. voltages derived from channel and 'grouper' faders. Switches select which grouper has control of each channel. In some cases the grouper is a separate dedicated fader, while in others the fader of one channel controls its own gain and that of others selected to the same control bus. Groupers can further be placed under control of other groupers, or of an overall master fader. It is now no longer necessary for the audio groups to tracks to have group faders, though level trim pots are usually provided. Any channels requiring to be controlled as a group are simply switched to any available grouper. There is a further splendid advantage not previously achievable: channels routed to different tracks may now be controlled with the same fader, easing problems of physical reach and simultaneous operation. The VCA was also the sole key to the introduction of fader automation for some years before the motorized fader (illustrated in Plate 5) became a viable alternative.

Currently available VCAs have a logarithmic control law, that is the change of gain is a constant number of dB per volt change of d.c. control voltage over almost the whole control range. This allows the fader to be a linear potentiometer and allows control voltages to be easily summed. In the early years, users wished to have the option to switch out the VCA when not using grouping or automation, and have the fader directly control the audio; hence the fader track had a semi-log audio taper, and electronic contortions were necessary to convert a d.c. voltage derived from such a track back to linear. Strangely, the obvious alternative of using a 'stereo'-type fader with one log and one linear track seemed rarely to be employed.

Plate 5. Motorized faders on computer-assisted mixing console (Photo: Neve)

The digital fader

Faders are available in which contact segments give the equivalent of eight on–off switches, thus producing 256 binary values over the travel of the slider. These values may conveniently be logged in, and returned from, an automation system. By a digital-to-analogue conversion, the VCA control voltage may be obtained. But the alternative is also offered of driving a multiple FET switch device incorporating, or switching in, resistors forming part of a passive attenuator. The units of attenuation may be, for example, 0.25, 0.5, 1, 2, 4, 8 dB, and so on. As the switch elements are either on or off, the result is an attenuator theoretically free of any non-linear distortion, and this is put forward as an improvement on the VCA. But if the steps are not small enough level changes may be perceptible as clicks, as in the case of the old-fashioned stud fader, and there is an inherent problem of FET switches injecting 'charge transfer' clicks of their own at each change, giving rise to what has been called 'zipper noise'.

Mixing circuits

After the microphone amplifier, the actual method of mixing the signals from channels is the next most critical area of design from the point of view of good signal-to-noise ratio. There are two main approaches, 'passive' and 'active' mixing. Passive mixing is possible in a small to medium-sized mixer, with each channel always feeding to the main output and a series resistor connecting each channel to a common point. The voltage produced at the common point is the source voltage divided by the number of sources. The mix point feeds into a voltage amplifier which restores the loss. The noise is naturally proportional to the amount of gain needed, which follows from the number of sources. When amplifier noise was not as good as it is today, a step-up transformer was sometimes used to improve the situation, exactly like a microphone input. But when sources are being switched on and off, as in the multitrack case, each source switched off must be substituted by a dummy resistance or short circuit, or else the mixing loss, and the level, will vary. So the noise is always 'worst-case'.

In the 'active' alternative, the mixing amplifier is an inverting type, with feedback returned to the input mixing point through the same value resistor as the inputs. This produces a current summing point which has almost zero impedance. The voltage gain from any source to the mix amplifier output is normally zero, though some gain can be produced if required. Sources may be connected and disconnected with negligible change of level. The noise produced by such a circuit varies with the number of sources connected and is minimum with only one source, though with a number of sources it will be the same as in the passive case. Hence its almost universal use despite some well-known design problems.

Group outputs

Following the track mix amplifier will often be found a further insert point with a switch, and a group overall level control before the line amplifier feeding the recorder. In the days of eight and sixteen tracks, these group controls were often main faders, though they tended to get little use. With 24 and more tracks, they have mainly become rotary trim pots. Some faders may be retained for their usefulness as subgroups in mix-down, odds and evens being again combined on to groups 1 and 2 and used as the main stereo mix, unless a separate stereo bus is provided. Auxiliary sends from groups may be provided in exactly the same way as from channels, feeding to the same auxiliary mixes. The line output will normally go to the recorders via a patch-bay (jackfield) and the record signal returning to the monitor input selection will be taken after the jacks, so that what is heard is always what is actually arriving to that track of the machine.

The mixing and output arrangements for an auxiliary output, echo, or foldback will be basically similar to that which feeds a tape track. An overall rotary level control will be provided (and in many cases a simple equalizer and insertion point) and in the case of a dedicated echo send a second insert point for tape or digital time delay.

Where there are several foldback mixes from channels and from tracks, there may additionally be a further combining matrix of rows of buttons, whereby different outputs to studio headphone feeds may each consist of a different combination of sources plus echo returns, external signals such as click-tracks, and very often a basic feed of the main stereo mix. Talkback can be superimposed on each headphone feed, usually reducing the level of foldback while it is in use.

The multitrack monitor system

During the recording of a multitrack tape, it must be possible to monitor the input or recorded signal on all tracks, and present this as a reasonable approximation to the final stereo balance on the monitor speakers. So for each track the following controls are provided:

(a) *Track level.* Usually a short-throw slide fader; sometimes a full-length fader if space permits.

(b) *Pan-pot.* This affects monitoring only.

(c) *Solo and cut switches.* These operate as described for the input channel. Solo here has no effect on recording, so may be operated at any time.

(d) *Monitor echo send.* A level control and selector switch enables echo to be sent from a track round one of the echo systems and returned (via further return switches and level pots) into the monitor system only.

(e) *Sync switch.* Depending on the remote controls provided with the multitrack recorder, this may or may not exist as part of the console. It enables the operator to decide whether he will hear the already recorded signal coming back from the machine's record head, or the input signal to the track. Automatic switching will transfer monitor back to input when the machine is put into record on that track.

(*f*) *Foldback send pots* (one or more per track). These feed the machine sync signal and/or the live input to the track to the artist headphones mix. When the machine drops into record, the sync signal disappears and the artist hears the live signal instead, if he was not already doing so. An output of the track monitor mix is taken before the main monitor volume control to a stereo recorder to permit a simultaneous reference recording.

Console main monitoring

A series of buttons is usually provided to select the input to the main monitor system between multitrack monitor mix, main stereo output, returns from each stereo recorder, cassette, disc player, and the like. There may also be positions to check each echo send and return, foldback sends, and external signals at the patchbay, such as from another studio. This selection leads to the master control of listening level, which may be a fader but is preferably a detented rotary control, so that the choice, or alteration, of reference listening level is a deliberate decision. A dim key with trim control is provided so that listening level may be brought down a pre-set amount to check balance at low level, or when using talkback or conversing in the control room, and then restored to standard level. Monitor mute is also provided, which is actuated when speaking idents on to tape ('slate'). Further buttons are usual to monitor stereo as mono, to mute one speaker, and to invert phase momentarily to one speaker if a phase error is suspected.

Switching is often provided to substitute alternative sets of monitor speakers for the principal ones. A pair of fairly small units is often placed on top of the console. These are high-quality 'nearfield' monitors; smaller speakers built into the console may provide a further choice, to simulate portable radios and to serve for intercom between control rooms.

Studio playback is provided for by a similar set of source selector buttons and overall volume control. Precautions are taken to prevent microphone signals being accidentally returned into a studio speaker.

Talkback

Talkback arrangements will vary widely in complexity, but one is likely to find provisions for:

Talk to studio on loudspeaker
Talk to each headphone circuit separately or all together
Talk to conductor's stand or another control room
Speaking identification on tape (slate).

In large music studios, provision will also be made for a conductor to speak to the control room, or to address the orchestra through the studio talkback speaker.

Metering

Level meters used in recording consoles are basically of two types, VU (Volume Unit) meters and PPM (Peak Programme Meters). The VU meter is an a.c. rectifier voltmeter, whose instrument has a specified ballistic (i.e. rise time and overshoot) behaviour when it is connected to the signal source through a specified value resistor. Its performance is defined by an American Standard specification, and it is important to realize that only meters conforming to this specification, and fed through the correct resistance, give readings that can be meaningfully compared on programme material. Not every meter having the usual VU scale does conform, particularly in semi-professional equipment, though all such meters will normally give consistent readings for 0 VU on continuous sine wave tone.

The normal sensitivity of a VU meter with its resistor (3.6 kilohms) is +4 dBu (1.73 V r.m.s.) for a reading of 0 VU. Standard line level for studio equipment is normally +8 dBu for peak recording level. The difference relates to the fact that the VU meter, due to its mechanical inertia, gives a lower reading on average programme material than on steady tone. Opinions vary as to the amount of 'lead' which should be allowed between tone and programme, from the above 4 dB to 6, 10, or even more. In fact, in relation to VU readings there is really no such thing as 'average programme material', and the permissible VU readings for different kinds of sound are something which is learned only by experience. Analogue magnetic tape is fairly forgiving as to the subjective effect of overload, but digital media are not, which strengthens the case for the peak meter. If a VU meter with resistor is connected across a 600 ohm source, it is possible to measure a small increase in distortion due to its presence. For this reason, and to permit setting of sensitivity to a desired value, VU meters are now commonly fitted with small buffer amplifiers.

The PPM (see also Chapter 25) has a drive amplifier and rectifier circuit which detects and applies to the instrument the momentary peak values reached by the audio voltage. It holds this value by charging up a capacitor, which then discharges through a high resistance. Thus the peak value of a short transient will be held long enough for the meter movement to reach the correct scale reading, and then fall back slowly, so that the eye can register the value reached without being confused by very rapid pointer movement.

A PPM (particularly of the all-electronic type) can be designed with virtually instantaneous rise time, but as certain transients are so short that if their full amplitude was registered they would produce a tendency either to under-record average levels or to disbelieve the meter, the charging time is deliberately slowed. In the BBC programme meter circuit this charge time is 2.5 milliseconds. PPMS are semi-logarithmic, that is the scale is more or less linear in dB (whereas the VU meter is basically a voltmeter). There are various PPM circuits in use in different countries, which vary as to the rise and fall times and the number of dB on the scale length.

In Europe for many years the standard precision programme meter was the so-called light spot meter. This is a moving-coil instrument of very low inertia in which the pointer is an image optically projected on to a scale. These gave a superb presentation for main programme output, but were too large and expensive for multitrack use. They have been superseded by 'bar graph' displays using either high voltage neon (plasma) columns or rows of very small LEDs. Backlit liquid crystal units are also coming into use. A 'peak hold' facility is easily added, allowing the highest value reached momentarily to be held for a few seconds, or to be held during a whole item until released. Column meters are also provided with Peak/VU switching, where the VU ballistics are electrically simulated, or even both indications displayed side by side.

Current practice is often to have some kind of column indicator for each track, with the main stereo output, or selected monitor signal, shown both on a high-quality column and on large conventional VU meters.

Console layout and ergonomics

Having reviewed the features required in a large console and indicated the very large number of manual controls called for, it will be evident that the layout and physical location of these controls require a great deal of intelligent thought. It is of little use to provide every possible flexibility of adjustment if this leads to a situation in which the operator can hardly reach controls which he needs to operate simultaneously, or if the number and layout of these controls cause operator confusion and mistakes when working under stress. Thus the art of panel layout may well be described as the intelligent choice of what to leave out, and the organization of what remains in the most comprehensible form.

Large music-recording consoles started out in a straight, long-table form organized in a more or less left-to-right way: first, all the input channels, then the groups with group master faders, then the track monitoring, then ancillaries. As more and more channels and groups were called for, operators had to roll their chairs up and down. For stereo listening, this was obviously a bad thing. So, first of all, the track monitoring and things like foldback were turned through 90° on one side. This also generated a useful space in the corner section to contain master monitor controls and auxiliaries such as compressors.

For ideal stereo monitoring, it was desirable for the engineer to sit centrally with the controls organized symmetrically on either side of him. Those controls requiring constant visual attention should be in the centre, those constantly being adjusted falling under his hands, and those requiring occasional adjustment should still be within arm's reach. This was the motivation for the development of the wrap-round console which had its greatest popularity through the 1970s and offered what was in many ways an optimum solution. But, though the angle sections of wrap-round designs generated even more usable space within arm reach, the demand for more input channels made the central straight section grow again. Wrap-round consoles were all custom-built, and the domination of the market even for large music consoles by quantity-produced 'straight' designs has forced users to forgo the ergonomic advantages. Automation has also reduced the need for large numbers of rapid 'live mixing' control moves. But the general ergonomic principles governing operators at control desks remain valid and must be remembered in any new designs.

The arrangement of meters and visual displays is a further area in which ergonomics seemed to suffer a temporary defeat. A strong case can be made for the arrangement of mulitiple meters of the conventional kind in some sort of rectangular block, so that they can be observed as a group with a minimum of head-turning. This was a viable tactic up to 16 tracks. For 24 tracks, one option was 12 meters selectable between tracks 1–13, 2–14, etc. on the basis that in the studio tracks are filled up sequentially. Alternatively, an 8×3 meter layout was possible, but in too many cases the worst choice—a single line of 24—was adopted. The coming of the vertical column meter has at least reduced this to the width of 24 channels, and given the additional possibility to provide the subsidiary display of a frequency spectrum or VCA fader settings rather than track levels, but the optimum display of many track levels, plus other information, has for a long time been the video screen, and at increasingly reasonable cost.

The 'in-line' console

The vast majority of current production multitrack consoles follow what might be called the accepted compromise solution to the ergonomic problems mentioned above. This line of development, which was introduced as a space and cost saver, has brought in some useful by-products of its own in the organization of the system. Perhaps its main drawback has been the exchange of console depth for console length (though more recently extreme length has returned as well!). The placing of the monitor controls in line with the channel inevitably called for some extension of reach, but the manufacturing convenience of construction of channels in one straight module at a very shallow angle has produced another 'worst-case' situation which users have come to accept. In most current layouts, it is possible to reach the input gain, and some equalizer controls, only at extreme arm reach or by standing up.

The significant features of the in-line channel strip have now become established more or less as follows: there are two parallel signal paths, usually known as 'channel' and 'monitor', corresponding to the separate modules described earlier. The 'channel' side is fed with microphone amplifier output, echo/effects device return, or tape return in mix-down. 'Monitor' receives tape track record, sync, or play signal, according to the machine switching. There may or may not be 'console master code' switches which force the inputs into preselected states, unless overridden by local switches. The output of the 'channel' side goes to the selection switching to tracks, and possibly a separate stereo output, with an optional pan-pot between odd and even tracks. The track (group) mixing and line output amplifiers for track no. 1 reside physically in channel strip no. 1, and so on; the back wiring provides that each mix amplifier picks up the right signal from the track select switching. Instead of 'group faders', rarely needed, there is a 'group level trim' pot to enable the overall level to track after mixing to be adjusted. This will normally be left at maximum unless many inputs to a track cause a build-up which might overload the tape.

The output of the monitor side goes directly via the 'main' pan-pot, close to the operator, to the stereo mix, which is also the feed to the main stereo recorder for simultaneous recording and for mix-down. There is a 'large' fader (the normal channel fader) which is driven by the automation system when in use, and a 'small' fader with shorter travel lever. When laying down tracks, the operator may choose which one will be in the input channel, the other controlling the monitor mix. In mix-down, the large fader will be used. If a large number of effects devices are in use and channels are used up, these signals may be brought back into the monitor side, through the 'small' fader, and added to the stereo mix, thus doubling the number of inputs. This is just the same as adding the monitor mix to the main mix in a separate-monitoring console. Each fader has it own solo and mute buttons.

Switching is provided so that the filters, equalizer, dynamics (compression/expansion/noise-gating—often provided at least optionally in each channel) can each be 'flipped' across the channel to monitor side as required. Also, as the demand for effects and foldback sends has steadily increased, as many knobs as can be physically accommodated are provided, with switches to allow each signal to be picked up before or after the fader in the channel or monitor side. The auxiliary mixes from the channels may be further subdivided on the way to the outputs, to give a maximum of separate sends.

Dynamics in the channel

Several designs now offer a compressor and expander or noise-gate in each input channel, with a flexibility comparable to a sophisticated rack-mounted unit. Switching also allows the filters or equalizer of the channel to be separated and placed in the side chain of the dynamics. A further option now offered is for a digital delay in the channel.

Because the group mix and output stages are in the channel strip, two other useful provisions are easily made. When 'one source to one track' recording is being done (a very common case) there is no point in routing the signal through unnecessary wiring and circuitry. A 'Direct' switch can take the channel signal from the fader straight to the output stage. And, if it is desired to have a fader in audio control of a track, or to re-equalize or compress the whole feed to that track, a 'Group' switch will substitute the normal channel input by the group mix signal, which will then pass through all the facilities of the channel (including the possibility of deriving auxiliary sends from this group) and then emerge from the track record output.

If the console, as is very commonly the case, has say 32 channel selection but only 24 tracks feeding to a recorder, a group of channels may be routed to, say, mix no. 30; channel 30 can then be put in the 'group' mode, and its output sent to, say, track 20.

Central system control

For many years, tape machine control boxes were built into any available space in consoles. With the number of remote switches and indicators increasing, this became impractical, and the mixing engineer tended to become surrounded by trolleys, with other boxes being placed on top of any faders or modules not actually in use. It is now becoming generally accepted that the console must contain all the essentials for running a sometimes very complicated session. So a central area is being designated for machine and automation management and log-keeping. As all these are related to the same time reference, normally a time-code on one of the tapes, it makes sense that one and the same electronic system, a smart computer, should deal with them all, and with an increasing amount of the housekeeping of large audio consoles.

Developing trends

As mentioned above, size, number of controls, component density, and heat output are the constant design problems as consoles have kept up with more demanding operational requirements. More ability to store and recall set-up and mix information in short and long term appears the main desire of the near future. At one point it seemed that the quantum leap to provide all these things, and incidentally eliminate many electronic design problems, was to digitize all audio at the earliest possible stage, and let the mixing console become one very fast, very clever computer in which the 'block diagram', and every kind of signal processing, became a matter of software algorithms. This has been shown to be possible, but is definitely not the only way, and certainly not the easiest. It has given rise to the term 'the virtual console', which is now being loosely applied to any kind of system in which the audio no longer flows through pots and switches behind a front panel.

Digitally controlled analogue audio

Entering the market as this is written, and discussed in Chapter 8, are designs in which fairly conventional audio circuitry (still constructed as individual input channels and groups) is separated from the panel controls which operate it, and driven by control signals along a data bus. In principle this could be done by a large number of wires carrying d.c., or by multiplexed d.c. values. In practice, a whole set of control values will be digitized and passed through encoders and decoders, and indications of status will be returned to displays in the same way. There is now no audio behind the control panel, and hence no question of fitting active and sensitive circuitry into the confined space of modules. The audio may be 'under' the console, but much preferably on PC boards of any convenient size or shape housed in standard racks, possibly outside the control room. These boards are laid out for optimum path length and isolation considerations. Digital and audio signals can be kept well apart, and the whole racks totally shielded from RF interference.

The control panel could still be of conventional design, but vast savings of space, coupled with the avoidance of cramped control layouts, are offered by the 'assignable' approach. This is already well established in the area of signal routing. Banks of buttons are being replaced by source and destination keypads, and whole console set-ups including auxiliaries are stored in memory for later recall. In the next stage, whilst those controls which the user feels still need to exist on a dedicated 'per channel' basis continue to do so, others (such as equalizer settings, dynamics, and auxiliary sends) will appear only once or twice on well-laid-out panels. At present it seems to be agreed that the full number of faders, one per input, should still be provided, though for some uses even this is open to debate. But the width of the fader top plate no longer depends on the layout and contents of a channel module, so it may come down to 25 or 20 mm, bringing more channels within comfortable reach. Above each fader there is a 'call' button, which, when touched, immediately places the master panels in control of the settings of that channel, and displays the existing settings on LED columns associated with the knobs, or on video or dot matrix displays. The controls and display remain 'connected' to the last channel called, until the call button of another channel is touched. The settings established in one channel may be copied into other channels.

The transmission of all instructions via a data bus means that the whole control patterns, or any part of them, may be stored by established techniques and recalled as often as required. This can mean per session, per scene of a programme, or per unit of time-code. The potential ability to have every element of mixing under dynamic automation control, thus giving the engineer an infinite number of hands and the memory to direct them, now exists and offers exciting prospects. Exactly what options are worth implementing will be established in the next few years, but it is clear that we shall gain a new ease of serviceability and updating, the chance of a return to more nearly ideal ergonomic layouts, the economic feasibility of custom control panels optimized for one or more specific applications, and visual displays which will transform the amount of useful information instantly available and comprehensible.

8

Console automation and digitalization

Martin Jones and Alan Jubb

The remarkable technical developments available in today's recording studio have proceeded hand in hand with the demands of producers and record buyers for a more sophisticated musical end-product. That sophistication may be employed to achieve a greater sense of reality in, say, an orchestral record, or it may be a totally new pop style, where the recording itself is the reality and the music depends on the recording studio for its performance. All such developments place greater demands on the techniques of the balance engineer. Recent electronic developments, particularly in the digital field, can simultaneously reduce the mental and physical effort required to carry out routine operations and give the balance engineer totally new tools to accomplish his creative task.

Remote control of gain

The discussion of analogue mixing consoles in Chapter 7 introduced the concept of group faders, which give the convenience of controlling the level of signals from several channels at once by routing the signals from those channels through a common mixing bus and group level control. A further control dimension is added by the voltage-controlled amplifier (VCA), which, as was described, is a variable-gain amplifier, the gain being controlled by an external d.c. voltage fed to the control input. A *VCA subgrouping* system includes a VCA in each channel, which is controlled by a d.c. output from the channel fader. In each channel there is also a facility for adding in an extra control voltage from a *submaster* or group fader, thus providing a remote control capability. A further input on each submaster control line comes from a *grand master* controlling all channels which are selected to a submaster.

One common arrangement is shown in Figure 8.1, where the channel fader is equipped with a selector switch (usually a thumbwheel) to select which submaster will control it (Figure 8.2). Unity (0 dB) gain through the VCA is usually given by zero control voltage, a typical scaling factor being 1 V control voltage per 10 dB of attenuation. Thus +10 V control gives 100 dB attenuation; further increases in control voltage produce no further effect because 100 dB attenuation is effectively the signal 'off' condition. This logarithmic (constant

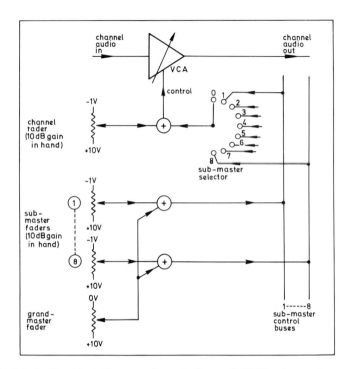

Fig. 8.1. Outline block diagram of a typical console VCA subgrouping system

dB per volt) control characteristic means that the attenuation given by the VCA is the total of the attenuation settings in dB on the channel, submaster, and master faders. Most VCAs will also provide up to 20 dB gain if required, the control voltage being taken negative to −2 V to achieve this gain. Thus the common requirement to have 10 or 15 dB gain in hand on the channel fader above the 0 dB line-up point is readily satisfied.

Whilst a conventional fader will always produce less signal degradation than a VCA, recent designs of VCA exploiting the latest techniques of transistor matching with IC technology can approach distortion figures as low as the rest of the console audio chain.

The use of VCA submasters enables overall control of a number of channel levels to be handled on one fader without mixing the audio signals. For instance, six vocalists may each have their own microphone and be recorded on separate tape tracks. A VCA submaster set up to control all six vocal channels can facilitate instant adjustment when, as often happens, all the vocalists sing louder in the recording session than they did at rehearsal. Without the VCA submaster, the individual channel faders would have to be adjusted, with the attendant danger of upsetting the relative balance between singers. Mute switches fitted

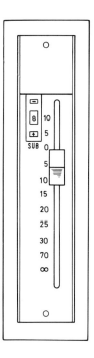

Fig. 8.2. VCA channel fader front panel, showing thumbwheel switch for selecting subgroup (courtesy Neve)

to VCA faders provide the additional facility of an instantaneous fast fade up or down. Such mutes can be particularly valuable for minimizing tape noise and extraneous sounds in the mix-down process, where tracks are brought in only when they have useful signals on them.

Console automation

Mix-down is a search for perfection. The very fact that the performers may have left the studio, with their various contributions on separate tracks of tape, leaves the producer and balance engineer an infinite number of different possible balances which could be chosen for the final mix-down. Every balance engineer has encountered the frustration, usually experienced in the small hours of the morning, of searching for that combination of fader levels which will give him the sound he achieved eight hours previously, and which was so nearly right!

The combination of remotely controlled fader settings with computer data storage allows fader movements to be memorized and replayed at will in sync with the tape. Such a 'console automation' system, exemplified by the Neve Necam 96, SSL Studio Computer, and AK Mastermix, enables the balance engineer to recall previous combinations at will, and use the best of various previous attempts at a mix together with just a touch of final adjustment to achieve the sought-after sound. Just to check his final mix, the balance engineer can instruct the automation system to replay it, whilst listening and watching to check that all the fader settings and changes are as required before recording on to the final master tape.

Automation features

Most large consoles can nowadays offer the option of automation. Some of the key features of a system are listed here:

(a) Data storage. All fader operations must obviously be synchronized with the music. One way of achieving this is to record the position data from the faders directly on to one track of the multitrack tape. An analogue audio tape machine is not, however, an ideal digital store and provides only capacity for a very limited number of mixes as well as a rather higher error rate than a separate memory device such as the floppy disc used in most systems. In addition to the inherent capacity of a separate disc store, the fact that it can operate independently of the audio tape greatly increases speed and flexibility in handling mix data. In order to limit the sheer quantity of mix data stored, it is usual to store only *changes* in fader positions instead of recording absolute positions continuously, thus gaining enormously in 'mix' capacity. If the tape is started somewhere in the middle of a mix, the computer looks back to the last record of absolute positions, then quickly reads all subsequent changes in order to work out what settings it ought to have now; this is only possible, of course, with a fast-access separate data store. Used in this way, a single floppy disc can accommodate hundreds of mix attempts. Even if one disc becomes full of data, it is a simple matter to carry on to another disc.

This use of a separate data store involves recording a synchronizing code on one tape track to relate mix data to tape position. The SMPTE time-code, or its EBU version, is normally used. This code, which originated in videotape editing and dubbing, uses a sequence of digital pulses designed for reliable recording on audio tape. It can be likened to a track representing sprocket holes in film, but is much more versatile, giving a time read-out in hours, minutes, seconds, and frames.

Any control movement recorded by the automation system will be written in store along with the time-code value when it occurred. Thus all control movements can be replayed at precisely the correct time.

(b) Fader display and update. The automatic replay of a mix becomes a balance engineer's tool rather than a mere novelty, with the addition of some easy method of changing or *updating* the mix as it is replayed. After all, the operator's reason for replaying the mix is in case he wants to *change* it in some way. Herein lies a particular challenge for the console designer: in many automation systems, the gain control is implemented only by means of a varying

control voltage on a VCA, the fader itself giving no visible indication of the channel gain at any instant.

Various techniques exist for updating channel gains during replay of a mix with VCA automation. One method is to switch the system to 'trim' status, having made sure that all relevant faders are set around the 0 dB mark. As the stored mix is replayed, if a change in level is required the fader knob is then moved as necessary. The number of decibels which the fader moves are added to, or subtracted from, the signal level depending on the direction of movement. This method has the disadvantage that the fader position then bears no relation to the absolute gain of the channel.

Automated VCA faders usually also incorporate a simple 'balance' indicator to show whether the fader knob is higher or lower than the actual gain set in the channel: a pair of LEDs is very common. When the fader knob is too high, the upper LED will light alone, whilst the illumination of the lower LED alone shows the fader is too low. Both LEDs light when the knob corresponds with the actual gain. When this position has been found, a 'write' button is pressed, and any necessary update in gain made by moving the fader. Only at this particular time can the engineer be sure that the gain in the channel corresponds with the fader position. When the fader is switched back to 'read', channel gain is once more under the control of the automation rather than the fader. Some systems include an 'auto takeover' mode which allows level to be manually updated during a section of a mix and then be restored automatically to stored data control as the fader passes through the point where VCA level and stored value match exactly. Some VCA automation systems also have the facility for displaying 'true' fader positions on bar-graph meters or VDU graphics, a useful aid to check exactly what movements are being replayed. Despite all such aids, the loss of the direct relationship between fader knob and replayed channel gain in a VCA automation system presents a difficulty for many balance engineers, particularly where updates to rapidly changing fader movements are required.

An alternative technique originated by Neve in the Necam system, and recently also employed in the Massenburg (GML) automation facility, is actually to move the fader. This 'robotic' approach recognizes that the fader knob is simultaneously a means of control and an indicator (see Plate 5, page 150). By incorporating a small motor and drive mechanism in the fader, the automation control signal actually moves the fader knob so that the balance engineer can at all times actually *see* as well as hear the system in action. The most natural way for the balance engineer to change any settings is to touch the relevant knob and move it to a new position. In order to allow this, the system incorporates touch-sensitive fader knobs: as soon as a knob is touched, the motor is switched off and the system is ready to 'read' new data. When the knob is released, the fader once more responds to stored position data. Thus button-pushing is eliminated and update becomes entirely instinctive, with fader knobs always in the 'right' position. A subsidiary advantage of the motorized fader is that channel gain can be controlled directly via an audio track on the moving fader, thus avoiding the cost and minor signal degradation of a VCA.

(c) The processor. Early automation systems used hard-wired logic systems. Before long, however, the amount of data handling required led to today's application of the minicomputer and more recently the microprocessor, where software is the heart of the system operation. The best automation systems have remarkably sophisticated 'multitasking' software systems which allow the many functions to be handled apparently simultaneously to the operator. Two floppy discs are usually used, one being a 'scratch pad' and the other a data disc. A mix attempt will be recorded first on the scratch pad. If the balance engineer then wishes to retain the mix, he presses a *keep* or *end* key on the control panel and the data file is transferred to the data disc and given a mix number. Should the data disc become full after a prolonged session, unwanted mix files can be deleted or, alternatively, the best mixes can be copied off on to a new disc.

The more recent systems, of which the Neve Necam 96 is a typical example, also allow direct replay of mix data from a 'scratch' memory without the need to transfer it to the data disc first. This speeds the process of achieving the optimum mix. If a mistake is made, it is only necessary to wind the tape back slightly, stop wherever required, and play it again. All the fader movements just recorded will be replayed and the mistake can be corrected manually on the relevant faders. The operator is thus freed from the rather regimented approach of keeping a number of mixes, mistakes and all, on the data disc simply in order to play and update them. Instead, mistakes can now be readily corrected 'on the fly'. This *intelligent rollback* facility exploits the fast data retrieval available from today's vast RAM memory and is particularly valuable in post-production dubbing work.

However easy it may be to correct mistakes, an essential feature of a good automation system is provision for the editing of stored mix data. Just as the tape of a performance will usually require many splices to combine the best features of several different recording sessions, or to cut out spurious material, so the best features of several mixes can be combined using off-line editing of data files. The 'merge' or 'join' operation in the Necam and SSL systems implement 'butt' editing. Complete sections of a mix can be 'spliced' together so that, for example, all the fader settings of mix 29 are used up to bar 36 followed by all the fader settings of mix 136 from bar 36 to bar 129, and so on. In addition, Necam provides the selective merge, allowing the combination of certain fader movements from one mix with other faders from a different mix over the same passage of music. For example, the string balance from mix 105 could be combined with the drum balance of mix 63 and the vocal balance of mix 78. The use of the 'merge' facility on mix information can often eliminate splicing of the final two-track master—a valuable time-saver.

(d) Control of tape machine. We have seen that mix data is inseparable from tape position if fader and mute changes are to be replayed at precisely the right time. Control of automated mix-down is also intimately connected with control of the tape machine: when starting an automated mix, the tape must be started at the same time as the data replay. It is therefore normal to integrate tape machine remote control and the tape position locator with the rest of the automation system. The integration of a synchronizer is also common, whether for linking two multitrack machines or audio and video for post-production dubbing. Provision is made for the operator to enter *labels* or *cue points* at particular points on the tape to avoid the tedium of entering codes in hours, minutes, seconds, and frames whenever a particular point on the tape is to be located. Such labels can be entered either on the fly or offline by entering the time-code value. They are numbered in sequence: label 1, label 2, label 3 – label 999, and may also be named and located by name or number.

The tape can also be located automatically to the start of a mix (also recognized by name or number). On being instructed to replay the mix, the tape automatically relocates at the start point and begins to play, with all the faders taking up their previous positions and implementing the recorded movements.

(e) Control panel and display. A good automation system can free the balance engineer from the more tedious chores, thus enabling him to concentrate on the most creative aspects of his task. Such potential benefits can, however, be nullified if the system control panel and display have not been appropriately designed. The balance engineer does not expect to program the automation system by typing out tedious instructions. The various functions must be available at the push of a button, and the system operations must be clearly displayed so that the engineer knows precisely what is happening at a given moment.

Plate 6 shows the Necam 96 with the control panel in the foreground having the various function keys used to gain immediate access to facilities such as *locate, start, play*, and the like. In addition, a numeric key pad and 'QWERTY' keyboard allow entry of number and name references. As might be expected, a simple text entry facility allows the typing of extensive supplementary notes on to the disc as required.

There are nine 'soft' keys, each of which can be programmed with any sequence of key-strokes. This powerful facility allows a whole series of complex actions to be initiated by just one key-push. Including the 'soft' key itself in the sequence allows indefinite repetition of the actions. All information is displayed on a colour VDU, which normally displays details of the mix being played and the present position within the mix. A whole variety of lists of labels, mixes, mutes, and so on, all displayed with relevant names and time-codes, can be called up at the touch of a key.

Plate 6. Neve Necam 96 automated console with control panel in the foreground (Photo: Neve)

Post-production dubbing and live applications

The post-production dubbing of film and videotape is facilitated by the provision of memorized switch closure 'events' for sound-effect cartridge machines. The ability to adjust precisely the timing of cues (say fifteen frames earlier than the first attempt) and to enter events 'off-line' before the dubbing operation starts can greatly increase the speed of the critical dubbing operation, which is frequently under enormous pressure of time. Channel mutes are programmable in the same way and can be trimmed accurately in time to bring up effects at exactly the right point.

The ability to recall a series of pre-set static mixes can find application in the 'live' situation. In mix-down, of course, the recording already exists and acts as a completely predictable time reference for the control of console functions. This predictability must inevitably be lacking in a 'live' performance, so that the contribution of automation is likely to be restricted to the manual recall of a series of 'snapshots' of different fader settings in much the same way as an automated stage lighting board enables the operator to recall particular combinations of dimmer settings. It is possible to recall a rapid sequence of different 'snapshots' stores to coincide with, say, a singer moving across a stage, requiring different microphones to be faded up and down quickly. The speed of transition between stores can be instantaneous, or can be at a programmed cross-fade rate. Alternatively, a separate fader can be used to achieve a manual cross-fade transition.

A useful capability is the pre-programming of events, stores, and cross-fades at time-codes taken by the dubbing engineer from the video edit list. Most effects and mixes can thus be called up at approximately the correct points in the programme, leaving the final dub just as a refining process. Such speed of operation is vital to meet today's short time-scales, and automation provides the means to achieve it.

Automation beyond the faders

Memory and automation can today extend further than the faders alone. The 'Total Recall' system pioneered by Solid State Logic (Plate 7) employs an

Plate 7. SSL SL 6000E Series automated console for stereo video with 'Total Recall' (Photo: Solid State Logic)

additional track on each potentiometer, and an extra pole on each switch, to provide positional information to the central processor. Control settings can thus be stored on floppy disc at will. As the controls are manual, there is of course no automatic reset, but a colour video graphic display (Plate 8) provides a clear indication of the memorized position and current position, thus facilitating manual resetting. The system has proved of value in restoring console settings at the continuation of a previous session.

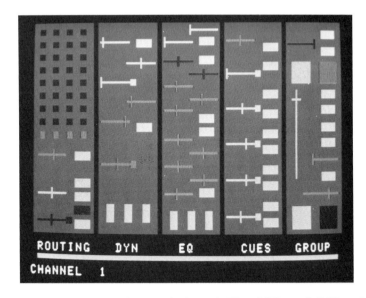

Plate 8. Total Recall display for console shown in Plate 7 (Photo: Solid State Logic)

To go beyond the manual resetting of Total Recall, it is clear that full automation of channel controls requires a solution to the task of automatically resetting over 1,000 potentiometers and possibly double that number of push-button switches. The push-button switch problem is readily solved by using non-locking buttons controlling electronic switches with LED indication of switch state. Thus the electronic switch and its indication can be operated either by stored data or the manual button.

The automatic resetting of potentiometers to the required accuracy, at least as good as 2 per cent, is an altogether more difficult matter, and in fact is best circumvented by first reducing the required number of rotary controls by recognizing that the operator can examine and operate only a very limited number of controls at one time. This *assignable* approach is used on today's most advanced consoles.

Assignable controls

The console shown in Plate 6 (page 168) is fitted with an assignable routing control panel, shown in the outline drawing in Figure 8.3. Here the individual channel-to-track routing buttons, traditionally found on the channel strips, have been centralized into a single set which is used by pressing a 'channel' or 'track' access button adjacent to each fader. Alternatively, channel or track number may be entered on the numeric key-pad. This assignable routing system is microprocessor-controlled and includes stores enabling different console assignments to be memorized.

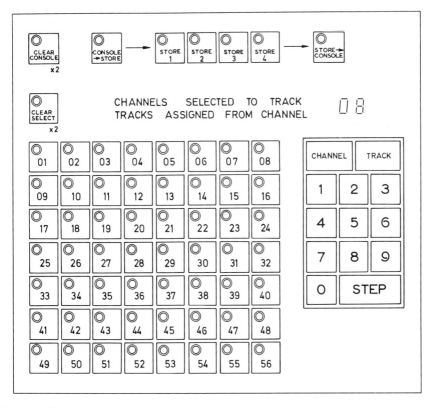

Fig. 8.3. Control panel for channel-to-track assignment system incorporating memory facilities (courtesy Neve)

Figure 8.4 shows how the assignable concept can be extended to the whole control console. In addition to the central routing panel, the assignable panel includes one set of each type of channel control: equalizers, dynamics, filters, cue and effects sends are all centralized. Access to a particular channel is made

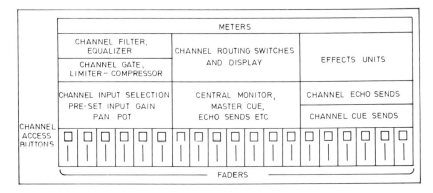

Fig. 8.4. Outline diagram of the assignable console concept

by pressing the access button adjacent to each fader. Thus the one set of memorized controls and displays is effectively moved from channel to channel as accessed by the operator. It is as though a sliding window were moved automatically to expose the required channel controls at the instant of pressing the access button, except of course that the controls come to the operator instead of vice versa. This has the advantage of enabling the operator to remain in the central stereo listening position whilst, say, adjusting the pan-pot on channel 47. This is clearly quicker than the conventional practice of dodging back and forth between an inaccessible control and the centre in order to check that the sound image is correct. In practice, a pair of assignable control panels may be fitted to facilitate two-handed operation and also offer the ability to compare settings on two channels.

The assignable control technique is applied to analogue consoles using VCAs and solid-state switching for digital control of audio. The full potential of automated assignable controls benefits from the flexibility now available in digital signal processing.

The digital mixing console

We have seen that the analogue mixing console can achieve a high level of performance both in technical and operational aspects, with a high degree of automation. Today's digital recording techniques do, however, raise the question of how far digital handling of the audio signal can improve the total audio system. The answer today, as evidenced by systems already in regular commercial use, is that digital mixing consoles and studio systems are destined to play an ever-increasing role in the audio industry.

Based on collaborative work with the BBC, the first commercially available digital consoles were designed and built by Neve, beginning with a digital tape transfer design for CD mastering in 1984, leading on to full-size multitrack systems, the first of these being at CTS Studios (Plate 9) and BBC Radio (Plate 18), the latter a mobile installation and described in Chapter 13.

Plate 9. Digital mixing console at CTS Studios, London (Photo: courtesy Neve and CTS Studios)

At the time of writing, digital signal processing (DSP) is more costly than the nearest analogue equivalent, and it is therefore useful to study the advantages presented by the digital approach:

1. The future of audio recording is digital. At the same time, an increasing amount of studio work involves transfer from one recording to another. Whether mixing down, sweetening, post-production dubbing, or just copying with a minor gain adjustment, an analogue mixing console used with digital recorders involves digital-to-analogue (D/A) and analogue-to-digital (A/D) conversion at every interface. Whilst conversion methods have improved greatly, they are still the weakest link in the digital audio system as far as distortion and noise are concerned. Their proliferation is therefore to be avoided. Digital signal processing in the mixing console allows direct connection to and from digital recording free from degradation by D/A and A/D conversion.

2. We have already recognized in this chapter the desirability of remote control of all audio processing, including not only gain control but also

equalization, compression, limiting, and suchlike. Whilst good performance is obtained from today's VCAs and solid-state switches, nevertheless digital control and sensitive analogue audio circuits of wide dynamic range are not comfortable bed-fellows. Analogue circuits tend to work best when their controlling potentiometers and switches are adjacent to the relevant electronics. Multiple stages of remote control can be distinctly unhealthy for the quality of an analogue system. DSP, on the other hand, is entirely controlled by numbers and therefore presents an ideal means of remote control.

It is this remote control aspect which is most immediately apparent to the user of a digital console. The control desk is fully assignable, whilst static memories of all controls provide complete reset of the console to recall automatically the settings in use at a previous session. Further 'snapshot' memories allow pre-programmed changes during a session in the same manner as a modern lighting switchboard. All data is stored on a removable floppy disc store, and of course the control data can be synchronized with SMPTE time-code to provide full mix-down/post-production automation of all controls.

3. A fundamental advantage in complex studio systems is the simultaneous simplification and indefinite flexibility of signal routing provided by the digital 'bus' system. This enables 128 different audio signals to sit on one 20-bit data bus. This is achieved by 'time-division multiplexing' (TDM), where each one of the 20-bit signals has its own time-slot on the bus relative to the sample clock pulse. This is illustrated in Figure 8.5. Thus, for example, channel 23 may be routed to track 34 by arranging for track 34 to 'look' at the bus at exactly that split second of time when channel 23 is present.

The remarkable advantage of this TDM system, which is now commonplace in modern telecommunication systems, is that the whole console system can easily be reprogrammed by the operator. This is so comprehensive that the

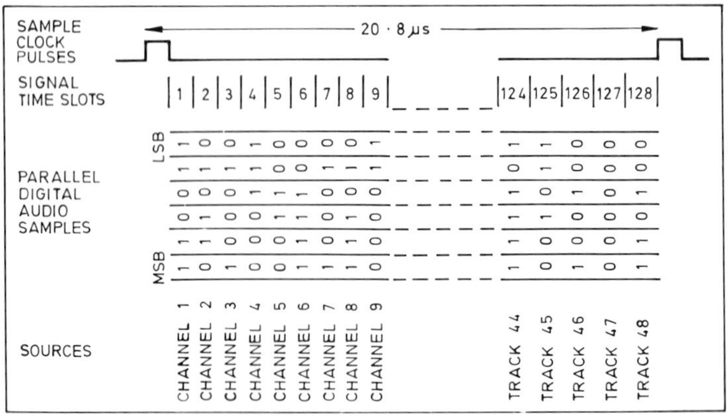

Fig. 8.5. Time Division Multiplexing (TDM), showing time slots on the parallel bus

mixer system can be effectively 'rebuilt' by the balance engineer to suit his particular application at the time. For example, processing for equalization, limiting, fading, compression, and so on can be built up in any order. Subgroups can be selected to feed further *ad hoc* subgroups in 'nesting' arrangements which would require a major rewiring job in an analogue system. Processing can then be included in subgroups as required, in addition to channel processing.

This flexibility is an important response of today's technology to the unique 'custom-built' requirement which was at one time *de rigueur* for any major studio. Today's hardware manufacturing techniques encourage standardization, the hand-built custom approach proving too costly for most applications. Now, with the flexibility of DSP, flexible routing together with appropriate control software restores to the balance engineer the ability to configure the ideal system for his task. Because this versatility is secured through the system software, the advantages of modern standard hardware manufacture are not sacrificed.

The large insertion jackfields necessary on analogue consoles are eliminated by digital signal routing. A dozen or so A/D and D/A converter pairs provide for the appropriate number of analogue 'effects' devices likely to be in use simultaneously. These patch points are then 'switched' into the required point in input channel, group, or output by means of the TDM digital routing.

4. The flexibility of DSP does not stop with signal routing. Signal processing benefits greatly, both in quality and scope. For example, functions such as equalizers which are particularly vulnerable to the imprecision of analogue component tolerance variations are completely accurate and predictable with digital processing. This helps particularly with accurate matching of stereo pairs in both frequency and phase response. DSP equalizers and dynamics controllers on present systems mimic accurately the characteristics of their analogue equivalents. For the future, however, new software programs promise some completely new effects.

One area which is complicated in the analogue world, and yet simplicity itself in digital, is straight time delay. This is used creatively for special echo effects and also for the more subtle restoration of phase coherence in a multi-microphone situation. The introduction of the appropriate amount of high-speed RAM into the digital signal path readily produces time delays adjustable from a fraction of a millisecond to several seconds.

We therefore see that there are powerful reasons for expecting a continuing trend towards digital processing in studios, and the rest of this chapter aims to give an overview of some of the practical aspects.

The digital studio system

A small DSP system such as a tape transfer console is a free-standing unit readily accommodated in the control room. The larger digital systems, however, involve processing units separate from the control console. These are normally housed in a separate equipment room, thus freeing listening areas from fan cooling noise and leaving only the compact control console to be accommodated in the control room.

Advantage can be taken of the structured system to install the elements of a DSP system in the appropriate places. Figure 8.6 shows a typical studio system embodying a digital mixing console. This illustrates the revolution which DSP brings about. The main system interconnections are via optical fibre cables, eliminating the usual anxieties of HF loss, earth loops, crosstalk, RF interference, and hum. Within the equipment room, the interconnections between processing and interface racks are made with ribbon cables carrying the 20-bit floating-point parallel bus which embodies the 128 time-slots used for TDM routing. The cross-connections between the racks enable the insertion of processing before or after mixing and also re-entrant mixing to create successive subgroups.

The fast arithmetic needed for channel processing (equalizers, dynamics, etc.) is carried out in the processor rack using high-speed bit-slice processors configured to be free from the usual bottlenecks of microprocessor architecture, and hence capable of carrying out on each processor board 10 million instructions per second. This power enables each processor board to carry out equalization, filtering, and dynamics control for two audio signals in the 20 μs time period available between successive audio samples. Also included in the

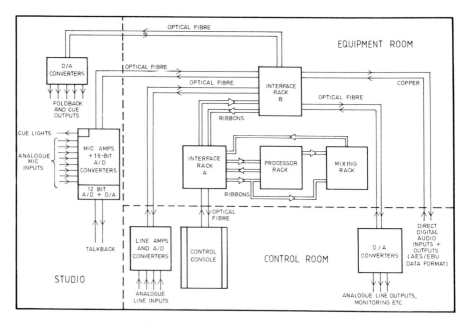

Fig. 8.6. Typical digital studio system

processor rack are a separate 'fader' processor board capable of 20 million multiplication sums per second and the delay processor board. This latter provides up to 2.7 s total delay which can be freely assigned between the 24 processing paths handled in each processor rack.

It is important to note that, within the processor rack itself, up to 28 bits are used. Despite the fact that the input and output signals in the system rarely need more than 16-bit resolution, much greater accuracy is provided within the processor. This is the equivalent of headroom within an analogue system and avoids overload whilst maintaining top-quality signal-to-noise ratio.

The mixing rack likewise uses up to 32 bits to perform the additions necessary to create the 128 mixes available on the output bus. Thus under no circumstances can the digital signal 'overflow' and so produce 'wrap around' distortion. Extension of the number of inputs and outputs on the system is simply achieved by adding more processor and mixing racks as required.

Digital audio interconnection

We take for granted the fact that analogue audio signals can be readily interconnected with twin-screened cable, and that the standardization on 0VU level ensures working results.

Digital audio interfacing is, as might be expected, more complicated to standardize. Fortunately, practical standards have been agreed under the auspices of the AES and EBU. This interconnection, known as the AES/EBU standard, uses the hardware standard RS422A, a differential two-wire serial transmission circuit long established by the computer industry. At the frequencies involved in the AES/EBU standard, transmission is reliable over 100 m of conventional twin-screened audio cable. Low-capacity data cable and/or signal equalization can considerably increase this transmission distance. Detailed discussion of the format lies beyond the scope of this book. The basic data format, however, was shown in Figure 3.29, which illustrates one subframe. Two such subframes are transmitted in each sample period, thus providing two-channel digital stereo down one pair of wires.

The channel code is of the *biphase mark* type, similar to SMPTE time-code, having virtually no d.c. content and being polarity-independent. Each subframe has 32 'time slots'. The first four are used for synchronization, and then follow 24 audio data bits (least significant bit first). After the audio comes the validity bit, which is normally zero and is set to one if the sample is defective. The user bit and status bit can carry information about the channel such as labelling, time-code, and so on. These are set to zero if not in use. Finally the parity bit provides for simple detection of transmission errors; it is set to either one or zero on transmission to make the number of binary ones in the frame even. Thus if an odd number of ones should arrive it is a clear sign of a transmission error.

The AES/EBU digital audio transmission standard is used by the major digital recorder and console manufacturers and is helping to facilitate the extensive application of digital audio systems in more and more studios.

Typical digital console control facilities

The scope of the facilities made possible by digital signal processing cannot be fully explored in the space available here. However, the following outline aims to impart a flavour of the ergonomic capabilities of the technique.

Plate 10 shows one of the two assignable control panels on a large digital console. The input gain, equalization, dynamics, routing, and auxiliary send controls are all included. The rotary control knobs operate shaft encoders instead of potentiometers. These encoders have no end-stops, the associated four-digit display providing a precise, clear indication of each control setting. Equalizer boost and cut use the popular up/down key method with calibrated LED bar-graph indication.

The faders use the 'Necam'-style robotic drive, enabling the knob to act as its own indicator. The access button has an LED to show which fader, and hence signal path, is under the control of the assignable panel. Normally the two assignable panels work in parallel. Sometimes, however, the operator finds it

Plate 10. Assignable control panel on a digital console—top left (Photo: Neve)

useful to lock a particular control function such as the equalizer on to a particular channel, so that, for example, he can ride EQ irrespective of any reassignment of the rest of the controls. A 'hold' button on each panel permits this locking; any further access will then be referred just to the second assignable panel. Stereo channels are readily handled on a single fader with either a single assignable panel or a L/R 'split' between the two panels.

Next to the access button on each fader is a four-character label display. This serves as an electronic 'scribble' panel and can be labelled by the central typewriter keyboard. The advantage of such electronic identification is that it follows the signal round the system, appearing on accessed controls, and routing diagrams on the VDU and even on the appropriate microphone input sockets in the studio.

Setting up the console is speeded by the 'copy' facility, where settings from one channel can be repeated on others, so that, for example, all relevant foldback sends can be set initially at approximately the correct level.

The group of keys towards the top of each fader includes the usual PFL, AFL (solo), and mute keys. The two further buttons in the group are less familiar. The 'soft' key is, as the name suggests, operator-programmable, with a range of different functions including patch-point switching or initiating an auto-fade. The 'source' button makes an important contribution to the power of the console by allowing the operator, if he wishes, to work with more audio inputs than the number of faders on the console. Any number of inputs can be assigned to a fader: these are then selected for control by that fader by stepping through with the 'source' button. For example, six vocalists' microphone channels can be assigned to one fader and mixed to a vocal group which is also assigned to that same fader. Using the 'source' button, the operator may choose to have that fader normally in control of the group, but may switch quickly to control an individual vocal mike if required. The label display on the fader indicates what it is controlling at any time. In the ultimate, all inputs could be assigned to one fader and control selected in turn! A whole bank of faders may usefully be reassigned together to control either live inputs or their corresponding multitrack tape returns, thus saving the space occupied by separate monitor faders.

In some applications, an extension of the assignable control panel principle is useful. This is the multi-function control where the actual purpose of a particular knob can be reassigned. Typically, two knobs are associated with each fader and a whole range of different functions (echo, foldback, pan, input gain, etc.) is selectable to those knobs. In this way the operator gains a view across the whole desk of, say, pan-pot settings instead of being limited to seeing just one channel at a time.

In these latest exciting applications of digital signal processing and control systems we see the main purpose of advancing console technology: to provide faster, better, and more rewarding creative facilities for balance engineer and producer.

9

Sound processing
Richard Elen

'Sound Processing' is an excellent catch-all phrase. Once the signal has entered the recording chain, and before it reaches the final medium—the Compact Disc, record, cassette, or whatever—virtually everything that happens to it can be described as 'sound processing'. Even level control is a form of processing. But, fundamentally, we are concerned here with techniques of altering the sound's *character*. This can be done in a number of ways, and the primary techniques to consider are those involving the frequency spectrum, dynamics and time and spatial localization.

Mixing consoles often contain a fair number of signal processing facilities, notably equalization, one of the most obvious forms of processing as discussed in Chapters 7 and 8. Some also offer control of dynamics, and some—like the Neve DSP—by providing programmable time delays, offer some control of the time domain. The common-or-garden pan pot offers basic control of spatial parameters. However, the more comprehensive forms of processing often require some kind of outboard equipment, generally rack-mounted. This, of course, gives the recording engineer a great deal of choice as far as signal processing is concerned. There must be literally hundreds of manufacturers of signal processors around the world, each producing devices which are capable of all kinds of sound manipulation from simple to complex. With so many possibilities available, this chapter can do no more than give a general overview of the techniques, without going into too much detail.

Equalization

Equalizers are designed to manipulate the frequency spectrum of a signal, giving prominence to certain frequencies or frequency bands, and reducing the amplitude of the signal in others. So why the term 'equalization'? Simply because, in the early days of signal transmission and recording, manipulating the spectrum of a signal simply for effect was frowned upon: the idea was to provide an essentially 'flat' frequency curve—why mess around with it? The equalizer arose as a means of correcting deficiencies in the frequency response—caused, for example, by imperfect microphones, transmission lines and recording equipment—to achieve this goal: to 'equalize' a signal to flat. This concept still exists in the way we refer to the adjustment of a tape machine to one of a number of recording 'equalization' standards—the idea is to get back from the machine what you put in.

Today, things are different. The equalizer, like many other areas of sound processing, has become completely integrated—in the minds of most recording engineers—with the idea of manipulating the sound for effect, to achieve a creatively more pleasing result. The original idea of 'capturing' a sound in the most accurate way possible has disappeared from many areas of recording, especially the recording of popular music, where the use of close-miking techniques and multitrack recording is an integral part of the creative process, and the concept of an 'original sound' waiting there to be captured is meaningless. In modern multitrack recording the 'original sound' can only be said to be what emerges from the speakers in the control room.

It is possible, however, even in the case of multitrack work, to break the use of equalization into two distinct areas. In the first, an equalizer is used to compensate for deficiencies in the signal arriving from the input to the console, particularly as a result of microphone placement. In the second, we find the resulting sound transformed by equalization to something that did not exist before. The areas, of course, completely run into each other, but they are worth examining separately.

The modern recording studio bears little or no relationship to an auditorium or concert hall with acoustics specifically designed to carry musical sounds to an audience. Together with multitrack techniques has developed the art of studio design, and in many ways both have fed off each other to direct the course of recording techniques in general. In the search for improved separation in the studio, acoustics have by and large become more controlled, and more 'dead'. This has required the use of microphones closer to the instruments they are capturing, often too close to allow the microphone to capture the subtlety of tone which would be present in a more 'open' recording environment. So when the sound from a close-miked instrument arrives at the console, it may not bear much resemblance to the sound that is actually going on in the room outside. Alteration of the frequency spectrum picked up by the microphone—and also of the dynamics—may be necessary to render a reasonable representation of what the instrument actually sounds like. Equalization can help in this situation, and generally the console equalizer will be sufficient to do the job.

On an orchestral session, this kind of manipulation may be quite sufficient as far as equalization is concerned (allowing for the idea that there is a need in many classical engineers' minds to compensate for the fact that the listener to a record will not 'be there' by making the sound just a little more exciting than the 'real thing'). On a pop or rock session, this is just the beginning. The engineer in such a situation will make a transition from using the equalizer to compensate for conditions to using it for creative effect—without even thinking about it.

Such modifications are, of course, entirely up to the production team at the time. But, in passing, it is worth making a few comments about the use of equalizers. In recording, just as in any other field, you seldom get something for nothing. The more extreme any signal processing the more the sound will—in some way, subtle or horribly not so—be degraded. An equalizer will emphasize noise in frequency areas that are boosted as well as the signal you want. It may affect the transients and other aspects of the 'clarity' of the sound, if only simply because the audio path has been extended by going through yet another set of electronics (and, in the case of a piece of ancillary equipment, no doubt a jackfield, a set of cables, and a few other odd bits).

There is thus a great incentive, despite the requirements for microphone technique imposed by a modern studio, to get the sound as right as possible before it ever gets to the console. It *is* worth experimenting with microphone technique. It *is* worth getting the right sound on the instrument 'out there', if it has the flexibility to do so, as do many modern instruments, especially synthesizers. All that work minimizes the 'traditional' role of the equalizer (or any other processing system, for that matter), that of getting the sound right at the console before you start messing with it, leaving you more room to use outboard devices *creatively* rather than simply to correct something you got wrong elsewhere.

Types of equalizer

Equalizers come in a great number of shapes and sizes, but in essence they all do the same thing: they allow the manipulation of the amplitude of selected parts of the frequency spectrum of a sound (see descriptions in Chapter 7).

At its most basic level, an equalizer offers a pair of controls: one to select the operating frequency and one to adjust the gain (and/or attenuation: some units, more commonly referred to as filters, offer only the latter). In such devices the unit will operate on a band of frequencies around the selected one, depending on the 'Q' of the tuned circuit employed. At the extremes of frequency, and in filters, it is most common for the frequency characteristics affected by the gain control to extend up (at high frequencies) or down (at low frequencies). This type of response is referred to as 'shelving' and is shown in Figures 7.5 and 7.6 (page 142). At other frequencies, a 'peaking' response is more usual, where the effect of the gain control is centred on the set frequency (Figures 7.8 and 7.9).

Originally, due to the complexity of the circuitry then required, it was most common to find a *switchable* frequency control, allowing selection of one of several frequencies. Today it is much more common to find 'sweep' equalizers in which the centre frequency of each band is infinitely variable between upper and lower limits. Often the bands overlap, and the combination of variable frequency and boost/cut makes this type of equalizer very flexible indeed.

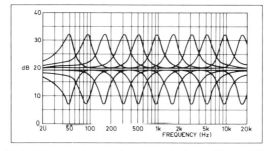

Fig. 9.1. Range of controls on a typical graphic equalizer

Sweep equalizers are often erroneously called 'parametric' equalizers. These—in which all the parameters are available for modification—exist, of course, but they offer more than a simple sweep EQ unit. Most importantly, they allow control of the 'tightness' or Q of the response curve, often with a multi-position switch or infinitely variable knob. At the extremes of the range, the Q can be adjusted to act on one narrow frequency band—tight enough, for example, to 'notch' out hum—or wide enough to have a very broad effect over a range of frequencies. This added facility offered by parametric units makes them exceptionally flexible, but equally they are more difficult to use effectively in haste, under the pressure of a session.

A particularly sophisticated type of parametric exists in which a computer is used to set up a complete full-range frequency response characteristic by allowing the engineer to 'draw', with a joystick control, the response curve required. The computer then generates the nearest approach to this curve by controlling a multi-band parametric EQ unit.

An alternative form of multi-band equalizer has been produced by one or two manufacturers in which the bands are deliberately allowed to interact, rather than remaining separate as on conventional units. The result is that both Q and overall frequency response can be modified with a remarkably small number of operator controls. These are very uncommon, however.

One of the most familiar of multi-band equalizers is the so-called 'graphic equalizer' (Figure 9.1). Here, a number of frequencies are available with amplitude sliders, enabling the engineer to set up an entire frequency curve, with the sliders displaying the approximate shape of the curve. The number of sliders—and thus the number of centre frequencies available—varies from half a dozen to as many as twenty-eight. The centre frequencies are standardized according to ISO recommendations. Graphics are somewhat of a double-edged sword, however. Although both easy to use and flexible, the large number of frequency bands controlled by such a unit can cause signal degradation especially as regards phase response. It is possible to design EQ units of all types with minimal phase errors, but this is not always seen in practice. The degree to which such effects are audible, however, depends on a large number of factors, notably the perception of the listener.

Time-domain processing

There is no simple name for this kind of signal processing. But time-domain effects are today a central part of the recording art, whether the effect be time delays, reverberation, flanging, or one of the more esoteric effects now available. Before modern digital delay processing systems came along there were tape machines to offer delay facilities—and, of course, real room reverberation is a time-domain effect.

Central to all these effects is the ability to take a sound and delay it, reproducing the sound—often at varying levels—once or a number of times. Heard with or without the original signal, the effect is exceptionally valuable.

Basic time-delay effects

At the bottom of all these effects is the simple time delay, and digital (or occasionally analogue) delay lines—which offer this facility flexibly and with great ease—are commonplace in the studio. At delay times of a few tens of milliseconds, delays can be used to 'double' a sound, creating an effect generally referred to as 'ADT' or 'Automatic Double Tracking'. This does not give quite the same effect as getting a musician to play or sing the same part twice, but it is very useful. Modern delay lines generally offer the facility to vary the delay with a low-frequency oscillator, adding a certain degree of 'detune' and time slippage which can liven up an effect that might otherwise sound somewhat mechanical. A delay of this order can also be used to split a mono sound into pseudo-stereo, and is the basis of a number of stereo synthesis devices and techniques.

Longer delays give the possibility of a 'slapback' echo-repeat (echo as distinct from reverberation) when heard with the original signal, as found on rock'n'roll records. Add a touch of regeneration—feeding a portion of the output back to the input—and the repeats can be made to last for some time. Some more sophisticated delay systems allow the length of the delay (and thus the time between repeats) to be controlled by an external signal—say a click-track or bass drum—so that repeats can be made to occur after a pre-determined number of beats. Some devices allow various 'taps' to be taken off the delay to allow multiple repeats (in the old days it was tape loops and a number of replay heads).

Make the delay shorter, and interesting things happen if the delay is heard along with the original sound: as the delay time falls within the lengths of time associated with audio waveforms, various cancellation and summing interference effects will be heard between the original and the delayed signal. We are now looking more at phase-related effects than separate repeats. Other things happen, too.

Phasing and flanging

At longer delay times, if the original and the delayed signal are split in stereo, our brains tell us that the sound source is in the direction of the original rather than the delayed sound (which is why the delayed signal in an ADT split left and right must be louder than the original to 'balance' left and right in apparent level). We interpret the delay as exactly that—the kind of time delay that happens because of sound reflections in the real world. As the delay decreases, however, the phase effects take over. If the delay between left and right is zero, we are listening in effect to two-channel mono. So the result of decreasing the delay to zero is that the sound pans across from one side (where the original is located) to the centre—phase-shift panning. If instead of using the original sound and a delayed sound split into stereo you used a sound delayed by a fixed amount on one side, and by a variable amount on the other, enabling you to sweep one delay *past* the other, the sound would pan wildly from one side to the other as the variable delay passed the setting of the fixed one. Listening to the same effect in mono, we have a very well-known effect born of the phase cancellations caused by the delay: 'phasing' or 'flanging'.

Exactly how this effect was discovered one can only guess. *When* it was discovered, and by whom, is similarly uncertain. The earliest well-known instance is the theme music to the film *The Big Hurt*, made in the mid-1950s. But there may be at least one example from the late 1940s. The familiar 'swooshing' effect was then rediscovered by more or less everybody in the 1960s: perhaps by Steve Reich in the United States: by Ken Townsend at Abbey Road with the Beatles; or by George Chkiantz for the Small Faces' 'Itchycoo Park'. The last example, however, is almost certainly the first time the effect was used under control.

In those days, phasing or flanging (the origin of the latter term is disputed, too) was done with tape machines. Later, devices based on notch filters were used to produce elements of the same effect. But it was with the development of delay lines that the effect became easily available with true repeatability in the studio. Today, it is a standard effect, and studio equipment can generally allow the effect to be controlled manually, by means of a low-frequency oscillator, or sometimes by the amplitude of the input signal. Generally, time-domain processing devices offer some or all of these effects.

Pitch-shifting and time-squeezing

In a digital delay system, the input signal is digitized and stored in memory. A short time later it is clocked out again and reconverted to analogue (unless you are working entirely digitally, of course, and are very lucky). The output will be a delayed version of the input if the rate at which it is clocked into memory is the same as the rate it is clocked *out*. Otherwise the pitch will be altered. Clock it out slower than it went in and the pitch will drop; faster and the pitch will rise. Chop up the contents of memory into slices and loop them, so that the signal lasts the same time whatever the clock rate, and you have a pitch-shifting device. In the old days, this was done with special tape machines, of which the Tempophon was the best-known. These had rotating heads on a drum which could run backwards or forwards with respect to the tape, at a wide range of speeds. The tape itself could also be speed-controlled, producing a range of effects, including speed change without pitch shift and vice versa. Today this can be performed with digital-delay-based systems, with or without the linking of the delay system to tape varispeed.

Reverberation

The most complex time-domain effect is that of reverberation. Natural reverberation is caused by the interrelation of a large number of reflections produced in an acoustic environment. After the original signal, there will be a pause followed by a number of distinct reflections: the sound being reflected, off the walls for example, and being picked up directly. Later, a complex series of multiple reflections will arrive at the listener, produced by sound having bounced off a number of surfaces first.

Figure 9.2 shows the kind of reflections (heavily simplified, of course) which produce reverberation effects. These can be simulated with a large number of delays (and delay taps) or via sophisticated algorithms involving memory storage. They can also be simulated by large sheets of metal fitted with transducers, as in the EMT echoplate and its successors; by springs fitted similarly with transducers; and, of course, by rooms and chambers of various sizes, which is how it was originally done. There is no doubt that modern sophisticated digital devices can simulate rooms very well—along with a large number of other effects—and it is the advent of microprocessor-controlled digital signal processors which has brought artificial reverberation down in size. Modern units are also quite affordable.

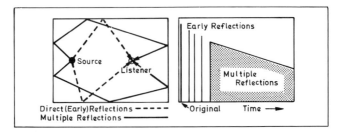

Fig. 9.2. Showing how reverberation is made up of direct (early) and multiple reflections

In addition to imitations of natural reverb, many of the more recent units can produce reverb effects, for example 'gated reverb' a sound fashionable in the early to mid-1980s (and now fully integrated into the overall repertoire of signal-processing effects), in which the reverb is cut off after a predetermined time.

Control of dynamics

The dynamic range of a recording system is simply defined as the ratio between the noise level at one end and the onset of distortion at the other. Almost all recording and transmission media have limits placed on their dynamic range by the technology, and several musical instruments and other sound sources encountered in the course of everyday studio life are capable of dynamics which exceed these limits to a greater or lesser extent. Even with modern digital systems—typically 16-bit in current studio applications—there are occasions when it is necessary to modify the dynamic range of a signal being recorded, though this is less necessary than it was previously.

In addition, it must be remembered that many of the media via which the finished recording will be heard possess considerably less dynamic range than can be recorded on the master tape. AM radio, for example, has the smallest dynamic range of any of the mass means of audio signal distribution, yet it is also one of the most important, certainly as far as popular music is concerned. FM radio has limitations, as do both conventional and DMM (Direct Metal Mastering) vinyl pressings (although the latter represents a fairly dramatic improvement over the former). Cassette tapes—particularly the pre-recorded variety—do not even get that far. Of all the current media, only Compact Disc offers the same dynamic range—potentially at least—as a digital master tape.

As a result, dynamic range control in the studio is a vital part of the recording process. Studio applications can be divided into three main areas: control of dynamics to enable 'difficult' material to be recorded or to survive the final medium; dynamics control for effect; and analogue tape noise reduction systems (the intention here, of course, being to increase the dynamic range of the medium).

Sitting on a fader, pulling it down during the loud passages and pushing it up during the quiet sections, is one of the most fundamental methods of dynamics control, and still one of the most effective. Manufacturers of compressor/limiters have spent many years developing equipment to do the job of fitting wide dynamic range material into a smaller space as well as a trained balance engineer can do on a complex live broadcast, for example. Here, the art is to anticipate changes in overall programme level and adjust the level gently so as to preserve the contrast between musical events. So-called 'gain-riding' is still a very useful method—indeed, in the multitrack environment it may well have increased in importance with the introduction of fader memory or 'console automation' systems which enable gain manipulation on the faders to be repeated until it is right, the system then remembering it for the rest of the mix.

Automatic gain control systems—compressors, limiters, and expanders—are some of the key tools in any studio, even where classical music is concerned. However, one of their primary uses is in the contemporary music field for effect purposes: to tighten up an errant bass drum or bass guitar, for example, or to enable a vocal to maintain energy and stay out in front however lacking in power the voice may be in certain registers.

The most common gain control element utilized in such devices today is the voltage-controlled amplifier (VCA) placed in the audio path, whose gain can be adjusted by a d.c. control signal derived from the input signal or, optionally in some units, from an external programme source (for example another track on the tape machine).

On the face of it, automatic gain control devices are pretty straightforward. Limiters and compressors reduce the gain in the audio path as the level rises above a pre-set threshold level; expanders reduce the gain as the input level falls. A limiter does not allow the output level to rise above a pre-set point. Simple, isn't it? But in practice automatic gain control devices are some of the most complex studio ancillary units for the novice recording engineer to operate successfully. There are a number of reasons for this.

Compression and limiting

Figure 9.3 shows a pair of compression characteristics. The gentler of the two, the 2:1 slope, shows that above the threshold setting (0 dBm in this case), an increase of 2 dB on the input results in only a 1 dB increase in the output level. The threshold setting for the 'infinity' slope—limiting, in other words—is +10 dBm. After this level is reached at the input, however much the input level rises, the output increases not at all. Typical compressor/limiters (often the two functions, which are essentially similar, as can be seen, are combined in one

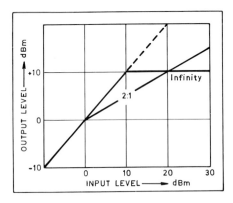

Fig. 9.3. Compressor/limiter characteristics

unit) usually offer a range of compression ratios. There will generally be an indicator or meter showing the difference between the input and output levels— the 'gain reduction'. A typical unit will have input and output controls as well as a compression ratio control. The threshold setting may well be fixed on simpler units—the effective threshold therefore being set by the input level—or it may be a separate control.

It should be noted from the graph that there is a point where the two lines intersect. Here, the gain reduction is the same, but at this particular input level the gain reduction has been achieved in two quite different-sounding ways. No real audio signal is constant, and the difference in sound between the two curves is dramatic. The softer compression retains much of the original dynamic range (half of it, to be precise), whilst the limiting characteristic simply squashes the dynamics altogether when the level at the input rises above a certain amount.

For this reason, limiters are often used to stop a signal dead, for example to avoid major distortion or even—in the case of disc-cutting applications— damage to the equipment. The threshold is generally set up 'out of the way' to catch wayward transients without affecting the normal course of musical events.

In compressor and limiter applications, it is important to determine the rate at which compression or limiting occurs, particularly when it comes to limiting. Often the attack and release times of the system are variable. To 'catch' transients with a limiter, it is important that the attack time is fast—to avoid too much overshoot—and that the gain is recovered rapidly after the transient has passed. In compression applications, however, for example 'tightening up' a bass guitar, a slow attack is often a good idea, as the deliberate overshoot at the front of the sound can add punch to the notes. Some units have an optional programme-controlled attack/release characteristic which allows the unit to set its own parameters according to the characteristics of the potential overload.

It is interesting to note one effects application of compressor/limiter systems, known as 'overlimiting'. It is often difficult to achieve on modern units, but the effect can sometimes be useful. In an overlimiting condition, the output level is squashed so hard by the limiting action that it drops below the threshold level: in other words, loud input signals (above the threshold) emerge at a lower level than quieter (below-threshold) signals. The result can be interesting.

The release time is also important. With a long release (or 'recovery') time, the signal level after a transient will take time to return to its original value. Quiet passages after a loud transient will be quieter than they would otherwise have been, thus reducing the overall average level. This should be watched, as it is the average level which determines the overall apparent loudness of the signal. Yet rapid attack and release times combined with a large amount of compression can sound quite horrifying, as various undesirable side-effects begin to creep in with fast gain changes. This is particularly noticeable on bass-end signals, where the compressor can begin to follow the excursions of the actual audio waveform, flattening it out. The result sounds like a form of distortion, which of course it is. But with some pop material it is surprising how much you can get away with before it becomes noticeable. If you wish to subscribe to the school of thought which forbids the peak level to vary beyond 5 dB for the duration of the song, this is the direction to head in: a careful compromise between gain reduction and rapidity of attack/release. The end result can, with care, sound much louder than it really is.

There are other undesirable side-effects of the compression process. It is very easy, for example, when one is compressing an entire mix, to end up with one dominant signal in the track (typically bass drum and/or bass guitar) pushing the rest of the track down when it plays. This can be uncomfortable on playback, but it is often difficult to know that it is happening when you lay down the mix, especially if you are listening at high monitoring levels and the ears are doing compression of their own. In circumstances like this, it is as well to listen briefly at a markedly lower level (or, if the producer objects, put your fingers in your ears) and watch for tell-tale signs. One of the most obvious is that changing the level of parts of the rhythm section by a very small amount appears to affect the overall balance dramatically.

Not only can a loud instrument in a full balance 'modulate' the rest of a track; a solo instrument out on its own can modulate the total system noise, especially if the compressor is right on the end of the chain. This shows itself as a 'breathing' or 'pumping' effect and is quite distasteful. As noise is particularly noticeable in the upper frequency ranges, solo bass instruments are the most likely to cause problems. There are a couple of ways round it: use a band-splitting compressor (in which separate gain control elements handle different parts of the frequency spectrum) if you can find one (they are usually found in broadcast applications, and seldom in the recording studio), or use a compressor where you can access the side-chain, the signal path in the unit that derives the gain-changing control voltage. Insert an equalizer in the side-chain and roll off the bottom end, thus ensuring that bass signals produce a minimal change in gain. Then, if possible and necessary, compress the solo instrument on its own.

Similar solutions are required in disc cutting where excessive high-frequency energy—in sibilants, for example—can cause problems. Here the traditional approach was to equalize the side-chain so that a compressor/limiter reacted only to high-frequency information. Again, the problem here is that the whole track is turned down to remove sibilance. An alternative approach used increasingly today is the band-splitting comp/limiter, which can treat the upper end of the frequency range separately without affecting other parts of the spectrum.

Comprehensive band-splitting compressor/limiter systems have wide potential applications for both of the instances described above, and they will no doubt become more common in the studio—as opposed to the specialist areas like disc cutting and broadcasting—as time goes by.

Expanders and noise gates

Expanders and noise-gates are, in simple terms, the inverse of compressors and limiters respectively. As can be seen from Figure 9.4, the effect of an expander is to *increase* the dynamic range by attenuating the output signal when the input level drops below a pre-set threshold. The attenuation is usually set by a control ranging from no attenuation to 'off'—infinity. A gentle characteristic will gradually increase the attenuation as the level falls; a harsh ratio—or infinity, as in a noise-gate—will simply reduce the output at a stroke the moment the input level drops below threshold (at a rate depending on the attack characteristic).

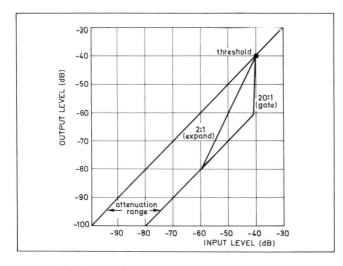

Fig. 9.4. Typical expander/gate characteristics

While expanders are quite difficult devices to use effectively, noise-gates are a very common and effective way of reducing the apparent noise level on multitrack, simply by turning tracks more or less 'off' when they are not playing. To do this effectively, of course, the gate must operate very fast, preferably in microseconds rather than milliseconds—otherwise transients will be cut off dramatically. Modern noise-gates, in fact, have tended to become more and more like basic synthesizer envelope generators: one very common unit has, in addition to input, output, and threshold controls, three further adjustments, labelled 'attack', 'hold', and 'release'. The time taken for each stage is independently adjustable, leading to a great deal of flexibility. The same unit allows optional access to the side chain (a 'key' input—very common in gating systems—to enable the opening and closing of the gate to be controlled by a *separate* signal, for example to tighten up a bass guitar by keying it with the bass drum) and has adjustable low-pass and high-pass filters in the side-chain to allow the keying signal to be tailored exactly to requirements. This is exceptionally useful, as it enables a complex signal, say part of a drum track with a lot of spillage, to be filtered so that only the desired components of the sound are used to control another signal. It is thus possible to separate parts of a track and treat them as separate entities: the snare, for example, can be isolated and given its own EQ and reverberation without affecting the rest of the drum tracks.

The selection of 'gating' and 'ducking' is also possible on several units, the latter allowing the keying signal to *turn down* the main audio path when a keying signal is present, thus allowing, for example, music programme to be attenuated automatically in broadcast applications when the presenter is speaking.

Noise reduction systems

Compressors and expanders are occasionally used together. It is a difficult business, as one tends to counteract the other, but there is one application where that is exactly what you want—as long as there is a tape path in between the two—and that is in noise reduction for analogue tape machines.

There have been several approaches to noise reduction over the past two decades, and it is interesting that Ray Dolby, whose Dolby A system was introduced in 1966, exactly twenty years later announced a new system— 'Spectral Recording'—at just the moment when many people in the industry were predicting the final eclipse of analogue tape recording systems by digital ones.

There were of course attempts at noise reduction before Dolby. The simplest— which relied on the fact that noise is more noticeable at the top end than in the bass—was a simple static pre-emphasis/de-emphasis system. You boost high frequencies on record, and cut them by the same amount on replay. This 'poor man's Dolby B', as one friend of mine once called it, does work (it has been used on FM radio for many years), but it has disadvantages when it comes to tape, which is at its most sensitive to overload at the high-frequency end. Static equalization curves were not the long-term answer.

One approach was to use a compressor on the record side, with an exactly complementary expander on replay. Such approaches are utilized in telephone systems (and, interestingly, by Soviet direct-broadcast satellite transmissions) to maximize the signal-to-noise ratio, but there they have the advantage that a control channel can be sent along with the audio (for example outside the audio bandwidth) to supply control data, ensuring that the input and output sides track successfully, because any error is doubly audible. This is impractical in current analogue recording applications.

The idea still sounds good, but there are other problems. One is that of overshoot on transients on the record side: in such cases the signal is *not* being effectively controlled by the compressor, and, however accurate the control information fed to the expander at the other end, it will be wrong. Then there is the question of modulation of one part of the signal by another, and the effects caused by throwing a single compansion system across the whole audio band.

Today, Ray Dolby's solution may seem obvious, but it is still a very clever approach to the problems presented by the analogue tape system. Dolby A is based around three primary factors:

1. Treating only the low-level signals in which noise is not masked;
2. Splitting the audio spectrum into four bands and treating them separately to avoid modulation effects;
3. Deriving a signal component which can be added to the direct signal on encode and subtracted from the signal on playback to maintain the integrity of the control signal, and enabling the same circuit components to be used for decode as for encode.

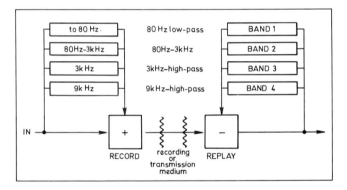

Fig. 9.5. Signal path in the Dolby A noise reduction system

The system also includes circuitry to limit transient overshoot in the compression stages.

Dolby A operates only on low-level signals: signal manipulation occurs below −40 dB. Above this level, the processing action is gradually removed and by −10 dB it is non-existent. The presence of a processing threshold, however, does mean that the system is sensitive to the input level. As a result, it is vital that a reference level is established on a tape-to-tape basis to ensure that encoding procedures carried out during recording are exactly undone in the playback stage. The later, consumer development of the Dolby system—Dolby B, which operates only on the upper frequency band, where noise is the most noticeable—also requires levels to be precisely correct, and this factor is one of the primary difficulties with the system.

In professional applications a 'Dolby level' must be established, and a Dolby reference tone must be included on the tape to permit alignment for subsequent deprocessing. (In consumer systems using Dolby B this facility is usually omitted—as is the ability to adjust levels easily even if you knew what they were—so many consumer products either start or end up incorrectly aligned, leading to loss of performance, particularly loss of HF information.)

In the early days, as Dolby rapidly became an international standard, there was a great deal of confusion as to how the Dolby reference level should be set, and this still continues to a lesser extent today. You were recommended to set operating levels in one of three ways: standard record level with Dolby level at 0 VU; elevated operating level with Dolby level at standard reference level; or elevated operating level *and* Dolby level. Over the past twenty years, tape technology has changed and so have normal operating levels, so it is always important to know what the Dolby level is on a tape, especially on an old recording, otherwise unpredictable results can occur.

Despite its noise reduction benefits—10 dB of noise reduction over the range 30 Hz–5 kHz and up to 15 dB at 15 kHz—and the fact that copies of encoded tapes could be made without decoding, producing an encoded copy with minimal additional noise compared to the master, many engineers were suspicious of Dolby A. There was a widely held belief—still existing today, to some extent—that Dolby 'changes the sound'. Some of this feeling could well have been the result of incorrect alignment in the early days; in other cases it may well have been that the reduction in noise level revealed faults in the recording that would previously have been masked. It is also possible for internal settings related to the processing bands in a Dolby processor to get out of alignment—a factor which cannot be corrected by the operator or even by a studio maintenance engineer—but this is unusual. It may be that some aspects of transient handling in the system, for example the overshoot protection circuitry, are capable of producing audible artefacts. But no firm conclusions have ever been reached, and as a result the alleged 'sound change' of Dolby A must be left to the individual engineer to judge.

While Dolby A continues as the primary noise reduction system in the studio to the present day, refinements were made to the consumer system. Dolby B operates on frequencies above approximately 500 Hz and offers around 10 dB of noise reduction. The newer Dolby C system gives almost twice as much. A later addition to the procedure—Dolby HX (for 'headroom expansion')—controls record bias and EQ according to the HF information, giving improved HF response, among other things.

In the professional field, other approaches were made to the problem of analogue tape noise. Some systems appeared and disappeared, like the Burwen 'Noise Eliminator', while at least one stayed around and still performs well under the right circumstances; the dbx system. This was developed by David Blackner and appeared on the market some time after Dolby. It suffered as a result of the fact that Dolby had already taken off—and also as a result of some inherent features.

The system utilizes a simple 2:1 compansion system coupled with pre- and de-emphasis (which is placed *before* the compression on record and *after* the expander on playback). This relieves some of the noticeable fluctuations in background noise which would otherwise occur in a wide-band compansion system. Figure 9.6 shows the basic features of the system. Another notable feature of the system is the use of true RMS level-sensing, rather than peak or averaging systems. This has the great benefit of representing the sum of all the signal components, irrespective of phase.

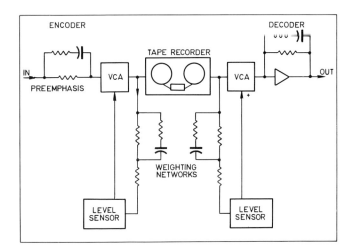

Fig. 9.6. Block diagram of the dbx noise reduction system

The dbx system provides up to 30 dB of noise reduction, but this is not achieved without a price. 'Pumping' and 'breathing' effects are not entirely eliminated, making it unsuitable for some kinds of programme material (although it is quite happy in many cases). In addition, when handling stereo programme, the two compansion channels cannot be linked. (This would upset the encode/decode process, as the system would operate on one channel under the control of signals in the other which may not be present in the same relationship on both channels.) The result is that the stereo image can 'wander' according to programme content. In many multitrack applications, however, it is entirely satisfactory. In addition, the simple compression characteristic adds headroom on tape to a useful degree.

The telcom c4 system, developed by AEG–Telefunken and now handled by ANT, came along late in the day and therefore benefited from hindsight as far as noise reduction system development is concerned. It can offer in excess of

25 dB of noise reduction, basically by combining the best elements of both Dolby and dbx. The spectrum is divided into four overlapping frequency bands whose sum produces a flat response, resembling Dolby in some ways. Each band, however, is treated by a simple 1.5:1 compansion characteristic, not unlike dbx, but with a gentler slope. The combination avoids a reference level— as dbx—but minimizes frequency-related modulation effects by means of the band-splitting (and the gentler slope).

One problem with band-splitting systems, however, can be the interaction of adjacent bands. In telcom c4 the bands overlap, potentially even more of a problem. It is important to derive a control signal on record which can be duplicated on playback. The telcom system handles this in an ingenious fashion. While the band-splitting in the audio path is generated by 6 dB/octave filtering, the control signal is generated using 12 dB/octave filters with the same centre frequency. The result is a control signal which does not suffer interference from adjacent bands, yet retains a smooth band overlap in the audio path. The combination is a good one, and while telcom c4 has suffered from arriving late it has gained a good following.

It is not, however, the last word in analogue noise reduction. Dolby has recently introduced a new system, Dolby Spectral Recording (or 'SR' for short). Arriving at a time when digital systems were poised to take over the top end of the multitrack market, but where sales were hampered by the lack of agreement on standards, the introduction of Dolby SR has enabled studios to put off the fateful decision between competing digital systems more or less indefinitely. Many studios are now likely to wait until a unified open-reel digital standard has been agreed before going further, because Dolby SR claims to offer a level of performance on current analogue recording machines which is audibly equal to, or better than, 16-bit digital. Owing something to the Dolby C consumer system, SR, rather than dealing simply with the activity below a certain level in a number of bands, instead develops a three-dimensional 'gain surface' which is a function of time, frequency, and the changing spectral properties of the signal. Figure 9.7 (courtesy Dolby Laboratories) shows the basic structure of the system.

The circuitry is mounted in a Cat 280 card, physically similar to the original Cat 22 Dolby A cards and capable of fitting into the same rack (both telcom and dbx units are also available in this format). In the record mode, the main activity of the system is to add gain to those areas in the frequency spectrum of a signal which contain low and medium-level components. On playback, exactly complementary degrees of attenuation are applied to these areas.

The input signal is first passed through a low- and high-frequency spectral skewing system which reduces the problems caused by signal components at the extreme edges of the frequency spectrum, where tape machine response can be uncertain. This is compensated for in the decode stage. There then follow three separate side-chains, dealing with high, medium, and low-level signals, the

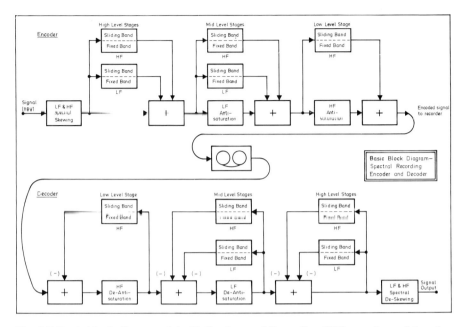

Fig. 9.7. Basic block diagram of the Dolby Spectral Recording (SR) encoder and decoder

output of each being summed into the main path. In each side-chain, the signal is split into LF and HF processing areas (with the exception of low-level signals, which are dealt with only at HF). Each subpath has sliding and fixed-band dynamic control, whichever is the most effective being used at any one time—a process which Dolby refer to as 'Action Substitution'.

There are three thresholds, -30, -48, and -62 dB. As the signal level drops below each of these, a separate gain control stage is brought into play, called 'Action Staggering' by Dolby. Behind the entire process is the fundamental idea of leaving the signal alone unless it needs treatment, and minimizing the treatment to exactly what is necessary.

There are other kinds of noise reduction which are worth a brief mention here. One type—exemplified by the MicMix 'Dynafex' unit— is a single-ended noise-reduction system: its acts on replay only. While basically an expander-based system, it is also frequency-sensitive.

One problem with expanders is that they can be unpredictable, and can produce side-effects. The entire signal level can ramp up and down at around the threshold level in a non-linear and disturbing fashion. Yet the principle is useful. Another approach to noise reduction—as utilized on some early cassette recorders by Philips, and referred to as 'DNL', or 'Dynamic Noise Limiting'— involved sensing the maximum frequency present in a signal above a pre-set threshold and generating a control signal used to adjust the 'knee' frequency of a low-pass filter, thus effectively 'turning down' the level above the maximum significant frequency. This can produce a dramatic apparent lowering of the noise-floor (the majority of noticeable noise being in the upper-frequency region), but it too suffers from problems. The apparent noise level can wander up and down according to the presence or absence of an upper-register solo instrument, for example. But the system is useful, and is available in some professional devices.

In the Dynafex, these characteristics—expander and frequency-sensitive HF roll-off—are combined in such a way that their side-effects tend to cancel out, or at least ameliorate, each other. The result is a unit with a simple threshold-setting control, the ability to gang channels for stereo, and a useful noise reduction capability when no other means are available. As it is sensitive to frequency and level, however, there can be some unwanted attenuation of low-level signals present in isolation, for example reverb decays, and this should be borne in mind.

All the systems so far discussed were designed to operate on the analogue tape path. There have, however, been a couple of attempts to tackle the problem of noise on vinyl discs. Here, the noise problem is more frequency-dependent than on tape, and there is a case for treating the problem in a slightly different way. The dbx system has been used virtually unchanged in this area with limited success, but CBS Laboratories decided in the late 1970s to develop a compansion system specifically designed for the disc medium. A frequency-biased compression curve was to be employed at the cutting stage, and domestic decoders would be available to supply the complementary expansion. Both in theory and in practice the system worked well, but it ultimately failed primarily because of the marketing strategy employed.

The system was called 'CX'—so-called 'Compatible Expansion'—and the failure of the system was due to the fact that CBS insisted that the compression was inaudible when un-decoded. The idea was that all records would ultimately be CX-encoded, and un-encoded discs would not be available (to avoid having to produce two versions of every album). If you had a decoder, you would experience the undeniable benefits of the system. But if you did not, said CBS, you would not notice the difference caused by the compression. Unfortunately, many people felt that they could.

Another approach to disc noise reduction is to try and reduce the audibility of clicks and pops on vinyl pressings. Such systems were at one time available in the consumer market-place, but professional systems of the type are often used to rejuvenate classic archive recordings for reissue. The technique is in fact a time-domain processing approach, but it is included here along with other types of noise reduction. In essence, the system relies on putting the signal through a short delay, slightly longer than the average click or pop. A sudden transient click is sensed by a time and level-dependent circuit (often with frequency-sensitivity as well) which is theoretically capable of discriminating between clicks and musical transients. When a click is sensed, the delay is either dumped completely (thus 'editing out' the click) and gradually restored, or a substitution is made with an immediately previous section of programme without the click. In both cases, the amount 'edited out' is very short, and as a result minimal side-effects are heard. The problem is in sensing pops and clicks accurately.

Spatial localization processing

Since the first days of stereo, engineers have been concerned with positioning signals in a sound-stage of one sort or another. Monophonic recordings, of course, have no spatial localization information available. But stereo and modern multi-dimensional systems offer at the very least the capability of placing a sound source along a straight line between the speakers.

In a true stereo system, for example a recording made with a Blumlein or crossed-cardioid microphone pair, the localization of sound sources is dependent on the original material. In this sense, stereo is simply a more realistic method of capturing what is going on. The same applies to dummy head or 'binaural' recordings where, to varying degrees, attempts are made to emulate the human hearing system. Binaural techniques recur every few years and are hailed every time as if they were something new; then they go away again. Some major advances in this field have been made in recent years, both in binaural recording, in the shape of Hugo Zuccarelli's controversial 'Holophonic' system, and in coincident microphone systems, like the 'Soundfield' microphone. They are not really 'sound processing' techniques as such, and will not be discussed further here.

The majority of current 'non-monophonic' recordings, however, whether made direct to two-track or via multitrack procedures, use a mixing console and multiple inputs. In this situation, it is necessary to position essentially mono sources in a sound-stage, usually a stereo environment created via two speakers, fed from two channels of information. This type of spatial manipulation is more accurately referred to as 'pan-potted mono' than as true stereophony, as the standard method of achieving localization is to control the relative levels of a given source between the two channels. A signal present only on the left channel will appear left; a signal present equally on both channels will appear centre-stage; on the right channel only it will appear hard right; and various combinations in between. The standard device to achieve this is the humble console pan-pot.

Localization by level

Pan-pot design is a surprisingly complex area, primarily because it is traditional—and necessary—to consider not only the stereo listener but also the listener equipped with mono listening systems. As a result, a pan-pot must produce both a respectable stereo effect and a minimal effect in mono—so-called 'mono compatibility'. A number of approaches are current in this area, and they differ in the 'law' by which the pan-pot acts in dividing the mono input signal between the two output channels across its travel, and whether the sum of the two channels is constant across the travel of the pot or not. The two basic laws are 'constant power' and 'constant voltage', and are discussed in Chapter 7.

A development of the basic pan-pot occurs in the form of the autopanner, in which VCA devices are used to control the relative levels of the two output channels, the control voltage being derived from a number of sources. Often these devices can handle two input channels, and the outputs behave in opposition to each other (so, for example, as one sound moves right, the other moves left). Autopanner control signals may be derived from a low-frequency oscillator, allowing a number of wild dynamic effects, from a push-button trigger, initiating a time-controllable pan from one side to the other, or in many cases from a pulse counter which can be fed with a click-track or other rhythmic signal to cause the pan effect to occur at musical intervals. Generally, the panning width can be defined on the front panel.

Sum-and-difference and phase-shift panning

An interesting development of level-based panning has now rather undeservedly fallen out of use, that of sum-and-difference panning. It can produce extremely exciting dynamic effects, including that of placing a sound beyond the width of the speakers, but its compatibility with mono is severely limited, to say the least. It relies on having available a sum-and-difference matrix encoder and decoder, and in these post-Blumlein days such things are hard to come by. The basic set-up is shown in Figure 9.8. A two-channel signal is fed into the encoder, and two signals, sum and difference, are supplied by the output. These are fed into console channels and level-controlled. They are also capable of being panned, but not directly to the stereo output; instead they are fed to a pair of groups (for example) which are fed into the decoder input. This would normally yield the original left and right signals, but in this case the left–right and level

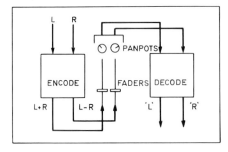

Fig. 9.8. Outline arrangement for sum-and-difference panning

relationships between the sum-and-difference pair may well have been scrambled, resulting in the feeding of variable proportions of anti-phase signals from one side into the other. The effect is very useful, and is found in some consumer portable stereo systems (in a pre-set fashion) to generate a 'wide stereo' effect.

The generation of anti-phase signals is just the start of a whole load of other possibilities. Level is only one of the ways in which our brains determine the direction of a sound source in real life. As a stereo localization system in recording, it suffers severe drawbacks, notably the fact that a sound can appear to move about in the sound-stage as you move between the speakers, on account of the fact that the relative level of a sound in the two channels is all that defines where it appears to be. Move to the left, for example, and the source will follow you, dramatically.

In real life, we use at least three systems to determine localization. Level is certainly one, but arrival time and phase are two other important considerations. Arrival time localization—or 'Haas Effect'—is noticeable when we ADT signals and split them left and right, as discussed above. The earlier sound will be the one we use to determine position, our brains interpreting the delayed signal as a reflection off some imaginary surface. In recording, this is less a localization system and more a nuisance, as in stereo ADT splits we need to enhance the delayed signal level to make it sound as loud as the direct: the 'spatial balance' and the level balance can differ significantly.

But, as was also discussed in the time-domain processing section, as the delay time is reduced, localization effects occur as the delay becomes measurable in terms of phase rather than gross time delay. Around the point where the two signals are nearly in phase, extremely dramatic panning can occur, extending beyond the speakers. Under control, this can be used to advantage, and at least one effects unit on the market uses phase-shift panning to create stereo effects. Once again, however, they are limited in their mono compatibility.

If level and phase are combined under control, we have a system which can emulate in the studio many of the characteristics of natural sound localization. Also, as a combination of level and phase cues can uniquely 'tag' the localization of a sound source virtually *anywhere* around the listener, we have the basis of a very powerful surround-sound system with good stereo and mono compatibility. Those cues can be used equally by the listener directly, or by a decoding system capable of deriving interrelated loudspeaker outputs to project the sound from the intended places.

Surround sound

Surround sound has had a chequered history. It was entirely natural to attempt to extend the 60° stereo sound-stage right around the listener, but it was difficult to do in practice. In the early 1970s, such attempts revolved around the idea that you could take four speakers instead of two and place them in a square around the listener, treating each side of the square as a stereo layout.

Unfortunately, such attempts had only limited success. 'Quadraphony', as it was called, relied on generating four individual signals, rather than the two associated with stereo. There were several problems with this approach. First, in the natural world it is only vaguely acceptable to reduce a soundfield impinging on the listener to four sources. Second, stereo operates successfully with the speakers placed so as to subtend an angle of 60° to the listener, not 90° as is the case with quadraphony. The result was a tendency towards 'holes' in the image between the speakers, although in some cases so-called 'discrete quad' was very impressive. Third, there were no four-channel transmission media available at the time (although some were developed, notably those using subcarriers and employing sum-and-difference encoding—as in FM stereo radio—on each channel of a stereo disc). So there was a need—to maintain compatibility with stereo and even mono once again—to develop matrixing systems to encode the four quad channels into two for stereo transmission and recover them at the other end ('4-2-4' systems). Regrettably, this is mathematically impossible.

However, matrix quadraphonic systems have survived in the film industry, in the form of Dolby Surround, a development of the more common original systems. They are capable of impressive effects in the cinema, though they are not at their best when trying to reproduce natural soundfields. Commercial consumer decoders are now available for this system, to decode home video releases derived from surround-encoded movie soundtracks.

Another fundamental problem with traditional quadraphonic techniques was that, particularly when quadraphonic mixes were being performed in the studio, the only method of synthesizing spatial localization was to use level-based localization only, generally with quad pan-pots. The disadvantages of level-only localization have already been discussed as regards the listening position in stereo; in quadraphony they are at least four times worse, and the listener is confined to a central position in the middle of the loudspeaker layout.

We have already seen that phase has a part to play in localization. Some recording systems—notably coincident-pair techniques—preserve many aspects of the soundfield, including both level and phase data, and the difference is easily heard in any situation in which coincident stereo pairs are combined with mono spot mics. If an orchestra, for example, is recorded with a coincident pair, it will be noted that the image is not only very stable as the listener moves about between the speakers, it is also capable of reproducing distance from the listener. A spot mic added into the balance to enhance a soloist, say, does not have these benefits, and will move about in a straight line between the speakers when the listener moves, in contrast to the orchestra.

This fact was used as the basis of a current surround-sound system developed in the UK in the 1970s. Called Ambisonics, it was originally designed to capture the natural soundfield and replay it—in three dimensions, with height if necessary—in an ordinary listening environment. Sound processing devices based on this principle are now available for mix-down applications, allowing the engineer to synthesize a soundfield in the studio, either for eventual surround-sound decoding by the listener, or simply as a means of creating stereo recordings with greater depth and image stability than is possible with conventional level-only localization techniques.

The basis of the Ambisonic system was derived directly from Blumlein's work in the 1930s on stereo recording. He used a pair of microphones, one an omnidirectional unit deriving the sum of left and right, and the other with a figure-of-eight characteristic, pointing left, and therefore deriving a difference signal. This sum-and-difference pair was then fed to a matrix decoder to derive left and right feeds. Ambisonics extends this technique into three dimensions, as shown in Figure 9.9. These signals can be generated by a 'Soundfield' microphone or can be synthesized from mono or stereo sources in a mix by a set of signal-processing devices. The signal is referred to as 'B-Format', and its four channels contain all the data required to pinpoint a sound source in three-dimensional space.

Of course this four-channel signal cannot be transmitted easily with currently available media. In addition, sum-and-difference signals are not in common use. So once again a matrixing system was developed to transmit as much data as possible via the channels available, while offering mono/stereo compatibility. The matrixing system is today referred to as 'UHJ', and it is a hierarchy of signal formats, each one being compatible with the one below it. Thus four-channel UHJ encodes all the spatial information, including height. Take away the fourth channel and you have three-channel UHJ, capable of high-definition

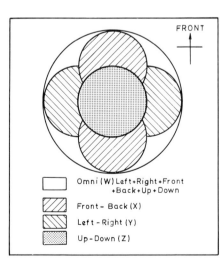

FRONT

Omni (W) Left+Right+Front
+Back+Up+Down

Front – Back (X)

Left – Right (Y)

Up – Down (Z)

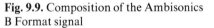

Fig. 9.9. Composition of the Ambisonics B Format signal

horizontal (or 'planar') surround. Take away the third channel and you have two-channel UHJ, the normal format for commercial applications.

Future developments in sound processing

Already, the processing systems described in this chapter are increasingly being handled digitally, either inside or outside the console environment. With the inevitable coming of all-digital recording systems, it will be possible to remove the conversion processes that often precede and follow such processors, especially as regards time-domain processors. Digital equalizers are already a reality, as are digital dynamic control systems. The tendency to digitalization means that signal processing in all its forms is increasingly a matter of number-crunching and computer power. Outboard processors already exist which offer a wide range of software-generated effects, and can be updated merely by inserting new ROMs or diskettes. This development will continue.

Control systems for signal processors are also increasingly available for computer access, either via RS232/422 serial data interfaces or via the high-speed MIDI (Musical Instrument Digital Interface) standard used in the vast majority of modern music synthesizers. This is inevitably leading, along with the development of 'tapeless' digital recording systems, to the integration of certain aspects of the music-making, recording, and signal processing chain in the modern recording studio. Already, signal processors can be interfaced both with music sequencers and with console automation systems.

Microphones will probably be the final link to be digitized, but once digital microphones are perfected there will be no need for the highly financed studio to use analogue techniques in any major form. Such an all-digital studio will not be cheap, however, and analogue techniques will not die out for some time. Neither will the need for engineers to be surrounded with large numbers of outboard signal processors disappear overnight, for the great advantage of individual units—whether they are centrally controlled or not—is that the user is not tied down to one manufacturer's signal-processing techniques, but instead can call on the unique sound-manipulating ingenuity of a wide range of manufacturers all over the world.

Until there is a single software-based system which does everything, and there is agreement on the basic input/output and control parameters required of signal-processing software for such a system—both rather unlikely at this point—engineers in studios the world over will continue to be surrounded by black boxes of one sort or another.

The new technology of signal processing has added to the repertoire of sounds available in the studio, and has made effects that were difficult to obtain now relatively easy. We are always looking for new sounds, and today's signal processors—and no doubt tomorrow's—indeed offer that. The technology of sound processing opens up even more creative potential.

But new sounds and facilities do not in themselves generate creative expression; they need to be handled and controlled by creative people. I am confident that it will never be the other way around. The technological capabilities of the modern recording studio are vast, but it is people—artists, engineers, producers, and everyone else—who bring the technology to life. It is the creativity of people that maintains the magic in the technology, and all these devices are simply the tools of the trade. When we find the technology forcing us to work in a way which does not suit the music, then it will be the machines that will have to change—and that is how it will be.

10

Loudspeakers and monitoring
Edward Veale

Studio monitoring is a very subjective and emotive subject. What we hear is the result of the process of hearing, and this is based upon our individual learning and experiences of different sounds and sound patterns. Because no two people are likely to have had precisely the same experiences, we all tend to interpret sound in different ways. For these reasons, it is difficult to gauge what another person is hearing or interpreting from a pattern of sound. Also, the response, texture, and quality of the sound reproduced by a loudspeaker is affected by the construction of the drive units, the enclosure within which the units are mounted, and the room or space within which the reproduction is heard. With so many personal and physical variations, it is little wonder that recorded sounds are given different interpretations by different people and, furthermore, that they actually sound different from one room to another. In fact, one may marvel that any similarity is achieved at all.

Over the past twenty years, the recording studio has moved from simple stereophonic and four-track recording to 46 tracks or more, analogue and digital. This rapid growth in techniques over recent years has placed varying demands upon monitoring systems. Single-source dual-concentric loudspeaker systems were once extremely popular, and, to some extent, they remain so. To satisfy the demands of the late 1960s (for ear-melting sound levels) twin-bass driver systems were introduced. About the same time, systems emerged which employed an efficient compression driver for the mid-range frequencies.

With the passage of years, measuring instruments have become more effective and better understood. The development of the microprocessor has enabled equipment to be designed and built which can, almost simultaneously, discriminate between the amplitude, phase, and time domain. This process is called Time Delay Spectrometry, or TDS (see also Chapter 4). In more recent times, with increases in the dynamic range of recordings, the benefits of advanced technology being applied to console design, digital signal processing and digital recording, the demands on studio monitoring systems have again changed, the latest requirement being a consistency of sound perspective over the full range of sound intensity. This latest demand, coupled with higher standards for definition in the stereo placement of sounds, has resulted in two developments coming to the fore: the nearfield monitor and the multiple-element soft dome monitor system.

The passage of years has also brought a better understanding of the behaviour of loudspeakers and how systems work when several drivers are housed in a single cabinet. The low-frequency output of systems can be improved by incorporating the enclosure into the building structure. Improvements in the transparency of the middle and high frequencies have been realized by co-ordinating the acoustical centres of the drivers, thus minimizing phase shift or delay between the associated frequency bands.

The demands which are placed upon monitoring systems by different sections of the industry also vary. Sound broadcasting, television, film, and video all have their particular needs. Sound broadcasting studios are most particular and selective about the monitors they use, and it is in this field that significant advances have often been made, particularly by the British Broadcasting Corporation. Within the other fields, the film industry is probably best organized, with frequency tailoring introduced to allow for the acoustic needs of the cinema auditorium and the optical transfer process. The particular demands placed on a recording studio monitoring system are greatest of all, in that it is required to reproduce sound in a manner which can be related to any other environment or reproductive system.

History of the loudspeaker

The loudspeaker can be traced back to 1925, when the first direct radiator dynamic device was developed by Chester Rice and E. W. Kellog. The theory of the direct radiator loudspeaker was first established in 1877 and discussed by Lord Rayleigh in his '*Theory of Sound*', Volume Two, published in that year. The mathematics of a direct radiator in an infinite baffle are presented in this book, but it was some forty-six years later before the first dynamic loudspeaker was actually developed.

In 1931 the first two-way system, described as a "divided range" system, was demonstrated by Frederick of the Bell Telephone Laboratories. Coaxial loudspeakers were developed to extend the frequency range of the single magnet/coil assembly. To overcome the problem of diminishing high-frequency response in the larger cone device, a smaller cone was introduced in the centre. The addition of this smaller cone improved the performance at the higher frequencies, and the introduction of a mechanical crossover arrangement enabled this to be effective from about 2 to 15 kHz.

The compression driver was later developed for public address work. The process of using a small diaphragm acoustically coupled to, and loaded by, a horn device produced a very efficient loudspeaker. There are two inherent problems with this device, distortion at the higher frequencies and an inability to reproduce low-frequency information. To overcome these problems, the compression driver was integrated into systems employing additional bass drivers and high-frequency units to extend their useful frequency range and take advantage of the efficiency they offered.

Dual-concentric devices were made popular by Tannoy and Altec in the 1950s. These comprised a cone loudspeaker for the bass frequencies, with a compression driver mounted on the back and feeding through a horn in the centre of the cone. These were compact, wide-range systems and offered great flexibility. They were much liked because the reproduced sound emerged from a single point; they are still produced and are to be found, for example, in current studio systems marketed by Tannoy and JBL under the UREI name.

The first purpose-built studio monitor was marketed by Cadac in 1970. This was a bi-amplified three-way system. It used the Altec 604 dual-concentric driver and a separate high-frequency array. The crossover was passive and designed to correct misalignment of the acoustic centres within the driver components. The design of the system also recognized the benefits of having short interconnecting leads between the amplifiers and speaker components, and later versions had the amplifiers mounted within the enclosures.

The electrostatic loudspeaker provides a presentation of sound unequalled by conventional moving-coil devices. Many systems were developed, but that by the Acoustical Manufacturing Company, under the 'Quad' banner, was the only one to become popular. Unfortunately, the electrostatic system cannot achieve the high sound levels demanded by most studio users, and so it never made much progress in the studio market, except for some classical music monitoring. A number of hybrid systems using cone-type bass drivers were developed, but these have not been taken up by the recording industry. However, there can be little doubt that the electrostatic loudspeaker has created standards by which the conventional system has to be assessed.

Since the mid-1970s there has been a significant growth in the number of studios engaged in professional sound recording, and it has become worth while for small, specialist firms to produce purpose-designed monitors; this is reflected in current product ranges and available systems. The 1980s have seen significant developments. Purpose-designed drivers have been produced for studio use and cabinet designs have advanced. A great deal of effort has been employed to overcome the problems associated with inefficiency, phase or time delay, frequency response, power handling, and distortion.

As well as a new breed of main monitor loudspeaker systems employing soft-dome drivers, smaller 'nearfield' systems were introduced to the market. Major advances in main monitor systems have been made, for example by Quested Monitoring Systems and Valley Audio. Both have introduced tri-amplified systems employing conventional and soft-dome drivers. Westlake has introduced a BBSM series of nearfield monitors which also dispense with compression drivers and are adaptable to a variety of applications.

Monitor uses

As already mentioned, the demands placed upon monitoring systems by different sections of the industry vary considerably, as do the acoustical qualities of the listening rooms. Broadcasters tend to favour small to medium-sized systems and build control rooms with the monitors placed to approximate a typical domestic environment. Film sound studios have their dubbing theatres designed to emulate the typical cinema. The recording studio is the most varied, and control rooms frequently sport three different monitor systems, selectable at the press of a button.

Broadcasting within the United Kingdom has been largely guided by the activities of the British Broadcasting Corporation, and many of their design practices have been embodied within the Independent Broadcasting Authorities Code of Practice for the control of Independent Local Radio. This Code of Practice document has become widely used and recognized as a reference for studio design and installation. It covers the requirements for the electrical systems and the studio acoustics.

The film industry has sought to improve the quality of film soundtracks by many new techniques. One has been to simulate, within the dubbing theatre, the environment experienced by the cinema audience, so that sound is mixed and equalized to optimize for such conditions. Electrical filters are provided to simulate the effect (or degradation) of the transfer of the soundtrack from magnetic to optical media. A great deal of work has been done by Dolby Laboratories to improve the quality of film soundtracks. This work extends to reducing background noise, increasing the dynamic range, and producing a stereophonic effect within the space available on the 35-mm optical soundtrack (see also Chapter 28). As a result of efforts to standardize the listening conditions in both the cinema and the dubbing theatre, the American National Standards Institute, together with the Society of Motion Picture and Television Engineers, produced a standard audio reproduction characteristic which was published in 1984 as ANSI/SMPTE214M. This stipulates the curve to which cinema auditoria and dubbing theatres are to be equalized (Figure 10.1).

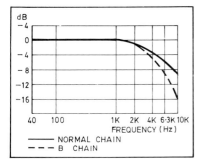

Fig. 10.1. ANSI equalization curves for cinemas and dubbing theatres

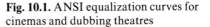

The sound recording studio, on the other hand, strives to attain excellence with no particular standards to guide those engaged in the design or operation. Because the recording industry is comparatively small, major advances tend to develop as a result of efforts by entrepreneurs or engineers who happen to design something which is appreciated by the studio users. As a result, trends in equipment and control room design tend to advance in definite phases and are more readily apparent than elsewhere.

It is because the recording industry is so small that, historically, most advancements have occurred as spin-offs from other sectors, and this is particularly true for monitoring systems. Only in recent years have loudspeaker drive units been specifically designed for studio systems and complete studio systems been developed uniquely for this application.

Studio monitors

To define the requirements of loudspeakers for studio monitoring, it is necessary to understand current design practice, the placement, use, and characteristics of the systems available, and also the working needs of the studio. The monitor loudspeaker is the link between the electrical information which represents the recording and the listener. The loudspeaker performs the opposite function to that of the microphone by turning variations in electrical signals into variations in air pressure which our ears can perceive.

The environments in which we listen to sound vary considerably in range and quality; from home to office, discothèque to theatre, motor car to concert hall, headphones (for personal listening) to piped music in hotels, and so on. All of these have different acoustical qualities which influence the sound that we hear from either live or reproduced music.

With the advent of electronic music synthesizers and keyboard equipment, developments in the electronic world, digital recording, and other advances which have been introduced to the recording chain, the demands placed upon the modern control room have grown considerably. Particularly with this in mind, we should not overlook the length of time that is devoted to making individual recordings and then refining and mixing these to produce the final master. Engineers and producers can spend many days concentrating on a single recording to obtain perfection. The overall environment and the quality of the facilities in the control room can either help or hinder this work.

The performance and the sound quality perceived from the monitoring system can be described in many ways. Many expressions are used by engineers or producers to describe sound quality, including such vague terms as transparency, harshness, definition, transience, darkness, lightness and aggressiveness. However, such terms often have different meanings for different people, and engineers involved with the technical design and manufacture of loudspeakers continue to strive for methods of measurement which will demonstrate a direct relationship between the subjective and the measured results.

These problems are further compounded by the advancements in digital recording which demand higher definition over the entire amplitude and frequency range, coupled with a wider dynamic range. This puts a greater strain, not only upon the power-handling capacity of the loudspeaker, but also on the design of the power amplifiers driving the loudspeaker, the crossover system, and every other link in the monitor chain.

Advances in measuring equipment have produced benefits for those engaged in product development by making available FFT (Fast Fourier Transform) analysers and TDS (Time Delay Spectrometry) systems. Such techniques now enable the measurement procedure to separate the loudspeaker from the room without the need for anechoic chambers, and to investigate these separately. Thus the actual response of the loudspeaker can be investigated in terms of frequency/amplitude/phase/time without the need for removal to laboratory conditions. Likewise the events within the room, either separately or in combination, can be investigated in greater depth. This has advanced our understanding of the behaviour of sound within the controlled environment and encouraged a better approach to design.

Whilst such equipment enables more investigations to be made in greater depth, the level of sophistication creates other problems: more information is produced and the control parameters of the measuring equipment have been enhanced to such a level that errors are easier to make and less easy to detect. Notwithstanding such advancements, it should not be forgotten that current measuring practices use a single microphone to receive information, which limits the amount of information which can be either received or processed. We, as mere mortals, have been given two ears which, coupled with the brain, perform analysis functions beyond the capability of even the latest measurement practices.

A considerable amount of information about the electroacoustic performance of loudspeaker systems is usually available from the manufacturer. Such information often includes frequency/amplitude response, power-handling capacity, impedance characteristics, distortion values, dispersion or directivity in terms of Q factors or polar plots, and, for complete systems, phase coherence (often referred to as time alignment). There is no standard method of expressing all such factors, although there are ANSI (American National Standards Institute), BSI (British Standards Institute), and IEC (International Electrotechnical Commission) standards which apply to some of them.

For these reasons the qualities of loudspeaker systems are difficult to quantify, and so this leads to personal assessments and preferences. Bodies such as the Independent Broadcasting Authority have set up panels of listeners to assess loudspeakers, and, from their judgements lists of acceptable products can be made. This demonstrates the problems that individual consultants and users can experience when asked to recommend a monitor system.

A further influence on the sound perceived from a monitor is the surrounding environment (room acoustics). There are varying ideas as to what constitutes a good room: these range from very dead to moderately live, with live-end: dead-end, and other special constructions to add variety. Add to this the effect that the building materials can have (especially on the low end) and the effect of the equipment (console, tape recorders, equipment racks, keyboards, etc.) on early reflections and diffusion, and the resultant effects are seen to be compounded and very complex.

It may now be realized how it is that some engineers and producers prefer certain types of monitor, and why it is that the same monitor can sound quite different between one location or studio and another.

One may be forgiven for thinking that there is a common standard for design in present-day studios, but this is not the case. For example, the designers of sound recording studios go to great lengths to ensure that the information delivered by the monitor loudspeakers is presented to the listener in the most efficient way possible and with the least amount of modification or room influence. This includes such techniques as mounting the monitors in such a way as to avoid energy radiated from the sides and back of the enclosure being reflected off the front and side walls and arriving at the listener at significantly different times. Such reflection problems do not appear to worry broadcasters, because their monitor loudspeakers are often intentionally placed at distances of one metre or more from all wall surfaces, and indeed this suggested placement is set out in European Broadcast Union Technical Recommendation R22-1985.

It must always be borne in mind at the studio that the recordings will ultimately be listened to in a variety of situations where the listening conditions may be very different. Popular music, for example, could be heard on loudspeakers or headphones, from a hi-fi system, in a discothèque, in a car, on television, or on a small personal radio. The engineer and producer need to be satisfied that the 'mix' will still be effective when listened to in any of these situations. To achieve this, it is common practice to have at least one or more alternative speaker systems on which the recording can be replayed. These range from the main installed monitor system to good domestic speakers and very small speakers representative of lower-grade systems. These small speakers are often referred to as 'nearfield' speakers, because they are usually positioned very near to the listener.

The attitudes of recording engineers towards monitors also varies. There are those who will work exclusively on the main monitors and make only occasional checks on the alternative speakers, and there are those who will do most of their work listening to a good-quality pair of hi-fi or near-field speakers, occasionally turning to the main monitors to hear how the mix sounds at very high level, or to impress visitors. There are also a few engineers who appear to have no difficulty in relating to the sound they hear from any monitor or speaker system, and who work with whatever system seems satisfactory to others on the session.

Most recording engineers will probably agree that listening to the mix on the main monitors at a moderate level enables the perspective of the sound to be most accurately assessed. Listening to the small 'nearfield' systems (often perched on top of the console meter housing) has the effect of reducing any room effects and creating a system response more compatible with in-car and other domestic listening environments.

Monitor positioning

The positioning and mounting of monitor systems is an important consideration. Obviously, they must be securely fixed to the main structure, and large obstructions are unwanted because these can affect the overall performance of the system and the quality of the sound presented to the listener.

In recording studios, the preservation of the stereophonic picture is of primary importance. Additional speakers are installed in control rooms where film work is done, to provide centre and surround-sound information, but these are secondary. The traditional equilateral triangle is always a good position from which to start, with the two loudspeakers subtending an angle of 60° to the listener (Figure 10.2). However, modern control rooms often dictate that a

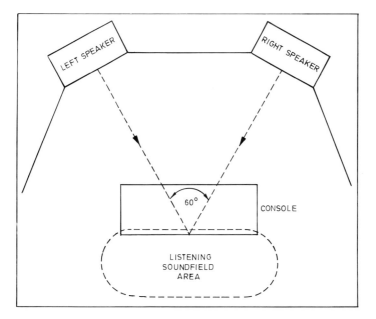

Fig. 10.2. Traditional 60° speaker layout for stereo monitoring, showing the listening soundfield area

different approach is necessary. In the larger control room, this traditional approach often reduces the designer's task but caution has to be exercised to ensure that the console position and the volume of space between the speakers and the console do not contribute to a poor bass response.

Whatever is done, whatever loudspeaker location is chosen, whatever the system, one thing is paramount: the quality of the sound presented to the listener in the main working area. This area is generally described as being equal to the width of the control console and extending from the seated position at the console to about two metres back. The height within which this area has to apply should be from about one metre to two metres above floor level. For convenience, this region is often referred to as the soundfield. The quality and texture of the sound presented to the listener within the soundfield will be affected by the type of monitor system selected, its location in the room, and the acoustics of the room.

Many control room designs are now created where the console is moved forward to the edge of, and sometimes into, the nearfield response of the main loudspeakers. The demand for space between the speakers to accommodate television monitors and similar, whilst still meeting the same needs for a suitable coverage angle, has meant that the traditional approach to layout has often to be abandoned or greatly modified. In other situations as we have said, a separate pair of small monitor speakers may be placed on top of the console itself (to simulate domestic playback conditions). This will generally produce a reduced listening sound-field area (Figure 10.3).

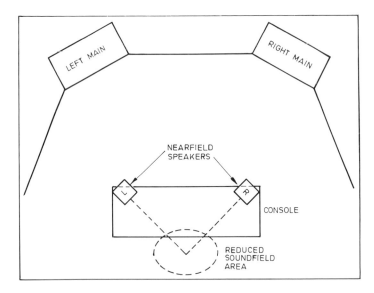

Fig. 10.3. Using small nearfield speakers reduces the listening soundfield area

A further influence on the effect of the soundfield is the elevation at which the monitors are mounted. This can be anything from the horizontal listening plane to an elevated position above, for example, a vision window. Thus the position selected for the monitor system will often be the result of a compromise between the space available, the coverage area required, and the type of system specified. To optimize the results within the soundfield, the designer normally contours the surfaces of the room and carefully selects and positions the acoustical treatments.

It is always a good design policy to reduce compromise wherever possible. In this regard, the monitor loudspeaker system can be selected to have characteristics which are complementary to the design needs. In this context, the coverage angles are important. These are related to the dispersion angles of the speakers and are often tailored by the designer of the system to direct the radiated energy into the desired space. This makes the system more efficient and can reduce room boundary effects.

In room designs which require the console to be close to the monitors, the required horizontal angle of coverage is greatly enlarged. Additionally, the ratio of distance between the loudspeaker and the nearest and furthest listening positions is considerably increased. This creates a demand for monitor systems which have an exceptionally smooth frequency response and wide angle of coverage. The soft dome radiators used in the latest breed of monitor systems are proving most suitable for these conditions.

With this interest in both monitor directivity and the listening soundfield, the dispersion characteristics of loudspeaker systems become significant in any calculations. This information is best obtained from a series of polar plots (see Figure 10.4) and to obtain sufficient information these plots should be made in one-octave increments in both the horizontal and vertical planes. Should any unexpected variations be observed in the horizontal or vertical results, then plots at a 45° angle should be performed; such plots will reveal any elliptical element within the dispersion field: this could cause a different sound to be presented at the extremities of the soundfield. Armed with an analysis of the prescribed speaker system directional performance, the required position and angle of the monitor system to the soundfield can be determined in relationship to the required soundfield.

Of great importance is the centre image, and this can be seriously affected when the distance between the two monitors exceeds the distance from the monitors to the listener (see Figure 10.5). Plots of the dispersion characteristics enable the angles at which the monitors are set to be adjusted so that any deficiency of the centre image is largely corrected. The sound intensity at the listening centre should remain constant when a signal is panned from left to right through the centre position. If variations exist, then the perspective and possibly the position of individual sounds within the stereo picture will change when reproduced on another system.

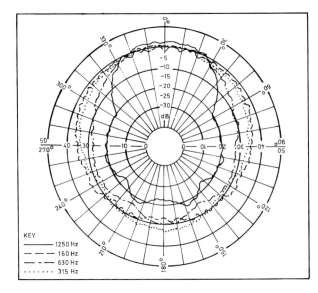

Fig. 10.4. Typical polar plot of a loudspeaker

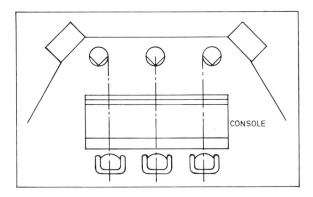

Fig. 10.5. Showing the image shift at different listening positions along the console. The characteristics and angle of the loudspeakers should be chosen to minimize this displacement effect

At frequencies below 400 Hz and particularly around 60 Hz, most speaker systems become omnidirectional, and energy is wasted by being radiated outside the area of interest. The design of some monitor systems has been adjusted to compensate for this reduction in on-axis amplitude at low frequencies by some form of low-frequency enhancement, and this may have to be catered for in choosing positions and layout.

A method which is often employed by designers to correct the effect of low-frequency fall-off is to recess the enclosure into the front surface of the room. This has the effect of increasing the area of the enclosure's front baffle and so preventing the low-frequency information being lost around the sides. This technique has the added benefit of eliminating any variations in frequency response which may occur in the listening area due to energy radiated from the rear of the enclosure being reflected by the front wall. These naturally arrive some time behind the original sound and give rise to phase errors which can cause cancellations and additions to the sound pressure at frequency-related distances.

Whilst building monitor systems into the front wall of the room can provide benefits in performance, care must be taken to prevent the construction materials from behaving as an extension of the enclosure. To induce vibrations into the air, the drive units vibrate mechanically, and some of this energy is induced into the enclosure or cabinet. If the cabinet is connected to the structure then these mechanical vibrations can be transmitted into the structure, and this must be avoided as far as possible.

Sound is conducted through building materials at higher speeds than in air, and a responsive surface elsewhere in the room can easily be excited and act like a speaker in its own right. Such effects often occur over quite narrow frequency bands, and when they do the information within the soundfield is blurred by the arrival of information which is different from the fundamental. These wavefronts may even arrive in advance of the direct sound and have a more confusing effect than normal acoustic reflections.

Isolation of the enclosures from the main structure is therefore very important (see Figure 10.6), and for optimum performance should be equal in all directions.

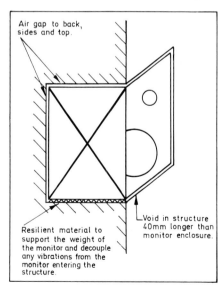

Air gap to back, sides and top.

Resilient material to support the weight of the monitor and decouple any vibrations from the monitor entering the structure.

Void in structure 40mm longer than monitor enclosure.

Fig. 10.6. The building-in of monitor loudspeakers to minimize transmission of sound energy into the main structure

It is of little benefit to use a suspension system which is soft or damped in one plane but rigid in another. Vibration from the enclosure will be transmitted into the structure in the more rigid plane and unwanted excitation of structural members will probably result. Free-standing monitors should be equipped with suitable stands. These should be as rigid as possible, to restrain movement, and be free of resonances. The manufacturer's recommendations for mounting should always be consulted.

Setting up monitors

The procedure for commissioning, checking, or setting up a monitor system should follow a standard pattern. A suitable procedure would be to check that each drive unit is working correctly and in the correct phase relationship to the other units, that the output of each section is adjusted for optimum performance, that crossover points are correct, and, finally, that optimum adjustment is made to any frequency-tailoring facilities which may be available.

In relationship to monitor speakers and frequency tailoring, there is a myth that should be dispelled: that monitor equalizers are a cure for all ills. They are not. In fact, if equalizers are wrongly used they can make the situation a great deal worse. During the mid-1970s it became the fashion to install equalizers on most systems, and it was not long before this became referred to as 'room equalization'. The fact is that rooms cannot be equalized by adjusting the electrical response of the monitor system. If acoustical problems exist, their character and effect will vary according to the location within the room where they are observed. Electrical equalization may appear to produce an improvement at one point, but the effects at other points may easily be exacerbated.

There is no doubt that equalizers have their place, and correctly used they can be of significant benefit. Few monitor systems are perfect, and a number of electrical problems can be greatly reduced, if not eliminated, by careful adjustment of the correct equipment. Electrical equalization of loudspeaker systems was made popular by the Altec Acoustavoice system. This was designed for public address installations and was developed as a convenient way to reduce feedback and improve acoustic gain and thus intelligibility within existing and new sound systems. It was not long before these equalizers found their way into the recording studio and were installed into monitor systems. With the growth in popularity, additional types of equalizers were produced by a variety of manufacturers. A wide range of equalizers is available, but those which meet the particular needs of monitor systems divide the frequency spectrum into about 27 bands at one-third octave intervals.

Adjustment of monitor equalizers needs to be approached with caution. There is considerable interaction between adjacent frequency band controls. For example, adjustment of three adjacent bands by the same amount of movement on each control will produce a result whereby the upper band will be affected to a greater degree than the lower. Also, the two bands immediately above the upper band will be affected. Adjustment should not be attempted without suitable checking equipment and some prior experience.

The following sequence, for which a real-time analyser should be used in conjunction with a pink noise source, may be followed:

1. Ensure that all the drivers are working.
2. Check that all the drive units within each system are in phase with each other and that both systems are in phase overall. If in doubt, reverse the phase of a suspect unit or system and compare the results.
3. Check and observe the sound pressure response of each monitor system in the nearfield and at several points within the listening soundfield. Note any significant deviations.
4. Select a microphone position on the centre line between the two monitors, and at a distance along the centre line where a reasonable average of the various observed patterns is found. If there are any peaks or troughs which are clearly the result of acoustic effects, ignore them.
5. Adjust the controls provided on the monitor systems, power amplifiers, and crossover units to obtain the best balance and smoothest response possible.
6. Replay a known musical recording over the monitor system and listen for any obvious defects. Note these defects and estimate the frequency bands in which they occur.
7. Return to the pink noise source and analyser and observe the response within the frequency bands noted. There may be peaks or troughs which need adjustment, and it is possible that an acoustical effect has masked the result of excessive adjustments carried out in step 5; should this be the case, then return the controls to a normal setting.
8. Repeat step 6.
9. If equalizers are installed, return to the analyser and pink noise source and further refine the response with the aid of the equalizers, taking care not to compensate wrongly for any acoustical effect.
10. Repeat steps 6 and 9 until optimum results are achieved.
11. Check compatibility and summation. This needs to be done by feeding the signal at a fixed level to both the left and right-hand monitors and switching the monitors on and off in turn. Note the mean response of the left-hand side and compare it to that of the right. Should there be any significant difference, adjust the overall gain until they are identical. Switch on both monitors and note the increase in sound level. A well-matched system in a reasonable acoustic environment will produce a rise of around 5 dB across the frequency spectrum. Should this not be the case, then phase errors within or between the systems should be suspected. With satisfactory results so far, a check should be made of the stereo picture. This is done by feeding the noise source to the monitors via a pan-pot and panning the signal from

left to right; the spectrum and the sound pressure level indicated on the real-time analyser should remain constant. This condition will occur only when the whole system is correctly matched; this includes the pan-pot, monitor systems, monitor angles and positions, as well as the room acoustics.

It is a good policy to check the performance of monitor systems periodically. Drive units do change their response with age and use. Systems used consistently for high-level monitoring will deteriorate much faster than those used for more moderate work. The time intervals between checks will need to be judged according to use. The monitoring system deserves to be as well maintained as any other piece of equipment within the recording chain, if best and truly consistent results are to be achieved.

11

Tape and tape machines: Analogue
Hugh Ford

The structure of magnetic tape

Magnetic tape is constructed using a base film to support the magnetic layer, or coating. This magnetic coating is applied on one side of the base film, whilst an additional non-magnetic coating is frequently applied to the reverse side. All modern magnetic tapes use polyester as the base film, marketed under a number of trade names such as Mylar from Du Pont or Melinex from ICI. Various grades of polyester, or more properly polyethylene terephthalate, are available from the manufacturers and have widely differing mechanical properties.

Figure 11.1 shows the typical dimensions of the cross-section of a standard-play studio recording tape, where the overall thickness is typically 55 μm, allowing 730 m to be wound on to a standard 267 mm NAB reel. In the long-play version, and other extended-play versions, it is common to reduce both the base film thickness and the coating thickness.

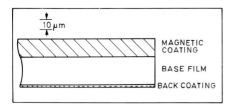

Fig. 11.1. Cross-section of a Standard Play tape with back coating

Studio recording tapes universally employ gamma ferric oxide (Fe_2O_3) as the main magnetic material, whilst recorders which operate at short wavelengths, such as video recorders and cassette machines, commonly employ alternative magnetic materials such as chromium dioxide (CrO_2) or pure metal pigments. Certain cassette tapes employ a mixture of magnetic materials, either in the form of multiple-layer coatings or 'doped' magnetic materials. Whilst such combinations do have advantages for short-wavelength recording, they have also suffered from instability of the magnetic characteristics.

In practice the magnetic coating cannot consist of the magnetic material alone, because, for one thing, it would not adhere to the base film. Furthermore, the surface properties have to be controlled so that the coating does not adhere to the recorder's heads and the tape does not deposit debris on the heads. A further factor is that the tape must not accumulate static electricity, not only because this might cause arcing, but also because static electricity interferes with the fast-winding performance of the tape. The requirements of these and other factors mean that the 'dope' used to coat the base film is a combination of a number of materials in addition to the magnetic material. Such additives include a wetting agent to assist with the dispersion of the magnetic material, a binder to secure the coating to the base film, anti-static agents, abrasives to keep the heads clean, lubricants to avoid sticking—all a rather complex piece of chemistry.

Other than surface properties and conductivity of the coating, the properties of the back of the tape have a considerable influence on the winding performance, with a smooth untreated back to the base film giving poor winding. Thus the base film may be designed to have different properties on its two sides, or a thin coating (2–3 μm thick) may be applied to control the surface characteristics and conductivity of the rear of the tape.

The manufacture of magnetic tape

The manufacturing process may be divided broadly into five operations:

1. Making the 'dope' for coating the base film
2. Coating the base film
3. Polishing or burnishing the coating
4. Slitting the final product
5. Testing.

In the process for making the 'dope', the magnetic oxide from the oxide supplier is typically a collection of acicular (needle-shaped) magnetic particles having a length in the order of 1 μm and width of 0.1 μm to 0.2 μm, as shown in Plate 11. In an ideal world, all the particles would have the same size and shape, because the magnetic properties of large and small particles are different.

The 'dope' for coating the base film is manufactured by mixing the oxide together with the other ingredients in a 'mill'. During the milling process it is important to do the minimum damage to the magnetic particles, whilst properly dispersing the oxide in the binder system so that a uniform coating may be applied to the base film. If the particles are damaged, the preponderance of smaller particles will lead to poor print-through. On the other hand, poor dispersion will give rise to poor modulation noise, poor surface properties in the final product producing debris on the heads, and possibly the migration of dope materials such as plasticizers to the tape surface.

It follows that the mixing or milling of the dope requires considerable care and that the choice of the mixing method is very important. The characteristics

Plate 11. Electron photomicrograph of iron oxide crystals as used in magnetic tape

of the oxides and coating materials used in professional audio tapes make them suitable for the traditional method of milling in a ball mill, whilst the more exotic formulations for high-performance videotapes, where the oxide loading may reach 60 per cent or more, dictates the use of alternative milling methods.

The ball mill comprises a drum mounted horizontally on a shaft, by means of which it is rotated. Within the drum are a number of metal or ceramic balls of varying sizes, depending upon the precise formulation being milled. During the milling process, the constituents of the dope are added, often one at a time, and the mill is rotated for the desired time at a given speed and temperature. The finished dope is thinned to the desired viscosity, filtered to exclude undesirably large conglomerates of particles, and passed to a holding tank before the coating process.

During the coating process, the dope is applied to a wide 'web' of the base film material in the form of a long roll which will typically have a width between 450 mm and several metres. Traditionally, the base film was trough-coated, where an open-bottomed trough of dope is located a small distance above the moving web of base film (Figure 11.2). With this method it is difficult to obtain an even and consistent coating thickness, partly because the base film thickness affects the coating thickness. This has led to the common use of gravure coating for professional audio tapes. Gravure coating is similar to a printing process, as shown in Figure 11.3, where a hard steel roller engraved with a herring-bone

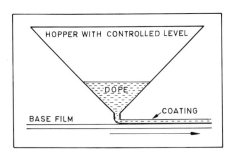

Fig. 11.2. Trough coating of the base film

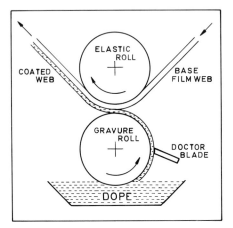

Fig. 11.3. Gravure coating

pattern is partially immersed in a trough of the dope which has been very finely filtered.

While the gravure roll is immersed, its engraved lines fill with dope, the excess dope being removed by a doctor blade to provide an accurate loading of dope. The dope loaded on to the gravure roll is then printed on to the surface of the base film, giving a coating thickness which is independent of the base film thickness and is directly related to the viscosity of the dope. There are a number of variations on the gravure process, but all leave a pattern in the coating which must be removed, if only for cosmetic reasons. This is accomplished by smoothing the coating by means of wipers or electromagnets, or by passing the partially dried coating over highly polished chromium-plated bars.

After the coating process, the magnetic particles are randomly aligned, and in order to obtain optimum tape performance all the particles must be persuaded to take up some more uniform alignment—longitudinally along the tape for audio purposes. This is done by passing the partially dried coated web over an electromagnet having a very uniform field in the desired direction of orientation. This is a critical process, as too-active orientation may disturb the surface characteristics of the coating.

Following orientation, the coated web is passed through a drying tunnel where the solvents used in the coating are evaporated, whilst the coating thickness shrinks to the desired value. After this the coated web is wound as a large 'jumbo' roll of tape. At this stage, the jumbo may be stored before the final polishing or burnishing process, which is usually known as calendering. This process not only polishes the tape surface to obtain an improved smoothness and high-frequency performance, but may also modify the physical properties of the base film.

During calendering, the coated web is passed under tension and pressure between highly polished rollers which may be made from a number of different materials and are commonly acting as high and low-temperature rolls. At this stage the physical and magnetic properties of the product are finalized, and all that remains is to slit the jumbo into the desired user tape widths. Whilst the permitted tolerances on the width vary slightly for different nominal tape widths, it is also very important that the final product be straight and clean, with undamaged edges.

In the common slitting process (see Plate 12), the web is accurately guided to a set of rotating steel knives at the desired spacing, as shown in Figure 11.4. Such a process inevitably damages the two edges of the tape in different directions, and proper maintenance of the slitting knives is vital if debris on the edges is to be avoided. From the slitter, the tape is wound under constant tension on to hubs or reels, after which it is boxed and bulk-erased.

Plate 12. Inspection of tape as it leaves the slitting stage (Photo: BASF)

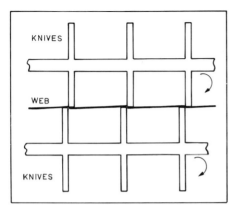

Fig. 11.4. Slitting

The mechanical properties

The basic mechanical properties of recording tapes are the tape width, thickness, and length. Whilst the length for a given size of reel is up to the manufacturer, the common lengths for a given reel size and type of standard-play tape are shown in Table 11.1. The length and time for long-play tape are × 1.5, and for double-play tape × 2.

TABLE 11.1. **Typical standard-play tapes**

Reel type	Reel size		Typical length	Tape time at 15 ips (38 cm/s) (minutes)
	(inches)	(cm)		
AEG	11½	29	3280 ft/1000 m	43
NAB	14	35.5	4800 ft/1463 m	64
NAB	10½	26.7	2400 ft/732 m	32
CINE	7	17.8	1200 ft/366 m	16
CINE	5¾	19.6	900 ft/274 m	12
CINE	5	12.7	600 ft/183 m	8

The maximum tape thickness and the standard widths are defined in the International Electrotechnical Commission IEC Standard 94-1, as shown in Table 11.2.

For some reason better known to themselves, tape manufacturers frequently specify other mechanical properties which are quite useless to the eventual user or machine designer. Such typical parameters are the yield strength and the ultimate tensile strength. Clearly, if the tension in a machine reaches these figures the tape is damaged for ever; but, because of the non-linear behaviour of different types of polyester, interpolation from these figures is impossible.

TABLE 11.2. **Standard tape widths and thicknesses**

Tape width		Tape thickness	
(inches)	(mm)	(inches)	(mm max.)
2.000 +0/−0.0024	50.80 +0/−0.06	0.0022	0.055
1.000 +0/−0.0024	25.40 +0/−0.06	0.0022	0.055
0.500 +0/−0.0024	12.70 +0/−0.06	0.0022	0.055
0.248 +0/−0.0024	6.30 +0/−0.06	0.0022	0.055
0.150 +0/−0.002	3.81 +0/−0.05	0.0008	0.020

Under operational conditions in professional audio recorders, the tape tension is a compromise between good head-to-tape contact, good tape winding, power consumption, and other factors. As a general guide, a tension of 70 g (2.5 oz) for 6.3 mm (quarter-inch) standard-play tape is ideal, with the tension being increased in proportion to the tape width.

The magnetic properties

The basic magnetic properties of recording tape are measured by plotting the applied magnetic field (H) against the magnetization (B), which provides a hysteresis loop as shown in Figure 11.5. Proceeding from a state of zero magnetization marked 'O', as the field H is increased (X axis) the magnetization (Y axis) increases to point A, beyond which the application of a larger field does not increase the magnetization. The magnetization at this point is known as the saturation flux (B_S). Decreasing the field to zero from point 'A' leaves a remnant magnetization called the remanence (B_R). As the applied field is reversed, the

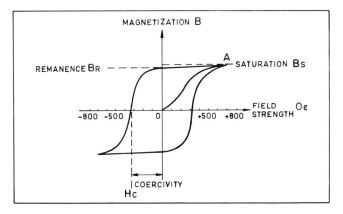

Fig. 11.5. The hysteresis loop

magnetization eventually falls to zero, at which point the applied field defines the coercivity (H_C).

Magnetic tape specifications commonly specify the coercivity H_C, the remanence B_R, and the squareness ratio, which is B_R/B_S and relates to the efficiency of the recording medium. Clearly, the coercivity (specified in oersteds or amperes/metre, where $1\ Oe = 79.58\ A/m$) relates to the ease of erasing a recording. This extends to the self-erasure in the recording process, which is a phenomenon that erases short wavelengths (high frequencies) more than long wavelengths (low frequencies) during the recording process. Thus there is a compromise in coercivity, as a high coercivity is desirable for good high-frequency performance, but too high a coercivity makes it very difficult to erase a tape.

Typical coercivities for professional recording tape are in the range 20–8 kA/m, whilst for compact cassette recorders operating at 4.76 cm/s ($1\frac{7}{8}$ ips), where the recorded wavelength is very short, there are four types of tape which have been standardized by IEC, as shown in Table 11.3.

TABLE 11.3. **IEC Cassette tape categories**

IEC type	Tape construction	Typical coercivity (kA/m)
I	Single-layer iron oxide	24–32
II	Single-layer chromium dioxide	34–57
III	Double-layer or doped	No requirements
IV	Metal pigment	72–96

It is logical that the remnant flux should relate to the maximum output available from a magnetic tape, and this is indeed the case at long wavelengths if the construction of the record head allows the full thickness of the magnetic coating to be penetrated. However, at shorter wavelengths the full depth of the coating is not penetrated and this relation does not hold.

Whilst the remanence is specified in milli-maxwells/millimetre (mM/mm), which multiplied by ten becomes nano-webers/metre (nWb/m) and represents the fluxivity per unit tape length, the retentivity cannot be directly compared. The latter is measured in gauss or milli-tesla, where $10\ G = 10\ mT$.

The electroacoustic parameters

The parameters of interest to the tape user and their effect upon the record/replay process may be summarised as follows:

Sensitivity. This relates the input to the recorder to the output for a stated input frequency. Figures quoted may refer to a specified reference tape.

Distortion. Three per cent harmonic distortion at 1 kHz (or 5 per cent at

315 Hz for low-speed machines) is related to a given recorded fluxivity as determined from a calibration tape. At high frequencies the tape saturation (the input level at which an increase of input does not produce an increase in output) is also related to a given recorded fluxivity.

It is also common to measure the third harmonic distortion at a specified recorded fluxivity and frequency of 320 nWb/m at 1 kHz or 250 nWb/m at 315 Hz.

Bias noise. The noise produced by a tape which has been recorded in the presence of bias without any audio input is referred either to the distortion as determined above at mid-frequencies or to a reference fluxivity.

Noise is weighted, that is the frequency response of the measurement is modified to correspond to the subjective effect of noise. Two weightings are in common use, 'A' weighting or CCIR Recommendation 468-3 weighting. The results of the two methods cannot be directly compared.

Direct current noise. Direct current noise is measured by the same method as bias noise, but with a d.c. current applied to the record head, and sometimes a different weighting is used. Direct current noise gives an indication of modulation noise, that is noise that is programme-related and not present in the absence of an audio signal input.

Print-through. Print-through, the layer-to-layer transfer of signals during storage, relates the recorded signal level at a given frequency to the level of the first pre-echo after storage at a specified temperature for a specified time.

All these parameters depend upon the tape speed, and they also vary according to the types of head used on the recorder. However, standard measurement conditions do exist. Another variable is the level of the high-frequency bias applied to the record head, which has little effect upon bias noise or print-through. It does, however, have a significant effect upon all the other parameters above.

The measured performance of a tape depends upon the frequency response of the record and replay amplifiers. Tape performance is normally measured using a constant record current. The equalization of the replay amplifier, that is the relation between the recorded fluxivity on tape, frequency and output voltage, is set to one of a number of standards which will be discussed later.

These effects are shown in Figure 11.6, where the top curves indicate the maximum output level (MOL) for 3 per cent third harmonic distortion at 1 kHz and the saturation at 14 kHz, versus bias. Increasing bias tends to increase the MOL, whilst reducing the high-frequency saturation. Thus a compromise is needed for satisfactory recorder performance. Lower down in Figure 11.6 it can be seen from the sensitivity curves that the frequency response of a recorder will also depend upon bias, because the relation between bias and sensitivity is not the same at all frequencies. This means that the frequency response of the record electronics must be equalized for a given type of tape at the operating bias current.

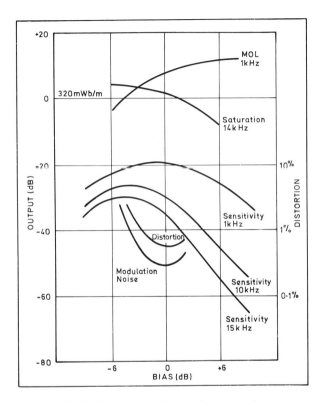

Fig. 11.6. Bias-related tape characteristics

Even more critical is the relation between distortion at a fluxivity of 320 nWb/m and the modulation noise, versus bias. These parameters have a distinct optimum bias, occurring at 0 dB in the diagram. When aligning a recorder for optimum performance, it is desirable to set the bias to this operating point, but most users do not have the equipment necessary to measure distortion or modulation noise. Instead, it is far simpler to record a tone whilst monitoring the replay output level and changing the bias level. This is the common method of setting the bias level.

Recorder manufacturers (and some tape manufacturers) often recommend a degree of over-bias: the bias is slowly increased until the peak of the output voltage is found and then further increased until the output voltage has fallen by a specified number of decibels.

In the past a 1 kHz tone was commonly specified, but, as can be seen in Figure 11.6, this part of the sensitivity/bias curve is rather flat, making the optimum bias point at about 1 dB over-bias very difficult to determine accurately. If a higher-frequency tone is used, such as 10 kHz, the curve at the optimum bias is much steeper, making accurate adjustment far easier. It is now common to adjust recorders to around 3 dB over-bias, using tones of 20 kHz at a speed of 30 ips, 10 kHz at 15 ips, or 5 kHz at 7½ ips.

Equalization and calibration tapes

Equalization is the process of modifying the frequency response of the replay amplifier, with a corresponding alteration of the frequency response of the record amplifier, to obtain a flat overall frequency response. The purposes of equalization are twofold, first to match the frequency distribution of the recorded signal to the capabilities of the recording medium, and second to obtain the maximum signal-to-noise ratio.

Because the MOL, high-frequency saturation characteristics, and the noise spectrum are related to tape speed, different tape speeds are optimized by different equalization characteristics. In all cases, high frequencies are attenuated in the record process, so that the recorded fluxivity decreases with increasing frequency. In the replay process, high frequencies are boosted to compensate, the cut/boost effect being introduced at lower frequencies for lower tape speeds.

In addition, some systems boost low frequencies during the record process and cut them in the replay process, in order to reduce power-line hum problems during replay.

To enable pre-recorded tapes to be replayed with a flat frequency response, it has been essential to standardize the replay equalization for any given tape speed. Unfortunately, more than one standard is in common use for some tape speeds. The equalization is expressed in terms of a time constant given by the expression

$$t = \frac{1}{2\pi f}$$

where t = time constant in seconds, and f = the 3 dB transition frequency in Hz.

Table 11.4 and Figure 11.7 illustrate the standard replay time constants in common use for each tape speed.

In order to simplify the adjustment of the replay chain of a recorder to any desired standard, calibration tapes for each standard are available. Such tapes contain recordings of a series of tones at a constant level for adjusting the replay chain to a flat frequency response. The frequencies of these tones are typically 31.5 Hz, 40 Hz, 63 Hz, 125 Hz, 250 Hz, 500 Hz, 1 kHz, 2 kHz, 4 kHz, 6.3 kHz, 8 kHz, 10 kHz, 12.5 kHz, 14 kHz, 16 kHz, 18 kHz, and 20 kHz for professional recorders.

In addition to these tones, calibration tapes have a standard reference level section and an azimuth alignment section. The standard-level section contains a mid-frequency recording at a specified fluxivity for aligning the metering on

TABLE 11.4. **Standard replay time constants**

Tape speed (ips)	Time constant (μs)	Standard
30	17.5	AES, IEC 2
30	35	IEC 1
15	35	IEC 1, CCIR, DIN
15	50 + 3180	IEC 2, NAB
$7\frac{1}{2}$	70	IEC 1, CCIR, DIN studio
$7\frac{1}{2}$	50 + 3180	IEC 2, NAB, DIN home
$7\frac{1}{2}$	50	NAB cartridge
$3\frac{3}{4}$	90 + 3180	IEC, NAB, DIN
$1\frac{7}{8}$	90 + 3180	IEC, NAB, DIN
$1\frac{7}{8}$	120 + 3180	Cassette (ferric oxide)
$1\frac{7}{8}$	70 + 3180	Cassette (chrome & metal)

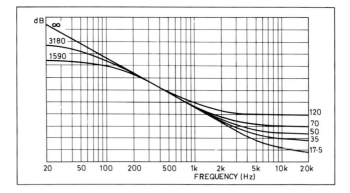

Fig. 11.7. Replay characteristics for some of the standards in use

recorders and setting Dolby level where the Dolby noise reduction system is to be used. In European calibration tapes, the level section is a 1 kHz tone at a fluxivity of 320 nWb/m as measured by the open-circuit method, whilst American calibration tapes commonly contain a level section of 400 Hz, 700 Hz, or 1 kHz tone, typically at a fluxivity of 185 nWb/m as measured by the short-circuit method.

This fluxivity is also known as 'Ampex Operating Level' and 'Dolby Level', and corresponds to 200 nWb/m when measured by the European open-circuit method. Other fluxivities may be encountered, and the most common of these are listed in Table 11.5.

TABLE 11.5. **Common tape fluxivities**

European fluxivity	USA fluxivity	Notes
510 nWb/m	470 nWb/m	Stereo format
320 nWb/m	295 nWb/m	30, 15, & $7\frac{1}{2}$ ips
280 nWb/m	260 nWb/m	Elevated operating level
250 nWb/m	230 nWb/m	$3\frac{3}{4}$, $1\frac{7}{8}$ ips, & cassette
200 nWb/m	185 nWb/m	Dolby/Ampex level
160 nWb/m	150 nWb/m	Cassette

The purpose of the azimuth alignment section is to set the vertical gap in the replay head at precisely 90° to the edge of the tape. Reference to Figure 11.8 shows that an azimuth error loss takes the form of a $(\sin x)/x$ plot, having a series of peaks at high frequencies. As azimuth alignment is carried out by moving the head to obtain maximum output, it would be easy to align a recorder accidentally to one of these peaks instead of to the correct optimum. This difficulty is overcome by the fact that the azimuth alignment section has a period of medium-frequency tone followed by a period of high-frequency tone. The recorder is first aligned using the medium-frequency, where severe azimuth errors are readily visible, and then by using the high-frequency section.

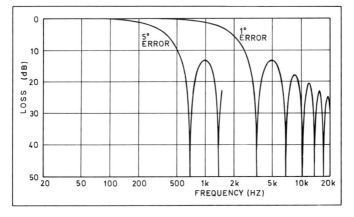

Fig. 11.8. Azimuth error for a 15 ips full-track tape

Tape recorder mechanics

At first sight, the recorder has only a small number of simple tasks to perform: to unwind the tape from a supply reel, pass it over the heads at constant speed with good alignment and head-to-tape contact, and then rewind the tape on to a second 'take-up' reel. Unfortunately, tape has a will of its own. Rather like one of those flexible steel tape-measures, if it is bent through an angle it tries to go in all sorts of odd directions. Furthermore, the tape is elastic and is easily stretched; wind it too loose on the reel and it forms concertina sections, wind it too tight and it permanently distorts.

As a consequence, the recorder has to provide accurate and consistent tension control at all tape speeds—which immediately implies difficulties in moving the tape at a constant speed. The fact that tape is unwilling to travel in a straight horizontal line while being led round bends means that the edges of the tape must be guided, particularly near the heads, where azimuth errors must be minimal.

Figure 11.9 shows the typical layout of a reel-to-reel machine. The tape is pulled continuously from the left-hand supply reel and passes over a spring-loaded arm before travelling to a roller, which may be a rotating guide having an inset slot of just over the maximum permitted tape width. To the right of the machine, a similar arrangement is used prior to the take-up reel, whilst the erase, record, and replay heads are grouped at the centre. This area commonly incorporates further tape-edge guides, which may be fixed steel posts with slots, again of just over the maximum permitted tape width.

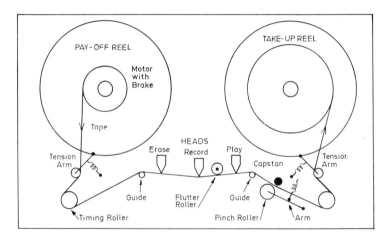

Fig. 11.9. Typical mechanical layout of a reel-to-reel tape recorder

The reels are usually driven directly by motors with solenoid-operated band brakes fitted to the motor shafts, the brakes being operational only when the tape motion has stopped. In less expensive machines, the motors may be a.c. driven so that they operate at constant torque rather than at constant tension. In this case the spring-loaded arms simply damp tape movement during acceleration and deceleration. More advanced machines use servo-controlled reel motors, with the spring-loaded arms fitted with tape tension sensors, and thus run at constant tape tension (see Plate 13). A further advantage of the use of servo control is that the tape tension is much better controlled during fast winding. Also, the fast winding speed can be held constant throughout a reel.

In simple machines the roller guides may act solely as guides, or possibly drive a tachometer disc to activate the tape time counter. However, more sophisticated machines have a separate roller guide which monitors the tape velocity and relays this information to the servo control microprocessor, which may also be fed with spool rotational speed to derive control information. This information may be used to activate regenerative braking of the reel motors during auto-locate functions, control tape tension during acceleration, and so on.

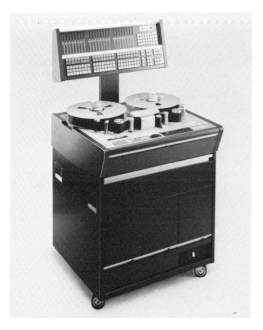

Plate 13. 24-track analogue tape recorder (Photo: Stüder)

Most machines control tape movement in the record and replay modes by means of a capstan against which the tape is held by a pinch roller which is itself mounted on a solenoid-operated arm. The capstan forms part of the capstan motor shaft, and may be made from steel or ceramic. A ceramic capstan has the advantage that it does not wear, but it can be more readily broken than a steel capstan.

Capstan motors in inexpensive machines are a.c. driven and are locked to the power line frequency, but more expensive machines frequently use d.c. servo motors fitted with a tachometer. These motors are phase-locked to a crystal-controlled reference frequency and may thus be driven at very accurate speeds irrespective of the power line frequency. In addition, such systems may be phase-locked to an external reference, permitting several machines to be accurately synchronized with each other.

Pinch rollers are typically made from an elastic material mounted on a metal core within which is a self-aligning ball-bearing which fits on to a spigot at one end of the pinch roller arm. High-quality machines use a cast-alloy arm hinged on a sleeve-bearing near its centre. At the far end of the arm, the pinch roller pressure is controlled by an adjustable spring which is tensioned by the pinch roller solenoid. The solenoid is engaged by passing a high current through its coil, the current being reduced once the roller has locked into its operating position to reduce heat dissipation in the solenoid coil.

Within the head area, the heads and guides may take the form of a plug-in subassembly (see Plate 35, page 430) or may be mounted directly on the recorder's chassis. In either case the heads should be firmly mounted whilst having provision for three mechanical adjustments: height, zenith, and azimuth. The zenith is adjusted so that the front surface of the heads is at 90° to the tape transport surface, the height so that the tape passes correctly in relation to the head pole-pieces, and the azimuth so that the tape edge passes at 90° to the vertical head gaps. The head pole-pieces may be manufactured from metal or from ferrite. The latter is more expensive but is almost immune from wear caused by the abrasive nature of the tape—iron oxide is used by jewellers for polishing in the form of jeweller's rouge!

Some machines also have a free roller just touching the tape in the head area. This is known as a flutter roller, and its function is to damp longitudinal vibrations set up in the tape because of its elastic nature.

The accurate passage of the tape over the heads relies on a mechanically stable tape transport. Therefore the more sophisticated recorders are based on a ribbed alloy casting, and not bent sheet metal as in cheaper machines. Such a casting can be precision-machined with reference faces to ensure accurate alignment to all the tape transport components, thus providing an extremely accurate and stable tape transport overall.

Whilst long-term tape speed variations depend upon the stability of the capstan motor, short-term fluctuations in the form of wow and flutter also depend upon accurate tape tension control and the precision of all rotating components in the tape path.

Tape recorder electronics

The electronics of any analogue recorder can be divided into three separate sections: the record amplifier, the replay amplifier, and the bias/erase oscillator. In multitrack machines, the record and replay electronics will be duplicated for each extra track, but there will usually be a single bias/erase oscillator, both for economy and to avoid frequency-beating between separate oscillators.

Figure 11.10 shows the block diagram of a simple professional recorder's audio section. The audio signal input is typically balanced with respect to earth to minimize the introduction of mains or radio frequency interference in the input cables. The signal circuit is then unbalanced and may be fed to some form of low-pass filtering to reduce the risks of radio frequency interference even further. A variable gain control is then included, allowing the input level to the recorder to be adjusted to match the output level for the given tape.

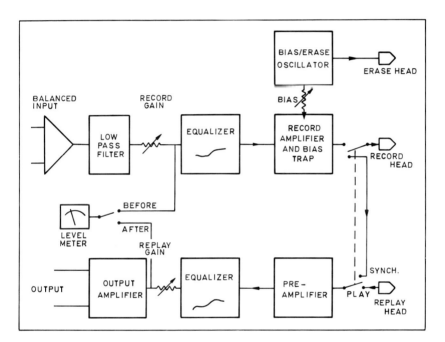

Fig. 11.10. Block diagram of the electronics in a typical recorder

The signal is then subjected to equalization, as already discussed. The equalizer section will have a high-frequency control to set the required high-frequency boost and may also, in the case of NAB equalization where a low-frequency time constant is used, have a low-frequency equalizer control. More sophisticated recorders include further equalizer networks operating at high to mid-frequencies to obtain an extremely flat frequency response, and may also include a control to compensate for phase shift in the record amplifier.

After equalization, the audio signal is mixed with the pre-set variable level of high-frequency bias before it is fed at constant current to the record head. Within this 'mixing' section is a bias trap to prevent the high-frequency bias from being fed back into the record electronics. This bias trap usually takes the form of an adjustable tuned circuit. The bias oscillator performs two functions.

It generates the high-frequency bias signal, of course, but it also provides a high-frequency signal to drive the erase head(s). Multi-channel machines will often have separate amplifiers and tuning controls for each track. An important feature of the bias/erase oscillator is that it must have minimal even-order harmonic distortion, because even harmonics magnetize the record head and increase tape noise. Also, to avoid problems with beating, the bias frequency should be at least five times the highest audio frequency.

Within the replay chain, the low-level signal from the replay head is fed to a pre-amplifier. This may be separate from the main audio electronics so that short leads can be used from the heads to avoid pick-up of interference. There follows the high and low-frequency replay equalization, which normally involves two adjustments with a further control allowing the replay gain to be set.

The final audio output may be balanced or unbalanced. Level metering is switchable between the input (after gain adjustment) and the output. Such switching may be manual or automatic, whereby the input is automatically monitored in the record mode and the output in the replay mode.

In multitrack machines it is desirable to be able to monitor the signal from the tape at the same physical position as the record head, so that a new track may be laid in precise synchronization with any existing tracks. For instance, a vocal track may be laid in synchronization with a backing track for subsequent mix-down. This mode of recorder operation is known as the sync mode and clearly requires that individual tracks of the record head may be switched to act as replay heads. This normally provides a degraded replay signal, because the record head gaps are usually wider than replay head gaps and the head design is different. Furthermore, in many machines the heads are simply switched to the standard replay electronics so that no special equalization is provided for the sync mode. However, in more expensive recorders a separate sync replay amplifier is provided with separate level and equalization controls.

Machine alignment

The alignment of recorders may be discussed under two headings, the mechanical alignment and the alignment of the record/replay electronics. The mechanical aspects must always be properly attended to before any attempt is made to perform the audio signal alignment.

First the machine must be thoroughly cleaned, paying particular attention to the heads and the tape guides. Deposits of the magnetic tape coating can usually be removed safely using cotton buds dampened with isopropyl alcohol, or products designed for computer disc maintenance. The use of other types of solvent may cause damage to the recorder or leave undesirable deposits; therefore the recorder manufacturer's recommendations should be strictly followed.

The next action is to demagnetize all metal components in the tape path, because magnetized surfaces will introduce excessive tape noise and possibly damage existing recordings. This demagnetizing should be done with a unit specifically designed for the purpose. Many of these have metal tips which should be wrapped in a soft covering such as adhesive tape before use, so that they do not create damage if they are brought into direct contact with the tape heads.

The demagnetizer should be switched on while it is a metre or so away from the recorder, and then passed slowly across all metal parts in the tape path before being slowly removed from the recorder and then switched off. Occasionally it may be very difficult to demagnetize ferrite heads. If the head block is removable, then the heads can be properly demagnetized by using a bulk eraser.

Following this demagnetizing procedure, the machine should be loaded with an unused tape and run in the play and fast-wind modes, while one is carefully observing the tape at the reels and guides. If the tape touches the surface of the reels or is seen to ripple at the heads or guides, it is probable that mechanical alignment is needed. Similarly, if starting or stopping gives erratic tape movement, the reel brakes or pinch roller may need adjustment; the recorder manufacturer's instructions should be followed in detail. If higher than usual wow and flutter figures are observed, this will also reveal the need to adjust the pinch roller mechanism.

Where the reel motors are electronically controlled, or the capstan is servo-controlled, adjustment of the controls in the electronics may be necessary. Again the recorder manufacturer's instructions should be followed, as the procedures vary widely from one recorder to another. Whilst some manufacturers suggest the use of spring scales for measuring tape tension, this is not a very satisfactory method and dynamic measurement using a Tentelometer™ is to be preferred.

Once satisfied that the mechanical performance is in order, the machine should be set to its lowest operating speed (or the speed to be used if time is short) and a suitable calibration tape loaded for alignment of the azimuth of the replay head. Accurate alignment in multitrack machines requires the use of a dual-trace oscilloscope or a phase meter to observe the alignment of the wave forms from the tracks at the two tape edges. The mid-frequency azimuth section of the calibration tape is first replayed, and the replay head azimuth adjusted for maximum output or exact phase alignment of the two output signals. This procedure is then repeated for the high-frequency alignment section of the tape.

Following this azimuth adjustment, the reference level section of the calibration tape is replayed and the replay gain control set for the desired output level. At this stage the metering in the replay mode should also be adjusted for correct indication of the desired setting. In the case of VU meters, the zero VU indication should normally be set to correspond to between 8 and 10 dB below the 3 per cent third harmonic distortion point for the tape type in use. In the case of peak indicating meters, such as the BBC-type PPM (peak programme meter), the peak indication (PPM 6) should correspond to the 3 per cent distortion point. Some organizations have their own internal standard for metering, to preserve compatibility between the levels on different tapes, but the above settings allow the maximum capabilities of particular tape types to be used.

Normally the next band on the calibration tape is the frequency response section, starting with a mid-frequency section of tone at the prescribed level and followed by short sections at other frequencies starting at the low frequency end. These tones are usually at 10 dB or more below the reference level to keep clear of saturation risks at the boosted end of the equalization curve.

Most calibration tapes are recorded across the full width of the tape. This will lead to quite large errors in apparent frequency response at low frequencies due to fringing at the replay head pole-pieces, but only minor errors at mid-frequencies (less than 1 dB at 1 kHz), which may generally be ignored. These errors depend upon the recorded wavelength and are therefore larger at high tape speeds. Furthermore, the errors depend upon the particular pole-piece design of the head and the contour effect, which gives ripples in the low-frequency response.

Unless one is familiar with these errors, or has access to a calibration tape pre-recorded for the track format in use, it is better to align the low-frequency replay equalizer using the record/replay process. An alternative is to use a flux loop, which is a wire loop placed in contact with the replay head and driven by an oscillator; but such devices are not commonly used in studios.

Having noted the machine's output level for the mid-frequency tone (often 1 kHz), the high-frequency sections of the calibration tape are then replayed and the high-frequency equalizer(s) adjusted for optimum frequency response. These procedures are repeated for all tracks at all the available tape speeds (or the speed about to be used) before setting about the record channel(s) alignment. As has been explained, the high-frequency bias level affects many parameters, so this is the first adjustment to be made. Bias is set while recording and replaying a high-frequency tone at a level well below tape saturation (and also well above tape and machine noise to avoid spurious bias pick-up in the outputs). A level 20 dB below the reference level is normally suitable. (Where separate sync replay amplifiers are fitted, they are aligned using the calibration tape in the same manner as for the normal replay chain.)

Whilst recording and replaying the desired high-frequency audio signal, the output of the replay channel is monitored on the meter and the bias is gradually increased from some low value until the output reaches a peak and begins to fall. The bias is then decreased until the peak output again falls, and is finally set to the desired amount of over-bias. This will typically be about 3 dB under the conditions listed in Table 11.6.

TABLE 11.6. **Common Conditions for 3 dB Over-bias**

Tape speed (ips)	Frequency (kHz)
30	20
15	10
$7\frac{1}{2}$	5

After the bias has been set for all channels at all tape speeds, the record equalization is adjusted for the optimum frequency response by sweeping the frequency of an oscillator applied to the input. Low-frequency record equalizers are not usually fitted, but the low-frequency equalizer in the replay channels may be set for optimum low-frequency response at this stage, whilst the record high-frequency equalizers are adjusted for the optimum high-frequency response.

The final adjustments in the record channels are to set the record gain controls so that the input levels match the output levels, and to set the metering so that the indication when monitoring the inputs to the recorder matches the indication when monitoring the outputs.

12

Digital recorders

Tony Faulkner

'Correct at the time of going to press' is hardly an expression one expects to find in a technical reference book, but it is appropriate for a chapter entitled 'Digital Recorders', where the situation remains unsettled and constantly shifting. Even the term 'tape recorder' begs certain questions, since there are already devices on the market which do not use tape and yet fulfil duties traditionally associated with magnetic tape recording.

Digital recorders first found their way into more than a few operational studios during late 1977, through two main routes. Firstly, out of the development laboratories of enterprising record companies (such as Decca and Denon) who were impatient to exploit the latest techniques and had sufficient manpower and budgets to manufacture in-house equipment for their own requirements. Secondly, early pre-production prototypes of commercial recorders were made available by manufacturers to selected studios prepared to act as guinea-pigs in the de-bugging of proposed designs, in exchange for which the studios gained experience in the latest technology without all the expense and aggravation of trying to construct and maintain their own.

The need for standards

Since these earliest days there have been many advances, not least in the reliability and robustness of systems. However, as always in the professional audio business, we are dogged with a multiplicity of standards, mostly on historical grounds rather than those of technical merit. These differences in standard are far more troublesome than those in analogue magnetic recording: for example, a Dolby-encoded analogue tape with NAB $50\,\mu s + 3180\,\mu s$ equalization is physically capable of being replayed on a non-Dolby recorder set to the IEC $35\,\mu s$ equalization curve. Maybe it will not sound precisely as intended, but the tape machine will produce an intelligible output. Most digital audio system incompatibilities produce total silence, or else random crackles.

In the case of digital, we face not only different physical kinds of videotape (U-Matic NTSC/PAL, R-DAT, Betamax NTSC/PAL, VHS NTSC/PAL, 8-mm NTSC/PAL, IVC 1-inch, even 1-inch C format), but also different encoding formats on the tape itself (Sony PCM1610/1630, R-DAT, JVC, Decca, Denon, EIAJ, Sony F1 pseudo-EIAJ 16-bit, Colossus, etc.). There are also two different philosophies of digital audio recording using video recorders. One is to record the data in pseudo-television picture form (such as on the Sony PCM1610/ 1630); the other is more efficiently to load encoded data directly on to the tape (such as Decca and R-DAT) keeping clear of the time-area in the immediate proximity of the head-cross.

Aside from the videotape-based rotary-head recording systems, which are at present by far the most common for stereo operation, there are at least five incompatible formats in regular use for recording digital audio on reel-to-reel tape (Sony/Studer/Teac 'DASH', Otari/Mitsubishi 'PRODIGI', original Mitsubishi, 3M, and Soundstream). Within the two most important and modern standards (DASH and PRODIGI) there are also additional sub-standards for different tape speeds, and 48 kHz or 44.1 kHz sampling rates.

One of the most exciting developments in digital audio recording is the use of disc-drives similar to those used with computers, but this will be another battlefield for standardization. Which kind of disc? Will a recording made on recorder A play back on recorder B? Full discussion of this topic will have to be postponed until a later edition of this book, when systems have become more established and the mists have cleared over what latest horrors of incompatibility face recording engineers.

An examination of the various options of digital tape recorders currently available to the recording engineer subdivides into whether multitracks (i.e. 24T, 32T, or 48T) or twin-tracks are under consideration. For multitrack, there is 'at the time of going to press' no real practical alternative to a large heavy reel-to-reel transport using special high-coercivity half-inch or one-inch digital tape (similar to high-grade videotape), and running at a tape speed of 30 ips (48 kHz operation).

For stereo, although disc recorders are now on the market, they are not yet a realistic option as one-for-one replacements for tape machines. Their role is primarily as erasable short-term storage for effects loops and sound effects, for, without banks of outboard disc-packs, storage time is limited (especially if more than two parallel tracks of audio are being stored at a time) and for the time being the cost of blank disc stock significantly exceeds the price of, say, blank U-Matic or R-DAT cassettes. The greatest advantage of a disc-based recorder is random access. It is frustrating on recording sessions when a performer innocently requests an instant comparison between, say, take 2 and edit take 128 in order to select his preference for a final choice to be edited. Such a comparison seems to take a nail-biting eternity, while everyone waits for the tape machine to spool through all the intervening takes. With a disc-based recorder, the jump from take 2 to retake 128 takes only a few seconds as the pickup lifts itself and moves across the disc in much the same way as a Compact Disc player is able to hop from track to track as directed.

Rotary-head or stationary-head?

Direct-to-digital disc stereo recording is not a realistic possibility at present for day by day studio work, and we should turn our attention to the two other main contenders—video-based (or more strictly 'rotary-head') machines, and stationary-head (i.e. deceptively similar in appearance to our old analogue reel-to-reel recorder).

The first big difference between analogue and digital recording is the bandwidth of signal which has to be stored on the tape. With analogue, we look for an audio-frequency response from, say, 20 Hz to 20 kHz to give high-fidelity performance, and it is precisely this bandwidth which we record on to tape in order to reproduce the required results. With digital recording, however, the signal on tape is in coded form. The bandwidth recorded on to digital tape using PCM (pulse code modulation) is generally much higher than with analogue recording, and is arrived at as a combination of the sampling rate (governing effective audio bandwidth in reproduced programme), number of bits resolution (effective audio dynamic range), plus the amount of interleaving and error protection/correction adopted (ability to correct tape faults and dropouts). Before the digital signals are loaded on to the tape through the record head, there may be some further processing/compression and spreading of the data over a number of separate tape tracks, but a typical figure of bandwidth requirement for 16-bit resolution, 48 kHz sampling rate, two channels, works out in excess of 1 megabit, which indicates immediately that digital tape recorder design is a science quite different from that of the old and familiar analogue machine.

The construction of a reel-to-reel transport (probably servo-controllable by external sync) suitable for recording and replaying such data is no easy task, and in the early days of digital recording several of the pioneers used commercial data recorders. (For example, Soundstream used Honeywell transports, and EMI chose SELAB.) Computer tape decks are not ideal for a sound studio, particularly for recording on location, where light weight is desirable. Furthermore, functions such as fast-forward/rewind can be distressingly slow, with accelerated and costly head wear, if there are no tape lifters.

Having determined that the use of commercial fixed-head data recorders could be viewed only as a short-term stopgap in the development of digital audio recording, the industry chose to go off in two opposing directions. One was to design suitable new dedicated stationary-head transports and sophisticated head-stacks, in the definite knowledge that the costly research and development would be essential in any case for making 24T, 32T, and 48T multitracks. The other direction still remains controversial (particularly among manufacturers and diehard studio engineers used to reel-to-reel designs): the use of helical-scan rotary-head video recorders to cope with the extended frequency spectrum, which is, by a happy coincidence, about the same as that required for recording television pictures.

Between 1977 and 1985, interest among studio and record company users concentrated very largely on rotary-head digital audio recorders for stereo, not least because of the *de facto* standard of the Sony PCM 1610/1630 for the majority of Compact Disc master-tape interchange (see Plate 14). The arrival also of a popular low-cost video-based consumer digital audio recording system

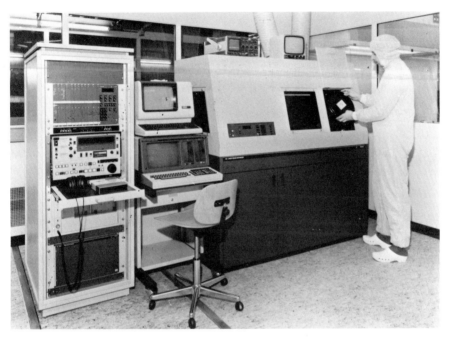

Plate 14. Digital mastering installation for Compact Disc tape-to-disc transfer stage, showing Sony 1610 digital audio recorder and U-Matic tape unit on rack at left (Photo: PolyGram)

(the famous Sony PCM F1, shown in Plate 15, and its sister products) served to endorse the concept of rotary-head recording in professional sound studios. In this respect, the R-DAT format promises to continue the line. From a purely practical point of view, there is much to be said in favour of using video decks for data storage:

1. The mechanisms are generally cheaper than fixed-head dedicated tape transports.
2. They are generally lighter than a fixed-head dedicated tape transport, an important consideration for the location recordist.

Plate 15. Sony PCM-F1 portable digital audio processor with AC power unit (Photo: Sony)

3. Spare parts and general servicing/maintenance are available in most places, because VTRs are used not only in sound recording studios but also in video studios, AV, schools, libraries, and so on.
4. Tape stock is widely available from non-specialist sources, and, since most formats are cassettes, they can be more easily protected against damage and accidental erasure.
5. Multiple copying systems call for a bay of standard or near-standard video recorders, and one central processor, not a bay of expensive machines with complete processors on board each recorder.

As might be expected, fixed-head machines (see Plate 16) have their own advantages:

1. Rapid razor-blade cut-and-splice editing is possible on the latest formats, within certain constraints.
2. Longer playing time than U-Matic video-cassettes.
3. Off-tape monitoring is available (not a standard feature of many rotary-head recorders, except Decca and R-DAT).
4. Variable speed/pitch replay is available over a wider range than most video-based systems, for special effects.
5. Servicing/maintenance compatibility with analogue multitrack reel-to-reel decks also probably installed in the same studio.

By far the most significant 'advantage' of the stationary-head twin-track digital audio recorder is its appearance. An excerpt from a sales-promotional brochure on stationary-head machines sums it up: 'THE SYSTEM—based on the familiar reel-to-reel design for both master and multitrack recorders. A system as easy and familiar to use as your analogue recorder, but it is digital.'

In my own specialist world of recording classical music on location, mixing straight to stereo whenever I can, I have a personal preference for the less

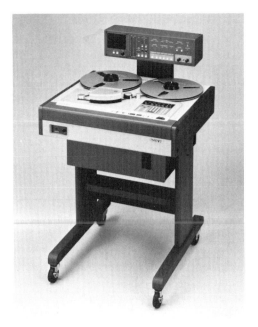

Plate 16. Two-track DASH recorder (Photo: Sony)

cumbersome helical-scan rotary-head machines, despite the necessity for electronic editing back at the home-base editing suite. With classical music editing, it is desirable to 'fine tune' joins until the least disturbing musical disruption is arrived at. After years of surgery on analogue 15-ips tapes, I should not relish going back to the razor-blade except for crude joins—the forbidden fruits of the subtleties and elegance of electronic editing have taken their toll. If you have an irresistible need for on-the-spot editing, then reel-to-reel is still your best option, but maybe not for too long, as disc-drive systems develop in sophistication. Electronic editing is also available for fixed-head recorders, but the instant appeal of razor-blade editing is undoubtedly a prime selling-point for such systems.

Analogue versus digital

When digital audio recorders (of all varieties, not just rotary-head or fixed-head) first came into more general use in studios, there was much discussion in audiophile circles about the sonic merits and/or demerits of digital audio. Some commentators greeted the 'New Age' with a blind euphoria for new technology whatever it might be; others branded it as the 'End of an Era', with nothing but disaster to follow. A trip to the attic to blow the dust off some old magazines uncovered practically identical commentary from the times when the LP supplanted the 78, and when stereo first came into the shops.

What is undisputable is that the medium of digital recording, with its domestic sister product the Compact Disc system, brings many challenges to established studio and hi-fi practices—not only the reduction in recorded hiss and wow/flutter which the specification sheet shows us. The crystal clarity of digitized sound is transparent not only to what we want to hear, but also to imperfections (technical and human) in the recording and reproducing chains which would previously have been diluted and/or masked by imperfections in the analogue recording process. After engineering a large quantity of digital albums, I have no doubts of the capabilities of the system, when optimized, nor any desire to 'wind the clock back' to analogue, although there have had to be some expensive changes in ancillary equipment.

From a purely sonic point of view, the main differences between old-style analogue taping and digital are:

1. Lack of tape compression of high-level peaks.
2. Increased linearity of low bass frequency response extension.
3. Increased audibility of high-frequency non-linearities in original source material.
4. Increased audibility of low-level acoustic non-musical noises, such as paper noises, chair squeaks, air-conditioner rumble, fluorescent light buzzes, outside traffic noise.
5. Increased audibility of low-level electronic non-musical noises, such as hum, radio breakthrough, noisy mixer circuits, noisy microphones, thyristor-dimmer breakthrough, poor-quality interconnections (noisy jackfields, etc.).
6. Extremely low 'no signal' noise-floor, much quieter than blank-leader analogue replay noise.

The less favourable implications of all the above are audible on many of the very first Compact Disc issues, and the engineers' lack of familiarity with the potential pitfalls explains most of the better-informed adverse commentary from critics when they first listened to CD at home. The prime area for change in a studio going over to digital audio technology, surprisingly, is not immediately to replace everything in sight to reduce noise, distortion, etc. It is actually far more important to optimize control room monitoring so that engineers can judge accurately what is coming off the tape, and decide for themselves what is in need of change or refinement.

It should be a source of shame to many studio owners that the monitoring conditions in their control rooms are inferior to the hi-fi systems which many members of the public have in their own homes. The biggest problem is ambient background noise from air-conditioning systems, fans on equipment, even humming motors installed in aquaria (!), to name just a few culprits. It is physically impossible for a balance engineer to make judgements on low-level subtleties when there is so much external noise. Yet domestic consumers (particularly those who enjoy headphone listening) spot low-level faults in master recordings which most engineers would have corrected had they been given the chance to hear them.

The next hurdle is the choice of monitoring. Many studios opted some years ago for ultra-efficient loudspeakers, primarily to achieve deafening playback levels with relatively modest power amplifiers, but few of these loudspeakers are designed for the minimum coloration which is expected as a matter of course among discerning domestic listeners. Most of these high-efficiency speakers exhibit response anomalies (despite the efforts of graphic equalization) and lack audible deep bass extension, except when listening at levels high enough to exhaust the engineer's usable powers of concentration within twenty minutes or so, and possibly lead to permanent hearing damage. Without re-examining your control room monitoring, the value of any changeover to digital technology is likely to be diminished considerably—with clients possibly able to tell more about their recordings at home on the hi-fi (or in their hotel room listening on a Walkman) than it is possible to hear in the studio control room. The audibility of differences between power amplifiers is a topic guaranteed to redden the faces of many conservative engineers, but the choice of the best possible amplification you can afford is likely further to enhance your studio's ability to generate the best possible recordings. A digital multitrack costs a very considerable sum of money, and it is important to budget for sufficient extra funds to optimize metering, monitoring, and ancillaries (such as replacing some of the old, dented, early transistor microphones) so as to be able to get the best out of your investment.

High operating levels

The lack of tape compression with digital recording brings problems in orchestral recording. With analogue recording it was common, if not unavoidable, to allow an occasional cymbal crash, say, to go slightly over the top in order to maintain an acceptably high average recording level; and, in any case, a certain amount of tape compression was going on at higher levels because of the physical nature of how analogue magnetic tape works. With digital audio, the transfer characteristic is linear up to the point of 'peak bits' or saturation, a point of clipping, where the system runs out of numbers to express the conversion from analogue to digital. The effect of hitting this digital end-stop is not quite as drastic as was originally feared, due to the filtering process, but it is still by no means as soft as with analogue. Therefore, in order to avoid clipping a cymbal crash, for example, the balance engineer must back off and reduce his overall recording level in anticipation of this one-off event. The net effect is that an analogue recording will sound louder overall, because the peak-to-mean ratio has been curtailed by the phenomenon of tape compression, and the average level raised. The digital recording may well be a closer approximation to the original, but the larger peak-to-mean ratio will cause more problems with inadequacies in the signal path and might sound less comfortable (for example, the power amplifier may have insufficient headroom to handle the peaks, once the average level has been set for comfort).

To give a specific example, during 1985 we prepared Compact Disc master tapes of exactly the same repertoire (Mozart Flute Concertos) for two different clients. One was an issue from edited original 15 ips non-Dolby analogue masters; the other was a new unadulterated PCM 1610 digital recording made without any gain-riding on the mixer–faders. Both the CD master tapes' loudest levels gave the same absolute meter reading as measured on the digital meters, but subjectively the two CDs sounded 3 dB to 6 dB different in volume. In fact the analogue transfer received a criticism in one of the hi-fi magazines for being at an 'unnecessary high level', a comment with which I would not agree, but which does emphasize the point.

Low operating levels

Just as there is a basic operational difference at high operating levels between digital and analogue audio recording, there is a whole new realm of problems at low operating levels. Contrary to uninformed speculation, digital audio is capable of resolving a great deal of low-level information both wanted and unwanted—such as traffic rumble, distant jet aircraft, creaking chairs, even a grumbling stomach in the case of one soloist I worked with a couple of years ago. With analogue magnetic tape, most of these effects are submerged wholly or at least partially in tape hiss and modulation noise. What you could still just discern in the background you could probably rely upon vinyl LP pressing noises to dispose of for you, unless it was very bad. With Compact Disc in the home, you have a whole new problem; now everybody can enjoy the slightest extraneous noise in the comfort of their front room. The question of what to do with the gaps between tracks becomes especially vexing.

In analogue days it was very simple: go to the end of the movement and edit a piece of blank leader-tape after the reverberation dieaway, and before the first squeak or word from the performers; measure the length of gap required and then cut into the start of the next movement, making sure not to slice off the front edge of the first note. Whilst it is perfectly possible to do exactly this with digital editing, there is one snag. The digital equivalent of blank leader-tape is a black hole of oblivion. Cutting straight out of hall ambience into total silence is unnatural and disturbing, and the sudden explosion into music out of absolute silence is equally alarming to the listener. One answer is to splice in some extra hall ambience, but this can be more difficult than it sounds because not only does it often fail to match, but also it is extremely rare for musicians to sit still and quiet even for the two or three seconds necessary for the natural hall reverberation to die away after the last chord. The overall outcome is that more time is often spent in digital editing suites compiling ambience gaps between tracks than is spent editing complete movements. Some studios opt for fast fades into silence, rather than a 'chop', but the effect of fast-faded ambience is unnatural and reminiscent of a maladjusted noise-gate when replayed on a system with reasonable dynamic range. So, when recording a digital album, be sure either to discipline your performers to sit still at the end of takes, or else record a full minute or two of them sitting still, which might with luck yield five seconds or so of usable room tone to use in editing.

Absolute phase

The significance of absolute phase is often disputed, but it would seem at least good engineering practice to try to get it right. With one of the widest-used professional Japanese digital audio processors, the absolute phase has spun like a top with the different generations of production. First the input/output Cannon sockets were wired to one convention, then they were reversed. Then new production A/D converter boards inverted the phase again. On replay, the phase of the headphone socket was correct, and the main output upside down, and then new D/A boards reversed the error! When it comes to evaluating the 'ultimate' in full bandwidth sound quality, absolute phase inversion is audible, and to a degree which would surprise sceptics who have not checked it for themselves. The Sony PCM F1, which was a revolution in its time, had an inversion in its record electronics, and the first step in fine-tuning its audio performance was to phase-invert its analogue line-in artificially in compensation. Such horror stories make it difficult for an engineer to know where he is, and the misery does not end there. One of the biggest-selling European CD players, often used for reference, itself has inverted output polarity.

Are 16 bits enough?

For domestic listening, it would seem that 16 bits of D/A resolution (especially with oversampling to sweeten the HF) are sufficient to give pleasing sound quality from CDs made from existing master tapes, and to span the practical replay dynamic range between living-room ambient noise-levels and the onset of neighbour intolerance or system overload. For professional recordists, however, an upgrade to 18 bits analogue-to-digital conversion and storage would be advantageous, especially for post-production, where level changes, equalization, compression/limiting, and sampling-frequency standards conversion (e.g. 48 kHz–44.1 kHz CD standard) could be carried out without significant degradation of the noise-floor of the final rounded-to-16-bit Compact Disc.

In the real world of recording live music, we are unable to take advantage of the full 16 bits' worth of A/D dynamic range promised by the mathematicians. There is currently no crystal ball commercially available to predict in advance peak volume levels of an orchestra. Therefore the setting of recording gain is based mainly upon informed guesswork on the part of the balance engineer, and most leave an arbitrary amount of headroom just in case of any surprises. The noise-floor of real-world A/D converters is also worse than that predicted by basic theory, because of the dither (noise added intentionally in the analogue circuits to minimize the crossover-like distortion around the zero crossing), and because of the non-linearities of practical commercial designs of converter.

Most of the fully professional digital recording and interfacing formats appear adaptable to an 18-bit original recorded word-length, some more easily than others. It is interesting to note that the existing Decca in-house recorders and processors, the later Otari/Mitsubishi 'Prodigi' reel-to-reel recorders, and the disc-based editor systems from Lexicon and Denon all boast word-length capacity immediately ready for accepting 18 bits or a couple more. The next step requires patience, waiting for suitable A/D converters to come on to the general market. Fortunately there are many areas of data handling, other than professional sound recording, where 18 bits' worth of A/D conversion would also be advantageous, and this will accelerate progress.

Before suitable 16-bit A/D and D/A chips became freely available for more modest PCM converters aimed at smaller studios and semi-professionals, various devices with less resolution came on to the market, most of which were really small-production-run laboratory prototypes disguised as production models. I have an old Sony PCM1 from 1977 in my attic which used a twelve-bit A/D converter with an additional ranging bit to give quasi-14-bit resolution. After that came 14-bit EIAJ linear processors from Japanese manufacturers including Sharp, Pioneer, JVC, Technics, Sansui, Technics, Akai, and Sony. The noise-floor of these 14-bit machines was obviously significantly higher than the 16-bit ones we have now got used to, and one way to increase the dynamic range to an acceptable level was to use an established professional audio practice—pre-emphasis, which is still with us largely as a legacy of the older machines.

Pre-emphasis

With pre-emphasis, account is taken of the typical energy spectrum of music programme. High frequencies are boosted on record, and attenuated on replay in mirror-image fashion (50 μs minus 15 μs shelving with the digital audio standard). This technique is already used successfully to improve signal-to-noise ratio, for example in FM broadcasting, RIAA LP disc-cutting equalization, analogue tape NAB and IEC equalization standards. Thus there is no thoroughly justifiable engineering reason why it should be dismissed so disdainfully by certain of the major record companies, and ignored by most professional recording equipment manufacturers, especially when low-cost permanently pre-emphasized 16-bit systems like the PCM F1 are acknowledged as producing excellent results. There are seven main advantages in opting for pre-emphasis in recording:

1. Additional resolution of between one-half and one whole bit, i.e. 3 dB to 6 dB better signal-to-noise ratio.
2. Spectral distribution of system noise, making it less toppy and consequently less annoying.
3. Improved replay resolution and dynamic range on cheaper Compact Disc players with less sophisticated D/A converters.
4. Unintentional over-recording (i.e. onset of clipping at or above peak bits) for A/D converters working with pre-emphasis 'in' tends to occur first at high frequencies, making for an HF saturation effect akin to high-frequency analogue tape-squash rather than the far more audible effect of low-frequency hard clipping.
5. Without pre-emphasis, the graph of distortion versus frequency shows increasing distortion (IM) with increase in frequency leading to more brittle subjective perception of sound quality. Pre-emphasis reduces this effect.
6. If master tapes are compiled from many different sources, including recordings transcoded from semi-professional converters such as the Sony PCM F1 (which has pre-emphasis permanently switched in, unless it has been modified), then it would be wise to stick to one in-house standard wherever possible.
7. Easy and automatic identification of the use of emphasis because of internationally agreed digital flagging of data for interfacing on master tapes, and on pre-recorded consumer products (Compact Disc, etc.).

There are naturally arguments against emphasis, which are outlined below:

1. With a small proportion of recorded material (for example a very close-miked drum-kit, or direct-injected synthesizer), the spectral distribution can deviate significantly from the text-book curve of natural music, and may include sufficient high-frequency energy to lose most of the advantages of pre-emphasis, because of the need to reduce the overall recording level in avoiding overload. None the less, the overall signal-to-noise ratio is likely to remain no worse than without emphasis.
2. A large proportion of non-Japanese professional studio equipment manufacturers have omitted the internationally agreed emphasis-flag recognition system from their products, at least for the moment, making it difficult to process emphasized tapes without internal modification to equipment.
3. Some early digital A/D:D/A commercial processor designs suffered from lack of headroom in the analogue circuits driving the A/D converters, which was audible as high-frequency distortion at levels approaching peak

bits when pre-emphasis was switched in. On listening tests, such overload would have been audibly unsatisfactory.

4. Once 18-bit A/D converters are installed in professional recorders, we shall have sufficient dynamic range not to need emphasis any more, and the extra complications of flagging and the like will have proved to be a short-term aggravation.

Interface and sampling-rate standards

The professional audio business has always been one where different record companies, studios, and equipment manufacturers have taken pride in their individuality when it comes to agreements and standardization. For large organizations with self-sufficient in-house research and manufacturing, the problems are not so great until they have to send one of their tapes to another country or company, or else they receive an outside tape to process. To some extent internal non-standard practices act like a 'Berlin Wall'—supposedly to protect those inside, but ultimately suppressing free exchange of ideas to the disadvantage of all. It is only now, after very many years, that most organizations (still not all, though) have settled on one agreed way to wire the humble three-pin XLR Cannon audio interconnecting plug. How long it will take for standardized digital audio practices to arrive is anybody's guess. Interconnection compatibility is obviously crucial in the healthy development of a range of digital audio products, and although there are two main agreed interface standards (the original in-house Sony format, which some others adopted to assure compatibility, and AES/EBU), many interfaces still tend to be individual, using obscure connectors, maybe intertwined ribbon-looms, some formatting LSB first, some MSB first, with or without sync pulses, and so on.

Another thorny topic is that of sampling rate. In the beginning of digital audio in the 1970s there were several different starting-points. Soundstream and 3M opted for 50 kHz, presumably because it was a simple, easily memorable number just over double the audible spectrum. The abandoned BBC/3M broadcast recorder collaboration operated at 32 kHz, a convenient multiple of the PO telecommunication frequency of 16 kHz, and adequate as double the present audio broadcast spectrum. Decca opted for 48 kHz, another convenient multiple of the telecommunication standard, and suitable as just over double the accepted hi-fi audio spectrum. The original Philips Compact Disc proposal was 44.3 kHz, and the Japanese quasi-video digital processors operated at 44.1 kHz or its drop-frame near-equivalent 44.056 kHz.

The choice of sampling rates for a system where the data is encoded on tape as a pseudo-TV picture is limited to certain 'magic' numbers which are permutations of video parameters, and 44.1 kHz is one such number. In an ideal world it would be considered slightly on the low side, since the Nyquist frequency, i.e. half the sampling rate, works out at just over 22 kHz, giving the analogue low-pass filters before the A/D converters a hard job to avoid aliasing whilst not disturbing the audio HF quality. Other sampling rates were adopted by various manufacturers for early prototypes, but their use was limited to inside the laboratory, or on exhibition stands, and it is not intended to catalogue them all here.

The final sampling rate for the consumer end, the Compact Disc, was agreed between Philips and the Japanese at 44.1 kHz, which coincides (not by chance) with the frequency of the video-based formats (such as JVC and the Sony PCM1610/1630) which became the prime formats for CD master-tape interchange. CD masters may obviously be prepared from recordings originated with other sampling rates on other machines, by transfer either via analogue to the A/D input of a 44.1 kHz processor, or else, more elegantly, digitally by means of a Sampling Frequency Standards Converter. Although commercial standards converters can perform very close to the theoretical optimum, there is a slight in-built degradation of signal quality. This would either be reduced, if the original recording had been 18 bits wide rather than 16 bits, or else avoided completely had the original been made at 44.1 kHz in the first place, rather than these unhelpful 48 kHz or 50 kHz sampling rates. The losses are a slight reduction in audio level (0.5 dB or so) and an increase in noise-floor. In any case, many of the 48 kHz recorders have analogue record anti-aliasing filters tuned to audio cut-off frequencies identical to those for 44.1 kHz machines, not taking advantage of the slight extension of HF response theoretically available by using a higher-speed sampling clock, even if such advantage were not to be lost in the standards converter anyway.

Upgrading to an integral multiple of the CD 44.1 kHz sampling rate (i.e. A/D 'oversampling' at 88.2 kHz, 132.3 kHz, or 176.4 kHz) would be worth while, however, since it would be possible to dispose of the steep analogue low-pass anti-aliasing filters on the outer edge of the audio band. Sharp analogue 'brick wall' filters tend to generate ringing, group delay, and phase distortion throughout the audio band, which may cause audible adverse side-effects. Oversampling at, say, 88.2 kHz would mean a much smoother analogue filter roll-off before the A/D converter, and the electronics necessary to standards-convert and filter the data digitally, removing audio frequencies over 20 kHz, would not be so demanding as that required inside a sophisticated non-integer sampling-frequency standards converter.

Differences in sound quality between various digital recordings have often been attributed to sampling rates and tape formats, rather than where they should be—the expertise and care of the designer of the analogue and digital circuitry within the processor itself, and, most important of all, the skill and imagination of the sound balance engineer confronted with all the exciting potentials of a total digital audio system.

13

Mobile recording units

John McErlean

The purpose of an integrated mobile recording unit fitted with all major items of sound control and recording equipment is to provide a comfortable, pleasing on-the-road version of a static control room. The main problem is to maximize facilities in a restricted space.

Mobiles range from simple panel van conversions, incorporating straight-to-stereo tape and/or line equipment, to purpose-designed high-specification articulated semi-trailers incorporating acoustic treatment, built-in multitrack and stereo recorders, computer-assisted control desk, and a host of peripheral equipment. Before commencing on esoteric and costly designs it is obvious that customer needs and aspirations, as well as the size of his budget, have to be evaluated.

The old carry-in idea with lots of portable units crammed into a panel van, manhandled into a venue, and connected together in a boxy backroom is still the cheapest method of providing mobile recording. However, this lacks not only creature comfort but also a repeatable defined environment, and is rarely satisfactory from an acoustic point of view.

Panel vans

Conversions of panel vans offer sensible solutions to the customer who does not require multitrack, environmental control, or lots of built-in equipment, but there is little that can be done to control the acoustic properties of the finished vehicle apart from some of the suggestions made here.

Vehicle shapes are subject to personal choice, but the choice of basic van should first be made on its physical dimensions, particularly the internal width and height. Few such vans have perpendicular sides, and a vehicle which has a maximum width dimension at control desk height has an obvious advantage in maximizing the size of the desk that can be installed. Internal height dimensions are critical for operating crew comfort; a vehicle in which a normal person cannot stand upright, at least in the central section, will be the source of constant frustration. It is recommended that an internal height of 2.2/2.3 m in an unmodified van will produce an adequate floor-to-ceiling dimension of 2.1 m in the central area of the fitted vehicle. Achieving this means obviously a high-top van with a metal rather than a fibre-glass roof to provide for strength, electrical screening, and the mounting of external fittings. Other factors which should influence the choice of vehicle are as follows.

Access doors

For safety, personnel access to the mixing area should be from the nearside or the rear of the van. The choice between a sliding or normal hinged door on the nearside depends on the vehicle manufacturer's options, but passing pedestrians may be somewhat surprised by a hinged door opening without warning. Door widths need to be great enough to allow installation of the control desk and other equipment.

Floor height

To allow easy ingress and egress, a low floor height is sensible, although the addition of a fold-down step in the vehicle skirt is usually straightforward for a reputable coachbuilder.

Spare wheel

Whilst the provision of a spare wheel is both normal and essential, the siting of the wheel can be a problem. It should ideally be stored externally, either under the floor or secured to a rear door to leave maximum internal space.

Van layout

The vehicle layout is dependent on its purpose, and by way of example only a stereo recording/broadcast van will be described (see Figure 13.1).

Although van dimensions preclude ideal stereo monitoring, placing the control desk either behind the front seats facing forwards or over the rear axle facing the rear can be satisfactory. Experience shows that the latter solution produces the best results. The control desk weight is borne by the rear suspension, providing a stable ride, and any vehicle wheel-arches can be 'lost' under the sides of the desk. The desk can be installed through the rear doors for ease of servicing. The area between the desk and the rear door can be covered with ribbed aluminium sheet for durability and to provide waterproof storage of cable drums and an undercover termination point for signal and power cables.

To increase the usable space in the van, the front seats can be changed to a rotating type which is lockable either in the normal driving position or facing into the vehicle. These seats can now provide work stations for producer and secretary. The remaining area of the vehicle can be used solely for technical furniture and personnel. Furniture built into the sides of the vehicle can house tape recorders, power control system, desk power supply, technical battery and charger (if required), and other associated equipment. Although technical a.c. and d.c. power systems are covered later, it may be noted that any technical

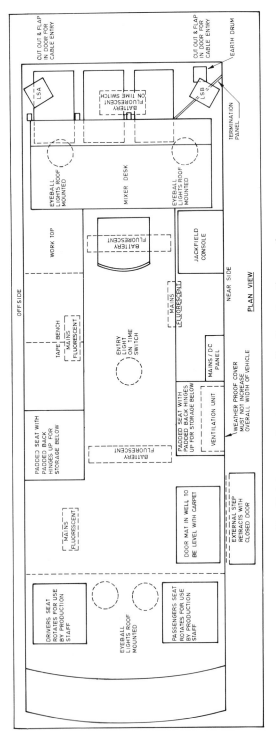

Fig. 13.1. Layout of a stereo recording/broadcasting panel van

batteries included in the vehicle should be installed outside, and a sliding ventilated battery locker can be built into the vehicle skirt by a reputable coachbuilder.

Construction details

Before any furniture or wiring fitments are installed, various measures need to be taken to improve the basic van. The steel panels used to form the vehicle will resonate at low frequencies (this can be shown by striking the van walls with a clenched fist). All panels, including the roof and door as well as the walls, need to be damped with purpose-made self-adhesive sound deadening material. This material should be affixed off panel centre lines to avoid frequency-doubling effects. Although space inside the van is limited, it is suggested that a flat wall surface is produced, because the vehicle-structured ribs are never ideally positioned for attaching fitments.

After any additional structural members necessary to support heavy items have been welded on, the vehicle walls should be lined with 6–10 mm plywood, with the void between this and the vehicle skin filled with mineral wool (rockwool) to improve sound isolation. Once the required fixed cupboards and equipment bays are complete, the walls need a hard-wearing decorative finish; carpet is suggested for this, as its acoustic properties and type specification (which are covered later) offer benefits. Further trimming details for the ceiling can be a matter of taste, but an open-weave fabric over mineral wool will provide a resilient surface.

Purpose-designed vehicles

These fall into two categories, rigid and articulated. A 'rigid' vehicle is one where the driving cab, engine transmission, and payload area are all mounted on a single chassis. An 'articulated' vehicle is signified where a prime-mover, or tractor, draws a trailer either by a drawbar or by the well-known 'fifth wheel' close coupling used by normal heavy transport vehicles. Drawbar trailers are capable of being moved on their built-in axles, whilst a close-coupled trailer has axles at the rear only and is supported at the front by the tractor rear axle or, when uncoupled, by a pair of landing legs. This latter type is known as a semi-trailer and is most commonly used by the heavy transport industry. Each type has distinct features, and thought needs to be given to the choice.

In the UK, government regulations (particularly the Motor Vehicle (Construction and Use) Regulations) control and restrict the vehicle designer. For example, all vehicles are limited to a width of 2.5 m, rigid vehicles to a length of 11 m, and articulated semi-trailers to a length of 15.5 m including the tractor. These dimensions are maxima and include all bumpers, rub rails, clips, etc. It cannot be emphasized strongly enough that ignorance of the regulations could prove disastrous and that a copy should be obtained from Her Majesty's Stationery Office before the design commences.

Rigid vehicles are based on commercial truck or coach chassis, and bodybuilders' drawings, which give dimensional weight information, are available from the various vehicle manufacturers. These show the designer which parts of the vehicle need to be accessible for maintenance and help to identify areas which cannot be utilized without penalizing the access. Truck chassis, for instance, often have a tilt cab, which folds forward to give access to the engine and gearbox. The bodybuilders' drawings will show an arc of tilt which should not be obstructed.

Coach chassis, apart from having awkwardly placed mid or rear engines, have restricted axle weights which can easily be exceeded with the type of technical equipment and vehicle techniques described here. Apart from this, coach chassis can offer a low chassis height and softer suspension, which may prove advantageous. The solution to the low axle weight capability is, at the design stage, to calculate the axle loadings and to have an extra axle added (common practice at the rear, but an additional steering axle at the front is a specialist matter).

Articulated vehicles have several advantages which will become apparent later, but the main one is that the vehicle can be longer and heavier in terms of the UK Road Traffic Act. Also, once the standard dimensions for fifth-wheel coupling are taken into account, much greater freedom is available from the trailer format.

Weight calculation

As an aside, weight calculation is amongst the most important design routines. An overweight vehicle is both illegal and unsafe, whilst an insufficiently laden vehicle will transfer the suspension 'bounce' to the equipment within. The method of calculation used successfully by the writer is as follows, and is equally valid for all types of vehicle.

The vehicle manufacturer's data will show the gross vehicle weight, maximum permitted axle loadings, the unladen vehicle weight, and its axle distribution. The proposed vehicle body-weight should be calculated from the wall, roof, and floor areas and the density of each area. This weight can be considered borne equally by each axle (unless very obviously different) and added to the basic vehicle axle loadings.

The remainder obtained by deducting this sum from the gross weight of both the vehicle and each axle will show how much *maximum* payload is available. Great care must now be taken to compile a list of all items to be carried on the vehicle; not just the control desk and tape machines but also technical batteries, air-conditioning plant, furniture, cable reels, etc. (A cable reel with 50 m of multi-pair cable can weigh 50 kg and ten of these amount to half a tonne!) By comparing items on this list and their respective positions to each axle, applied mathematics can be used to calculate moments about each axle, multiplying the distance from the axle by the item weight. It may be noted that an item located behind the rear axle will have a positive moment (i.e. loading) on the rear axle but a negative one (i.e. lifting) about the forward axle.

This mathematical process is rather tedious, and greatly aided by a microcomputer programme, but will highlight any glaring errors in axle and vehicle loading and will aid the basic vehicle chassis choice. However, if all the calculations show a gross vehicle weight of say 10 tonnes, do not be tempted to buy a 12-tonne GVW chassis, but instead choose a 14/16-tonne GVW one. This will provide not only a margin for error and some 'spare' capacity for future additions, but also ensure that the vehicle is not underpowered. Remember, few transport vehicles operate at 100 per cent gross vehicle weight for 100 per cent of their life. Unlike technical vehicles, they run empty occasionally; also remember the times you've cursed a struggling underpowered truck on a mild gradient.

Now, armed with an idea of how much things weigh and their effects—and having made a choice of favoured control desk, tape machines, and other technical equipment—the designer is ready to combine these and other vehicle-related systems into the desired finished mobile. Before considering the finer points of layout and finishes, vehicle-related systems must be considered. It is very important that the vehicle should 'sound' right, particularly at the mixing engineer and producer seating positions, and that everybody should feel comfortable within the vehicle no matter what the ambient conditions are outside. Also, power systems, termination panels, and storage areas need to be thought about. Accordingly, acoustic properties, air-conditioning, a.c. and d.c. power systems, and the provision of storage will now be discussed, in that order.

Acoustic design

Many learned papers have been written on acoustics relating to buildings but few have been specific on vehicles. The same principles can be applied, however, with attention to related detail on the two facets, insulation and response.

Insulation

Sound insulation, particularly at low frequencies, always presents a problem in vehicle design as the vehicle is subject to size and corresponding weight restrictions. As can be deduced from the above with regard to vehicle weights, the heavier the basic vehicle the less the payload that can be carried.

Sound insulation is dependent on wall surface density (mass per unit area), and, although a restriction of wall surface density increases the vehicle's payload, it also reduces the degree of sound insulation which can be achieved; also, the need to restrict wall thickness, thereby increasing the internal volume, precludes the use of a double-leaf construction. (The term 'wall' implies all vehicle surfaces including roof and floor.)

Wall construction

The wall construction chosen for a recent series of sound vehicles (see Figure 13.2) offers substantial improvements over previous vehicles. The construction is in a 'sandwich' form. The outer surface is 15 mm-thick glass-reinforced plastic-faced plywood followed by a 25 mm layer of mineral wool infill, a layer of heavy flexible material-loaded plastic on a fabric backing (barrier mat), a further 25 mm layer of mineral wool, and a 15 mm internal plywood wall. The internal wall is faced with sound absorbers and carpet. Structural strength is provided by horizontal and vertical aluminium 'top-hat' sections built into the sandwich.

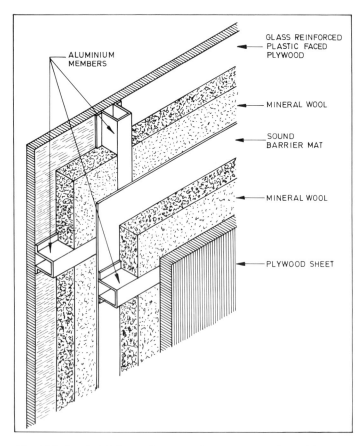

Fig. 13.2. Sandwich form of construction for a recording vehicle wall

The choice of mineral wool rather than rigid foam avoids the disadvantage of a dip in insulation which may occur in the mid-frequency range due to combined material resonance. The barrier mat provides a useful increase in mass per unit area without substantially adding to the wall thickness. This type of construction needs to be continuous around the operational area and any air-conditioning ductwork or air-handling unit situated outside the operational area.

Doors

External personnel doors are a particular problem, giving sound leakage paths which assume greater significance with the improved sound insulation given by the vehicle's wall construction. Double, or preferably triple, seals under moderate compression are necessary over the entire door perimeter. Door catches and locks should be chosen so that they do not interrupt or damage the seals.

Windows

Windows should be avoided, as not only do they take up valuable wall space and present a hard reflecting surface, but they are difficult to install while providing the necessary isolation. A small window in the door(s) is, however, a good idea for safety. This window (150 × 300 mm) can be constructed with a proprietary sealed double-glazed unit on the outside and an additional single-glazed pane flush with the inside face of the door.

To complete the sound insulation measures it should be ensured that vehicle skirt panels and any vehicle sub-panels are braced and adequately damped to prevent sympathetic vibrations from being conducted into the vehicle structure and thus into the interior. Also, any cable ducts should be adequately pugged with linen bags containing dry sand, other cables or pipes filled with mastic or similar material. As with static installations, the places where the acoustic skin is perforated should be minimized and chosen carefully. These combined measures have been used on recent high-specification vehicles and produce isolation figures of greater than 42 dB averaged between 100 Hz and 2.5 kHz.

Acoustic performance

For a mobile recording vehicle to be successful, the perceived sound inside, especially near the control desk where the mixing engineer and producer sit, must be closely controlled and designed to emulate the best that static control rooms can offer.

The physical dimensions inside even the largest mobile are very limited; the internal height is limited by the maximum overall height desired for the vehicle and the height of the chassis from the ground; the overall legal limit of width to 2.5 m reduces, with the acoustic isolation measures outlined above, to approximately 2.3 m; length is determined by which type of vehicle is chosen (rigid or articulated) and the chosen vehicle layout. This small enclosure size produces problems, particularly in the lower frequency ranges. Firstly, there is the effect of room modes (eigentones) which are more widely spaced than in larger static control rooms. The result is to make an overall acceptable characteristic difficult to achieve, due to variations in sound quality and reverberation time from place to place. Secondly, the space restrictions preclude the use of bulky low-frequency absorbers which would be effective in low-frequency control.

Another problem is that the monitoring loudspeakers are closer to the walls than in a static control room, and acoustic irregularities are caused by reflections from wall-mounted enclosures, such as cupboards, bays, and benches. Some of the problems can be minimized by placing a dividing wall across the operating area, effectively separating the interior into control and recording areas, and by expanding the width of the control area on site. These measures were taken with the BBC's Digital Control Vehicle (see Plates 17 and 18), providing an amazing transformation of listening conditions compared with other vehicles.

Also, extensive acoustic treatment on the walls and built into the ceiling will help control the listening conditions. Design reverberation times of 0.3 sec from 250 Hz upwards have been used for recent large mobiles. The acoustic treatment used has taken the form of low-frequency and all-band studio-style modular absorbers sited on the side and end walls (as well as on the ceiling) to control the eigentones effectively. The ceiling absorbers are unobtrusive, as they form

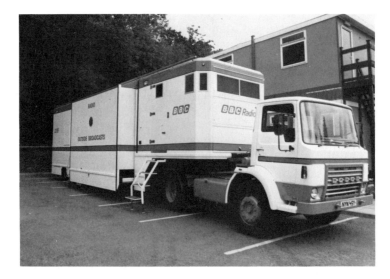

Plate 17. Digital recording vehicle, showing the expanding wall sections in the extended position (Photo: BBC)

part of an integrated design with air-conditioning ducts and grilles and electrical modules containing fluorescent and incandescent eyeball-type down-lights.

Wall-mounted absorbers have to be placed carefully, as reflections from the hard front panel can produce edgy or tinny sound quality. In a vehicle where walls and ceiling may be within one metre of the sound control position, it is necessary to place the absorbers where they will not cause specular reflections from the loudspeakers. Surfaces within the vehicle from which troublesome specular reflection would occur need to be covered with a material having sound-absorbing characteristics which do not rely on 'averaging' between areas of high and low absorption. Conventional all-wool (or at least 80 per cent wool) Wilton carpet, without underlay, is used for this and has the advantages of being visually attractive and hard-wearing.

To mitigate the high-frequency reflections from the control desk, the ceiling area immediately over the desk should be covered with a long-haired shag-pile carpet. The floor needs to be covered with a hard-wearing robust covering, for obvious reasons, and a haircord carpet will suit whilst ensuring that the high-frequency response of the vehicle will not be too damped.

Following even this type of treatment, it has been found that the control area can still sound bass-heavy and that some limited monitor equalization is necessary. This appears best set up by ear initially using graphic equalizers, before a permanent equalizer is installed. A simple bass roll-off of 10 dB at

Plate 18. Neve DSP digital console in the BBC vehicle shown in Plate 17 (Photo: BBC)

50 Hz on a 6 dB/octave curve, with two or three shallow notches at higher frequencies to reduce any sound colourations caused by specular reflections, is all that is usually required.

Monitoring loudspeakers are a matter of much argument and personal taste. The only point to be recommended is that, to achieve a stereo image which is good and stable, the speakers and listening position should form the classic equilateral triangle as far as possible. The loudspeakers should be placed close to the side walls (accepting the other problems of doing this). Special trapezoidal-shaped cabinets assist in this, and a recent version of the BBC-designed LS5/8 bi-amped loudspeaker was formulated especially for sound Outside Broadcast vehicles.

Vehicle choice

Rigid vehicle chassis, even the specially designed ones used for fire-engines and the like, can still be restrictive. Articulated semi-trailers can overcome some of these limitations. One of the problems in use of a rigid vehicle is mechanical breakdown. If the tractor of an articulated unit fails, then, at least temporarily, another can be hired. Also, a replacement tractor can be used when the normal unit is in for maintenance.

In large organizations, with their own transport as well as electronic maintenance engineers, almost inevitably the transport engineers have the mobile placed over a pit before the electronic engineers arrive, on the rare occasions when the vehicle touches base. This often leads to the electronic equipment on a rigid vehicle leaving for its next show without equipment faults being rectified, whereas an artic can be simultaneously maintained.

Other advantages of the artic mentioned earlier, increased length and weight, can be significant in the provision of storage and creature comfort areas as well as permitting the weight penalties of acoustic isolation construction. Figures 13.3, 4, and 5 show layouts of mobiles based on truck, coach, and articulated trailer chassis respectively. The truck layout is of a workhorse mobile without multitrack, whereas the coach and artic both offer the concept of large automation-assisted consoles, multitrack, and stereo tape machines.

Figure 13.6 also shows an articulated vehicle, but a very special one, the BBC Digital Control Vehicle (see Plate 17). This vehicle houses a Neve DSP digital control desk (Plate 18), digital multitrack and stereo tape machines, and a BBC NICAM digital distribution system. This very exciting vehicle has a number of points of interest apart from the digital system. To provide an ideal working environment for the assessment of digital audio, the normal control room dimensions of a mobile were judged unsatisfactory in terms of volume. A novel system was evolved where the sides of the vehicle in the control room area were made to expand by 600 mm on each side (see Figure 13.7) increasing the volume of the control area from 20 m^3 to 30 m^3. This was achieved on each side with a

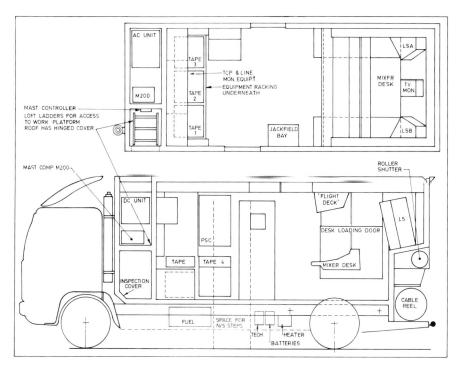

Fig. 13.3. Layout of a truck for sound recording

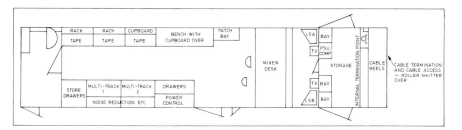

Fig. 13.4. Layout of a coach for sound recording

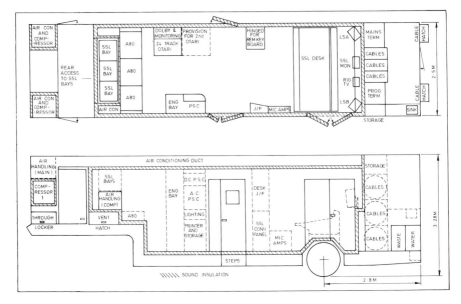

Fig. 13.5. Layout of an articulated trailer housing an automation-assisted control desk, multitrack recorders, etc.

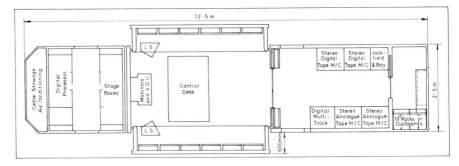

Fig. 13.6. The BBC's first all-digital control vehicle

pair of hydraulic rams moving the complete side section, which was supported on seven slide mechanisms. Two continuous compression seals around each side, in both the retracted and expanded modes, ensured acoustic isolation. Figure 13.8 is a side view of the Digital Control Vehicle showing an acoustic separate area, constructed as a cab where all the processing equipment is housed, with only a pugged cable duct connecting into the control area. An isolation average of 62 dBA exists between the two areas.

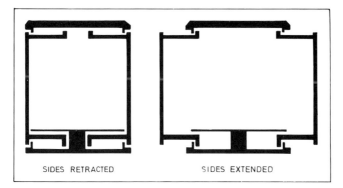

SIDES RETRACTED   SIDES EXTENDED

Fig. 13.7. Section through BBC digital vehicle, showing how the sides can be extended on location

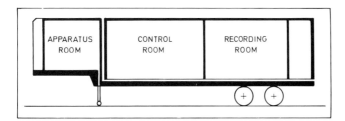

APPARATUS ROOM   CONTROL ROOM   RECORDING ROOM

Fig. 13.8. Side view of BBC digital vehicle, showing how two separate acoustic areas have been built

Suspension

Technical equipment finds it difficult to survive the hard life of mobile recording, even when permanently installed in a vehicle. The vehicle suspension system is critical in providing a good 'ride', and it is recommended that an air suspension system is provided for the rear axle(s), particularly if the control desk is situated above. In fact, deliberately siting the control desk over an air-suspended rear axle is a good policy; the weight of the desk is borne by the suspension, where there is always the greatest load-carrying capacity, and a soft ride is provided.

Tape machines are best installed so that accelerative shocks to the motors are taken vertically, not laterally, by the motor bearings. Also, the machines themselves need to be securely bolted or strapped in place, as should all items carried in the operational area. The damage caused to finishes and equipment by a loose microphone stand, let alone a multitrack machine, has to be seen to be believed.

Another advantage of air suspension, particularly on a trailer (where compressed air is provided by the tractor via a flexible hose) is that it can be evacuated on site; the suspension will then sit on its bump stops providing stabilization. For levelling, a trailer can be uncoupled from its tractor, the suspension evacuated, and the front end lowered on the landing legs until the vehicle is level. A word of warning though—do not allow the driver to couple tractor to trailer by reversing at speed (a common 'transport' trick). This will not succeed due to the difference in height between tractor and lowered trailer, and damage will result.

Levelling

On the subject of levelling and stabilization, the addition of simple mechanical jacks at each corner is useful to stop the vehicle rocking on site. This will relieve distracting motion when somebody enters or moves around in the vehicle. On-site convenience will be aided if these jacks have several coarse adjustment slots, with a screw section attached to a broad foot piece for fine adjustment.

Storage and creature comforts

Storage space on vehicles is always at a premium. Inside, small and large cupboards for the storage of tapes, instruction manuals, paperwork, tools, spares, and similar should be carefully planned around an ergonomic equipment layout with the intention of providing as many cupboards as possible. The customer needs to be consulted as to any specific requirements and the size of internal divisions. The catches on the cupboards need to be simple in operation, strong, and not prone to opening in transit and allowing the contents to fly out.

Outside storage also needs to be comprehensive. Apart from lockers housing stabilizing jacks, technical batteries, air-conditioning compressors, and similar vehicle system hardware, unallocated space needs to be provided for all sorts, shapes, and sizes of equipment. Large areas with full-size doors, big enough for a person to stand in, will hold PA speakers, large stands, extra cable drums, equipment transportation trolley, and the like. Smaller lockers built into available spaces will have a variety of uses, and, if possible, a through locker arranged across the vehicle will house a ladder for access to venue cable entries and for slinging cables. Locker doors should clip back close to the vehicle body for public safety and ease of access, with gas struts aiding the raising/lowering of horizontally hinged doors.

Since many cable drums (multi-pair signal, single XLR-XLR , CCTV camera, and mains power) are needed to cover even the simplest show, storage and ease of use must be considered. Other than multi-pair cables and high-current mains cables, most cable drums are reasonably small, so that skirt lockers can be arranged to house them. The two former cable types require purpose-built storage as they are both large and heavy. Several multi-way cables will be needed to service the long runs of multi-mic set-ups, so easy-to-use storage is necessary. A useful mechanism has been devised, by one of the leading UK sound vehicle coachbuilders, which mounts each multi-way drum on a frame supported on a pair of sliders. This frame can be latched into a recessed locker or slid out and locked in position, enabling the cable either to be unreeled *in situ* or the complete drum removed and transported to a remote point.

Mains cables can be similarly treated, or, for space saving and ease of rewind, a d.c. motor-powered reel can be built in. A type of reel used successfully recently was developed by a proprietary manufacturer from one of his fire-engine hose reels! Alternative locations for this large cable drum storage can be seen in Figures 13.4 and 5. Both locations are similar in that cables are reached via the rear of the vehicle. This allows safe access wherever the vehicle is parked.

Cables slung across a roadway, and maintenance of any roof-mounted aerials or aerial bases, will require climbing on the vehicle roof. A loose ladder placed against the vehicle side is likely to be unsafe on uneven or sloping terrain. A fixed ladder attached to the vehicle solves this problem, but, to comply with the UK's Health and Safety at Work Act, the ladder should fold close to the vehicle when not in use, and some means of preventing unauthorized climbing should be provided.

If space and finance permit, as shown in Figures 13.4 and 5, consideration can be given to some creature comforts. Apart from air-conditioning (covered elsewhere in this chapter), these include a sink with hot and cold water, for freshening up and removing the inevitable grime of cable running, and a water boiler (which can also provide the hot washing water) to make tea or coffee, a refrigerator, and somewhere to hang wet clothes and muddy boots.

The provision of a water system requires some comment regarding health safety. The storage of fresh and waste water is fraught with difficulty, and the simplest solution is to use two equal-volume plastic jerrycan containers, clearly marked and not interchangeable, so that as the fresh water container empties the waste container fills; the two-containers thus have to be serviced together. Water can be sucked from the fresh water container by a suction-valve-operated electric pump, and delivered either to the cold tap or to the water boiler. A small caravan-style stainless steel sink with appropriate plumbing connected to the waste container will complete the system.

Air-conditioning

One consequence of good sound isolation is that it prevents natural air-flow through the vehicle. This, with the heat gain deriving from equipment and people, means that some environmental control is necessary. Solar gain is small due to the high U value of the wall build-up, and, although calculable, can be almost ignored.

An air-conditioning system needs to be capable of providing stable comfortable working conditions for the number of people expected to work in the mobile, as well as coping with the power dissipation of the technical equipment and the lighting. The modes of operation necessary are 'cooling', 'heating', and 'ventilation', with thermostat and humidistat control. It is essential that the air-conditioning plant is properly planned, normally by a specialist working in conjunction with the coachbuilder. Obviously, the specialist will need all details of power dissipation, occupancy, and problem areas to provide a good system.

A reasonable basic specification for a system in the UK is for the 'cooling' mode to provide reduction in average air temperature inside the vehicle body to 21°C dry bulb at 45 per cent relative humidity, when all the technical equipment is switched on, the vehicle is exposed to summer sunshine on a windless day, and the external shade temperature is 30°C. A differential of at least 9°C should be maintained up to an external shade temperature of 40°C. To avoid draughts, the temperature of the air leaving the ducts should be no more than 5.5°C cooler than the average air temperature inside the vehicle. Filters, 95 per cent efficient at 5 μm and easily removed for servicing, should be fitted. Also, as a draught precaution, air pressure in the vehicle with all doors closed should be slightly higher than external air pressure. A 10 per cent bleed of fresh air should be introduced to prevent stale odours and stuffiness.

The 'heating' mode is similar to the 'cooling' except that the system should now be capable of maintaining 21°C dry bulb, 45 per cent relative humidity when the external temperature is -5°C, 100 per cent relative humidity. Electric heater batteries in the supply air-flow achieve the necessary climatic effect. The 'ventilation' mode is useful where limited mains power is available. In this mode, the compressor and heater batteries are disabled and the air-handling unit is used purely as a fan for moving air through the vehicle. For the 'cooling' and 'heating' modes to work correctly, the vehicle doors need to be closed, and continual opening and closing of doors will cause shortcomings in system control.

The silencing of the plant is of prime importance, and care should be taken in mounting the air-handling unit and the compressor, with anti-vibration mounts used where necessary. Silencers should be installed in the supply and return air paths, to prevent motor and fan noise being coupled into the duct system. A noise-level specification should be agreed, noting that possible beneficial masking effects of air-conditioning noise in a building do not apply in the much smaller environment of a vehicle. Compressors and fans should be mounted outside the acoustically isolated operational area, and, apart from anti-vibration mounts, the coolant pipework should have flexible sections inserted at both ends to prevent noise transmission into the body. It is important that liquid coolant does not enter the compressor, and a sump heater with delayed start-up may be necessary.

On the basis that continued noise is less noticeable than intermittent noise, and to prevent the start-up surges on the mains supply which will upset some technical equipment, the compressor must run continuously. To achieve this, the compressor needs to be fitted with a hot gas bypass system or preferably a secondary evaporator and diverting control valve. The latter system provides a more constant load to the compressor, prolonging its life, but its mode of operation and the control gear requirements are quite complex and outside the scope of this book.

Safety devices such as high and low-pressure cutouts and de-icing thermostats should be fitted. The evaporation condensate should collect in drip trays which self-drain to the outside. These drip trays need to be of sufficient volume that condensate does not leak into the vehicle when it is parked off-level.

The air ducts must be adequate in cross-section, avoiding sharp turns and restrictions which cause turbulence and noise and reduce the air-flow. The ducts should be as long as possible and, for maximum noise attenuation, lined with underfelt formed in a corrugated fashion. Simpler lining, such as fire-retardant foam, may be used on longer ducts, but, on fire safety grounds, foam should be avoided wherever possible. A lined duct presents a fairly high impedance to the air-flow, and care should be taken that internal panelling is positioned so that air is prevented from taking low-impedance paths and bypassing the system.

Supply grilles need to be of a low-noise flush-fitting type with volume control dampers, and consideration should be given to air extraction from the main body and also directly above any particular heat-producing equipment. All grilles should be checked for sympathetic vibration and acoustic damping. The ideal place for control gear is with the power control switchgear described in the next section.

Before leaving the subject of air-conditioning, other items of environmental comfort need mentioning. The first is a diesel-fuel-fired coach heater. This simple device is useful as a source of heat, both in vehicles with and without air-conditioning or electric heating, but for different reasons. The reason for a source of heat in the former is straightforward, but in the latter it may seem superfluous. The use of a diesel-fired coach heater in an air-conditioned vehicle is to keep moisture out overnight, or to provide some warmth in the vehicle before the power supply is connected. Incidentally, the unit is best fed from its own tank, as, although fuel demand is low, it could be embarrassing to run the engine fuel tank dry; also, the heater can be run on rebated (i.e. cheap domestic fuel oil) rather than diesel road vehicle fuel.

The second useful item is the ventilator fan. In vehicles, such as panel vans, without air-conditioning a ventilator fan can be useful to clear stale air. Unfortunately, most of these units tend to be noisy and are therefore not really compatible with sound control mobiles. Recently, the author discovered a variant on the ventilator fan theme. This unit, made by a Japanese company, incorporates a heat exchanger coil whereby the exhaust air pre-warms ingoing air, supplying this by a two-speed fan motor. The unit has two ports, one for input and the other for output, and is impressively quiet in operation. When mounted resiliently on the vehicle and two separate 600 mm ducts formed, each lined with corrugated underfelt, the system is very quiet and certainly satisfactory for a budget mobile.

Second air-conditioning system

A second system with 'cooling' and 'ventilation' modes can become necessary where technical equipment power supplies or an automation system computer produce high heat loads, or have integral noisy cooling fans leading to the necessity of an acoustically isolated enclosure to house them. The basic ideas expressed above for a personnel area system still apply, although the noise criteria can be relaxed provided that sound isolation from the equipment housing to the main area is good. Fresh air bleed is not necessary; a recirculating air-flow is adequate. The 'cooling' mode still requires a continuously run compressor, for the reasons outlined above, but care should be taken with the system specification to avoid 'hot-spots' in the equipment, and also overcooling, which could cause condensation inside the equipment.

The 'ventilation' mode is for use in minimum power situations where the computer is bypassed and switched off along with other unnecessary equipment. In this mode the compressor is unpowered, and the recirculating system ducts are converted to 'total loss', with flaps allowing fresh air to be sucked in by the air-handling unit fan through an outside grille, passed over the equipment, and exhausted directly back to the outside.

Power systems and lighting

Both d.c. and a.c. systems are necessary on sound recording mobiles and will be discussed in that order.

Direct current systems and lighting

Direct current power is required to operate battery lighting, rigging lights, alarm systems, control and ignition of diesel coach heater, powered cable drums, and standby power for technical equipment having a low voltage input as well as a pneumatic mast compressor (if fitted). Internal battery lights will be useful in the absence of power on first arrival at site, or on derig, and also to produce minimum power demand at limited venues. For this application, experience has shown that fluorescent-type lamps are most suitably powered on an automatic changeover circuit, from technical batteries to a d.c. power supply powered by a.c. mains. This arrangement allows a single on–off switching arrangement adjacent to entry doors, and neatly avoids duplication of d.c. and a.c. switchgear, chokes, and the like associated with fluorescent lighting. Also, d.c. fluorescents radiate less radio-frequency interference than their a.c. counterparts.

Rigging lights, mounted so that they shine on termination panel areas, entry doors, storage lockers, and around the perimeter of the vehicle, will provide safety and security. Many types of lamp unit are available, but none are designed for the purpose, and consequently they are not entirely satisfactory. Recent vehicles have been fitted with reversing lamps set on an angled bracket within the dimensions of the vehicle cant rail. These lamps have been the most satisfactory, requiring no adjustment on site and providing a very good light coverage down the side of the vehicle and a few feet out from the side. Additionally, a powerful rotatable work lamp adjacent to the fixed ladder is useful for shining along the roof and up at buildings or highlighting a required area.

Alarm systems, warning of doors or hatches opening in transit, over-temperature of equipment, fire, or unauthorized persons, are sensible precautions. Door warning and intruder alarm can both be achieved with micro switches. Mechanical switches are difficult to align in view of vehicle movement and they also suffer from corrosion. However, magnetic feed switches are quite satisfactory, being tolerant of line-up, robust, and corrosion-proof. The use of magnetic switches does require care in mounting, avoiding close proximity to steel-work which will reduce the effectiveness of, or even defeat, the switch. An alarm indication panel visible from the outside of the vehicle, with a composite mutable audio and visual indicator in the driver's cab, will provide useful identification of a problem. Over-temperature alarms for equipment are fairly self-explanatory, and fire detectors, or, more accurately, ionization-chamber smoke detectors, are straightforward domestic types installed in all compartments where fire, due to electrical or human failing, can start.

Diesel coach heater manufacturers supply the necessary data with their products, as do other equipment manufacturers, to design these control systems. In budget mobiles, the technical equipment can have the option of battery input. This can be especially useful at venues where no a.c. power is available; of course, battery tape machines are then also needed, and monitoring may have to be done on headphones! Installation and component specification details are similar to a.c. systems and are covered below.

Batteries and charger

The source of supply for the d.c. power system will be battery. A pair of series-connected lead-acid 12 V 100 AH batteries with an associated charging system is all that is required. The batteries themselves need to be superior to ordinary automotive units, as the charge/discharge cycle is a series of deep discharge and heavy charge. A semi-traction battery has been found to survive the experience due to its construction comprising greater amounts of lead.

The batteries must be installed in a ventilated enclosure to disperse charging gases; siting them in a vehicle skirt compartment open to the outside air will be satisfactory. The compartment should allow for easy maintenance and be painted with an acid-resisting paint in case of spillage. The batteries need to be charged, when the vehicle is powered, by a mains-powered automatically regulated charger. The charger should have an output of at least 10 amps and must not overcharge the batteries when switched on for long periods.

It will also be useful if the technical batteries are charged from the vehicle alternator when the vehicle is in motion. If the vehicle alternator is of insufficient output, or a different voltage to the technical batteries, then it may be possible to fit a second engine-driven alternator. An automatic changeover system should be provided to prevent the batteries being charged from two sources.

Alternating current power systems and lighting

The a.c. power requirements of a sound recording mobile are varied and complex. A simple low-budget mobile will run on a single 13 amp input, whilst a fully equipped high-specification mobile will need approximately 50 amps. (The previously mentioned Digital Control Vehicle was originally calculated, based on manufacturers' maximum data, as requiring 180 amps or approximately 50 KW.) The measures to be taken to cover safety, diversity, and the ability to run basic facilities on minimum power require considerable thought.

The prime consideration is the safety of people operating and associated with the mobile. In the field, power earths can be questionable and only large venues may have a low-impedance earth available. At large, regularly visited venues negotiation with the owners or management company should lead to the provision of a supply point of sufficient capacity with low-impedance earth; often direct connection to the supply bus bars will be possible. The power control system needs to incorporate an earth loop impedance tester, for checking the incoming supply before connection to the mobile, and built-in sensors for deviation in 'earth' potential.

On the basis that saving lives is more important than saving a recording or broadcast, devices which are now known as Residual Circuit Breakers (RCCB), previously called Earth Leakage Circuit Breakers (ELCB), should be connected in series with each power input to the vehicle and with any power takeoff provided for use with external equipment. This device monitors the current in live and neutral conductors; any imbalance of more than 30 mA integrated over a 30 msec period will cause the device to trip and disconnect the supply. If calculations show that a normal standing earth current of 30 mA or more will be set up by equipment (for example, switching mode power supplies in the control desk), then an RCCB will not be satisfactory. Additionally, experience shows that RCCBs have a tendency to trip with 'spikes' on the supply. If this is not acceptable, a bypass switch could be used during actual recording, but this removes any safety precautions.

An alternative system to the RCCB is a proprietary system with current transformers in the live and neutral lines, and a processing circuit which provides an aural and visual alarm when a pre-set limit has been exceeded. This system has been used successfully in several recent mobiles and provides an excellent indication on an ammeter of standing current deviation, with a lamp and mutable buzzer giving the alarm at the pre-set limit. The system requires a closely defined power and earthing system, which is necessary anyway to avoid circulating currents, common impedances, and a generally 'clean' earth for the technical equipment.

Earthing

Earth connections are needed to all exposed metal surfaces (except those trim plates and fittings screwed to the wooden body with no possibility of power connecting to them), conduits, boxes, and mounting racks. Also, earths are required to vehicle chassis (best connected where any vehicle battery is joined to the chassis), technical battery negative terminal, incoming mains connectors, and technical equipment earth system. All these earths should be flexible, of the correct cross-sectional area, and individually connected to a single point. This must be the only point where earths join, and is known as a 'star' system. Sub-branches from each star leg are acceptable provided no loops are formed.

Additionally, for use where a venue has no supply earth or where the earth is not low-impedance, an earth spike should be supplied and connected to the central point of the star earthing system. This spike can be driven into the ground and kept moist to provide a reasonable earth, the longer and broader the better, but practicalities often limit the spike to a 1 m long 25×25 mm section passivated steel rod.

Power distribution and systems

The total load of all equipment installed in the vehicle must be calculated, with an allowance for extras. Ignoring apparently insignificant small loads will be regretted in service.

The loads should be listed and split into distributions such as technical, general services, and air-conditioning. Careful planning and switching of these distributions will allow for a high current input powering all systems and changeover switching to lesser current inputs powering reduced facilities at low-power venues. For example, if the 'ventilation' mode of the air-conditioning is run from the 'technical' or 'general services' distribution and high-demand technical equipment (such as a multitrack recorder) run from the 'air-conditioning' distribution, then, at a low-power venue, switching off the 'air-conditioning' distribution will allow the mobile to function, albeit in a limited form.

Each mains input should be fed through waterproof connectors and flexible cable. Phase indication to guard against live/neutral reversal should be installed. A pair of series neons, one green connected to the live and one red connected to the neutral with the common point connected to earth, will show an inversion. Voltmeters and ammeters are also useful to show supply and load parameters.

The use of more than one supply phase is not recommended, but, providing the loads are kept separate and adequate monitoring provided with safety in mind, there is no reason why a system cannot be devised. The BBC's Digital Control Vehicle has three power inputs, each capable of a 60 amp load, to cope with the high demands. The power system has been designed so that the vehicle can run on one, two, or three phases, dependent on available supply.

Miniature circuit-breakers (MCB) of the magnetic type are recommended as the fuse element in each distribution, for two reasons. Firstly, they repeatedly trip on overload currents at defined points and do not suffer the metal fatigue failures which seem to affect wired fuse links subject to vehicle motion. Secondly, MCBs double as switches for deliberately isolating circuits for load shedding or servicing.

The circuit configuration recommended is a double-pole MCB feeding each distribution, with single-pole MCB feeding individual subcircuits or items of equipment. The type of MCB should reflect the fusing diversity, ensuring that a subcircuit MCB fails before its distribution MCB, and also the type of load. Various delay curves, to cope with inrush currents and motor start characteristics, are available and need to be chosen to suit manufacturer's data.

MCBs are also available, and are recommended similarly, for d.c. power control systems. A power control cabinet housing all the ammeters, voltmeters, RCCBs, MCBs, alarm devices, etc., with d.c. systems separated by a metal barrier from a.c., is recommended for a tidy installation. An electrical engineer or specialist company will be able to advise, design, and construct such a control cabinet.

However, in view of the vibration caused by vehicle motion which all the wiring and fittings will be subject to, suitable precautions need to be taken to ensure that connections do not work loose, and a few pointers are necessary in component choice and installation. Where possible, crimped stud and spade terminals should be used, particularly on power control cabinet components; screw terminals and soldered joints should be avoided. If screw terminals have to be used, say on socket outlet plates, then some form of anaerobic liquid should be used to 'lock' the threads. Metal conduit or trunking should be used, with any sharp edges over which cables pass protected by grommets or plastic edging strip. Ducts should be formed for multiple cable runs with a.c. and d.c. power separated by a metal barrier, and all circuits should be run as 'pairs', that is line and neutrals must be run together; common neutrals are not acceptable. If the mains supply subcircuits are run as on the ring main principle, the earth conductor must not be included in a ring. These two latter points will help avoid hum loops being generated inside the vehicle.

Obviously, adequate power outlets should be available where needed to avoid trailing cables inside the vehicle.

Lighting

As mentioned under 'Direct Current Systems and Lighting', it is recommended that switchable fluorescent light be designated on a changeover supply from d.c. to a.c. These fittings can be used in all compartments, except the small lockers, to provide general high light levels.

For more intimate operational light, eyeball fittings recessed into the ceiling around the acoustic treatment will provide light sources which can be aimed at specific areas, such as tape machines, engineering bay, and the like. Over the central desk similar fittings or spotlights can be used. Incandescent lighting is recommended for operational purposes, because, although its power consumption is higher than fluorescent, dimmers can easily be provided. Dimmer types should be chosen for minimum radiation of radio-frequency interference.

Technical equipment and systems

The heart of a mobile is its technical equipment, which must be capable of coping with all the production demands made of it. The vehicle must be as flexibly and fully equipped as possible, with spare space for the addition of equipment on a temporary basis neatly and well engineered. Attention must be paid to the provision of as many permanent facilities as possible. The more basic facilities like equalization and dynamics which are built into the control desk the better, as valuable space would be taken up with these common requirements on outboard racks.

Also, narrower desk modules will allow more of them to be fitted inside the restricted width of the vehicle (see Plate 19). As noted before, the internal width with acoustic isolation build-up will be approximately 2.3 m; this will house 56 60-mm modules or 64 35-mm modules, allowing for desk framework. The useful desk width can be maximized by omitting end cheeks, or the wall build-up can be relieved in the desk area, though this of course will provide lower isolation.

All equipment should be examined for robust construction, tidy well-supported cable forms, and retention of components and subassemblies. Good-quality connectors must be used, gold-plated if possible. Poorly located boards with edge connectors tend to 'saw' their way through the mating connector in

Plate 19. Mobile recording vehicle, showing control and monitoring area (Photo: BBC)

transit and should be avoided. For a simple mobile, a 25-8-2 desk is likely to be satisfactory, whereas in a large mobile a 48-32-4 desk could prove limiting. One solution to this problem is to provide a fixed submixer adjacent to the main desk to cope with the overspill.

Mobiles are often co-sited with TV or PA companies using a common mic rig, and it becomes necessary to decide who supplies phantom power and has the primary signal and who has split feeds. It is wise to arrange that the mobile control desk has individually switched phantom power per channel, with some form of indicator of the presence, or absence, of phantom power, no matter what the source. Mic signal splitting is occasionally the source of argument over who has the primary feed; it is not wise just to parallel feeds, as a fault on one will reflect directly on to all the others, apart from the obvious impedance mismatch. A system with a straight through route for the primary feed and a transformer coupled with resistor buffers for the other routes (normally two will be sufficient) works well. The transformer will not pass phantom power and therefore the primary route supplies it. The transformer needs to be selected with the source and load impedances and the dynamic range of signal levels in mind. A splitter must work equally well on the least sensitive dynamic microphone, through capacitor microphones, to the high-level output of synthesizers. Also, the breakdown of flash-over voltage between primary and secondary windings of the transformer with associated wiring and connectors needs to be considered. Some safety regulations insist on the complete unit surviving a 4,500 V flash test! This could be critically important in a mobile operating under adverse weather conditions or near power installations. A recent large mobile includes this type of splitter permanently installed on all seventy incoming mic lines, as well as a number of portable units for additional or alternative on-stage splits.

Signal cables from the performance area to the mobile need to be robust mechanically and electrically. Multi-core microphone cables terminating in a converter box will save much time and frustration compared with single-pair cables. Specially developed multi-way cables with a thick plastic outer sheath and an internal overall electrical screen enclosing individually screened 'quad'-type inner cores are strongly recommended for use in the hazardous environment met by mobiles. Braided, or at least lapped, screens should be chosen in place of foil to minimize handling noise. A 'quad'-type inner array, wired as a pair, very effectively reduces the thyristor dimmer noise that plagues a mobile operating near lighting rigs. The multi-pin connectors used also need to be similarly robust. Military specification types with gold-plated contacts and positive cable clamp and lock mechanisms are expensive but are worth while in minimizing contact problems and maximizing cable survival. Obviously, multi-way connectors are not suitable for all circuits, and a number of single-pair and screen connectors of both gender for miscellaneous circuits will be useful.

The mobile ends of the cables need to connect to an easily accessible 'termination panel' close to the main cable storage. If a number of cables can be run from the vehicle simultaneously rigging time will be greatly reduced. It is recommended that this panel be on the rear face of the vehicle, protected by a door or weather-proof roller shutter against road dirt. The rear of a vehicle in motion is a low-pressure area, and road dirt will be sucked against the vehicle and permeate all but a well-sealed compartment. Recent large mobiles have had all or part of the termination panel installed in a walk-in storage area to protect the connections still further, and also to provide an undercover plugging area for the technical staff. Vehicle internal wiring connecting the termination panel to the desk patch-bay (jackfield) through a properly planned and accessible cable duct can have a lower specification than the external cables. The internal wiring must be flexible to cope with vehicle motion, but individual or multi-way foil-screened cables will be satisfactory.

Even on small mobiles the desk patch-bay is the interconnection point for incoming and outgoing circuits, internal tie-lines for tapes, reverberation, flanging, and similar units and a host of desk input, output, insert circuits. As space is limited, especially as the patch- bay needs to be close to the control desk operator, using normal 6.3 mm B-gauge telephone-type jacks means that either the patch-bay is reduced in size and facilities or it has to be divided. The latter is usually unsatisfactory and so a method of achieving the former must be found. Fortunately, mini or bantam 4.4 mm jacks solve both problems. Patch rows with 48 or even 56 bantam jacks can be fitted on a standard 19-inch panel. Reported reliability problems with bantam jacks have now been solved by a new product from a UK manufacturer.

It is recommended that as much normalling (innering) as possible is included on the patch-bay to avoid trailing cords and movement noise on low-level circuits. For earthing reasons, circuits leaving the patch-bay should be wired as three-wire with the screens interconnected only at one point, usually at the patch-bay itself. Great care needs to be taken to avoid earth loops and spurious earths, particularly on low-signal-level (less than $-20\,\mathrm{dBV}$) circuits. Jacks themselves need to be mounted on insulating material to break earth continuity between individual jacks and the frame, except where the desk manufacturer advises otherwise.

Many control desks have the option of transformer or electronically balanced inputs/outputs. At the risk of fuelling controversy, the author recommends that microphone inputs are transformer-coupled, with longitudinal stop filters, as even with special cables high common-mode voltages can be generated in the cables of a mobile rig. It is almost impossible to predict the electrical/magnetic conditions which will be met at each and every possible mobile venue. Some manufacturers have produced very impressive figures, supported by 'golden ears' judgement, for their electronically balanced inputs, but the risk factor for a mobile desk is too great. Internal, and therefore predictable, circuits to tapes and other equipment are ideal candidates for transformerless techniques, but the transformer coupling should be repeated for any circuit that supplies signal outside the vehicle, including all line-send amplifiers for any output sent by PTT line. In the UK, British Telecom is very strict about connection to any part of its network, so any intended line-send amplifier should be checked for compliance with BT's regulations. The distribution amplifiers can usefully be employed as common buffers for all equipment requiring a feed of desk output, such as stereo tapes, audition cassettes, and external monitoring.

The type of tape machine is again a matter of preference, as most modern types are independent of supply voltage and frequency, both of which can be unsure at remote sites. If any video or simulcast work is envisaged, then centre-track time-code is necessary. Any multitrack recorder and associated noise reduction system needs to be selected bearing in mind size, weight, and compatibility with relevant automation and synchronizer systems as well as capacity to handle large-diameter spools to give longer recording times. Larger mobiles will carry two multitracks for continuous recording or to provide a greater number of tracks by synchronizing the two machines (see Plate 20). A synchronizer with a time-code generator will be useful for pre-striping the tape without tying up the automation computer to generate time-code.

Reverberation and other modern digital signal processors have already been mentioned in terms of patch-bay space, but the siting of these units can present problems. Either they can be installed in an engineering bay with all the

Plate 20. Mobile recording vehicle, showing 2-track and 24-track recording area (Photo: BBC)

distribution and line-send racks and myriad remote controls wired to the desk, or the units can be housed in an operationally more statisfactory position. Small racks can be accommodated under the control desk edges, providing you have not craftily hidden the wheel-arches there. Alternatively, a 'flight deck' arrangement placed over the control desk and built as part of the ceiling can be used. This is quite useful as it is close to operator and safe from accidental damage and inadvertent reset, although a bleed of air may be necessary for cooling.

Comprehensive monitoring and direct tape-to-tape dubbing systems which are completely independent of the control desk are great savers of time and aggravation. A stereo tape system needs to be arranged so that each tape machine can be lined up independent of whatever the other machines or the control desk are doing. A similar system for the multitrack(s), without the dubbing facility, will also be useful. The system designed for some recent mobiles incorporates a microprocessor-controlled switching system with miniature relays as the signal-switching element. This has proved very successful, as hard wiring is minimized and reduced to printed circuit board/connector wiring only. The oscillator used for tape line-up must have a very low output impedance capable of supplying a constant voltage to a low-impedance load— two 32-track tape machines, with all tracks paralleled, may present a load as low as 160 ohms.

A sound mobile intended to work with TV or video companies will need a video system to interface with them. Also, a CCTV system, enabling the vehicle operator and producer to see the artists, is almost essential and need not cost a lot.

Basic video facilities needed include tie-lines from the termination panel, video patch-rows, distribution amplifiers with integral equalizers, and a simple switcher for routing to a colour monitor. This colour monitor can be the same one as for CCTV, and if a TV tuner is required this can be a separate device routed as a source to the switcher. A video cassette recorder, suitable for professional cassettes (if possible, capable of acting as master to a synchronizer), will complete the system.

Communications are also vital, not only between the mobile and artists, but also to stage technical personnel and PA/TV companies. Control desks developed for studio work usually incorporate sufficient talkback to cues and studio loudspeaker circuits to cope with artist communication, but extras will be needed for other functions. A radio talkback system (beware problems of frequency allocation and power output) will be useful in communicating with mobile personnel on stage or around the venue, with switched talkback input from the desk microphone(s) and 'back contact' input for cue purposes.

Additional talkback circuits, fed as above but pluggable on the patch-bay to termination panel tie-lines for onward connection as necessary, should be adequate for most requirements. If a customer requires anything more complex, then a purpose-designed communications system will be necessary.

Reverse talkback into the mobile is also needed. This can be achieved using existing control desk provisions or via additional low-quality self-powered loudspeakers. A simple multi-input talkback mixer can be useful to avoid too many small loudspeakers cluttering up and confusing the operational area, although some people prefer a number of RTB loudspeakers to provide directional coding of talkback source.

In a short chapter, it is impossible to cover all aspects of mobile recording vehicles, let alone their use and inherent problems. In closing, the author would like to thank his colleagues who have assisted him with work on mobiles, in particular E. W. Taylor of BBC Research Department for his work on acoustic design and related problems. The author would also like to thank the Director of Engineering, British Broadcasting Corporation, for permission to publish.

Reference
Taylor, E. W., *The Acoustic Design of Outside Broadcast Vehicles*, BBC Research Department Report Number RD 1984/3.

14

Maintenance

Malcolm Atkin

As the audio industry has matured, there has been a great increase in the number of small manufacturing companies producing an ever-wider range of equipment for studio use. This in turn has meant a changing role for the maintenance engineer. He may no longer be asked to build an in-house mixing console, but he will be expected to have wide experience ranging from antique musical instruments to the merits of the latest softwear updates. He will also be the person whom everyone calls upon when things go wrong.

A professional studio should have a fully qualified technical engineer available at any time that a session is in progress. Whilst breakdown cover can be provided by mobile service engineers, this should not be a substitute. A true recording studio is always being modified and re-equipped as tastes and methods change, and a full-time engineer who has intimate knowledge of the installation and operation of all the equipment in the studio is a tremendous asset to the company.

Basic requirements

All studios require a separate service area, preferably with natural light and on the same level as the studio to allow free movement of machinery. Adequate deep-bench area at waist height will be required for each engineer, with plenty of power outlets and patch access through the more common connector systems of the studio to central music sources, oscillators, monitor systems and the like. If space permits, specialized service areas for items like tape machines are very useful and a good monitor system is essential for checking out equipment. All workshops will require some metalwork facilities, and if possible these should be sited in a separate area with a solid bench and vice. A good selection of tools will be required for panel and box manufacture. If more ambitious projects are envisaged, a pillar drill, fly press, small grinder, and a selection of hand power-tools will prove invaluable.

Up-to-date manuals should be maintained for all equipment. All modifications should be noted at the relevant point. Where more than one manual of the same type exists, master copies should be clearly marked. Diagrams or sections which are used frequently should be copied and filed separately so that the originals are kept in good condition.

Trade magazines are a valuable information source and should be filed and continuously updated. Modern reference and text-books will also be very useful.

The spares holding in any studio will be subject to many considerations. The first of these is obviously financial, since heavy investment here will have to be at the expense of something else in the studio. A fine balance has to be struck between availability and accessibility from manufacturers' stock and the omnipresent danger of excessive down-time. Even the best maintenance team cannot be expected to repair faulty assemblies immediately, so the spares holding in many areas is quite obvious. Experience is the best guide as to what should be kept. A careful log of all faults will soon help to show which areas need most careful attention to stock levels.

General electronic spares are best kept in wall-mounted storage systems. Specialized items for specific equipment are best stored separately, so that the spares kit can be carried to the equipment if required.

Electronic test equipment

The test gear required for a studio workshop would consist of most of the following items:

1. *Audio function generator.*
2. *Counter timer.*
3. *RMS voltmeter*—a good-quality high-impedance meter calibrated in dB is a useful reference item.
4. *General-purpose multimeter*—some modern meters incorporate dB scaling, and hand-held counter versions are invaluable for circuit board check-out.
5. *Oscilloscope*—to cope with modern digital equipment; a minimum bandwidth of 50 MHz is required.
6. *Bench power supply*—capable of supplying ± 30 volts.
7. *Spectrum analyser*—an accurate analyser is an expensive item but very useful in many areas, especially for checking loudspeakers and microphones. A pink-noise source will be needed.
8. *Audio analyser*—an expensive bench item which can feature many of the above. Whilst very useful, it should not be provided to the exclusion of single-feature test equipment.
9. *Distortion analyser*—again a fairly expensive item, probably not as useful as most of the above, and may be featured in other analysers.

A well-equipped workshop will also contain most of the following items:

1. *Test tapes*—essential to the line-up of tape machines; should cover all equalization standards, speeds, and tape widths. These tapes are expensive and

should be used only as a reference. Before running a test tape on a machine, the heads should be de-magnetized and the tape path cleaned. Each project should have tone runs made from these tapes for daily checks. With care, multiple-tone tapes can be made for use in copy rooms and the like to reduce the use of master tapes. Test tapes should be stored in a cool secure place well away from stray magnetic fields.

Computer software on floppy disc systems should all have back-up copies made and be stored as above. Working copies of these programs should be generated at regular intervals to minimize failures. Software in EPROM form should also have back-ups available.

2. Complex console strips will require the use of *custom electronic test jigs* for testing or repair without recourse to the console facilities. An example is shown in Plate 21.

3. *A microphone test jig*, consisting of a speaker inside an anechoic box, with fixed connections for all types of microphone, will enable comparative response tests to be made in conjunction with a spectrum analyser. To this end, the frequency response of all microphones should be logged when purchased.

4. *A variable mains transformer* can be very useful in the repair of old equipment. Sometimes a fault condition can be noticed and corrected before full power is applied.

5. *Accurate spring gauges* are required for setting tape tension. Some transports require the use of a Tentelometer, a proprietary mechanical meter. If hand

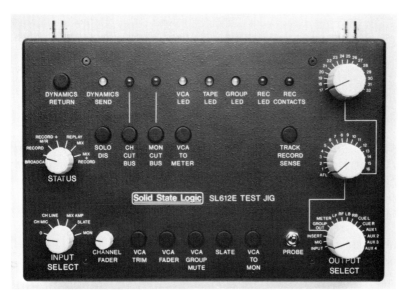

Plate 21. Solid State Logic test jig allowing bench testing of all logic and audio functions of individual modules (Photo: SSL)

lapping of heads is carried out, lapping blocks and realignment jigs will be needed.

6. Some manufacturers supply *extender cards* for their equipment. These are essential in many cases to access card assemblies whilst still in circuit. Extenders should be obtained for all relevant studio equipment.

7. *A vacuum de-soldering station* is a useful addition. Repair of high-density digital boards requires very careful handling to prevent damage to components and board pads. LSI circuits directly soldered to the circuit board are almost impossible to remove by any other method.

8. In order to connect test equipment to all other studio systems, *interconnecting leads* of all types are required. As most test gear uses BNC connectors, this problem is considerably reduced. A lead rack holding test leads of a uniform length on a convenient wall space will prove both tidy and time-saving.

Hand-tools

Every technical engineer requires a comprehensive set of hand-tools. These tools are often personal property and are usually best selected by each engineer, as individual preferences vary widely. As well as a good selection of general tools, a studio engineer will also require specialized cabling tools and a basic set of metal-work tools.

A good tool kit will contain most of the following items: sets of flat-blade, cross-point, and jewellers' screwdrivers; temperature-controlled soldering iron; set of BA and metric spanners and Allen keys; wire cutters—several sizes; pliers—general and long-nose; wire-strippers; sleeve-strippers; sleeve-expanders; internal and external circlip pliers; small torch; inspection mirror; small hacksaw; steel ruler; set square; scriber; files—various; small hammer; centre punch.

Communication

As in all businesses, good communication is essential if a studio is to provide an effective service to its clients. A studio maintenance department is no exception to this rule and must therefore have well-established methods of communication within the department and to the other areas of the studio operation. Since technical engineers are not primarily employed for their business skills, these procedures are best kept as simple as possible. As many studios operate shift systems, a diary is an invaluable method of logging session requirements and problems. An order book is also very useful for logging spares deficiencies as they arise, so that re-ordering can be a routine function not requiring a stock control meeting!

Control-room log-books are also an invaluable method of communication. The log-book should be constantly used by both the balance engineer and the technical staff to note faults, modifications, and routine line-ups. As a diary, it should note any special requirements of the day, and a constant dialogue should be encouraged.

Routine procedures

Most of the following procedures can be performed by an assistant engineer, since they consist largely of aural and visual checks. A few minutes checking before the start of a session can save a lot of aggravation later, since a known problem can often be bypassed until a repair can be effected.

Tape machines

As the prime function of the studio is to record, the performance of the tape machines is paramount and should be checked first. Obviously at the start of any set of sessions the tape machines should be subjected to a rigorous line-up procedure using a tone reel containing tones at 1 kHz, 10 kHz, 100 Hz and a record pad. Usually the studio will have been left set up from the previous day's work, and the following checks should be sufficient to spot most problems. (Checks should be performed only after the equipment has been allowed to warm up.)

Analogue. 1. Carefully clean all audio head assemblies and guides with pure isopropyl alcohol or a recommended head-cleaning fluid. Care must be taken to prevent excess fluid getting into bearings, etc.

2. Play the tone reel and observe the level at 1 kHz at the machine meters, noise reduction systems (if used), and console meters from both the playback and sync heads of the machine. If possible set up a roughly equal mono mix from all tracks and note the level.

3. Observe the tape carefully in the play mode. It should show no tendency to 'ride' on to any of the guide systems. Special attention should be paid to the travel over the head assemblies.

4. Play the high-frequency tone from the tape and again check levels. The mix set up at the 1 kHz tone will still read approximately the same level if the azimuth is correct. Note that EQ and effects returns in the system will distort this check.

5. Ensure that all the cue sends are cut and noise reduction systems bypassed, then set the desk oscillator to 1 kHz at the standard operating level and route to all multitrack sends. Observe the meter level on all console sends.

6. Set the multitrack to read input and again observe the level on all recorder input meters.

7. Set up the record pad (a sample of tape from the same batch as the master tapes) on the tape machine, zero the machine clock, and record 1 kHz tone on all tracks for at least one minute. Observe the level returning from tape on the machine meters.

8. Leave the machine in record mode, set the oscillator to 10 kHz, and carefully observe the level returning to the desk. In analogue machines some transport problems become very apparent at this stage.

9. Set the desk oscillator to 100 Hz or lower and again observe the returning level at the console. Secondary gap effects on analogue machines may prevent an exact level match unless the send frequency has been carefully selected, and so this should be used only as a guide.

10. Finally, return to the beginning of the record pad and deselect the desk oscillator. Initiate record on all tracks to erase the previously recorded 1 kHz tone and listen carefully to each track individually at a high monitoring level, remembering to lower the volume between each track select. Many problems related to erasure, biasing, tracking, and system noise will quickly become apparent. Even if no other checks are made before a recording session, a test similar to this should be performed. Any noise reduction systems should now be switched back in and checked.

Digital. On digital storage media, cleanliness is even more important. A very small amount of dirt can cause an uncorrectable error. As with analogue machines, heads and guides should be cleaned at the start of the session and at convenient times during the session. Cotton gloves should be worn if the tape needs to be handled, as perspiration can cause problems.

Machine performance can be simply checked at the start of a session by recording pink noise on all tracks and observing the error correction indicators on playback. These indicators should be checked constantly during the session, as excessive correction will eventually lead to muting. Recordings should be copied immediately if a problem is detected.

Other areas
1. Check control room diary/fault book.
2. Check desk power-supply indicators if fitted.
3. Check amplifier and computer installations for signs of overheating.
4. Check headphones and monitor systems with music. Fresh ears will sometimes hear substandard reproduction not noticed at the end of a long day.

Periodic procedures

As well as the daily performance checks outlined above, the whole control room and studio should be subjected to regular service procedures. In a busy studio these will have to be fitted around the booked sessions. A good manager will ensure that preventative maintenance is not allowed to be left for too long and that adequate time is allocated for it.

Tape machines

The easiest solution is to carry a spare machine. Since this will be invaluable for editing, copying, slaving, and extra tracks, as well as providing a very quick method of fault-finding, there is a strong case for its inclusion in every professional studio. Servicing is then a matter of finding suitable periods when the spare machine is not required and removing it to the service area. Periodic checks should be performed as follows:

(a) *Head assemblies*. On analogue machines, a constant visual check should be maintained for signs of uneven wear due to wrap or zenith problems and gap breakup on ferrite heads. If a bad wear pattern is allowed to persist, a very expensive head will need to be replaced long before its rated life. Heads should also be checked regularly for high-frequency spacing loss and lapped when a problem is detected. Note that manufacturers' alignment jigs are essential when refitting heads. Some assemblies also feature flutter idlers. As their name suggests, these idlers can induce flutter if bearings are not maintained.

Most head assemblies will gradually become magnetized if left unchecked, with a resultant loss of high frequencies due to erasure. It is therefore essential that all head assemblies are demagnetized on a very regular basis. Care must be taken to move the degausser slowly at all times in the vicinity of the heads, or the head could end up being more magnetized due to a sharp movement. All master tapes and test tapes should be moved well out of the way before using one of these tools, and the tape machine must be switched off to prevent the replay electronics being damaged.

Head assemblies on digital machines should not be touched, as they are set to a much finer tolerance and can be set up only by the manufacturer. Degaussing of these heads is not normally required.

(b) *Transport*. Many transports have pinch roller systems which push the tape against a capstan motor to control absolute speed. These assemblies need regular inspection and cleaning to ensure that they do not cause tape tracking problems. Tape tension should also be checked regularly since a small drift can have dramatic consequences on the sound reproduction. Digital tape, being much thinner and more fragile, requires greater tension control from the transport. Hence even greater care must be exercised when setting up these machines.

(c) *Electronics*. The alignment of the tape machine electronics is necessary to compensate for variations in manufacture of the magnetic tape used on the machine, as well as the more usual processes of wear and ageing. Thus the electronics are subject to far more routine adjustment then other items. As well as the rudimentary checks mentioned above, there is a strong case for checking sensitivity and bias on a regular basis, especially if tapes from different batches are being used on the same set of sessions. As the heads wear, the resonant circuit on the erase head will change, and realignment for optimum erase depth is required on an occasional basis. If the master bias oscillator frequency is adjusted for any reason, then all bias trap circuits must be checked. Digital machines also require regular checks in many areas to ensure a standard performance, and these should be performed in accordance with the manufacturer's specification.

Monitor systems

Being the acoustic interface between the electronics and the human ear, the control room monitor systems are exposed to constant subjective analysis by all present. A modern studio monitor usually requires multiple power amplifiers, both passive and electronic crossovers, and nowadays many studios also utilize $\frac{1}{3}$ octave equalizers for further control. The loudspeaker itself is a very fragile item and can be damaged by even moderate abuse. This can be further aggravated by a badly set-up system. Adjustment should be attempted only with a clear understanding of the strengths and weaknesses of the whole monitor chain. An accurate spectrum analyser is an essential item for setting up the system but should be used only in conjunction with critical listening tests on known material.

Consoles

The modern music recording console is a very complex system containing several hundred front panel controls and switches. It is therefore inevitable that faults may occasionally be present for some time before they are noticed. For this reason, the whole console should be periodically tested in an orderly fashion and every function and indicator exercised. In addition the following checks should be made:

1. Noise measurements from every strip should be checked against the specification.
2. Meters and gain structure should be checked against an external reference.
3. Faders should be checked for smooth operation and visually inspected for the ingression of various solids and liquids.
4. Power supplies should be checked for correct voltage and trip operation. A console's performance can be severely compromised and damage can occur through incorrect power rails.
5. Computers for automation and general data storage are now commonplace and complete digital systems a reality. If the computer is maintained in a properly air-conditioned and dust-free environment, then these systems

can be extremely reliable. Floppy-disc storage systems should be regularly cleaned and the whole system occasionally checked by running diagnostics programs.

Microphones

Microphones are at the boundary between the recording system and the sound source, and as such are subject to the same vagaries as loudspeakers. A microphone can be rejected for no other reason than that it does not sound right. Microphones are extremely fragile devices and should be treated with great care. Capacitor microphones are very sensitive to dust and spittle, which can give rise to a severe loss in level. This type of microphone should be regularly inspected and the capsule occasionally cleaned with distilled water, exercising extreme care. Any wrinkling or rupture on the capsule surface will probably compromise its performance and can be repaired only by the manufacturer.

Ribbon microphones contain a large permanent magnet and again are very fragile. Do no carry two in the same hand or leave near magnetic tapes. Storage should be in separate compartments. Repair of some types can be effected but ribbon replacement is again best performed by the manufacturer.

The third main category is dynamic microphones. These are probably the most robust and are very popular in high-risk areas. Consequently most problems are due to physical damage. Apart from reassembling the pieces, capsule replacement by the manufacturer is usually the only answer.

Leads

Connecting leads are one of the mainstays of any studio. They are used in all areas to customize the whole set-up to the session's requirements. Since leads are in essence very simple pieces of equipment, there can be few problems more frustrating on a session than having to cope with faulty leads and connections. All microphone leads, machine looms, and ancillary looms should be visually checked at frequent intervals for signs of damage, and connector clamps securely tightened. Regular testing for continuity on leads in high-risk areas, such as microphone leads, should be performed. A simple test facility in the studio will prove very useful. Console patch bays usually utilize GPO or bantam jack systems. Due to the high insertion force and contact method, the patch jacks used in these fields are usually made from unplated brass. Regular cleaning is therefore essential to maintain these cords in a usable state.

As well as the standard looms and leads, every studio soon collects a myriad of interconnecting leads to cope with different clients' personal equipment. Storage of these can be a problem since some will be only rarely used. Whenever possible these leads should be made a standard short length to enable them to be hung straight on a cable rack.

Custom equipment

One of the more interesting tasks for the technical engineer is the construction of specialized equipment for the studio. Today manufacturers provide a very wide range of equipment for the audio industry. However, a manufacturer can only respond to a sizeable demand, and a creative studio environment will soon discover the need for something not available commercially. Projects of this nature can provide very worthwhile innovations; however, careful consideration should be given at an early stage to the cost, time required, and eventual usefulness.

Another inevitable consequence of a wide choice of manufacturers is a lack of common standards. This means that the studio in many cases has to provide the interface. This is a more common area for custom-made equipment and can provide the technical engineer with ample scope to exercise his talents.

Reliability

Since the repair of unserviceable items is one of the main tasks performed by a technical engineer, a clear understanding of the main causes of failure is essential. Reliability is the subject of many text-books and is a major consideration during the design of any equipment. The problems facing a technical engineer are of a different nature. Until all else fails, he must normally assume that the design engineer has done his job correctly; previous experience is usually the greatest asset when identifying the causes of malfunction. Most components follow what is colloquially referred to as the 'bath tub' law (see Figure 14.1). Failures usually occur in the first few hours, or after a number of years. In the interval between, the equipment is usually very reliable, as indicated in the diagram.

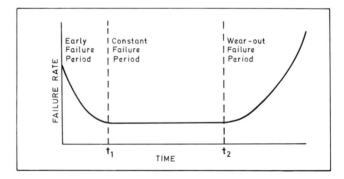

Fig. 14.1. The 'bath tub' curve, showing the periods when maximum failure rate may be expected

Active electronic components

Curiously enough, if the design of the electronics is good and the equipment is thoroughly soak-tested by its maker, then this is one of the more reliable areas. Unfortunately, it is also the area which can cause the most problems, as failures can be quite subtle, often not appearing until the equipment has warmed up for hours, and then sounding faulty to only the most fastidious ears.

Passive components

Again this is usually a very reliable area, with the notable exception of capacitors. These have a definite shelf-life, after which they should be discarded. Capacitors in old equipment which has been left switched off for a long period will also be highly unreliable. Equipment in such a state should be gradually brought up to full power by using a variable transformer on the mains input.

Electromechanical components

Switches, connectors, relays, loudspeakers, disc drives, and the like all come under this heading by virtue of the fact that they all have moving parts. Problems due to wear, contact corrosion, metal fatigue, arcing, and so on are a major cause of failure and can occur at any time due to use or abuse. Troubleshooting is usually quite easy although repair can sometimes be very awkward.

Solder

In common with most metals, solder is prone to fatigue. Its widespread use in the field of electronics is due to its low melting-point and good conductivity. However, it is mechanically very weak, and every joint must be supported, usually by the use of a printed circuit board or support pillar. Excessive vibration (plenty of that in the average studio), loose nuts on switches, and similar problems will very quickly cause failure of solder joints.

The other main problem with solder is the phenomenon known as the 'dry joint'. This is due to oxidization of the surface of the component pin and/or board prior to soldering, or lack of flux during soldering. This gives rise to a solder joint where surface tension prevents a true weld. Unfortunately, this can sometimes give rise to a joint which initially looks and performs perfectly. Progressive oxidization can then cause a high resistance and fault condition long afterwards.

The third problem is one of temperature. A low-temperature soldering iron will cause the flux to burn off prematurely, giving rise to all the problems mentioned above. When the solder does finally melt, it will make a very crystalline joint, and there is a very real danger that the component will have been damaged.

Other facilities

As well as the actual recording systems, every studio requires a complex electrical and air-conditioning system. Whilst the audio technical engineer should not be expected to undertake installation and full maintenance of these systems, he should have a clear understanding of their operation.

Electrical

All electrical systems should be installed and tested by a qualified electrician. Insurance cover may well be invalid if current regulations are not strictly adhered to. These regulations now require that all exposed metal surfaces are locally bonded to earth. This can sometimes be at odds with the audio requirement to have only one earth connection, to prevent induced hum loops. Great care must be taken at all times that both these requirements are fully met. Most professional studios have a separate technical earth rather than relying on the supply authority's connection. A high-impedance earth can be the root cause of many studio technical problems and should occasionally be checked. There is also a legal requirement to provide an emergency lighting system, adequate fire alarm system, and fire extinguishers. These should be regularly checked and logged. If any filming or video shoots are envisaged, there will be a heavy power requirement for lighting. Suitable outlets at an accessible point would be very useful.

There is a tendency amongst lighting design engineers to install banks of thyristor dimmers. Whilst these can be successfully installed in a studio and can look extremely decorative, great care should be exercised in the siting of all such cable runs, which must be installed in earthed steel conduit or mineral cable.

Most mains-borne interference can usually be removed by an isolating transformer on the main control-room power feed in conjunction with a radio frequency filter. Mains voltage regulation should not normally be necessary, with the possible exception of location work. If heavy voltage fluctuation is a problem, there is probably a good case for a generator.

Air-conditioning

An effective air-conditioning system is expensive to install, maintain, and run,. Since a failure in this area will quickly bring a studio to its knees, the technical engineer should have a working knowledge of its operation and protection systems. Much money can be wasted in a system which has been incorrectly designed, operated, or maintained.

One of the acoustical requirements of a studio control room is a very quiet environment, isolated from external noise sources. This is usually achieved by the use of heavy lagging, isolated structures, and sealant, all of which give rise to a room perfectly sealed against heat dissipation. Coupled with 10 kW of heat from machinery and lighting, this calls for an air-conditioning design which needs to work irrespective of the external temperature. A system with spare capacity will soon pay dividends.

Any plant room should be visited daily to ensure that no pumps or compressors have tripped. The water or air send and return temperatures should be noted, together with pressure readings from compressors etc. Standby systems such as pumps need to be rotated regularly and filters cleaned or renewed.

RECORDING TECHNIQUES

15

The spoken word

Derek Taylor

At the outset it should be said that all microphone balancing is an art or a technique, not a science. It is impossible to lay down hard-and-fast rules. If you say something must always (or never) be done, the next day some combination of programme requirement/studio acoustic/equipment characteristic will prove that the only practical solution is the exact opposite. The only criterion is: will it sound right to the listener? The only way of being sure is to try something and listen. This may take time, and this chapter is designed to help to obtain the desired result more quickly by using well-tried methods and avoiding some of the pitfalls. In practice the method adopted will be controlled to a large extent by the facilities and time (that is to say money) available.

A single voice

The simplest form of programme likely to be encountered is a single voice, as in a talk or story reading. The object should be to produce an accurate representation of the person's voice, not iron out all voices to a standard 'good quality'. The best plan with a new speaker is to go into the studio and have a short conversation to put him at his ease, and listen to the character of the voice.

The studio should have a reverberation time in the order of 0.25 to 0.4 sec at all frequencies, with an even decay. Also, it should not be too large, something in the same order as an average living-room. A large studio, even if it is dead enough, sounds wrong. The impression of size is given by the timing of the first reflections; the longer these are delayed the larger the studio sounds. Acoustic screens can help in such a case. Arranged round the microphone, they may not have any significant effect on the total reverberation time but they will provide an earlier first reflection.

The microphone type is not critical provided it has a smooth frequency response. Avoid bright-sounding microphones as they often have resonances in the upper-middle and top registers which emphasize sibilance. Some microphones which sound good on orchestral strings are very unpleasant for speech. At the same time, working too close to a pressure-gradient microphone (i.e. a ribbon or any microphone with a figure-of-eight polar diagram) will produce bass tip-up which can alter the character of a voice and reduce clarity. This bass tip-up effect is much reduced with cardioid microphones and absent from omnidirectional microphones, as explained in Chapter 6.

As far as microphone mounting is concerned, the choice is either a table stand or suspension from the ceiling or a boom. If a table stand is favoured, strict precautions must be taken against mechanically transmitted bumps and rumble. Movements of the speaker may produce very little airborne noise but considerable mechanical interference. Also, structure-borne noise, such as footsteps in another part of the building, traffic, or tube trains, can be a problem. The stand should be as solid as possible to provide inertia and there should be no loose joints or spigots to cause clicks and rattles. There should also be effective mechanical decoupling between the stand and the microphone. Flexible swan-necks are quite effective for lightweight microphones. In studios rigged permanently for speech, such as news studios, a more elaborate set-up is often used, with the swan-necks mounted via shock absorbers on to a low steel frame bolted to the floor. They then protrude through a hole in the table without touching it. It is probably simpler to avoid these problems by suspending the microphone over the table from a boom with elastic cables.

The type of table and accessories, such as script racks, can have a significant influence on the sound quality and ruin an otherwise good studio. Any hard objects can reflect sound up into the microphone, but they will only reflect sounds whose wavelengths are shorter than the dimensions of the reflecting surface. Thus the bass frequencies are not affected, but the higher frequencies are reinforced with a slight delay, or phase shift, and often produce a harsh quality.

Tables should be as acoustically transparent as possible; a satisfactory construction has proved to be a wooden frame covered on top with perforated steel (approximately $\frac{1}{4}$-inch holes closely spaced) covered with loudspeaker cloth (Figure 15.1). An $\frac{1}{8}$-inch thick layer of felt or plastic foam under the cloth can increase its stability; the cloth must be fixed only at the edges, as any movement on the steel may cause rustling noises.

Script racks or lecterns should also be acoustically transparent, but they are a doubtful asset. It is important that the speaker should speak directly into the microphone, and a rack may help him to keep his head up and not read into the table, but the script can also cause HF reflections, and the angle of the rack may direct the reflections into the microphone. It is better to encourage the speaker to hold the script up at the side of the microphone so that he can speak directly into it and simply divert his eyes to the side to read.

The main factors in the balance of a single voice are perspective and volume, and both are a function of the distance from the microphone. The perspective is the ratio of direct-to-indirect sound being picked up—the further away the more indirect sound is received. However, this is also a function of the polar diagram of the microphone (see Chapter 6). A figure-of-eight will pick up less reflections from the studio walls, ceiling, and so on than an omni-

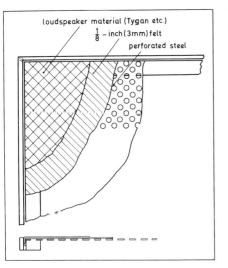

Fig. 15.1. Construction of an acoustically transparent talks table

loudspeaker material (Tygan etc.)
$\frac{1}{8}$ – inch (3mm) felt
perforated steel

directional microphone, as it is live on only two faces. Thus the ribbon will sound closer.

Very close working for speech should be avoided (except for special effects in drama). The technique of modern singers who handle microphones like ice-cream cones should be actively discouraged. A good working distance is about 45–60 cm, and even this is too close for a ribbon microphone unless the bass tip-up is countered by a filter to roll off the bass. Any close working tends to emphasize the mechanical processes of speaking giving rise to teeth clicks and lip-smacking; also, the sheer weight of breath can cause blasting and popping of the microphone, especially on the explosives—Ps, Bs, etc. A windshield can help with the latter. If the speaker has a weak voice, it is generally better to increase the microphone gain than to allow him to sit too close to the microphone.

Electronic frequency correction is best kept to a minimum. As mentioned, a high-pass filter may be essential when using a ribbon microphone, but, with a very woolly voice the addition of a presence hump can improve clarity; conversely, some reduction of the higher frequencies, such as a presence dip, can help a very sibilant speaker, but discretion must be used.

Interviews and discussions

The term 'balance' is more applicable where two or more voices are involved. For interviews it is more natural for the two people to be facing one another, and if their voices are of similar volume and have no unusual characteristics a ribbon microphone placed between them will serve very well (Figure 15.2). The figure-of-eight polar diagram will accommodate the two speakers whilst being

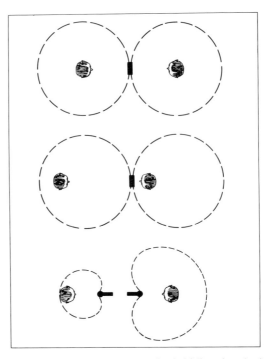

Fig. 15.2. Two evenly balanced voices can use a single bidirectional microphone (top). If one voice is louder, the distance can be adjusted (centre) or separate cardioids can be used (bottom)

dead to the rest of the studio, and will therefore reduce any ambient noise. If the volumes of the voices are not well matched, however, the microphone can be placed nearer to one speaker than the other, but there is a limit to how far this can be done as there is the danger of excessive bass on one voice. Also the perspectives will change. In this situation two cardioid microphones arranged back to back are more satisfactory. The perspectives will be better maintained, as the microphones can be placed at the same distance from each speaker, any bass tip-up is greatly reduced, and the compensation for volume is done electrically.

A cardioid microphone can be used for round-table discussions. It can either be hung with the dead side upwards, which will reduce ventilation noise from the ceiling, or stood on the table. It is even better in a well in the centre of the table, which will reduce problems like script rustles, but of course it may then be subject to bumps if the table is knocked or kicked. A word of warning regarding cardioid microphones may not be out of place here: many microphones sold as cardioid are only so over a restricted frequency range. They are frequently omni in the bass and single-sided in the top, getting narrower as the frequency increases. Therefore, if you are going to work around a cardioid, as distinct from into the front, it is better to arrange the microphone either a little above mouth level, if hanging, or below if table-mounted. This avoids working in the areas where the level is likely to vary with frequency.

As with two-voiced programmes, a single microphone works well if all voices are of similar volume or if all speakers are experienced broadcasters; if not, then a multi-microphone set-up is needed. One cardioid microphone per person is sometimes used. Some news studios have a large D-shaped table with room for a presenter and news-reader on the straight side and up to six contributors round the curve, each with his own microphone. This is a rather elaborate solution, and having a large number of microphones open together in a small studio can cause problems of increased ambient noise, and also phasing due to a voice being picked up by more than one microphone.

Whenever more than one microphone is used at a time, great care must be taken to ensure that they are in phase, otherwise the voice will take on a thin and distant quality. This can cause complications if mixed polar diagrams are involved, as the two sides of a figure-of-eight or a hypercardioid are in opposite phase. Therefore, for example, if a cardioid microphone is placed in the field of the back of a ribbon both microphones may pick up the same voice, but out of phase.

Panel games and quizzes before an audience present problems of their own. The main possibilities are either a long or horseshoe-shaped table with the question-master in the middle and the team split equally either side, or two tables facing each other on either side of the stage with the question-master on one and the team on the other. This is useful if there is a guest artiste who appears for only part of the show, as he/she can share the question-master's table. For the team, one microphone between every two artistes is a practical alternative to everyone having their own. Picking up questions from the audience is best done with a hand microphone on a trailing cable, or a radio microphone passed to the questioner by an assistant. Attempting to pick out one person in an audience with a rifle microphone is often unsatisfactory.

Actuality interviews using portable gear are best conducted by holding a cardioid microphone vertically at about chest level between the interviewer and the interviewee, somewhat nearer to the latter. The habit of some interviewers of holding the microphone first to their own mouth and then thrusting it in the face of their victim for the reply, is disturbing to the person concerned and usually produces a lot of handling noises from the microphone. This sort of technique should be adopted only in cases where the background noise (traffic, machinery, etc.) is excessive and it is not practical to move to a quieter venue.

As stereo portable tape recorders are now common, two tie-tack/lapel microphones can be used, one on each track, and then the interview balanced later in the studio. The two tracks can either be mixed to mono or, if it is going into a stereo programme, the two tracks panned a little way left and right of centre. An interview full left and right would sound too wide apart.

Drama

The balance engineer's job in drama is to provide the actors with a suitable environment which will convey to the listener the impression that the action is taking place in the locations indicated by the plot. This aural scenery is created partly by the acoustics and partly by effects, and within this setting the actors must be able to make convincing moves.

The most important factors in the acoustics of the settings are the reverberation time and the size of the location. To cope with all types of dramatic productions, the studio needs to be fairly large—around 30,000 cubic feet—and the acoustic treatment varied to give different reverberation times in different areas, with curtains to shut an area off if required. A separate very dead or anechoic room leading off the main studio is very useful for outdoor scenes but must be fairly large. Typical reverberation times are 0.2–0.3 sec for the dead end, 0.5 sec for the normal part, and 0.7–0.8 sec for the live end. It is a great advantage if the live end has a carpet which can be rolled back for live scenes or laid to deaden it down and give a bigger normal area. Portable acoustic screens with one reflecting and one absorbing side can be used to modify the studio acoustics and give a larger number of different sets.

Some productions have been recorded partially or completely on location, but this can be very costly, especially in time, and in cash terms if the cast is large. The results can be very good, but finding locations without unwanted extraneous sounds is very difficult. In addition, monitoring conditions are likely to be rather primitive, and if faults are found during the subsequent editing session, repeats may be difficult or even impossible to arrange. Much of television is recorded on location, but in radio drama the entire story has to be conveyed to the audience in sound terms. In television most of the information is in the picture, and unfortunately sound quality has sometimes to be sacrificed. Location pictures may end up with studio sound.

Mono drama

In mono drama the most useful microphone is a ribbon. Its figure-of-eight polar diagram means that actors can face each other, which is more natural and comfortable for them than standing side by side. Also, having two dead sides means that the studio can be made to give the impression of much greater size than its physical dimensions dictate. The reason for this is that our judgement of distance is determined by the ratio of direct-to-indirect sound; the more indirect the further away the source appears. Thus anyone standing close to the microphone in the dead field will not be picked up except by reflections from the studio walls, and consequently will sound very distant. If he then backs away from the microphone and circles round on to the live side, he will appear to have made a long straight approach. To produce the same effect on an omnidirectional microphone would require three or four times the studio space. For normal speech, the actors should not work closer than about arm's length from the microphone, and should step back or turn off slightly when using a very loud voice. However, for very intimate scenes or 'thought voices' they may work much closer, down to three or four inches. In this case it is essential to work across the microphone instead of straight on to it, to avoid popping and blasting. It may well be worth while rigging a cardioid with a windshield close by for the actor to turn to for thought-voices.

A cardioid microphone suspended with the dead side upwards is often used for scenes involving a large number of actors, especially in fairly live acoustics such as courtrooms. This gives much more room to work, and very long approaches and recedes are not usually required.

Artificial reverberation or 'echo' may be required, and a room is often preferred to a plate, as the latter tends to sound metallic on speech. Echo rooms of course take up valuable accommodation, and a reverberation device within the cubicle has a great attraction. As has been said before, the impression of size is determined by the timing of the first reflection; it is therefore desirable to be able to delay the reverberation signal for a large location. Adding straight reverberation will work for a small cell, but for a convincing church some delay is required. A simple way of introducing delay is to feed the echo chain via a tape machine. Switching tape speeds will give some control of the length of delay, or a loop can be pulled out between the record and replay heads and taken round a jockey pulley. In this way distinct repeat echoes, as for mountains, can be produced.

Digital reverberation/delay devices are now on the market and provide a much more elegant solution; in theory almost any acoustic can be synthesized. It may be thought that with such a device a dead studio and one microphone should be all that is required. However, this is not likely to get the best out of the cast, as experienced actors make their moves and project their voices to suit the acoustic, and they require their acting area defined. This may mean only a few hard screens round a microphone in the dead part of the studio for a drawing room, and another microphone in the live side using the whole area for a church; much of the engineer's job of dynamic control will then be done for him.

A typical set-up is shown in Figure 15.3. The requirements of the script are: living-room, outdoor, car interior, office, and courtroom. For this a figure-of-eight microphone on the dead side will suffice for the living-room. The outdoor must be as dead as possible, and is therefore on the same side of the studio but surrounded by soft screens for more absorption. There is no need to use screens on the dead sides of the microphone, and those on the live sides must be angled so that any reflections from them are dissipated into the dead studio and not back at the microphone. No two screens must be parallel, otherwise standing waves will be set up.

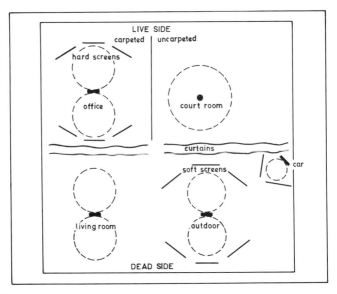

Fig. 15.3. Typical layout for mono drama in a live end/dead end studio with movable screens

The car interior must sound small and boxy, so there must be a reflecting surface very near to the microphone. A good plan is to screen off a corner of the studio and place a ribbon microphone with one live side close to the wall (but not quite parallel to it), with the actors sitting side by side on the other face. The office would be on the live side of the studio with hard screens to reduce the size of the location. If this proves to be over-bright then soft screens should be used.

The courtroom could be the majority of the live side with a suspended cardioid microphone. If this is not bright enough, artificial reverberation can be added, but for a long scene this may be tiring to listen to. It may be better to rig another cardioid or omni microphone high up for atmosphere and crowd reaction and add any necessary reverberation to that. The reverberation times achieved will almost certainly not be those found in real locations, but they should provide suitable contrasts to give the right impressions to the listener.

Sound effects

The addition of background effects will heighten these impressions, especially on outdoor scenes. However, too much reliance must not be put on them. The technique of using only one acoustic and just adding different backgrounds is very unconvincing and distracts from the action of the play.

Effects are divided into two groups, recorded or spot. Spot effects are those done in the studio during the action of the scene, such as doors, crockery, pouring drinks, telephones, and so on. Recorded effects are backgrounds and sounds which cannot conveniently be accommodated in the studio, such as express trains. At one time spot effects were used to simulate sounds which could not be got into the studio, like lead shot on a drum for sea-wash, the thunder sheet, wind machine, and the like, but with the reduction in size and weight of mobile recording gear there is less necessity to fake effects, and with the improvements in transmission and reception it is more difficult to pass them off on the listener.

There may be a temptation to record all effects and play them in from tape or disc, or dub them in afterwards, but it is much better for the actors and much easier to get the perspectives right if spot effects are used when appropriate. The timing of an effect is vital and can turn high drama into farce if mistimed. A good spot effects operator works with the actor and positions himself either alongside or in the same perspective on the opposite side of the microphone, and the scene is acted out naturally. A separate spot microphone should be avoided if possible, as it tends to alter the studio acoustic and distort perspectives when it is faded up; it also divorces the spot operator from the action.

Doors are difficult to make sound convincing. If they are built into the wall for the sake of solidness, they are nearly always in the wrong perspective and sound wrong anyway as there is no room beyond them. Portable doors, on the other hand, are much more convenient and easier to get into the correct perspective but tend to sound flimsy.

The choices of the source of recorded effects and the system of recording depend largely on the time and resources available. Given access to a good library of recorded effects and only a limited time to complete the programme, the choice is obvious. However, if effects can be recorded specially for a particular programme the end-product should be superior. Again, where time is important, effects recorded on disc have the advantage. Given gram decks with a good groove-location system, it is much quicker to find a particular spot on a disc than to spool through a reel of tape. Additionally, storage of large quantities of material is easier on disc, but they must be renewed at frequent intervals to avoid surface noise and scratches. Tape cartridge or cassette systems have a great appeal in theory, but not much practical use seems to have been made of them. This is largely due to the length of time required to make up a set of cartridges for an individual production, or the mammoth storage problems if a library is composed of cartridges. One 7-inch $33\frac{1}{3}$ r.p.m. disc may easily contain twenty or thirty possible starting-points. If each tape cartridge has to start from the beginning, this means twenty or thirty cartridges.

Whichever system is employed, it must be flexible and fast enough to enable the effects to keep pace with the action. It is no good having all the effects in rigid order and duration, with the cast having to wait for cues to allow the effects to happen, for the whole flow of the play will be lost.

Gunshots are very difficult to balance; they either overpeak or, if held back, sound very flat and lack dramatic impact. It is probably better to pre-record them. The microphone gain can be set at normal level and the gun fired about ten feet from the microphone. This will overpeak and distort but the tape will saturate and act as a limiter. When the tape is replayed, it will not need to be held back so far and will give a longer sound with more impact. Some artificial reverberation can also help. Of course a limiter can be used, but this will require experimentation with cutback and recovery times to get the most convincing result.

The usual method of cueing the actors is by cue-light, but where very quick reaction to an effect is required, as with a shot or a series of reactions, it may be easier to use foldback and let the actor react naturally. If the foldback loudspeaker is situated on the dead side of the microphone, and the level kept fairly low, it will not affect the microphone balance. Foldback is also useful for telephone calls where one actor is on the main microphone and one on a distorted microphone in another part of the studio. In this case it may be better to put foldback on to single headphone earpieces.

Stereo drama

Much of what has been said about mono drama also applies to stereo, but stereo does bring its own problems. Most of these are in production rather than technicalities, especially when the programme must be mono/stereo compatible. This compatibility is very important in broadcasting as it must be assumed that the majority of the audience will be listening in mono. Many will be listening on portable transistor receivers or car radios, and only a small proportion of them will be sitting centrally between two stereo loudspeakers giving their full attention to the play. Thus, although directional information will heighten the enjoyment of the production, it must not be essential to the understanding of a situation. Also, stereo gives the listener greater powers of discrimination than mono (the 'cocktail party effect'), and dialogue which is perfectly audible in stereo may be drowned by effects or studio crowd in mono.

The transmission system in use is compatible from the point of view that the stereo listener hears two channels (A—left and B—right) and the mono listener hears one carrying both sets of information (A + B). This is achieved in simple terms by modulating the main carrier with A + B, or M as it is usually called, and a subcarrier with A − B (or S). If a sound is central in the stereo picture it will be equal in both channels and thus, when they are added, will form M (in practice 3 dB up); when they are subtracted, they will cancel completely and produce no S signal. A sound fully left or fully right will produce equal M and S signals. On the other hand, an out-of-phase signal will not produce any M and will be inaudible to the mono listener. Thus the system is compatible, but the programme material may not be, as any phase shifts will tend to cancel. This explains one of the reasons for the preference for coincident microphones rather than spaced pairs in broadcasting. The spaced pair relies largely on phase shift for its effect. With the coincident pair all sounds arrive at the same time (in the horizontal plane anyway) and the stereo effect is produced purely by volume differences, and is therefore potentially more compatible.

The acceptance angles for coincident microphones of different polar diagrams are shown in Chapter 6 (Figure 6.11). It will be seen that a pair of crossed figures-of-eight gives an acceptance angle of 90°. A sound on the X axis will be picked up only on the A microphone, as it is on the dead side of the B microphone, and vice versa on the Y axis. A sound in the centre is picked up equally on both, or in other positions more on one microphone than the other. However, if the sound source is moved round to one side beyond the 90° arc, it will be picked up on the front of one microphone and the back of the other, and so be out of phase. Normal stereo will be produced in the back 90° arc but the left and right directions will be reversed. Working in the out-of-phase angles must be avoided as this will produce cancellations in mono and unpredictable location in stereo.

Crossed cardioids have no back lobes, and therefore there is no out-of-phase area. The useful angle is shown as 180°. This is the full extent of the stereo picture from one loudspeaker to the other. Using the greater angle of approximately 270° will give perfectly acceptable quality but no more width; the level will fall off the further round you go. The area at the back will give a very distant perspective, and the sound is liable to jump from one side of the picture to the other rather suddenly. Hypercardioids give an angle between figure-of-eight and cardioid, about 130°.

The different acceptance angles can be very useful, so variable polar diagram capacitor microphones with two capsules in one case are favoured. However, two mono microphones mounted with their capsules as close together as possible with their axes at 90° are perfectly satisfactory. The fact that the stereo effect is dependent on the polar response means that the two capsules must be very accurately matched at all frequencies. This of course makes the microphones expensive, and even with good microphones the angles should not be taken on trust but should be checked in the studio, as the dead sides are often not true to the theoretical shape and reflections from the studio walls etc. can modify the angles and give a lop-sided working area. In drama the crossed cardioid is the configuration most often used, as it gives the maximum working area. The main thing the actor has to remember is that to move in a straight line across the stage he has to walk in a semi-circle.

Coincident pairs must always be lined up, whether they are in one case or two. To ensure that the gains are equal, the microphone axes must be turned in line, and while an assistant is talking in front of the microphones the engineer listens to the S signal (i.e. both outputs on one loudspeaker but out of phase with each other) and adjusts the gains of the two channels for the null point. The monitoring should then be restored to stereo (in phase), and, with the microphones still facing the same direction, the assistant should walk slowly round the microphones talking continuously. His voice should stay in the centre of the stereo picture. It will become more distant as he passes the dead side (S), but if it moves from side to side the polar diagrams of the two microphones do not match.

With the microphone axes reset to 90°, it is as well to check at which points the voice becomes fully in each loudspeaker. The angle found on crossed cardioids may well be greater than the theoretical 180°, due to inaccuracies in the cardioid pattern. This does not matter as long as the actors are aware of the limits of their stage. Alternatively, with variable polar diagram microphones, the angle can be narrowed by setting them towards the hypercardioid condition.

Working in stereo is more demanding in terms of the studio itself. Much more room is required for approaches and recedes as the dead side cannot be used as in mono. It is very difficult to get a good open-air sound as the stereo microphone reproduces the studio acoustic much more accurately, and thus very large, very dead studios with no ventilation or outside noises are required. Such a studio is unlikely to be found in practice and the best has to be made with what is available. The actors can help a lot with distance by pitching their voices as if projecting, but not using much actual volume. Turning away from the microphone and talking into a soft surface can also help.

Great care must be taken with spot effects to ensure that they are in the same position and perspective as the associated voice. Footsteps may prove difficult, as coincident microphones are usually mounted one above the other, so the sounds from the floor reach the bottom capsule before the top one. This produces a time delay which gives the footsteps a slight off-set. Generally speaking, the greater discrimination given to the listener by stereo means greater realism is needed for spot effects; faked effects become all too obvious.

Recorded effects should of course be recorded in stereo, but these may not always be available. There are methods and devices whereby mono recordings can be used and produce a reasonably convincing result. With crowds, good results can be obtained by pre-recording and taking several copies of the same crowd, starting them from different points in the duration of the effect, and panning them to different places across the sound stage. There are electronic 'stereoizing' devices which rely on introducing some degree of phase shift. These work quite well on some types of effect but not on others, and it is a matter of trial and error, always bearing in mind the need for mono compatibility.

With any stereo effects, care must be taken to get the width in correct scale with the perspective. For example, a horse and cart passing in the far distance would be a point source, and a mono effect panned across would be quite appropriate. However, in the foreground the horse has two pairs of feet and the cart two sets of wheels and would take up most or all of the sound stage. Thus with stereo effects used in a different perspective to the original recording, width and off-set controls are required on the stereo channel to enable the effect to be narrowed and moved. Of course, if two ganged mono channels are used, the width and movement will be controlled on the pan-pots. In fact an effect can start distant and narrow on one side, come closer and wider in the centre, and narrow down and fade out on the other side, but this does require more than the usual complement of hands, so some pre-recording would be indicated.

At one time nearly all radio drama was performed live, and the studio techniques were developed to this end. With the introduction of tape recording and editing, and the added complexity of stereo, there was a move towards rehearsing and recording each scene, not necessarily in sequence, and compiling the production in the editing room as with film. However, with the stress on economical use of facilities and time, there is now a move back to the continuous performance with perhaps difficult sections pre-recorded and played in.

Binaural stereo

In recent years there has been renewed interest in dummy head recording brought about by experiments in Germany to produce a standard artificial listener for evaluating auditorium acoustics. The idea of placing two microphones in a dummy head has been used on and off since the 1920s or even earlier, but only as a source of loudspeaker stereo. During the German experiments, however, some startlingly realistic all-round sound was obtained on headphones, especially those of the open type.

Coincident microphone stereo depends for its effect on a difference in volume between the two channels, derived either from the polar response of the two microphones or a mono source electrically divided between the channels. In binaural stereo, two omnidirectional microphones are placed ear-distance apart, separated by a suitable baffle to give the correct time difference. When reproduced via headphones, each ear receives the sound with a time difference which varies with the angle of the sound source, and only a very small volume difference. Thus the basis of binaural stereo is much nearer to natural hearing and produces a very realistic sound. The quality and realism can be so true that first-time listeners often refuse to believe that the headphones are working and have to take them off to be convinced.

However, although side location and perspective are good, frontal perspective is poor for many people. The usual complaint is that the frontal image either collapses into the listener's head or even moves round behind. A minority of people do get full 360° soundfield and in tests can accurately plot the moves made by the actors in the studio. From statistics taken from listeners' letters received following BBC transmissions of binaural programmes, it seems that although only 26 per cent reported an all-round effect (62 per cent had a front hole or rear bias, 12 per cent did not mention direction), 80 per cent enjoyed the binaural effect and only 0.7 per cent were distressed by it.

The reasons for the differences in directional perception between individuals are not clear. Any sounds on the centre line will have equal time of arrival at the ears, and therefore confusion will result unless other factors can be brought in to resolve it. If it cannot be resolved, the brain puts the sound inside the head towards the back, as with mono on headphones. What these factors are seems to vary from individual to individual, and they probably have their origins in the learning processes from infancy. Sight undoubtedly plays a significant part: most people have difficulty locating sounds in fog or in a wood at night, for example. It is probable that slight head movements are used in normal locating to modify the arrival times in a sort of scanning action, but as the microphones are fixed this facility is lost.

Very accurate models of the head and ears have been made for microphone mounting, but the directional information has not proved significantly better than two microphones spaced by a simple baffle, and the quality and frequency response is degraded. Using a live human head and lodging small microphones in the outer ears may give better quality but no improvement in direction. Interestingly, experiments using extremely small microphones placed in the ear canals right up against the drums produced better results for the person involved but not for others.

One microphone set-up often adopted uses a 10-inch diameter Perspex disc with a rod through it, a little off-centre, and two electret lapel microphones mounted ear-distance apart on the rod on either side of the disc. This gives a simple, light, and unobtrusive arrangement which in practice gives at least as good results as the more elaborate and scientific designs.

Effects and music must also be recorded in binaural. If mono is used, the sound is in the middle of the listener's head; even stereo effects, although they may have some width, can only move a short distance beyond the ears and are confined to a band across the head. Binaural effects perspectives can stretch into the far distance.

Edits tend to show up much more than usual, as an angled cut interrupts the background ambience in one ear before the other and can cause a sudden sideways jump and back again, so vertical cuts must be used. Therefore mixing or dub-editing is often employed instead, although the less equipment the signal has to go through the better the quality. From the broadcasting point of view, if the binaural system could be improved in the frontal area it would be ideal, as it would produce all-round sound which could be transmitted over a stereo network without modification.

16

Classical music
Adrian Revill

The techniques involved in recording classical music are different from those used to record other types of music, and this is largely because the philosophy behind the recordings is different. The record industry uses the term 'classical music' to encompass many styles, not only the music of Mozart and Haydn but also large-scale Romantic works of Wagner, twentieth-century orchestral music, and a growing catalogue of early music. All of it was originally conceived for public performance, and there is behind every recording of classical music the idea of a kind of perfect performance captured to give the listener the effect of a perfect seat in a concert hall. The producer and engineer keep this in mind, even when hundreds of takes need splicing together from sessions recorded in a London church which has never seen an orchestra before; it is not necessary to recreate the occasion to represent it. Although for some the only way of achieving the desired result is to adopt the purist approach, with a single microphone and long continuous takes with no editing, the majority of classical recordings are not produced in this way. They employ various microphone techniques, and, to understand how these have evolved, it is necessary to consider the parameters which make up the sound of a classical recording.

Sound characteristics

Figure 16.1 shows a straightforward orchestral layout with the simplest microphone technique: one coincident pair in position *A*. Consider the result of recording a reasonably long passage. On playing it back, a number of characteristics of the sound will be noticed. Probably the most obvious one will be *perspective*. Is the overall effect that the orchestra is too close and too dry, or too distant and indistinct? Is it all in the same perspective or are some of the sections closer than others? The next feature to be noticed will probably be width or *spread*. Are the violins cramped up in the centre of the picture, or so widely separated from the basses that the notorious 'hole in the middle' is apparent? Further listening might reveal a passage where the woodwind is playing a musically important part but it is not clear because the strings are too prominent; this is a problem of *balance*. Throughout the playback, the listener will consciously or unconsciously register the overall *sound quality*. Is the bass

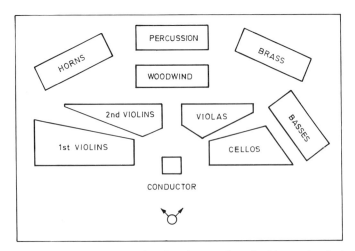

Fig. 16.1. Normal orchestral layout, showing the use of a coincident pair of microphones

full and firm, do the top strings sound harsh or edgy? Would the terms boxy or smooth be applicable? All these factors are interrelated; it is perfectly possible to make a fine recording with deficiencies in one or other of them, but *quality* is the most important parameter in classical music recording, and will be considered first.

Quality

When discussing recording quality, we can assume that the technical deficiencies of the medium which were once inevitable are now of secondary importance. The recording machines should be virtually perfect, the mixing desk will have a flat frequency response, and the microphones will be the very best available. The most important factors which influence recorded quality are not so amenable to engineering solutions. The single most important contribution is probably the acoustic of the recording studio, and very few venues are capable of producing top-class recordings even in the best of circumstances. Many buildings which have made successful recording venues were not built as studios—town halls such as Brent and Walthamstow, churches such as All Saints, Tooting, and former church buildings such as St John's in Smith's Square and Henry Wood Hall are examples. Excellent recording acoustics can be found in unlikely places, but generally they will be large buildings considered a little too reverberant for live performance, and they will rarely be built of concrete and glass. The other most important contribution to recording quality will be the quality of the musicians, since only a great orchestra will produce the quality of sound required to make the best recordings. On many occasions, the engineer and producer can worry about the microphones, fuss about their position, and make many changes at the start of a session, only to notice that the quality improves as the musicians 'warm up'; the playing becomes more secure and the actual recorded sound quality starts to improve.

Certain technical deficiencies will adversely affect quality, of course. The microphones must be chosen not only for their on-axis frequency response, but should produce a uniform response off-axis as well, since the reverberant soundfield will contribute much to the overall effect. Equalization of microphone channels can play a part, and microphone positioning must be sensible.

Perspective

In the simple recording envisaged earlier, we may have been concerned that the orchestra sounded too close. Opinions differ about perspective, but generally classical recordings are made with a reasonable amount of reverberation. If this is overdone, orchestral detail may be blurred and the impact lost, but the very dry recordings produced in the early days of the industry reduced the scale of the performance, making the orchestra sound small and reducing the apparent dynamic range. The recording venue plays an important part here too. For example, large concert halls may have long reverberation periods but sound relatively dead in the stage area, so that microphones placed close to the stage will produce a dry unreverberant sound, whilst the loudest musical passages excite the main reverberation of the hall, causing the perspective to shift. It is frequently necessary to rig 'space' or reverberation microphones towards the back of the hall, and there are several possible configurations (see Figure 16.2).

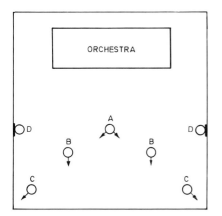

Fig. 16.2. Adding space microphones: (A) backward-facing coincident pair, (B) back-facing cardioids, (C) spaced omnis, (D) pressure zone microphones on wall

Any of the normal stereo types can be used, including a backward-facing coincident pair, spaced cardioids, omnis, or pressure-zone microphones. The space microphones should in themselves produce a balanced sound, and should not be too distant, or time-delay effects will make satisfactory blending into the mix difficult.

As important as the overall perspective are relative perspectives, and the general aim with an orchestral recording will be a realistic gradation of perspective, with, for example, the woodwind sounding rather more distant than the strings. The single microphone pair used in the first example (Figure 16.1) can therefore be moved backwards or forwards to produce the desired effect; moving further back will produce a more reverberant result, with more uniform perspectives. The dangers of moving the microphone too close are that, whilst the strings may be brought into the correct perspective, the instruments towards the rear of the orchestra will be disproportionately distant.

Spread

As the single coincident microphone is moved backwards and forwards, the apparent width of the orchestra will change. The usual aim is to fill the sound stage with an even spread of orchestral sound, whilst the positioning of instruments and groups of instruments is unambiguous and credible. Using the single microphone pair, the spread, perspective, and balance are closely related, and they all depend on the position of the microphone and the polar diagram selected. Usually a compromise position has to be sought.

Balance

This is not necessarily the most important parameter in recording classical music, despite its predominant concern to the engineer and often the producer. For purely orchestral music and an orchestra with good internal balance, a satisfactory recorded balance is not particularly difficult to achieve. Indeed, if only single coincident microphones are available, there is little one can do to affect it. If the microphone is placed too close, then the nearer instruments will be overbalanced relative to the more distant ones, but at a reasonable compromise position deficiencies in balance can only be improved by the musicians themselves. This is where the notion of 'natural balance' comes in, although it is a term to be viewed with suspicion. Recording balance may not be 'natural', in the sense that techniques are adopted to change the balance which would be heard by a listener seated in front of the orchestra. Very often the acoustics of the recording venue will influence this. The recorded balance should sound realistic and give the correct musical prominence to orchestral sections or soloists. It is always worth checking by listening in the studio, if serious adjustments seem to be demanded, but it is certainly not the experience of the record industry that placing one microphone in the 'best seat in the house' necessarily produces the best recordings. The most obvious case of the difference between recorded balance and natural balance would be that of songs with orchestral accompaniment. In the concert hall, the vocal part would often be covered by the accompaniment to the extent that at times the voice may be inaudible or the words unintelligible. To reproduce this balance on record would be unacceptable, and, since recordings began, techniques have been adopted to give unnatural prominence to the soloist. In the early days, recordings almost obliterated the accompaniment, but they were sold on the name of the prima donna rather than the composer. To some extent the tradition lingers on, although the famous Decca recordings of Wagner's *Ring* made by John Culshaw in the 1960s were characterized by a full orchestral sound supporting the vocal lines, which resulted in recordings that sounded exciting, satisfying, and also natural, and which perhaps influenced taste away from over-dominant soloists.

Recorded balance is a major preoccupation of the engineer and producer, and the following sections will describe techniques which have been evolved to control balance, but which at the same time affect all the other parameters which make up the sound of classical recording.

Single microphone pair

Once the decision is made to employ a single coincident-pair microphone technique, the only decisions remaining are the choice of polar diagram and the distance from the sound source. As the polar patterns are switched from cardioid to figure-of-eight, the stereophonic image widens and the amount of reverberation, picked up on the back of the microphones, increases. As the microphone pair is moved away from the source, the stereophonic image narrows, the amount of reverberation increases, and the perspective of the whole recording will change. Very often a suitable compromise position and setting of the polar responses can be found. The height of the microphone pair can also be chosen to optimize the balance. Normally a height of 3–7 m is typical, with the intention of reducing differences in perspective between the rear and forward sections of an orchestra by increasing the height. However, an improvement in balance can adversely affect quality, since, for example, violins do not sound their best from directly above and a warmer tone can be picked up from a height nearer to that of the instrument. Thus it can be seen that all the parameters of the recording, perspective, spread, balance, and quality are interrelated, and that they should all be considered when any alteration is made in the microphone's position or polar response.

It can also be seen that certain deficiencies cannot be corrected with this technique, and the use of additional microphones is often required. Before these are considered, mention should be made of non-coincident microphone techniques.

Spaced pairs

Although some recordings are produced with non-coincident pairs of microphones, spaced a few centimetres or sometimes a couple of metres apart, the approach will be similar to the coincident technique described above. A different approach, using much wider spacing, is shown in Figure 16.3.

One of the earliest methods of producing stereophonic recordings of classical

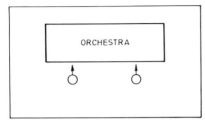

Fig. 16.3. Spaced pair

music used a widely spaced pair of microphones. This is still the basis for more complex layouts, but in itself it rarely produces satisfactory results. The stereo imaging is imprecise and frequently the effect is of no definition in the centre of the sound stage, giving a 'hole in the middle'. The advantage of the technique, however, is the presence and attack coupled with width, which makes the recording superficially more impressive and glossy than coincident microphone techniques. Indeed, unless considerable care is taken, a single coincident pair can produce a recording of the normal orchestral layout which favours the middle of the orchestra in balance, spread, and tonal range. The spaced-pair technique produces recordings of almost exactly opposite character, which verge on an extreme reproduction of width and tonal balance with undue prominence given to the back desks of violins and basses (not usually the best players in the orchestra).

A more commonly employed layout is the use of three microphones, where the centre one fills in the 'hole' and acts as a pivot for the main pair. In this layout it is common to use omnidirectional microphones for all three, or sometimes cardioid microphones for the outer ones with an omni for the centre. It is worth noting that the centre microphone has to be very carefully mixed into the picture, otherwise it can reduce the width by an unacceptable amount.

Hybrid techniques

Starting with a single coincident pair, it is a natural step to add one or more 'spot' microphones to enhance soloists or important orchestral sections; it is a short step from this to a technique which attempts to cover all the important sections of the orchestra with individual microphones in addition to the main coincident pair. Figure 16.4 shows a typical microphone layout for a large-scale performance.

In producing a balanced result, the engineer will often use the coincident pair as a kind of camera to suggest the orchestral positions. The outputs of the mono spot microphones are then panned to the same positions in the picture, and their levels increased until their contribution is just audible. With care, this technique can produce recordings with very clear spatial definition and very accurate control over the balance. Perspectives need to be carefully checked, to avoid giving too much prominence to less important sections, but the recording

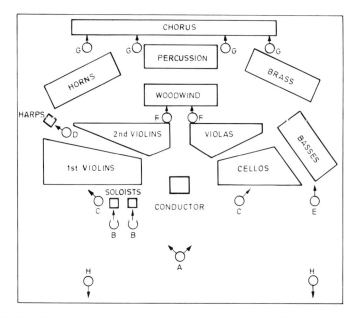

Fig. 16.4. Hybrid microphone technique for large-scale work: (A) main coincident pair, (B) solo microphones, (C) string reinforcement, (D), (E) examples of spot microphones, (F) spaced pair on woodwind, (G) chorus microphones, (H) space microphones

quality, although open to criticism on theoretical grounds, can also be superior to that produced by single microphone techniques.

Concern is often expressed that such an approach can give tonal distortion, due to the phase cancellation between different microphones which are picking up the same source. In practice this rarely seems apparent, probably because not only are the sources separated by a large number of wavelengths' distance but the reverberant soundfield is extremely complex, so much so that a mathematical analysis is impossible. Quality can suffer, however, by injudicious choice of microphones, and it is necessary to choose types which have a very good off-axis frequency response.

Critics of multi-microphone techniques can point to a body of evidence: recordings spoilt by crude mixing, faulty balance, and distorted perspectives. Certainly, considerable skill is required of the engineer, but the technique is extremely flexible and capable of instant control from the sound mixing desk. For this reason it is very commonly employed for live radio and TV broadcasts as well as for specially mounted studio recordings. In its favour it can be said that many of the best recordings of classical music issued in the last two decades use the above technique or a similar one derived from spaced microphones—and therefore a truly multi-microphone approach.

Multi-microphone technique

In the layout shown in Figure 16.5, no main pair or cluster is used, the sound being built up from a number of mono microphones positioned over sections of the orchestra. Coverage depends on the layout, and is most effective when engineer and producer have full control over the seating arrangements, so that closed-circuit recording sessions are often engineered in this way. The sound picture is built up by careful balancing of the microphones on each section according to musical requirements, and the spatial balance is achieved by the addition of spaced pairs or trios. The two parameters interact, however, and care should be taken to ensure that microphones are at similar distances from the sections with similar microphone amplifier gains. Typical heights will be between 2 and 3 m above the musicians, and once again omnidirectional microphones are frequently used, especially for the string sections.

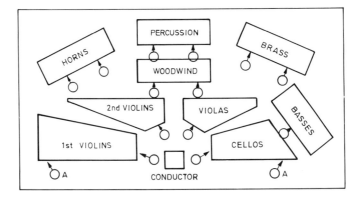

Fig. 16.5. Multi-microphone technique: note that the microphones all face outwards, and the wing microphones (A) are often omni

It is possible to cover straightforward orchestral recording with about a dozen microphones, but the technique is capable of considerable expansion. The CBS quadraphonic recordings produced in the 1970s used up to eleven microphones on the woodwind alone. Nevertheless, it is impossible to mike up each individual pair of musicians, as one would in a TV or light music studio, and less than twenty microphones is the norm. The technique has been evolved for classical orchestral music, is very usable for operatic and choral recordings, and can be adapted for modern symphonic music. The remainder of this chapter will look into different categories of classical music and suggest microphone techniques which are appropriate.

Orchestral music

As seen above, a coincident technique, a hybrid technique, or a multi-microphone technique are all capable of producing highly satisfactory results. The music to be recorded remains the most popular section of the record catalogue—from Mozart and Beethoven through to Stravinsky—and the aim will be to produce the effect of large forces smoothly blended. The control of dynamic range will have to be undertaken carefully, but on the whole this is not the most difficult type of music to record.

Chamber music

From string trios to wind octets, this category of music is in itself wide. A typical challenge can be the recording of a piano quintet (piano, 2 violins, viola, and cello), as shown in Figure 16.6. Despite the small forces involved, such a

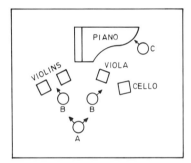

Fig. 16.6. Piano quintet: (A) main coincident pair, (B) possible spot microphones, (C) possible piano microphone

combination can produce very difficult problems of balance and perspective for the engineer. Chamber music in general is not easy to record, since deficiencies of balance are immediately and glaringly obvious, variations in perspective are very apparent, and the positioning needs to be accurate and convincing. A simple coincident microphone technique should be tried if possible, but it is frequently not totally effective. It must be said that the presence of a grand piano in any combination of chamber music proportions usually presents a problem, since much of the repertoire was conceived for instruments producing less volume than those used today. The piano is frequently both too loud and too distant, and a hybrid or multi-microphone technique is frequently needed to achieve a satisfactory result. Thus Figure 16.6 shows a main coincident pair A, in combination with possible spot microphones B and C.

The position of the musicians is extremely critical. They will have spent long hours practising together, and for the producer or engineer to move them around to suit the microphones will simply result in an inferior performance. It is essential that the musicians are seated so that they are comfortable, have good lines of visual and aural communication, and can produce the standard of performance which is the basis of the record.

Pianoforte

As mentioned above, it is not always easy to record a grand piano. In Figure 16.7 position *A*, the tail balance, is frequently the most effective approach, giving a good tonal balance from an instrument with the lid open. Coincident microphones in position *D* can also produce good results, and sometimes a combination of mono microphones at *B* and *C* with a coincident pair at *D* is effective. It is often necessary to use such a set-up to minimize the distortion of perspective which can occur where the top two octaves of the instrument sound more remote, more reverberant, then the middle and bass.

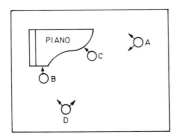

Fig. 16.7. Piano: showing some possible microphone positions

Voice and piano

Figure 16.8 shows a typical layout for recording a singer accompanied by piano. It is usually necessary to introduce a solo microphone *B* and to balance this against the main pair at *A*. For certain passages, piano microphones at *C* and *D* may also be needed. The problem with these layouts is one of separation, which is sometimes not helped by a soloist who does not wish to see any microphones nearby, or who moves backwards at times to lean on the piano.

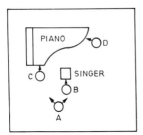

Fig. 16.8. Piano and voice: (A) coincident pair, (B) solo spot microphone, (C) and (D) possible piano microphones

Early music

The move towards 'authentic' performances of early music solves certain problems for the recording engineer and producer. Early music was probably not intended to produce the same smooth blend to which we have grown accustomed with nineteenth-century composers. It may have been that the different tonal qualities of the instruments were exploited for dramatic effect, or to clarify the part writing. Authentic performances will use instruments with gut strings played with lighter bows, which sound different from the more frequently encountered modern variety. Also baroque wind instruments sound very different from their modern counterparts, so that the engineer should approach the recording with an open mind. However, the forces employed will have been chosen so as to eliminate problems of balance, and this may suggest that a more simple microphone technique can be employed. Yet the recording should not be too distant or else the clarity and articulation of the performance could be lost, and the distinctive character of the sound might not be fully reproduced. A hybrid or multi-microphone technique has produced many very effective recordings in recent years of baroque music. For recordings of earlier, Renaissance music, a similar approach may be required, with the very unusual and distinctive qualities of the instruments contributing their own balance problems.

Modern music

There is a considerable catalogue of modern orchestral music now on record. Recording techniques need to be sophisticated for the venture to be sucessful, and the engineer and producer require an open mind since the tonal effects intended by the composer are very often unusual and extreme. The dynamic range is also often very difficult to control, and can be made more difficult by the large size and ungainly nature of the score. It is helpful for the composer to contribute to the discussions of balance—the only category of 'classical' music where such help is usually available!

General considerations

Dynamic range

The wide dynamic range of classical music poses particular problems for the recording engineer, for although modern digital media can record and reproduce the full range encountered, satisfactory records for home listening will not be produced without some restrictions. The aim is to give the effect of a wide range, without either the pianissimo passages being inaudible behind domestic noise or the fortissimo passages causing distress or offence. In the past, engineers were taught to control the range using a carefully marked-up score which, from rehearsal or a previous take, had settings noted to accommodate the loudest passages. The main fader setting was then carefully reduced in the bars leading up to the climax so that, without further alteration, the peaks just reached maximum permissible level. This does not often produce the most convincing results, and more experienced balancers will adapt the technique to incorporate 'potting the peaks', that is acting like a musical compressor by reducing gains actually during the loudest passages.

Live performances

The recording, or radio or TV broadcasting, of live classical music performances places a number of constraints on the techniques adopted. There is usually no possible control of seating or orchestral layout, and microphones need to be unobtrusive (or, for opera, invisible). Microphone booms are rarely acceptable, so that vertical microphone stands and slung microphones are normal. Because of its foolproof nature, the single coincident-pair technique is often a good start, and a hybrid technique based on this is that most commonly employed. Space microphones need very careful positioning if they are to capture reverberation without audience noise. Since retakes are impossible, it is frequently necessary to use multitrack recording to cover balance problems caused by accidents, or by the changes in acoustic when an audience is present. At rehearsal, when the concert hall is empty, the mix will be different in many respects from that needed for the actual event. For instance, considerably more reverberation, natural or artificial, is almost always required.

Mixing classical music

Whatever technique is employed, the actual process of mixing classical music for a satisfactory balance is not the same as that used for other types of music. Despite the label on a channel stating '1st Violins', the channel or track when 'soloed' will appear to have most of the orchestra on it as well—often louder than the violins. Mixing becomes a process of carefully balancing the outputs of several such sources with intentionally poor separation, and it is only when pairs, or groups of channels, are balanced spatially that the intended picture is built up. Little equalization is needed, but artificial reverberation often helps the closer microphones to be mixed in without distorting perspectives. Artificial reverberation has even been used to good effect on recordings from St Paul's Cathedral.

Throughout the recording, the score should be guiding the eye and ear, and all alterations should be made with careful attention to the interaction of balance, perspective, spread, and overall recorded quality: a demanding business.

17

Popular music

Mike Ross

For the purposes of this chapter I shall describe the guidelines for recording popular music, which falls into two main categories: (*a*) orchestral music with rhythm section as used for easy-listening albums, TV background music, and television commercials, and (*b*) small ensemble rock and pop groups aimed at the popular music charts. This chapter could in no way be described as definitive, as the methods and ideas of today's producers and engineers vary considerably, but I shall try to describe the basic approach, which can be modified to your own requirements.

Setting up the recording session

The engineer should have some prior contact with the record producer or arranger, or in some cases the musicians, before the start of the session, to assess the type of music which will be recorded and the approach required. Most producers have a preconceived idea of how they would like the finished recording to sound, and they will try to impart these ideas to the engineer, who will then set up the studio and equipment accordingly. The engineer should also establish how many tracks on the multitrack recorder the producer wishes to use at the initial recording stages. In most cases where every section of the orchestra is recorded at the same time, all tracks can be used because overdubbing will not be necessary, although it may be wise to keep at least one track free for any last-minute change of heart.

In the case of working with pop or rock bands, only a few tracks are used during the initial stages of recording, and much overdubbing of electronic keyboards, guitars, and vocals will take place during the latter part of the session. Therefore the more tracks left open for overdubbing the better. This will make the engineer's job easier at the mix-down stage, avoiding the need for sharing tracks, which results in several sounds on the same track requiring different amounts of echo and equalization.

The engineer should also establish with the producer what kind of recording equipment should be made available. During the last decade the main standard has been 24-track analogue recording at a speed of 30 ips using the Dolby noise reduction system, although many producers and engineers prefer to record without Dolby. Instead they use a higher recording level, sometimes as much as 6 dB above the standard operating level. As much overdubbing is required by rock bands, it soon becomes apparent that more tracks are needed, so a second 24-track recorder is sometimes brought into the studio. This second machine is synchronized to the first recorder using time-code recorded on one track of each machine. This time-code is read by a synchronizer such as the Audio Kinetics Q-Lock which locks both machines together in perfect sync.

If the use of a second multitrack recorder needs to be avoided for the sake of time or expense, a second option known as 'track bouncing' is open to the engineer. Two or more recorded tracks can be mixed together by replaying these signals from the sync heads of the multitrack machine through the recording console, adding equalization if necessary, and re-recorded on to any available spare tracks. The original tracks can then be erased and used again for overdubbing. It should be noted that this process results in a generation loss, so signals of a wide dynamic range should not be re-recorded in this way, as tape noise will be increased. The most favoured approach to this system is when recording vocalists who perhaps need to record several vocal parts which require triple-tracking. Once all the parts have been recorded, using as many as nine tracks, these can then be bounced down to two available tracks in a stereo picture, leaving nine tracks available for future overdubs.

Digital recording techniques are now becoming more common as producers and engineers are being made aware of the advantages, such as the lack of tape noise and saturation problems often found with analogue equipment. There is also greater track availability in the 32-track digital recorders now being used, and the 48-track recorders soon to become available. In fact, track availability is not so important in digital multitrack recorders, as track bouncing can be performed many times due to the lack of tape noise and generation loss.

All this equipment information should be confirmed with the producer before the session commences, ideally several days ahead, so as to allow the studio time to organize availability. On the day of the recording session, everything should have been well prepared, as time wasted is money spent, especially when working with professional musicians working on a set fee for a three-hour session. Correct preparation ahead of the session combines to create an easy and relaxed recording environment.

Studio layout

In an effort to obtain maximum separation for every section of the orchestra and each instrument of the rhythm section, it is frequently necessary to adopt a multi-microphone technique, using directional microphones with each microphone or series of microphones being fed to its own track on the multitrack recorder. The orchestra used for popular music usually consists of four main sections: no. 1 strings, no. 2 woodwind, no. 3 brass, and no. 4 rhythm (made up of drums, bass guitar, electric guitar, piano, electronic keyboard, and percussion). It is important for musical and recording purposes that the members of each main section are seated together in their own separated parts of the room.

The major problem with recording large orchestral works is excessive leakage between instruments. Brass and drums, due to their extreme dynamics, can cause the most serious problems, leaking into the microphones above the string section and causing the drums and brass section to sound 'distant' and lacking in focus. For this reason, the drums are often set up inside an isolation booth. The drummer will then wear headphones or 'cans' so that he can hear the other members of the orchestra. A talkback arrangement should be organized for communication between the control room, conductor, and drummer. The brass section is separated from the rest of the orchestra by high acoustic screens. It is not possible to isolate the brass section completely as they need to retain a certain open acoustic quality, not always possible when using isolation booths. It should also be noted that, with the drums in the isolation booth, the other members of the orchestra will need to hear them, and the engineer will organize folding back the drums into the headphones worn by the orchestra.

Figure 17.1 shows a typical seating plan for a popular orchestral session in a modern recording studio. It will be seen that the string section is set out in the live area of the room. Although artificial reverberation can be added at the mixing-down stage, it is more beneficial to achieve reverberation acoustically, resulting in a much larger string sound with the minimum of players. Of course, it should be remembered that a certain lack of control is experienced when working this way, so finer points of balance and sound considerations should be settled at the time of recording, and not during the mix-down.

Brass, as mentioned earlier, is separated from the string section with floor-to-ceiling acoustic screens. French horns can sometimes benefit from being placed in the live part of the studio, bearing in mind that some degree of leakage will occur between the strings and horns. By careful inspection of the musical score, it can soon be ascertained whether this is permissible. The woodwind section can be set up behind the strings, as their acoustic dynamics do not cause great concern with regard to any possible leakage. Also, by using the live area for the woodwind instruments, it is possible to set microphones to a high position above the players, avoiding the 'breathy' and 'edgy' tone, and the key noise so often heard on woodwind. Live rooms or areas are always advantageous in that microphones can be used at much greater distances than is possible when working in damped conditions, where close miking is necessary to achieve maximum clarity.

No recording studio is perfect, and complete separation is impossible unless the various sections of the orchestra are overdubbed individually. If time allows, it is sometimes possible to overdub the strings separately. The brass and rhythm sections usually take a recording break, during which time the string sections

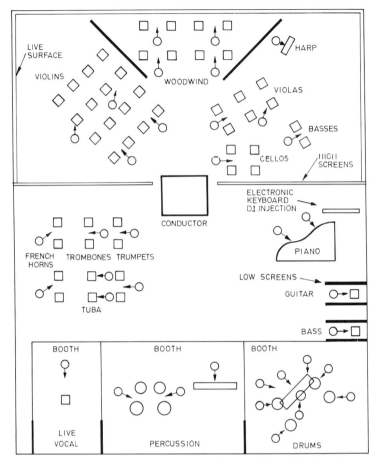

Fig. 17.1. Orchestral seating plan for popular music recording of rhythm, brass, strings, etc.

will be recorded with each player listening to the pre-recorded brass and rhythm tracks via headphones. Unfortunately, this is time-consuming, and the earlier approach of recording everyone at the same time is usually adopted.

The rock band

The favoured drum sound as heard on many records is usually of a live quality and cannot be achieved using the isolation booths. As only a few instruments are being recorded, the live section of the studio is available for recording the drums. Here the engineer can use ambience as well as close microphones.

By careful balancing of these, a large live drum sound can be achieved. It

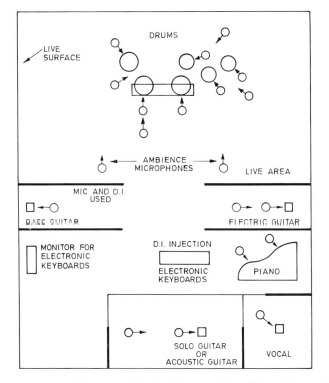

Fig. 17.2. Rock group studio set-up, showing live recording of drum kit, and isolation of electric guitar in case re-recording is needed at a later date

should also be noted that each one of the microphones will be recorded on to a separate track. These can then be remixed at a later stage, adding echo, equalization, and gating if necessary.

In Figure 17.2 it can be seen that it is important to screen the bass and electric guitars, as well as the keyboards, to prevent leakage into the ambience mikes at the live end of the studio. A guide vocal is recorded at the same time as the basic track. This guide vocal will have to be placed in the isolation booth as it may be erased and later re-recorded, so any leakage on to other tracks must be avoided. As the musicians are separated into different parts of the studio, they cannot hear each other comfortably, so they will listen to a rhythm mix with vocals in the foldback headphones.

Figure 17.3 shows the layout for a small ensemble group where clarity is of the utmost importance. Each instrument plays into its own microphone, positioned very close. A dry sound will result, but echo can be added at the mix-down stage. This method does permit a degree of separation between each instrument over the live studio sound. This layout is normally favoured by small

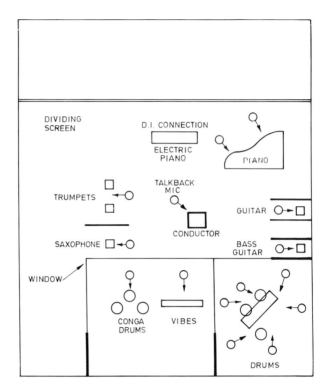

Fig. 17.3. Small ensemble studio set-up when a dry controllable sound is needed

jazz groups, or for recording rhythm sections which will have brass and strings added at a later session.

It is important to remember when there is a conductor that he will need to be able to see everyone, and vice versa.

Rigging for the recording session

All rigging for the session is usually carried out several hours ahead of commencement. Choosing microphones for particular instruments and sections of the orchestra is a matter of personal preference, but certain types of microphone have been found through experience to be preferable. As a general rule, a dynamic microphone is used on drum-kits and electric guitars, and capacitor microphones are used for acoustic-sounding instruments such as strings, brass, woodwind, acoustic guitars, piano, etc. The electronic keyboards and bass guitar are normally direct-injected into the recording console using a DI transformer. The following is a list of microphones commonly used for recording drum-kits:

Bass drum	Electrovoice RE20
	AKG D12E or 20E
Tom-toms	Shure SM57
	Sennheiser MD421U
	Beyer M201
Snare drum	Shure SM57
	Beyer M201
	AKG C414B
	Neuman KM84
Overhead cymbals	AKG C414B
	Neuman FET47
Hi-hat	AKG C414B
	Neuman KM84
	AKG 451
Ambience	PZM
	B & K 7006
	Neuman U87 (omni)

A pair of ambience microphones may be used if recording in the live end of the studio.

There are two methods of recording an electric guitar. Firstly, for the guitar which is playing a basic rhythm pattern as part of the musical arrangement, a good-quality dynamic microphone can be placed 15 cm from the loudspeaker cabinet, with the guitarist making adjustments for level, EQ, etc. on his own amplifier. This results in a very satisfying guitar sound for the basic rhythm section approach. Secondly, when working with rock groups where the guitar sound is an integral part of the song, a much more spectacular sound needs to be found. This requires a double microphone approach, miking the cone very close with a dynamic microphone and then, some 3 or 4 m away, using a capacitor microphone such as a U87 or FET47 as a room microphone. The microphone angles and distances can be adjusted to produce an ambient sound, but not before much experimentation has taken place.

Recording the bass guitar requires direct injection into the recording console, although some engineers prefer to mike the bass guitar amplifier too and mix the direct sound with the live sound; most bass guitarists prefer their sound to be directly injected. In fact, when most bass guitarists arrive at the studio they no longer have an amplifier with them, and even if they are carrying an amplifier it is only for the purposes of monitoring. Due to the wide dynamic range of the bass guitar, it is sometimes necessary to use compression on the original recording, thus preventing any overloading problems.

Now we come to the easiest instrument of the orchestra to record, the electronic keyboard, where the sound is self-contained within the instrument and good-quality output terminals are provided for direct injection into the recording console. In many overdubbing situations, the keyboards can be set up inside the control room. This has the advantage of giving the musicians a very good monitor mix via the monitoring loudspeakers, and good communication with the producer and engineer. Various sections can be discussed and recorded at the same time. There will, from time to time, be occasions where the electronic keyboards have to be set up inside the recording studio, perhaps for better communication with other musicians. As the electronic keyboards are directly injected into the recording console, it may not always be possible for the musician to hear what is being played, so a small monitor loudspeaker will be provided for him in the studio. The level of this monitor speaker should be kept to a minimum, as any leakage into other microphones would prevent re-recording at a later stage.

Recording piano usually requires two microphones. One is placed near the low strings and the other near the top strings, sometimes as close as 15 cm above the strings, with the piano lid in the half position. This produces a very transient sound which is suitable for today's pop music. It is important, however, to ensure that each note played should sound in the same perspective. While one is listening carefully to what is being played, the two microphones can be moved to different parts of the piano. If a percussive effect is required, the top microphone should be moved fairly close to the hammers, and if a warmer sound is wanted the microphones should be moved more towards the tail end of the piano.

There are no rules about this, and it is worth experimenting. For a natural piano sound, the lid should be fully opened and a pair of microphones placed in a semi-arc in front of the piano, some one or two metres away from the sounding-board or lid. By carefully moving the microphones along the arc from the top to the bottom of the piano, the required sound can be found using a pair of good-quality capacitor microphones.

For recording the string section, the players will sit in arrangements of two at a desk, with the desks placed one behind another. An average string section consists of ten first violins, eight second violins, six violas, four cellos, and two double basses. A system of using two microphones per section should be employed. The first microphone is set up directly over the first violin or leader at a minimum height of approximately two metres above the instrument; this will be suitable for any solos played by the leader and will also be sufficiently close to record the first three desks. A second microphone is placed directly above the fourth desk, and this will pick up the rear end of the section. This same method applies to the second violins, violas, and cellos. The double basses will usually be close-miked, as most of the reverberation from these instruments is picked up on the high-string mikes. The close microphones will be fed into the string mix, allowing the engineer to produce a tight bass sound. Good-quality capacitor microphones are always used for recording string sections, such as the Neuman U87, KM84, or U89; the AKG 414 can also be used where a bright sound is required.

A typical brass section used in popular music recording has four trumpets, two tenor trombones, one bass trombone, tuba, and four French horns. A close balance on trumpets and trombones is difficult to control, but it will help if the players are prepared to co-operate by leaning into the microphone on quiet passages of music and sitting back for the louder passages. Without this co-operation from the players, the engineer would need to make drastic changes of level during the recording. A system of using one microphone for each pair of players is employed, with the bass trombone and tuba having a microphone each. French horns should be miked from behind, although if they are placed where their sound will reflect from a wall or reflective screen a microphone can be placed in front, thus recording the reflected sound.

Woodwind players, like the rest of the orchestra, usually sit in pairs. A typical section would be two flutes, two oboes, two clarinets, and two bassoons, with a microphone placed between each pair. The players are positioned in two rows, with flutes and oboes on the front row, and clarinets and bassoons at the back. Woodwind players often change instruments during the session: the producer or arranger will cue the engineer where these changes occur.

Once all chairs, music stands, and microphones are placed in position, the engineer must check that each microphone is working correctly and that the fader positions correspond to their proper microphones. Each microphone should be checked with audio, either by an assistant speaking into the microphone or by a form of click which can be generated from a digital metronome via a loudspeaker.

Most importantly, each microphone should be checked to ensure that they all operate in the same phase. If microphones are used out of phase, problems will occur when mixing down to mono or when recording with stereo pairs. If a microphone is discovered to be out of phase, a simple remedy is to reverse the phase at the console channel by using the phase reverse switch.

All communication circuits should be checked and headphones audibly tested. Talkback facilities between engineer, producer, and conductor must be tested, as well as the drummer's communication in the isolation booth. Before each session commences, all tape machines should be realigned and all tape heads cleaned. In the case of a large recording studio, this job is carried out by the technical department, but in a small facility this will be undertaken by the engineer or his assistant.

The recording session

In the case of a multitrack recording session, the balance engineer will adopt a scheme of allocating instruments to various tracks. The edge tracks, 1 and 24, are most vulnerable to damage or misalignment, so these are not normally used for the basic initial stages. A typical track arrangement for an orchestral session is shown in Table 17.1:

TABLE 17.1.

Track 1	Spare
Track 2	Bass guitar
Track 3	Bass drum
Track 4	Snare drum
Tracks 5 and 6	Stereo mix of tom-toms and overhead cymbals
Track 7	Hi-hat
Track 8	Electric guitar
Tracks 9 and 10	Stereo piano or electronic keyboards
Tracks 11 and 12	Stereo woodwind mix
Track 13	First violins
Track 14	Second violins
Track 15	Violas
Track 16	Cellos
Track 17	Basses
Track 18	Trumpets
Track 19	Trombones and tuba
Track 20	French horns
Track 21	Harp
Track 22	Percussion
Track 23	Guide vocal
Track 24	Spare.

In the case of a rock band, the track split will favour greater track availability for the drum-kit, and tracks will also need to be made available for the recording of drum-machine codes and SMPTE time-codes for second machine synchronizing. A typical track split for a rock band is shown in Table 17.2:

TABLE 17.2.

Track 1	Spare
Track 2	Bass guitar DI
Track 3	Bass guitar amp
Track 4	Bass drum
Track 5	Snare drum
Tracks 6 and 7	Stereo mix of tom-toms
Tracks 8 and 9	Stereo mix of overhead cymbals
Track 10	Hi-hat
Tracks 11 and 12	Stereo drum ambience
Track 13	Electric guitar
Tracks 14 and 15	Stereo electronic keyboards
Tracks 16–21	Open for vocal overdubs, guitars, or keyboards

Track 22	Guide vocal
Track 23	Code from drum machine or electronic keyboard for possible re-recording at a later time. By connecting this code back to the drum machine, the internal electronics can be triggered into action to repeat the same drum pattern in time with the recorded piece of music. The various elements of this pattern can then be updated while remaining in sync with the multitrack recording.
Track 24	SMPTE time-code to enable the multitrack to be synchronized to a second multitrack should the musicians require more tracks at a later date. This second multitrack is known as the 'slave machine'.

The engineer's first priority at the start of a recording session is to work on the drum sound and balance as quickly as possible, because as the drummer is in an isolation booth the rest of the musicians will need to hear him in their headphones before they can play. Sometimes the drummer is asked to arrive thirty minutes before the session starts in order to do this, enabling valuable time to be saved during the session.

Once a drum sound has been achieved, the musicians can begin running through while the engineer listens to and balances the remainder of the orchestra, starting with the rhythm section. The drum sound will already have been established, so the bass and electric guitars, and various electronic keyboards, will be added. This rhythm mix will be heard through all the headphones in the studio. The other sections of the orchestra are added to the rhythm section, starting with the brass section, woodwind, French horns, and finally strings and harp. As the various members of the rhythm and orchestral sections are being recorded on separate tracks, the finer points of balance will be carried out at the mixing stage, so a good monitor balance is the main priority. Echo will also be added to the monitor outputs to enable the producer to get a feel of how the final record will sound. (The monitoring channels are not recorded.) Once a satisfactory balance and echo setting are achieved, the only thing left is to go for a perfect musical performance, leaving the engineer to keep an eye on the recording levels. Some pre-mixing is undertaken during this initial recording stage, and it is important that the engineer keeps an eye on the brass section, as brass players are constantly moving from open to muted sounds with as much as 10 dB difference in level.

As mentioned earlier, doubling of instruments occurs, particularly with woodwind, and quite large changes of level can appear between different instruments. Also, one needs to keep a careful eye on the percussion. Timps, vibes, xylophone, and various Latin American instruments require constant changes of level. The producer or arranger can help by careful cueing at the appropriate moment.

As well as being concerned with these complexities, it is one of the engineer's duties to ensure that a good headphone mix is achieved. In most cases, the control-room monitor mix sent through the headphone circuits will be sufficient, but often the musicians will ask for an entirely different balance, usually for more bass and drums. A separate foldback mix will have to be set up. The drummer, on the other hand, will really need to hear only the orchestra and not himself. This complicates matters, as two foldback circuits have to be set up; in some cases three or four foldback circuits are needed. In a typical recording session today, the engineer can spend as much time balancing foldback circuits as recording the orchestra.

One of the engineer's other duties is to look after the digital metronome, or 'click-track' as it is better known. This provides a fixed tempo in beats per minute which can be varied. Listening to this click on headphones enables the musicians to maintain the same tempo throughout, without speeding up or slowing down. The click-track is particularly important during film soundtrack recording, where a piece of music has to fit into a predetermined number of frames. A constant problem when using clicks is that, if the headphones are too loud in the studio, the clicks will leak into the microphones. The engineer may therefore be required to turn up the click track during the loud passages and down again during the quiet moments. In a two-track recording situation, where the engineer is balancing straight to a two-track tape machine, it would be impossible for him to balance the orchestra live, alter the click levels, and balance the foldback at the same time, so another pair of hands is often employed. (The producer takes on the role of looking after the clicks!) All this, of course, applies to the typical three-hour recording session using session musicians.

When working with rock groups the atmosphere is much more relaxed, as there is no time limit on starting or finishing. Sessions sometimes go on well into the night. Here much experimentation takes place, with musical ideas constantly being recorded and re-recorded.

Equalization on the recording session

It should be emphasized that equalization should not be used without first trying to achieve the desired result by moving the microphone or changing to a more suitable type. It should also be noted that certain microphones have peaks in their response, and careful selection of the microphone for various instruments reduces the need for excessive equalization. The main use of equalization during live recording is to remove unwanted frequencies which are above or below the required signal. A low-frequency cut-off on the strings microphone is often needed to remove low-frequency leakage from the bass guitar and piano. When close-miking strings for the purposes of preventing such leakage, a harshness is often heard in the mid-range. A slight rolling-off of mid-frequencies will eliminate this, and achieve the same result as raising the microphones without the extra leakage that this would produce. Also, a slight high-frequency boost will add brilliance to the string sound. Lower-mid equalization is sometimes added to the violas and cellos to give more body or richness. Brass often benefits from a slight mid-lift, somewhere in the region of 5–7 kHz. Equalization is always a matter of personal taste, so definitive rules on this subject are impossible. Certainly there are no hard-and-fast rules for recording drum-kits. The most important points are to make sure the kit is properly tuned, and that all loose fittings have been tightened. The front skin of the bass drum is nearly always removed, and the inside of the drum filled with a blanket or cushion, pushed up against the back skin, with a microphone placed inside the drum.

This sometimes results in bass tip-up, an increase in the lower frequencies. It can be cured by cutting the extreme low frequencies and lifting the recording level, thus making the bass drum sound tighter and firmer. Lower mid-frequencies can then be added to make the sound 'crack'. Tom-toms and snare drums are recorded with the microphones positioned very close to the edge of the skin, working at a minimum distance of possibly 5 cm. Tom-toms and snare drums often 'ring' when heard via microphones, thus creating a lower and upper harmonic as the drum is hit; by applying small pieces of masking or gaffer tape to the skin, this ring can be reduced or eliminated.

Snare drums often benefit from a lift in the high or middle frequencies. In extreme circumstances where a snare drum is difficult to record, it may have to be changed. Many drummers carry two snare drums, so it is worth listening to both. Some drummers also remove the bottom skins of their tom-toms, so the microphone can be placed inside the drum from underneath. The same problem with bass tip-up sometimes occurs, so the cutting of lower frequencies will make the sound brighter and firmer. If the cymbals and hi-hat are of good quality, no special equalization is necessary, though some low-frequency cut-off may help, as well as equalization in the upper frequencies. When working with professional session musicians, these problems will not often occur, as their kits have been specially tuned and treated for recording work. The problem invariably arises when working with rock drummers whose kits are tuned for live work.

When recording live, a problem is often experienced with the acoustic guitar. Because of the quiet nature of the sound, the gain of this microphone is turned up to such a high position that most of the surrounding sounds near the guitar will leak into it. Acoustic guitars are usually isolated in studio booths, with a microphone like the AKG 414 positioned about 30 cm away from the main hole of the guitar; sometimes two microphones can be used in stereo. Bass tip-up will probably not occur at this distance. However, when miking very close, bass tip-up can cause severe problems, and cutting frequencies below the 200 kHz region is essential.

When recording vocals, again there are no set rules, as the human voice is so variable. If the artist has a good voice, all that is needed is a high-quality capacitor microphone, with no equalization and no compression, just a slight lifting or reducing of the odd word or phrase. Good microphones favoured for vocal recording are the Neuman U87 and AKG 414. Many engineers are still using the Neuman U47 with its valve pre-amp and believe this to be the best vocal microphone, though it is sadly no longer manufactured.

Sibilance is sometimes a problem with vocalists, and also popping on letters 'P' and 'B'. A way round this is to ask the vocalist not to over-pronounce the letter 'S' and to sing across the microphone. However, this is not always practicable, as the singer has many other things to think about. A pop shield can be used on the microphone to protect the diaphragm from the wind generated by the letters 'P' and 'B'. Many of the commercial pop shields are unsuitable, as a reduction in high frequencies can occur. A makeshift pop shield can be created cheaply: a wire coat-hanger with a stocking stretched over it is suspended in front of the microphone. This does not affect the high frequencies, and is a method adopted by many studios.

A De-esser device can also be used to take away unwanted sibilance. When working with a vocalist with a wide dynamic range, microphone compression will have to be used, though care should be taken not to reduce the dynamic range to such an extent that the singer sounds 'squashed'. It is also important not to ask for too many repeat takes, so it is usual to keep all the takes. Each separate vocal performance is recorded on a separate track. Then, when four or five takes have been recorded, these can be played back and the best parts of each noted by the producer. The best sections can then be bounced down to a separate track, to build up the final vocal performance.

Where orchestral sections are sharing microphones or tracks, as in the case of the brass, it may be necessary to ask the trumpets, trombones, and horns to play separately to ensure that the microphone is picking up all the elements of the section in proper balance. The engineer can, for example, request the brass to play a built-up chord. He can then quickly detect which member of the section is blowing away from the mike and which member is blowing too close; and a slight adjustment of seating arrangements can quickly eliminate any problems. It is also important that the players remember their positions.

Overdubbing

The most favoured form of recording today is overdubbing. In an overdubbing situation, the engineer can experiment with types of microphone, position, and ambience. With only one or two musicians to worry about, there is plenty of time to experiment. Ambience and a feeling of depth are very important parts of a recording, giving the listener the feeling of actually being at the performance. What most engineers are striving for is the natural live sound. Strings are definitely at an advantage when overdubbed, as the engineer can move the microphones as far away as possible to achieve a large string sound without the close-miking harshness. Sometimes, when working in extremely good acoustics, only a stereo microphone is necessary, thus giving a natural sound which may be impossible to achieve when recording the whole orchestra together. Brass too can benefit from overdubbing, as microphones are taken away as far as possible, eliminating much of the valve and wind noise. These experiments with distancing microphones from instruments can only be carried out, of course, when working in a live acoustic. A dead room will almost certainly muffle the instruments. The use of reflective panels in a dead area can sometimes reduce this muffling quality.

Today it is becoming more and more the trend to build a live area in a studio, and some major studios are now completely live. When working in an overdub situation, the score can be recorded in sections. The first eight bars of the music can be recorded first; then, on playing back these eight bars to the musicians, the record button can be pressed at the start of the ninth bar. The musicians will then start playing from this point until a musical error is heard. The tape will then be spooled back to the ninth bar and the process repeated.

This process of 'dropping in' will continue until a perfect musical performance has been recorded. This operation is usually carried out by the tape operator. When all the recording and overdubbing is complete and recorded on the multitrack machine, we are now ready for the mixing-down process.

The mix-down

This is another area of recording where no rules apply—the final sound is down to the taste of the engineer, producer, and artist. Many hours are consumed with this task—even days. Before attempting the mix-down, the engineer has to establish what special effects are required by the producer. Will the vocals or guitars need to be harmonized? What kind of digital delay is required, or special echo facilities? Finally, how are we mixing-down—analogue or digital? The two most popular tape formats in use today are 30 ips half-inch non-Dolby analogue, or Sony 1610 or 1630 digital. With the advent of the Compact Disc, current trends predict that most recordings will very soon be mixed down to the digital format, though some engineers and producers still believe that the analogue sound is more punchy, and have little faith in the digital format.

Today's multitrack recordings have become so musically complex that it is impossible to mix these recordings manually. Manual mixing, by moving faders at predetermined points to alter musical dynamics or emphasize a certain point in the arrangement, can be an extremely laborious task, the operator having to remember thirty or forty different moves during one three-minute segment.

To make the mixing process easier, and to avoid having to remember so many different moves, the recording can be mixed in eight-bar segments. Once all the segments have been mixed, they can be edited together to form the final three-minute piece of music. Some modern recording consoles have facilities for automated mix-down, which has taken over from the old-fashioned manual approach. The electronic applications of automated mix-down will not be discussed here, but it is important to remember that a suitable facility for the recording of automated data should be made available, either by using two tracks of the multitrack tape machine or a floppy-disc drive unit, or an analogue tape machine synchronized to the multitrack recorder. It is important that this data track runs simultaneously in sync with the segment of music which is to be mixed.

Another important thing to remember about automated mix-down is not to build each track one at a time. A better starting-point is to establish a rough mix which will give the engineer and producer an overall picture of how the final recording should sound. Once this rough mix is established, and everyone is happy with the degrees of echo and equalization of the various instruments, the delicate art of balancing the finer points can be undertaken. This rough mix can now be 'written in' to the automation. Once completed, this first stage can now be read back, and by turning the recording console into update mode we can now change the picture of this rough mix. Each section can be treated individually. Perhaps the bass guitar needs to be pushed in certain areas of the song, or the guitar solo needs lifting. The producer may decide to accent the brass in certain areas to make the arrangement more punchy. He may also wish to simplify the arrangement by keeping the strings out until the second chorus is established, thus building the song as it progresses.

Most importantly, the vocalist may need to be pushed in certain sections which are being lost. This process can take many hours, as the engineer and producer are trying to come up with something that sounds interesting and which could possibly make or break the record. Each subsequent change in the arrangement or balance is achieved by constantly updating the data track. By recording the original data on to a second track, the update information can be added to this second track at the same time as the transfer. This process can be repeated many times, backwards and forwards, i.e. track bouncing, with each bounce containing new updated information. Small segments of updated information can also be 'dropped in' to the data tracks, so avoiding the problem of running the tape from the start of the recording each time an update is required. If a remix is required at a later stage, this data information can be used to reset the recording console to the exact point where the last mix left off. Not all automated consoles memorize EQ and echo settings, and so it becomes necessary to note these details for each mix and keep them with the tape box.

Sampling

Another important aspect of mix-down is sampling. This simply means locking a musical sound from another source, like a snare drum beat or bass drum pattern, into a digital memory or sampling unit. This memory can then be edited to play only the duration of the locked-in signal required; the memory can be triggered by the unwanted original snare drum beat. On the final mix-down, it is only the sample drum beat that was locked into the memory which is heard. By using this system, a new drum sound can be achieved by using drum samples from another source. This method of sampling is often carried out during the recording session itself, with good snare and bass drum sounds locked into the memory. The drummer will simply trigger these sounds with his own drum patterns or beats.

The result of this sampling process does ensure a tighter consistent sound throughout the recording than is sometimes humanly possible. Many engineers have their own library of drum samples—sounds which they have collected from various sessions—and this can save much time on recording sessions.

Electronic drum machines, like the Linn 2000, can also be triggered in the same way, thus dispensing with sampling. A popular unit in use for sampling at many recording studios today is the AMS DX15 80S microprocessor-controlled delay line. This is a versatile machine which enables the engineer to carry out digital delay effects, harmonizing, and the lock-in sampling function. The unit also has the facility for changing the pitch of the locked-in sample.

'Spinning in', as it is known, is also a popular system of recording, saving much time and trouble at the recording session. Providing the sampling device has a long enough memory, the first chorus of a song can be sampled and, by switching in the sampling memory at the appropriate time during the start of the remaining choruses, this sampled chorus can be recorded on to the multitrack recorder at the start of each chorus section. This enables the artist to record only one chorus, with the remaining five or six spun in using the sample. The sampled chorus will stay in sync with the original rhythm track, as the sampling device is not speed-conscious. Sampling and spinning in can be used for virtually any sound or instrument. This may sound like cheating but it saves many hours of studio time, thereby keeping budgets down and enabling more recordings to be made. It can be argued that this form of recording produces very bland music, but this is a matter of taste.

Echo

Using echo on mix-down has now become extremely complicated, with as many as five or six different echo units being used at the same time. Gone are the days when only a single echo-chamber was used. On a modern mix-down session, the engineer could have at his disposal up to two stereo echo plates, a Lexicon 224X, AMS RM16, Lexicon PCM 70 or 60, and also up to three or four AMS units for harmonizing, delay effects and sampling. The reason behind using such a complex array of echo facilities is that most modern recording sessions are based on the overdubbing principle, with each sound recorded separately and thus lacking ambience and delayed leakage in the studio.

To give the impression that all the musicians are playing together, an ambience has to be created by artificial means; simply adding echo does not achieve this effect. By using digital delay lines and short-decay echo effects, the blend of instruments can soon sound as though they were recorded at the same time. Stereo harmonizing on vocals and guitar solos can be very effective. A slight change in pitch, either up or down the octave, can add a three-dimensional effect in the mix. When mixing drum sounds down, it is often necessary to use noise-gates. If the noise-gate is correctly set up, it will open when a loud signal is received and close again when the signal stops. This enables the track to be opened at the precise point of impact. Then, when the drum is not being played, the track will be closed to eliminate any leakage or noise from other elements of the drum-kit.

This results in an extremely tight and clean drum sound. Noise-gates can also be used on electric guitars to eliminate amplifier hiss and hum when the guitar is not being played, and even between notes during quiet passages. Noise-gates are useful for effects, notably on brass tracks, clipping the decay of an instrument at an earlier point, thus creating a very tight and clipped brass sound. Often noise-gates are used on room ambience and echo return to give the effect of hearing the echo only at the point of impact. This puts the instrument concerned into a large acoustic without the problems of echo decay overlapping into the next portion of the song.

Equalizing is always carried out at the mixing stage, although there are two schools of thought on this subject. One insists that most equalizing should be carried out during the recording session, and the other insists on recording everything flat and equalizing at the later stage. There are of course advantages with either method. Equalizing during the recording does give you the option of changing microphones and moving positions, rather than resorting to excessive equalization. Recording everything flat and equalizing at the mixing stage does give the option of delaying your decisions—in this very fickle industry, engineers have to change ideas from one day to the next. The positioning of the various tracks in the stereo picture is usually left to the engineer and producer to decide. It is normal practice to place the bass drum and bass in the middle, with stereo drums panned left and right. Rock band stereo positioning can change from song to song, as most of the important sounds are played on guitars and keyboards, so positioning will be conditioned by the musical arrangement.

The orchestral layout follows a standard orchestral pattern, with the highest strings placed on the left and the low strings on the right. Horns appear left and the brass right, with woodwind centre. There are no rules, however, so the producer can decide for himself, though where the orchestra has been recorded in stereo this has to be obeyed on the final mix-down. Moving an instrument recorded on the left hand to the right can cause problems by leaving the remaining leakage on the left-hand channel.

People often ask, 'How do you start mixing down?' The most popular method is to start with the rhythm section; once a good rhythm balance has been achieved, the vocal can then be added. Once happy with the balance, strings and brass can be added to the picture. Another favourite technique is to put the vocal in first and then add the instruments.

One of the most serious problems during mixing down is running out of gain. This is often caused by engineers and producers constantly pushing things up— the old maxim of 'let's have more of that, and more of this'. Sometimes it can be a lot easier to take something down to hear something else louder. What should also be realized is that adding EQ to an instrument may also increase the level.

Another important point to remember when mixing down is that most of the record-buying public are not listening to the recording on control-room monitors. It is important to monitor the mix-down on domestic loudspeakers at low levels. It will soon be noticed, when playing the mix on domestic loudspeakers, that the bottom end will have substantially decreased, and also some reduction in high frequencies will be experienced. This can be corrected by the engineer, so that the bottom and top ends of the mix can be heard better on domestic loudspeakers. When the mix has finally been completed and everybody is happy with the results, cassette copies will be made for the producer, artist, and engineer to take home and listen to on their own speakers. Later, if everybody concerned is happy with the results achieved on their own equipment, the tapes can be handed to the record company.

A remix is often needed, especially if the mix was carried out late at night or during the early hours of the morning when the ears were not quite so fresh. It can be unwise to mix late at night, and sometimes a break between the recording and mix-down process is advisable to avoid the unnecessary expense of remixing. If, however, a remix has to be done, the automated data which has been recorded can still be used, only the tracks which need to be altered being updated. It is important to remember that any outboard equipment used is not logged on the automated data, so the engineer must write down any settings before leaving the studio.

Tape presentation

Finally, it is important for the engineer and tape operator to label all tapes correctly: all technical information should be marked on the tape box, together with song titles, artist, producer, client, etc. The tape should carry a set of reference tones—all recorded at the standard operating levels at the time of the mix-down—so that the cutting or transfer engineer can line up his tape machine to match the original machine.

Where noise reduction is used, such as Dolby, the original Dolby tone should be on the tape. With analogue recordings, all titles should be leadered, using white leader tape to indicate the front of a recording and red to indicate the end. Sony 1630 and 1610 digital recordings should have all titles electronically edited, using blank space between tracks. Time-code should be recorded on the analogue track, and the start and stop time-code numbers of each separate recording logged on the tape box.

18

Electronic music
Jonathan Gibbs

Since the tentative beginnings of electronic music at the turn of the century it has been hoped that the electronic manipulation of sound might, in theory, offer the composer the most glorious opportunities to explore new forms of musical expression. But there have been major stumbling-blocks. The penalties have been the long hours spent slaving over a tape editing block, turning crude physics-laboratory waveforms into pleasing sounds, programming sluggish computers in low-level languages to perform tasks they were not designed to do. For the professional composer of electronic music those long hours have been a significant barrier, because, unlike the composer for conventional instruments, he has to be intimately concerned not only with the music the instruments will play but also with the very design of the instruments themselves. Too often that has meant a struggle, and if it takes him a day to create one really good note it is inevitable that integrity must suffer.

But within the last decade the technology of electronic music has exploded, and it is now expanding so fast that it is quite impossible to stop and say, 'This is the state of the art'. What is a problem today will be solved tomorrow, only to bring up a new set of problems. We now have cheap synthesizers and controllers which can, with care, begin to realize some of the dreams of electronic music—to create any sound imaginable or unimaginable, to make that sound worth listening to, and, most important in the professional environment, to do it quickly. The lead time between conception and realization of a sound is reduced to insignificance. That is good news not only for the accountants but also for the talented composer, because he need not waste time on the approach that is not going to work, but can go for the approach that will.

This technological explosion has brought machines which are not only cheaper, more flexible, and easier to use, but which also offer a much greater variety of sounds. In addition to the subtractive-synthesis family, in which voltage-controlled oscillators generate raw waveforms such as square and saw-tooth which are then filtered and shaped, there are also sampling devices, which make digital recordings of live sounds and then play them back through the keyboard; frequency-modulation devices, in which sine-wave oscillators are arranged to frequency-modulate each other; additive synthesis, in which the amplitude envelopes of harmonics can be individually adjusted; and wavetable synthesis, in which the initial waveforms of subtractive synthesis are more elaborate and can be changed through time. And there are even large computer systems which combine all these processes in one machine.

The sounds not only have greater variety, but they can also be more attractive. In the small-scale environment of individual notes, the ear is bored quickly and needs continuous changes of pitch, volume, and timbre to find those notes interesting. This can easily be proved by making a single-cycle loop in a sample of, say, an oboe, and then comparing that loop with the sound of the real thing. The sampling synthesizer may be giving a perfect copy of one cycle of oboe tone, but the minute changes in quality which the oboist naturally makes give his note far more interest than that unvarying electronic loop. But greater control of a synthesizer's parameters, using bend-wheels, key pressure, and the like, coupled with more complex note envelopes, means that synthesized sounds can now be much richer than before. More significantly, they can break away from the limited ideals of perfectly imitating well-designed instruments of the orchestra into much more progressive ideals of developing new instruments.

MIDI: advantages and disadvantages

The most significant development has been the ability to link together this considerable armoury of synthesizers with the Musical Instrument Digital Interface, or 'MIDI'. This is the internationally accepted set of protocols for communication between synthesizers and peripheral devices, based on a serial communication line operating at 31.25 Kbaud. It is virtually *de rigueur* on all new electronic instruments, and there are even kits to transform grand pianos into generators. At its simplest level, it means that playing a note on one MIDI synthesizer will send out three eight-bit bytes from the 'MIDI out' socket on the back of the machine, which may be routed to the 'MIDI in' socket on another machine and so tell it to play the same note at the same velocity, that is hit with the same force. When the note is released, another three bytes are sent, to tell the second machine to release its note.

While this in itself may not seem all that significant—after all, organists have been linking Great and Swell manuals for years—the real power of MIDI becomes evident when that 'note on, note off' information (and a whole lot more besides) can be stored in a sequencer. Once that raw data is available in the sequencer, it may be edited and modified, new material may be generated by manipulation within the sequencer itself, and whole pieces may be built, not as fixed individual acoustic tracks on a multitrack recorder but as files of data on a computer disc, so that every performance is first-generation, and there are infinite possibilities of changing and improving that performance.

The MIDI standard means that machines from different manufacturers can talk to each other. Also built into the specification are 'System Exclusive' protocols for individual machines from the same manufacturer to store and communicate data about, for example, the make-up of a particular voice, or a rhythm sequence, or a particular sample. So, in theory, the musician can go to a studio, which is equipped with the right synthesizers and sequencers, carrying just a box of floppy discs or a few ROM cartridges, which contain both the music and the sounds.

It is not only synthesizers which respond to MIDI. There is a whole generation of treatment devices—reverberation, harmonizing, delay, and all the other peripheral 'black boxes'—which can be made to change their parameters according to standard MIDI instructions. There are even mixers which respond to MIDI, although the speed restrictions of that 31.25 Kbaud make full automated control of substantial numbers of mixer channels a highly complex proposition. However, it is certainly possible to control the peripherals from that floppy disc, as well as the synthesizers.

It would be wrong, though, to suggest that MIDI is the answer to every prayer. When it can be so successful at controlling music synthesizers, there is a temptation to run absolutely everything with MIDI. Although the speed as originally specified is quite adequate for musical performance (and initial gloomy prophecies about propagation delays have largely proved false), it is pushing it to the limits to expect it to control larger systems such as professional mixing desks in real time. This is simply because MIDI is very slow when transmitting continuous control movements. MIDI information can be recorded only in a digital storage system, such as a sequencer, because the frequency is too high for analogue multitrack tape. Therefore, when MIDI data for electronic instruments is being recorded alongside analogue tracks of live instruments, the sequencer must rely on control tracks on the multitrack (either time-code or dedicated pulse trains) to run in sync, and those control tracks may be extremely vulnerable. In particular, a few pulses missed through dropout in a dedicated pulse train will throw out the sync from that point on. Great care is needed, therefore, when recording sync tracks of this kind, to ensure that enough level gets on to tape to give good reproduction, without risking crosstalk to adjacent tracks. It is wise to switch out any noise reduction, which may corrupt frequency-shift-keying pulse trains.

Although there are 'song pointer' commands built into the MIDI specification, which should theoretically mean that a piece can be started from any point by first sending the sequencer an instruction to tell it where to start, the slow response of floppy-disc-based systems with limited RAM means that, in practice, every time a piece is run in sync with the multitrack it has to be started from the beginning. MIDI has no handshaking, so the sequencer has no way to confirm whether it has got to the right start-point or not. There are hard-disc-based systems (such as the Synclavier) which overcome these problems, but at present such systems are much more expensive than the smaller floppy-disc machines. The other alternative is to hold all the data in RAM, as in some of the sequencers based on microcomputers (such as the Apple Macintosh) which have relatively large RAM storage.

A further disadvantage of MIDI systems is that, as in all data communication, the data is vulnerable, particularly when using floppy discs. The first law of floppy discs is that they will always choose the most awkward times to corrupt—just when you have finished three hours of intensive programming and have not yet 'backed up'—and that corruption is potentially far more disastrous than a spot of dropout on analogue tape. Naturally, the manufacturers are more interested in developing 'user friendliness' for the more exciting parts of their software, and backing up discs may well be a tedious business. Nevertheless, keeping regular backups of work is absolutely essential, as anyone who has learned the hard way will verify.

MIDI has been developed for the world of conventional chromatic music based on the keyboard, and anyone wishing to work with more adventurous ideas of microtonal or macrotonal music will find it sadly lacking, because the smallest pitch change definable on most MIDI synthesizers is one semitone. Although the full MIDI specification is admirably thorough, there are plenty of manufacturers who have cut corners and failed to implement it to the full.

Despite these drawbacks, MIDI has the huge advantage that it is a recognized standard, and there are thousands of devices on the market which adhere to that standard. Even if MIDI itself is superseded (and no doubt it will be), those machines will be around for some time. Also, with such commercial pressure behind it, the drive to make MIDI a universal recording studio data transfer language is huge; possible developments already under discussion include a form of MIDI time-code to replace SMPTE, and much faster data rates.

MIDI in practice

MIDI devices are usually fitted with three five-pin DIN sockets, labelled MIDI IN, MIDI OUT, and MIDI THRU (see Figure 18.1). MIDI IN is the input, and goes straight to the sound generation or modification circuits of the device; MIDI THRU sends out a perfect copy of what comes into MIDI IN, buffered with an opto-isolator, so that further devices may be daisy-chained; MIDI OUT sends out MIDI information which has been generated locally by the device itself, from its keyboard for example. Note, therefore, that MIDI OUT does not normally carry the data coming into MIDI IN; it is not a 'mix' of input data and locally generated data. It is inadvisable to make very long daisy-chains of instruments using THRU connections (say more than three), because the opto-isolators used may cause cumulative rise-and-fall time errors in the data. Cables connecting standard MIDI devices should not run longer than 15 m without a repeater. If the device does not have any means of local generation—a synthesizer without a keyboard, or a peripheral such as a reverberation unit—

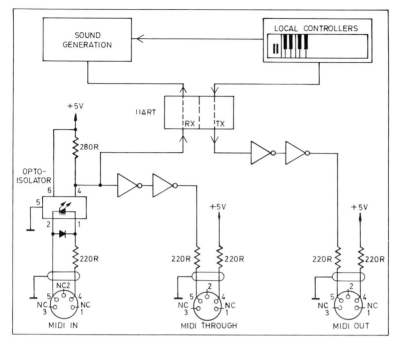

Fig. 18.1. Basic MIDI connections

then it may not need the MIDI OUT socket. Some devices do not implement MIDI THRU.

The MIDI system allows for 16 channels. This means that data intended for several different devices may be sent down the same cable to all those devices in a daisy-chain, or in parallel, but only those which are set to respond to the correct channel will hear the data meant for them. It is possible, for example, to set up a 'mother keyboard' such that the lower part of the keyboard sends out data on a channel dedicated to a bass-line synthesizer, whilst the upper part sends data on another channel. If a receiver is set to OMNI MODE, however, it will hear all incoming data on its cable.

MIDI messages

MIDI messages are of two basic types: *channel messages*, which will be heard only by devices set up to receive that channel (or to receive all channels, in omni mode) and which include the fundamental 'note on, note off' messages; and *system messages*, heard by all receivers regardless, which include data such as synchronization clocks. (System messages will be explained later, in connection with sequencers.) If a receiver has no use for the incoming data it will ignore it. Synchronization clocks, for example, mean nothing to a synthesizer, but may be relevant for a sequencer or drum machine. It is clearly important that, if channels are being used, the right devices are set to the right channels. The specification states that on power-up a receiver should default to omni on/poly on mode, that is to say it will hear all incoming channels and play polyphonically. However, it is expedient for some devices (such as racked modular banks of synthesizers) to default to specific channels.

The MIDI data itself is divided into two groups, *status bytes* and *data bytes*: a receiving device will know the difference because status bytes have bit 7 set, i.e. are greater than 127. A complete listing is given in Table 18.1 at the end of this chapter. When a receiver hears a particular status byte, it can make decisions about whether to act on it—is this data on my channel? Is it relevant to me?—and, if necessary, listen out for further data bytes before acting. So, for example, if a synthesizer on channel 1 hears a status byte which says 'Note start on channel 1' (i.e. hexadecimal number $90, decimal 144), it will listen out for two further data bytes, which will define the key number and the key velocity.

There are eight principal categories of channel information. These are *note off* and *note on*, which may also define a velocity (that is how fast the note on the keyboard is depressed or released). Such velocity information can be used by the receiving synthesizer to control level, for example, or harmonic 'brightness'. *Polyphonic key pressure* and *channel pressure* send information about how hard the note is being pressed after it has reached the bottom of its travel (after touch); polyphonic key pressure deals with individual notes, channel pressure with the whole keyboard as one. *Program change* messages call up different voices (pre-set sounds) in the receiver; in peripherals such as reverberation units, they may call up different pre-set settings. *Pitch bend change* messages echo the movement of bend wheels or levers used to shift the tuning of the whole instrument, although different synthesizers may impose different scalings on that data. *Control change* messages carry changes in controllers such as pedals, wheels, and switches. Each controller has a number, and certain numbers have been generally accepted as linked to certain common controllers. A list is given in Table 18.2 at the end of this chapter. The last category of channel information is *mode change*. In practice it may be tricky to use, because transmitters cannot know what state a receiver is in, but in theory it allows a transmitter to control how the receiver will respond to its transmission data. In *omni on* mode, the receiver hears all channels; in *omni off*, only one specific channel. In *poly on* mode, it distributes incoming notes polyphonically up to the limit of how many voices it can play at once. In *poly off* mode it either plays one note at a time regardless (omni on), or it assigns incoming channels monophonically to individual voices (omni off). In practice, most contemporary synthesizers are polyphonic, and there should be few problems about mode. One additional command in this category is the *local control on/off* command, which controls whether or not the receiving synthesizer's local keyboard can talk to its sound-making circuits, or relinquish control entirely to incoming

MIDI. In some cases performance will be more reliable if the local processor does not have to waste time paying attention to its local keyboard.

When a large number of MIDI instruments and peripherals are in use, it becomes impracticable to keep replugging MIDI leads every time you need to change the arrangement. To help with this problem, there are MIDI matrix switching-boxes available which work like solid-state MIDI jackfields, routing different inputs to outputs. It is also possible to use MIDI 'brains', units designed to overcome the problem that, for example, one machine's pedal controller has a different control number from another machine's. The unit might be set up to change the control numbers automatically.

Clearly, a good knowledge of how MIDI works, and what it can and cannot do, is as essential to the electronic music studio engineer as is his knowledge of signal paths in a mixing desk. But what of the synthesizers themselves?

Analogue synthesis

'Analogue' has come to be a generic term applied to all synthesizers which make sounds in a similar way to Robert Moog's classic first voltage-controlled synthesizer, using the basic tools of oscillators, filters, amplifiers, and envelope shapers. In fact, of course, current versions incorporate digital technology both for control and sound generation, and there is plenty of cross-fertilization between 'analogue' functions such as filtering and digital functions such as sampling; however, the terminology of analogue synthesis has become the universal language in the field.

The older machines need a 'CV' (control voltage) from a keyboard to define pitch, and most take a logarithmic scale of 1 V/octave. This voltage is (notionally) applied to a voltage-controlled oscillator, VCO, which produces one of several waveforms—usually square, saw-tooth, pulse (in which the mark-to-space ratio may often be voltage-controlled), triangle, or sine. Some machines, such as the PPG Wave, allow greater control over this initial waveform. The user may create his own waveform, or even use a succession of different waveforms which course through as the note sustains.

This waveform is then filtered in a voltage-controlled filter, VCF. The principal controls here will be *cut-off frequency, Q*, or *resonance* (which gives a variable peak at the filter cut-off frequency and may even drive it into oscillation), and *envelope* parameters. Envelope generators have at least four elements: *attack time*, the time it takes to reach the initial attack level; *decay time*, the time it takes to decay to a holding sustain level; the *sustain level* itself; and *release time*, during which the envelope dies away after the note is released (hence 'ADSR'). An envelope is active as long as a gate voltage is present, which will usually be taken from the keyboard, and it enters the release phase once the gate voltage drops. More modern envelope generators may have more than these four elements, with perhaps two or more initial decay sequences.

After filtering, the signal passes to a voltage-controlled amplifier, VCA, in which another envelope generator defines the overall amplitude shape of a note. The other principal components of an analogue system are low-frequency oscillators or LFOs, which generate sub-audio waveforms to introduce effects such as vibrato and tremolo; noise generators, for white or pink noise; ring modulators, which combine two input frequencies to produce a sum-and-difference output frequency; and sample and hold generators, which take a sample of an incoming voltage and then hold that level until the next clock pulse arrives, so producing stepped voltage changes. All these classic terms may be conveniently applied to most synthesizers.

Early analogue synthesizers allowed all the elements to be interconnected with patch cords, and a specific arrangement was called a patch. More modern equivalents allow all parameters and routings to be stored digitally as a voice number, and later recalled and edited.

This type of analogue synthesis is basically subtractive—the harmonics in a rich waveform are filtered out to varying degrees. With *additive synthesis*, such as that offered by the CMI Fairlight Mk II Page 4 or (more limited) the Yamaha DX7 Algorithm 32, sounds are built by giving harmonics individual envelopes, rather than by filtering. To work usefully, however, the phase relationship between harmonics has to be controllable as well as their relative levels, and this facility is uncommon. Additive synthesis may give interesting results when a Fourier Analysis is made of a sampled sound, and the results used to 'rebuild' the sound using oscillators. Such facilities are naturally to be found only on the more expensive computer synthesizers.

FM synthesis

When the output of an LFO is applied to the control voltage input of a VCO, the result is vibrato. If the frequency of that vibrato is increased, so that it is comparable with that of the VCO carrier itself, and if the deviation of the carrier frequency is also increased, then sideband frequencies are produced, including 'negative frequencies' which are perceived as positive frequencies with reverse phase; the result is a dramatic change of tone colour. If, further, the modulation frequency and the deviation are varied dynamically, then remarkably 'unsynthesized' sounds occur. These principles were developed in the late 1960s by Professor John Chowning of Stanford University, and he subsequently took his ideas to Yamaha of Japan. The outcome was the Yamaha DX range of synthesizers, one of the most significant steps forward in easily accessible electronic music. For those interested in imitative synthesis, it is possible to produce extraordinarily lifelike sounds, especially with bells and brass.

The DX synthesizers allow six sine-wave oscillators (termed 'operators') to be interconnected on one of thirty-two different algorithms, such that cascades of modulator–carrier relationships may be formed, or arrangements where operators are simply mixed. Each operator has its own envelope generator, and may give a frequency which is either fixed or which tracks the keyboard. There are several methods of controlling the output level of each operator, and thus the deviation of any carrier it is acting upon, in addition to its envelope generator: the level may be made sensitive to key velocity, to aftertouch, to various controllers, to an LFO, or to the position of the key on the keyboard. Pitch control is more limited, to the bend-wheel, LFO, or a master pitch envelope.

There are a great number of parameters to be adjusted in a DX synthesizer, and they are accessed by the now common method of selecting the parameter to be edited with a push-button, and then using a data-entry slider or up/down buttons. By using Systems Exclusive MIDI commands these operations can be done remotely, and there are several 'DX editor' software packages available for microcomputers fitted with MIDI interfaces to make the job easier, with graphic representations of envelopes and so on. These may be useful, since processes such as softening a sound, which is easy on an analogue synthesizer (just reduce the filter frequency), can involve adjustments to several operators. Indeed, developing sounds with an FM system is often a more challenging affair than with an analogue system, because there may be several ways of approaching the same problem, and predicting the result of a change is not easy. As with many other modern synthesizers, whole patches may be stored on non-volatile media such as floppy disc, solid-state cartridge, or tape, using further System Exclusive MIDI commands.

Sampling

A sampling synthesizer is one which makes a digital recording of a sound and then replays it at appropriate pitches on triggers from an input source, such as a keyboard or incoming MIDI. From digital recording theory it is clear that the higher the sampling rate, and the greater the resolution (the 'number of bits'), the better the sample. The first sampling synthesizers, such as the Fairlight Mks. I and II, used eight-bit resolution and sample rates up to about 33 kHz; later machines use twelve- or sixteen-bit resolution, helped by compansion, and sample rates which reflect those in the parallel technology of straight digital recording. Improvements in this area are directly dependent on developments in memory technology.

Samples of simple percussive events are fairly easy to use, because the incoming trigger (from keyboard or MIDI) just 'fires' the sample at the appropriate pitch, which then plays through to its conclusion. But, for sustained notes, the sample must be able to continue playing as long as the note is held down. This means making a 'loop' in the sample, whereby a defined section of the sample will be played repeatedly as long as the note is held. To avoid hiatuses, the end of the loop must be at the same instantaneous level as the beginning, and the loop must be long enough not to be uncomfortably recognisable. In an effort to make loops less noticeable, some machines offer 'backwards–forwards' looping, where instead of shuttling from the end of the loop to the beginning the looped section is played backwards to the beginning, then forwards again. Other options include automatic looping, where the machine itself selects suitable zero crossing points to define the loop.

The simplest sampling synthesizers offer merely the ability to make digital recordings and define loops. More advanced machines give the user the opportunity to modify the samples, and to mix or edit together different samples. It is here that the opportunities exist to create innovative new sounds from natural sources, and develop the concepts of *musique concrète* outside the limitations of classic tape manipulation. Techniques borrowed from analogue synthesis, such as filtering and envelope shaping, or even from word processing, such as 'cut and paste', are currently being applied to sampling.

Digital recording is a memory-intensive business, and the cheaper machines which rely on floppy-disc storage have limited sample lengths. Unlike a digital recorder, a sampling synthesizer needs effectively instantaneous random access to the recording. But bigger synthesizers like the Fairlight and Synclavier, which use hard-disc storage or, in time, even more advanced fast-access systems, can offer very long sample lengths, so that the conceptual division between a 'sample' and a 'finished recording' is merely semantic. Here the worlds of synthesis and digital recording begun to blur, and a sample may in effect be a whole piece.

One specialized division of the sampling family is the drum machine. While older versions used analogue resonant circuits and noise generators to simulate percussion sounds, modern drum machines employ samples of real instruments which have been carefully recorded using all the best studio tricks. The sounds may then be triggered by drum pads, by MIDI, or from a sequencer which is part of the drum machine itself. When such machines are driven by MIDI note on/note off commands, each sound is allocated to a specific note or set of notes: sadly, there is little agreement about which MIDI notes should trigger which standard sounds, although the better machines allow the user to set up a patch.

Sequencers

Sequencers bridge the gap between music as it is notated, with bar lines, note lengths, and expression marks, and music as it is played, with LSI chips. They store and replay not sounds but the instructions required to make those sounds, in a form which makes sense to the musician. In addition, they may be able to print out a score in standard musical notation.

The data is put in to a sequencer in one of two ways: real-time recording and step-time recording. With real-time the composer sets the sequencer running, probably with a click to give the timing, and plays a MIDI keyboard; and MIDI data is then recorded 'live'. It may subsequently be edited, to clean up mistakes, or even quantized, to bring fudged notes into correct timing. With step-time recording the notes, note values, and other parameters are entered by hand, directly into the sequencer itself.

For certain kinds of repetitive work, such as rhythm sequences, it is easier to build individual bars and then assemble those bars into complete pieces. This philosophy is usually found in drum machine sequencers. Here a bar or number of bars will be repeatedly played, and the composer can keep adding new material to the loop until it is complete. That 'sub-sequence' is then compiled with other sub-sequences to form the final track.

Most serious MIDI sequencers borrow the 'tracks' concept from multitrack tape machines and allow several different tracks to be recorded in parallel. The MIDI data for each track may then be sent out from physically separate MIDI OUT sockets (as with the Yamaha QX1) or mixed on one socket, with different MIDI channels assigned to each track. It is also possible to drive more than one sequencer in synchronization using special MIDI messages. So, for example, a rhythm sequence can be built with a drum machine, which is then slaved to a master sequencer which provides the rest of the music. The *system common* MIDI messages are used here: synchronization clocks, which are prescribed at 24 clocks per quarter-note (crotchet); the *start* message, which makes the slave play its sequence from the top as soon as it receives clocks; the *continue* message, which makes it resume playing from wherever it happens to be, again on receipt of clocks; and the *stop* message. *Song select* MIDI messages allow different sequences to be selected, and *song pointer* messages direct the slave to a particular start point in the sequencer. The data number which is transmitted after a song pointer status byte is the number of elapsed clocks since the beginning of the sequence, divided by 6. So, to point to the second bar of a sequence in 4/4, for example, the song pointer number would be $(24 \times 4)/6 =$ 16; that is 4 crotchet beats elapsed at 24 clocks per crotchet, divided by 6.

MIDI sequencers are locked rather strongly into the concept of bars (or measures, as they are often called). This is fine for straightforward songs, but for a composer of incidental music for TV or film it is highly unlikely that the 'hit points' he wants to use as the skeleton for the cue will fit nicely on to a regular 4/4 beat. He is therefore faced with the prospect of either disregarding bar lines completely—which will create a havoc of unreadable tied notes if the music is to be printed out—or building in tempo changes in the sequence to 'pull' the bars into the skeleton. As yet there is no sequencer which allows the composer to 'draw in the bar-lines' after the music has been recorded—but no doubt it will come.

Sequencers offer software designers ample opportunity to show off their talents at graphic presentation. The more basic dedicated machines just give numbers on an LCD display to show note pitch, duration, start time, and velocity; others use VDU displays either to show the music in proportional representation (with blocked-out lines on a musical stave, the length of which shows the duration), or in full musical notation, including all the Italian marks. The latter are clearly limited by the resolution of standard VDUs, and need movable 'windows' on the score.

Synchronization can be a big headache for TV and film music composers: in closed systems such as the Synclavier there are few problems, but composers using sequencers alongside multitrack tape machines have to lay down control tracks which incorporate any tempo changes necessary, and then use those control tracks to drive the sequencer. The whole system has then to be linked to time-code. This is an area to which the manufacturers are currently giving a great deal of attention, since so much electronic music is used for incidental scores for TV and film, and there should be rapid developments.

Music computers

Virtually all modern synthesizers incorporate microprocessors and could therefore be called dedicated 'computers', but certain larger systems (such as Fairlight, Synclavier, and the PPG Waveterm) reserve the title Music Computer because they set out to offer complete music systems. They give complete studios in a box, needing only loudspeakers, and offer all types of synthesis together with sequencing, synchronization, and even final digital mastering. The music computers in use at the research establishments such as IRCAM, Stanford, and MIT have not yet made an impact on commercial electronic music, though this may well change. The IRCAM 4X, for example, allows the composer to build systems using software modules rather than hardware. Such ideas are already penetrating the mass-production market.

At the other end of the scale, the personal computer market has taken a very great interest in electronic music, not only for editing DX sounds but also for sequencing and data storage. More sophisticated programs are available for machines such as the IBM PC and the Apple Macintosh which offer complete MIDI control systems, together with score print-outs, although the sound chips used in these machines are not up to standard for serious sound creation. When linked with dedicated MIDI synthesizers, however, such systems may be very powerful indeed. One outcome of this market development has been that more and more people are able to afford to set up small 'bedroom studios' where material can be prepared, ready to be given the final gloss in the professional recording studio. As a result, the boundaries between what is 'professional' equipment and what is not are increasingly blurred: while there is a clear difference in performance between a studio tape machine and a domestic one, a MIDI sequencer package for a home computer may well be more useful to a composer than a dedicated machine with a much higher price-tag. Good software is good software, no matter what it runs on.

Looking ahead

It is significant that in the 'outboard peripherals' market more and more machines are appearing which offer not, say, reverberation alone or harmonizing alone, but sound processors which can be set up to perform any of the usual outboard tasks. Under the influence of the big mainframe systems currently found only in the research establishments, it is possible that these ideas will come to sound synthesis as well, and the present dividing lines between synthesizer, sound processor, mixer, and recording machine will evaporate. This is already happening in the very big systems.

Electronic music is now firmly in the hands of software designers, and it is to be hoped that they can continue to make equipment easier, clearer, and more friendly to use.

TABLE 18.1. **MIDI messages**

Status byte	followed by data bytes	Description
Channel messages—for specific MIDI channel reception		
1000 nnnn	key number	Note off event (nnnn = channel number − 1)
	key velocity	Middle C = key number 60
1001 nnnn	key number	Note on event
	key velocity	Velocity 0 = note off
1010 nnnn	key number	Polyphonic key pressure/after touch
	pressure value	
1011 nnnn	control number	Control change (see notes)
	control value	
1100 nnnn	program number	Program change
1101 nnnn	pressure value	Channel pressure/after touch
1110 nnnn	LSB	Pitch wheel change
	MSB	
System Common messages		
11110000	none	Start of System Exclusive message
11110010	LSB	Song position pointer
	MSB	number of MIDI beats into song, where MIDI beat = 6 MIDI clocks
11110011	song number	Song select
11110110	none	Tune request
11110111	none	End of System Exclusive message

TABLE 18.1. (*continued*)

Status byte	followed by data bytes	Description
System Real-time messages		
11111000		Timing clock
11111010		Sequence start
11111011		Sequence continue
11111100		Sequence stop
11111110		Active sensing
11111111		System reset

TABLE 18.2. **MIDI control numbers**

Control number	Function	Control number	Function
0	Undefined	68–95	Undefined
1	Modulation wheel or lever	96	Data increment
2	Breath controller	97	Data decrement
3	Undefined	98–121	Undefined
4	Foot controller	122	Local control on/off
5	Portamento time	123	All notes off
6	Data entry	124	Omni mode off (all notes
7	Main volume		off)
8–31	Undefined	125	Omni mode on (all notes
32–63	LSB for controllers 0 to 31		off)
64	Damper pedal (sustain)	126	Mono mode on (poly mode
65	Portamento		off)
66	Sostenuto	127	Poly mode on (mono mode
67	Soft pedal		off)

Notes on Controllers: Control numbers 0–63 are for up to 32 continuous controllers, such as wheels or sliders. The MSB values are given after control numbers 0–31; corresponding LSB values, if required, are given after control numbers 32–63. Controls 64–95 are for switches. Controls 122–7 are reserved for Mode messages.

19

The role of the producer

Phil Wainman

For many years, when a problem has arisen in the studio, I have often wished I could refer to an imaginary 'Producer's Handbook' which had the answers to everything from machine breakdowns to people with similar ailments. Thus I see my chapter in this book as being perhaps more along the lines of a 'Dr Spock of Record Production', something that reflects my own experiences through the years, rather than a tome on the dos and don'ts of recording, mixing and cutting.

A painting analogy is probably apt as, like an artist with his raw materials—paint, oils, brushes, and canvas—the record producer begins with a song, a piece of music, someone to sing it, someone to play it, and some studio time, in the same way as a painter would begin with a blank canvas. The challenge is to produce work interesting enough to attract an audience.

The dictionary definition of 'produce' is 'to bring forward or show for examination', and of 'producer' it says 'a person producing articles of consumption or manufacture'. I have heard the role of a producer in the record industry being likened to that of a director in the film world, and I suppose that is true in that a record producer has to be creative, efficient, and something of a psychologist (as does a director), but I would add other elements. After all, a producer is working within the framework of a song which leaves room for interpretation, whilst a film director has to work more closely with his original material in the form of a script.

What a producer needs

First I would say that a record producer has to have infinite patience. He has to have discipline (definitely an asset with some bands) and responsibility, and the ability to pick a good song, together with the ability to add an element of surprise to that song (when he gets into the arrangement and production of it) in order to end up with a record which stands out from the hundreds of others.

Production is a very human part of the music business. It's very personal, and the producer should be able to contribute artistically to the end-product. Record production is all about people and working together, and I think you can actually tell when a record has been put together by people who all enjoyed the process. Conversely, you can hear if there has been friction, musically.

If you can get all these elements together, including of course a hit song, you should be in pretty good shape. It all sounds great, doesn't it, but there is a minus side which you should think about carefully if producing is your professional aim.

You will have almost no social life! So, if your social life is important to you, perhaps you should reconsider your career. You have to be prepared to give up so much in the way of a personal life that you sometimes wonder why you're doing it. If you have a family, they will need to take second place to your work, at least until you are a track-record producer and have the luxury of being able to pick your projects. It is not uncommon to work 16-hour days which leave you feeling jet-lagged and completely out of sync with what is going on in the outside world. Music is one thing and the 'normal', conventional way of living is another. So you have a choice—either you continue with your social life, friends, family, or whatever, or you become a record producer!

I began producing in the 1970s, and I was lucky to get a start then, because the music business was a very different animal from the one it has become in the 1980s. Also, I was fortunate to be around when so much was happening musically. The Beatles were strong influences and from America had come Motown. Those records and sounds are still being emulated today. I was beginning to get noticed as a writer and player, having come off the road touring as a drummer in France, Germany, and Scandinavia, to join The Paramounts (who were later to become Procul Harum).

As a writer, I had been demo-ing my own songs for some time and had begun the laborious business of treking around the record companies trying to get my songs recorded by bands who already had record deals. I had been doing some session work too, which helped to get me in the door to the A. & R. departments.

A. & R. (Artists and Repertoire) men are basically the people who sign talent to record companies, whether it be in the form of finished masters or new bands needing development. Some young artists are quite often signed to a music publisher simply because the writers have shown some potential. A good music publisher plays an active role in the development of young talent. He can help structure the act and subsequently open doors to the relevant A. & R. department.

In the 1970s, production was all about the strongest-willed person; it was whoever shouted the loudest. I think it was that, coupled with my reputation in the studio for coming up with ideas for sounds, arrangements, and song structures, that really gave me my first production break.

The song was 'My Au Pair', and was a rewrite of 'Little Games', a title of mine which the Yardbirds cut when Jeff Beck and Jimmy Page were in the line-up. It was a minor American hit for the band; I really liked the melody, so I decided to change it a bit and go in with an orchestra and take a very different approach. Obviously the costs of working with an orchestra were and are much higher, and I needed the talents of an arranger. I knew what I wanted to end up with musically, and I could hum the parts, but, as I said, an orchestra is expensive and you must have a written arrangement for the musicians to be sure of getting all the orchestral parts down in one session. However, I still needed a budget in order to get into the studio in the first place.

Luck plays a large part in this business and I had a nice slice of it handed to me at just the right time. I met a man who wanted to get into the music business and he agreed to finance my project—as long as I would produce a particular girl singer on the same session.

We agreed to work together, and I went ahead and cut both my song and his. Both titles were released and although they did not make the charts they gave me a working introduction to the record companies. As I mentioned, I had worked for a lot of them as a session player, but now they saw how enthusiastic I was about getting into production and I began to get regular work as a producer.

Getting started

In some ways it is much easier to get a start today. Home recording set-ups are relatively easy to put together, both from a technical and a cost point of view, and many writer-producers start in a domestic situation working with their own portastudios, guitars, synthesizers and songs.

These songs may then be heard by A. & R. departments, who may say, 'OK, we believe you've got something here; the ideas are great but the technical quality is not good enough.' In these circumstances the record company will probably let the writer-producer loose at a professional level in a proper studio with good equipment, state-of-the-art desks, monitors, effects, etc. Before you know where you are, you are on your way to producing; remember that hits can be created in your home set-up too. In fact, going back to the 1950s and 1960s, although recording was far less sophisticated then, a spate of 'garage band' hits came out, mainly from America, and here in Britain too there have been chart records that started life as home-recorded tracks. Thomas Dolby and Dave Stewart certainly came up the portastudio route, as did many others, because it is a way for germinal writer-producers to express themselves with little capital investment.

The other road to record production is via a professional studio, beginning as a tea boy and working up through tape copier, tape operator, assistant engineer, to engineer. Provided you have the other qualities I mentioned earlier, you should soon start contributing creatively to the sessions you are working on. Then, if you are lucky, you will get to work with a particular act as co-producer, maybe working on the B-side of the next single. If the record company likes what you have done with the track, you might be offered a band to produce by yourself.

I think the engineer-producer probably has it easier than the writer-producer in these early stages, as the engineer has already got all the tools to hand. He just needs to prove himself by growing up in a professional environment.

I can appreciate both types of producer and I believe the differences add colour to the chart. I am primarily a musician and a writer, and therefore I like getting involved in the material itself, working closely on the arrangements with the band. I tend to rewrite lines sometimes, put in key changes and breaks, and generally work as another writer within the band to develop their songs. Of course I will take a look at the technical side too. I like to look at it objectively, through the ears of a potential record buyer, but I think that an engineer-producer sees a different picture. He thinks mainly about creating different colours with sound and may not look at the musical details of the songs as much. Providing there is somebody in the band who is a good writer, the engineer-producer can complement him and that can work very well.

Hits and budgets

The only way record companies can survive is to have hit records. That is of course stating the obvious, but it is very unlikely that a record company would sign an act just because it loved the music. A band or a singer must also look good; the image is very important. Above all else the record companies are looking for hits, and they have to feel that any act they sign has all the ingredients. The choice of the right producer for a new signing is very important, as he is expected to become part of the team and deliver that potential.

Second only to the material, the main concern for a producer is the budget. Record sales fluctuate from year to year; budgets do the same, and the recording is only a part of the whole process of making an act successful. Once the recording is completed, the company has to invest heavily in marketing. For instance, a video to promote the record on television can often cost far more than the recording itself.

If you are asked by an A. & R. department whether you think you can bring a particular single or album in for a certain budget amount, and you say that you can, you have to stick rigidly to that figure. Otherwise you will find that you lose credibility as a producer (and in some cases money) no matter how wonderfully creative you may be in the studio.

So it is important to evaluate exactly what you have got to work with before committing yourself. How much are you going to need for recording time and for mixing time? Is the band going to need additional musicians, booked on a session basis? Can they handle their own backing vocals, or do you feel you might like to add, say, a girl vocalist to the voices you've got, to change or brighten the sound? Are you going to need to hire in specialist players, synth programmers, and the like? What about an arranger?

All these different things have to be looked at, and it may be an idea to budget each area separately. Whether you actually use or need them or not, you are developing your credibility with the company.

Remember, there are ways to save money too. A lot of the work can actually be done before going into the studio. Working out the routine of the song is very important, because you can usually tell early on whether you have got it right; it is also cheaper to work things out in a rehearsal room rather than in high-cost studios. If you find the band can handle their own backing vocals, it might be worth spending some time working out what everyone sings, so that, when you are in the studio, you can do all your back-up vocals in the shortest time possible. Routining outside the studio also gives you a chance to get to know the people you are going to be spending a lot of time with; you can also find out how temperaments interact and whether there are musical weaknesses in the band which need covering by session players.

I can recall working for the first time with a certain group in Edinburgh. I had gone up there to cut some exploratory tracks and to get to know them, when I became aware that they were in fact checking me out. The leader seemed to keep coming up with the silliest questions, but I knew my time to turn the tables on him would come.

When it came to his vocal overdub, his tuning left plenty to be desired— either he was very flat or the track was very sharp! I told him that there was a well-established technique I often used to overcome this problem. We would record him whilst he was standing on a chair, and this would help him to hit the high notes. We did a take, and then I told him that he was now singing too sharp, but that if he bent his knees a little, it would be about right. He really fell for it, by which time the rest of us were in hysterics. This evened the score and certainly helped to break the ice. After that, of course, we became firm friends and subsequently worked together for some years.

Another way to cut costs if you have agreed a tight budget, is to work in less expensive studios to record, and then work in more upmarket ones when it comes to mixing. It is a question of how much you have to spend.

In any case, you will not be expected to come with a budget at the first meeting when you are called in to discuss the project. A. & R. men are used to producers taking time to evaluate the situation before committing themselves; but when you have, you must be responsible for the recording from start to finish. It is not just a question of going in there and being one of the boys having fun making records. You have got to remember the money side and be as cost-conscious as possible.

Once you have delivered the record and perhaps remixed it because the A. & R. man does not think you have got quite enough voice in one spot (or there is not quite enough bass throughout), the marketing machine takes over. Marketing includes press coverage, sales, and promotion. The record company will aim to get the record higher on the chart than the competition. This means air-play and television exposure, and their ability to achieve this is also part of your responsibility. You should have taken care to avoid any reasons for air-play not being forthcoming—bad language, say, or plagiarism, or out-of-date references.

The recording session

Let us look at the recording process in more detail. If you are working with a straight rock band, the best way is to start with the rhythm section; alternatively, with today's electronic techniques, you may start right from scratch and lay down a time-code which will govern your timing. I personally prefer to work with the musicians, as I think that ideas will come from the rhythm section as they actually begin playing. It also means there is a basic element of feel to the track. The bass player may come up with something to complement what the drummer is doing. (The producer can also have his input, and soon the pattern will begin to emerge.) The chemistry between the musicians and the producer during the actual session improves things to my mind. It is certainly more human and less mechanical. However, having said that, there is a lot to be gained from tracking individual instruments in certain situations. It is part of the producer's responsibilities to work out which is the best method for any given situation.

It is a good idea, too, to lay a guide vocal at the same time as you are putting down the rhythm track, as the musicians get a feel for the song. Certainly, once you have got the basics, you must include a guide vocal, as it is around this that you are going to build all the other musical lines towards the finished production. Next you should look at the backing voices, if any. Use as many tracks as you need, then bounce them down to stereo pairs in order to retain as many tracks as possible for other overdubs, synths, guitars, brass, or whatever. Finally, lay the lead vocal—the icing on the cake.

During the sessions you may find that the band are coming up with ideas for arrangements, instrumentation, or interpretation, and of course their ideas should be discussed and tried. You will get situations where you completely disagree with each other, and then it is a question of knowing where to stop, which is where psychology comes into play. You have to know how strongly the band feel about their ideas and whether you can use them, elaborate on them, or adapt them, or whether you have to insist on taking your own route; but remember that time is money. It is sometimes a fine line you have to tread when dealing with this kind of situation. Diplomacy comes with experience, as does dealing with a temperamental artist.

It is your responsibility to get the best vocal performance from an artist, again knowing where to stop. It is pointless continuing if the singer's voice is strained after two or three hours working on the same title. It might be that you just take a break from that and do some other overdubs, coming back to the lead vocal at another time. However, if you are very close to the right sound, then you should continue and capture the performance at that moment. The trick is knowing when you have it. You have to know when enough is enough, and say, 'We've got it. I'm very happy with that one.'

The best way of working with a band depends on what sort of band it is. If there are one or two writers in the line-up, they may feel that they need constantly to bounce their ideas off someone else. This someone else could be another member of the band, which would make them pretty self-contained, but it is more usual for that other person to be more objective about the whole unit—and then it is important for them to record with a producer at the helm.

A producer's role with a solo recording artist is somewhat different in that there are only two people to make the decisions. The song is the key here, as its direction and feel will dictate what type of track you are going to be looking at recording. You will certainly need a rhythm section, but you may be looking at a piece of work which cries out for orchestral backing, so you have to plan your sessions accordingly. You may decide to use a rhythm section which is an integral unit, either a band in their own right or a nucleus of musicians who regularly work together in recording studios or backing solo singers on live gigs. There your approach will probably be similar to that used in recording a group line-up. However, if you are thinking in terms of an orchestra, you may wish to hand-pick your rhythm section for certain individuals, to make up the total picture you have in mind. In any event, you will need to lay down a guide vocal early on and plan your overdubs around that, be they brass stabs, guitar solos, or a fully arranged orchestral session featuring string, brass, percussion, etc.

Sometimes fate can take a hand, turning something bad into something good. On one occasion, my multitrack tape was at one studio, whilst my forty-piece string section and I were at another. I had asked the studio holding the tape to have it biked over to me, but, for one reason or another, the multitrack arrived one hour after the musicians had left. In the meantime, however, I did have a $7\frac{1}{2}$ ins copy of the track with me and so I played that to the string section and recorded their parts straight to quarter-inch stereo. Then, when the multitrack finally arrived, I spun the strings into spare tracks. There was a bonus in that the strings phased with the original track, giving it a unique overall sound which I would not have got otherwise.

With a solo artist, too many people tend to look 'middle of the road' and play safe. Of course you have to get into the songs, to see what you have to work with, but then you should go to the extreme and try to be different. Try to create something which will stand out from the rest of the current chart releases. It is often worth trying something really weird and wonderful if your budget will run to it. But do remember that you and the artist are both in there to come up with a hit record, and you have to consider what he is trying to bring out in his material. If you push him or her too hard, you may find yourself with a difficult artist on your hands. You will then be better off taking five minutes or so to cool off and talk—always outside the studio, and never in front of the other musicians or studio staff.

The tack to take in this situation is to say, 'It's in both our interests to come up with a recording and a performance that is better than average, and that is the reason why I am pushing you.' You may even have a word privately about the singer's interpretation or diction.

Finally, let us look at the self-contained artist or one-man band. If you have a writer who sings and plays guitar or synths, he will be able to programme his own machines. In this situation you would definitely begin with a time-code on click-track, from which you would develop a drum pattern. Against this you would track all the other instruments, laying them one on top of the other. It has become fashionable to work this way, and it is certainly cost-effective. For myself, I still prefer to work with a band, as I find there is a tremendous amount they can give me. I then become part of a team, rather than a producer working in a purely mechanical fashion where most of my input would be at the mixing stage.

Live albums

Live recording is another area you need to understand in order to be a successful producer. As an artist's recording career progresses, he will inevitably want at some time to record his material in concert. I would say that the main thing you have to remember is that you are not going to be able to stop the band in mid-set, in order to re-record something you could not get right first time. The most important thing is to make sure that all the microphones are working and conveniently placed for the band, so that nothing handicaps the live performance, and leads are not going to be pulled out or anything knocked over by accident.

You, as the producer, are usually stuck in a vehicle outside the venue, and once the show starts your only method of seeing what is going on is via a TV monitor; the rest of it is very much an aural exercise. I remember, when making a live album with Sweet, that I got myself out of trouble by ensuring that I had plenty of ambient mics around. On that particular date I ended up with some mics not working, and the ambient mics really saved the day. Of course, if it is necessary, you can add a little sound sweetening in a remix room later.

The engineer

When it comes down to it, the producer has to be the final arbiter, either in the studio or on a live recording date, but someone equally important to the project is the engineer. I have one rule I always try to adhere to. Do not get in his way. Of course you are directing the session, but once you have established what it is you are looking for let the engineer get on with his work. The producer has to look at things objectively, remembering the potential buyer's ear. If something sticks out as being really wrong, then you have to do something about it. Other than that, you should give the engineer his head and let him contribute, rather than suppress him. If there is a particular sound you want or, for instance, you need more tracks and think the solution is to bounce down (which of course it very often is), listen to him, be guided by him; that is what he is there for.

At the moment we are looking at two different trends in engineering. There are those from the old school who are able to handle a complete line-up of musicians, though they are getting fewer and fewer. A lot of the younger engineers are very contemporary in their approach to modern-day recording, in that they are used to synthesizers for everything, and you virtually never see a live musician playing an acoustic instrument on their sessions. Everything is plugged in, and, with a lot of engineers today, if you say 'We have a live drummer today', they may have a problem in knowing how to mike up a real kit. Choose your engineer according to the type of session you are producing. If you have an orchestral session, look for an engineer who can handle that, and conversely, if you have an electronic set-up, look for an engineer who is used to working with that format.

Some of the larger studios do get large line-ups, more particularly for film music, and these studios are able to train youngsters accordingly. However, line-ups are generally getting smaller, due to budget limitations, and those smaller line-ups are often used in conjunction with synthesizers.

I personally do not think that the industry is doing enough to address this problem, but, with costs escalating for live line-ups, the only alternative is to use synths, and this seems to be the route many are taking.

The mixing session

Never say, 'We'll sort it out in the mix.' If it's wrong, it's wrong; and it's going to take twice as long to do it later. So do make sure you have everything you need on the tracks before you finish your actual recording. When you feel you've got to the point where you have everything on the tracks, it's time to begin your mix.

Mixing, again, is all about personal taste, and you can mix in thousands of different combinations. First decide on the vocal interpretation you want. You might decide to use a chorus from one track, a verse from another, and a second chorus from yet another. There are really no dos and don'ts in mixing, but basically the vocal track has to have first consideration as you need to be able to hear the voice to determine what the song is actually all about. Apart from that, you need a bottom end, a top, and various degrees of middle. If you bear in mind our painting analogy when you are mixing, you are actually painting a sound picture. When you look at your picture it must have perspectives, and this is important to understand. You may be sitting between a pair of speakers, listening to the detail: the detail is important, certainly, but you have to remember that you must make the overall sound of the record as interesting as possible.

At this stage, you may decide to use some ancillary equipment to enhance a particular sound on a vocal or instrumental line. You are trying to deliver three minutes or so of excitement, and this sometimes means taking a chance to try something wild. Provided you have got it right on the basic tracks, you can afford some experimental trickery with the new digital equipment available.

There are areas of recording which I have deliberately not covered, specifically because I consider them to be marketing tools, or passing fashions. One example is the 12-inch EP version of the standard 7-inch single. At the moment there is every chance that your multitrack tape will be shipped across the Atlantic for a currently hot American remix specialist to make his input. It might be that you have the 7-inch and he has the 12-inch credit. I think it is just a passing phase.

EP's are considered to be good value and can therefore motivate purchase. As, at present, any record with a playing time of less than 20 minutes is counted as a single, an EP release, plus the 7-inch version and an extended 12-inch club mix with maybe one other title, can certainly help not only to sell records but also to build the artist.

Finally, your work as a producer on any given project is not finished until you have delivered the master in the formats that enable the record companies to produce the sound carriers to be sold to the buyers. At one time this meant only cutting the master on to lacquers for black vinyl production, but with the advent of new technology you now have to consider CD and cassette production too.

You will master directly from tape to lacquer for the production of black vinyl records. With CD you must first prepare a production master on a digital format. You must make sure that the production master for vinyl is not used for this, as there are compromises made for vinyl production, which are not necessary for Compact Discs. For instance, there can be a loss of top in the vinyl production process which you have to compensate for in the cutting. This does not happen with CD, where the digital production master and the subsequent disc will sound identical to the finished mix.

Take care too, when deciding the running order for an album, that the general level from title to title is the same. With cassettes, the running order may differ from the album version so that the two sides are equally balanced in terms of running time.

It is advisable to make friends with the cutting engineer, and to be present at every first cut of your production. Do take his advice; he will be experienced and aware of the needs of the production departments at particular record companies, pressing plants, etc.

And there you have it: a potted guide to production. Of course there is much more that I have not talked about. It would be impossible to cover every eventuality; every artist and every session is different; each recording studio has its own little quirks; every A. & R. man his own ears. If you have decided to make record production your career, grab every chance you can to talk to people with experience and a love of their craft. At the end of the day, you will only learn by your out-takes and by making the most of every opportunity that comes your way. See you in the charts.

THE CONSUMER PRODUCT

20

The role of post-production
Ben Turner

Why post-production?

After a recording leaves a studio, there is a general assumption that a magical change occurs, transforming the master tape into cassettes, records, and Compact Discs. In fact, this metamorphosis is the result of a considerable post-recording production process. Examples of this process include editing, re-equalization, and the 'harmonizing' of tapes from other sources for compilation. In addition, a tape will need to be mastered in some form; a bin-master recorded for cassette duplication; lacquers cut for LPs; and a tape-master prepared for CDs. This Chapter will explore some of the differing and important roles that modern post-production technique has to offer and, at the same time, outline some of the decision-making processes which every post-production engineer has constantly to employ.

Selection of tapes

Finding the most suitable tape for a job is not as easy a task as may at first be thought. Record companies do not have a good reputation for keeping an accurate record of the many types of tape that they own, or even of where these tapes are physically located. To be fair, however, it can be difficult to tell the difference between a master, a safety copy, a production master, a copy of this production master, and so on. In this context there is need for dialogue between the engineer and the record company. After all, a record company relies on an engineer's assessment of a tape's recorded quality, as this cannot be determined merely by looking at it! On the other hand, the engineer needs to have definite guidelines on which he can judge the suitability of a tape.

One example may serve to illustrate some of the almost legalistic complexities which can arise: a record company sends over the tape of a new release for CD pre-mastering. The project is urgent, as the artist involved has suddenly become very successful. The tape turns out to be a non-Dolby 15 ips copy, recorded in Japan, of a tape recorded from a film sound-track. There is a fair amount of quiet material on the tape, submerged in an ocean of tape hiss. The record company sends a replacement copy but is growing impatient. This second tape turns out to be a copy of the version first sent! Further enquiry reveals that no other tapes are easily available except from Japan.

What should the engineer do? Should he stick his heels in and insist that he is provided with a better tape? Or should he plough on, regardless of the tape hiss? Neither decision will serve the client's best interests. The company will either miss the release date or, if unwilling to do so, come later to regret releasing a poor-quality, and therefore uncommercial, version of the album.

In some ways it has been the historical carelessness, by both record company personnel and post-production engineers, in using the first tape to come to hand which has led to difficult situations such as these. With the arrival of CDs, the importance of actually finding the 'correct' tape with which to work has become particularly significant. All concerned need re-educating in taking the greatest possible care to search out the most suitable tape to serve a particular purpose.

Compilation of tapes

Compilation takes two forms: either that of compiling new material (e.g. tracks for inclusion in new albums), or that of compiling previously released material (e.g. 'Best Of . . .' albums). The processes are broadly similar, although each requires a slightly different emphasis.

When dealing with new material, supervision of the post-production session is usually carried out by the producer, the artist, or a member of the record company's A. & R. department. This person should ideally know the material musically, and should also know in what order the tracks are to be placed, how long he wants them to last, what the maximum running time is to be, and so on. Constructive dialogue between engineer and client is of vital importance. To give one example, some people may refer to what one calls 'editing' as 'cutting', and to what one calls 'fading' as 'editing'.

Important matters for discussion between an engineer and client include, for instance: where a fade should start and how long it should last for; the length of time to be left between one track and the next; whether a cross-fade from one track to another is required, and so on. At times, an engineer may need enormous reserves of patience, while those around him debate the theoretical virtues, or otherwise, of a specific solution. In all such cases, the engineer should suggest adopting a practical trial-and-error approach. If the timing of a fade, for instance, is unlikely to 'work', a practical demonstration will be more informative than any discussion.

With either form of compilation, if re-recording of material is to take place one of the first decisions to be made concerns the format upon which to record. One example would be where the majority of the tracks for an album have been recorded at 15 ips, but one track has been recorded at 30 ips. Should the 30 ips track be 'downgraded' to 15 ips, or the 15 ips tracks transferred to 30 ips? Again, if some tracks are analogue and some are digital, should the digital material be 'downgraded' or not? Finally, if two different digital formats have been used, a production decision has to be made (probably on engineering advice) on which format to record the final compiled master.

The second decision will concern the amount of 'correction' which ought to be made to the individual sound quality of each track. For instance, tracks on an album should be related in level to one another, but this relationship can depend on the relative EQ of each track, since level and EQ are somewhat interdependent. The engineer may have an instruction to alter level but 'not to touch' EQ. Yet, since perceived level depends partially on the balance between bass and treble, to adjust the relative level of tracks without altering their EQ can be a futile exercise. Similarly, if one track has been heavily compressed and the following are not, level-matching may be impossible without resort to some compression of the latter track.

At present, the normal practice with new material is that it will be re-recorded, or simply edited, on to one format in the correct running order and with appropriate fades. This is the task of a specialist compilation engineer, or it may be carried out at either the analogue cutting or CD pre-mastering stage.

With compilation of older material, the work is most efficiently carried out by the specialist engineer, who is likely to be left to his own devices. He must therefore develop a sense of those approaches which best serve the interests of the client. He will re-record the material with all appropriate EQ and level correction. This saves time and also eases problems for the mastering engineers later in the post-production chain. The days of physically taking tracks out of masters in order to 'make up' a compilation—disregarding the fact that they may or may not have noise reduction, and that lining-up requirements may differ—have now, thankfully, passed.

Editing

Often tape needs to be edited, either to put together a complete performance from several takes of the same material or, as is more the case with pop music, to bring a certain track within a specified length of time.

Format is a crucial consideration. There is a choice between razor-blade editing (analogue or digital) or electronic editing (VTR or hard-disc-based). Cost considerations will be a major influence, the price of razor-blades being infinitesimal compared with the cost per hour of electronic editing. The decision about which format to use will also be based on the original format of the material in question, and on the type of editing which is to be carried out. For instance, if the material has been originally recorded on to analogue tape at 15 ips, it may not be cost-effective to transfer to a digital VTR format. The complexity and difficulty of editing classical music means that, in this case, electronic editing (see Plate 22) is now used almost exclusively. Pop music will

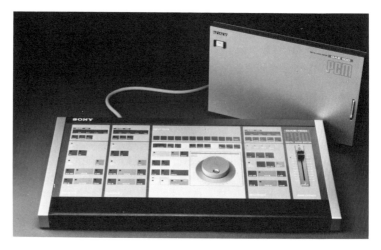

Plate 22. Digital editing controller (Photo: Sony)

generally be edited using the same format on which the stereo mix-down has been recorded.

All these decisions are essentially pre-production in nature, but, as has been stated before, informed engineering advice can be of the utmost importance. To give one further example: editing 12-inch mixes, where spontaneity is an important feature, is a nightmare on VTRs. This is partly due to the difficulty in isolating sections of music quickly, and partly because of the relative slowness of the whole editing procedure.

Once again, during an editing session, a major problem can be that of communication between the engineer and client. Many people are used to the physical handling of tape, but electronic editing means, of course, that this is not possible. Therefore, when dealing with 'invisible' tape, it is all too easy to become confused between two sections which sound the same, either within a take or between similar takes. Here heavy reliance on SMPTE time-code readers or similar is necessary.

Establishing a common vocabulary between engineer and client early on in the editing session is useful; discussing the difference between 'in-point' and 'out-point' is an obvious but good starting-point. Another communication device is for the engineer to keep the client fully informed as to exactly why he is performing particular procedures, such as recording sections of silence, or changing tapes at a particular time. Such advice is also relevant to razor-blade editing. It is wise on this type of session to ascertain whether a master should be spliced or whether a copy should be made first, as well as whether unwanted sections are to be kept or destroyed.

With all types of editing, at the start of an editing sequence one should always begin with the most obvious procedure, bearing in mind that Murphy's Law may well ensure that the least likely place at which to edit is the one which actually works in practice. It is up to the engineer to engage in useful dialogue with other parties in deciding on the choice of an editing position. At the same time he should always consider, if possible, more options than those suggested.

One problem which often occurs is that a splice is audible after the edit has been carried out. The essential point, in these circumstances, is that the engineer must be seen to be doing something of a constructive nature. He should never play an edit endlessly in the vague hope that some miracle will occur to make it inaudible. One solution with electronic editing is to remember that a cosmetic change to an edit may produce complete satisfaction.

With editing, the main qualifications are practice and experience, which themselves comprise the best form of instruction. In fact, experience builds up on itself, and no amount of theoretical work will prepare the engineer to meet those unique situations where creative imagination can be the key to success.

Areas of responsibility

Within the audio community, one major question which is often asked is to what degree, and at what stage, a recording should be tailored to match the medium for which it is intended. How far should an engineer bring his skill to bear on what may be interpreted as someone else's area of responsibility? Thus, if a recording engineer is using a 16-bit digital recording format, should he make allowances for the fact that the system's dynamic range of up to 96 dB is well outside the effective range of a vinyl disc or cassette? Should he control the amount of high-frequency content? Should he be concerned that the vinyl record cannot cope with large amounts of out-of-phase low-frequency content?

One possible approach at the time of recording is to ignore all those problems which might occur later at the mastering stages. This may mean, paradoxically, exercising an intelligent non-interference. It would, for instance, be unwise for a recording engineer deliberately to add overall compression to a rock album in the hope that this will help the vinyl mastering engineer to cut the album 'louder'. This sort of interference may be more damaging than helpful.

On the other hand, it would be foolhardy for a recording engineer to ignore vocal sibilance or excessive rumble. Rather than leaving correctable faults such as these to be dealt with by the post-production engineer, a recording engineer can usually remove them by modifying the equalization on individual channels on his mixer. Otherwise, a subsequent engineer may be forced to add EQ over an entire stereo mix in his attempts to minimize original recording problems, with the overall sound quality suffering as a result.

The question of dynamic range serves as another example here. Many engineers ignore this question, believing that on a Compact Disc, for instance, a wide range is not a real problem, and that it is up to the consumer buying the CD to provide the environment in which the whole dynamic range is audible.

But, leaving that aside, what is the vinyl or cassette mastering engineer to do when given a tape with a huge dynamic range? Presented with an unfamiliar digital master, the mastering engineer could turn out to be unsympathetic towards the musical content. He might be short of time, although at a mastering session with no producer present the engineer should ideally play a tape from beginning to end before committing himself. Even then, he might have no idea of the producer's philosophy about dynamic range. For instance, should the engineer apply manual level adjustment, use a compressor, or . . . what? Under these circumstances it is negligent *not* to provide the mastering engineer with relevant instructions, a negative request being just as informative as a positive one (e.g. 'Please do not use compression on mastering'). At the very least, an engineer or producer should provide the mastering engineer with precise information as to where peak levels are, where unexpected percussive effects occur, and so on.

Compact Disc pre-mastering

It is the CD pre-mastering stage which brings together all the various elements of what should ideally happen at the post-production phase. This is not to imply that either vinyl or cassette mastering is not equally important, but, as a CD is to all intents and purposes an accurate reflection of what was on the finished tape master, this master *has* to be of the highest quality. A CD should always strive to be transparent, giving the listener the impression that he is listening to a musical event as it in fact happened, not after it has been transferred from tape to tape, equalizer to equalizer . . . and so on. In other words, violent fades should be avoided, hiss should be manipulated so that it does not become obtrusive, cross-fades should be imperceptible, and level from section to section should be set so that the listener should not feel inclined, while a disc is playing, to change the volume at any time.

We can probably best illustrate some of the processes which may occur at the pre-mastering stage by giving hypothetical examples (based on real-life situations). Remember that at the moment most pre-mastering is carried out using the Sony 1610/30 system and the associated DAE 1100 electronic editor.

Suppose that, in our role as pre-mastering engineers, we are presented with a 1610 EQ'd production master (see definition below) of a pop album. There is no indication of the source from which this tape has been copied, nor has the record company or producer indicated any particular policy to be adopted during mastering.

We start the tape and notice two clicks during the first track, at the end of which hiss is audible as the fade comes to an abrupt end. The advantages of mastering using electronic editing techniques and an associated fader now becomes obvious. To begin with, the clicks can be simply edited out. The fade can then be improved by editing at a point before it begins and recording a perfected version, after any necessary practice. An added bonus of 'helping' the fade will have been the reduction of the hiss at the end of the track.

Some people may argue that all intervention of this nature is misguided. There is of course no right or wrong; an engineer will have to decide whether a 'fault' is the result of carelessness (as may have been the case with the cut-off at the end of this track); whether a fault is something that the original engineer had no influence over (the hiss in this case); or indeed whether any intervention at all will detract from the original nature of the programme.

The next track begins with a loud chord but is then followed by a quieter passage—and hiss—after which there are more loud chords. This situation presents a classic dilemma, for by 'helping' the fade at the end of the previous track we have accustomed the listener to 'quiet' programme. If we were now to ignore the hiss on this new track, we would spoil the effect achieved on the previous one.

There are several courses of action that can be taken. We could ignore the hiss completely (it may not be a 'problem' at all); a low-pass filter could be used; the gain could be reduced; or indeed both gain reduction and filtering could be utilized. Having carried out a particular course of action, it may then be best to restore the reduction of treble or of gain by using editing techniques: in other words, we stop at the first loud chord after the hiss and edit at this point, thereby restoring, at exactly the right point in the music, the gain or equalization back to normal. If on the master there had been a crescendo back to full volume, then obviously a gradual restoration to normality would have been in order.

We now continue, and find that before the start of the next track the origins of the original master are laid bare—print-through is clearly audible. In this instance we must surely take some action, possibly by judicious use of a fader.

It is important here to make a slight digression. Noise and hiss are obviously disturbing features on CDs, but so too is digital silence. This is most noticeable on classical material which is recorded, often as not, in a lively ambient atmosphere. If, between movements of a piece, ambience is faded to nothing, the result can be quite disturbing to the listener. To a greater or lesser extent, this fact holds true for all types of music, and it may be true to say that the more hissy or ambient a recording is then the more important it becomes to keep this background 'noise', of whatever sort, as consistent as possible. The writer has indeed on occasion *added* hiss or ambience to classical CDs during those silences where a hard-hearted engineer had previously been over-eager with a digital fader between movements.

The lesson to be learnt perhaps is that, when one is faced with print-through and other similar 'faults', one must be careful to reduce the gain, or use filters, only by just as much as is necessary to avoid detecting the fault at high listening levels.

Having been at pains to point all this out, in the following track we come across a seemingly contradictory situation. In this case there is an instance where the music stops suddenly, is followed by hissy silence for a few moments, and then suddenly starts again. At this point, the musicians presumably wanted to hear 'studio silence', not hiss; but we have seen above that introducing absolute digital silence here might be even more distressing. Bear in mind that there is a distinct difference between 'classical music silence', which in fact is usually quite noisy, and pop music's 'manufactured' silences. Devices such as gates or expanders are therefore not terribly useful at this stage. When applied over an entire stereo mix, it can be difficult to set up the required gain reduction, attack, and release times so that they react 'musically' with material.

The electronic editor's manual fader is again a vitally useful tool. The ability to rehearse manual gain reduction, for example, or manual addition of treble filtering at such problematical moments is of enormous value. In this particular case, one would therefore consider lowering the gain by just enough to reduce the perceived hiss level, so that the audible effect is that of things having become quiet but not actually silent.

Perhaps it seems that this concentration on noise and silence has been unduly emphasized, but it is attention to such details which provides one contrast between good and bad discs. If the consumer does not notice fades, hiss, or 'silence', then one's endeavours can probably be adjudged to have been a success.

We now come to the end of the first side of the LP, and another production-oriented CD problem occurs. How long should the gap between the end of side one and the beginning of side two be on the CD? Indeed, what action should be taken if some or all of the tracks on the album are cross-faded; should the break between sides also be cross-faded, in order to match in with the rest of the album? Each case has to be decided on its own merits—and preferably with advice. In any case, the ability to carry out cross-fades with efficient matching of levels is a technique with which all pre-mastering engineers should be familiar. At the time of writing, this is normally possible only in the analogue domain, but no noticeable degradation of the signal should occur if a second digital processor is used, the F1 format being useful here.

Another advantage in being able to cross-fade 'at will' is with an album of a live performance. This is an obvious instance of a case where the break between sides *has* to be cross-faded. But, in addition, a little judicious mixing of applause—from other moments in the tape—over those terribly audible joins between tracks which one often hears on live albums can give a CD the powerful impression that it has been thoroughly remastered.

We can now go to the end of our master. The tape has been rewound—and the telephone rings! The record company coolly announces that it wants an extra track to be put at the end of the CD. The tape is sent over, and we find that it has been recorded, mixed, and mastered at different studios to those of the album. The 'sound' of this final track will therefore be completely different to the other tracks. Another problem is therefore provided: should the sound be left as it is, or should the listener be persuaded that this additional track *is* part of the album and should thus sound 'the same' as those tracks preceding it? Advice will again have to be sought.

We have been considering here the technique of pre-mastering which is particularly relevant when dealing with material that has been previously mastered. The digital pre-mastering engineer is given a unique opportunity here. All other mastering engineers have to work in real time. If they make a mistake, they normally have to decide whether the mistake will prove to be noticeable, and go back to the beginning of the side in question, or carry on. As we have seen, the pre-mastering engineer can rehearse short sections until perfected, and continue only when he is satisfied. Such techniques will also be applicable when mastering tapes straight from a recording studio, when music-editing and conversational skills may also be required!

PQ encoding

One of the most important tasks facing the CD pre-mastering engineer is accurately notating the beginning and end points of each track. These timings are taken from the SMPTE time-code which should be present on all 1610/30 tapes. It is possible, when using an electronic editor, to find these timings to an accuracy of one SMPTE frame, that is to within $\frac{1}{30}$th of a second. Such timings are then written into a PQ editor which 'translates' them into a code which is then normally recorded on to the master U-Matic tape (see Plate 23). This operation is known as 'PQ encoding'.

The CD disc's subcode has room for eight different subcode channels: PQRSTUVW. The P channel designates the start of a track. R–W will be used for other information such as graphical displays. The Q channel contains such data as the total running time of the disc, the emphasis status, and any designated ISRC (International Standard Recording Code) for each track, and also has a facility for 'blocking' the digital output of a CD player. When a tape is mastered, the PQ code is encoded along with the programme content on to the master disc, so that whenever a CD is played the player can read this information from the disc, telling it exactly where tracks start, whether they have emphasis, and so on.

The act of finding the starts and ends of tracks appears to be a simple operation but in fact opens up yet another grey area for debate: the question of 'offset'. When accessing individual tracks, CD players mute the audio output, search for the new track, unmute, and start to play. The time taken to unmute varies with each model of CD player, with 'earlier' models generally taking longer than present-day machines. This unmuting time should not be confused with the time taken for a player to *search* for the new track, nor is it relevant when the player plays consecutive tracks (when the audio does not mute at all).

Plate 23. Subcode processor used in preparation of digital master tapes for Compact Disc production (Photo: Philips)

The problem is this: when entering the PQ data, one must obviously allow for the demute time. In other words, the time entered as the start of a track has in fact to be deliberately set too early. At the moment there is no international standard to define how long the offset should be, one of the obvious areas for discussion being whether one should allow for 'worst case'. Take the example of an opera, where the music is continuous but the producer wants individual arias to be given separate track designations. If we set the offset for each track to, say, one second, then on a fast unmuting player we will hear almost the last second of the previous number. If we offset by only one-sixth of a second (this being the shortest recommended time), then there is a good chance that 'slow' players will clip the beginning of the selected track. Although the latter case is the most objectionable, the former can be almost as annoying.

The offset problem has been aggravated by the fact that up until now most CD factories have recommended their own offset timing, whilst some pre-mastering facilities are now using their own PQ editor and thus have to decide on a certain offset time for themselves. Should the mastering facilities follow their own judgement, and upon what *technical* criteria should they make their decision? Conversely, why should factories dictate such matters when their only task is to replicate the customer's product? Such matters as cross-fade points and the timing of pauses between tracks are artistic matters, and should no doubt be left to competent pre-mastering engineers who are in close contact with either the record company or producer. The conflict is that most CD factories regard pre-mastering as an integral part of manufacture and therefore feel they have some right to judge the 'correctness' of any outside PQ editing.

There are signs that the major record companies are adopting their own in-house standards for such matters as offset timing, and are therefore insisting that their CD manufacturers must follow suit. Independent companies, it would seem, must make decisions based on limited information and despite the conflicting interests of others. Small wonder then, that these companies avoid making any decision—obliging the CD pre-mastering engineer yet again to decide important matters of policy.

Production Masters

It is now normal practice, at least in British and American vinyl-cutting rooms, to make a copy of the master tape which reflects the changes of level, EQ, vari-speed, reverberation, and so on that the mastering engineer, producer, and artists have decided to make during the cutting process. This copy of the master tape is known as an 'EQ'd production master', and this is the copy which is used for subsequent copying jobs such as cassette mastering, export copying, and, as we have seen, sometimes for CD pre-mastering. Although we have seen that these changes are perhaps best carried out—at least from the point of view that they can be perfected—at the CD preparation stage, there is still enormous debate with regard to the quality and indeed suitability of EQ'd PMs, which centres around two main issues.

The first of these is the question whether the changes being made to the sound of the original master, in order for programme to be physically cut into a lacquer disc, are so drastic that large-scale compromises are likely to be made to the sound of the original material. These compromises would take the form of high-pass filters, elliptical equalizers, high-frequency limiters, and so on. In these days of high-powered cutting amplifiers and computer-controlled lathes, these compromises are in fact few and far between. As a rough guess, about 90 per cent of album EQ'd production masters do *not* contain changes significant to that medium alone. For instance, even when cutting albums with long playing times, it is normal practice for the cutting level to be reduced to a minimum before high-pass filtering is introduced. On the other hand, it is true to say that, in the earlier days of cutting pop albums in stereo, there does seem to have been wide-scale monoing of low-frequency content, and it is for this reason that EQ'd PMs of this era should be used with caution.

The second objection to EQ'd PMs has been that one is dealing with a tape *copy* rather than an original master. When we are referring here to an analogue copy, there is no denying that some degradation of quality will have taken place in the copying process. Even in the all-digital domain, the use of sampling-frequency converters, to give one example, will lead to some degradation.

The reply to these criticisms of PMs—if one *has* to be offered—is best given in purely pragmatic terms. Of course, ideally, the original master should be used to make copies from, to make bin masters, and for CD pre-mastering. But, on the other hand, there are the obvious physical dangers in using an irreplaceable master. It is also true to say, having seen the sorts of changes that can be made to a master at the post-production stage, that at least in pop music a master ready for production copying cannot exist without the original master itself having been copied in some form.

Theoretically it *is* possible to notate all the changes which are made, and to keep these notes with the master. But, with no two studios having identical equipment, precise replication would be impossible. Another problem would be at cassette duplicating plants. No criticism is implied, but it is probably fair to state that most cassette mastering facilities do not have the esoteric equipment which is found in modern analogue cutting rooms, with which they could match the artistic changes made to a master. Nor would a producer probably want to supervise personally three mastering sessions—album, cassette, and CD—possibly at three different locations.

We can therefore see that the EQ'd PM is normally not the unspeakable aberration of the audio community which we have all been warned against using. Indeed, in many instances, the use of such a tape is unavoidable.

However, the inescapable conclusion is that, practically speaking, the CD master tape proves to be the most demanding and revealing medium for which to cater. Once a tape has been prepared for CD, digital copies can be made for other media. Therefore any necessary compromises which need to be made can be confined to one medium without compromising another. Indeed, with the advent of other domestic playback sources such as Digital Audio Tape (DAT), unless a standard finished master is derived at an early stage a sort of tape anarchy will break out, with rogue copies being duplicated erroneously, as is not unheard of even now with regard to CD mastering.

Copying

It is an unfortunate fact of life that tape copying has never been considered to be a specialist post-production function. This is a pity, because the inaccurate copying of tapes can, with a single careless throw of a switch, negate all the careful work that has gone into preparing a tape.

For various reasons, copying is seen by most studios as a junior's task. Little or no training or, just as important, reasoning is ever given to this junior. If copying is to be so relegated, we could at least give our junior the best chance of 'getting it right'. To deal with analogue tapes first:

1. High-quality tape machines must be used, and must be well maintained

and checked. Junior may not realize what wow is, until a tape slows to an unexpected halt in the middle of a track.

2. Tape stock should be of high quality. The use of left-over lengths of tape for album copies is unacceptable, as they may come from different batches with resulting differences in bias and so on.

3. Each reel of tape to be recorded on should be individually biased and EQ'd. Junior may not know the precise electronic reasons for so doing, but may perform these tasks more intelligently if he or she is given a rough idea of what bias does—and an idea of what programme sounds like on a tape which has been lined up incorrectly.

4. All tapes should have a selection of tones recorded at the beginning of the reel. Almost mandatory are a tone at 1 kHz, with left/right identification, a high-frequency tone (10–12 kHz), low-frequency (40–100 Hz), and Dolby tone if applicable. Ideally, there should be two low-frequency tones, say 50 Hz apart, as it is in this area that analogue machines show the greatest variation. Junior should be urged not to make individual sections of tone too short, as tempers get somewhat frayed when trying to line up a tape where a tone disappears just as an adjustment is about to be made.

5. Lining up tones from the tape to be copied should be carried out with scrupulous care, ensuring especially that Dolby tones read correctly on Dolby meters. Junior should perhaps be told to line up tones to an accuracy of 'plus or minus nothing'. (For a discussion of azimuth, which is also relevant here, see below.)

6. The actual level recorded on the copy will depend on many factors. Whilst one is careful here to respect the personal philosophies of engineers with regard to level, perhaps a few pointers could be set.

  (a) Care should be taken if the level recorded on to tape is elevated within the record machine. An inexperienced engineer may be content to see meters making frequent contact with the end-stops in the mistaken belief that there is always 'something in hand'.

  (b) Although ideally a tape should be copied at the same level as the master, there may be occasions where additional gain is required or else the gain needs to be lowered. An inexperienced engineer will need guidance relating to when he should intervene with level control. He may not appreciate that, with classical music for example, one may have to leave the level 'dangerously' high at peaks in order for there to be sufficient level at quieter moments to outweigh tape hiss.

7. Obviously, when copying, the use of as little electrical equipment as possible in the path between tape machines should be encouraged. Indeed, the best copies are made with the output of one machine connected directly to the input of the other. However, the ease of so doing should not disguise the need for the provision of some sort of console to provide monitoring facilities, gain manipulation, supply of line-up tones, mono/stereo switching, line-in/line-out

switching, and so on. In other words, if copying is to be done with the maximum fidelity an engineer must be provided with all the appropriate facilities with which to do the job.

8. One problem which has probably led to more 'faulty' copies being made than any other is carelessness with Dolby encoding and decoding. In order for level changes to be made to encoded tapes, it is essential that the encoded tape is 'destretched' (i.e. de-Dolbyed) before level variation is applied, and it is vital that correct calibration of replay tones is carried out at this time. Level variation can then be carried out subsequently, and the resulting programme can then be re-encoded if so required.

Although Dolby and other noise reduction devices are powerful tools, the havoc that they can wreak in inexperienced hands can be little short of disastrous. One might also add that, when noise reduction is being used and Junior is to listen off-tape from the record machine intelligently, then his room should be equipped with an additional decoder, so that, as with all copying, sensible remarks about the tape being copied—such as extraneous noises, hum, hiss—can all be noted down.

9. With every copy, a conscious decision should be made whether to copy with noise reduction or not, rather than the decision being left to whim. In other words, it seems nonsensical for a studio to adhere strictly to a 'no noise-reduction policy' without regard for the eventual use to which the copy will be put.

10. One of the first lessons on introducing a person to the job of tape copying is the 'reading' of tape boxes. The clairvoyant connotation here is most suitable, because the lack of relevant information given with most tapes (analogue or digital) *has* ceased to amaze the most hardened professionals. In the 'early days' of digital it was not uncommon to play a half-inch master on an analogue machine only to find the result puzzlingly silent . . . and then for the digital truth suddenly to dawn.

11. One can introduce at this time the importance of selecting the correct tape equalization on the replay machine, and can also discuss which characteristic should be used on the recording. Here again, as with noise reduction, there may be a standard 'in-house' recording equalization. Common sense should prevail, however. Although the equalization on most tape machines is switchable, it is regarded as being courteous—if nothing else—to copy 15 ips tapes for the USA with 'NAB' and tapes for the BBC with 'IEC/CCIR', to give just two examples.

It is at this point that one can begin to impart to the learner something about a 'sixth sense' which is so important to all engineers. This is the sense which tells an engineer that most tapes emanating from the United States are *likely* to be 'NAB' if they are not so described; that tapes which sound suspiciously 'bright' may have been subject to noise reduction even if not so notated on the tape box and even if they are without the identification tone; that some

Continental studios may line up Dolby tone to the 'DIN' mark on Dolby meters, and so on *ad infinitum*.

12. Many of the above comments are relevant to making analogue copies either from or to the digital domain. One further point is relevant to the analogue domain, but can be of crucial importance to the digital.

One of the first complaints about early CDs was of poor mono compatibility at high frequencies on some discs. Whilst the effect of 'time-shared' A to D converters was obviously one culprit here, what no one seemed to consider was that the problem could be an entirely human one. And so it has turned out to be. One small turn of a screwdriver or spanner on the replay head of the analogue mastering machine could have been a revelation to some CD pre-mastering engineers.

The term 'azimuth' refers to the angle at which the replay head (or any other head on a tape machine) sits in relation to the tape passing longitudinally across it. If on replay this angle is not set at precisely that at which the tape was recorded, high-frequency cancellation will occur. This cancellation is most noticeable when a two-channel recording is replayed in mono.

The correct adjustment of azimuth is obtained when playing the high-frequency tone recorded as part of the line-up sequence on the master tape. This adjustment is most easily carried out by using a phase meter, by looking at a 'Lissajous' display on an oscilloscope, or by combining the two channels on to a single meter and adjusting for maximum amplitude.

Once the adjustment has been carried out on tone, it is vital that a check is made on actual programme by listening alternately in stereo and mono. The reason for carrying out this further check is that, on multi-generation copies, the azimuth between tone and programme may differ, this in itself being due to an incorrect setting on a previous copy. The effect of incorrectly set azimuth—and the effect to demonstrate to the novice—is of 's' sounds becoming 'sshh' sounds, lack of brightness on cymbals and snare drum, and a general 'clouding over' of sound.

It should be clearly understood that, at the time of writing, if an analogue tape is transferred into the digital domain with an incorrect azimuth setting, nothing can be done to correct the fault while remaining solely in the digital domain.

13. Obviously the copying of digital tapes within the same format is a relatively easy task. This should not necessarily absolve the copying engineer from attentiveness during the copying process. Digital processors have been known to manufacture 'one-off' glitches and clicks, or even mute the audio output, without indicating that they have done so (static shocks being a common cause of this).

On VTR-based systems, where random access to various parts of a tape can be a tedious process, it is especially important that track and side timings are given. These timings should always be referred to the SMPTE or other code wherever possible.

Strictly speaking, a full line-up of tones is not necessary on digital tapes, although a 1 kHz tone is useful. This tone is normally equivalent to 0 VU or whatever the in-house line-up level is. This calibration is helpful at subsequent analogue copying or mastering stages. A high-frequency tone is also theoretically useful, as this shows up any possible fault in the mechanical emphasis relays which are present on some processors. Finally, as BNC video leads seem to have an even greater propensity for becoming reversed than do jackfield plugs, a left/right identification is valuable.

14. We can make a summary of many of the above points by pleading for as much information as possible to be put on tape boxes and labels. This information should include:

Date;	Engineer's name;
Address of studio;	Telephone number;
Name of client company;	Catalogue number;
Name of artist;	Title of album (if relevant);

Source of tape (e.g. 'copied from 1610 master' or 'stereo mix from 24-track');
Description of tape (e.g. 'CD tape master' or 'copy for radio');
Total time of track, side, or disc;
Level and frequency of line-up tones.

Supplied with, or included on, the tape box should be a complete list of track titles, takes, individual timings, and other relevant information: producer, location of recording, and so on. This information should also contain notes about all defects such as clicks, dropouts, hum, hiss, etc. which may be on the tape.

Analogue tapes should show in addition:

Speed;   Equalization;
Type of noise reduction (if used).

Digital tapes should show:

Type of processor;   Sampling frequency;
Emphasis status;
Type and length of tape (if manufacturer's labels are not used);
Whether tape has been verified (VTR systems).

Conclusion

The post-production engineer's prime responsibility is to produce finished material of the highest possible quality, whether this is a three-minute tape for one-off broadcast use, or an expensive 75-minute CD tape master. In either of these cases the standard of craftsmanship should be the same, with the greatest possible care being taken at all times and with all types of material.

It is human nature to consider that one's own role, as a link in a creative chain, is that of the highest importance. Any engineer responsible for post-production could claim such a place of responsibility in the creative hierarchy. After all, this engineer may be the last person with any creative control who listens to a product before its release to a potentially vast audience. If one were to be honest, however, the real nature of the role of post-production is to be invisible. The situation of a post-production engineer is not unlike that of a Victorian child, but in this case not only should he never be heard; his very presence should be undetectable.

21

Disc cutting
Sean Davies

A disc-recording machine consists of a turntable, a screw shaft (the leadscrew), and a carriage to which may be attached an electromechanical transducer (the cutter head). The leadscrew causes the carriage to travel along a radius of the turntable, and a chisel-shaped cutting tool fixed to the cutter head may be used to cut a groove in the surface of a blank disc placed on the turntable (Plate 24). The turntable normally rotates at a constant speed, and, if the same is true of the leadscrew, then a spiral of constant pitch will be cut in the disc. In practice the leadscrew speed is not constant but is altered to produce a variable-pitch groove, for reasons which will be apparent later.

Plate 24. Modern disc-cutting lathe with video camera attached to microscope for groove examination (Photo: Neumann)

The cutting stylus is made from artificial sapphire (fused aluminium oxide) or from diamond, and is ground to extremely fine tolerances (Figure 21.1). Up until the early days of microgroove (LP) recording (around 1953) most studios used a slab of specially formulated wax as the recording medium, upon which a sharp-edged cutting stylus could give a quiet groove and excellent high-

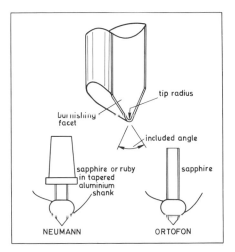

Fig. 21.1. Two types of cutting stylus, showing the chisel-shaped tip

frequency response. Unfortunately, the electroplating process used in the preparation of the metal master disc gave noisy results with wax, so the recording medium is now a blank disc with either a lacquer or copper coating into which the groove is cut.

The groove

Information is stored by causing the cutting stylus to move whilst it cuts the groove. For a single-channel (monophonic) signal this movement could be either lateral (Figure 21.2a) or vertical (Figure 21.2b) with respect to the plane of the disc; commercial mono discs always use the lateral system. The deflections of the groove are an analogue form of the electrical signal fed to the cutter head, but the conversion is deliberately made non-linear in terms of the recorded signal level relative to the input signal.

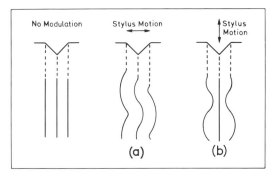

Fig. 21.2. Stylus motion in mono recording could be (*a*) lateral or (*b*) vertical

Consider a sine wave of constant frequency and amplitude (Figure 21.3). If this wave is taken to be the motion of a reproducing stylus as it traces a groove, then the maximum or peak velocity of the stylus (V_{max}) occurs as it crosses the centre or zero line. Now $V_{max} = 2fa$, where f is the frequency and a is the amplitude. If we maintain V_{max} constant while f is increased, then it is obvious that a will decrease. The effect is illustrated in Figure 21.4 for three different frequencies, each with the same V_{max}.

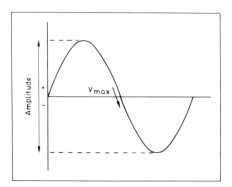

Fig. 21.3. Sine wave: showing that maximum velocity occurs as the signal crosses the zero-amplitude line

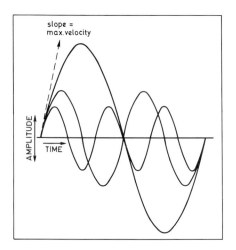

Fig. 21.4. Sine waves for three different frequencies having the same maximum velocity

Conversely, with reducing frequency, a must increase. The maximum allowable amplitude is governed by: (a) the space available between adjacent grooves, and (b) the ability of the reproducing stylus to follow the deflections. The minimum allowable amplitude is governed by the noise level of the system. In practice the velocity of the cutting stylus is attenuated for frequencies below

1,000 Hz and boosted for frequencies above. The amount of boost and cut related to frequency is known as the recording characteristic and has been standardized for some years on the RCA New Orthophonic curve, now known variously as RIAA, IEC, or BSI (see Figure 21.5).

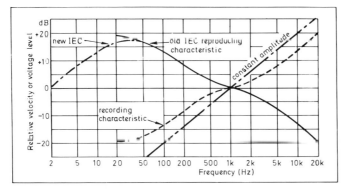

Fig. 21.5. Comparing the standard recording characteristic with the constant-amplitude line, and also showing the IEC reproducing characteristic with and without the more recent bass roll-off recommendation

For correct reproduction of the original signal, the reproducing system must incorporate a network known as the playback equalizer which gives an inverse or mirror image of the recording characteristic. Two points are worth noting: (*a*) noise inherent in the storage medium (e.g. granular and particle noise in the pressing) is attenuated by the HF section of the playback equalizer, and (*b*) low-frequency disturbances such as turntable rumble, vibrations, impulses, and induced mains hum are all boosted by the LF section. It is for this reason that the recording characteristic reverts to constant velocity at the extreme LF end.

The recorded level may be expressed in terms of stylus velocity, and it is here that disc recording has an advantage, in that there exists an absolute optical method of measurement of stylus velocity; that is it is not necessary to play the disc. The method is due to Buchmann and Meyer, and consists in observing the width of the band of light reflected from the groove walls. The width depends on the groove velocity regardless of frequency or disc diameter (but depends on the turntable speed, which is of course constant). The light used for inspection must have parallel rays and be at an angle of 45° to the disc surface, as must the observer (Figure 21.6).

Thus a cutting stylus designed to yield a constant-velocity cut would show a constant-light bandwidth. An ideal method for calibrating a system incorporating the RIAA curve is therefore to feed the test tone signal to the cutting amplifier via a precision attenuator which may be set to give the inverse of the RIAA at each selected frequency (above 1 kHz). The cut should then show a constant-light bandwidth.

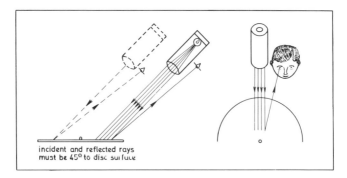

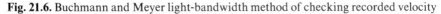

incident and reflected rays
must be 45° to disc surface

Fig. 21.6. Buchmann and Meyer light-bandwidth method of checking recorded velocity

The Stereophonic Groove

One of the prime requirements of a two-channel stereophonic transmission or storage system is that there should be negligible exchange of information between the respective left and right channels (crosstalk). Although total isolation is not possible in practice, the system should be designed to get as close to this ideal as practicable. In an ideal mechanical system, motions acting at 90° to each other would be non-interactive: a cutting stylus could thus carry one channel of information by moving in the plane of the disc (lateral) and the other by moving vertically. Picture a modulation cross placed within a section of the groove (Figure 21.7); by rotating the cross through 45°, the two channels are represented by motions upon the inner and outer groove walls respectively. This system was patented in 1932 by A. D. Blumlein (of the Columbia Graphophone Co. and EMI), and forms the basis of all stereo discs issued today.

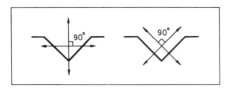

Fig. 21.7. Stereo recording: comparing the lateral/vertical method (left) with the 45/45 method used in practice

An important feature of the 45/45 system is the compatibility achieved with mono (lateral) discs, since lateral stylus movement represents equal in-phase signals on the two channels.

Variable-pitch recording

From early days, disc-cutting lathes were provided with a means of varying the speed of the leadscrew relative to that of the turntable, usually by a precision gear train. The recording engineer decided what pitch to set by consulting a chart showing playing time against pitch. Once set, the pitch was constant for the duration of the side. Since the maximum stylus amplitude allowable depends automatically on the space between adjacent grooves, the maximum recording level was also governed by the playing time of the programme. It will be clear that, when the amplitude of the cutting stylus is appreciably less than the maximum allowable (during quiet passages in the music), the groove pitch is unnecessarily wide, leading to a waste of disc surface area (Figure 21.8a). The ideal solution is to adjust the pitch continually so that the prevailing programme amplitude is just accommodated without intercutting (overlapping of grooves).

Although such a system was proposed quite early (a patent was taken out by the Parlophone Co. in 1929), it was not until the use of magnetic tape as an intermediate recording medium around 1954 that a working application was possible. The reasons for this will be clear from the following: in Figure 21.8b, the pitch A is known as the basic pitch and allows only a small (approx. 10 μm) space or 'land' between unmodulated grooves. The third turn contains a signal of such an amplitude that the pitch must be increased to a value B in order to preserve the same land between the peak amplitude and the previous groove. Assuming the signal to be symmetrical and no further signals ensuing, the pitch must be maintained at value B in order for the next (fourth) turn to clear the signal. Then, if no further signals occur, the pitch can revert to value A. The change in pitch from A to B implies an acceleration of the leadscrew and hence of the carriage, which latter often has an appreciable mass. Now force = mass $\times$ acceleration, and so if the new pitch B had to be reached at the same time as the signal arrived at the stylus, infinite force would be demanded of the leadscrew drive motor.

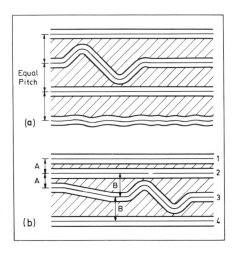

(a)

(b)

Fig. 21.8. Example of groove spacing: (a) showing waste of disc surface area when the recorded amplitude is less than the groove pitch allows, and (b) how, in variable-pitch recording, an increase in pitch from A to B to accommodate a large-amplitude signal must be maintained for the ensuing turn of the disc

To avoid this in practice, the tape is passed across a preview head (position 1 in Figure 21.9) whose amplified output controls the speed of the leadscrew motor: the playback head at position 2 feeds the audio signal to the cutting amplifier (see Plate 25). The distance d between the two heads is chosen so that the time taken for a signal to traverse the distance at a given tape speed is equal

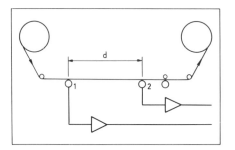

Fig. 21.9. Use of a preview head on a tape machine for variable-pitch recording: the preview head (1) precedes the playback head (2) by a distance d

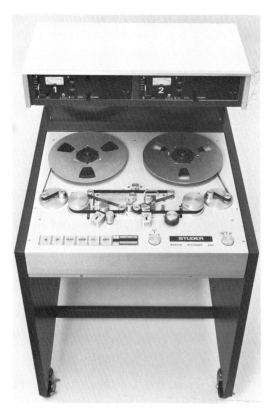

Plate 25. Two-track tape playback unit with separate prelistening heads and choice of tape paths for varigroove tape-to-disc transfer (Photo: Stüder)

to half a revolution of the disc at the given turntable speed. Alternative tape paths are provided for the various combinations of tape and disc speeds, as may be seen in Plate 25.

With stereo grooves, the signals are frequently asymmetrical, that is there is a vertical component reaching a maximum in pure vertical motion of the stylus, representing equal anti-phase signals. Such motion could cause the stylus to leave the disc completely on the upward swing. The obvious solution is to have a deeper basic groove. However, we should find ourselves in the same situation as with fixed pitch—having a waste of space at anything other than peak amplitude. Therefore, in addition to varying the groove pitch, we should vary the depth of cut when required by the phase content of the audio signal. Of course extra depth implicitly requires extra pitch, even before the modulation movements of the stylus are considered, so a complex signal-processing circuit derives the relevant information from the tape preview head (L R difference signal), (right signal for outer groove wall); and the playback tape head (left signal for inner groove wall) from which the required combination of groove depth and pitch is fed to the cutter-head mounting assembly and the pitch motor.

It is worth noting that, with variable pitch and depth cutting, the space taken up on the disc is governed by the programme content, and hence the playing time and maximum recordable level are interrelated in a different manner from that found with fixed pitch.

The cutting head

The cutting head is an electromechanical transducer whose action is best understood by considering the electromechanical system of equivalent units which are set out in Table 21.1.

TABLE 21.1.

Electrical quantity	Equivalent mechanical quantity
EMF (voltage)	Force
Current	Velocity
Inductance	Mass
Capacitance	Compliance
Resistance	Frictional resistance

Figure 21.10 shows a simple moving-coil cutter head and Figure 21.11 its equivalent circuit. To obtain a constant velocity-versus-frequency characteristic from the head, the system should be stiffness-controlled (stiffness is the inverse

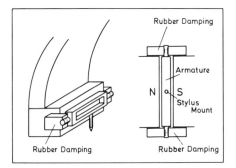

Fig. 21.10. Simple moving-coil cutter head

of compliance), which, by electrical network theory, implies that the system must operate below its resonant frequency, so that the latter should therefore be as high as possible. This may be achieved by reducing M_1 and M_2 and increasing R_1, but there are practical limits to the masses involved, and increasing R_1 reduces the overall sensitivity of the system. An alternative approach was

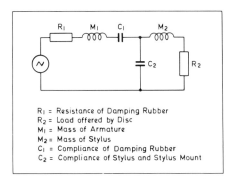

Fig. 21.11. Equivalent circuit of the moving-coil cutter head

adopted by A. Haddy of the Decca Recording Company in the FFRR head, which used a very high magnetic flux to obtain high sensitivity (a 25-watt drive amplifier was sufficient to give full modulation of a 78 rpm disc), but the moving system resonance was around 1 kHz. The variation in R_2 due to disc diameter was small when cutting a pre-warmed wax blank, but became severe when cutting lacquer. C. Windebank (also of Decca) added feedback which was derived from the motion of the system (as opposed to flux linkage from the drive coil field). This enabled a constant-velocity response to be obtained irrespective of grades or makes of lacquer disc. A further benefit of motion-derived feedback is that the rubber damping, with its temperature-sensitive drawbacks, may be disposed of, since the feedback loop provides its own electromagnetic control. The response of such a head with varying degrees of feedback is shown in Figure 21.12.

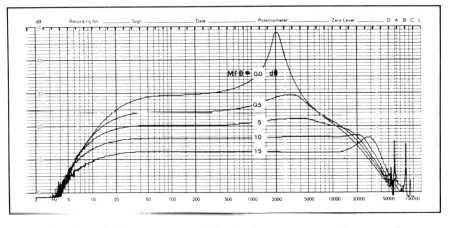

Fig. 21.12. Effect of different amounts of feedback on cutter overall response (courtesy Ortofon)

For stereophonic cutting heads, two main systems are in use, the Ortofon and the Westrex/Neumann (Figure 21.13). In both types it is important to position the stylus tip at the apex of the triangle of movement. It will be seen that another requirement is that the mass of the moving parts below the coil systems should be kept as low as possible for two reasons: (a) since force = mass × acceleration, the power required at high frequencies is largely determined by the total mass of the moving system, and (b) the above-mentioned parts are below the feedback coils, hence non-linear behaviour (e.g. elastic deformations, subsidiary resonances) will not be reflected in the feedback signal.

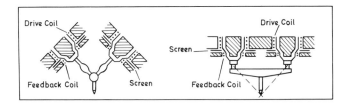

Fig. 21.13. Comparing the Ortofon (right) and Westrex/Neumann types of stereo cutter drive systems

The Recording Amplifier

The main components of a typical recording amplifier are shown in Figure 21.14. Points to note are: (a) the feedback section must have a very wide bandwidth (e.g. 10 Hz–150 kHz) in order to avoid phase shifts in the operating

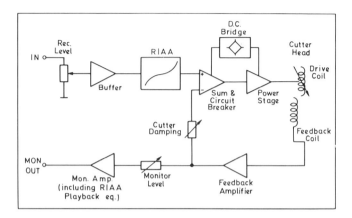

Fig. 21.14. Block diagram of typical recording amplifier

range of the cutter head which could cause the feedback to become positive at some frequencies and thus produce instability or continuous oscillation (in a first-order time-constant circuit the phase shift is 45° at the 3 dB point); (b) the output stage must be capable of delivering sufficient power to the head after the programme has been subjected to the recording characteristic. Since power doubles every 3 dB, there may be considerable demand on the power stage at frequencies around 10 kHz (where the boost is 13.7 dB) with modern recording techniques. The power available from a transistor output stage depends upon the load impedance, which in the case of a cutter head is predominantly inductive, hence rising with frequency. A network inserted between the output stage and the cutter head converts the latter's impedance to an apparently resistive load as seen by the output stage; nevertheless, powers of around 500 W r.m.s. are required from the amplifier.

The cutter head cannot stand such a power continuously, so a protection circuit is necessary. In modern designs this takes the form of a small (c. 200 mV) d.c. potential applied to the drive coil; since copper has a positive temperature coefficient, the resistance of the drive coil is an accurate indication of its temperature, and the voltage drop across the coil is compared with 200 mV in a bridge circuit. When the difference exceeds a pre-set safe value, a circuit breaker interrupts the drive coil connection. The bridge imbalance may also be used to drive a meter indicating the instantaneous temperature of the coil.

Half-speed cutting

It has long been known that the subjective quality of an audio system is greatly improved by its transient response, that is its ability to follow a rapidly changing signal. Amongst the benefits of a rapid transient response are: (a) clean high frequencies and clarity of detail, and (b) precise and stable stereo imaging. In disc cutting, transient response is primarily governed by the ability of the cutter head to move the stylus rapidly over a large distance (relative of course to the groove dimensions). From the previously cited relationship $f = m \times a$, and since acceleration $= dv/dt$, it follows that a high-power cutting amplifier with a good power bandwidth (or slew rate) will be required. A typical modern design has a slew rate of 60 V/sec. There is, however, a limit to the amount of power the cutter head can handle before damage occurs, so simply increasing the cutting amplifier power does not bring indefinite improvement.

On the other hand, suppose that the required acceleration rate was halved: this would be equivalent to quadrupling the amplifier power while not endangering the head. By playing the master tape at half its recorded speed, all frequencies are halved, and, if the disc is then cut at $16\frac{2}{3}$ r.p.m., a normal spectrum would be heard when playing the disc at $33\frac{1}{3}$ r.p.m. Modifications must be made to the equalizing networks in both the tape playback and disc-cutting amplifiers, whilst the wavelength effects on the tape at low frequencies must be corrected by special equalizers. The undoubted advantages of half-speed cutting are realized only when the master tape contains high-quality transient information, and when sufficient care is taken in the subsequent manufacturing stages.

Direct Metal Mastering (DMM)

A recent innovation has been the replacement of the lacquer-coated disc by a metallic blank. During the 1960s a video disc system was developed jointly by Decca in the UK and Telefunken–Decca (Teldec) in Germany, using a vertical cut groove on a disc rotating at 1,500 r.p.m. ($\frac{1}{25}$th playback speed). The tendency of lacquer to relax from its recorded condition, particularly at short wavelengths, rendered it unsuitable as a master medium. Good results were obtained, however, by cutting directly into copper plated on to an austenitic steel substrate. The Teldec video system was marketed in Germany, but, with its restricted playing time of only ten minutes, it failed to secure a sufficient market in competition with the tape-based video systems.

The technology developed for this direct cutting into copper showed interesting features for the audio disc, and a commercial system was offered under licence by Teldec in 1980. Georg Neumann of Berlin then introduced a modified version of the company's VMS 80 lathe and SX 74 cutter head for the new process (the VMS 82 and SX 84)—see Plate 26. The essential features of the system are as follows:

The blank disc. An austenitic stainless steel blank 0.8 mm thick is prepared to a high degree of flatness and surface finish. High-purity copper is then plated on to one face of the blank to a thickness of 100 μm. The resulting disc must be

Plate 26. Close-up of disc-cutting lathe employing Direct Metal Mastering on to a copper-coated disc (Photo: Neumann)

cut within a comparatively short period (a few weeks) as the copper undergoes structural changes which would result in a poor signal-to-noise ratio.

The lathe. Additional power is required in the turntable drive motor, and the removal of the copper swarf requires an air-flow which varies with the depth of cut (hence weight of swarf). Owing to the virtual absence of material flow or relaxation, there is less need to allow a wide spacing between adjacent turns of high and low-level modulation, although the effects of creep in the vinyl pressing itself must still be allowed for.

The cutter head. In the electrical analogy of a simple cutter head (Figure 21.11) the loading of the disc R_L was assumed to be resistive. Whilst this simplification works well enough for a lacquer disc, we have to examine R_L more rigorously for a copper medium.

In the case of copper, C_L assumes a significant value, leading to a resonance at a frequency determined by the combined circuit elements. Two important facts should be noted: (*a*) for a constant rotational velocity of the disc, Z_L will vary according to the position of the stylus on a radius of the disc surface, and (*b*) the energy required to feed the resonant circuit comes from the turntable motor in rotating the disc. This implies that a recorded 'signal' could occur with no programme input to the head.

In practice such an oscillatory signal has been found useful where the depth of cut changes (as in most stereo material). By suitable design of the relevant head parameters, the oscillatory frequency is placed around 75 kHz; when increasing the depth of cut, a chiselling action occurs which is somewhat similar to that of a pneumatic drill. The stylus has reduced polishing bevels, resembling the sharper profile used in wax recording, and is not heated.

The electronics. The internationally agreed cutting angle of 22° was designed to allow for the lacquer spring-back effect, but this effect is absent in copper. A physical adjustment of the cutting angle on copper is not feasible for mechanical reasons, so an electrical circuit placed before the drive amplifiers introduces a wave shaping which simulates the correct angle. Increased depth of cut places severe energy demands on the system, so the audio programme is controlled to keep the vertical excursions within pre-set limits. In other respects the drive electronics are essentially unchanged.

Processing. Since the copper surface is electrically conductive, it does not need to be silvered as lacquer does (see Chapter 22).

Summary comparison between copper and lacquer

Benefits from copper

1. No material relaxation at short wavelengths.
2. Negligible pre/post echo.
3. Considerable cost savings by avoiding silvering.
4. Absence of the noises which originate in the silvering process.
5. In-house quality control of the blank disc. (Since the copper blanks must be used within a few weeks after plating, it is normal for these to be grown in a specially assigned bath at the factory associated with the cutting room. The latter is thus freed from dependence on outside lacquer manufacturers.)

Benefits from lacquer

1. Universal acceptability in processing plants.
2. No dependence for blanks on one particular factory.
3. No implicit restrictions on the phase content of the recorded programme. (As already mentioned, a stereo groove may contain modulation causing stylus movements in any plane from lateral through to vertical, which may have amplitudes of the order of 150 μm. Whilst there is no problem in cutting such depths in lacquer, copper cannot permit such vertical excursions, and hence the phase content of the programme may need to be modified. The audible effect of this will depend on the original microphone technique, being greatest, for example, in coincident pair recordings.)

The control console

Ideally a master tape should be transferred straight on to disc with only a cutting level control intervening. However, corrections may need to be made either to yield a better finished pressing or because the producer has second thoughts on hearing the tape some time after the mixing session. A typical console is shown in Figure 21.15. During cutting, the cutter-head feedback signal, suitably equalized, is fed to the monitoring circuits, and this greatly assists in quality control of the lacquer or copper master (which cannot be played before processing).

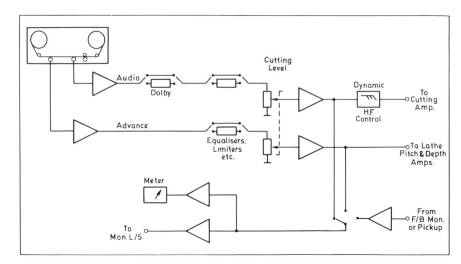

Fig. 21.15. Block diagram of typical cutting chain, showing only one audio and advance channel

Special signal processing

Apart from the familiar filters, equalizers, limiters, etc., the modern disc-cutting console may contain some units not found in the usual studio mixing console. It has been seen that excessive power can damage the cutter head, especially when associated with high-frequency signals. One solution would be to attenuate the HF section of the programme, but this would lead to an audible degradation of the programme quality. The solution adopted is to pass the signal through a low-pass filter, the cut-off frequency of which is normally above the audible range, but a pre-adjustable control circuit allows that frequency to come down very rapidly so as to attenuate a troublesome HF signal to within safe limits. Immediately the dangerous signal has passed, the filter cut-off returns to its supersonic value. The action of such a filter is inaudible, when properly used, and it allows a higher overall level to be cut as well as reducing HF distortion which might arise from pickup tracing difficulties.

Most pickups, especially the cheaper types, have greater difficulty in tracing vertical signals than lateral ones. It follows that it is advisable to restrict the vertical motion of the cutting stylus in high-amplitude passages as long as this does not introduce audible effects. If the two channels of the stereo signal A and B (for left and right) are put through a sum-and-difference network, the resultant two signals will be: (a) the Sum or Middle signal, and (b) the Difference or Sides signal. It is the Difference signal which contains the stereo information, so it is this signal which causes vertical movement of the cutting stylus. If the Difference signal is passed through a low-frequency limiter, and the two M and S signals are recombined to obtain A and B again, the resultant groove cut will have a reduced vertical content. The only audible effect would be a narrowing of the stereo image at low frequencies when the limiter is working, but since low frequencies are not very directional the effect usually passes unnoticed. A better solution, of course, is to try to avoid large-amplitude anti-phase signals in the original recording.

Cutting from digital tapes

Two-channel digitally recorded master tapes are increasingly being used as a production medium for analogue disc mastering, as well as providing the master for cassettes and Compact Discs. Since most current digital recordings are on a tape system which allows only one playback position, it is not possible to provide a groove control signal from a preview head in the manner already described for transfer from analogue tapes. Depending on the tape format and the hardware involved, the replay signal may be fed through a delay system, either via an analogue interface or directly in the digital domain (see Plate 27). The delayed signal forms the audio input to the cutting stylus, whilst the output from the normal digital replay head is fed via a D/A converter to the groove

Plate 27. Digital preview unit for varigroove cutting from digital tape masters (Photo: Stüder)

control circuitry of the lathe. In fact, such a system is already finding use for cutting from analogue tapes too, since the console may be reduced to two channels, with the delay taking place after all signal processing is completed. This is particularly useful when using dynamic control such as limiting, as it is difficult to get four limiters/compressors to track when in a different time domain.

Whatever digital system is employed, it is vital that the replay electronics are designed to give impulse-free muting when the error correction capability of the system is exceeded. Some early systems produced violent impulses from severe tape dropouts, causing a signal akin to a gunshot to be fed to the cutting amplifier at full level. Destruction of the cutting head almost always resulted. The low background noise level of a digital recording may show up the noise floor in a cutting system, leading to a need for improvements in the feedback section of the cutting amplifier, the choice of stylus/lacquer combination, and swarf removal noise.

To the cutting room specializing in classical music work, the advent of digital tapes has not been so very dramatic, since many classical recordings have always been presented in the form of a directly recorded analogue two-track tape whose performance does not differ greatly from the digital counterpart. On the other hand, a pop or rock master mixed down on to digital from a digital multitrack may contain unexpected waveforms: the high HF energy content of an electronic keyboard, for example, will come through without the gradual smoothing effect of analogue generation losses. Since the frequency range of a good cutting head exceeds that of most digital systems (e.g. 10 Hz–25 kHz for disc compared with 20 Hz–20 kHz for digital) there is no inherent problem, but the cutting engineer must be careful not to cut a waveform which cannot be traced by a typical domestic playback cartridge.

Some digital recording systems are based on video recording techniques. When using a video playback machine without a special editing or cueing device, it is difficult to locate the programme start accurately. Therefore a rather large number of blank turns may be needed at the start of the disc cut. Since digital recordings are inherently free of pre/post echo (print-through on analogue tapes), it may be necessary to allow increased groove pitch in places according to the programme dynamics; some lathes can do this automatically.

It is a great help to the cutting engineer to be given the timing of the occurrence of peak signal level on the tape, since it is not possible to spin the tape past the heads whilst listening for the loudest section, as with analogue. Checking track by track while a video machine goes through a tape is very time-consuming. Where possible, an analogue version of the recording (for example on the audio track of a videotape) is most useful for location and fault tracing.

With the proliferation of incompatible digital recording formats, it is essential that full details of the system employed be given, not only with the tape itself but in all paperwork relating to it. Then the cutting room can make sure to have the correct playback system on hand for the booked time. Even a seemingly minor error in description can make a tape unplayable.

Finally, although the digital recording cannot theoretically suffer from deviations in frequency response or unpredictable distortion levels, it is useful to record a frequency run at the start of a tape, as with analogue. Aside from malfunctions in the digital domain, there is always a D/A converter followed by analogue circuitry which requires a regular check to ensure uniform quality.

The playback process

The playback pickup cartridge is functionally an inversion of the cutting head, in that it provides an electrical output from a mechanical actuating force. Interactions occur between the moving system and the groove/disc material in essentially the same way as with the cutter head, and it is desirable to place the pickup resonant frequency above the working range. Another resonance occurs at low frequencies where the compliance of the cartridge assembly combines with the relevant parameters of the pickup arm to give a resonant frequency of between about 5 and 15 Hz.

A form of distortion known as the *pinch effect* occurs because of the effective narrowing of the groove when the cutting stylus is not at right angles to the tangent of the disc (Figure 21.16). The resulting vertical modulation appears at the output terminals at twice the frequency of the recorded signal. Another

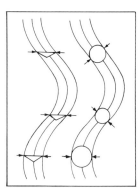

Fig. 21.16. Pinch effect: showing (left) how the cutting stylus inscribes a groove of varying width, and how this causes the replay stylus to ride up and down twice in each cycle

form of distortion arises from the finite dimensions of the playback stylus. When the tip radius equals the recorded wavelength, no output is possible: this is known as the *extinction frequency*. As the wavelength of the recorded signal approaches this value, the reproduced distortion rises rapidly. One solution, used on most good-quality pickups, is to employ a stylus ground to an elliptical

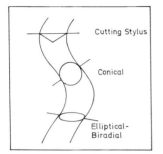

Fig. 21.17. Stylus shapes: showing that an elliptical stylus more nearly resembles the cutter contour, with consequently less distortion on playback

(or similar) shape presenting the major axis transverse to the groove (Figure 21.17). Attempts have been made in the past to introduce recorded 'pre-distortion' in anti-phase to the expected playback distortion, but this can work only for a given playback stylus profile and in other circumstances may degrade the quality.

Ideally, the pickup cartridge should traverse a radius of the disc, following the path of the cutting head. However, it is normally mounted on a pivoted arm which results in the stylus following an arc (Figure 21.18). This introduces *'tracking error' distortion*, but careful design of the relevant arm geometry can reduce this to insignificant levels.

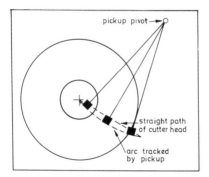

Fig. 21.18. Tracking error occurs with a pivoted pickup arm since it tracks along a curved arc instead of following the straight radial path of the cutter

Practical points

Many problems in disc rooms arise from tapes being improperly prepared and/or insufficiently documented. Since a disc cannot be stopped and restarted during a cut, there must be no changes during the programme which cannot be corrected while running; these include different azimuths as a result of different recording machines being used, different Dolby levels, or different recording curves such as NAB and IEC. A frequency run, and a Dolby tone (if used), should be put at the head of at least the first reel in a set. The playing time should be clearly stated, and, if the programme has a wide dynamic range, it is most helpful to indicate where the peak level occurs.

When cutting master lacquers, the stylus tip should be cleaned using a piece of pith soaked in acetone before every side; a stylus should be discarded when the groove walls show a smudged appearance on the curvatures of modulation. When changing makes or batches of lacquer disc, a test cut should be made using different amounts of stylus-heating current; it will be found that there is an optimum value at which the groove noise is a minimum. Similarly, the strength of swarf suction should be adjusted to give minimum noise while listening to the feedback signal at a very high monitoring level. It will be found that the angle of the swarf tube nozzle makes a considerable difference. When using a feedback-type cutter head, the stylus must never be lowered on a stationary disc with the head connected, as this could cause system instability and damage the head.

22

Vinyl disc processing
Jim Hughes

So well established is the practice of disc record manufacture that this chapter nearly became called 'Beyond the Melba Stone'. For the curious, the 'Melba Stone' was laid by Dame Nellie Melba in 1907 during the building of the old Gramophone Company's factory at Hayes in Middlesex. The stone has since been moved and now stands in front of the modern automated vinyl disc and tape record factory of EMI M. & D. Services, through whose courtesy the following account of vinyl disc processing took shape.

Although the lateral-cut moulded disc is the longest-surviving form of audio software, its deeply rooted manufacturing technology has been continuously updated throughout the years, keeping pace with progressive developments, and today the vinyl disc is a precision moulding made under specialized mass-production conditions.

Manufacture of the vinyl disc may be divided broadly into three main stages:

Preparing the moulding tool;
The moulding operation;
Packaging the record.

Quality assurance is built in at each stage, and the process starts after the programme from a master tape has been cut into a recording blank such as the 'lacquer', which has long been the traditional medium for cutting microgroove records (see previous chapter).

Lacquers, sometimes misnamed 'acetates', consist of plasticized nitrocellulose suitably lubricated and then coated on to a flat aluminium substrate. It is from these that moulding tools are made with the object of producing replicas in the form of vinyl discs, as faithful to the original as commercial practice will allow.

The moulding tool is conventionally referred to as a stamper and takes the form of a nickel negative replica of the lacquer master, from which it is prepared by a series of electroforming operations.

Silvering the lacquer

In order to electroform, it is first necessary to make the lacquer surface electroconductive. Therefore, after embossing an identity code into the lacquer and roughening the centre area to prevent label rupture during moulding, it is cleaned and wetted in an aqueous phosphate surfactant solution. Subsequent processing quality depends upon the effectiveness of this initial cleaning in removing all residual plasticizer from the cut surface before silver is applied.

Silvering is done automatically by rotating the wet lacquer beneath a series of jets angled in such a way that the solutions sprayed from them reach to the bottom of the cut groove. Each of these jets operates in sequence to clean, sensitize, and rinse the surface. Finally, two jets operate simultaneously spraying ammoniacal silver and glucose formaldehyde solutions until a continuous film of metallic silver about 0.1 μm thick has been deposited by chemical reduction.

The nickel master

The surface of the lacquer is now electroconductive and suitable for growing a metal master. To do this, an electroplating bath of nickel sulphamate is used, with nickel pieces as an anode and the silvered lacquer as the cathode. The lacquer is rotated in the electrolyte and first subjected to gentle pre-plating to deposit a thin layer of nickel without distorting the recorded groove. Current density is then raised and plating continued for about 3–4 hours until a nickel master of fine crystal structure and about 400 μm thick has been grown on to the lacquer.

As the nickel is also deposited around the edge of the lacquer locking the two parts together, it has to be trimmed away on a circle-cutting machine before the master is stripped from the lacquer by hand. After separating, the master is washed in solvent spray to remove residual traces of lacquer which may be adhering, and then the silver film, which has now been transferred to the face of the master, is removed chemically before growing a positive. It is possible to play the master using a stirrup stylus (having a V-shaped tip), but normal practice is to examine the surface visually, making sure that all silver has been removed and that the master is in good condition.

The positive

The process of growing a positive from the nickel master is the same in principle as growing a nickel master from the lacquer except that, as the original and the replica are now both metal, the pre-plating technique used with the soft lacquer may be omitted and high current density used throughout. One other essential difference is the need to film the surface of the master so that the two metal parts can be separated after electroforming. Before the master is placed in a plating bath, it is again cleaned and a molecular colloidal film applied to its recorded face.

After completion, parting is achieved by inserting a small stripping knife at the edge between the interfaces and then, without hesitation, separating in one complete movement to make sure that the recorded surfaces are not damaged by re-contact.

The positive, as its name implies, is the first exact replica of the recorded lacquer, and, like the lacquer, it will have fine 'horns' at the top of the groove thrown up by the cutting stylus. As these are easily damaged, debris from them can cause problems later and the nickel positive provides the first opportunity for their removal. This is done mechanically by working a fine abrasive across the face of the positive for thirty seconds whilst rotating at high speed, then washing away the debris with petroleum spirit.

Several stampers will be grown from a positive, so it is important to make further quality checks before proceeding. Besides a careful visual inspection, the positive is given an audio check with subsequent repair of minor groove blemishes if necessary. The positive is also the starting-point for making 175 mm records with inked or 'painted' labels, which is described later.

The stamper

Last in the generation of metalwork is the moulding tool itself—the stamper— which is electroformed from a positive in much the same way as the positive is grown from the nickel master. Then the two metal parts are held in a vacuum chuck and separated ultrasonically at the filmed interface (see Plate 28), resulting in a negative replica of the lacquer master in the form of a ductile low-stress nickel stamper about 300 μm thick. Another visual quality check is made and a film of flexible PVC is then immediately applied to the front of the

Plate 28. Vacuum-ultrasonic separation of nickel stamper from the positive (Photo: EMI)

stamper, giving protection to the delicate recorded surface during the subsequent finishing processes. This film remains intact until removed in the press just before the record is made.

The next operation is to punch a hole in the exact centre of the stamper, essential if 'swingers' (i.e. off-centre records) are to be avoided at the moulding stage. The stamper is held securely on a vacuum bed and centring is accomplished optically by punching the hole when a rotating image of the concentric groove projected on to a screen passes across the centre of a target.

At this stage the stamper has a mirror-like finish on the front face and a matt irregular surface on the back which, if left intact, would impress its pattern through the nickel shell and deform the recorded surface when subjected to the pressures of moulding, resulting in high surface noise and roar. It is therefore necessary to polish the back of the stamper. This is done automatically using four air-driven abrasive heads, each with progressively finer grit to give a consistent finish.

Finally, the stamper, which up to now has existed as a flat disc, is formed to shape in a hydraulic press, and is now ready for fitting into a mould block to provide records of the required profile.

Direct Metal Mastering (DMM)*

The technique of cutting into a copper blank instead of the conventional lacquer (described in the previous chapter) has simplified the methods of preparing a moulding tool as well as provided the end user with very considerable advantages.

As the starting-point for vinyl disc manufacture, the copper master is already in effect equivalent to a nickel positive in being the metal part from which a stamper can be grown directly.

The flow diagram in Figure 22.1 compares the manufacturing sequences of the lacquer and Direct Metal Mastering systems, showing how silvering, dehorning, and subsequent debris removal are omitted, with an eventual improvement in quality because replication losses inherent in these operations are eliminated.

Once the copper master has been cut, there is a choice of two routes through to the stamper. First, the copper may be put into the plating bath each time it is required to grow a stamper (see Plate 29). Alternatively, where several stampers are needed quickly, it becomes necessary either to cut a number of copper masters or, preferably, to process via nickel positives grown from a copy master. Both systems retain the advantages of direct metal mastering.

Copper blanks may be prepared on site as required, using a bright stainless steel substrate about 800 μm thick. High surface finish of the flat face to be

*Trademark of Teldec Schallplatten GmbH, W. Germany.

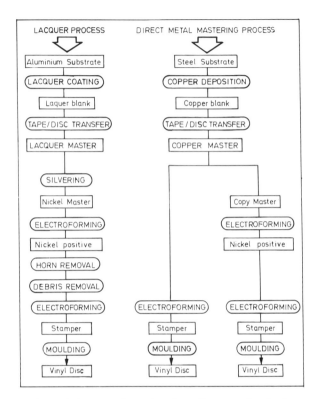

Fig. 22.1. Comparison of the manufacturing flow diagrams for the lacquer and DMM processes

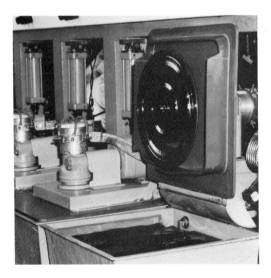

Plate 29. A copper master in position above a plating bath ready for electroforming a nickel stamper (Photo: EMI)

plated is important, and to achieve this the discs are lapped with diamond slurry, great care being taken to ensure the absence of scratches and other blemishes likely to flaw the plated surface. Cathodic cleaning of the steel surface in an alkali phosphate solution is followed by anodic acid etching of the face to be plated and flash plating with nickel to provide a key for laying down the copper to about 100 μm thickness (Plate 30). This then needs to be dichromate-passivated to prevent oxidation. Two types of plating bath are suitable, either an acid copper or a pyrophosphate copper, and each has certain advantages. The acid copper system tends to have superior levelling and is useful where faster deposition is needed, but the less aggressive pyrophosphate bath can produce blanks with a longer shelf-life before cutting and a better signal-to-noise ratio.

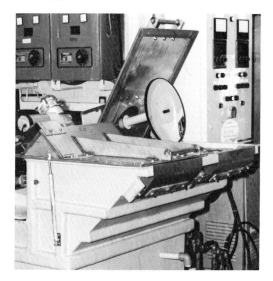

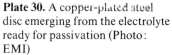
Plate 30. A copper-plated steel disc emerging from the electrolyte ready for passivation (Photo: EMI)

The benefits obtainable from direct metal mastering were stated in the previous chapter on disc cutting, but, looking at them again from the aspect of the vinyl disc manufacturer as well as the consumer, they may be summarized as follows:

Manufacturing reliability is higher;
Unlike the lacquer master, it is possible to produce matrices directly from the copper master;
The DMM process results in significant plating economies;
Up to 15 per cent more playing time per side;
Virtual elimination of pre-echo and post-echo;
Reduction in both rumble and surface disturbances;
Up to 10 dB improvement in signal-to-noise ratio.

The processes described in preparing the moulding tool, whether from a lacquer or a copper master, are primarily those of electrochemistry, and need controlling to make sure that the resulting metalwork is of correct crystal structure, hardness, and ductility. Besides the checking of the end-products for these properties, frequent tests are made assessing electrolyte concentration, its pH, and the balance of additives. Maintaining solution purity is essential, to ensure the absence of suspended matter and soluble contamination. Therefore, in addition to continuous filtration, the electrolyte is subjected to low current deposition for removal of unwanted cations.

The moulding tool or stamper having been prepared, it is now ready for use to press out the required numbers of vinyl discs. Before this can be done, however, it is necessary to have available the plastic material from which to mould the record.

The record material

The vinyl disc of today is made from rigid PVC based on vinyl chloride/vinyl acetate copolymers, with an average molecular weight of about 47 K and vinyl acetate content in the region of 15 per cent. Some early record materials were formulated on vinylidene chloride copolymers. In some parts of the world, extender resins were incorporated to improve mouldability or reduce costs, whilst at other times there has been extensive application of polystyrene, mainly for 175 mm records. Addition of non-compatible surfactants has also been tried, to obtain an anti-static record. However, this has usually been abandoned, mainly because of cost coupled with a lack of consumer response, or of deterioration resulting from the moisture sensitivity of the moulded groove surface because of the hydrophilic nature and incompatibility of the anti-static agents themselves.

The situation has settled down into two main processing systems founded on granular compound or powder dry blend. The former material is normally prepared by gelling, milling, and dicing after the material has cooled, or alternatively by feeding to a compounding extruder and lace cutting or hot cutting at the die: such material requires to be heated again before moulding the record. Powder blending, on the other hand, has its initial dispersion during high-speed mixing and is subsequently fed to an efficient extruder at the press side, where a second dispersion is obtained and the extrudate presented to the press preheated ready for moulding. This has obvious economic advantages. Whatever system is chosen, dispersion of the raw materials is essential to obtain full efficacy of the stabilizing, lubrication, and pigmenting systems.

Formulation balance is fundamental to success and it is necessary to provide sufficient thermal stabilization to cover all aspects of processing. This, in addition to compounding and moulding, should allow for reprocessing surplus material in the form of flash or rejected records. Earlier practice tended towards over-stabilization through the use of comparatively large amounts of lead-based compounds, having the advantage of long-life processing but the disadvantage of plate-out of non-compatible degradation products on to the surface of the record. Modern technology prefers the use of low-toxicity materials, such as fatty acid alkali metal synergistic stabilizers, added in small amounts but sufficient to provide for necessary material recovery options.

Lubrication is another intrinsic requisite, necessary during compounding or extrusion and release of the disc from the mould, and for better wear performance of the record. To some extent, fatty products liberated from the thermal stabilizer provide a measure of lubrication, but in order to maintain a controlled situation a purpose-designed chemically stable lubricant is added such as a micronized esterified wax derived from lignite.

Pigmentation is a further requirement, and records are by convention black. This is normally brought about by the addition of a fine-channel carbon black, though dyes have also been used for the purpose. Any pigment put into the mix will make its contribution to the steady surface noise character of the record, and this will be directly attributable to the fineness of the pigment and its dispersion. Furthermore, such blacks must be free from iron or other substances which might initiate premature thermal breakdown of the polymer. Where dyes are used for black or other coloured records, they are required to be colour-stable both to heat and light, and to chemical changes within the record compound.

Flow modification of the plastic mass is also desirable to ensure complete filling of the inter-stamper cavity when moulding the record, with consequent avoidance of 'airmarks' or non-fills in the groove. This is usually accomplished by adding a high-molecular-weight, lower-acetate PVC copolymer to the mix. The choice and quantity of this will largely depend upon the type of equipment and processing conditions, but for an effective result the secondary polymer must remain as a separate phase and not be taken into solution during processing.

Control of particle shape and size distribution of the polymers used in airveyed powder blend systems is particularly important, as the presence of excess fines tends to result in a high concentration of additives on the increased surface area presented by the finer polymer, causing problems of plate-out and bloom during the moulding of the record. Quality assurance requirements are embodied in the specifications for polymers to avoid this happening, as well as in the specifications for all other raw materials. Nevertheless, on-site checks still have to be made when polymers are received, particularly to avoid the presence of moisture, which can cause other moulding problems, and to make sure that the material is free of contaminations such as sand and rust particles which would be likely to damage the stampers in the press. Before proceeding to mould the disc, the label used to identify the record's content has to be considered.

The record label

The apparent simplicity of paper record labels conceals special technology designed to facilitate processing under automated record-moulding conditions, as well as to guarantee a high standard of commercial presentation. Labels consist of a paper substrate with information printed on the front face, usually by offset lithography. A requirement common to all labels, however pressed, is that the paper should have ample strength to meet the shear forces experienced during moulding, as label failure at this stage (for whatever reason) means a rejected record.

Specialized handling techniques associated with modern vinyl disc production have in turn led to continuous development and standardization of both papers and printing inks. Choice of paper is influenced by the moulding systems used, but additional features which have to be taken into account, apart from strength, are as follows:

Good print surface and fabrication, capable of being punched, drilled, or lathe-turned without loose debris which could become trapped in the groove during pressing.

Predrying at high temperature without curling, excessive strength loss, or discolouration.

Air permeability: where labels are transferred by suction, air porosity should be low and remain so after drying.

Typical papers consist of a cellulose fibre base, each side coated with chalk-china clay mix in a flexible casein and synthetic latex binder, balanced to minimize curl during drying. Such coatings also have good opacity, and unlike uncoated paper they prevent vinyl bleed into the substrate during pressing, resulting in a moulded label of superior appearance.

Apart from printing well, the inks have to be colour heat-fast and have good release from the mirror-finish nickel shell against which they are impressed during moulding, as any residual ink transfer produces a ghost image on subsequent records in a run and major failure can result in cumulative breakdown of labels.

At the present time, drying of labels is necessary before moulding: one reason for this may be shown by examining the effect of the natural presence of moisture in the paper base, which is likely to be between 5 and 12 per cent, depending upon ambient humidity. If this is not reduced before presenting the label to the press, the moulding temperature of 165°C will cause instant conversion to steam while the label is in intimate contact with the nickel stamper. Steam generated in the closed mould can result in severe groove non-fills near the centre of the record, as well as affecting the label itself by plasticizing the paper coating and ink surfaces. This would make them mouldable, with consequent sticking to the stamper and label delamination on withdrawing the record.

Predrying of labels is done by conveying them (spaced apart on rods through their centre holes) through a circulatory air oven for one hour at 165°C. Air impinging on the labels rotates and disorientates them, balancing out minor grain curl tendencies and dislodging loose paper fibres. Moisture removal at this temperature covers both adsorbed and some molecular water, and, with the paper almost reaching the onset of carbonization, advantage is taken of lower moisture pick-up hysteresis when the labels are again exposed to ambient conditions. Oven treatment also results in ink film degradation reducing thermoplasticity, largely through polymerization, oxidation, and distillation of the more volatile binder fractions. After emerging from the oven, the labels are sealed whilst hot into high-density polyethylene bags, ready for use at the press.

An alternative to using paper labels is to print the information directly on to the record just after it has left the mould. Some Continental manufacturers produce 300 mm records in this way, with attractive labels printed in two or three colours. In the UK, direct printing techniques are mainly used for the 175 mm record, which is then often described as having a 'painted label'. This method has an important advantage as it provides a rapid turn-round of product where quick response to demand is needed, such as with fast-moving pop records. Delays in waiting for paper labels to be printed, punched, dried, and fed into the mould are avoided, as the label information is processed at the matrix stage early in the production chain.

The method is to etch photographed title copy into the nickel positive using a photoresist, the film of which also protects the recorded area from the etching solutions (Plate 31). Every stamper grown will then be titled in relief, and every record made will come from the mould already titled in recess without a paper label having been used. All that now remains is to colour the land of the label area. This is done as the disc leaves the press, by passing it through transfer

Plate 31. A nickel positive with photographed title copy etched into its surface ready for growing a 175 mm record stamper (Photo: EMI)

rollers coated with a metallic ink to give a brightly coloured label with the design in black (Plate 32).

Plate 32. Immediately after leaving the mould, a 175 mm record with recessed title information passes through transfer rollers coated with metallic ink (Photo: EMI)

Moulding the vinyl disc

With all three components ready—the stampers, the record material, and the labels—the record can now be made. The vinyl disc is made by thermoplastic moulding, which, unlike a thermosetting process, means that the record needs to be cooled in the mould. The method of moulding is much the same whether material is fed to the press in the form of granules or powder blend, but both have to be rendered plastic by heating before presenting to the mould. Powder blend requires further dispersion of additives, however, which is done in a small compounding extruder next to the press.

The general principles of moulding a vinyl disc, which may be classed amongst the most critical mouldings made in any plastics material, can be shown by the example of compression-moulding a 300 mm record. This is done on a microprocessor-controlled press specially designed to withstand continuous working to accurate tolerances, and fitted with two thermally balanced steel mould blocks channelled for rapid steam heating and water cooling. The two stampers used to form the record need to be fitted one on to each block, but before this is done both stampers and block need to be prepared. The reason for this is that, to take advantage of the longer stamper life made possible through modern technology and improved production techniques, it becomes necessary to retard the onset of fretting corrosion in order to obtain high-quality pressings consistently throughout the whole of the run. Corrosion is due to slight movements of the metal interfaces held in contact under heavy stress, resulting in detritus forming behind the stamper which can impress its pattern into the moulded record, thus increasing audio rumble.

With a press working continuously under production conditions, the mould block requires thorough cleaning using a molten wax preparation every time a stamper is changed to remove corrosion by-products and prevent degradation reaching unacceptable limits. Good surface condition of the blocks is maintained by lapping periodically and rubbing down. Abrasives are avoided as the resulting damage provides a nucleus initiating corrosion development. After an anti-fretting agent is applied to the polished back of the stampers, they are clamped to the blocks, surface contact is secured by vacuum, and finally the protective film is removed from the recorded surface.

Dried labels are then taken from their moisture-proof bags and loaded into magazines positioned in front of the extruder nozzle at the press. Sufficient extrudate for a record, plus about 15 per cent extra to allow for flash escape from the mould, is discharged into a preform cup, the lid and base of which are formed by the label magazines. With a label from the magazines adhering to its top and bottom, the preform is moved forward into the mould cavity and positioned centrally on the stamper fitted to the bottom mould block, which by now has reached a temperature of about 165°C (Plate 33). The mould is closed and pressure of about 150 kgf/cm^2 is applied, causing material to fill the mould cavity, with excess leaving as flash. Then the mould is immediately cooled

Plate 33. A vinyl preform with two labels positioned centrally on a stamper fitted to a mould block ready to mould a 300 mm record (Photo: EMI)

rapidly, the record is carefully removed, and the flash is trimmed away. Vinyl discs made in this way, at about 180 an hour, are inserted automatically into bags as soon as they are trimmed to give immediate protection and avoid any handling of the record. The bagged records are positioned horizontally in a box, with a flat separator between every fifth pressing, where they remain until the initial effects of entropy have stabilized. Apart from quality assurance attendant upon the process up to this point, quality control is effected by statistical sampling followed by visual, physical, and audio checks on discs as they are moulded.

The 300 mm disc now appears to be made exclusively by compression moulding. The smaller 175 mm record can also be made by this means, either in single or double moulds, or alternatively it may be injection-moulded; recent developments in injection-moulding machinery have created continuing interest in this method of manufacture.

Whatever method is used for moulding, there is always the need for the recovery and recycling of surplus material. This may exist either in the form of flash or records which have been scrapped for a variety of reasons. Material is generally reused for 175 mm records, but it must be clean and free from contamination. Flash can be recovered in its entirety, as can discs with 'painted labels' printed in a compatible vinyl ink, but records with impressed paper labels require the centre to be discarded before recovery.

There remain two types of record which, although neither is suitable for scrap recovery, fall within the broad category of the vinyl disc. The first is the PVC film record, at one time popular as a mailing sampler, which is not moulded but has the groove embossed into the surface of the film with limited and somewhat variable results. The other is the compression-moulded picture disc, consisting of two large-diameter printed labels each encapsulated between PVC film, with an embossed groove and a solid stock core. This is in effect a five-component pressing, but a simpler three-component version may be made by printing a picture on each side of a single sheet of paper and moulding one face in a clear colourless vinyl mix, with the other side embossed into PVC film. All types of record have to be packaged in some way, and a brief survey of this aspect will complete this description of the manufacturing process.

Packaging the record

The primary technical function of packaging is to protect the contained vinyl disc. At the same time, the packaging has become fundamental and integral to the commercial appeal of the product. Both needs have to be accommodated, and specifications must allow for printing, specialized finishes, or any novelty packaging which may be called for—particularly by the fashionable pop record market—without compromising quality standards. Other aspects to be taken into account are the properties necessary for handling by the disc manufacturer, transit and short-term storage, consumer usage, and long-term storage. Packaging itself assumes different forms according to the type of record being protected, but if falls into two essentially different categories, that which comes into intimate contact with a recorded surface and that which does not.

The bag noted earlier, into which a 300 mm record was inserted at the press, comes into the first category and consists of paper with or without a polyethylene film liner. Important features for automatic handling include air permeability, low electrostatic properties, good slip, close stable dimensional tolerances, a low scratch and damage index (as the material is coming into contact with a record), and freedom from anything being transferred to the disc. Such a bag may be printed and varnished, and it will certainly contain an adhesive to stick either the seams or the film liner. All these substances must be free from migratory agents capable of attacking an enclosed record during storage, and the adhesive bond must remain intact.

Into the second category comes the outer packaging to give further protection, such as jackets and album boxes. Not coming into contact with the actual record, a wider range of durable boards of various types may be employed, but dimensional stability is a prime essential as distortion of such packaging can induce record warp. Similarly, the structural design of jackets must provide correct support to keep records flat by containing the cold flow of the moulding material, either when packed in single jackets or within the structure of a composite pack.

Shipment of discs in bulk is usually done in heavy-duty boxes, having the contents stored vertically with adequate but not excessive side pressure. Packaging and boxes are designed around the product to reduce internal movement and avoid transit damage to both the boxes and their contents.

Stringent packaging requirements laid down by the disc manufacturer are carried forward to benefit the consumer. They are in effect subjected to a practical life-test in the field, the results of which may find their way back to the manufacturer in diverse ways and can eventually modify the specification.

Practical long-term storage concerns preventing deterioration of the disc while it is in possession of the consumer, and, in addition to the features mentioned earlier, packaging design has to take into account cold flow properties of the moulded record. The preference is for vertical storage and an evenly distributed sideways pressure at reasonably constant temperatures consistent with normal living conditions.

True long-term storage, however, such as for archival purposes, is not easily predictable and is difficult to design into a commercial product like the vinyl record. With the introduction of new information carriers, the future of the vinyl disc is presently the subject of much discussion, but, whatever it may be, groove-cut discs in various forms have already been around for well over eighty years, the vinyl disc itself, almost incredibly, for nearly forty of those years, and in this respect at least it appears to have the durability for continued existence.

23

Tape duplicating

Gerd Nathan

The vital link between the creators of sound recordings and their prospective customers is the so-called software manufacturer. It is his task to manufacture and supply faithful replicas of any given recording in the format required, such as vinyl discs, cassettes, or Compact Discs.

In theory, the sound from any software format should be precisely the same as that from the original recording. In practice, however, this is rarely possible, because each software format sets its own particular technical limits. For instance, very high recorded levels at low frequencies on vinyl discs will almost certainly cause the customer's pickup to jump during playback, particularly if the groove excursions contain large vertical components. On the other hand, any attempt to record excessive levels at high frequencies on cassette tape is very likely to result in distortion and a dull sound. It will therefore be understood that the sound from the replica will usually differ very slightly from that of the original, and that, furthermore, these differences will not be the same for all software formats. Consequently, software replicas in different formats derived from the same original may well show small but audible differences, yet each format should, within its own technical limits, give the best possible account of the original recording. It should be noted that any attempt to unify the sound for all formats will inevitably result in a mediocre sound, because each format will be subject not only to its own technical limits but also to those from all the other formats. We thus have the choice between standardized mediocrity or diversified excellence.

The successful emergence of the cassette as a high-fidelity consumer product was largely due to an early recognition of its technical limits, and to a concerted effort by raw-material suppliers and software manufacturers to minimize the effects of these limits as far as possible. Over the last decade we have witnessed a dramatic improvement in the quality of domestic cassette players, cassette tapes, and cassette housings. Cassette players now have better tape transports, resulting in better track alignment and azimuth during playback; cassette tapes have become more tolerant to high-level high frequencies and are less hissy; last but not least, cassette housings are moulded to closer tolerances with consequential improved tape guidance during playback. These are just some of the factors which have placed the cassette 'on the map' as a hi-fi format.

General principles

No manufacturer can survive unless his production process is viable and his prices are acceptable to his potential customers. One way of achieving this goal is to keep non-productive processes such as quality control and administration to an absolute minimum, while still supplying reliable product of adequate quality to the consumer. The successful manufacturer will therefore have a highly reliable, possibly automated, production process, and will use raw materials which are of consistent and adequate, rather than variable and high, quality. In other words, he would rather use cassette tapes and housings which are consistent irrespective of batch or time of delivery than aim for top quality or low price, because not only does variability of raw materials play havoc with automated mass-production machinery, but it will also necessitate the use of extra non-productive personnel for incoming inspection of raw materials and for quality control of the finished product. It is vital to avoid the incidence of random faults in any mass-production process, because no level of quality control short of 100 per cent will prevent faulty product reaching the customer. Within these confines, it is the task of the cassette manufacturer to match the sound of his cassettes as closely as possible to that of the programme material supplied to him.

The programme material

The sound quality of cassettes can only be as good as that of the programme material received by the cassette manufacturer. Unfortunately, he rarely, if ever, has access to original recordings and must therefore rely on the duplicates which are supplied to him. These duplicates represent the starting-point for cassette manufacture, and it cannot be emphasized too strongly that they need to be of the highest quality.

Duplicates are supplied as either 'copy masters' or 'mother tapes'. A copy master is, as its name implies, a 1:1 copy of the original recording. A mother tape, on the other hand, is a tape on which the sound has been especially equalized, if necessary, to accommodate the technical limits of the cassette system; it has been fully monitored and is ready to be played on the high-speed playback machine (the 'sender') for copying on to the high-speed record machines (the 'slaves') (see Plate 34). A 'QC copy' is a tape identical to the mother tape which has been recorded at the same time but which has not been monitored. It is used either for comparison purposes when the mother tape is not available, or as a replacement mother tape, provided it is first monitored for random faults such as dropouts. The installation of senders and slaves is generally known as a 'high-speed duplicating system', or simply as a 'high-speed duplicator'.

Plate 34. High-speed senders with loop bins (left) and slaves (right) (Photo: Ablex Audio Video)

From Figure 23.1 it will be seen that the mother tape is an essential part of cassette manufacture. However, the preparation of a good mother tape requires equipment which is more usually found in recording studios rather than in factories. For this reason, the starting-point for most factories is the mother tape rather than the copy master or the original. Preparation of the mother tape is dealt with in Chapter 20, but at this point it is important to note that close technical liaison between mother tape and cassette manufacturers is absolutely essential if major disasters are to be avoided.

Liaison between manufacturers of mother tapes and cassettes

The mechanical and electroacoustic properties of the tape used for making mother tapes must be carefully agreed between mother tape and cassette manufacturer. If the tape is known to be reasonably consistent from batch to batch, it is sufficient to specify the particular brand and its type number. Its mechanical properties must be suitable for repeated playings on the high-speed sender and its associated tape reservoir (the loop bin); after repeated playings, the recording must not change in any way (e.g. loss or gain in high frequencies, increase in tape hiss), and it must not shed debris or leave any deposits on the

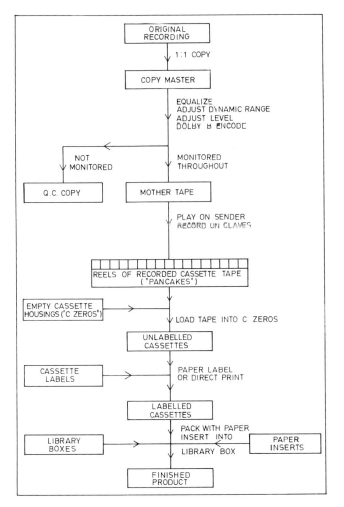

Fig. 23.1. The process stages in pre-recorded cassette manufacture

playback heads of the sender. If it does, there is a good chance that random and uncontrollable dropouts of sound will occur on the finished cassette. It goes without saying that the electroacoustic properties of the tape must be very consistent, so that all mother tapes can be played back at identical settings on the high-speed sender.

So much for the tape. There are, however, several technical parameters which are under the control of the mother tape manufacturer and which must be subject to technical liaison and agreement. It is important, for instance, that the recorded tracks on the mother tape should coincide exactly with the gaps of the playback head of the high-speed sender. If they do not, the signal transmitted

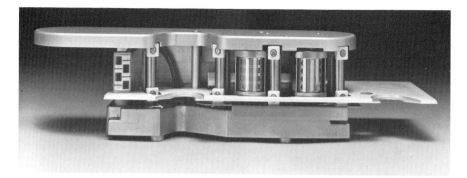

Plate 35. Head block of recorder for making mother tapes for cassette duplication (Photo: Stüder)

to the high-speed slaves will not only be too low in level, but will also be accompanied by unnecessary noise. In other words, track alignment between mother tape and the high-speed sender playback head must be very precise (see Figure 23.2 and Plate 35).

Fig. 23.2. Track misalignment

Another frequent source of error is an angular deviation between the recording on the mother tape and the gaps of the sender playback head. Under these conditions, the sender playback head will be unable to detect and transmit high-frequency signals from the mother tape to the slaves, and in consequence the resulting cassettes will sound dull. This error is known as an 'azimuth error' (see Figure 23.3).

Most large-scale production machinery tends to be somewhat inflexible, and the high-speed duplicating system is no exception. Setting and resetting of track

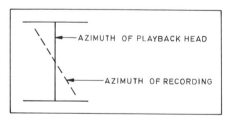

Fig. 23.3. Azimuth error

alignment, azimuth, frequency response, and gain tend to be long and tedious operations and will, in consequence, lose valuable production time. It is therefore highly desirable that a calibration tape be shared between the mother tape and the cassette manufacturer in order to ensure compatibility between the mother tape recorder and the high-speed sender. Such calibration tapes are best made on the recorder that makes the mother tapes, so that test conditions are as close as possible to production conditions. The use of full-track calibration tapes is not recommended because of fringing errors at low frequencies. The provision of a high-frequency (say 10 kHz) test tone on each mother tape, recorded at the same time as the programme, will give an excellent current check on azimuth compatibility. In these ways, deviations are detected at an early stage and can be rectified with minimum interference to production.

In order to ensure the minimum amount of unwanted noise on the final cassette, it is usual to employ the Dolby B noise reduction system. It works by compressing the dynamic range of the original recording during tansfer to the mother tape, thereby achieving a higher signal-to-noise ratio during the quieter parts of the programme. The dynamic range is later restored to that of the original recording by means of expansion on the customer's cassette player, while still retaining the improved signal-to-noise ratio achieved on the quieter parts of the programme. It is, however, a strict condition that the overall compression/expansion (sometimes referred to as 'encoding and decoding') process results in a gain of precisely unity at all frequencies. Unless this condition is met, the sound from the cassette will not be representative of the original recording.

In order to achieve this unity gain at all times, it is highly desirable that each and every mother tape be provided with a test tone recorded at Dolby level, which at the same time provides the cassette manufacturer with a convenient check on the gain setting of his own high-speed equipment.

The use of the Dolby B noise reduction system means that the cassette manufacturer must work to a constant gain, and this in turn means that peak programme levels on the mother tape need to be such as to avoid saturation on the cassette tape. Depending on the cassette tape in use, peak programme levels on the mother tape should lie 2–6 dB above the Dolby reference level.

To summarize, therefore, close liaison between mother tape and cassette manufacturer is essential and agreement must be reached on the mechanical and electroacoustic properties of tape, track alignment, azimuth, Dolby B encoding level, peak programme level, calibration tapes, and the test tones on mother tapes.

The high-speed sender

The sender is basically a tape player which plays a tape over and over again at high speed. In order to do this, the tape must be in the form of an endless loop for which a reservoir must be provided. This tape reservoir is generally known as a 'loop bin' and can be either horizontal or vertical. In either case, the tape passes from the playback head via capstan and tape guides into the bin, and from there out again via more guides and a second capstan, back towards the playback head. The capacity of the loop bin must be great enough to store some 50 minutes of programme, which means a tape length of well over 1800 ft (500 m) for mother tapes recorded at $7\frac{1}{2}$ ips (19 cm/s). The tape width is usually 1 inch (25.4 m) or $\frac{1}{2}$-inch (12.7 mm).

The speed of the tape across the playback head of the sender is either 240 ips (6.1 m/s) or 480 ips (12.2 m/s), and at these high speeds it is essential that head-to-tape contact is maintained. This is usually achieved by dual capstans of slightly different diameter, ensuring a constant tension across the playback head. Any intermittent head-to-tape contact is likely to lead to uncontrollable variability of high frequencies on the cassette.

Tape guidance must also be carefully controlled. It can be affected by the tape tensions outside the dual capstans, the positioning of the tape guides, the zenith of the playback head, and, last but not least, the accuracy of slitting of the tape. The effects of poor tape guidance can be, for instance, poor track alignment with consequent loss of signal level; up-and-down movement of the tape across the playback head, resulting in periodic variability of recorded level on the finished cassette; azimuth variation, which can cause high-frequency variability and image shift on the finished cassette; edge damage to the mother tape, which invariably results in its premature rejection for serious mechanical damage.

Wear on the playback head is not normally a problem on the high-speed sender, although periodic inspection is certainly advisable. Grooves worn into the playback head can cause poor head-to-tape contact and can also, in severe cases, adversely affect tape guidance. As with any tape player, frequent checks should be made on the gain, frequency response, and azimuth of the high-speed sender, so that these parameters conform to the values as agreed with the mother tape manufacturer. It is always good practice to check the test tones of the mother tape.

Apart from repeatedly transmitting complete programmes to the slaves at high speed, the sender is also activated to start and stop a very low-frequency signal, which is recorded by each slave between the end of one programme and the beginning of the next. The activation is usually achieved by a piece of transparent tape inserted between the end and the beginning of the programme on the mother tape, which, as mentioned before, is in the form of an endless loop (see Figure 23.4). The low-frequency signal is known as a 'cue tone' and serves to locate the inter-programme gaps when the cassette tape is later loaded into cassette housings.

It is also important to keep an eye on environmental conditions. If the humidity in the duplicating room is too low, the build-up of electrostatic charge will lead to erratic running of the tape on the sender and in the bin; if it is too

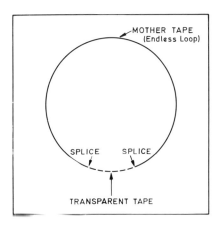

Fig. 23.4. Activation of the cue tone by transparent tape

high, the oxide from the tape may start clogging the gaps of the playback head, and this will cause random and uncontrollable dropouts on the finished cassette. It is, of course, desirable that all tape is stored under good environmental conditions, but it is essential that no tape is ever subjected to violent environmental change just before it is used. It should always be stored for a minimum of 24 hours in the environment in which it is to be used.

The cassette tape

The question of tape properties is discussed in Chapter 11, and here it will suffice to list those parameters which are thought to be desirable for cassette tape in particular.

In common with all other raw materials for large-scale manufacture, it is essential that the cassette tape has constant properties, no matter when it was made or how long ago it was stored. These properties may not be the ideal properties, but for mass production it is preferable to have consistency, even if it means a marginal sacrifice in quality. It should, of course, have low basic noise and exhibit low distortion at mid-frequencies, while at the same time being capable of accepting relatively high recorded levels at high frequencies.

Good slitting is very important, because it will not only affect the way the tape transports on the slave but will later also profoundly influence the quality of wind in the finished cassette. Badly slit tape can easily cause cassette jamming. In order to achieve good head-to-tape contact at all times, the recorded side of the tape should have a fair polish, but it should be noted that too high a polish can cause unsatisfactory tape transport in cassette players. Bearing in mind the low tape speed ($1\frac{7}{8}$ ips, 4.76 cm/s) and low tape tension in a cassette player, the tape should be flexible and show little or no sign of longitudinal or lateral curl. Cleanliness is another factor, the absence of which will lead to uncontrollable random faults such as dropouts, build-up of oxide on tape guides, contamination of capstans, pinch rollers, etc. Tape exhibiting debris or head-clogging should be avoided at all costs.

Cassette tape is usually supplied on reels or on hubs. Reels have the advantages that the tape edges are, at least in theory, protected while the tape is in transit and there is no risk of the tape coil disintegrating as it could do when wound on a hub. It is indeed a sad sight when a hub drops out of the centre of a 3 km coil of cassette tape! A hub, on the other hand, also has great advantages. The tape is less prone to edge damage when being recorded on the slave, and any defective tape is noticed more easily before it is used. Moreover, hubs are much more compact and disposable than reels, and thus save costs on internal and external transport. It is, however, particularly important not to subject tape on hubs to rapid environmental changes, because this can cause the wind to fall apart.

Cassette tape should be supplied with a minimum of packing consistent with mechanical safety. It saves costs on packing materials and their subsequent disposal.

The high-speed slave

The slave is a tape recorder which records many miles of cassette tape at high speed. The speed is usually either 60 ips (152.4 cm/s) or 120 ips (304.8 cm/s). The duplication ratio, i.e. the programme time at normal speed divided by the programme time at duplicating speed, varies from one establishment to another, but is generally either 32:1 or 64:1. Table 23.1 shows how these duplication ratios are achieved in practice. The first figure is in ips, the second in cm/s.

TABLE 23.1. **High-speed duplication speeds**

Duplication ratios	Mother tape speed: ips (cm/s)	Sender speed: ips (cm/s)	Slave speed: ips (cm/s)	Cassette speed: ips (cm/s)
32:1	$7\frac{1}{2}$ (19.05)	240 (609.6)	60 (152.4)	$1\frac{7}{8}$ (4.76)
64:1	$3\frac{3}{4}$ (9.5)	240 (609.6)	120 (304.8)	$1\frac{7}{8}$ (4.76)
64:1	$7\frac{1}{2}$ (19.05)	480 (1219.2)	120 (304.8)	$1\frac{7}{8}$ (4.76)

The slave is normally fitted with two two-track record heads, one for each side of the cassette. It is of interest to note that the slave records one side in the same direction as the programme, whereas the other side is recorded in the reverse direction. As with the sender, the tape tension across the record heads is normally controlled by a dual capstan system. The tape tension outside the dual capstan system is critical, particularly on the take-up side, where it controls the quality of wind of the recorded tape. Since the width of cassette tape is only 0.150 inch (3.81 mm) and its overall thickness is only of the order of 0.6 mils

(15 μm), tape tensions, including instantaneous tensions, must be kept as low as possible (say about 30 g) if tape stretch is to be avoided.

The wavelengths of signals recorded on the cassette tape are very small indeed, because the playing speed of the cassette is low ($1\frac{7}{8}$ ips, 4.76 cm/s). For a signal frequency of 10 kHz, the wavelength is less than 0.2 mils (5 μm), and this means that the recorded azimuth must be as near perfect as possible. The smallest deviation in azimuth will result in large losses of high frequencies on playback of the cassette tape, and these losses will be compounded by the Dolby decoder on the customer's cassette player.

The Dolby B noise reduction system has been one of the most important contributory factors in establishing the cassette as a 'hi-fi' medium. At the same time, however, it has imposed very severe disciplines on the pre-recorded cassette manufacturer. As mentioned previously, perfect programme reproduction in the customer's home is achieved only if the overall gain of the combined Dolby B encoding/decoding process is exactly unity at all frequencies within the frequency range over which the Dolby B noise reduction process operates. If it is realized that the encoding process is performed on the mother tape, and that the decoding process does not take place until the customer plays the cassette at home, the difficulties of meeting and maintaining the unity gain criterion may be appreciated. Since the Dolby B system operates only over the upper part of the audio frequency range, it is of vital importance that the high frequencies of the original programme material are accurately preserved throughout the entire cassette manufacturing process.

One cause of high-frequency loss is the inability of conventional cassette tapes to accept and retain high frequencies at high levels. In other words, the cassette tape behaves as a limiter for high frequencies, thus introducing non-linearities to the frequency response, which are later accentuated by the customer's Dolby B decoder. One method of overcoming this defect is to use a (generally more expensive) cassette tape specially designed to accept and retain high frequencies at higher levels, such as, for instance, chromium dioxide tape. It is very important that such tapes are recorded to the same characteristic as conventional tapes, i.e. to the $3,180 + 120$ μs curve: see Figure 23.5. The use of the $3,180 + 70$ μs curve is not recommended, because, for a given recording level, it wastes some of the hard-gained high-frequency headroom of the tape (4.4 dB at 10 kHz). Incidentally, it would also make life more difficult for the customer by introducing a dual playback standard for pre-recorded cassettes.

A second method of overcoming high-frequency loss due to cassette tape limitation is the installation of the Dolby HX PRO process (see Plate 36). This is designed to increase the high-frequency headroom of cassette tapes by varying, as a function of frequency, the bias (pre-magnetization) current through the record heads of the high-speed slaves. This device therefore enables the cassette manufacturer to enhance the high-frequency performance of conventional cassette tapes, but it requires capital investment as well as subsequent

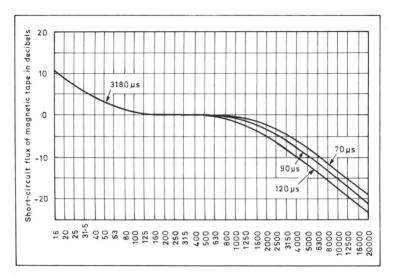

Fig. 23.5. IEC standard playback characteristics, showing the difference between the conventional 120 μs curve used for both ferric and chrome pre-recorded cassettes and the 70 μs curve used for home recording on chrome and metal blank cassettes

Plate 36. Master tape recorder electronics board with Dolby HX Pro processor unit (Photo: Stüder)

monitoring in order to ensure correct operation. It does have the advantage, however, that its benefits are obtained on any playback machine, since it is a record-stage process only.

High-frequency losses can also be caused by poor adjustment of the high-speed duplicator. In particular, correct azimuth setting of the record heads of the high-speed slaves is absolutely vital and must be checked frequently. At the same time, gain and frequency response of each slave must be measured and corrected, if necessary. It cannot be emphasized too strongly that unless these requirements are met the Dolby B decoder on the customer's cassette player cannot perform correctly.

It is normal practice to check these parameters by feeding an oscillator to the slave and measuring the output from the recorded tape by means of a test playback head mounted on the slave. While serving as a quick check, this method is not usually sufficiently accurate for setting the slave up precisely. It is better to measure the recorded tape on a real-time reel-to-reel player, which, in turn, should also be checked frequently by an approved calibration tape. A list of suppliers of such approved calibration tapes will appear in parts 2 and 3 of Publication 94 of the International Electrotechnical Commission.

Overall performance of the duplicating system should also be checked periodically. This is carried out by playing a calibration tape on the sender, recording the signals on each slave, and assessing the recording on a reel-to-reel player. This is the test method which most closely resembles production conditions, and which also takes into account any deficiencies in cabling between the sender and the slaves. It is a very effective method but somewhat long and tedious, and so it is not particularly popular with engineers or production personnel.

As with all tape transports, correct tape guidance is of paramount importance, and this applies particularly to cassette tape, due to its small size. Up-and-down movement of the tape will cause considerable level changes, which will be compounded by the customer's Dolby decoder. Edge damage to the tape must also be avoided at all costs, because the outer recorded tracks contain the left-hand channel of each programme; if edge damage occurs, the cassette will suffer from intermittent output from the left channel with consequent image shift. Severe edge damage will cause erratic winding of the tape inside the cassette, which, in turn, can cause it to jam.

In view of the vast lengths of new tape which pass over the record heads of slaves, it is vital that frequent checks are made for head wear. The first signs of head wear usually manifest themselves by an inability to record high frequencies at high levels. If frequency response measurements (see above) are made at a fixed recorded level, say x dB below the Dolby reference level of 200 nWb/m, the deviation from flatness at the high-frequency end can be used as a measure of head wear. By the time a record head shows visual signs of wear, it has probably produced many somewhat inferior cassettes.

It was mentioned above that the mother tape, via the sender, starts and stops a low-frequency oscillator between programmes. The signal from this oscillator needs to be recorded on the cassette tape at a fairly high level with a minimum of distortion. The fundamental of the signal is inaudible (it is usually around 5 Hz at cassette playback speed), but the overtones generated by distortion can be a nuisance. In some factories, this cue signal is actually cut from the tape while the cassette tape is being loaded into cassette housings.

Cassette assembly

The machine which spools the recorded cassette tape into cassette housings is known as a 'loader'. Modern loaders are fully automatic in that they accept long lengths of recorded tape plus empty cassette housings (known as 'C-zeros') and combine them into finished but unlabelled cassettes. The loader is fitted with a device which detects the low-frequency signal (the cue tone) that was recorded on the slave between programmes. Detection of the cue tone causes the loader to stop spooling at the right place, so that the leader tape from the C-zero can be spliced accurately to the cassette tape. The cue detector must sense the cue tone reliably while, at the same time, rejecting any low-frequency components which may emanate from the programme. If it does not, more than one programme could be spooled into one housing, or the loader could stop and splice in the middle of a programme.

Loaders must spool cassette tape very fast, while at the same time treating it gently. Any jerking during acceleration or deceleration of the tape could easily cause the tape to become stretched and have disastrous effects on programme quality. All edge damage to the tape must also be avoided.

Cassettes are labelled by one of three processes. The oldest process was rather messy and employed a form of glue. The two processes favoured nowadays are either heat seal or solvent. Heat-sealed labels have a heat-sensitive layer on their back which will stick to the cassette housing when heat is applied to the label. In the solvent process, the surface of the cassette housing is softened, and the label is applied to the softened surface. The solvent process has the disadvantage that fume-extraction apparatus must be installed over the labelling machine, as the solvent is toxic.

Programme information can also be printed directly on to the cassette housing, but the final appearance of the cassette is generally considered to be inferior to its labelled brother. Direct printing requires a good and uncontaminated cassette-housing surface, which must be free from all mould-release agent. This process, however, has the distinct advantage of making the cassette manufacturer totally independent of outside suppliers of printed labels. Moreover, it can effect large cost savings by eliminating label storage and the scrapping of labels surplus to requirements.

Most cassettes are packed into standard library cases, together with their relevant paper inserts. It is obviously important that both the labels and the paper insert should correspond to the programme that has been recorded on the cassette tape. This packing process is usually fully automated, and for this reason it is important that the dimensional characteristics of cassette housing, paper insert, and library case conform to close and agreed tolerances. Non-standard methods of packaging should be discouraged as far as possible, because they usually have to be carried out by hand or require heavy capital investment.

It is highly advisable that the finished product is stored in good conditions: temperature should be moderate to reduce any tendency for print-through between adjacent tape layers and consequent pre- or post-echo. For obvious reasons, the strengths of any magnetic fields in the storage area should be as low as possible.

Quality control

Quality control is a necessary but non-productive, and thus non-profitable, activity. For this reason, the aim should always be to create a highly reliable production process to give a high level of confidence. Preventative maintenance to machinery, regular performance checks, and reliable raw materials all contribute to the establishment of this confidence. Above all, the incidence of random faults should be kept to a minimum at all times. By their very nature, they are difficult to detect and, when detected, are difficult to relate to any particular shortcoming of the production process. Time and money spent on the prevention of random faults are usually an excellent investment. Generic faults, on the other hand, are more easily detected and remedied. They include faults like damage to mother tapes, permanent absence of one channel, or wrong programme.

Direct comparison of the cassette to the mother tape (A/B test) should form the basis of all assessment. If the mother tape is still in the duplicator, the QC copy (see above) may be used instead of the mother tape. If the cassette manufacturer has matched the sound of the cassette exactly to that of the mother tape, he has succeeded in his task.

The principle of A/B testing is a very important one, because it uses the ear as detector in preference to meters and other electronic gadgetry. Bearing in mind that the customer buys a cassette in order to listen to it, it seems only right that quality assessment of the product should reflect that requirement. Meters, oscilloscopes, and other equipment are excellent aids, but the final arbiter of cassette quality must always, ultimately, be the human ear.

Conclusion

No two cassette manufacturing plants operate in the same manner, with the same materials, or with the same machines. The principles involved in the manufacture of good cassettes are, however, universal and include good planning, regular preventive maintenance and performance checks, reliable raw materials, good communications, and, last but not least, good ears and a high level of common sense.

24

Compact disc processing

Gerald Reynolds and Jonathan Halliday

The new technology of digital, optically read discs has given rise to a manufacturing process of a new order of complexity. The Compact Disc is a precision moulding carrying detail of truly microscopic size, yet at the same time it is a mass-produced product. Figure 24.1 indicates the main dimensions and features of the disc. As a further indication of the relative complexity of producing CDs than LPs, it may be mentioned that the CD tracks are a mere 1.6 μm wide, whereas LP grooves are about 125 μm (see Plate 37).

The process contains more separate stages than LP manufacture, it requires much more stringent standards of cleanliness, and skilled scientists rather than technicians are needed to run it. Above all, the CD mastering process is the key

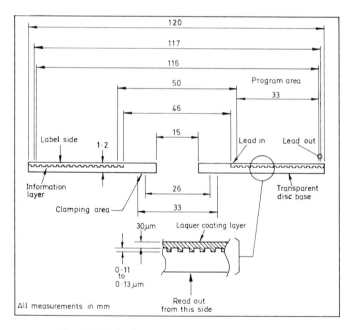

Fig. 24.1. Principal CD dimensions and features

440

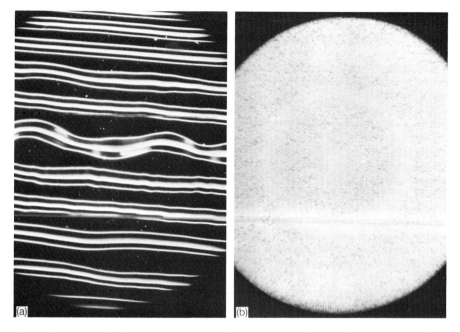

Plate 37. (a) detail of LP grooves magnified 60 times; (b) detail of Compact Disc information pits magnified 300 times (Photos: Nimbus Records)

to the whole, and without the understanding that comes from having control of its own mastering system, a pressing plant is poorly placed to judge the quality of the discs it is making.

This chapter describes the various processes which occur, firstly in the mastering system and secondly in the CD pressing plant itself (see Figure 24.2).

Glass master preparation

Whereas an LP is cut by a stylus in a coating of so-called lacquer on a metal substrate (as described in Chapter 22), a CD is etched by the exposure to laser light of a coating of photoresist (a light-sensitive material) on a glass base. This coating (unlike that on an LP lacquer) is normally prepared in the premises where the mastering is done.

The glass base is an exceptionally finely ground and polished disc, which must be prepared to a standard of surface finish considerably in excess of that regarded as good enough for laser-quality optical components, notwithstanding the greater size of the disc. This disc, after scrupulous cleaning, is coated with a layer of photoresist. The equipment used to do this is akin to that used in the semiconductor industry, where similar materials are used. However, the coatings used in semiconductor manufacture are usually several microns thick and are

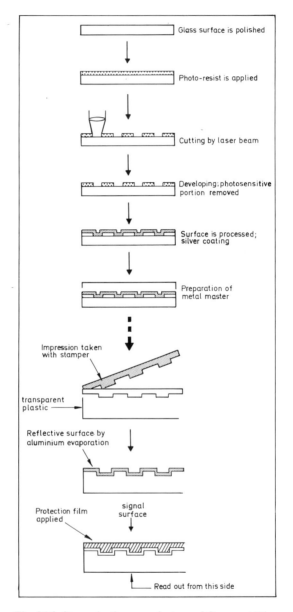

Fig. 24.2. Stages in the manufacture of Compact Discs

applied to silicon wafers not more than 80 mm in diameter, whereas for CD the coating is only 0.12 μm thick and the glass disc is typically 240 mm in diameter. Moreover, the coating thickness (which can be measured by ellipsometric methods) is not allowed to vary by more than a few per cent over the central playing area. Suffice it to say that a number of exacting problems have to be solved before arriving at an apparatus adequate for preparing CD master discs under production conditions.

Master tape inspection

Prosaically, before proceeding to the actual laser mastering stage it is wise to perform a careful check of the condition of the incoming digital master tape. In some cases, the customer requests that exact PQ editing (the setting of track start and stop times) be done by the laser mastering facility, or he may provide an analogue tape which has first to be transferred to a digital format. Even where, as is preferred, PQ editing has already been done by the customer, or by one of the various independent studios offering this service, the tape still has to be checked for audible playback faults (dropouts) arising at the time of playback, since these are cause for rejection if they occur during laser mastering. It has to be said that the reliability of available digital tape systems has lagged behind that of the CD process itself, and that unrepeatable tape dropouts are a frequent source of rejects even with the most carefully checked tapes.

Audible dropouts which are actually recorded on the tape as a result of some previous step in the editing process are, of course, strictly the responsibility of the customer, but a reputable CD manufacturing organization will make a point of bringing such occurrences to the customer's attention in case he had overlooked the faults and wants to take some corrective action.

Encoding

The pattern of dots and dashes recorded on the disc represents the digital signal which was taken off the master tape, but the format in which this signal is encoded is different from that on the tape. During laser mastering, therefore, the signal on the tape is played back, decoded in the normal way with error correction by the PCM tape processor, and then re-encoded into CD format by the specialized electronics of the CD encoder. Simultaneously, a stream of subsidiary (subcode) data carrying continuous track-timing information derived from the customer's 'PQ' data is fed via the encoder to the laser beam recorder, where it takes its place amongst the audio signals recorded on the disc.

The properties of the CD encoding format are remarkable. The audio data, taken in units ('blocks') of 24 eight-bit bytes representing 6 samples of (two-channel) information, is first expanded to 32 bytes by the addition of 8 error protection bytes, derived from and related to the audio data, in two stages, separated by an extensive interleaving or dispersing of the data in time. The added error protection bytes ensure that, when the disc is eventually played, the decoder can to a large extent detect and correct for erroneously read information by deducing what it should have been. The interleaving, and the reciprocal de-interleaving in the player, has the virtue that erroneous information due to localized faults on the disc is dispersed in time before it reaches the decoding stage, so that the job of correcting it is made easier. The error correction is such that faults up to a certain magnitude are completely corrected and are totally inaudible. Only when this threshold is exceeded is anything untoward heard.

In a later stage of the encoding process, these 32 eight-bit bytes, together with one byte of subcode data, are transformed into the same number of 14-bit words separated by three-bit 'merging' patterns. These words are then fed serially (bit by bit, 4.3 million bits per second) to the laser beam recorder, where they are used to turn the laser light on and off while it is focused on the rotating master disc.

Superficially, the effect of replacing the eight-bit bytes by 14-bit words appears to have been one of increasing the amount of information to be recorded. In actual fact the 4.3 MB/sec data rate is a misleading fiction, because the 14-bit patterns which are used are carefully selected according to certain criteria, one of which is that there are never less than three identical bits in a row. The 'merging' bits are likewise chosen such that this remains true wherever one pattern joins up to the next one. So the highest modulation frequency which is ever actually present on the disc is only about 700 kHz, which is less than it would have been if the eight-bit bytes had been recorded directly. Meanwhile, certain other virtues have been gained, notably that the average mark/space ratio of the recorded signal remains close to unity. This means that the line of pits on the disc presents, in aggregate, a uniform appearance to the optical pickup in the player—hence the performance of the servo which is used to follow this track when playing the disc is more constant than it would otherwise be.

Laser mastering

It is one thing to track a line of pits in the player correctly, but another to generate that line in the first place. The degree of mechanical and electronic stability of the laser beam recorder has to be such as to lay down a spiral track on the glass disc with a pitch of 1.6 μm (and uniform to within a fraction of that amount) while covering the playing area of the disc (radii 23–60 mm). This is done by rotating the disc while the focused beam of laser light moves across it. Meanwhile the master tape plays in real time, and the light is interrupted in accordance with the bit-stream coming from the encoder. The disc rotates with a constant linear velocity (1.3 m/s) at the point where the light is focused, which means that the rotational speed and the speed of radial motion are both curious functions of time. Slight variations in the track pitch and linear velocity are allowable, and can be utilized in order to 'squeeze' extra-long playing times on to a CD without the music reaching outer radii on the disc which would be diffcult to mould. It is preferred not to use such extreme values, however, because other parameters of the disc then begin to be more critical.

Developing

Next the coated disc, having been exposed to the laser light, is developed in a process basically akin to photographic developing. Those areas which were exposed dissolve away to leave pits in the surface; the intervening areas remain unaffected. After rinsing and drying, the developed master is vacuum-coated with silver to make it electrically conductive. It is then ready for the plating stage.

Plating

The silvered glass master is placed in a nickel electroforming bath (electroforming is fast nickel-plating, producing a 0.3–0.4-mm-thick deposit of nickel in 2–3 hours), and a metal master is grown.

This metal master is then separated from the glass master, and after cleaning to remove all traces of non-metallic matter it is passivated and once more placed in the bath to grow a metal positive or mother. The purpose of the passivation is to ensure that the mother can subsequently be separated from the metal master. The metal master is a negative replica of the developed surface of the glass master, so that the mother is once again a positive copy of it.

After separation, the mother is again cleaned and passivated and used to grow a nickel stamper, carrying a negative replica (bumps instead of pits) of the original developed glass master's surface. From the original master several mothers can be grown, each yielding a number of stampers. Each stamper can then be used to mould several thousand discs.

The electroforming technique is largely similar to that used in LP manufacture (see Chapter 22), but with several additional requirements:

1. Extreme cleanliness of the plating solution, all chemicals and water, and a very clean working environment.
2. The stamper must be flat, and its thickness must be uniform to within a few microns over its whole area.
3. The back of the stamper (the electroformed surface) must be prepared to a very smooth finish.

Moulding

Several different processes have been proposed for the mass replication of CDs:

1. The '2P' (photopolymerization) process (used for videodisc)—takes 20–30 seconds—uses an expensive substrate and requires several finishing processes (centring, centre-hole punching, and edge trimming).
2. Compression moulding (Polygram, Hanover)—takes about 20 seconds—also requires centring, centre-hole punching, and edge trimming.
3. Injection moulding (most CD manufacturers)—takes 10–15 seconds—makes a mechanically finished disc.
4. Stamping (DocData prototype)—takes some 2–5 seconds—uses an expensive, difficult-to-make substrate, and requires centring and centre-hole and outside-edge punching.

The material used to make CDs is a special grade of polycarbonate, chosen to combine mechanical and optical properties. PMMA (acrylic resin) in fact has much better optical properties but is sensitive to moisture, and so is used only for balanced, double-sided discs such as videodiscs, while other plastics so far proposed have been unsuitable on grounds such as lack of rigidity or transparency. The purity of the polycarbonate has to be excellent, and all drying and handling of the raw granules must be done in very clean conditions. Optical discs have presented material suppliers and equipment manufacturers with a level of difficulty not encountered elsewhere. Small specks of contamination which would go unnoticed in any other moulded part can render a CD useless.

Whereas most plastic mouldings are complex in shape in order to provide rigidity, the deceptively simple flat disc, which appears so easy to mould, has created a new kind of tightrope for man, machine, mould, and material. The conditions which will produce good discs fall within a very small tolerance. Whatever the method used, the moulding process must accurately reproduce the pits in the surface of the disc while maintaining very low stress in the disc as far out to the edge as possible. To do this, the plastic must be processed at temperatures not far short of those at which it starts to degrade. We have to remember that each CD has on its surface a microstructure of pits as fine as the densest integrated circuits, yet it is twenty times larger in area than the latest VLSIs. Even so, this structure (containing 600 megabytes of information) is mass-produced at the rate of one every 10–20 seconds. It is not surprising that only a few companies have engaged in the manufacture of CDs.

The importance of stress in the discs is that it causes birefringence; in other words, the light passing through the disc is split into two (polarized) components for which the disc appears to have slightly different thicknesses. The reading laser beam in the player looks at the pits through the thickness of the disc. So the players, especially those using circularly polarized optics, have difficulty in focusing on the pits at all. Such problems due to the disc are aggravated by problems in the player—for example, many players of Japanese origin have badly set-up tracking servos, which result in difficulties in playing. Unfortunately, the disc manufacturer has to make allowance for the worst players.

Only two of the replication methods listed above have been of commercial importance in manufacturing CDs. One is the compression moulding process used by Polygram. Here the disc is formed very much like a 7-inch single. Hot plastic is injected at the centre of the mould space between two stampers, one with information pits and the other plain. Both stampers are formed at their edges to create a restriction. At a chosen moment, injection ceases and the mould halves move together, compressing the plastic till it extrudes through the restriction to form a flash (excess material). Since the stress is worst at the edge of a moulded disc, trimming off the edge of an oversize disc is an elegant way of overcoming the stress problem. The centre hole is not fully moulded at this stage, and each disc has to be accurately centred and punched later on.

The waste of material, long cycle time, and need for extra processes introduce their own problems, for each stage brings with it the risk of extra rejects. However, this process was the first CD mass-production method to be used in Europe.

The Japanese and all subsequent European manufacturers have instead favoured injection moulding (see Plate 38). Its advantage is that the disc comes from the machine in a fully formed state. Only one, flat, stamper is used, and

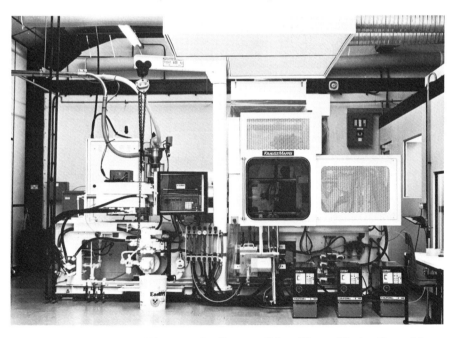

Plate 38. Injection moulding press for Compact Discs (Photo: Nimbus Records)

the other half of the mould has a highly polished face. The mould is closed against the stamper and then hot plastic is injected into this cavity very quickly (sometimes in as little as a tenth of a second). Once the plastic has cooled enough, the centre hole is punched (still within the mould), and the mould then opens for the finished disc to be extracted (Plate 39).

Whichever process is used, the moulding must be performed under clean room conditions, for the disc is very vulnerable to dust and dirt until it has been metallized. The stamper likewise has to be protected from dirt.

Plate 39. Robot extracting CD from injection moulding machine—note centre hole and outer edge of disc are already formed (Photo: Nimbus Records)

Metallizing

Although the disc as it leaves the moulding machine already carries all the information in the form of pits in the surface, the familiar rainbow colours are only dimly apparent, and a reflective layer must be applied to the information side of the disc before it can be read by a CD player. The usual method of metallizing is vacuum deposition, either evaporation or sputtering. Metallizing still creates an inconvenient bottleneck in an otherwise readily automated process. Truly continuous vacuum metallizing systems are only just coming into use, and some form of batch process will be used for most of the discs produced in the next two years.

In the simplest form of batch process, the discs are loaded on to jigs in a large cylindrical chamber (Plates 40 and 41). As soon as the chamber door is closed, large pumps begin to evacuate the space. When a sufficiently high vacuum has been reached, the jigs are moved around heated tungsten filaments which have been loaded with high-purity aluminium wire. The aluminium melts and then

Plate 40. CD pressing being loaded on conveyor prior to entering the metallizing vacuum chamber (Photo: Nimbus Records)

Plate 41. Discs being loaded into the vacuum metallizing chamber (Photo: Nimbus Records)

evaporates, depositing itself on the waiting discs. The whole process takes 20–40 minutes, depending on the equipment used, its cleanliness, and the condition of the discs to be coated. Only a fraction of this time is occupied by the actual evaporation.

In the next step towards a continuous process there are three linked chambers: a load lock, a process chamber, and an unload lock. Jigs carrying discs are placed in the load lock, and when this has been pumped down to a sufficient vacuum a valve opens leading into the process chamber. The jigs now pass one at a time past a sputtering source, from which atoms of aluminium are ejected by a low-pressure gas discharge, and then through another valve into the unload lock. In this way the discs are coated serially. Afterwards, both valves are closed and the coated discs can be unloaded from the unload lock while the next batch is going into the load lock. This is still a batch system, but it wastes less time in loading and unloading. A greater fraction of the total time is spent doing the actual metallizing.

Most of the development effort on truly continuous or 'in-line' metallizing has been concentrated on 'air to air' systems, so called because the discs go direct from normal air into a high vacuum to be processed, one at a time, and again emerge direct into the air. In principle, these machines are ideally suited to serve injection-moulding machines which produce discs at a steady rate. In practice, a sizeable buffer or marshalling area must still be provided in case of breakdown of the in-line metallizer and for when it has to be serviced. Such machines have to include valves and seals which must operate as fast as twenty times a minute. Most of these systems are of such a size as to cope with the output from three injection-moulding machines, and this puts a very high premium on reliable continuous operation. The speed of an in-line system is dictated by the slowest stage in the process, whether it be the loading and unloading robot, the time taken to outgas the discs, or the time spent depositing the aluminium.

In all vacuum systems the discs have to be outgassed sufficiently and pumped down to a high enough vacuum, or the adhesion and reflectivity of the aluminium will be poor.

Recently a new type of continuous metallizing, namely wet metallizing (which has been used for some time with videodiscs), has entered production trials. If this succeeds and can be shown to produce good adhesion and reflectivity without a high penalty in terms of material costs and effluent creation, then it will provide an attractive alternative to vacuum metallizing.

Lacquering and printing

A layer of lacquer is next applied over the metallized layer, so that the information pits are completely sandwiched between the plastic of the disc and the lacquer. This is essential to ensure that the microstructure of the pits and the delicate and easily corroded aluminium layer are protected. Once sealed in, the information layer is safe from any but the most careless handling. The label information is then printed over the top of the lacquer.

These final processes, whilst they have no bearing on the functional performance of the disc, present the first aspect of it to be seen by the buyer, and because of the smooth, shiny appearance of the disc even very small blemishes in the lacquer or print are readily visible. It has been a common experience amongst CD manufacturers that these secondary processes cause almost as much trouble, and as many rejects, as the technically more advanced parts of the mass-production process.

Testing

It is essential to test a wide variety of parameters of the disc, all of which can affect its playability. These include both average error rates and worst-case errors, stress (birefringence), quality of metallizing, centring, and flatness. These tests are made on samples at regular intervals during each production run, including a complete computer display of the playing errors present. In this way, any systematic fault or deterioration of the stamper can be traced and suspect discs rejected. All testing of error rates during manufacture must be directed at giving early warning of levels of error which are well below those which would cause any direct playing problem but which, if left, may reduce the safety margin for individual disc faults or for the effects of dirt and damage in the home.

All discs in most CD plants also undergo a full visual inspection for individual disc faults, for example black specks in the plastic or defects in the metallizing, lacquering, or printing. Many of these faults can be detected with some success by automatic inspection methods, which allow more properties of each disc to be tested to a uniform criterion. However, some types of fault which are easily seen by a trained tester cannot be recognized by a machine. Therefore in practice an automatic testing machine has a 'good', a 'bad', and a 'maybe' output, and has to be backed up by skilled human testers who can check those discs placed in the third category.

The assessment of disc faults has caused some general confusion, especially the use of the 'block error rate' (BLER for short). The CD system standard specifies that the average BLER should be less than 3 per cent, i.e. 220 erroneous data blocks per second, when measured over a ten-second period. This is merely one of many parameters which are specified, and its function is to give an indication of the general quality of the disc. It does not have any direct relation to the audibility of faults on the disc, which are a function of the worst-case errors after de-interleaving rather than of the BLER. A BLER exceeding 3 per cent does not necessarily give rise to any audible fault, nor does a low BLER guarantee that there will not be audible faults, for such faults are largely caused by localized defects which do not show up strongly in the mean BLER. It is now possible to buy a CD analyser which operates in conjunction with a professional CD player and produces, amongst other things, a histogram of the BLER taken over consecutive ten-second periods. However, it has always to be remembered that ten seconds is a long time when playing a disc, and that this mean BLER does not yield any very specific information about anything.

Packing

The final stage of manufacture is to bring together the disc, the jewel box, tray, booklet, and inlay card. This can be either a labour-intensive process or a capital-intensive one, depending on the degree of automation used. The jewel box has been criticized as being difficult to open, yet if anyone can invent a better package which retains the advantages of quality, protection of the disc, and the ability to display information on four of its six sides, CD manufacturers and public alike will be delighted.

ALLIED MEDIA

25

Radio broadcasting

Dave Fisher

In a short space it is very difficult to do justice to so wide a subject as broadcasting. Therefore I shall try here to describe the differences between broadcasting and the rest of the sound recording industry.

The following differences are generally true throughout broadcasting:

1. Broadcasting can be live. This means that studios, equipment, and operational procedures need to be designed for the possibility of live programmes, even though many programmes are recorded.

2. The absolute technical quality of a programme may take second place to its production 'feel', particularly if it is live. For instance, audience noise (including applause) at a live concert may add more than it detracts from a live transmission of a concert.

3. There is a need to generate a feeling of a 'network', in which many individual programmes combine with one another to produce a harmonious whole. This may mean that there is a need for a 'network style' and general agreement about levels of modulation.

4. The technical requirements of the transmission chain, especially that of medium wave, dictate a limit to the frequency response and the dynamic range of the programme; in some circumstances, such as the BBC's external services, the audience may be listening under the very worst reception conditions, conditions which are completely outside their control. Once again it will be better to ensure that the programme is audible and intelligible rather than that it is flat from d.c. to 20 kHz within 0.5 dB!

Studios for network radio

Radio studios come in almost every size and shape, from talks studios, just big enough for a round-table discussion with half a dozen people, to music studios of concert hall proportions, capable of accommodating a symphony orchestra. To aid communications between everyone involved in a programme, especially when programmes are live, each studio will have at least one clock. All the clocks in a studio centre are driven from the same master, to ensure that they remain in exact synchronism.

Each type of studio will have facilities to suit its needs. For example a talks studio will have an acoustically transparent table and a reverbation time of about 0.3 sec; a drama studio will have live (long RT) and dead (short RT) areas, and means of producing 'practical' (spot) effects, like a supply of water to simulate a stream or the sound of someone washing dishes, a set of different stairs (wooden, concrete, carpeted, etc.), effects doors with every conceivable lock, catch, or bolt, and any other props necessary for the type of drama recorded there.

Personnel

Generally speaking, in broadcasting the title 'engineer' is given to someone who repairs or builds equipment, or at least to someone who is trained to do so. The title 'operator' is normally given to people who use the equipment to make programmes. Depending on the style and complexity of a radio programme, there will normally be one or two operators (one mixing and the other operating tape and grams), the producer, and any other production staff.

Control rooms

A modern broadcast studio control room (sometimes called a 'cubicle') looks much like that of a modern recording studio, with two exceptions. There will be record players ('grams') so that records can be transmitted, and there will be more quarter-inch tape machines than in most recording studios.

Grams

To the broadcaster, discs not only offer a ready and cheap source of programme material, they also allow much quicker changing than tape, since no spooling is necessary. This means that when sources have to be changed in very rapid succession, for example sound effects in drama, discs are preferable to tape.

Grams suitable for broadcast use need to be of high technical quality, and must be easy to cue up, so that a record can be started quickly, without wow or rumble, at a precise cue point. Normally there will also be a fader built into the machine.

To cue up a disc, the turntable is started (normally with the fader closed!) and the stylus placed on the disc by hand at about the correct place (there may be a display showing which groove the stylus is in to aid cueing). When the cue point is reached, the turntable is stopped and then turned slowly backwards and forwards (normally by hand) until the exact point is found. The disc has now to be turned back by a fraction of a revolution (normally a quarter to a third) to allow the turntable to get up to speed before the cue point. Obviously this process puts unusual strains on the cartridge, and one that can resist back-cueing without damage is essential.

If the operator has memorized the position of the label at the cue point, then he can open the fader quickly just before the required cue point is under the stylus. This method ensures that surface noise, starting rumble, starting wow, or unwanted programme is not transmitted. Some players mute their output for a short time after the start button is pressed to achieve the same result. Inevitably, they are prone to clip the start of the required programme, or unmute too early. For the time being, at least, a skilled operator is far superior to the machine. Some modern broadcast record players do this back-cueing automatically, and will even allow you to rehearse starting the disc then automatically recue the disc to the memorized cue point.

Compact Disc

The same cueing requirements apply, of course, to Compact Discs. Professional players allow back-cueing, the storage of a large number of cue points, and rapid recueing and starting but are expensive compared to domestic machines. However, when items are to be played from the start of a track or from an index point, a domestic machine may be suitable.

Tape machines

The control rooms of most broadcast studios will have at least two or three quarter-inch tape machines, and a drama or news studio may have more. Tape machines will be used to play inserts into the programme was well as to record the studio output. The machines will normally have monitoring (headphone, LS, meter—almost invariably a VU meter), and a replay fader so that, if necessary, the levels can be controlled by the tape operator. Music (and sometimes drama studios) will have multitrack machines and mixing desks of the same type as a recording studio.

Mixing desks

Channels facilities, routing, and groups will be very similar or identical to those found in a recording studio. The main differences are:

(a) *Desk inputs.* The circuits from microphone points in the studio will terminate on a source jackfield, rather than being hard-wired to a desk channel input, (though they may be normalled to channel inputs). This source jackfield will also contain other necessary sources, such as tape machine outputs, grams, and outside sources. An outside source (or OS) is a circuit from a central area in the studio complex where sources external to the studio, such as outside broadcasts (OBs) or other studios, can be routed into the studio to form part of its output. The source jackfield allows flexibility, because the desk can be laid out to suit the programme and unused sources can be removed from the desk.

(b) *Clean feeds and cue programme.* A contributor in a remote studio (for instance, a politician in Birmingham contributing to a news programme originating in London) will need to hear what is going on in the studio. He therefore needs a sort of foldback. Generally, however, a simple feed of the studio output will suffice, and is technically simpler to arrange. This feed is known as cue programme. If the contributor is very remote (say if the politician were in America and contributing to a British news programme by satellite) he would find his own voice coming back to him over cue programme very disconcerting (indeed he would probably find it impossible to speak—try attempting to record your voice on tape whilst listening to the machine output on headphones). Furthermore, if the feed from the main studio back to the remote studio must be listened to on a loudspeaker rather than headphones, then there is a danger of howlround. The problems of delays over long circuits and of howlround can be greatly reduced, if not always eliminated by the use of a clean feed (in America this is often called 'mix minus').

A clean feed is simply a feed of the desk output but without the source to which it is being fed back. This is rather easier to say than to achieve, because each source requiring a clean feed needs a different mix. A large news or current affairs studio may have to generate up to ten such independent feeds. The normal arrangement is to use one desk group for all the outside sources and then send back to each source a feed of all the other OSs and the non-OS groups. This is often achieved in a separate matrix. For international exchanges, if each broadcasting authority sends the other a clean feed then each can add its own announcements or commentary, whilst sending to the other all 'international sound' such as music or effects. In this way they exchange programmes yet keep their own announcements or commentary.

Where a clean feed is clearly unnecessary, such as with the feed to the studio headphones or to a reasonably close source, it is normal to send cue programme. This has the advantage that, when the source is faded up by the master studio, people in the remote studio can hear their own output, which is both reassuring and allows cues such as 'And now over to the London Weather Centre' to be given over the air if the programme is live. Furthermore, especially if the source is a remote OB, this can reduce line costs because the feed of cue programme can be obtained off-air from a portable radio receiver.

(c) *Visual monitoring.* Transmitters not only clip suddenly but can be damaged by being overmodulated. In the early days of broadcasting it was necessary, therefore, to monitor visually the peak level of the signal. Modern transmitters are protected by fast-acting limiters on their inputs, but peak monitoring is still necessary if the balance leaving the studio is not to be changed by a remote limiter. Additionally, the broadcast signal passes through many pieces of equipment between the studio and the transmitter which must not be overloaded.

When the signal for stereo transmission reaches the transmitter, it is coded into M and S form before being modulated on to the RF carrier; for mono transmissions (e.g. medium and long wave) only the M signal is used. There are, therefore, four separate signals–A, B, M, and S—that must be monitored in the studio to ensure that no signal will cause overmodulation. The most convenient way of providing this is by two twin-pointer PPMs, one for A and B with red and green needles, and one for M and S with white and yellow needles. The readings of twin-pointer meters are much easier to interpret at a glance than those of separate meters.

Much useful information can be gleaned from these PPM readings. For instance, for normal stereo material A and B will be approximately equal, and S will normally be 4 to 8 dB less than M. If S is consistently higher than M, then the signal is phase-reversed; if S is zero, then the signal is either mono or very narrow, and so on.

The characteristics of the meter are defined in BS 5428–9: 1979 and IEC 268–10A. The British Standard allows two different scale designs; the one normally used in this country is arbitrarily numbered from 1 to 7 (see Figure 25.1). Zero level or O dBu produces a reading of 4, and there are 4 dB between each scale mark. For the marks to be roughly equispaced, the meter must be driven through a logarithmic amplifier (see Figure 25.2); additionally, the drive amplifier must detect the peak level of the input signal and produce a fast rise-time; a slow fall-time makes the meter easier to read.

The standards specify an integration time of 10 mS, and a fallback time of 3 sec. These values have been chosen after many years of experience. Although

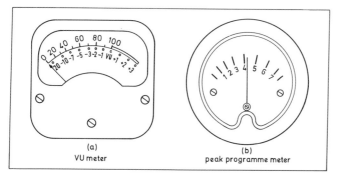

(a)
VU meter

(b)
peak programme meter

Fig. 25.1. Comparison of VU meter and PPM scales

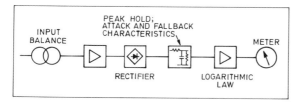

Fig. 25.2. Block diagram of a typical PPM drive amplifier

a shorter integration time would produce more accurate peak readings, the modulation would be unreasonably low; the chosen value allows very short peaks which should not produce audible distortion to pass. This does, however, mean that some very spiky waveforms may beat even a PPM. Care must therefore be exercised when recording instruments such as clavichords or harpsichords.

The integration time is defined by the CCITT as the duration of a tone-burst which produces, across the integrating capacitor, a voltage which is 80 per cent of the peak voltage of the applied signal; this is produced with a CR time-constant of 2.5 mS. The fallback time is the time taken for the reading to fall from PPM 7 to PPM 1 when the signal is suddenly removed. The peak level which may be sent to line is $+8$ dBu, that is PPM 6.

(d) *LS monitoring*. In addition to desk out, the speakers can be switched to a feed of cue prog (that is the output of the destination to which the studio is routed), feeds of each radio network, incoming OSs etc. To make mono monitoring more realistic, the speakers can also be switched to monitor a mono version of the studio output on only one loudspeaker, usually the left one. To check whether or not a source that sounds out of phase really is—without phase-reversing the source because the possible phase reversal may not have been noticed until the source has been put on air—the speakers can also be put out of phase with one another.

(e) *Line-up tone*. To ensure that all levels are set correctly, each source will send line-up tone at a standard level (see later) to its destination before it sends programme. So that tone can be sent whilst the studio is rehearsing, without interrupting the rehearsal, it is normal to be able to switch the line leaving the studio away from the desk output to a feed of standard-level tone (see Figure 25.3). Provided that the loudspeaker and PPM monitoring can be switched between the desk and the line output, this allows rehearsals to continue whilst sending tone.

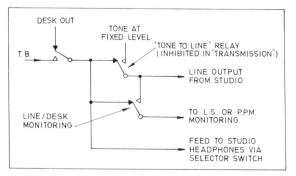

Fig. 25.3. Switching of tone and talkback to line

(f) *Foldback and AER*. Foldback will be similar to that in a recording studio. Acoustic Effects Reproduction (AER) is a system which feeds tape or grams into a studio loudspeaker rather than to a desk input channel.

AER is necessary because a sound effect played in from tape or grams will only sound correct if it matches the acoustic of the rest of the studio action; otherwise it will probably sound too close. The easiest way of achieving this, and simultaneously of controlling the perspective is to use AER. An example is making a record sound like background music in a restaurant, or making a background noise than could not reasonably be produced live in the studio (such as countryside or weather effects) fit behind dialogue.

(g) *Ergonomics*. The desk will be much easier to use if it has plenty of space to hold a script; the script space is usually a shelf which runs the length of the desk between the operator and the faders.

Some broadcasters use faders that fade up when pulled towards the operator, that is they work in the opposite direction to faders on a recording desk. This method has the advantage that the operator can place the heel of his hand on the script tray; this is far more comfortable for the inevitable hands-on style of mixing necessary in broadcasting. It also has the advantage that faders which are accidentally knocked by the script or the operator's sleeve are knocked closed rather than open. Although it may seem back-to-front to someone used to conventional faders, it soon becomes quite natural.

Studio communications

Much useful information can be exchanged between a producer or operator and a studio presenter by hand signals or suitable facial expressions through the studio observation window; looks are almost always more concise than words. Nevertheless, there are some things which can only be put into words, so talkback from the control room to the studio (interrupting the desk output) is provided.

To provide a fast and secure means of communication, each source is linked to its destination by a telephone circuit called a control line. This control line is established each time a source is routed to a destination, no matter whether the connection is made manually or by a switching system. A studio going on air with, for example, three outside sources will have control lines to each OS and one to its destination which can also be picked up in the central area.

Green cue lights are used to cue studio action—effects or speech—and are quicker and more concise than talkback. Cue light use can be quite eloquent. Steady for 'Go steady', flicker for 'Go quicker' is an old convention. The studio red lights can usually be switched on locally, as in a recording studio, and also remotely by a continuity suite. When the studio is on air, it is important that some of its facilities are disabled. For instance, it should not be possible to send tone, even accidentally, from an on-air studio; nor should talkback be routed to studio loudspeakers unless all the studio microphones are faded out. These interlocks are provided automatically by putting the studio into transmission; the opposite condition is rehearsal, indicated by blue lights in and around the studio; these conditions are selected from the mixing desk.

Providing that the studio is in rehearsal, it is convenient to replace the main output with talkback when the talkback key is pressed, as shown in Fig. 25.3. This provides a type of slating, and allows all destinations to hear talkback without the need for a separate circuit. Obviously this facility must be disabled when the studio is in transmission.

Pre-transmission checks

Before going on air, it is important that the continuity suite (which assembles the network from studio and pre-recorded tape sources) and the studio perform the following checks:

1. *Control line*

It must be possible to ring and speak in both directions.

2. *Routing*

Continuity needs to be sure that it is making checks with the correct studio. It can ask the studio to cut its tone and check that the tone arriving in the continuity suite cuts simultaneously; the studio can identify itself and its programme by using rehearsal talkback.

3. *Level*

The studio should send tone to the continuity suite at a known level. In the days when all studios were mono, 0 dBu tone was sent. If it arrived at continuity at 0 dBu then all was well; if it was more than about 2 dB out then there was a fault which merited investigation. If it was within about 2 dB then correction at the destination was in order. With the coming of stereo there was a problem. Every destination, whether stereo or mono, needed to be able to line up with any source, whether it was stereo or mono. It is easy enough to feed the M output of a studio to mono destinations and the A and B outputs to stereo destinations, provided that the source and the destination are in the same building; but what if a mono version of a stereo source is made at a remote point? Because (in the BBC system) the M signal is derived by adding together the A and B signals, and then attenuating the result by 3 dB (see Figure 25.4), the level needed on A and B to produce 0 dBu on M is −3 dBu. Therefore, if stereo sources send −3 dBu tone on each leg not only will M PPMs everywhere read 0 dBu (as in mono days), but the M tone will be 0 dBu no matter whether it is generated in the studio or at a remote point. There is then no need to

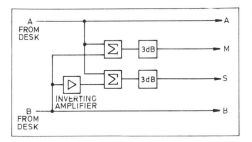

Fig. 25.4. Derivation of M and S
signals from A and B

distribute the M output of the studio; the M output of a stereo studio and the only output of a mono studio will be at the same level. If all this seems over-complicated, remember that the majority of radio listeners are probably listening on medium or long wave, which is unquestionably mono.

4. *Red lights and buzzers*

These are only provided for internal sources such as a studio but not an OB. The buzzer is used from studio to Continuity to confirm that the red lights are on, and to indicate the end of the programme.

5. *Clocks*

The continuity and studio clocks should be in sync; Continuity and studio should agree an on-air time and a programme duration.

6. *Cues*

The studio must check that it is receiving the correct cue programme. In and out cues (words or music) etc. must also be arranged/checked.

Central area

This is often called the control room (the studio control room is then called a cubicle); however, to keep confusion to a minimum I shall call it the central area. The outputs of all the studios are routed to the central area. This is rather like a telephone exchange, providing communications and routing between all technical areas. Routing a source to a destination involves a large number of different circuits (stereo music, control line, cue prog, red lights, buzzer, etc.) and would be time-consuming if each had to be plugged up by hand. Although manual over-plugging is provided for seldom-used sources or for emergencies, remote-controlled switches that switch all these circuits simultaneously are obviously more convenient. Relays, uniselectors, and code bar switches have all been used in the past; modern installations use electric matrices.

The central area also has extensive monitoring facilities, and can examine the signal at every point in its progress through the broadcast chain. In addition, it receives programme from OBs and remote sources, and sends programme to transmitters, other organizations, and remote destinations such as regional studio centres.

Incoming circuits

Most remote sources arrive by land line (known as a music line), though an increasing number are on digital links. From an OB site, the music line will go to the nearest BT telephone exchange. The programme is sent from exchange to exchange until it arrives in the central area of the broadcast centre via circuits known as local ends, where it is equalized and has its level restored. The line-receiving chain is shown in Figure 25.5. The U-links are the demarcation line between BT and the broadcaster. The rep coil (a high-quality 1:1 transformer) maintains accurate line balance; this ensures that minimal line noise and interference are present in the signal after equalization.

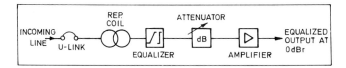

Fig. 25.5. Incoming line equipment block diagram

The equalizer is rather different from that on a control desk. It must have a response which is accurately predictable and repeatable. To make line-testing easier, it must also have an input impedance (of 600 ohms) which does not change with frequency or the equalization setting.

To set the equalizer, the frequency response of the line is first measured with a meter (also of 600 ohms input impedance). The frequency response graph so obtained is then compared with the known response of the equalizer using a transparent mask. When a good fit has been found between the line response and one of the equalizer's responses, the necessary settings of the equalizer controls can be read off the mask. If the equalizer is now connected in place of the meter, the response of the line will not be affected. The output from the equalizer will therefore have a flat frequency response, because its response is the inverse of the line's. If the equalizer is purely passive, its output level will be low, and indeed it is normally attenuated to a standard level (−45 dBu). An amplifier restores the signal to the same level as it set out.

Outgoing circuits

Outgoing music lines are fed via a Line-sending amplifier, rep coil, and U-links. The line-sending amplifier either has variable gain or a fixed gain of 10 dB followed by a variable attenuator. Programme is sent to line at up to +10 dBr, that is with programme peaks of up to +18 dBu. Programme is sent in this way between buildings, to other organizations or broadcast centres in other towns or countries, and to some transmitters. The BBC has, since the late 1960s, used a digital PCM system to feed programme to its main VHF transmitters (see later).

Continuity suites

In the early days of broadcasting, the signal from a studio was routed directly from the central area to the transmitters. Unfortunately, this led to the problem that there was no one to take overall responsibility for the programme content of the network, and so continuity studios were designed. Each continuity has an announcer who links contributions from all the sources into an integrated network, and who carries executive authority for the content of the network. The announcer is able to fade out any incoming programme if he feels that it is unsatisfactory for any reason. For some radio networks, like Radio 3 or Radio 4, this is still the major function of Continuity.

A continuity suite consists of a small studio, with a self-drive desk, microphones, grams, and cartridge machines (see Figure 25.6). The control room that goes with the continuity studio has facilities to select outside sources to which it has extensive communications links; pre-recorded programmes can be played in from tape machines.

The programme which leaves a studio is routed via the central area to a continuity suite, where it can be monitored and controlled; the continuity and studio exchange pre-transmission checks. About 10 seconds before the start of the programme, the continuity operator will flash the red lights of the studio; the studio will answer with a buzz. When the studio is faded up on the continuity desk, the operator will send a steady red light to the studio.

Since the continuity studio can play records, pre-recorded tapes, NAB cartridges, and now Compact Discs, it is quite capable of originating its own programmes. Therefore many disc programmes come directly from a continuity. This poses a new problem, in that continuity cannot rehearse one programme whilst it is on air originating another. There may now be a need, therefore, to switch the network between different continuities. Continuity still remains, however, the last point of operational control within the broadcast chain.

The 13-channel PCM system

The output from the continuity suite returns to the central area, where it can again be monitored, and is then sent by an extensive system of circuits to the transmitters. Distribution can be by BT music line, but is more likely to be digital. The BBC's distribution to main VHF transmitter sites is via their so-called 13-channel PCM system.

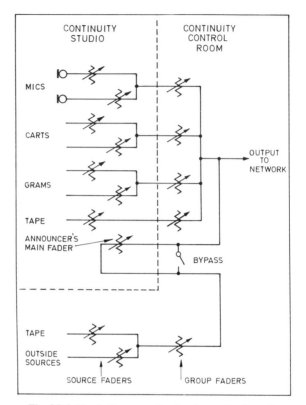

Fig. 25.6. Block diagram of a simple continuity suite

This system, put into service in the late 1960s, codes 14 separate signals (13 high-quality audio circuits and one data circuit) and combines them by time division multiplex on to one bearer circuit (either a BT coaxial circuit or a SHF radio link). Each of the audio signals is sampled at 32kHz and coded using 13 bits per sample. By the standards of professional digital audio, this may not seem like a high-quality system. The frequency response of broadcast signals is 15 kHz, so 32 kHz sampling is perfectly adequate; the programme fed to the coder has already undergone the normal broadcast level control, and therefore has a much smaller dynamic range than many commercial classical recordings. This control of dynamic range has always been necessary, because many people are listening under adverse conditions, such as on medium wave, or with high background noise levels. So, although a 13-bit system has a S/N ratio which is 18 dB worse than a 16-bit system, the higher noise level is masked by the higher levels of quiet passages. Recently, the use of NICAM coding has allowed an increase in the number of channels and an improvement in the sound quality.

Modulation

Before the programme arriving at the transmitter can be radiated from the aerial, it must be modulated on to a radio-frequency carrier.

Amplitude modulation

The simplest form of modulation is AM (amplitude modulation). It is used for the long, medium, and short wavebands. The amplitude of a radio-frequency sine wave (called the carrier) is changed in sympathy with the amplitude of the modulating signal (in this case the audio programme). The result is known as the modulated signal or the envelope (see Figure 25.7). If the peak level of the programme exceeds that which just causes zero amplitude of the modulated envelope, then the demodulated signal in the receiver will be clipped. The use of PPMs for programme control and a fast-acting delay line limiter at the transmitter prevent this happening.

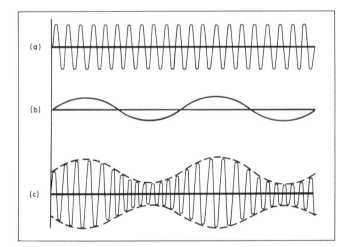

Fig. 25.7. Amplitude modulation: showing (*a*) the unmodulated RF carrier, (*b*) the AF modulating signal, (*c*) the amplitude-modulated signal

If a sine-wave tone is used to amplitude-modulate a carrier, then the output of the modulator will contain three frequency components: the carrier and two sidebands (see Figure 25.8). The sidebands are spaced from the carrier by the frequency of the modulating signal. If, for instance, a 200 kHz carrier is amplitude-modulated by 3 kHz tone, the lower sideband will be 197 kHz and the upper sideband will be 203 kHz. The output from the modulator will therefore contain 197, 200, and 203 kHz. The bandwidth of the modulated signal is therefore twice that of the modulating signal, so audio with a bandwidth of 15 kHz would take up 30kHz of 'air-space'. In order to fit more channels into

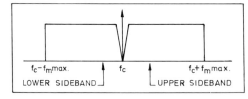

Fig. 25.8. Spectrum of an AM signal

the medium wave broadcast bands, the bandwidth of each broadcast signal is therefore reduced, by international agreement, to about 5 kHz.

Frequency modulation

AM suffers from impulsive interference, because any stray pulse within the bandwidth of the modulated envelope will be demodulated by the receiver as a click. If the amplitude of the modulating signal is used to change the frequency rather than the amplitude of the RF carrier (Figure 25.9), then most of this interference can be eliminated in the receiver, because the receiver has only to detect the instantaneous frequency of the carrier; the interference, which tends to change the amplitude of the carrier, can be removed by limiting. The amount by which the frequency of the carrier is changed is called the deviation. In Band II the maximum deviation used is 75 kHz (this corresponds to PPM 6, or +8 dBu).

If, therefore, a 1 MHz carrier was frequency-modulated by a 3 kHz sine wave to a deviation of 75 kHz, the carrier frequency would rise sinusoidally from 1 MHz to 1.075 MHz, fall sinusoidally to 925 kHz, then return to 1 MHz. Since the modulating frequency is 3 kHz, this whole sequence would be repeated 3,000 times per second.

If an RF carrier is frequency-modulated, an infinite number of sidebands is

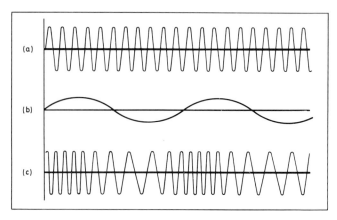

Fig. 25.9. Frequency modulation: showing (*a*) the unmodulated RF carrier, (*b*) the AF modulating signal, (*c*) the modulated signal

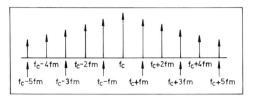

Fig. 25.10. Spectrum of an FM signal

generated, each separated from the next by the modulating frequency (see Figure 25.10). Clearly this presents a major problem. Luckily, the distortion produced by discarding the more extreme sidebands is small. In practice, therefore, the bandwidth needed for an FM system (or RF Channel) is $2 \times (f_m + f_d)$. For a mono signal on band II this is $2 \times (15 + 75) = 180$ kHz.

Stereo broadcasting

FM broadcasting on band II (VHF 88 to 108 MHz) started long before stereo broadcasting. The transmission system adopted for stereo had therefore to be compatible with the previously existing mono system. The easiest way of achieving this is to transmit not A and B (the signals corresponding to left and right) but M and S, as is done with the universally adopted Zenith GE pilot tone system described here.

The S signal is first amplitude-modulated on to a 38 kHz carrier (see Figure 25.11), with the carrier component of the envelope suppressed (this is called Double Sideband Suppressed Carrier Modulation, or DSBSC). This envelope therefore contains only two sidebands and is contained between 23 and 53 kHz (see Figure 25.12). This signal can therefore be added to the M signal without any overlap of frequencies. In order to demodulate the signal, the receiver must be able to identify the phase of the 38 kHz (suppressed) carrier. Therefore a

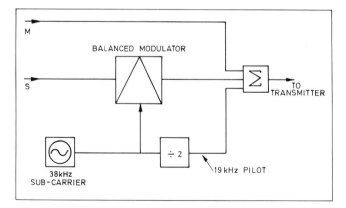

Fig. 25.11. Block diagram of a stereo coder

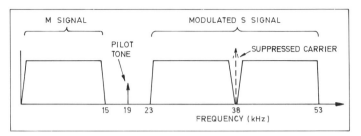

Fig. 25.12. Spectrum of a Zenith GE modulated stereo signal

low-level 19 kHz pilot tone is added, and this composite signal is used to frequency modulate the RF carrier: 90 per cent of the peak deviation is now due to audio information and only 10 per cent to the rest of the transmitted information.

In the receiver, the 19 kHz can be used to re-generate the 38 kHz carrier, reinsert it, demodulate the S signal, and then matrix it with M to produce A and B. However, a useful feature of DSBSC is that its phase changes by 180° when the modulating signal passes through zero. This change of phase means that the 19 kHz pilot tone can be used to identify positive and negative half-cycles of the S signal. A very simple method of decoding is therefore to regenerate 38 kHz from the pilot tone, and use this to switch the composite signal between the left and right outputs of the decoder.

Local radio

Local radio uses many of the methods and techniques pioneered in network radio. Since it is on a smaller scale, its programme chain is technically less complex, but otherwise similar. Most local radio studios are similar to the continuity suites described above. The studio can be used with its control room for complex programmes or can be self-drive for simpler ones. There are often two studios, each self-drive, either of which can be used with a control room and a news studio. Either studio needs to be able to 'seize' the transmitters so as to go on air. This allows one studio to rehearse whilst the other is on air; at the programme junction when they are to swap, the on-air studio can release the transmitters and the other take them.

A more sophisticated method, often used between network continuities, is for the incoming studio to take the on-air studio as a source, fade it up, and check that the output levels of both studios are identical. If the transmitters are now switched to the incoming studio, there will be no change as far as the listener is concerned, but the incoming studio can either fade out the outgoing studio, or just face up its own microphones and let the programme presenters have a two-way handover conversation (provided the outgoing studio listens to the correct cue programme).

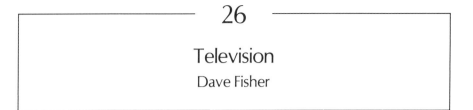

26

Television
Dave Fisher

The broadcast chain in television is in many ways similar to that in network radio. To some extent, of course, pictures add an extra constraint, because in general the pictures and sound must match one another in perspective at least. This is not to say that the pictures or sound must be compromised, but rather that there is the extra challenge of making them fit together harmoniously.

Television principles

Scanning

An image of the scene is focussed on to a photo-sensitive layer in the camera tube. It is easy to imagine this as a mosaic-like set of 200,000 or so elements (Figure 26.1). These elements cannot be sent to a monitor simultaneously (without the use of 200,000 separate cables!), so they are sent sequentially, using a scanning system, which produces a single signal whose voltage at any instant represents the brightness of the scene at some point in the mosaic. The elements are scanned from left to right and top to bottom. Each row of elements produces one line of picture signal. When all the elements have been sent, the process starts again at the top. To portray movement without jerkiness it is necessary to send at least 24 complete sets of elements per second. This is called a picture or frame. In practice, the scanning is done with an electron beam which is scanned from left to right at high speed (15,625 times per second) and simultaneously from top to bottom at a much slower speed. To reduce the flicker produced by scanning, a system of interlace is used, in which half the lines are scanned on the first journey down the image and the other lines are filled in on the next

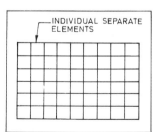

Fig. 26.1. Mosaic-like structure of picture elements

INDIVIDUAL SEPARATE ELEMENTS

journey (Figure 26.2). Each vertical scan is now called a field, so in the 625-line system there are 625 lines each frame, and 2 fields per frame. The line frequency is therefore 15.625 kHz, the field rate is 50 Hz, and the frame or picture rate is 25 Hz. The electron beam used for scanning returns quickly from the end of one line or field to the start of the next; this is called flyback.

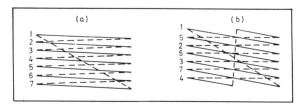

Fig. 26.2. The interlace system: showing (a) a seven-line non-interlaced raster, (b) a seven-line interlaced raster

Synchronization

To ensure that the receiver reassembles the picture in the same order as it was split up by scanning, extra information is added at the start of each line and each field. This information consists of synchronizing pulses. So that a receiver can reliably detect the difference between picture information and sync pulses, picture detail is sent as a positive voltage (black is 0 V and peak white is 0.7 V) and sync information as a negative voltage (-0.3 V), as shown in Figure 26.3.

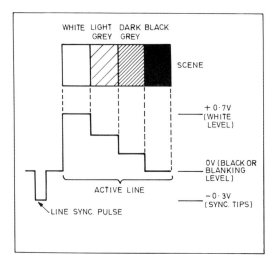

Fig. 26.3. Showing one line of video produced by scanning the scene above

In the receiver, the electron beam which scans the phosphor in the CRT to reconstruct the picture cannot flyback instantly. If there was picture information whilst flyback was in progress, annoying spurious lines would be displayed. To prevent this, the signal is blanked, i.e. muted for part of each line and field. In the 625-line system, line blanking is 12 μs out of a total line time of 64 μs, leaving 52 μs of active line (Figure 26.4); field blanking is 25 lines per field, leaving a total of 575 active lines per frame (Figure 26.5).

Before syncs are added to the signal, it is referred to as a picture or non-composite signal; after the addition of syncs it is called a video signal. The word 'video' therefore refers to an electrical signal

Colour

Using a prism it is possible to split white light into the familiar spectrum from red through orange, yellow, green, blue, and indigo to violet. Almost all visible

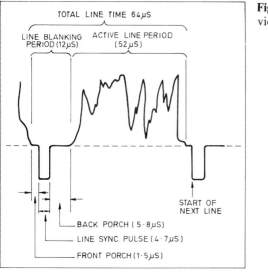

Fig. 26.4. Line timings for a 625-line video signal

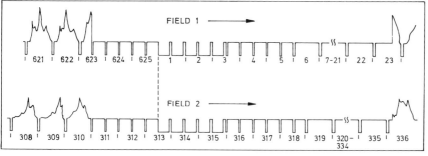

Fig. 26.5. The field-blanking interval

hues can, however, be analysed into or synthesized out of a mixture of red, green, and blue—the primary colours. In the colour camera, therefore, the light from the scene is split by a dichroic block into three separate images, one red, one green, and one blue (Figure 26.6). Each image is focused on to a different camera tube, each scanned with synchronous rasters, so that the camera produces three separate outputs, one red, one green, and one blue. The scanning of each tube must be adjusted so that the three pictures fit together exactly when reproduced. This is called registration.

The three parameters of a colour are hue, luminance, and saturation. Hue is the essential property of a colour which distinguishes it from all other colours, e.g. red and green are different hues. Luminance or brightness is the quantity of light. Luminance is an objective unit (like level in sound); brightness is the subjective sensation produced by light (like loudness in sound). Saturation is the purity or richness of a colour. Highly saturated colours contain only the dominant hue; desaturated colours like pink can be made by adding white light to a saturated colour.

Display tubes

In a colour monitor, the display tube produces a separate electron beam for each of the three primary colours. The electron beams are arranged so that the beam produced by the red input hits only phosphor that glows red, and so on. The inside of the screen is coated with alternate spots or lines of the three phosphors. To prevent any beam hitting the wrong colour phosphor, a perforated metal plate just behind the screen puts all phosphor except the correct one in shadow. This metal plate is called a shadowmask or aperture plate. At normal viewing distances, the eye cannot resolve the separate colours, so the tube can reproduce all the colours which can be synthesized from the three primary colours.

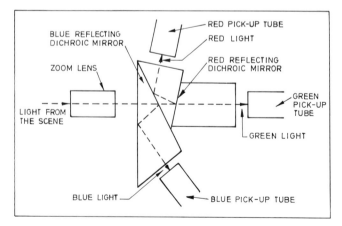

Fig. 26.6. Dichroic block used in the camera to analyse the incident light into its red, green, and blue components

Bandwidth

Fine detail in the scene will produce the highest-frequency video. The finest detail which can be reproduced will be limited by the bandwidth of the transmission system. A bandwidth of 5.5 MHz produces adequate detail, and so R, G, and B each have a bandwidth of 5.5 MHz, as do monochrome transmissions. It would be impracticable to transmit the three separate RGB signals (in any case, colour was introduced after monochrome and replaced it). The colour transmissions must therefore be coded so that one 5.5 MHz channel carries all the colour information (see Figure 26.7), and meets the following requirements:

1. *Compatibility*. The colour transmission must produce an acceptable picture on existing monochrome receivers.
2. *Reverse compatibility*. A monochrome transmission should produce a satisfactory black-and-white picture on a colour receiver without any modification to the receiver.
3. *Bandwidth restriction*. The colour signal should not occupy any more bandwidth than a monochrome transmission.

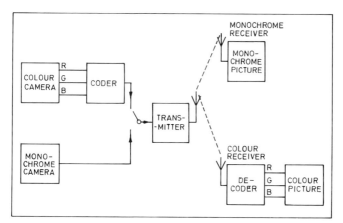

Fig. 26.7. Compatibility and reverse compatibility: a colour transmission must produce a satisfactory picture on a monochrome receiver, and vice versa

Studios

Television studios, like radio studios, come in a large range of sizes. Unlike their radio counterparts, however, television studios are more likely to be either general-purpose (their use limited only by what will fit into them) or 'News and Current Affairs'. To allow studio equipment, especially cameras, to move smoothly around the studio, the floor is covered in heavy-duty lino and is very flat. Cameras are mounted on pedestals or cranes to give increased mobility.

Microphone booms

A boom is the basic method of dialogue pickup in a television studio. The Fisher boom is the most versatile. A microphone mounted on a boom can follow artists around the set, and control the perspective (simply by positioning) to suit the action and the pictures; it does all this whilst out of shot.

The Fisher boom has a microphone mounting which can be remotely controlled from the platform. The microphone cradle can be swivelled from side to side (panned) and up and down (tilted). The whole arm can be moved from side to side (swung) and up and down (lifted and lowered), and can be extended or retracted (racked in and out). The platform on which the operator stands can be raised and lowered, and the whole thing, mounted on wheels, can be tracked or steered around the studio floor.

The microphone is usually a cardioid: an omni would pick up too much studio noise and be difficult to get close enough without being in shot; a figure-of-eight would rumble too much when moved. The ideal position of the microphone should be achieved without the mic being in shot, and without casting shadows into shot. The boom operator therefore needs to be able to see a picture monitor during rehearsals, so that he can tell how close to the wind he is sailing, and reproduce a satisfactory position when on air.

Lighting and boom operation are very closely related; a good boom operator needs to understand both. The simplest situation is 'one man to camera'. The keylight, a hard source of light, casts shadows with hard, clearly defined edges; the filler, a soft source of light, casts shadows with a soft, fuzzy edge. When the boom is in the position shown in Figure 26.8, the hard shadow of the microphone cast by the key light is cast out of shot, on the floor at camera right.

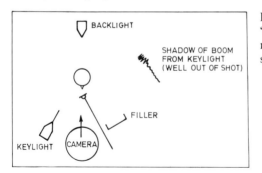

Fig. 26.8. Simple lighting plot for 'one man to camera', using a boom microphone on the same side of the set as the soft filler

Microphone cables

The dimmers used to control the brightness of the studio lights use SCRs (usually Triacs). They work by switching on the current to the lamp part way into each half cycle of the mains (Figure 26.9); the longer the switch-on is delayed, the dimmer the lamp will be. This method has the advantage that it is

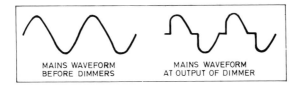

Fig. 26.9. Waveform distortion of the mains by a triac dimmer

very efficient, but the disadvantage that it generates large amounts of AF and RF energy. To prevent this causing interference to microphone circuits (the interference is very wide-band, being harmonics of 50 Hz, and extends well into the medium waveband) well-balanced circuits, good desk channel input transformers, and star quad cable are needed.

Star quad cable has four tightly twisted conductors within the screen (Figure 26.10). The object is to ensure that the same amount of interference is induced in each leg of the balanced circuit. Provided this is the case, the desk input transformer will balance out the induced e.m.f. and there will be no resultant interference. The cable is wired so that diagonally opposite conductors are connected together at both ends of the cable. An interfering field therefore needs to be very close to the cable to induce a different e.m.f. in each leg of the circuit. The tight twist helps to ensure this.

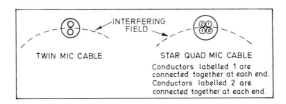

Fig. 26.10. Comparing twin and star quad cables

Radio microphones are often used for documentaries and current affairs. They allow the use of a personal mic without the inconvenience of a trailing cable. A battery-powered transmitter, small enough to fit into the hip pocket, allows any microphone to be used. Frequency modulation is used with a maximum deviation of 75 kHz.

The control room suite

Lighting and Vision Control Room
The camera outputs are fed to the lighting and vision control room, where remote controls allow vision operators to control the black level, optical iris and fine colour gain of each camera. The outputs of each camera can thus be

Plate 42. Production gallery in Studio 4 at BBC Television Centre (Photo: Link Electronics)

matched so that when cameras are cut between there is no difference in the exposure of the picture or of its colour balance.

The control room also houses the lighting control desk, which is normally computerized to allow the recall of the large number of lighting cues necessary, particularly in light entertainment.

The RGB outputs of each camera are then fed to the apparatus room, where they are coded into composite video and distributed to monitors and the vision mixer.

Production Control Room

The director, sitting in the PCR, can see the output of each vision source to the studio (Plate 42). These include cameras, VT machines, TK machines (these convert film into television pictures), slide scanners, electronic caption generators, OBs, and other studio outputs. He is responsible for the production once it is in the studio. So that his directions can be heard by everyone involved in the programme, whether in the studio, the other control rooms, or at an outside source, he has an open talkback system known as Production Talkback (PTB).

The vision mixer (in Britain a person as well as a piece of equipment; an anomaly avoided in America by calling the equipment a video switcher) can cut

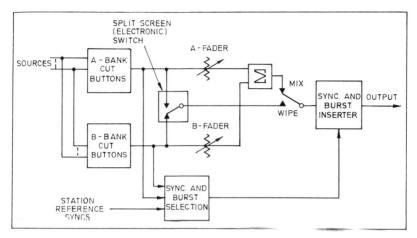

Fig. 26.11. Block diagram of a simple A–B vision mixer

between any of the sources available to the studio (Figure 26.11). To be able to superimpose sources, or to wipe between them, requires that they are synchronous with each other and with the studio. To be synchronous, the sync pulses of each source must arrive at the vision mixer simultaneously.

The timing of video sources is a rather complex business. The sync pulses must arrive within 50 ns of each other, and the burst phases must be within 1.3 degrees of each other. Although the sync timing requirement can be met by cutting cables to the correct length (5 ns represents about 10 m of cable), the colour requirement cannot (1.3° of subcarrier represents about 16 cm of cable, and it is not practicable to cut all the cables in a studio to within 16 cm of 'correct'). Some sort of manual or automatic adjustment is therefore necessary before any colour source can be considered synchronous.

Technical supervision of outside sources, including communications, line-up, and synchronism, is usually co-ordinated from the production gallery.

Sound control room

The SCR, or sound gallery, is in the charge of a sound supervisor who is responsible for all sound aspects of the programme and also mixes the programme. He will be assisted by a tape and grams operator who is usually responsible for the whole balance of tape or gram items. TV sound desks are normally larger than radio desks; forty or fifty channels is a common size. Otherwise the technical facilities are similar.

Though TV sound is at present transmitted in stereo only by using the transmitters of a radio network, new TV sound desks are usually stereo, and it is likely that TV sound transmissions will be stereo-capable in the near future.

Ancillary desk facilities such as clean feeds, foldback, etc. are similar to radio, although more facilities are generally required. Outputs for public address are also necessary when a studio audience is present. This facility is similar to foldback, available from desk channels or groups, but may incorporate fader backstop switching so that the PA feed can be pre-fade (which has, for instance, the advantage that the PA howlround point does not change if a channel feeding PA is opened further on air than it was in rehearsal), and yet the feed of that channel to PA is automatically cut when the channel (or group) is faded out.

Studio communications

The problem of keeping every source and destination in close contact are manifold. There are therefore many different communications systems in use.

Red lights: indicate transmission, and are switched on locally when recording.
Blue lights: indicate rehearsal, i.e. the studio is in use (and therefore admission is restricted) but the output is not on air or being recorded.
Buzzers: are used from video tape (VT) and Telecine (TK) to the studio. The advantage of a buzzer is that it requires less concentration on the part of a hard-pressed director than a voice channel would; the disadvantage is that only 'Yes' (one buzz) or 'No' (two buzzes) can be sent.

Talkbacks
These include:

(a) *Production talkback*: An 'open' system (i.e. no switch needs to be pressed to energize it). PTB originates from the production desk (director/producer, production secretary, production assistant) and is distributed to everyone involved in the production (cameramen, outside sources, SCR, L & VCR, apparatus room, etc.). Note that the sound supervisor will be listening to PTB on a loudspeaker, and may therefore have difficulty in detecting induction of talkback on to programme sound. For this reason, the studio's destination is often the area responsible for ensuring that there is no such induction. Although PTB is the prerogative of the director, some other operational positions, such as sound supervisor or lighting director, can also speak on it.

(b) *Sound talkback*: The sound supervisor has a sound crew (boom operators, tracking foldback operators, PA operators, etc.) on the studio floor that he must direct. They, of course, also need to hear the director. Sound talkback therefore normally carries PTB, but when the sound supervisor presses his STB key the STB distribution is switched away from PTB to the output of the sound supervisor's talkback microphone. A blip of tone is sometimes added to STB whenever the sound supervisor presses his STB key, to help those listening to

STB to identify the different voices that may be speaking on it. A similar arrangement is available in lighting to direct lighting staff (like follow-spot operators) on the studio floor.

(c) Reverse talkback: Reverse talkbacks are intercoms which allow an individual to reply to the source of some talkback; for example, camera reverse talkback allows cameramen to reply to the director; sound reverse talkback allows boom operators to reply to the sound supervisor; outside source reverse talkback allows VT or TK operators to reply to the studio (normally the director).

Programme sound: This is a feed of the output of the sound desk (as opposed to studio output, which is fed from after the tone relay). Programme sound will, for instance, allow a cameraman to time a track or a pan to music if he can mix it with the other signals in his headphones; though for most programmes he will not need it. Boom operators listening to prog sound will be able to hear their own microphone when it is faded up, and will therefore be able to position it more accurately.

Intercoms: Talkback channels generally allow one person to speak to a large number of people. Often an individual will want to speak to another individual: for example the sound supervisor may need to discuss a boom shadow problem with the lighting director. Intercoms permit such person-to-person conversations whilst the programme continues.

Control lines: As in radio, control lines will link every source with its destination; in addition there will be control lines to central areas.

Cue dots: Cue dots are small black-and-white striped rectangles inserted into the top left or top right of a broadcast video signal, either by a network control room or a master control, to indicate the proximity of a programme junction. Their advantage is that, because they are radiated from the transmitter, everyone who watches the transmitted output can see and therefore act upon them. For instance, a remote OB can get cue programme off-air using a receiver and still see the cue dots which will cue them to start their programme. In the BBC, the cue dot appears 30 secs before the start of a programme, disappears at 10 secs to go, reappears at 5 secs to go, and disappears again when the source is cut to by network control. ITV companies use them to indicate coming commercial breaks.

On even the simplest programme, all these communication systems will be available (with the exception of cue dots if the programme is not live). Indeed the communications involved in a programme are often much more complex than the programme sound.

Videotape recording

Professional VT machines are much more complex, and much larger, than their domestic cousins. They are generally located some way from the studio, under the charge of a specialist operator.

A video signal has a bandwidth which extends from d.c. to 5.5 MHz; unfortunately, using conventional magnetic recording, it is theoretically possible to record only about 10 octaves. If the video is first modulated on to an RF carrier, the number of octaves that the video signal occupies will be reduced, but the modulated signal will contain much higher frequencies than the original video. Frequency modulation is used, because variations in head-to-tape contact cause changes in the level of the replayed signal; these amplitude changes can then be removed by clipping (just as impulsive interference is removed from FM transmissions) provided the modulation system is FM.

So, after modulation, the signal will contain fewer octaves (and therefore be recordable) but contain very high frequencies. To record the modulation products, an extinction frequency of up to 20 MHz is necessary. This in turn implies tape-to-head speeds of about 90 m.p.h. The only practical way of achieving this is by the use of rotating heads, which scan the tape at relatively high speed, whilst the linear speed of the tape remains similar to audio tape machines. There are two realizations of these principles, transverse scan (quadruplex) and helical scan; C Format is the most common of the helical scan formats.

Transverse scan (quadruplex)

This format, the first professional format, was invented by Ampex and launched in 1956. It uses two-inch tape running, on 625-line systems, at 15.625 inches per second (the original monochrome 525 version runs at 15 ips; the strange 625-line speed is a consequence of converting the format for European use). There are four heads, equispaced around the edge of the head drum, which is mounted at right angles to the plane of the tape (Figure 26.12). The tape is sucked by vacuum into a shaped guide which keeps it in contact with the head drum.

On the 625–line 50-fields-per-second system, the drum rotates at 250 rev/sec (15,000 rev/min), so that the heads record nearly vertical video tracks across the tape (Figure 26.13). Each head is in contact with the tape for 114° of the head drum rotation, so that there is an overlap when two heads are both in contact. On replay, an electronic switch selects the output of each head in turn; the switching is done during line blanking, and so is not visible on the picture. After the audio tracks have been recorded (erasing part of the vision tracks) there are 18 video lines per track; either 15 or 16 of these are used on replay.

The video input is frequency-modulated before being recorded on the tape; the carrier frequencies produced are: sync tips 7.16 MHz, black level 7.8 MHz, white level 9.3 MHz. Two audio tracks are recorded longitudinally along the

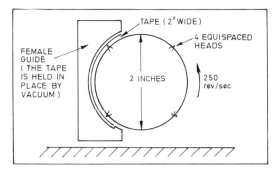

Fig. 26.12. Head drum assembly in the quadruplex video recording system

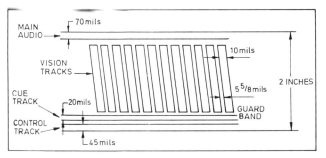

Fig. 26.13. Track layout in the quad system

tape. The main audio track is near the top edge of the tape; the cue track (which is of lower quality and intended only for cue or edit information) is recorded near the bottom of the tape. The cue track, although of inferior quality, can be used for clean effects to be used later during editing, but is not suitable for stereo use with the main audio track. A third longitudinal track, the control track, records a 250 Hz signal derived from the head drum rotation, and on replay enables the correct relationship between linear tape speed and head drum rotation to be maintained; this ensures that, on replay, the vision heads accurately scan down the previously recorded tracks. To maintain sound-to-picture synchronism, the same audio head is used for both record and replay.

On replay, to produce stable colour pictures and in particular pictures which can be made synchronous at a studio mixing point, electronic time-base correction must be applied to the off-tape signal. The tape and head drum speeds and the position of the tape in front of the heads (so that the off-tape signal can be aligned with the station reference pulses) are controlled by servo systems which cannot, of course, react instantaneously. A quad machine therefore requires about five or six seconds to lock up; to be sure that its output is synchronous with reference pulses, the machine is allowed a run-up time of

10 sec, and must therefore be run by the director 10 sec before its output is needed. There are machines which lock up faster than this, such as the Ampex AVR 1, which has a spec of 4 frames.

C Format (helical scan)

The C Format was produced by collaboration between Ampex and Sony in the late 1970s, and European machines on this format were available in 1979. The tape, which is 1 inch wide, is wrapped around the head drum in a helix (Figure 26.14). The head rotates in nearly the same plane as the tape movement, and records vision tracks which are at 2.5° to the edge of the tape. With this format it is possible to stop the tape and replay one vision track over and over again. Since each track is one video field, a still frame can be produced with suitable (and quite extensive) signal processing. Similarly, by moving the tape on replay more slowly than it was recorded, slow motion is possible provided that the head can be made to follow the vision tracks.

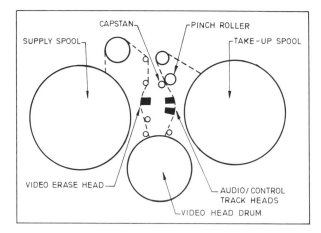

Fig. 26.14. Mechanical layout of a C Format tape deck (Ampex VPR2)

The vision head can be deflected at right angles to the recorded track by a servo, which ensures that it retraces the recorded track, even in slow motion or still frame. Additionally, some tracks can be omitted or repeated to make the vari-speed output synchronous with reference syncs. The ability to replay still and slow motion is a major production advantage, particularly for sport. Once again FM is used for the video signal; the frequencies are: sync tips 7.15 MHz, black level 7.68 MHz, white level 8.9 MHz. Unlike the quad format, there are separate video record and replay heads, mounted at 120° to one another on the head drum (Figure 26.15).

Since the record head cannot be in contact with the tape for a whole field (with a single-head omega (Ω) wrap machine there is always a small gap, called

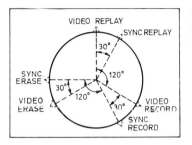

Fig. 26.15. C Format head drum, showing positions of heads (the sync heads are not normally fitted on machines used in Europe)

the format dropout, when the head is out of contact with the tape between the end of one track and the start of the next), the gap is arranged to be in field blanking; on replay the period of the format dropout can be replaced from the reference pulses. Some broadcasters (mainly American) felt that they wanted to record the whole field, so the original version specified a sync recording head, mounted 30° in advance of the main record head, to record the period of format dropout (Figure 26.16). Most European broadcasters have decided, however, that this facility is not essential, and there is therefore an option which allows the fitting of a fourth audio track which uses the area of the tape otherwise occupied by the sync tracks.

There are at least three audio tracks on a C Format machine. Unlike quad, all tracks are of the same quality. Tracks 1 and 2 are adjacent to one another and can be used as a stereo pair. Track 3 is used for SMPTE/EBU time-code in editing, but can be used for another audio signal if time-code is not required. Track 4, only present if the machine has the fourth audio track option, is particularly useful for editing or dubbing. The control track is between audio 4 (or the sync track) and the bottom edge of the vision tracks.

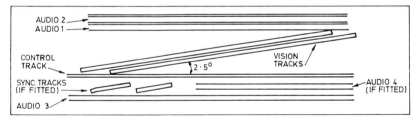

Fig. 26.16. C Format track layout: track widths are respectively audio 0.03, control 0.022, and vision 0.006 inches

VT editing

Although quad tape can be cut edited, this is now very rare. Most VT editing is done by dubbing from one machine to another. If only two machines are available, this only allows pictures to be cut together, although sound can be mixed by off-laying it on to a quarter-inch machine or a spare track, playing in the laid-off sound in sync with the original action, and cross-fading from it to the play-in machine whilst recording the result on the record or edit machine. If three machines are available (two play-in and one record), then sound and picture mixes are possible.

Edit points can be located manually or by using SMPTE/EBU time-code (which was originally developed for this purpose). Each machine needs time to lock up, so will be parked ten or fifteen seconds before the edit point. The out-point can be found by playing back the previously recorded material on the record machine, then spooling the machine back by the pre-roll time; when using time-code this cueing up will be done automatically.

The in-point can now be found on the play-in machine and the machine recued. The two machines are started (the play-in machine is either started remotely by the record machine, or by the editing equipment reading time-codes from both machines). At the edit point, the monitoring is switched from the output of the record machine (which is at present in replay) to the output of the play-in machine, thus rehearsing the edit. If it is satisfactory, both tapes must be reset to their original pre-roll positions, and the operation repeated. This time, however, the record machine will be switched automatically into record at the edit point, joining the new material on to the old.

After the VT editing has been completed, multitrack and video cassette tapes (usually U-Matic) can be made for post-dubbing (see Chapter 27).

Telecine (TK)

A Telecine machine produces a video output from cine film. Many systems are possible, but the best results are obtained from continuous-motion machines.

In an optical projector, a frame of the film is registered in the gate, the frame kept stationary, the shutter opened, and a static image of the frame projected. The shutter is then closed, the film advanced by one frame, and the next frame shown. To reduce the effects of flicker, each frame may be shown more than once. A continuous motion TK machine, however, uses the motion of the film to produce some of the vertical scanning, and has the advantage that the picture is steadier and the wow on Commag or Comopt prints is considerably less than with an intermittent motion machine.

Light from a CRT raster is focused on to the film. The light which passes through the film is split into RGB components and then converted into three electrical signals by photoelectric cells. The signal, after processing, is coded into normal composite video. To produce a correctly interlaced output, there must either be two optical paths (the twin-lens machine) or the raster must be moved between fields (the Hopping Patch method). A number of other types of TK machine exist, but these are the most common.

Films shot specifically for TV will usually have sep mag sound, that is the sound will be recorded on a separate piece of stock of the same gauge as the picture (for example 16 or 35 mm) coated over its whole width with magnetic oxide. The sep mag sound is run on a separate machine, in sync with and locked to the TK picture mechanism. Film shot for TV will be shot at 25 frames per second, and run at the same speed; film shot for the cinema will be shot at 24 frames per second but, using this type of TK machine, must be transmitted at 25 fps, and will therefore be about 4 per cent fast. A TK machine, like a VT machine, needs time to get up to speed when started. TK machines are normally run from a '10' on an Academy leader; since the machine will run from '10' to the start of picture in about 8 sec (it depends a little on the type of machine), TK machines are normally run 8 sec before they are needed at a studio mixing point.

Central area

There is the same need in television as in radio for a central area to equalize, route, and monitor sources and feed them to the correct destination. For each source in TV there will be video, main sound, at least one control line, cue programme (both sound and video), PTB, and perhaps intercoms, remote controls, buzzers, reverse talkback, control signals for the automatic correction of synchronism, red lights, clean feeds, extra sound or vision circuits, and many others. The single word 'source' implies all these circuits. As in radio, uniselectors, relays, code bar switches, or solid-state switches can be used for the routing of sound and communications signals, but solid-state matrices are generally necessary for video because of the bandwidth needed.

Additionally, the TV central area (often called a central apparatus room CAR) needs to generate the pulses necessary for scanning and coding. Seven separate signals are necessary (mixed syncs, mixed blanking, field drive, line drive, vertical axis switch, burst gate, and colour sub-carrier). Such a set of seven pulses is called a pulse chain. These signals, needed by each source within the studio centre (and often called station syncs or reference syncs), are generated by a sync pulse generator (SPG).

The SPG may be in the CAR and the seven separate outputs distributed by line to each source. Alternatively, a locking signal (normally a feed of sync pulses with colour burst, called 'black and burst' or 'colour black', can be generated in the CAR and distributed to each source, which then genlocks its own SPG to the reference (genlocking simply means that an SPG produces pulses which are synchronous with another video signal (the reference)). If sources were not locked to a central reference, they would not be synchronous at mixing points, and could not be mixed between. Incoming and outgoing circuits to and from the outside world (like OBs, transmitters) will terminate here.

Continuities

As in radio, there is a need to link programmes together into a network. This will be done in a master control or network control room, which selects and cues sources in a similar way to radio. The associated continuity studio or presentation area will house an announcer or presenter, who may be in or out of vision, to provide linking and breakdown announcements. Pre-transmission checks with the source will be similar to radio, with the added complication of video and the need to check its synchronism if the source is to be mixed to. Additionally, since a studio that is about to go on air is likely to have its opening titles on VT or TK, and will therefore need to run them some seconds before the on-air time, the studio needs an accurate cue from network some seconds before network takes the studio. In the BBC, for instance, this facility is provided by cue dots which give accurate 30, 10, and 5 sec cues.

Distribution to transmitters

The video signal may leave the studio centre by microwave link or by coaxial line. The sound may leave by BT line, or can be combined with the video signal using a system called sound in syncs (SiS). Sound in syncs is used by the BBC for distribution of BBC1 and BBC2 and by the IBA for Channel 4. It is also used by the EBU for international sound, and is available for OBs.

Sound in Syncs

SiS has three major advantages:

1. It is cheaper than a separate sound circuit.
2. It eliminates the possibility of operational errors pairing a video source with the wrong sound source.
3. Being digital, it is of better quality over long distances.

In the original mono system the sound signal is sampled at twice line frequency (31.25 kHz), giving an audio bandwidth of about 14 kHz. There are 10 bits per sample. Alternate samples are stored for half a line, and then two samples are inserted into each line sync pulse. If the mean level of the pulse train changes between samples, the effect on the video could produce 'sound on vision'. To keep the mean level near the back porch more constant, and reduce the likelihood of sound on vision, the pulses of alternate samples are inverted, and all samples are sent with the least significant digit first. The samples are preceded in each sync pulse by a marker pulse; there are therefore 21 pulses in each sync (Figure 26.17). Each pulse is shaped to be sine-squared, has a half-amplitude duration of 182 ns, and has negligible energy outside 5.5 MHz.

To reduce the quantizing noise, the signal is pre-emphasized and companded (Figure 26.18). After pre-emphasis, a 15.625 kHz pilot tone is added to the

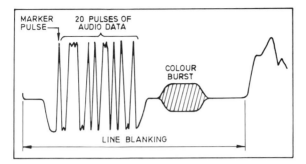

Fig. 26.17. The line-blanking period, showing the SiS pulses in the line sync pulse

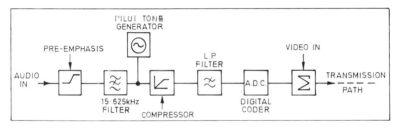

Fig. 26.18. Coder for Sound in Syncs

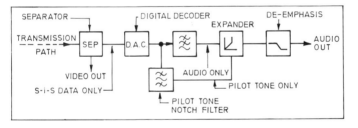

Fig. 26.19. Decoder for Sound in Syncs

signal, which is then compressed. At the decoder (Figure 29.19) the pilot tone is extracted from the signal (because the intervening link is digital, the pilot tone will have undergone no phase or attenuation distortion) and used to control an expander, so that the expansion is an exact mirror image of the compression. The overall performance has a signal-to-noise ratio which is slightly better than a 12-bit system without companding. A stereo system of SiS has been designed. This system uses 14-bit NICAM and a quaternary (four-level) coding system instead of binary in order to fit all the necessary information into the time available in a sync pulse.

At the transmitter the SiS signal is decoded and removed from the video signal; SiS is not radiated from the transmitter. The video is amplitude-modulated on to a UHF carrier using vestigial sideband modulation; this simply means that only part of the lower sideband is radiated. This saves bandwidth, so allowing more transmitters in a given frequency range. Receivers compensate for the vestigial sideband by their IF response.

The sound is frequency-modulated on to a carrier locked to and 6 MHz higher in frequency than the vision carrier; the maximum total carrier deviation is 50 kHz. The total channel bandwidth, that is the frequency difference between adjacent sound or vision carriers, is 8 MHz (Figure 26.20).

The BBC has developed a system which will allow a stereo digital bitstream to be radiated from the transmitters in addition to the present signals, though this is not in service at the time of writing.

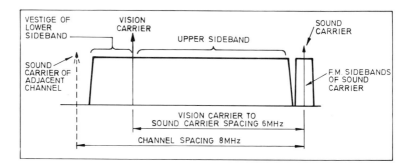

Fig. 26.20. Spectrum of a UHF television channel

PSC and ENG

Portable single camera shooting and electronic news gathering are developments of the late 1970s. With the introduction of broadcast-quality cameras which are battery-powered and sufficiently small to be hand-held, many broadcasters have seen the advantage of using them instead of film. Unfortunately, portable VTRs are either of inferior quality to the professional formats described above, or are expensive. In either case they are heavier and more bulky than the film equivalent, and have the disadvantage that the cameraman is attached to the VTR by a cable. With film, the lead joining the cameraman to the sound recordist was done away with years ago by using crystal sync. Whilst the cable is probably not too inconvenient in PSC, it can be a great nuisance in ENG, where the cameraman and recordist may need to move very fast (and maybe in a crowd) to follow the action, or even to escape from danger.

Nevertheless, ENG and PSC have a number of advantages to the broadcaster:

1. Videotape cassettes (high-band U-Matic is normally used) are cheaper than film stock and can be reused.
2. There is no time lost in film processing.
3. The pictures can be replayed on site and can, if a satellite or other link is available, be returned to base more quickly than film.
4. Film degradation of the signal is eliminated; the signal is generated in the form that it will eventually need to be in for transmission (video).

Unfortunately, the sound quality of U-Matic is much inferior to the film system using a portable quarter-inch recorder (usually a Nagra) and sepmag. Moreover, the editing and dubbing of film has been custom-designed and standardized by the film industry so as to make it very flexible; for the present at least ENG and PSC sound has not reached that level of sophistication; no doubt it will in the future.

27

Video

Trevor Webster

It might be supposed that sound for use with pictures is produced in much the same way as sound by itself, for radio or records. Although there are obvious parallels, and some of the same equipment is used, the differences are in fact very considerable. There are basically two ways of recording moving pictures, either of which can be used to originate programmes for subsequent TV broadcasting or videotape distribution. Firstly, they can be recorded directly on to light-sensitive film inside a film camera. Secondly, they can be picked up by an electronic television camera (a video camera) and fed as an electrical waveform (the video signal) down wires to a videotape recorder. Although each system has borrowed techniques from the other, it is still largely true that the type of camera used tends to dictate the way in which the production is organized, and also the most appropriate sound techniques. In this chapter I shall deal with those sound techniques which accompany shooting with video cameras. I shall then go on to describe some aspects of post-production.

Video in television broadcasting

Naturally, the biggest users of video-originated material are the major broadcasting organizations. Public service television broadcasting is about fifty years old (BBC TV began in 1936), and for about the first twenty-five years was mostly a 'live' medium. It is true that some programmes were 'telerecorded' on to film, but, from an operational point of view, they were recorded 'as live' using three, four, or even more cameras. This imposed great discipline on all the sound and vision operations involved, since they all had to be performed in real time with no opportunity for retakes. Live broadcasting has certain disadvantages, amongst them the need to play safe, avoiding anything too likely to go wrong. It does have the advantage, though, of producing highly skilled professional operations with very high productivity, and it is largely the tradition of long continuous 'takes' which makes television operations distinct from those of film, where one shot at a time is the rule.

Most productions start from a script (or score) which primarily represents the sound element rather than the visual one, and it is generally true that most of the production information is carried in the sound. Not many programmes are worth watching without the sound, whereas in the days when transmission breakdowns were more frequent it was quite common to continue in sound-only until the vision could be restored. When sound and vision are present together, however, there is little doubt that vision is the dominant sense, and it is actually nonsense to consider the two contributions separately. Experience has shown that only when the sound and pictures work together is a production successful. They need to be regarded as complementary, supporting one another, rather than as radio with added pictures, or as silent film with added sound.

But the organizational needs of the different disciplines—sound, camera work, lighting, etc.—are very different and often difficult to reconcile in a practical situation. The preferred sound coverage can make satisfactory lighting impossible, or vice versa; sound or lighting can make it impossible to shoot; the set design can make everybody's life a misery, and so on. It can be seen that television is a collaborative art, and careful planning of all the elements is essential. The successful sound man will need to learn something of the unique problems encountered by lighting directors, cameramen, designers, and directors.

Planning

The type of planning involved varies with the type of production. A one-off drama will have to be planned in considerable detail, with heads of sound, lighting and cameras meeting around the table with the designer, director, and production manager as well as make-up and wardrobe designers. Ground plans and elevation drawings of the studio or location, and of the proposed 'sets', will be studied carefully and perhaps modified as interrelated problems are discussed. Scale models are often made, to show what the set will look like in three dimensions. Considerable negotiation may be needed to formulate a production plan which will work for everybody. All those present (sometimes called the 'realization team') are aware of their individual needs but also of their dependence on each other, and relationships of great trust often form between the members of the team. This explains why the same people are seen to work together time after time.

A major light entertainment production, whether variety or comedy, is planned in a similar way to drama. Other kinds of programmes require a different approach. Current affairs programmes, for example, cannot be planned in such detail because the exact nature of the material is not known until the last minute. In this case, a cover-all plan has to be made which will deal with any situation within certain overall limits. For example, an interview area may be designed which can be used for any interview involving up to, say, eight people. A demonstration area may be used to show objects on a table with a small number of people standing around it. Standard lighting and sound arrangements can be devised which will cope with any situation within those criteria. Detailed requirements are communicated as soon as they become available, sometimes while the programme is actually on the air. In some ways this calls for more detailed mental planning than when the precise situation is known in advance. Another example of this situation is in sports coverage. The overall format is predetermined, not least by the rules of the game, but the details of the action have to be dealt with as they arise.

Each type of programme is slightly different—children's, educational, music, the various kinds of outside broadcasts—and all have their separate planning requirements, but the sound supervisor (or audio director) must leave the meeting with a clear idea of how the various problems will be solved. Once a programme has been planned, it is possible to calculate the requirements in terms of staff and equipment.

Staff and equipment

The sound staff on an ordinary programme can vary in number from about three to twelve. All except the most junior will have some special skill in addition to their general expertise. One will perhaps specialize in recording, editing and playing-in of music and effects, using vinyl disc, tape, various kinds of cartridge, and digital sources including Compact Disc and the new computer hard disc systems (of which more later). Others will specialize in boom operating, radio microphones, Public Address control, etc.

The equipment used can vary greatly. A wide range of microphones is used, partly for their particular sound quality and partly for their directivity. Unwanted sound is a particular problem in television studios and at many outside locations. Often forty or fifty people have to be on the set. Just the sound of their breathing can be a problem. Microphones are therefore as useful for what they exclude as for what they pick up. This also applies with in-vision orchestras, where the layout of the instruments may suit visual requirements better than those of sound. The worst situations can usually be avoided nowadays (like open brass blowing straight into the strings' microphones) because producers understand the importance of good sound, but without directional microphones we would still be in big trouble.

Probably the most usefuo piece of equipment on the studio floor (from a sound point of view) is still the television microphone boom. It is often underrated by people outside the industry, but is enormously mobile and has the great advantage of instantaneous control by an experienced operator. It can follow an actor who has walked to the wrong place, or a singer who cannot find his floor marks. It can immediately adjust the balance between two contributors or turn its back on some unwanted, unexpected noise. In the hands of a skilled operator, and with a carefully chosen directional microphone, it is a wonderful machine.

New operators can be trained to follow a person who is walking in figures-of-eight talking all the time. A skilled operator can do this with ease, and keep the person 'on mic' the whole time, by co-ordinating five different hand movements so that the microphone can be moved left or right, up or down, and in or out (the boom arm is telescopic). The mic can also be 'panned' and 'tilted' in its cradle. In confined spaces, or out on location, the 'gun mic' and hand-held boom ('fishing rod') are more usual, but their manœuvrability and useful range are comparatively limited

As well as booms, the full range of microphone stands is used, and microphones are sometimes slung from lighting and scene hoists, attached to the scenery, concealed among 'properties' in the set, or even fitted inside imitation books or other devices. Sometimes they are concealed on the person or, if they are unobtrusive, allowed to show. The small electret capsules have long been considered acceptable 'in shot', except on drama productions, and the new-generation ones are smaller than ever. Often these 'personal' mics are used in combination with a radio transmitter in a pocket or pouch, or hidden in the artist's costume. On many modern radio mic systems the output of the associated receiver can have a quality and reliability approaching those of cabled mics, but there are pitfalls for the unwary. Multi-path concellation, resulting in a momentary loss of signal at the receiver aerial, can have distressing results and, in some cases, the shielding effects of cameras and other equipment can cause dead spots in certain areas of the studio and enormous variations of RF signal level. These problems can usually be overcome by the use of 'diversity systems', which automatically switch between two receiver aerials (or aerial–receiver combinations) in order to select the best signal from moment to moment. For example, Audio Engineering's well-established Micron system combines the outputs of two receivers if their levels are not more than 3 dB apart. When they differ by more than this, it silently selects the best one. More recent is the development of some quite sophisticated compander systems. The audio is compressed in the transmitter and expanded in the receiver, giving clean audio at much lower RF levels. There is, of course, an eventual cut-off level below which the thing will not work at all, and the sudden transition from beautiful clean sound to complete loss of programme can be disconcerting to say the least.

Where the artist needs to have great mobility, radio mics provide a unique solution. Often they are used in conjunction with radio talkback, which allows the director to talk into the artist's ear-piece by a separate radio system operating in the opposite direction. It is quite common to use six or more radio mics at the same time on different artists, with separate radio frequencies and separate pairs of receivers fed from two aerials. Indeed, on some outside broadcasts (such as golf coverage) where large numbers of people are spread over very large areas, the number and variety of radio systems employed is almost beyond belief. The successful operation of such a rig involves careful planning and highly specialized skills.

Television studios

Television studios have a very high capital cost and are almost always designed as general-purpose studios, that is they are not dedicated to any particular type of programme. For this reason they are designed to be acoustically fairly dead, on the basis that it is easier to add reverberation than to take it away. Where reverberation is needed, it is created artificially, using one or more of the many digital devices now available. Indeed, the whole range of special effects devices finds a use in modern television production.

Sound desks used in television are often quite large, sometimes having more than eighty channels. The principles are described elsewhere in this volume, but one feature may be worthy of special mention. A problem which arises in drama is the matching of sound to picture when the two ends of a telephone conversation are intercut. Let us say that actor A is in a telephone box which is supposed to be on a busy street, and actor B is in his flat with the sound of somebody taking a shower in the next room. Whenever the viewer is given a shot of A, he needs to hear A normally along with the traffic effects from outside; but if B speaks, B's voice needs to be distorted in line with the dramatic convention of telephone conversations, and the shower also needs to be distorted and very much quieter. If we are then given a shot of B, the situation is reversed. B and the shower noise will be clean, whilst A and the traffic noise will be distorted. In other words, the sound is constantly being changed to match the picture cuts. It is very difficult to perform this operation manually, because the picture cuts may not be at exactly the same points as rehearsed and may even fall in the middle of a speech. (There are many reasons for these variations, mostly to do with slight variations of the actors' performances.) The solution to this problem is to use a set of effects units (simple top and bass cut circuits) which can be switched automatically from the vision mixer (vision switching apparatus). This simple device gives very convincing results. Even if the vision mixer operator makes a mistake, the sound will make a matching mistake, and this strangely enough is far better than the sound being 'right' but contradicting the pictures. This example typifies the peculiar philosophy of sound and pictures working together.

Music has its own special problems. Sometimes a performer is asked to sing and dance at the same time, or to perform in vision a song which was produced for record distribution in a very complex way over a period of several days in a recording studio. If the performance cannot be recreated live for the cameras, it is necessary to pre-record the sound and play it back to the artist in the television studio or location so that he can 'mime' to it. It is sometimes assumed that the original released recording will provide the ideal sound balance for miming, but this is often not the case. In a straightforward song with solo singer and orchestral backing, the cameras will concentrate on the singer, often using close-up shots. In this situation our brains tell us that we should hear more of the singer, and consequently we may consider that the orchestra is too loud. If we switch off the pictures, we hear that the balance is actually correct in sound-only terms. So the balance must be adjusted to match the pictures, and to this end it is sometimes useful to keep the vocal on a separate track so that moment-by-moment adjustments can be made when the shots are seen.

In the case of classical orchestral music, it is the music which dictates the shots. It makes no sense to have a close-up of the violins when the music is featuring the brass section. But even when the pictures are showing the lead instrument or section there is still a feeling that the balance is wrong. The featured instrument sounds too quiet. Over the years, there have been many arguments about whether or not the balance of classical music should be adjusted to take account of this visual effect. There is of course a purist view, that the music should not be changed in any way and that the picture director will just have to make his own arrangements. I favour the opposite view, however, that it is the perceived effect which matters. Television programmes are not primarily aimed at blind people, and to offer a sighted audience something which seems subjectively wrong surely cannot be right. The problem is very complex, however, and involves careful consideration of perspective and reverberation as well as balance. A number of 'spot mics' can be used to increase detail and clarity in the balance, without the need for rapid perspective changes. Twenty years ago, it was quite noticeable that TV sound supervisors responded to the problem by using a closer perspective than was popular at the time on radio or published records. More recently the fashion has changed, so that radio and records often aim for a perspective similar to that of TV, though usually achieved with fewer microphones and often in a better acoustic environment.

Communication circuits

In addition to the programme chain, the sound supervisor has control of a large number of communication circuits (as discussed in Chapter 26). Some of them provide communication between the various operational groups in the control rooms and studio. These are essential to every production and are used from day to day, usually without much attention. Other facilities can be used in many different ways to give 'talkback', intercom, or telephone communications both within the studio and to remote contributors. An important feature of broadcast television is its ability to take contributions from a number of sources many miles apart, apparently as easily as if they were in the same studio. This relies on the ability to offer adequate communications and the correct programme feed to each one. For example, if six groups of contributors in six locations are having a discussion, each group will need to hear the other five on a loudspeaker (but not themselves, or there would be a great danger of feedback). The special feed to each of these loudspeakers is called (in Britain) a clean feed or (in USA) a mix minus, and all these feeds are provided from a matrix in the sound control room of the master studio. In a similar way, calls from the public telephone system can be put on the air, the remote contributor hearing the whole mix minus himself down the telephone.

Video editing

I said earlier that for the first twenty-five years television was mostly live. In the second twenty-five years, as videotape machines have become more plentiful and more sophisticated, television has become much more a recorded medium, with the notable exceptions of sport, news and current affairs. The problem of live programmes is having to perform all operations in real time, but the ability to record and edit programmes has brought a new problem. It is now common to record a sequence several times, and later to edit between the takes to use the best bits of each. Since sound and vision are edited together (they are both recorded on the same piece of tape), the editing of pictures can have a serious and detrimental effect on the sound. This is less true in music shows, where the editing points will in any case be determined by the music, but in drama situations any sound effects and background music which were played in 'as live' are likely to cause problems at the edit. They will either be re-edited (along with the dialogue and pictures) into a form which was not originally intended, or will severely restrict the contribution which the VT editor is able to make to the programme.

Since the late 1960s it has increasingly been necessary to leave off the effects and background music at the recording stage and to add them later, after the pictures have been edited. This is usually called video post-dubbing or, in the USA, audio sweetening. It is distinct from film dubbing in many ways, most notably because much of the sound is already recorded (at the same time as the pictures) on a single track. This includes all the live dialogue and the natural effects—those noises which the actors make as they move about the set. It may indeed include many noises which are not required, and which must be removed before the production is ready for public viewing. Some of the original sound will have to be treated, and a great many additional sound effects may have to be added in order to create the impression, for example, that two sheets of tile-patterned hardboard and a little steam are actually the corner of a large, busy Turkish Bath. Dubbing also gives the advantage that the background music need not be written and recorded until after the pictures have been edited to length. Thus the composer can judge the precise mood and duration required. In the days of live drama, the composer had to guess these from a reading of the script, and an operator had to play the tapes with the live performance, after editing them during rehearsals to match as closely as possible the pace of the action.

Early systems of dubbing were very crude, using such equipment as was to hand. The edited programme was simply replayed from one videotape machine and re-recorded on to another, the sound being fed via a conventional mixing desk (Figure 27.1). Sounds were added and removed in real time. This was still essentially a 'live' operation and involved an element of operational risk if difficult things were being attempted. There were no synchronous tracks for track laying or pre-mixing in the manner of film dubbing, and all material except the original sound had to be played in entirely by the skill of the operators. Not only was the system limiting in terms of the creative contribution which sound could make, it was also remarkably expensive to run. This was because of the very high cost of broadcast videotape machine time, of which this system was very wasteful. For reasons of economy, any new system of dubbing would have to be 'off-line', that is the operation would have to move out of the videotape department and away from expensive broadcast-quality pictures. The BBC 'Sypher' system which came into operation in London early in 1974 is typical of the best off-line systems. It relies on the use of time-code, an eight-digit code which identifies each individual frame of picture in a 24-hour period. With 25 frames per second in British television, this represents well over two million separate addresses. Time-code is now well known and widely used in the recording industry. It is originated in a time-code generator (a kind of electronic clock) which gives an audio output (an unpleasant burbling noise). This can be fed down a cable and recorded on tape just like any other audio

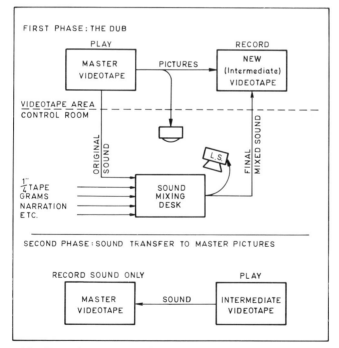

Fig. 27.1. The two phases in videotape-to-videotape dubbing

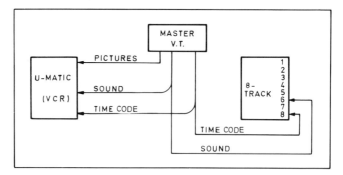

Fig. 27.2. Sypher phase 1: transfer to Sypher tapes

signal, or it can be fed into a time-code reader which then gives a digital display of the time, updated every twenty-fifth of a second. As a recording on tape, it is sometimes compared with the sprocket holes in film, but of course sprocket holes are all exactly the same, whereas time-code addresses are all different. If two tape machines with recordings of time-code are played into an appropriate interface unit (a synchronizer) it is possible to derive a control signal which will drive one of those machines into synchronism with the other and keep it there. This time-code synchronization system is at the heart of off-line dubbing systems like 'Sypher'.

Sypher

The Sypher operation begins in the videotape area, after the programme has been edited so that visually it is complete. The edited master is replayed and the sound and time-code are copied on to two tracks of an eight-track sound recorder (tracks 6 and 8 in Figure 27.2). At the same time, the pictures and time-code are copied on to a semi-professional videotape machine—a low-band U-Matic. The sound is also copied on to one of the U-Matic sound tracks, but this is not capable of giving the desired transmission quality and will be used only as a guide.

The second phase in the Sypher operation is conducted in a dedicated suite using only the U-Matic and eight-track tapes (Figure 27.3). They are time-code-locked in synchronism as described above. The pictures from the U-Matic are fed to a picture monitor and the sound from the eight-track is fed to one channel of a sound mixing desk. (For simplicity a mono programme is being considered.) The U-Matic machine is controlled remotely from the mixing desk and the sound machine follows it in either play or spool. In spool mode the two machines are not actually in lock but within four or five seconds of pressing the play button they become synchronous and a light indicates this condition to the sound mixer. It is now possible to rehearse the first part of the show repeatedly,

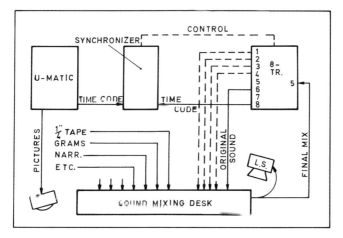

Fig. 27.3. Sypher phase 2a: the dubbing operation

by simply playing and spooling back, until the results are satisfactory. The final sound is then recorded on to another track of the eight-track tape, alongside the original sound. In practice almost every attempt is recorded and, if unsatisfactory, recorded over at the next attempt. The first successful pass is therefore the only take preserved. This recording continues from the beginning of the show until something goes wrong with it. The tapes are then rewound by a few seconds and played. By pressing a balance (comp-check) button, the mixer can compare the level and balance of the last good part of the recording with the level and balance set up on the desk faders for the same section of programme. This ensures that there will be no step (in quality or level) on going into record again. This process of running the tapes back, going into play mode, balancing, and dropping into record is sometimes known as 'rock and roll', and it continues until the whole programme is completely re-recorded.

If parts of the programme are too difficult to get right in a single pass, the mixer may resort to track-laying (Figure 27.4). Some element of the sound, let us say the music, is recorded on to spare track 1. The original sound is monitored during this process as a guide. After rewinding, the original sound and the music can be monitored while (say) narration is recorded on to track 2. All three tracks can then be monitored while some spot effects are recorded on to track 3, and so on. The levels are not critical at this stage, only the timing. When sufficient tracks have been recorded, the mixer can once again rewind the tape and mix the newly laid tracks with the original to produce the final mix, which will be recorded, as before, on to the final mix track.

If a large number of tracks is required, an additional 24-track recorder with a time-code striped tape can be locked to the system using an additional synchronizer. One track will be needed for the time-code, but that still leaves 23

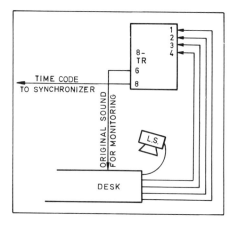

Fig. 27.4. Sypher phase 2*b*: track laying

for the audio, and in principle there is no limit to the number of machines which can be locked in. The time-code on these extra machines need not have identical times to the master machine, as an 'offset' can be used. For example, the master picture and sound programme tapes may start at 10 hours, 10 minutes, 10 seconds, 10 frames, (i.e. 10:10:10:10), and the extra machine time-code may start at say 14:56:25:19. This problem would be solved by selecting a time-code offset of 04:46:15:09 in the synchronizer. Thereafter the machines would behave exactly as though they had the same time-codes. The same technique can be used for synchronizing quarter-inch tape machines, which may have extra heads to give an additional time-code track (centre track time-code).

The third phase of the Sypher operation is carred out back in the videotape area (Figure 27.5). The U-Matic tape is now discarded and the eight-track tape is synchronized with the master pictures. The videotape machine is then put into 'record audio only' and the final sound is recorded back on to the master videotape ready for broadcast.

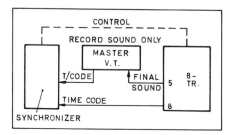

Fig. 27.5. Sypher phase 3: transfer to master

Time-codes

The great technology explosion of the last ten or fifteen years has made as great a contribution in video dubbing as anywhere in the industry. Advanced cueing and mixing systems, using time-codes as triggers, have made very accurate work possible by taking it out of real time. Thus a very difficult operation, where several things have to be done in the space of half a second, can now be programmed into the computer over a period of a minute or two. This actually saves time because many attempts would be needed to achieve an acceptable result in real time. Here is an example. Suppose that an actor in a period piece has ad-libbed a word which is out of period. If this is not noticed at the time, an acceptable alternative word may have to be substituted at the dub. After recording the new word on quarter-inch tape, the following critical operations are necessary:

1. Play the quarter-inch tape of the new word at exactly the right time.
2. Play a quarter-inch tape of background atmosphere to match the original at exactly the right time. (This may be no more than one second long.)
3. Play a quarter-inch tape to simulate any sounds of movement which were under the original word.
4. At precisely the right moment and the right speed, mix from the original sound track to the three quarter-inch tapes.
5. At precisely the right moment (perhaps only six or seven frames later) mix back.
6. Stop all three quarter-inch machines.

If all the levels, equalizations, and reverberation are correct there is a good chance of success, but steps 1 to 5 may need to be accurate to one frame. It is a tall order for human operators, but much easier if those five critical events can be initiated automatically at predetermined time-codes.

Computer-assisted mixing

Computer-assisted sound mixing is useful because some programmes require a very complex mix, and even simple programmes often have one or two short but very difficult sections. Computer assistance is not always fully understood by those who have not had an opportunity to use it. The computer does not actually try to produce a mix without the aid of the sound mixer. Instead, it carefully notes some or all of the operations which he performs during a mix attempt, and it is capable of repeating them automatically on a subsequent pass of the same material. If, in practice, the first attempt to mix a section of the programme is satisfactory, then the computer need not be used. Also, if the first attempt is completely hopeless, there is little point in using the computer to recreate it. Most of the time, however, the first or second attempt at the mix will be fairly successful—only one of two things may need to be corrected. A further (manual) attempt at the mix may still not be perfect, however, because all the operations have to be performed correctly in the one pass. Frequently, the sound mixer will correct the previous faults but make a mess of something which he got right the first time. With computer assist, however, the previous mix attempt is repeated exactly by the computer, and the sound mixer is able to take control of those elements which he needs to change. This is a truly liberating experience because it allows him to concentrate fully on small but difficult elements of the mix. If the mix is still not quite right, the sound mixer can repeat the process, working from either his new updated computer mix or the old one which he used last time. He can repeat the process as many times as necessary, gradually refining the mix until he is satisfied with it. Only then will he re-run the final computer mix and record the audio on to the final track.

On some systems it is possible to store the computer data of a large number of mix attempts, so that they can be replayed and compared before a final choice is made and the final audio mix recorded. In such systems it is usually possible to combine the best sections of two or more 'data mixes' without even playing the material through. There are two approaches to this. In the first one, certain timed sections are chosen from each mix and the data from those sections is made into a new mix. This allows the mixer to choose (say) the first thirty seconds from mix 1, the next forty from mix 3, and the rest from mix 2. These can be combined to make mix 4. The second approach is to take some faders from one mix and other faders from another. Thus the rhythm balance from mix 2 might be used with the front-line balance of mix 1. Although the value of these more esoteric techniques is not evident until one attempts an 'impossible' mix, computer-assisted mixing has improved productivity as well as product quality. At the same time, it has reduced the length of many sessions with the spin-off advantage that less-tired directors and sound supervisors are able to make better programme decisions. Another, less desirable result has been the enormous rise in the capital cost of dubbing facilities. Small companies are therefore unable to support their own in-house facility and are using the facility houses which have sprung up to meet the need. This is a logical development, because at the highest operational level dubbing costs can only be kept down by spending increasingly large capital sums and then using the facilities efficiently every day.

Future trends

It is interesting to contemplate the possible future trends in video post-dubbing. Two very recent developments may give clues. The first is a new kind of automated sound desk which the BBC has specified and ordered. This system will combine VCA (voltage-controlled amplifier) technology with computer-driven faders to give a unique range of operational modes. It may well be that the BBC, always in the vanguard in the video dubbing field, will again be setting trends with this new desk. The second clue comes from the emergence of systems which record sound digitally on computer hard disc (Winchester discs). One example of this is the AMS Audiofile. This device, already in service with the BBC and others, is one of the most exciting developments in recent years and potentially one of the most influential. The Audiofile records sound digitally on Winchester discs. It has its own built-in synchronizer and offers very fast time-code synchronization with any video player. It has several simultaneous output channels which can be cued either from time-code or manually, in the latter case with virtually instantaneous start. Quite apart from the obvious quality advantages of digital sound, such devices promise major advantages from built-in digital editing and track looping. If they are used for synchronous track laying, it is quite easy to track-slip (time-slipping one track in relation to another)—you cannot do that with an eight-track!

It is quite possible that a large Audiofile will completely replace the eight-track in some future systems. Indeed, it may well be that, within a few years, we will see the video equivalent of it, not giving transmission-quality pictures perhaps, but able to hold an hour of working-quality pictures on some kind of high-volume 'instant access' digital store. This would have several real advantages. Spooling time, even from the beginning of the programme to the end, would be no more than a few milliseconds. The first and third phases of the off-line dubbing operation could probably be done at several times speed without any loss of quality, and with consequent hardware and operator savings. In the same way that we now see the paperless office and newsroom, we may be heading for the tapeless video dubbing suite early in the next decade.

28

Film

Eric Tomlinson

When one realizes that the film industry was largely responsible for many of the present-day recording techniques (multitrack and practical stereo, for example), although in a somewhat rudimentary fashion, it is surprising that it has taken so long for good-quality sound to arrive at the local cinema. The film-going public is no longer prepared to accept mediocre sound reproduction, as nearly every home today boasts some sort of hi-fi system, and people have come to expect better quality. During the early 1970s, Dolby Laboratories became interested in film sound, and one of their first tasks was to persuade cinemas to re-equip with modern sound systems which would include the ability to decode and replay stereo optical soundtracks. This, coupled with the optimization of cinema acoustics, made it possible for blockbuster films to have a real impact on the audience.

Given this situation, the problem of recording music specifically for film should no longer exist. The engineer can plan his recording without 'adjusting' the sound and having to make allowances for the deficiencies once inherent in the average provincial cinema. Now every recording should satisfy the demands of any medium. In fact most soundtrack albums are taken directly from the original, and often end up being released on Compact Disc—the ultimate test.

Feature film production can be split into three main segments. These are pre-production, production, and post-production. Sound recording in the film industry, with the exception of the musical film, takes place on two occasions, at the time of photography (production), and after photography is completed (post-production) During production, the recording will consist of original dialogue and effects whilst during post-production it will comprise post-sync dialogue, effects, music (scoring), and dubbing (re-recording).

Floor and location recording

When sound was first introduced into films around 1928/9, a form of interlocking sound and action was required to maintain lip-sync. The simplest method would have been to record both on to the same piece of film, as is the case today with the soundtracks on a video recorder or the release print of a film. However, full control of the sound can be achieved only if the sound is separated from its associated action. Consider the often-used editing technique of sound preceding or following a cut or scene change, and you will realize that this would not be possible if action was always accompanied by its associated sound. So, once separated, some interlock system to maintain lip-sync is necessary, and the system most commonly used today for original dialogue recording is the Neo-Pilot pulse. In this system, a reference frequency, usually 50 or 60 Hz, is recorded on two narrow tracks equally displaced about the centre line of the single audio track on a portable quarter-inch tape recorder.

The machines most used are the Nagra 4.2 and the Stellavox SP 8 or SU 8. The signals on the two tracks of the Neo-Pilot system are recorded 180° out of phase to each other and are aligned in level to achieve maximum cancellation when scanned by the full-track audio replay head. For rushes (dailies) viewing, editing, and re-recording (dubbing), the original quarter-inch tapes are copied (transferred) to sprocketed magnetic film, and this is where the Neo-Pilot pulse plays its part. The pulse recorded on the tape is now derived from the divided down output of a crystal (very stable) source, and the camera motor is referred to a similar crystal reference and is therefore running at a very precisely defined film speed. During transfer, the pulse replayed by the reproducing machine is compared with the motor speed reference for the magnetic film recorder (usually the mains frequency) and the two are locked together by a synchronizer (resolver). This is a bare outline of the most common method in use at the present time, though there have been other systems and in the future, no doubt, SMPTE/EBU time-code will predominate.

Original dialogue for films is usually recorded monophonically, as experience has shown that dialogue is more acceptable if it emanates from the centre or near-centre of the screen, whilst stereo information, music, and effects may emerge from left, centre, or right of screen, or from the ambient (surround) speakers in the auditorium. The film sound recordist will therefore generally use only a stereo recorder for recording sound effects or for two-track recording. This kind of two-track recording is used, for example, to record on-screen lines on one track, and off-screen lines on the other, or where 'silent playback' is used. This technique is employed where artists are fitted with minature receivers and the playback signal is fed to them, enabling them to hold a conversation with another voice on one track, and their responses to be recorded on the other. A big advantage here is that the new dialogue recording is clean of the playback, a big help to the editors.

It is the responsibility of the film sound recordist to record the best possible dialogue, very often under far from ideal conditions. Also, if he is involved at the pre-production stage, he may advise on ways of improving the acoustic environment. On exterior locations, it may be impossible to achieve usable sound, as one always seems to be near a motorway or the flight-path of an airport. (There are very few really quiet places left in the world.) However, in a film studio he will find a much more controllable situation on the sound-stage (floor recording), although even here sets are becoming noisier. Electronic lighting, which is both electrically and acoustically noisy, is coming more into use; camera noise has not been entirely eliminated—all these can create problems. In the early days of sound, when microphones were less directional, extraneous noise had much more attention paid to its elimination at source than happens now.

The sound man's main task during original dialogue recording is to maintain high artistic and technical standards; in so doing he should consider the recipients of his efforts. This does not just mean the cinema audience, but the editors who will assemble the tracks, and the dubbing mixer responsible for combining the many tracks which will go to make the final print. It is worth mentioning here that as accurate a log as possible must be kept at all times, as it may be many months before the project is eventually completed, and new personnel may be handling the final dubbing.

The maintenance of artistic standards is mainly the province of the director, and interference by the sound recordist can easily lead to a clash between recordist, director, and artist, unless diplomatically handled. The most frequent reason for intervention by the sound mixer is where artists are allowed to overlap each others' lines unnecessarily, unless specifically required (as in an argument). This should be avoided, as it can lead to many problems at the editing stage, and the editorial department relies upon the sound mixer to ensure that this does not happen.

The actual method of recording will often involve more than one microphone and in most cases the microphone will move with the action. Hidden microphones and radio microphones can be used, but one must be aware that they can give rise to perspective problems, and so they should not be used without pre-planning. Much of the responsibility for good-quality sound falls on the shoulders (or rather the arms) of the boom operator. It will be realized that the requirement to record usable sound often means a more directional microphone, which makes the boom operator's job even more difficult; only a slight error or delay in favouring the speaking artist will result in noticeable 'off-mic' quality. Thus the sound recordist is in the hands of the boom operator, who in turn is relying on the director of photography not to light him out of the shot.

Technical standards are maintained and improved by careful selection, intelligent use, and good maintenance of sound recording equipment. In the mid-1980s a typical sound recording kit comprised two recorders with crystal sync or time-code capabilities and accessories, a mixer, ten or more microphones including say four radio microphones, a vast collection of windshields for interior use and basket types for exterior use, with high-wind socks to go over the baskets in very windy conditions; and also rain covers, as the sound of rain on a windshield can be recorded with irritating fidelity, microphone poles of various lengths for exterior use, with possibly a Fisher microphone boom for studio use, connecting cables, cases, and covers.

Post-production

When the work of the location sound recordist for a particular film is over, the responsibility for sound is transferred to a studio where most of the post-production work will be carried out. Here, after the director and editor have gone through the selected takes, a decision will be made as to which sections will have to be re-recorded (post sync), either to improve the performance or because of extraneous sounds. It is now that the sound mixer has to call upon all his skills so that the dubbing mixer can combine satisfactorily the many tracks he will eventually receive. First he must watch the film with the original sound, in order to assess the acoustic. He will then decide on microphone placing, acoustic screens, either hard or soft, curtains, or whatever he feels necessary to recreate the atmosphere and acoustic of the scene. Then the film is run for the artist, who will hear his original performance in earphones and will attempt to re-enact the feel of the scene. Technically, this operation is known as looping, which goes back to the time when each section to be replaced was physically cut out of the film and made into a loop, so that the artist could have several attempts at re-recording. Now, however, the operation has been simplified, and thanks to the world of computers, the complete edited reel can be run with the original dialogue in sync and the facility of being able to drop in and out of record at pre-set positions to enable the artist to re-record his lines. Many takes are possible by utilizing multitrack film recorders, and the film and guide track can be rewound at up to ten times the normal film speed. This system is known as ADR (Automatic Dialogue Replacement). The advantages here are that the director, the editor, the sound man, and, of course, the artist can see the finished result of their work straight away, and make any necessary changes.

Sound effects

Still very much in the area of post-production are sound effects. Although over the years a vast library of effects has been compiled, most film-makers still prefer to record specifically for each movie. Once again the ADR system is called upon, and in a specially designed room with many different floor surfaces the footsteps artists, as they are known, work through the projected film scene by scene, recreating every footstep, body fall, glass breaking, door slam, kick, punch, or even kiss! An interesting point here about the floor surfaces is that they are designed to cover almost every possible floor covering that could be found. This makes it possible for the artist to move from scene to scene, from carpet to tiles, grass to gravel, etc., all in one continuous take. There will also be a comprehensive effects box, having door knockers, bells, telephones, and door locks and catches, to which is added almost daily any device which makes a potentially useful noise. Once again, the recordings are made on a multitrack film recorder, selected takes being transferred out and passed on to the editorial department to be cut into the dubbing tracks.

Music recording

The layout of the orchestra, choice of microphones, use of acoustic screens or separation booths is very much a matter of personal taste, and of course will depend on the style of the music and its instrumentation (see Plate 43). Usually, if time permits, the score is discussed with the musical director, who will explain his requirements, and this assists in the decision-making. If time is not available prior to the recording session, and this is very often the case, then there is no alternative but to adopt the 'better safe than sorry' method and start out with many more microphones than would at first appear necessary. The reason for this is purely the speed of working. A film score can be an unusual and sometimes an unmusical object. It has to assist the mood of the film without really being heard, but it must also be able to take over completely and, thanks to the improved dynamic range of the whole system, make a considerable impression on the audience. This is where the many microphones can help. The producer, director, editor, and all who have helped create the movie are completely in the dark as to the music they are about to hear for the very first time (apart perhaps from a piano demonstration). They are not always able to explain musically just what is needed to help any particular scene, but by liaising with the musical director and engineer it is possible to close in on a particular section of the orchestra to give just the required touch of magic to satisfy their requirements. This is where the similarities between recordings for disc and a film soundtrack move apart. Although many very successful albums have been

Plate 43. Studio 1 at CTS Studios, London with screen in position for film music recording session (Photo: CTS Studios)

made from film soundtracks, it is usually only after a complete remix to remove these accented sounds, and to raise the level of a section which had been written to accommodate a dialogue scene, or to lower the level where in the film it had to fight through an explosion or, even worse, music's biggest enemy, helicopters!

The soundtracks ultimately end up in the dubbing theatre in a three-track format (still the most popular), although in some cases, and especially for more rock-orientated scores, Dolby stereo four-track is preferred. The original recording would be on two-inch multitrack tape, with either a 50 Hz pulse or time-code, or both, printed on to two of the tracks. With projected film it is usual to use the 50 Hz pulse, whereas the time-code interlock would be used when the musical director is working to a video monitor.

The synchronizing of music to picture is the job of the musical director, working very closely with the music editor, and they can call upon many aids to make the task easier. If one assumes that the picture is to be shown on a large screen projection system or on a video monitor, then these aids are as follows:

1. *Click-track*. An electronic metronome, which generates a click at a pre-set tempo, and which is fed to the MD or the whole orchestra via headsets. This click can, by using simple mathematics (or more usually a set of tables), be arranged to dictate the exact beat of music which has to be accented to cover a particular scene or change of mood. This click-track is arranged to run in sync with the picture, and can also be started at a required number of clicks before music starts in order to give a count-in to the musicians. In some cases, it is possible to project the elapsed time on to the screen, to give yet further assistance to the MD.

However, this fixed-tempo click-track cannot meet all requirements. Music is not necessarily played at one tempo throughout a cue, so one of the following might be used:

(a) Use two click generators, and cut from one to the other as required. Not an ideal way, but it can and does work.

(b) Build a variable click-track by cutting together the various tempi needed for the particular cue. This is a laborious task, but is nevertheless accepted and is absolutely accurate.

(c) Use an all-singing, all-dancing Click Generator Computer, which can be programmed to accommodate all the accelerandi and retardi that should ever be required.

2. *Punch holes*. A system mainly used in the USA and known as the Newman system (after the composer Alfred Newman). It consists of a series of diagonal streamers scratched into the working print of the film, running from top left to bottom right of screen and usually lasting two seconds. The streamers terminate in a series of punch holes, producing a bright flash on the screen to coincide with a particular sync point. This sync point can be used to indicate a change of

tempo or musical mood, to ensure that the music is 'on-time', or simply that the hero kisses the heroine. Combined with this system, the MD may utilize a simple 60-second clock, which is preferred as it does not dictate any particular tempo by flashing on and off as would a digital display.

The dubbing theatre

The dubbing theatre could warrant a complete book to describe the workings in this most magic of all areas, where the film eventually takes shape and the production team sees the final result of its efforts. Under a cover of perpetual darkness, skilled technicians go backwards and forwards over the same section of film until all are satisfied. There are usually three sound mixers handling a feature film, each with their own section. One looks after sound effects, another the dialogue pre-mixes, and the supervising dubbing mixer handles the overall mix including the music. There is no limit to the number of tracks which can be combined to make a complete soundtrack. Many pre-mixes may be necessary in order to bring the number of tracks used in the final mix to a workable total.

The musical film

Every musical film will present its own set of problems, but it is nevertheless necessary to follow certain basic rules. Long before the shooting starts, the musical numbers—either songs or dance routines—will be recorded on multitrack, edited where required, pulsed, time-coded, and/or transferred to 35 mm film to become the original masters. From these masters, tapes for floor playback, cassettes for the actors and actresses to study and rehearse to, mono soundtracks on 35 mm for the editors will all be made. It is vitally important that some form of synchronizing is retained from the very start of production because to 'chase sync' later on can be an extremely expensive and not always successful operation. Floor playback is now always supplied from tape, and a multitrack machine is becoming more popular. It will usually be in eight-track format, which can give good control over the balance of the musical arrangement, making it possible to solo the vocal lines and thereby assist the artists. At the shooting, the playback tape (having been marked with many starts) is played from the required section by the floor playback operator. He will also ensure that the tape is running at the correct speed, by resolving the pulsed playback tape. Loudspeakers are strategically positioned around the set, audio feeds are sent to a central distribution system and split as required. Many films now employ simultaneous video recording on set, in order to check immediately, and they also require an audio feed. The music editor, who is ultimately responsible for sync, may need an earphone feed, as do any of the special effects personnel.

The task of the sound mixer at this stage can become very exacting, for his dialogue will have to match any sung line, previously recorded in an ideal studio situation. Here he is on a noisy set, attempting to record clean dialogue, usually as a lead into or out of a song, and he usually finds a great difference in acoustic. By close co-operation with the music mixer, this difference can be minimized, and if all the dialogue recording is of the highest possible quality a good dubbing mixer can combine the live and pre-recorded sounds so that the join is undetectable.

When shooting is finished, the original music tapes are remixed for maximum visual and stereo effect, transferred to magnetic stock, and supplied to the editors. Some time later, the underscore will be planned, and recorded using the devices mentioned previously (click-tracks, etc.).

The foregoing should be regarded as only a brief glimpse into 'sound in the film industry'. It is an industry where complete chaos would reign without maximum co-operation by everybody. Technicians are employed to do their own job on a particular production, but they must always bear in mind the many other creative aspects of the film, and fully understand the duties of the other specialists on the crew. This can make the film industry a most satisfying place in which to work.

APPENDICES

Appendix I: Units

The SI system of units (Système International d'Unités) is an extension and refinement of the traditional metric system (MKS=metre, kilogramme, second) and is moving towards world-wide acceptance. The main features of SI can be summarized as follows:

1. There are six basic units:

Quantity	Unit	Symbol
length	metre	m
mass	kilogramme	kg
time	second	s
electric current	ampere	A
thermodynamic temperature	kelvin	K
luminous intensity	candela	cd

NB Symbols for units do not take the plural form.

2. Fractions and multiples of units are normally restricted to steps of a thousand. However, the full list of possible fractions and multiples would include the following:

Fraction	Prefix	Symbol	Multiple	Prefix	Symbol
10^{-1}	deci	d	10	deca	da
10^{-2}	centi	c	10^2	hecto	h
10^{-3}	milli	m	10^3	kilo	k
10^{-6}	micro	μ	10^6	mega	M
10^{-9}	nano	n	10^9	giga	G
10^{-12}	pico	p	10^{12}	tera	T

3. Various derived SI units have special names, including the following:

Quantity	Unit	Symbol	Definition
energy	joule	J	$kg\ m^2/s^2$
force	newton	N	$kg\ m/s^2$
power	watt	W	J/s
frequency	hertz	Hz	$1/s$
electric charge	coulomb	C	$A\ s$
electric potential	volt	V	W/A
electric resistance	ohm	Ω	V/A

4. Other derived units include the following:

Quantity	SI unit	Symbol
area	square metre	m^2
volume	cubic metre	m^3
	(also litre = 1 cubic decimetre)	$(l\ or\ dm^3)$
density	kilogramme per cubic metre	kg/m^3
velocity	metre per second	m/s
pressure	newton per square metre	N/m^2
	(or pascal)	$(Pa = N/m^2)$

517

Table of conversions

Length

1 thou = 25.4 μm	1 μm = 0.04 thou
1 inch = 25.4 mm	1 mm = 0.039 inch
1 foot = 304.8 mm	1 cm = 0.39 inch
1 yard = 0.9144 m	1 m = 39.37 inches
1 mile = 1.609 km	1 km = 0.62 miles

Area

1 sq. in. = 645.2 mm^2	1 mm^2 = 0.00155 sq. in.
1 sq. ft. = 0.093 m^2	1 m^2 = 10.764 sq. ft.
1 sq. yd. = 0.836 m^2	= 1.196 sq. yd.

Volume

1 cu. in. = 16.387 cm^3	1 cm^3 = 0.061 cu. in.
1 cu. ft. = 28.317 litres	1 litre = 61.023 cu. in.
1 pint = 0.568 litres	= 0.0353 cu. ft.
1 gallon = 4.546 litres	1 m^3 = 35.315 cu. ft.

Weight

1 oz = 28.35 g	1 g = 0.0353 oz
1 lb = 453.59 g	1 kg = 35.274 oz
= 0.4536 kg	= 2.2046 lb

Appendix II: Standards

The following lists show only a selection of the more relevant standards published at the time of writing. Readers are recommended to check on the existence of further standards, or more up-to-date reissues, with the issuing authority.

(*a*) *British Standards* (British Standards Institution, 2 Park Street, London, W1)

BS 204: 1960   Glossary of terms used in telecommunication (including radio) and electronics

BS 661: 1969   Glossary of acoustical terms

BS 1568: Part 1: 1970   Specification for magnetic tape recording equipment, Part 1. Magnetic tape recording and reproducing systems, dimensions and characteristics

BS 1568: Part 2: 1973   Cassettes for commercial tape records and domestic use, dimensions and characteristics

BS 1568: Part 3: 1976   Eight-track endless-loop magnetic tape cartridge

BS 1928: 1965   Specification for processed disc records and reproducing equipment

BS 2498: 1954   Recommendations for ascertaining and expressing the performance of loudspeakers by objective measurements

BS 2750: 1956   Recommendations for measurement of airborne and impact sound transmission in buildings

BS 3383: 1961   Normal equal-loudness contours for pure tones and normal threshold of hearing under free-field listening conditions

BS 3638: 1963   Method for the measurement of sound absorption coefficients (ISO) in a reverberation room

BS 3860: 1965   Methods for measuring and expressing the performance of audio-frequency amplifiers

BS 4197: 1967   Specification for a precision sound level meter

BS 4297: 1968   Specification for the characteristics and performance of a peak programme meter

BS 4847: 1972   Method for measurement of speed fluctuations in sound recording and reproducing equipment

BS 4852: Part 1: 1972   Methods of defining and measuring the characteristics of disc record playing equipment. Part 1. Disc record players

BS 5428: Part 1: 1977   Methods for specifying and measuring the characteristics of sound system equipment

(*b*) *German Standards* (Beuth Vertrieb GmBH, 1 Berlin 30, Burggrafenstrasse 4–7)

45510   Magnetic sound recording: terminology (1971)

45511/1   Tape recorder for recording on magnetic tape 6.3 mm (0.25 in.) wide: mechanical and electrical specifications (1971)

45511/2   Tape recorder for three- or four-track recording on magnetic tape 12.7 mm (0.5 in.) wide: mechanical and electrical specifications (1971)

45511/3   Tape recorder for four-track recording on tape 25.4 mm (1 in.) wide: mechanical and electrical specifications (1971)

45512   Magnetic tapes for sound recording
         Sheet 1: Dimensions and mechanical properties to be stated (1968)
         Sheet 2: Electroacoustic characteristics (1969)

45513   Sheet 1: DIN test tape for magnetic tapes for 76.2 cm/s tape speed (1968)
         Sheet 2: Ditto 38.1 cm/s tape speed (1967)
         Sheet 3: Ditto 19.05 cm/s tape speed (1966)
         Sheet 4: Ditto 9.5 cm/s tape speed (1968)
         Sheet 5: Ditto 4.75 cm/s tape speed (1972)
         Sheet 6: Ditto 3.81 mm (0.15 in.) wide and 4.75 cm/s tape speed (1972)

45514   Sound recording and reproduction, magnetic tape apparatus: Spools (1961)

45520   Magnetic tape recorders: measurement of the absolute level of the magnetic flux and its frequency response on magnetic tapes (1973)

45521   Measurement of crosstalk in multitrack tape recorders (1963)

45523   Remote control by signals from magnetic tape recorders (1968)

45524   Evaluation of the tape speed of magnetic tape recorders (1968)

45536   Monophonic disc records M.45 (1962)

45537   Monophonic disc records M.33 (1962)

45538   Definitions for disc reproducing equipment (1969)

45539   Record reproducing equipment: directives for measurement, markings, and audio-frequency connections, dimensions of interchangeable pickups, requirements of playback amplifiers (1971)

45541   Frequency test record St.33 and M.33 (1971)

45542   Distortion test record St.33 and St.45 (1969)

45543   Crosstalk record St.33 (1969)

45544   Rumble measurement test record St.33 (1971)

45545   Wow and flutter test records 33 and 45 rpm (1966)

45546   Stereophonic disc records St.45 (1962)

45547   Stereophonic disc records St.33 (1962)

(c) *American (NAB) Standards* (National Association of Broadcasters, 1771 N. Street, NW, Washington, DC 20036)

Disc recordings and reproductions (1964)
Cartridge tape recording and reproducing (1964)
Magnetic tape (reel-to-reel) recordings and reproductions (1965)
Audio cassette recording and reproducing (1973)

(d) *International Electrotechnical Commission (IEC) Recommendations* (1 Rue de Varembe, Geneva, Switzerland)

IEC Publication 50   International electrotechnical vocabulary
IEC Publication 94   Magnetic tape recording and reproducing
IEC Publication 98   1964   Processed disc records and reproducing equipment
IEC Publication 268   Sound system equipment

(e) *International Organization for Standardization (ISO) Recommendations* (1 Rue de Varembe, Geneva, Switzerland)

R131   Expression of the physical and subjective magnitudes of sound or noise
R357   Expression of the power and intensity levels of sound or noise
R532   Procedure for calculating loudness level

Appendix III: Bibliography

General

Bekesy, G. von, *Experiments in Hearing* (New York, 1960)
Davis, D. and C., *Sound System Engineering* (New York, 1974)
Fletcher, H., *Speech and Hearing in Communication* (New York, 1953)
Gelatt, R., *The Fabulous Phonograph* (London, 1956)
Langford-Smith, F., *Radio Designer's Handbook* (London, 4th Ed. 1954)
Olson, H. F., *Music, Physics and Engineering* (New York, 2nd Ed. 1967)
Pohlmann, K. C., *Principles of Digital Audio* (Indiana, 1985)
Lord Rayleigh, *Theory of Sound* Vols. I and II (London, 1896, republished 1960)
Read, O. and Welch, W., *From Tin-Foil to Stereo* (New York, 1959)
Seashore, C. E., *Psychology of Music* (New York, 1938, republished 1967)
Tremaine, H. M. (Ed.), *The Audio Cyclopedia* (New York, 1974)
Wood, A., *The Physics of Music* (London, 1947)
Winckel, F., *Music, Sound and Sensation* (New York, 1967)

The Studio

Beranek, L. L., *Acoustics* (New York, 1954)
Beranek, L. L., *Music, Acoustics and Architecture* (New York, 1962)
Gilford, C., *Acoustics for Radio and Television Studios* (London, 1972)
Knudsen, V. O., *Architectural Acoustics* (New York, 1952)
Mankowsky, V. S., *Acoustics of Studios and Auditoria* (London, 1971)

The Equipment

BBC Monographs (various titles)
Eargle, J., *The Microphone Handbook* (New York, 1985)
Frayne, J. G. and Wolfe, H., *Elements of Sound Recording* (New York, 1949)
Gayford, M. L., *Acoustical Techniques and Transducers* (London, 1962)
Godfrey, J. W. (Ed.), *Studio Engineering for Sound Broadcasting* (London, 1955)
Robertson, A. E., *Microphones* (London, 2nd Ed. 1963)
Spratt, H. G. M., *Magnetic Tape Recording* (London, 2nd Ed. 1963)
Stewart, W. Earl, *Magnetic Recording Techniques* (New York, 1958)
Sturley, K. R., *Sound and Television Broadcasting* (London, 1961)

Techniques

Bernhart, J., *Traité de Prise de Son* (Paris, 1949)
Blumlein, A. D., British Patent No. 394325 (1933)
Burroughs, L., *Microphones: Design and Application* (New York, 1974)
Culshaw, J., *Ring Resounding* (London, 1967)

Douglas, A., *Electronic Music Production* (London, 1973)
Eargle, J., *Sound Recording* (New York, 1986)
Franssen, N. V., *Stereophony* (Eindhoven, 1962)
Burrell Hadden, H., *High Quality Sound Production and Reproduction* (London, 1962)
Howe, H. S., *Electronic Music Synthesis* (New York, 1975)
Nisbett, A., *The Technique of the Sound Studio* (London, 3rd Ed. 1974)
Oringel, R., *Audio Control Handbook* (New York, 4th Ed. 1972)
Runsten, R. and Huber, D., *Modern Recording Techniques* (New York, 1986)
Woram, J. M., *The Recording Studio Handbook* (New York, 1982)

Manufacturing Processes

Guy, P. J., *Disc Recording and Reproduction* (London, 1964)

Allied Media

Alkin, G., *Sound with Vision* (London, 1972)
Alkin, G., *TV Sound Operations* (London, 1975)
Hilliard, R. L., *Radio Broadcasting* (New York, 2nd Ed. 1974)
Johnson, J. S. and Jones, K. K., *Modern Radio Station Practices* (Belmont, California, 1972)
Millerson, G., *The Technique of Television Production* (London, 9th Ed. 1972)
Wysotsky, M. Z., *Wide-Screen Cinema and Stereophonic Sound* (London, 1971)

Appendix IV: APRS information sheets

No. 1. Procedure to be taken when tapes are submitted for transfer to master lacquers or direct playback disc (January 1974)

(a) The tape box must indicate:

1. Client/Artist/Title.
2. The speed. Minimum speed 19 cm/s ($7\frac{1}{2}$ ips).
3. Full-track mono, half-track mono, or two-track stereo, etc.
4. The duration of each item; the total playing time including spacers.
5. The recording characteristics: IEC, NAB, etc.
6. Speed and size of disc to be cut.
7. Disc matrix reference number (if applicable).
8. Any other information, i.e. if stereo XY or MS or quad etc.; state if Dolby system used.

(b) Leaders, spacers, and trailers

1. *Beginning* 2 m (6 feet) of leader tape white or green must be joined to the beginning of the tape to within 12 mm ($\frac{1}{2}$ inch) of the programme.
2. *End* 2 m of red trailer must be joined after the reverberation ends.
3. *Spacing:* Where scrolls are required on the disc a minimum of four seconds (unless otherwise specified) of white spacer must be inserted at the desired position in the tape.
4. Tapes must be wound trailer end out.
5. Spacers must be matt side to head to reduce static.

(c) Recommendations

1. Spool and tape box should be identified with each other.
2. For half-track recording, use new tape and ensure *all* the width is fully erased before recording.
3. If Dolby system used, add 30 sec of Dolby tone at start of tape.
4. At the start of a tape a 30 sec band of 10 kHz tone should be inserted at a level of at least 10 dB below peak programme level for head alignment, followed by a 30 sec band of 1 kHz tone at peak programme level.
5. Standard play tape of 0.052 mm ($1\frac{1}{2}$ mil) base thickness is normal, though tape of 0.035 mm (1 mil) may be acceptable.
   Double or triple play tape is not acceptable.
6. Recording levels should be in accordance with accepted commercial standards and relative to a standard test tape.
7. A cue sheet containing content and duration should be supplied with each tape.

No. 2. Recommended conditions for custom pressing

(a) Minimum requirements for lacquer masters submitted for processing

1. Only discs manufactured specially for processing should be used.
2. Studios are recommended to make themselves familiar with the requirements of BS 1928:1965 and AMD 856.
3. Cutting styli made to comply with the requirements of BS 1928:1965 and AMD 856 must be used.
4. It is recommended that should the first attempt fail, a fresh blank be used. Do not turn blank over.
5. For 30 cm (12 inch) pressings a 35 cm (14 inch) recording blank should be used. For 18 cm (7 inch) and 25 cm (10 inch) pressings reference should be made to the processing factory before cutting blanks to confirm which size of blank best suits the factory's equipment.
6. Discs for processing must be without drive holes or labels.
7. Titles or numbers should be lightly scribed on the edge of discs.
8. Master lacquers must not be played.
9. Recorded levels should agree with normal commercial practice.

(b) Handling and packing of lacquer masters

The container—preferably metal—for transporting the masters should be free from dust. Discs should be space packed, i.e. with a bolt through the centre hole and at least one spacer between each disc, each spacer to be not less than 1.6 mm thick. Where several discs are packed the bottom one should be face up and all others face down. The whole stack to be bolted firmly. The lid should be sealed with adhesive tape to prevent entry of dust.

(c) Processing and pressing instructions

Full information must be given in an envelope securely attached to the outside of the container. The instructions should include:

1. Details of contents of container; matrix numbers and size.
2. Name of cutting studio.
3. Name of client studio.
4. Any observations by the cutting engineer which will assist the manufacturer's quality control.

Where the cutting studio is itself the client studio, the following additional information should be included:

5. Whether full or half process is required.
6. Order number for pressings.
7. Source of labels.

(d) Limits of responsibility

1. Whilst every care is taken with discs received for processing, the factories do not normally accept any responsibility for damage that may occur during the various operations or processing. If a faulty master lacquer is submitted to the pressing

factory, re-processing is chargeable; if processing is faulty, normally re-processing is free of charge, but the client must provide a new master lacquer.
2. Stampers made by the factories from lacquer masters remain their property and will not in any event by deliverable to the customer. (Note: The lacquer masters are not returnable.) 'Masters' and 'Mothers' (positives) remain the property of the customer, and are stored at the customer's risk. As processing charges are usually contributory, an extra charge is made if 'Master' or 'Mother' plates are handed over to clients. *It is recommended* that they be kept for two years after the date of the last order, after which factories reserve the right to dispose of them.

(*e*) The above are subject to the manufacturer's own terms of business.

No. 3. Copyright and sound recording (January 1968)

The Copyright Act, 1956 and the Dramatic and Musical Performers Protection Acts, 1958 and 1963, give monopoly rights to certain classes of copyright holders, enabling them to restrict the use of their works.

1. *Authors and composers* (and publishers, arrangers, etc.) can refuse permission for their works to be published, performed in public, or recorded.
2. *Musicians and actors* (and even speakers, if they are using a script or text as opposed to speaking impromptu) can refuse permission for their performances to be recorded.
3. *Gramophone recording companies* (and private recording studios) can refuse permission for their recordings to be copied.*
4. *Broadcasting organizations* (sound and television) can refuse permission for their programmes to be recorded (except by a person for his own private and domestic use—when the permission of any copyright holders and performers is still required).

These separate restrictions add up to a formidable maze of copyright difficulties. Unauthorized recording 'off the air' of a broadcast of a musical gramophone record, for example, would mean the infringement of several copyrights at once.

Briefly, recording studios should take action on the rights of these four categories of copyright holders as follows:

1. *Authors and composers*

Most British copyright holders have appointed the Mechanical Copyright Protection Society Ltd., Elgar House, 380 Streatham High Road, London, SW16, to act as their agents. MCPS can therefore issue a licence granting permission for recording, subject to certain conditions:†

(*a*) The studio must compile a monthly list of copyright music recordings, giving enough information for the copyright owner to be identified, i.e., title of work, publisher, composer, etc. Forms on which these returns can be made are available from MCPS.

---

*The owner of the mechanical copyright in a recording is the studio or person who made the recording. However, where a person commissions the making of a recording and pays for it, that person is entitled to hold the copyright—in the absence of any agreement to the contrary.

†Members and Associates who participate in the APRS Copyright Scheme can, by paying a single annual fee, avoid the need to make separate applications, returns and royalty payments to MCPS—where up to 25 copies are concerned.

(b) The studio (or client) must pay a royalty of $6\frac{1}{4}\%$ of the retail selling price (less tax) of each record with an agreed minimum payment per copyright work. (This assumes that the recording is made in this country and not from an imported master, and that the musical works have previously been issued on a commercial gramophone record in the UK.)

(c) The studio (or client) must affix a royalty stamp to all copyright recordings. These stamps are supplied free of charge by MCPS as required.

(d) The studio (or client) must ensure that the label bears the words—in bold type— 'REPRODUCTION, RESALE, BROADCASTING OR PUBLIC PERFOR-MANCE PROHIBITED WITHOUT LICENCE'.

2. *Musicians and actors*

An artist has no copyright in his performance (whether live, broadcast, or recorded) but he is protected against having it re-recorded, broadcast, or filmed.

The studio (or client) must ensure that he has the written consent of every artist, amateur or professional, whom he wishes to record.

3. *Gramophone recording companies*

Re-recording of gramophone records is expressly forbidden without the permission of the recording company or studio concerned. This permission is rarely granted, and if it is the full royalty is still payable to MCPS.

4. *Broadcasting organizations*

Except where recordings are made 'for private purposes', off-the-air recording is only possible when prior permission has been granted. The studio (or client) must obtain this permission and in addition that of any artists or copyright holders concerned.

5. *Public Performance*

Recording studios are sometimes involved in outside events where sound recordings are reproduced over loudspeakers. This constitutes a public performance, which is forbidden without a licence, by the warning notice printed on all record labels.

Where records are used for this purpose, the performance involves both the musical work and the copyright recording. Therefore two licences are usually required, the first from The Performing Right Society Ltd., 29–33 Berners Street, London, W1, in respect of the musical works, and the second from Phonographic Performance Ltd., 62 Oxford Street, London, W1, who act on behalf of most British record companies for that purpose.

GLOSSARY

Glossary

Absorption	1. Damping of a sound wave on passing through a medium or striking a surface. 2. The property possessed by materials, objects, or media of absorbing sound energy.
Absorption coefficient	The fraction of the incident sound energy absorbed by a surface or material at a given frequency and under specified conditions. The complement of the sound energy reflection coefficient under those conditions, i.e. it is equal to 1 minus the sound energy reflection coefficient of the surface or material.
a.c.	Abbreviation for alternating current, which periodically reverses its direction, as opposed to d.c. (direct current).
Academy roll-off	Control of the upper frequencies in terms of total response heard by the audience in a cinema, to minimize the effect of unwanted random noise in the system.
Acetate	Alternative term for Lacquer disc.
Acoustics	1. The science of sound. 2. Of a room or auditorium. Those factors that determine its character with respect to the quality of the received sound.
ADC (analogue-to-digital converter)	Circuit whose output is a digital representation of an analogue input.
ADT (Automatic Double Tracking)	Duplication of a voice or instrument track with a delay of a few milliseconds to increase the impact or simulate the effect of more performers (see Double-tracking).
Advance	Sound is printed on film, and scanned, at a point in advance of the picture aperture by an amount equal to 20 picture frames for 35 mm optical track, 26 frames for 16 mm optical, and 30 frames for 16 mm magnetic. NB 35 mm striped films such as Cinemascope and 70 mm prints are scanned for sound after picture.
Aerial	(American: Antenna.) Wire or system of wires supported at a height above the ground for the purpose of radiating or of collecting electromagnetic waves.
Alignment	The process of positioning tape heads and amplifier pre-sets for optimum tape performance.
Ambience	The combination of reverberation and background noise which characterizes the sound in a given hall or studio.

Ampere (amp)	Practical unit of electric current.
Amplifier	A device in which an input signal controls a local source of power in such a way as to produce an output which bears some desired relationship to, and is generally greater than, the input signal.
Amplitude	Of a simple sinusoidal quantity. The peak value.
Amplitude distortion	That part of non-linearity distortion which is an undesired variation of gain or sensitivity with change of signal level.
Amplitude modulation (AM)	Modulation in which the amplitude of the carrier is the characteristic varied.
Analogue (Analog)	Electronic signal whose waveform resembles that of the original sound (cf Digital).
Anechoic	Without echo. An anechoic chamber is a chamber or room where walls are lined with a material which completely absorbs sound.
Antenna	(See Aerial.)
Aspect ratio	Proportion of height to width.
Atmosphere microphone	Microphone placed at some distance from the performers to pick up the general ambience.
Attack time	Time taken for a limiter or compressor to produce the necessary gain change.
Attentuation	Reduction in current, voltage, or power along the transmission path of a signal.
Attentuation distortion (or amplitude/frequency distortion)	An undesired variation of gain or sensitivity with frequency.
Audio frequency (AF)	(Low frequency, deprecated): Rate of oscillation corresponding to that of sound audible to the human ear (i.e. within the range from about 20 to 20,000 Hz).
Auto-locate	Tape machine facility giving fast location of chosen points on the tape.
Azimuth	The angle between the gap in a tape head and the longitudinal axis of the tape (should be 90°).
Backing	Accompaniment, as when a group of vocalists record a 'backing track' to which the soloist listens on headphones when recording.
Back-tracking	The production of a composite recording by combining live sound with a previously recorded backing track.
Baffle	General expression for wall, board, or enclosure carrying a loudspeaker. The purpose of the baffle is primarily to

separate the front and back radiations from the cone or diaphragm which would otherwise cancel each other.

Balance — Placing of artists, speakers, or other sources of sound in relation to a microphone or microphones, or vice versa (hence 'balance test').

Balanced line — Programme cable in which the twin signal wires are both isolated from earth and are suitably terminated so as to be at equal potential but opposite polarity.

Band — Portion of the recorded surface on a disc separated by a marker space or scroll.

Bandwith — The interval between the cut-off frequencies or -3 dB points in a response curve, expressed in octaves or as a frequency difference in hertz.

Beats — The periodic variations of amplitude resulting from the addition of two periodic quantities of the same kind but of slightly different frequency.

Bel — A scale unit used in the comparison of the magnitudes of powers. The number of bels, expressing the relative magnitudes of two powers, is the logarithm to the base 10 of the ratio of the powers. One bel equals 10 decibels.

Biasing — The superposition of a magnetic field on the signal magnetic field during magnetic recording. This additional field may be alternating at a frequency well above the signal frequency range (HF bias). Alternatively, the additional field may be stead (d.c. bias).

Bias trap — Low-pass filter in tape replay circuit designed to attenuate any high-frequency bias present.

Bi-directional — Type of microphone having a figure-of-eight directivity pattern.

Binaural hearing —
1. Normal perception of sounds and/or of their directions of arrival with both ears.
2. By extension, the perception of sound when the two ears are connected to separate electroacoustic transmission channels.

Bit — Contraction of the words 'binary digit' (a '1' or a '0'). A number of bits assembled together, often 4 or 8, is called a 'byte'.

Blimp — Soundproof cover device for a camera. Later models of studio camera are 'self-blimped', that is they have a double skin suitably insulated.
NB The term 'silent camera' is a misnomer as it refers to a camera which can be used only for making silent films and is usually very noisy.

Boolean algebra	Branch of logic in which operators such as 'AND', 'OR', 'NOR' are used in place of mathematical signs.
Boom	A mobile carrier for a microphone which includes a movable arm from which the microphone is suspended.
Break jack	A jack arranged to break the normal circuit when a plug is inserted.
Buchmann and Meyer pattern	The pattern formed by the spread of reflections from a modulated groove when a parallel beam of light is caused to fall normal to the surface of one or the other wall, and when the groove is viewed from the direction of the light source. It is used as a measure of the maximum modulation of either wall of the groove in the calibration of the performance of recorders, and for the measurement of levels on test records.
Bulk eraser	Electromagnet designed to erase a reel of tape in a few seconds.
Bump	Colloquial term for making an interim reduction of, say, four tracks to two to make room for more material on a multitrack tape (also called 'Jump').
Burnishing facet	The portion of the cutting stylus directly behind the cutting edge which smooths the groove.
Bus bar	Common earth or other contact wire.
Butterfly head	Type of multitrack head with a flared guard band to give improved crosstalk performance.
Cans	Colloquial for headphones.
Capacitance	The magnitude of the capability of an element, or a circuit, to store electric charge. Measured in microfarads (μF).
Capacitor microphone (sometimes called Condenser or Electrostatic)	Type of microphone in which the signal is generated by the variation in capacitance between the diaphragm(s) and a fixed plate.
Capstan (American: Puck)	Drive spindle of tape machine.
Cardioid microphone	Class of microphone having a heart-shaped directivity pattern.
Carrier	The wave which is intended to be modulated.
Cartridge	1. Easy-loading magazine of magnetic tape; generally refers to the Eight-Track Stereo format.
	2. Disc reproducing head.
Cassette	Easy-loading magazine of magnetic tape; generally refers to the Philips Compact Cassette format.
CCIR	Comité Consultatif International des Radiocommunications: International standards organization.
Chip	American term for swarf (q.v.).

Chromium dioxide (CrO$_2$)	Magnetic tape coating permitting higher levels at high frequencies than the conventional ferric oxide.
Clapperboard (or slate)	Primitive but efficient system for simultaneously giving an identification to the picture camera and an audible and visual synchronizing point at the start or finish of a filmed section or 'take'.
Clean feed	Version of a programme signal which omits one source (e.g. voice, to allow overdubbing in another language, etc.).
Clipper	A device for removing fast transients above a prescribed level. Normally used in conjunction with a limiter if it is to be inaudible.
Clipping	Form of distortion due to severe overloading.
Cocktail party effect	The faculty of selecting one stream of information out of a number of voices speaking at the same time.
Coincident	Refers to microphone arrangements in stereophony. Two microphones are said to be coincident if they are placed immediately adjacent to each other so that any differences in the times of arrival of the sound are negligible.
Colouration	Change in frequency response caused by resonance peaks.
Compandor	A combination of a compressor at one point in a communication path for reducing the volume range of signals, followed by an expander at another point for restoring the original volume range. Usually its purpose is to improve the ratio of the signal to the interference entering in the path between the compressor and expander.
Compression moulding	The process of forming a disc by compressing a quantity of suitable plastic in a cavity.
Compressor	Means for reducing the variations in signal amplitude in a transmission system according to a specified law.
Concentric (Finishing groove)	The closed circular groove which succeeds the lead-out groove.
Concert pitch	System of music tuning based on a frequency of A = 440 Hz.
Continuity studio	A small studio from which an announcer, supervising the running of a sequence of programmes, makes opening and closing announcements, and interpolates interlude material when required.
Copy master	1. Reserve or replacement metal negative produced from the positive for use as a master. 2. Identical copy of any master tape: should indicate type of master from which copy was made.
Crossfade	To fade in one channel while fading out another in order to substitute gradually the output of one for that of the other

	(e.g. to create the impression of a change of scene). Hence 'crossfade' (noun).
Crossover frequency	As applied to a dividing network. That frequency at which equal power is supplied to each of two adjacent frequency channels.
Crosstalk	Form of interference caused by break-through of signals from one circuit or tape track to another.
Cutter head	A recording head with cutting stylus for electromechanical or mechanical recording.
Cycle	Of a periodic quantity. The sequence of changes which takes place during the period of a recurring variable quantity.
Cycle per second (c/s)	Unit of frequency, now generally superseded by hertz.
DAC (digital to analogue converter)	Circuit for converting a digital word into the corresponding analogue signal.
Damping	That property of a circuit which tends to cause decay in amplitude of oscillations or reduce resonant peaks.
dbx	Proprietary noise reduction system.
d.c.	Abbreviation for direct current, which flows in one direction only, as opposed to a.c. (alternating current).
Dead studio	Studio having very little reverberation.
Decibel (dB)	A unit of transmission giving the ratio of two powers. One-tenth of a bel.
De-emphasis	A change in the frequency response of a reproducing system, complementary to pre-emphasis.
Differential amplifier	Device designed to amplify the difference between two signals.
Diffraction	Form of interference by means of which longer-wavelength sounds effectively bend round obstacles.
Digital	Refers to signals which have been converted from the normal 'analogue' form to a series of coded pulses.
DIN	Deutscher Industrie Normenausschus: German standards organization.
Direct-cut	Method of recording straight to disc without a tape stage.
Direct disc	Lacquer recording blank which is intended for reproduction without further processing.
Direct injection	Process of recording a guitar or other electronic instrument by feeding the electronic signal direct to tape instead of via a microphone.
Directivity pattern	Graph showing the response of a piece of equipment such

as a microphone at all angles in a given plane—sometimes called a polar diagram.

Distortion	The unwanted change in waveform which can occur between two points in a transmission equipment or system.
Dolby	Noise reduction system named after its inventor, Dr Ray Dolby. Dolby 'A' is used in professional tape mastering; Dolby 'B' and 'C' are simpler systems used for example in domestic cassette recorders.
Doppler effect	The change in the observed frequency of a wave caused by time rate of change in the length of the path between the source and the observer.
Double-tracking	Overdubbing a voice or instrument 'playing along' with a previous track of the same musical line (see also ADT).
Drop-in	Process of inserting a recorded sound by playing up to a chosen point and switching one or more tracks to the record mode.
Dropout	Momentary loss of signal caused by a fault in tape coating, or dust etc.
Dubbing	1. The combining of two or more recordings into a composite recording. 2. The recording so obtained. Misnomer sometimes used to describe 're-voicing' (in the original or a foreign language) the dialogue spoken by an actor appearing on the screen.
Ducking	Process of automatic compression, e.g. when the announcer's voice signal causes the level of music to be attenuated.
Dummy head stereo	(German: Künstkopf Stereo.) System of recording using microphones placed in the ears of a model head (or of a wearer).
Dynamic range	Of a programme. The range within which its volume fluctuates. (The term is applied to the original sounds and to the electric currents produced by them.)
Echo	Sound which has been reflected and arrives with such a magnitude and time interval after the direct sound as to be distinguishable as a repetition of it.
Echo chamber	A reverberant room, containing only a microphone and a loudspeaker, through which an output from a studio or hall is passed in order to allow a variable degree of reverberation to be added to the direct output from the same source. The microphone output is combined with the output of the programme source and controlled in volume to give a desired degree of reverberation.
Editing	Process of cutting, rearrangement, and selection of recorded material.

Efficiency	Of mechanical or electrical plant, the ratio (expressed as a percentage) of the output energy in the required form to the total input energy.
Eigentones	(German.) Resonances set up in a room or enclosure at frequencies determined by the physical dimensions.
Electret	Non-conductor which has been given a permanent electrical charge: used in microphones and other transducers.
Electromagnet	Coil of wire, possibly having a core of soft iron, which behaves as a magnet only while a current is passing through it.
Electron	Smallest charge of negative electricity which may exist by itself or as part of an atom. (From the Greek 'elektron' = amber.)
Electronic crossover	Frequency—dividing circuit using split amplifiers rather than passive circuits.
Envelope	Graphical representation of the changing amplitude of a complex wave.
Equalization (EQ)	The process of modifying the amplitude/frequency response in a recording and reproducing system to produce flat overall characteristics, minimize noise, or give an artistic effect.
Erase head	The component in a magnetic recording system that obliterates previous recordings so that the recording medium may be used afresh.
Expander	Means for increasing the variations in signal amplitude in a transmission system according to a specified law.
Farad	Unit of capacitance, which for convenience is subdivided into one million microfarads (μF).
Feedback	The return of a fraction of the output of a circuit to the input. *Note*. Feedback may be either positive or negative, i.e. tending to increase or decrease the output.
Figure-of-eight	Polar response shape of a bi-directional microphone.
Film speed	1. Scale of sensitivity of photographic emulsion. 2. Rate of film travel, related to 24 frames per second. NB For television, in order to avoid stroboscopic effects, the nearest multiple of mains frequency is used. In Europe this is 25 frames per second, which raises the pitch of reproduced sound by a noticeable amount. For films commissioned for television, the speed of 25 frames/sec is adopted.
Filter	Electrical network composed of inductors, capacitors, or resistors, or a combination of these, designed to discriminate between currents of different frequencies.

Flanging	Coarse phasing effect like that obtained by placing a finger on the supply spool of a tape machine (cf. Phasing).
Fletcher and Munson curves	Set of equal-loudness graphs showing frequency-dependent behaviour of human hearing.
Flip-flop	Device having two stable states used, for instance, as a binary counter.
Floating	Not connected to any source of potential.
Flutter and wow	Undesired forms of frequency modulation introduced by the recording/reproducing process; for example, by irregular motion of the recording medium. *Note.* 'Wow' usually refers to the range of fluctuation frequencies between about 0.1 Hz and 10 Hz and is perceived as pitch fluctuations. 'Flutter' usually refers to fluctuation frequencies above about 10 Hz.
Flutter echo	A rapid multiple echo of even rate.
Flux density	Measure of the concentration of an electric field or magnetic field. (Magnetic flux density is measured in lines per square centimetre, or gauss, or webers per metre of tape width.)
Foldback	Process of feeding microphone or tape signals to headphones or loudspeakers as a cue to artists during recording.
Formant	A band of frequencies in the spectrum of a complex sound which may be associated with a resonance in the mechanism of the production of the sound. *Note 1.* Vowel sounds may possess more than one formant in different parts of the spectrum. *Note 2.* The term may also be used in relation to musical instruments.
Frequency	Of a periodic quantity. The rate of repetition of the cycles. The reciprocal of the period. The unit is the hertz (Hz).
Frequency correction	(See Equalization.)
Frequency modulation (FM)	Modulation of a sine-wave carrier in which the instantaneous frequency of the modulated wave differs from the carrier frequency by an amount proportional to the instantaneous value of the modulating wave.
Fringe effect	Misleading increase in low-frequency output when a full-track test tape is used on a multitrack machine.
Fundamental frequency	The highest common factor of a series of harmonically related frequencies in a complex oscillation.
Fuse	Wire or strip of metal connected in an electric circuit so as to act as a protective device by melting, and thus interrupting the circuit, if the current exceeds the maximum safe value.

Fuzz	Deliberate use of distortion for special effect with electronic guitars etc.
Gain	1. The ratio of the output load power to the input power. 2. The ratio of the output and input voltages, or currents, under specified conditions of impedance termination. *Note.* In this case the terms should properly be 'Voltage gain' and 'Current gain' respectively.
Gap alignment	The adjustment of the magnetic gap in relation to the magnetic medium. (*a*) Azimuth alignment. The adjustment of the orientation of the magnetic gap in relation to the direction of motion of the magnetic medium. (*b*) Lateral alignment. The adjustment of the magnetic gap parallel to the plane of the magnetic medium and normal to its direction of motion. (*c*) Pole face alignment. The rotation of the contact surface in a plane at right angles to the direction of motion of the magnetic medium in order to effect satisfactory contact over the full length of the gap.
Gate	Special amplifier circuit which has zero output unless the input level exceeds a chosen threshold level.
Gramophone record	A processed copy of a disc recording from which sounds may be reproduced by a mechanical or an electromechanical system.
Graphic equalizer	Frequency correction device giving selective control in narrow bands and having slider controls which indicate the approximate response curve chosen.
Groove	In a mechanical or electromechanical recording. The track inscribed in the recording medium by the cutting or embossing stylus.
Groove shape	The geometric form of the cross-section of a groove. It is defined in terms of the radius of the bottom of the groove (bottom radius) and the included angle between the walls of the groove (groove angle).
Guardband	Spacing between tracks on a multitrack tape.
Gun microphone	(American: Rifle microphone.) Type of microphone employing a long tube and being narrowly directional along the axis.
Haas Effect	An effect concerned with the apparent location of the source when the same sound is heard from two or more sources (as in a public address system). Within certain limits of the relative intensities of the separate sounds, and of the time intervals between their arrivals, the sound appears to come from a single source, namely that from which the sounds first arrive even though the later sounds are more intense.

Harmonic	A sinusoidal oscillation having a frequency which is an integral multiple of a fundamental frequency. A harmonic having double the fundamental frequency is called the second harmonic and so on.
Harmonic distortion	A constituent of non-linearity distortion, consisting of the production in the response to a sinusoidal excitation of sinusoidal components whose frequencies are integral multiples of the frequency of the excitation.
Headroom	Amount of increase about the working level which can be tolerated by an amplifier or tape etc. before the onset of overload distortion.
Helmholtz resonator	A resonator consisting of a cavity in a rigid structure communicating by a narrow neck or slit to the outside air. *Note*. The frequency of resonance is determined by the mass of air in the neck resonating in conjunction with the compliance of the air in the cavity.
Hertz	Unit of frequency ($=1$ cycle per second).
Hill and dale recording	A mechanical or electromechanical recording in which the modulation is perpendicular to the surface of the recording medium.
Howlround (Howlback)	Instability in a sound reinforcement or other system when feedback is allowed to build up between the output and input.
Hum	Low-frequency noise at the a.c. mains frequency and its harmonics.
Hunting	Fault condition, where the transport mechanism or motor is alternately reaching synchronous speed and falling back again in rhythmic fashion.
Hybrid transformer	Type of transformer having two secondary windings with minimum crosstalk between them; used to split signal to 'echo send', for example.
Hypercardioid	Class of microphone having a directivity pattern intermediate between cardioid and figure-of-eight.
IEC	International Electrotechnical Commission: International standards organization.
Impedance	That property of an element, or a circuit, which restricts the flow of an alternating current. Measured in ohms.
Inductance	The magnitude of the capability of an element, or a circuit, to store magnetic energy when carrying a current. Measured in henrys.
Injection moulding	The process of forming a disc by injecting a liquified plastic material into a die cavity.

Insulator	Substance or body that offers a very high resistance to the flow of an electric current and may therefore be used to separate two conductors from each other.
Intensity	Of a sound, the objective strength of the sound expressed in terms of the r.m.s. pressure in dynes per square centimetre (or bars)—more recently in newtons per square metre or pascals—or in terms of the power in watts per square metre (cf. Loudness).
Intermodulation distortion	A constituent of non-linearity distortion consisting of the occurrence, in the response to coexistent sinusoidal excitations, of sinusoidal components (intermodulation products) whose frequencies are sums or differences of the excitation frequencies or of integral multiples of these frequencies.
Internal balance	Placing adopted by the performers in a musical combination in order to secure a satisfactory relationship between the sounds produced by each of them, as heard in the studio or other place of performance.
ISO	International Organization for Standardization.
Jack	A device used generally for terminating the permanent wiring of a circuit, access to which is obtained by the insertion of a plug.
Jump	(See Bump.)
Kilo (k)	Prefix signifying one thousand.
Künstkopf stereo	(See Dummy head stereo.)
Lacquer disc	A disc for mechanical or electromechanical recording usually made of metal, glass, or fibre and coated with lacquer compound. It may be coated on one side (single-sided) or both (double-sided).
Land	The uncut surface between adjacent grooves.
Lateral recording	A mechanical or electromechanical recording in which the groove modulation is perpendicular to the motion of the recording medium and parallel to its surface.
Leader	Uncoated tape, usually white, spliced to the beginning of a recording tape.
Lead-in groove	The length of plain groove that starts at the periphery of the record and the pitch of which is greater than normal recording pitch.
Lead-out groove	The length of plain groove which succeeds the recorded surface and the pitch of which is greater than the normal recording pitch.
Level	Intensity of a continuous tone used for test purposes (measured in decibels by comparison with the standard

reference level, or zero level, of 0.775 volt r.m.s. which is equivalent to a power of 1 milliwatt in a resistance of 600 ohms); colloquially, intensity of programme output or of noise. Hence 'level test'.

Limiter	Device for automatically limiting the volume during programme peaks so as to prevent accidental overmodulation of a transmitter or overloading of other equipment. (As the volume applied to the input of the limiter increases, the volume at the output increases linearly up to a certain critical point, after which a further increase in input volume produces a much smaller increase in output volume. When the applied volume exceeds the critical value, the device necessarily introduces amplitude distortion, but ought not to introduce excessive non-linear distortion.)
Lissajous figure	Locus of displacement resulting from two signals applied at right angles. The form of ellipse obtained indicates relative phase.
Live	1. Programme broadcast or recorded at the time of its performance to an audience (as distinct from a studio recording). 2. Studio having a comparatively long reverberation time, and therefore tending to give a brilliant acoustic effect (cf. Dead studio). 3. Connected to electrically sensitive part of a circuit.
Logarithmic scale	Scale of measurement in which an increase of one unit represents a tenfold increase in the quantity measured.
Loudness	An observer's auditory impression of the strength of a sound.
Loudspeaker	An electroacoustic transducer operating from an electrical system to an acoustical system and designed to radiate sound.
Magnetic field	Field of force in the vicinity of a permanent magnet or an electric circuit carrying current.
Magnetic tape	Recording medium in the form of a plastic tape (e.g. cellulose acetate, polyvinyl chloride, polyester), coated or impregnated with magnetizable powders.
Masking	1. The process by which the threshold of hearing of one sound is raised due to the presence of another. 2. The increase, expressed in decibels, of the threshold of hearing of the masked sound due to the presence of the masking sound.
Master	A recording, in edited or approved form, from which copies can be made.
Matching transformer	A transformer designed for insertion between two circuits having different impedances to reduce the reflection at the junction and increase the power transferred.

Matrix	1. Generic term applied to all processing electroforms. 2. Circuit designed to mix or separate electrical signals.
Matrix number	Serial number engraved or embossed on the lacquer or subsequently on the metal parts.
Matt backed tape	Type of recording tape with a dulled finish to facilitate proper winding, even on open hubs.
Mega (M)	Prefix signifying one million.
Memory	Device which can be made to store the value of a signal presented to it.
Micro (μ)	Prefix signifying one-millionth part.
Microgroove	A groove of which the unmodulated width at the top is less than 0.076 mm and which is intended to be played with a stylus having a tip radius less than 0.025 mm.
Micron (μm)	One-millionth of a metre.
Microphone	An electroacoustical transducer operating from an acoustical system to an electrical system.
Milli (m)	Prefix signifying one-thousandth part.
Mixer	An apparatus by means of which the outputs of several channels can be faded up and down independently, selected individually, or combined at any desired relative volumes.
Modulation	The process by which the essential characteristics of a signal wave (the modulating wave) are impressed upon another wave (the carrier wave).
Modulation noise	In a recording and reproducing system. That part of the total noise which varies with signal amplitude.
Monaural hearing	The perception of sound by stimulation of a single ear.
Monitor	1. (Verb) To check the technical quality of a transmission. 2. (Noun) An apparatus for comparing the technical quality of a programme at one point in the transmission chain with that of the same programme at another point and for giving an alarm if there is any significant difference between the two.
Monophonic (mono)	A transmission system in which, at some point, only a single signal exists.
Mother	Electroform produced from the master.
Moving coil	Of a microphone, loudspeaker, etc. depending for its action on the movement of a coil in a magnetic field.
Multiplexer	Circuit in which information from many sources is switched in a defined order to be sent to a single destination.
Multitrack master	A multitrack session tape prepared for mix-down.

Mumetal	An iron alloy used in tape heads and for magnetic screening.
NAB or NARTB	National Association of Radio and Television Broadcasters: American standards organization.
NAB operating level	Equivalent to 0 VU.
Neopilot head	Improvement on the original Piloton system of sync pulse in which two thin tracks are positioned at the centre of the tape (where they are more reliable) recorded in opposite phase (push-pull) and so do not reproduce in a full-track scan.
Newton (N)	Unit of force.
Noise	Sound which is undesired by the recipient. Undesired electrical disturbances in a transmission channel or device may also be termed 'noise', in which case the qualification 'electrical' should be included unless it is self-evident.
Noise gate	(See Gate.)
Noise rating curves	An agreed set of empirical curves relating octave-band sound pressure level to the centre frequency of the octave bands, each of which is characterized by a 'noise rating' (NR), which is numerically equal to the sound pressure level at the intersection with the ordinate at 1,000 Hz. The 'noise rating' of a given noise is found by plotting the octave band spectrum on the same diagram and selecting the highest noise rating curve to which the spectrum is tangent.
Noise reduction	Process using gain control devices to improve the signal-to-noise ratio. (See DBX and Dolby.)
Non-linear distortion	That part of the distortion arising in a non-linear system (i.e. a system whose transmission properties are dependent on the instantaneous magnitude of the excitation) which is due to the non-linearity of the system.
Normalled jacks	Sockets on a jackfield having permanently wired interconnections.
Notch filter	Bandpass filter tuned to a very narrow frequency band.
Octave	1. A pitch interval of 2:1. 2. The tone whose frequency is twice that of the given tone.
Ohm (Ω)	Practical unit of resistance or impedance.
Ohm's Law	Fundamental generalization describing the flow of direct current in an electrical circuit, by stating that the magnitude of the current is proportional to the potential difference, provided the resistance is constant. The practical unit of potential difference, the volt, has been so chosen that 1 volt is produced across a resistance of 1 ohm when 1 ampere is flowing through it, so that: $$\text{Current (amperes)} = \frac{\text{p.d. (volts)}}{\text{resistance (ohms)}}.$$

Omnidirectional (or Non-directional)	Equally sensitive in all directions.
Open circuit	Circuit which is not electrically continuous and through which current cannot therefore flow.
Operational amplifier	Ideal amplifier whose principal properties are infinite gain, bandwidth, and input impedance.
Optical sound track	A narrow band, usually on cinematograph film, which carries a photographic record of sound.
Original master	A fully prepared first-generation tape in final format (i.e. an edited session tape or mix-down of multitrack master).
Oscillator	Apparatus for producing sustained oscillations, usually by means of positive feedback between the output and the input of an amplifying valve or transistor.
Out-takes	Retained non-master material (edited or not edited).
Overtone	A component of a complex wave which may or may not be an integral multiple of the fundamental.
Pad	A network of resistors designed to introduce a fixed loss, or for impedance-matching purposes.
Pan	To shift a sound image as desired between the positions occupied by the loudspeakers in stereo or quadraphonic reproduction.
Pan-pot	(Panoramic potentiometer.) Ganged volume control used in panning.
Parabolic reflector	A light, rigid structure which reflects sounds to a focus at which a microphone is placed.
Parametric equalizer	Frequency correction device which allows both the frequency and the bandwidth of the boost or cut to be selected.
Pascal (Pa)	Unit of pressure = 1 newton per square metre.
Patch	To connect reserve equipment by means of flexible cords and plugs, so that the connections to the normal equipment are automatically broken by break-jacks.
Peak Programme Meter (PPM)	An instrument designed to measure the volume of programme in a sound channel in terms of the peaks averaged over a specified period.
Peak value	Of a varying quantity in a specific time interval. The maximum numerical value attained whether positive or negative.
Phantom power	Method of sending d.c. supply to a capacitor microphone by connecting the positive side to both signal wires of a balanced line and the negative to the screen.
Phase distortion	Form of distortion in which wave trains of different audio

frequencies travel with different group velocities, owing to the characteristics of the medium (e.g. a landline).

Phasing — Trick effect obtained by splitting a signal to two tape machines or networks and introducing a time delay in one of them (cf. Flanging).

Pilot tone — A signal wave, usually a single frequency, transmitted over the system to indicate or control its characteristics.

Pink noise — Random noise signal having the same amount of energy in each octave (cf. White noise).

Pitch —
1. That attribute of auditory sensation in terms of which sound may be ordered on a scale related primarily to frequency.
2. Number of grooves per inch.

Plane wave — A wave in which successive wavefronts are parallel planes.

Polar response — A plot of the variation in radiated energy with angle relative to the axis of the radiator. Similarly used for receivers and microphones.

Post sync — Recording of music, effects, or dialogue to synchronize with a previously filmed picture.

Potentiometer (colloquial: pot) — Potential divider or variable attenuator used, for example, to control the volume of a programme.

Pre-echo — The undesired transfer of a recorded signal from one groove to another.
NB Post-echo can also occur.

Pre-emphasis — A deliberate change in the frequency response of a recording system for the purpose of improvement in signal-to-noise ratio, or the reduction of distortion (see also De-emphasis).

Prefade listening (PFL) — Listening to a programme before it is faded up for transmission or recording; technical facilities provided for this purpose.

Presence — Degree of forwardness in a voice or instrument achieved by boosting in the frequency region 2–8 kHz.

Pressing — Moulding of thermoplastic material produced from the stamper by the application of heat and pressure and subsequent cooling.

Pressure gradient operation — Method of responding to sound signals in which the sound wave has access to both sides of a microphone diaphragm.

Pressure operation — Method of responding to sound signals in which the sound wave has access to only one side of a microphone diaphragm.

Print-through — The undesired transfer of recorded signal from one layer to another of the recording medium when these layers are stored on spools.

Production master	An equalized or otherwise modified copy of the original master for production purposes.
Proximity effect	Increase in low-frequency response which occurs at distances less than about 1 m from pressure-gradient-operated microphones.
Public Address (PA)	Arrangements of microphones, amplifiers, and loudspeakers used to reinforce speech or music over a large audience area.
Pulse code modulation (PCM)	Modulation in accordance with a pulse code.
Q-factor	A measure of the sharpness of resonance.
Quadraphony	System of recording and reproduction using four channels and four loudspeakers in an attempt to recreate a 360° soundfield around the listener.
Quantization	A process in which the range of values of a wave is divided into a finite number of smaller subranges, each of which is represented by an assigned or 'quantized' value within the subrange.
Radio microphone	Type of microphone incorporating a small radio transmitter to give reception at short distances without the need for cables.
RAM (random-access memory)	Memory designed so that the location or 'address' of a given piece of information is independent of the information stored.
Recording head	A transducer whereby the state or configuration of the recording medium is changed in conformity with the signal.
Recovery time	Time taken for a limiter or compressor to return to its quiescent state on removal of the high-level signal.
Rectifier	Device for transforming an alternating current into a direct one.
Reduction	The mixing from a multitrack recording to produce a mono, stereo, or quadraphonic recording as a production master.
Reflection	A return of energy due to the wave striking some discontinuity in its supporting medium.
Register	Device which can store a certain number of bits, usually only temporarily (cf. Memory).
Relay	A device, operated by an electric current, and causing by its operation abrupt changes in an electrical circuit (making or breaking the circuit, changing of the circuit connections, or variation in the circuit characteristics).
Release time	(See Recovery time.)

Reproducing head	A transducer whereby the signal is re-created from a recording.
Resistance	That property of a substance which restricts the flow of electricity through it, associated with conversion of electrical energy into heat. Measured in ohms.
Resonance	A condition resulting from the combination of the reactances of a system, in which a response to a sinusoidal stimulus of constant magnitude reaches a maximum at a particular frequency.
Reverberation	In an enclosure. The persistence of sound due to repeated reflections at the boundaries.
Reverberation time	Of an enclosure, for sound of a given frequency. The period of time required for the sound pressure in the enclosure, initially in a steady state, to decrease, after the source is stopped, to one-millionth of its initial value, i.e. by 60 dB.
Re-voicing	Post-synchronization in the same language as the original but with a different artist.
Ribbon microphone	Type of microphone in which currents are generated by the movements of a metal ribbon suspended in a magnetic field.
Ring modulator	Device which may be used to produce sum and difference frequencies of two signals applied to the input.
Rise time	The interval between the instants at which the instantaneous value of a pulse or of its envelope first reaches specified lower and upper limits, namely 10% and 90% of the peak value unless otherwise stated.
ROM (read-only memory)	Memory having fixed contents which cannot be altered, used to hold microprocessor programs, tables, etc.
Root mean square (r.m.s.)	Of a varying quantity. The square root of the mean value of the squares of the instantaneous values of the quantity. In the case of a periodic variation, the mean is taken over one period.
Rumble	Low-frequency vibration mechanically transmitted to the recording or reproducing turntable and superimposed on the reproduction.
Rushes	First prints (usually made overnight or at speed) from any new material for a film. Usually screened in a preview theatre.
Safety master	Copy of a master recording made for protection purposes.
Scale distortion	Loss of fidelity when the sounds from a large concert hall, for example, are reproduced in a small listening room.
Scroll	Portion of the recorded surface where the groove pitch has been increased to mark the separation of two successive bands of recording.

Sel-sync	The adding of live sound to a spare track to synchronize with recordings on a multitrack tape or film by the temporary use of other tracks of the record head for replay.
Sensitivity	Of an electroacoustic transducer. The ratio of the response to the stimulus under specified conditions. *Note*. This is usually expressed in decibels relative to a reference sensitivity.
Separation	Degree to which individual microphones reject unwanted voices or instruments and give effective control of the desired source.
Session tape	A reel of original recorded material: can include both master material and out-takes.
Signal-to-noise ratio	The ratio of the magnitude of the signal to that of the noise, usually expressed in decibels. *Note*. This ratio is expressed in many different ways, for example, in terms of peak values in the case of impulsive noise and in terms of root-mean-square values in the case of random noise, the signal being assumed sinusoidal (see also Weighted noise).
Sine wave	Waveform of an alternating quantity which varies according to a simple harmonic law, so that the amplitude at any instant is proportional to the sine of the quantity: $2\pi \times$ frequency × time (the time being reckoned from the instant when the quantity is zero and becoming positive in sign).
Slate	Term used for recording spoken 'take' numbers or cues on tape by analogy with the chalked cues on a film clapperboard.
Slope	1. Steepness of the sloping part of a response curve: usually stated in dB/octave. 2. A plotted slope derived from input and output amplitudes and stated as a ratio (e.g. 1:1 a conventional amplifier, 20:1 a limiter).
Solenoid	Form of electromagnet permitting remote operation of switches etc.
Sound pressure level (SPL)	The sound pressure level of a sound, in decibels, is equal to twenty times the logarithm to the base 10 of the ratio of the r.m.s. sound pressure to the reference sound pressure. In case of doubt, the reference sound pressure should be stated. In the absence of any statement to the contrary, the reference sound pressure in air is taken to be $2 \times 10^{-5} \mathrm{N/m^2} (= 20 \ \mu\mathrm{Pa})$.
Sound reinforcement	(See Public address.)
Splicing tape	Special dry adhesive tape used in butt editing of tape recordings.
Spot effects (Hand effects)	Sound effects created in a studio where the scene of which they form part is taking place.

Stamper	Metal negative, produced by electroforming from the positive or mother and used for the production of pressings.
Standing waves	An interference pattern characterized by stationary nodes and antinodes.
Stereophony	A process designed to produce the illusion of a spatial distribution of sound sources, by the use of two or more channels of information.
Stripe	A narrow band of magnetic material applied as a coating on cinematograph film and which carries the sound record. (Further similar bands are frequently applied to the film for control and other purposes.)
Stylus	The needle, generally diamond or sapphire-tipped, in a cutterhead or pickup cartridge.
Subjective	As judged by the senses: opposite of objective, i.e. measured.
Swarf	(American: chip.) The material removed from the recording blank by the cutting stylus.
Swinger	Record in which the hole is not at the exact centre of the groove spiral.
Sync facility	Feature on some tape machines permitting individual tracks of the record head to be switched to act as replay heads, for example to provide synchronous foldback to artists during overdubbing.
Synthesizer	Device used in electronic music giving flexible control of the pitch, timing, and tonal quality of signals.
Take	Recording of whole or part of a musical item. Thus a long work or one which is difficult to perform might consist of many 'takes' to be edited together.
Talkback	A circuit enabling spoken directions to be given from a studio control cubicle or television control room, or from a production panel to a studio, or other programme source, for the purpose of directing a performance or rehearsal.
Timbre	That subjective quality of a sound which enables a listener to judge that two sounds having the same loudness and pitch are dissimilar.
Time constant	Shorthand method of specifying the values of resistor and capacitor to be used in a frequency correction network by reference to the time taken for the voltage across the capacitor to fall to 37% (approx.) of its original value through the resistor. Equals the product of R and C: stated in microseconds (μs).
Tracing distortion	Non-linear distortion due to the different shapes of the cutting and reproducing styli.

Tracking error	The difference between the curved path followed by a pivoted pickup and the straight radial path of the cutter.
Tracks	Regions of the tape of specified width scanned by the tape heads.
Transducer	A device designed to receive oscillatory energy from one system and to supply related oscillatory energy to another.
Transferring	Copying by re-recording on a different medium.
Transformer	Component having two coils of wire, the primary and secondary, whose length (number of turns) are in a fixed ratio to permit voltages to be stepped up or down and circuit impedances to be matched for maximum power transfer.
Transient	A phenomenon which occurs during the change of a system from one steady state to another.
Transmitter	Equipment for converting the audio-frequency electric currents corresponding to a programme into a modulated carrier wave which can be radiated by an aerial.
Truth table	Convenient method of tabulating the output condition of a gate or system for every combination of inputs.
Unidirectional	(See Cardioid microphone.)
Variable-area	System of optical recording in which the modulation varies the area through which light is transmitted.
Variable-density	System of optical recording where the width is constant but the transmission factor is varied. This system has largely fallen into disuse with the increased popularity of colour film.
Varigroove	The technique of varying the groove spacing in relation to displacement amplitude of the cutting stylus.
VCA (voltage-controlled amplifier)	Amplifier whose gain is controlled by an external d.c. voltage.
Velocity	Distance travelled in unit time (e.g. velocity of sound in air at $20°C = 344$ metres per second; velocity of electromagnetic waves (light and radio) = 300,000,000 m/s).
Velour effect	Difference in performance of a magnetic tape when it is run in the opposite direction; caused by asymmetrical distribution of the magnetic particles in the coating.
Volt	Practical unit of electrical pressure or of electromotive force, of such a magnitude that if a pressure of one volt is applied across a resistance of one ohm, a current of one ampere will flow (see Ohm's Law).
Volume	Intensity of programme, or of noise, expressed in decibels relative to a standard reference volume or zero volume, according to the readings of a programme meter, the

characteristics of which must be specified in order to define the volume accurately (see also Level and VU).

VU (Volume Unit)   A unit for expressing the magnitude of a complex electric wave such as that corresponding to speech or music. The volume in volume units is equal to the number of decibels by which the wave differs from a reference volume.

VU meter   A volume indicator the specification of which is given in American Standard 'Volume Measurements of Electrical Speech and Program waves', C16.5-1942.

Watt   Practical unit of electrical power equal to one joule per second. (In a d.c. circuit the number of watts is equal to the product of the volts and amperes; in an a.c. circuit it is equal to the product of the volts and amperes multiplied by the power factor.)

Waveform   The shape of the graph representing the successive values of a varying quantity.

Wavelength   Of a sinusoidal plane progressive wave. The perpendicular distance between two wavefronts in which the phases differ by one complete period. Symbol λ.
Note: The wavelength is equal to the wave velocity divided by the frequency.

Weber   Unit of magnetic flux.

Weighted noise   The noise measured within the audio-frequency band using an instrument which has a frequency-selective characteristic.

White noise   Random noise signal having the same energy level at all frequencies (cf. Pink Noise).

Wow   (See Flutter.)

Zero level   Standard of reference used when expressing levels. (The zero level generally chosen is one milliwatt, which corresponds to a voltage of 0.775 volt r.m.s. across a resistance of 600 ohms.)

Index

DATE DUE